TIM KELLEY'S
FISHING GUIDE

OFFICIAL GUIDEBOOK TO COLORADO & WYOMING FISHING

HART PUBLICATIONS, INC.
DENVER, COLORADO

TIM KELLEY'S
FISHING GUIDE
The Official Colorado & Wyoming Guidebook

Founded by Tim Kelley in 1954

Seventeenth Edition

DONALD HART
Editor & Publisher

DICK PROUTY
Managing Editor

GEOFFREY O'GARA
Associate Editor

SCOTT ROEDERER
TOM LENTZ
JEAN TREADWAY
Contributing Editors

DICK BEARD
Advertising Manager

VILMA BOUBELIK
Production Manager

SYLVIA DETTERMAN
MELISSA REISCHMAN
Production Assistants

MARC CONLY
Art Director

DOTTIE SPARLIN
Distribution Manager

IVY HIMSCHOOT
BOBBIE PASSMORE
Typesetters

ISBN 0-912553-01-4
Copyright © Hart Publications, Inc. 1985
P.O. Box 1917
Denver, CO 80201
Telephone 303/837-1917

All contents of Tim Kelley's Fishing Guide are protected by copyright. Permission to reprint, copy or duplicate any portion other than brief excerpts of less than 150 words for review purposes requires the written permission of the publisher.

Preface

This edition launches the fourth decade of Tim Kelley's Fishing Guide books. One would think that by this time nearly every fishing spot in Colorado and Wyoming would have been identified—after all, they're not likely to move.

True, many of the more than 3,000 lakes, streams and reservoirs have been described before. But we keep finding new places—dozens of 'em—and different fishing situations. The quality and kind of angling in one place will improve or deteriorate. Lakes once stocked no longer are, or they're stocked with cutthroat instead of rainbow, or you can now get a boat in the water. Warm water fishing is becoming increasingly popular.

The ongoing challenge is public access. Landmarks are destroyed or changed; roads and trails are relocated, washed out or buried in landslides. Government regulations and laws have closed old mining and logging roads and 19th-century railroad rights-of-way to vehicles. So, all too often, you can't get there from here the way you used to. Even dependable maps can't keep up to date. But lake by lake, stream by stream and reservoir by reservoir, we've checked 'em out. And we've had a tremendous amount of help in doing it.

However, the core of the book still belongs to Tim Kelley, the late University of Colorado geography professor, who, with his wife Rae, spent many seasons traveling his beloved West in pursuit of fish and information pertinent to catching them. The information has been updated, verified and reorganized.

State fisheries personnel in Wyoming headed by John Baughman and in Colorado by Eddie Kochman have been helpful beyond measure. We've also had input from professional guides, ranchers, tackle shop operators and fellow fishermen. Particular credit is due Jim Blecha, Robert Pollock, Scott Roederer, Tom Lentz, Bruce Hill, Everett Pierson, Jim Hekkers, Russ Bromby, Dale Lashnitz and the publisher, Don Hart, who believes in fishing and a good book on where it is and how to get to it.

We rarely venture opinions on how to fish or what to use. There are too many variables. We wonder why people, who invest so many weekends, holidays and vacations in fishing (let alone equipment and paraphernalia), don't take fishing lessons. People who know how to fish catch the fish. It's said that 10 per cent of the fishermen catch 50 per cent of the fish and 80 per cent of the fishermen catch 50 per cent. Ten per cent don't catch fish. Many tackle shops, Trout Unlimited and the Bass Federation are able and willing to increase your fishing success and enjoyment with a lesson or two.

Descriptions of major stream drainages begin with an overview. Then creeks and lakes at the headwaters of the main stream high in the Rocky Mountains are described.

As major tributaries join the primary stream, the tributaries and their associated lakes and creeks are described from the headwaters of the tributary down to where it joins the primary stream. Then discussion of the mainstream resumes.

We believe in and recommend using maps with the Guide to make the most of those precious hours of fishing. We've added a chapter on maps and guides and where to get them. We've added a list of tackle shops this year, most of them mentioned from personal experience or by recommendation of fellow fishermen. Certainly, the list is incomplete, but it's a beginning and we hope it's helpful.

We call attention to our advertisers and suggest you patronize them to enhance your fishing expeditions. Their participation in the Guide has helped keep the Guide reasonably priced.

Most of all, we wish you good fishing. It's out there in both states, and there's lots of it, temperamental though it may sometimes be.

Dick Prouty

If you're in the market for an outboard motor, you've got a choice. You can buy an outboard with a big name. Or you can buy an outboard with Mariner's economy, durability and reliability. We can't tell you which choice will be more comfortable for you. But there's one thing we can tell you. When a storm's coming up and you're a long way from shore, you'd better have more than a name to get home.

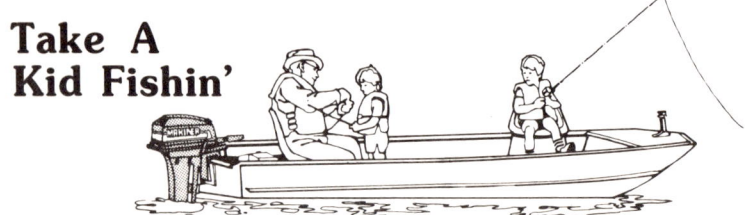

Take A Kid Fishin'

Invest With A Winner: If you're currently a marine dealer or thinking of becoming one, you owe it to yourself to consider the retail opportunities available with Mariner Outboards.

Proven Growth Record: Mariner is a division of the Brunswick Corp., one of the world's foremost manufacturers of recreational products. We didn't sell our first motor in the U.S. until 1976, yet we're already one of the top four brands in a retail marine business that totals over $8 billion annually.

Products That Perform: Mariner Outboards have a reputation for reliability. After you sell them, they don't come back. We offer a complete line of outboard power options from 2 thru 200 horsepower, plus six electric models.

Opportunity Is Knocking. Are You Listening? Our dealer organization is growing rapidly, but we still need representation in a number of areas. So there may be an opportunity for you to share in our growth and success. To find out, call Joe Masek at 308/436-2143.

Masek Distributing
1320 - 10th Street
Gering, NE 69341
308/436-2143

Table of Contents

COLORADO FISHING	**13**
Gold Medal Waters	17
Wild Trout Waters	17
Record Fish	18
PLASTIC LURES WORK	**20**
RIO GRANDE	**24**
Clear Creek	27
South Fork Rio Grande	31
Sanchez Reservoir	33
Conejos River	33
SAN LUIS VALLEY	**40**
Saguache Creek	40
SOUTHWEST RIVERS	**44**
San Juan River	45
Piedra River	50
Los Pinos River	50
Vallecito Reservoir	51
Southern Ute Indian Reservation	52
Animas River	53
DOLORES RIVER	**58**
SAN MIGUEL RIVER	**62**
GUNNISON RIVER	**66**
Tomichi Creek	66
Cochetopa Creek	67
Taylor Reservoir	68
Texas Creek	69
East River	72

ANTHONY F. CANNOVA
TAXIDERMY & SCULPTURE STUDIO

1984 NATIONAL TAXIDERMY CHAMPION

- Fish Woodcarvings
- Natural Skin Mounts
- Bronze Reproductions
- Fiberglass Reproductions

Experience Since 1967

Near I-25 and University Blvd.
1685 SO. CLAYTON ST. • DENVER, CO. • 80210 • (303) 744-0147

Blue Mesa Reservoir	75
Lake Fork Gunnison River	76
Lake Cristobal	78
Cebolla Creek	78
Morrow Point Reservoir	80
Cimarron River	80
Crystal Reservoir	81
Black Canyon of the Gunnison	81
North Fork Gunnison River	83

WHITE RIVER 89
Lake Avery	91

FLAT TOPS WILDERNESS 94
Trappers Lake	95
Wall Lake	96
South Fork White River	98

YAMPA RIVER 101
Stillwater Reservoir	103
Mandall Lakes	103
Steamboat Lake	108
Williams Fork River	109
Green River	111

NORTH PLATTE RIVER 115
Grizzly Creeks	117
Delaney Butte Lakes	118

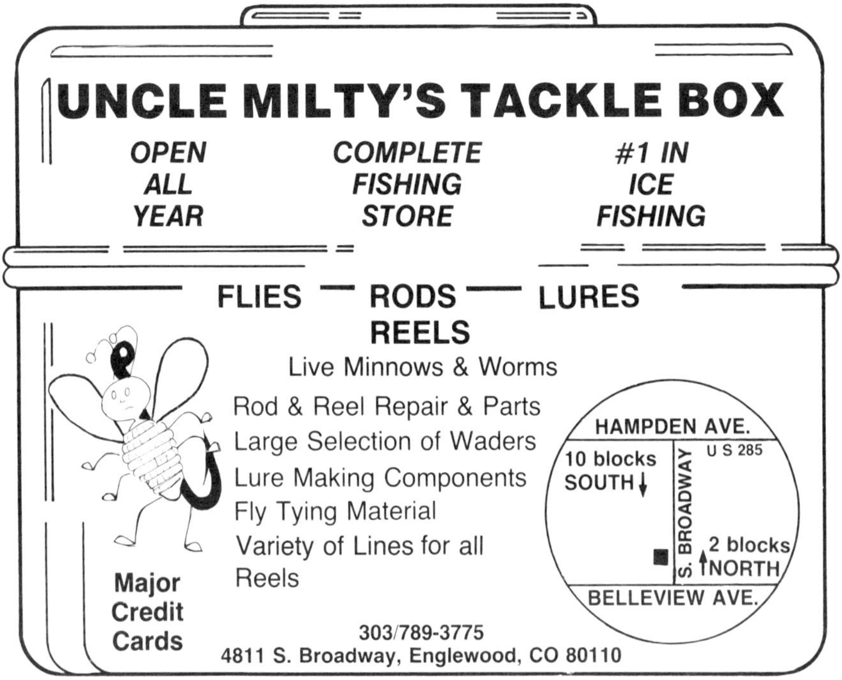

UNCLE MILTY'S TACKLE BOX

OPEN ALL YEAR

COMPLETE FISHING STORE

#1 IN ICE FISHING

**FLIES — RODS — LURES
REELS**

Live Minnows & Worms
Rod & Reel Repair & Parts
Large Selection of Waders
Lure Making Components
Fly Tying Material
Variety of Lines for all Reels

Major Credit Cards

HAMPDEN AVE.
10 blocks SOUTH ↓
U S 285
S. BROADWAY
2 blocks ↑NORTH
BELLEVIEW AVE.

303/789-3775
4811 S. Broadway, Englewood, CO 80110

Lake John	119
Illinois River	120
Big Creek	121
Encampment River	121

LARAMIE RIVER 123
    Chambers Lake 123
    Rawah Creek 125
    Hohnholz Lakes 126

CACHE LA POUDRE RIVER 127
    Long Draw Reservoir 128
    Joe Wright Reservoir 128
    Red Feather Lakes 131
    Horsetooth Reservoir 131

ROCKY MOUNTAIN NATIONAL PARK 133
    Big Thompson River 135
    West Side of the Park 137

ARAPAHO RECREATION AREA 139

COLORADO RIVER 142
    Grand Lake 143
    Lake Granby 144
    Fraser River 145
    Blue River 148

Dillon Reservoir 149
Gore Wilderness Waters 152
Green Mountain Reservoir 154
Derby Creeks 156
Eagle River 159
Gore Creek 163
Roaring Fork River 166
Fryingpan River 169
Rifle Gap Reservoir 175
Grand Mesa 179

ARKANSAS RIVER 188
Turquoise Lake 190
Twin Lakes 192
Clear Creek 193
Cottonwood Creek 193
Texas Creek 197
Sangre de Cristo Fishing 197
Pueblo Reservoir 201

SOUTH PLATTE RIVER 205
Antero Reservoir 208
Spinney Mountain Reservoir 209
Elevenmile Reservoir 209
North Fork South Platte River 212
Chatfield Reservoir 215
Cherry Creek Reservoir 217

METRO DENVER FISHING 222

FRONT RANGE STREAMS 231
Clear Creek 231
South Boulder Creek 236
Barker Reservoir 239
Brainard Lake 239
Middle St. Vrain Creek 240

EASTERN COLORADO FISHING 243
Boulder Reservoir 245
Loveland Area 246
Bonny Reservoir 248
Nee Noshe Reservoir 251
Trinidad Lake 252

26 lb. Rainbow — Flaming Gorge

Del Canty's
Museum Quality Taxidermy

Fish Only

37 Years Experience

Del Canty's Lunker Hunter Systems • "Backpacking Gear"
3 pound Fishing Float • 13 oz Bivouac bag • 3 pound River Float
4 pound Backpacker Boat • Light Raingear • Rods
Reels • Waders • Swim Fins • Flies etc.

Visit our fish museum at the following address:
Del Canty's   4039 Highway 91   Leadville, CO 80461
303/486-0769

TIM KELLEY'S FISHING GUIDE 11

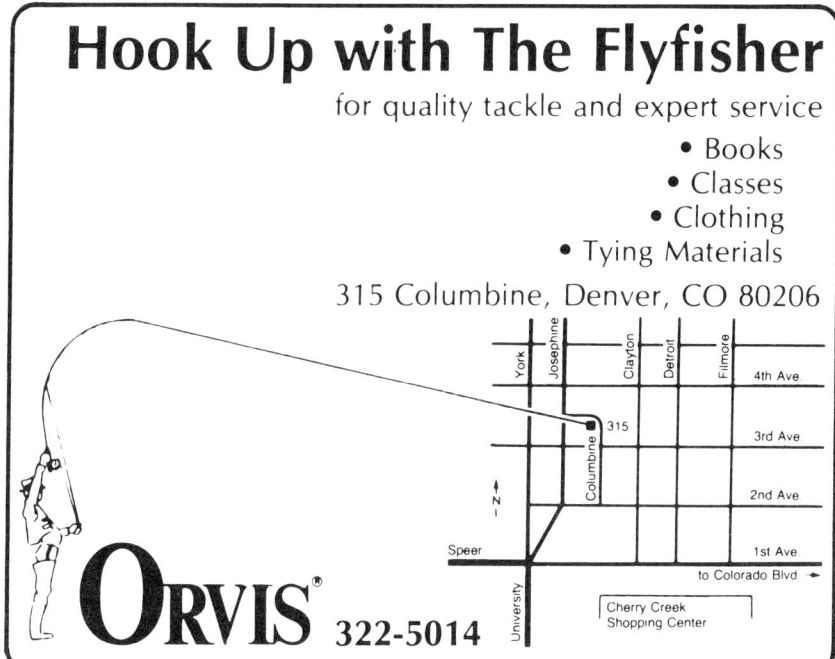

ICE FISHING	255
WYOMING FISHING	**257**
Record Fish	261
WEATHER IN THE WEST	**262**
FLY FISHING PATTERNS	**264**
BEAR RIVER	**267**
WIND RIVER	**268**
Brooks Lake	270
Torrey Creek	272
North Fork Popo Agie River	274
Sinks Canyon	276
Louis Lake	278
Wind River Indian Reservation	278
Boysen Reservoir	281
BIGHORN RIVER	**284**
Bighorn Lake	286
Nowood River	287
Medicine Lodge Lakes	289
Shell Creek	290
Shoshone River	292
Buffalo Bill Reservoir	293
Clarks Fork Yellowstone River	294

YELLOWSTONE NATIONAL PARK ... 298
  Snake River ... 300
  Heart Lake ... 301
  Lewis River ... 301
  Madison River ... 302
  Firehole River ... 304
  Gallatin River ... 305
  Yellowstone River ... 306
  Yellowstone Lake ... 308
  Gardner River ... 312

SNAKE RIVER ... 316
  Jackson Lake ... 318
  Gros Ventre River ... 321
  Grey's River ... 323
  Palisade Reservoir ... 324

GREEN RIVER ... 328
  Fontenelle Reservoir ... 330
  Flaming Gorge Reservoir ... 331
  Upper Green River ... 333
  New Fork River ... 336
  Fremont Lake ... 337
  Bridger Lakes ... 338
  Boulder Lake ... 340
  Big Sandy River ... 343

SWEETWATER RIVER ... 347

NORTH PLATTE RIVER ... 349
  Saratoga Area ... 353
  Snowy Range Lakes ... 353
  Seminoe Reservoir ... 357
  Miracle Mile ... 357
  Pathfinder Reservoir ... 358
  Alcova Reservoir ... 360
  Glendo Reservoir ... 363
  Laramie River ... 364
  Grayrocks Reservoir ... 364

NORTHEAST WYOMING ... 368
  Crazy Woman Creek ... 369
  Piney Creek ... 370
  Lake DeSmet ... 372
  Goose Creek ... 372
  Keyhole Reservoir ... 375

MAPS & GUIDES LISTINGS ... 378

COLD WATER FISH ... 393

WARM WATER FISH ... 397

SELECTED TACKLE SHOPS ... 401

INDEX OF ADVERTISERS ... 402

LAKES & STREAMS INDEX ... 403

Colorado fishing is fine trout or bass on line

Many years ago a small wooden plaque held an unobtrusive yet revered place on the wall of a sportsman's study. Picked up in a roadside knick-knack/souvenir shop by a longtime and treasured fishing companion, it was a gift with symbolic value beyond price. The words on it read: Allah does not deduct from a man's allotted time those hours spent in fishing.

It's true.

Nowhere could it be more true than beside the waters of Colorado mountains and prairies. Medical studies show blood pressures drop, hearts assume a decaffinated beat and workday worries become their faraway selves as one takes up rod and reel and goes fishing.

Benefits beyond catching fish are reaped annually by nearly a million men, women and children who actually hook some 24 million of their Colorado quarry. While all kinds of statistics are conjured up, the net result is the same: fishing in Colorado is better than it was even a few years ago—by about 6 million fish annually. And it could be getting even better.

Improved fishing is attributed to better fish management programs by the Colorado Division of Wildlife (DOW) plus increased numbers of reservoir fisheries and warm water fishing holes. For example, Spinney Mountain Reservoir on the South Platte River opened in 1983; McPhee Reservoir on the Dolores River at Cortez was being filled and stocked with hundreds of thousands of trout in 1985. The Denver Water Department has opened Cheesman Reservoir to limited fishing and the City of Aurora manages a prime urban fishing pond at Quincy Reservoir.

The DOW also is endeavoring to improve the quality of fishing through regulations limiting the use of bait, setting size limits and restricting the numbers of fish destined for the frying pan. It encourages catch and release angling, as do local trout and bass organizations.

There's a reason for the rules. Artificial fly and lure requirements, for example, mean fish are less likely to swallow the hook than if it were concealed in bait. Thus the undersized fish has a better chance to survive its release and to grow and be caught again.

Keeping fewer fish and setting 16-inch

"Colorado Springs' Full-Service Dealer"

Cross Country • Pathfinder
Midas • Auto-mate
Motor Homes
Road Ranger • Alpenlite
Starcraft
Travel Trailers

"One-Stop Service"

Coach • Engine • Drive Train
Parts & Accessories
Propane • Dump Station

303: 596-2716

4815 E. Platte Ave. (Hwy. 24)
- 5 Miles East of I-25 -

minimum sizes can help a trout reach maturity so it can reproduce naturally and let nature improve the fishing as well as the hatchery.

Bass fishing is getting "hot," especially at Nee Noshe, Navajo, Pueblo, Trinidad, Bonny and other reservoirs. The future is bright for this "flatland fishin'."

The largemouth, smallmouth, white and wiper bass are rivaling the mountain rainbow, cutthroat, brook and brown trout for sheer fishing pleasure. All this adds up to a $500-million industry that's the backbone of Colorado tourism. Yes, it's fishing, not big game hunting or skiing that's the number one outdoor recreation expenditure. And, fishing is truly a lifetime pastime.

•

It's popular to think fishing in the "olden days" was fabulous. Sometimes it was. Yet raising and stocking trout began in 1882 when 24,000 trout were stocked and another 40,000 were sold to private fisheries, according to DOW. Today more than 4.5 million catchable size (8-10 inch) fish are stocked from 14 hatcheries. Two more hatcheries are in the works—at $6 million each.

Thousands of additional fish are bought and stocked by private land owners who understandably post no fishing signs beside their ponds and streams. Many a mountain lake has trout because of a guide or outfitter packing fishermen in on horseback wants to be sure there are trout for his customers.

•

Fishing licenses today are $11—a bargain when compared to what else can be obtained for the same price. Yet, they'll be increasing in price to help offset higher hatchery, stocking and other fish management costs of around $5 million a year (not bad for a $500-million return).

As far as Colorado fishing is concerned, it's a man and nature cooperative venture.

•

One of the changes in western angling in recent years is a decided increase in expert anglers. These are men and women who know fish and their behavior, insects and their life cycles, how to read the waters of streams and lakes and are cognizant of what's going on in nature. They've mastered fly or spin tackle, often tie their own flies (sometimes at streamside) and have responded to the considerable challenge of fishing masterfully.

The result is **they catch a lot of fish.** They also let most of 'em go to be caught again, though it's good conservation to dine well if the lake or stream populations are sufficient to keep angling at a high level.

Why don't fishermen who invest lots of energy, money, weekends, evenings and vacations in their pasttime take fishing lessons? There are golf lessons, tennis lessons, handball lessons, etc. It would seem some fishing lessons from a local expert or tackle shop afficianado would reap joyous benefits to last decades. Yet the outdoor observer sees anglers angling where there is little chance of success or none at all. The folks at the local Bass Federation chapter or the Trout Unlimited people also are more than generous with sharing their enthusiasm and know-how. They can add a dimension to fishing that's priceless. The tough luck fisherman might ask himself: Do I know how to fish? Or, better yet: Am I catching fish? And then respond accordingly.

•

One thing that would help Colorado fishing is for Colorado fishermen to attend the September Colorado Wildlife Commission meeting at which rules and regulations are set. The current emphasis on cost-consciousness isn't always in the interest of better fishing or maintaining good fishing habitat. While fish management director Eddie Kochman can be ingenius in stretching dollars and staff, there is a limit to what can be done. Of particular concern is looking ahead and planning for the fishing three, four and five years from now. It needs some bucks if there is going to be good fishing.

Federal participation and dollars are declining. The Colorado General Assembly is squeezing too. It's time for anglers to get to the commission, find out what's going on, the consequences of various decisions and start putting in their two cents worth. The fish organizations can't do it all.

One thing's sure, Kochman and his people are more than willing to tell what they see in Colorado's fishing future and they encourage fishermen to get involved.

As Eddie says, "If we said we'd close the fishing season, people would line up from here to breakfast to do something about it. But day by day and piece by piece we're having to fight being set back. It would be nice to get public understanding on what's going on and to realize it's their fishing that's on the line."

Meeting dates are published in the newspapers. The commission's address is 6060 Broadway, Denver, 80216.

COLORADO DIVISION OF WILDLIFE
6060 Broadway
Denver, CO 80216
303/297-1192

Northeast Regional Office
317 W. Prospect
Fort Collins, CO 80522
Phone: 303/484-2836

Northwest Regional Office
711 Independent Ave.
Grand Junction, CO 81501
Phone: 303/243-3395

Southwest Regional Office
2300 S. Townsend
Montrose, CO 81401
Phone: 303/249-3431

Southeast Regional Office
2126 North Weber
Colorado Springs, CO 80907
Phone: 303/473-2945

Pueblo Regional Office
1202 B W. 13th
Pueblo, CO 81003
Phone: 303/545-2216

DOUBLE LIMITS ON RAINBOWS AT 13 LAKES/RESERVOIRS

Beginning with the 1985 season, fishermen could be seeing double rainbows. A special Rainbow Trout Stamp is available for $11 which permits the angler to take a double limit—16 instead of 8—of the scrappy fish from 13 designated lakes and reservoirs.

The stamps are available where fishing licenses are sold and are attached to the fishing license.

The 13 waters with double limits allowed with a signed stamp in possession are:

Big Eggleston Lake on Grand Mesa in Delta County
Carter Lake in Larimer County
Chatfield Reservoir on the Jefferson/Douglas county line
Green Mountain Reservoir in Summit County
Home Lake (Sherman Lake on some maps) in Rio Grande County
Horsetooth Reservoir in Larimer County
Jackson Gulch in Montezuma County
Ruedi Reservoir on the Eagle/Pitkin county line
Spring Creek Reservoir in Gunnison County
Trinidad Reservoir in Las Animas County
Twin Lakes in Lake County
Williams Fork Reservoir in Grand County
Willow Creek Reservoir in Grand County.

The double limit rainbow stamp program is experimental for 1985 only and may or may not be extended pending a review of the results. See the current fishing regulations.

16 TIM KELLEY'S FISHING GUIDE

photo courtesy Scott Roederer

COLORADO GOLD MEDAL TROUT STREAMS

Streams designated "gold medal" by the Colorado Wildlife Commission provide outstanding angling opportunities for large trout. These designations are given sparingly and represent the highest quality aquatic habitat.

Currently, only 161 of 8,000 miles of trout streams are designated gold medal. Signs identify stretches of streams that are considered of high enough quality to receive the special designation. These areas may change as fishing conditions change, with some sections being deleted and others being added.

Arkansas River: from the stockyard bridge below the town of Salida downstream to Fern Leaf Gulch (28 mi).

Blue River: from Green Mountain Reservoir Dam downstream to the confluence with the Colorado River (16 mi).

Colorado River: from Windy Gap Reservoir downstream to the confluence with Troublesome Creek (20 mi).

Fryingpan River: from Ruedi Reservoir Dam downstream to the confluence with the Roaring Fork River (14 mi).

Gore Creek: from Red Sandstone Creek through the town of Vail to the Eagle River (3 mi).

Gunnison River: from the upper boundary of the Black Canyon of the Gunnison National Monument downstream to the confluence with the North Fork of the Gunnison (26 mi).

Rio Grande: from the upper boundary of Coller Wildlife Area northwest of South Fork downstream to Farmers Union Canal east of Del Norte (22.5 mi).

Roaring Fork River: from the confluence with the Crystal River downstream to the confluence with the Colorado River (12 mi).

South Platte River: from Cheesman Reservoir Dam downstream to the confluence with the North Fork of the South Platte (19.5 mi).

WILD TROUT WATERS

Selected lakes and streams managed by the Division of Wildlife offer anglers the challenge of catching wild fish. DOW has stocked those waters with trout raised entirely within their natural environment, rather than a hatchery.

West of the Continental Divide

Colorado River: from the upper end of Gore Canyon downstream to the town of State Bridge (16 mi).

Fraser River: from one mile below the town of Tabernash downstream to one mile above the town of Granby (5 mi).

Blue River: from Green Mountain Reservoir Dam downstream 2.5 miles.

Roaring Fork River: from the Hallum Lake in the town of Aspen downstream to Woody Creek Bridge (7 mi).

Gunnison River: from the upper boundary of the Black Canyon of the Gunnison National Monument downstream to the confluence with the North Fork of the Gunnison (26 mi).

East River (Gunnison County): from its confluence with the Taylor River upstream to the bridge at the Roaring Judy Fish Hatchery.

Cochetopa Creek: within the Cochetopa (Coleman) State Wildlife Area, 38 miles southeast of Gunnison on Hwy 114 (4.5 mi).

Los Pinos Creek: within the Cochetopa (Coleman) State Wildlife Area (2 mi); 10 miles west of North Pass on Hwy 114.

Emerald Lakes: located in the Weminuche Wilderness area (279 ac), on the Lake Creek tributary of the Los Pinos River.

Trappers Lake: located in the White River National Forest, Flat Tops Wilderness Area, 40 miles east of Meeker.

East of the Continental Divide

North Platte River: from the Routt National Forest boundary downstream to the Colorado-Wyoming state line (5.3 mi).

Laramie River: within the Hohnholz Lakes State Wildlife Area (2.5 mi) along Hwy 10 just south of Wyoming border.

Cache la Poudre River: from the Monroe Tunnel, 5.5 miles west of Ted's Place, downstream to the Poudre Valley Canal headgate (4.3 mi). And from Hombre Ranch, 1.7 miles above Rustic, downstream to Grandpa's Bridge (4.2 mi). Also from the Poudre Fish Rearing Unit, 2 miles east of Kinikinik, downstream to the confluence with Black Hollow (4.7 mi).

North St. Vrain Creek: from the confluence with Horse Creek downstream to Button Rock Reservoir (8.5 mi).

Middle Fork of the South Platte River: within the Tomahawk State Wildlife Area, 1 mile northwest and 2 miles southeast of Garo on Colo. Hwy 9 (3 mi).

South Platte River: from the confluence with Beaver Creek downstream to the South Platte Arm gauging station, 0.2 mile above Cheesman Lake (9 mi). And from Cheesman Reservoir Dam downstream to the Wigwam Club (3 mi).

Tarryall Creek: from the Pike National Forest boundary (3 mi downstream to the confluence with the South Platte River).

Arkansas River: from the confluence with Gas Creek south of Nathrop through Brown's Canyon to Four Mile Creek (6 mi). From below Texas Creek, east of Cotopaxi, downstream to 1.5 miles above the village of Parkdale (14 mi).

Conejos River: from the Menkhaven Ranch downstream to the Aspen Glade (Forest Service) campground (4 mi).

Lake Fork of the Conejos: from the headwaters to the natural dam at the outlet of Rock Lake (3 mi).

Cascade Creek: six miles east of Cumbres Pass from its headwaters to the confluence with Rio De Los Pinos (2.5 mi) alongside the Cumbres and Toltec Railroad.

Osier Creek: seven miles east of Cumbres Pass from the headwaters to the confluence with Rio De Los Pinos, same vicinity as Cascade Creek (2 mi).

COLORADO RECORD FISH

Compiled by Colorado Division of Wildlife

Species	Year	Location and County	Weight lbs.	oz.	Length (inches)
Trout					
Rainbow	1972	South Platte River, Park County	18	5¼	32
Brook	1940s	Unknown	7	10	
Brown	1972	Vallecito Reservoir, La Plata County	24	10	37.6
Native	1964	Twin Lakes, Lake County	16		
Grayling	1974	Zimmerman Lake, Larimer County	1	7	15
Mackinaw	1949	Deep Lake, Garfield County	36		42
Splake	1976	Island Lake, Delta County	18	15	32
Golden	1979	Kelly Lake, Jackson County	3	12	22.5

Species	Year	Location	Length	Weight	Score
Whitefish	1982	Roaring Fork River, Garfield County	5	2	18.75
Salmon					
Kokanee (Angling)	1979	Eleven Mile Res., Park County	5	12	24.5
(Snagging)	1978	Eleven Mile Res., Park County	6	3½	26.5
Catfish					
Channel	1973	Nee Noshe Res., Kiowa County	33	4	41.5
Black Bullhead	1980	Farm pond, Las Animas County	4	10	22.5
Blue	1976	Private lake, Lincoln County	10	1	32.75
Pike					
Northern	1971	Vallecito Reservoir, La Plata County	30	1	48.5
Perch					
Walleye	1973	Cherry Creek Res., Arapahoe County	16	8	34
Sacramento	1974	Banner Lakes, Weld County	1	14	13.25
Yellow	1983	Private pond, Larimer County	2	5	14.8
Bass					
Smallmouth	1979	Smith Reservoir, Kendricks Lakes Jefferson County	5	5	20
Largemouth	1979	Stalker Lake, Yuma County	10	6¼	23.25
White	1963	Blue Lake, Bent/Kiowa counties	4	7	18
Striped	1977	North Sterling Res., Logan County	10	4	27.02
Rock	1979	Ramah Reservoir, El Paso County	1	1¼	10.6
Drum	1978	Lonetree Reservoir, Larimer County	17	3	31
Bluegill	1981	Ramah Reservoir, El Paso County	1	11	10.25
Carp	1973	Cherry Creek Res., Arapahoe County	22		32
Sunfish (Green)	1973	Stalker Lake, Yuma County	1	1	10.6
	1982	Pond, Delta County	1	1	10.2
Tench	1977	Cherry Creek Res., Arapahoe County	2	8	17.5
Sauger	1980	CF&I Reservoir #3, Pueblo County	3	1	20.5
Crappie					
White	1975	Northglenn Lake, Adams County	4	3¼	17
Black	1980	CF&I Reservoir #3, Pueblo County	3		17.02
	1981	Ketner Lake, Jefferson County	3		

Fishing for whoppers with plastic lures

by Tom Lentz

The shad began its dive for the bottom. For 10 seconds it dove, then leveled off above the sandy bed of the shallow cove. Surrounded by the black water of a November night, it moved toward shore—60 feet distant. Sixty feet is a great distance to a two-inch shad.

The big walleye was not yet hunting. A 10-inch channel catfish dissolving in its gut stayed pangs of hunger. Something was coming, swimming along the sloping bottom toward shore. Goaded by stimuli that had for millenia led her species, the walleye turned toward the source. The hunter began to hunt.

The shad was only halfway to the shore when it vanished. Approaching the quarry quartering from the rear, the hunter had paced, caught and engulfed the prey. The shad, caught in the maelstrom created by the hunter's flaring gill covers, had been sucked in an instant into the toothed maw.

A jolt, initiated by the sudden attack of the big fish, traveled up the line, through the rod and into my hand and arm. Belatedly I set the hook into a slack line. I reeled frantically to recover the slack. A tightening sensation in the line triggered a second and third hook set. The steel hidden in the plastic shad found a point of solid purchase in the hunter's jaw.

Hooked securely, the walleye yielded begrudgingly to the constant pressure of rod and line. Presently, the fatigued fish was eased onto the sandy beach of Standley Reservoir near Arvada. The predator was soon to move up the food chain. Diner became dinner.

Weighing almost 7 pounds, it was the latest in a series of large fish to succumb to a powerful prescription for an angler's malaise—soft plastic lures.

PLASTIC LURES WORK

Soft plastic lures can be divided into worms, grubs and shad. The lures are soft to the touch. Their similarity to the living tissue of food organisms increases their effectiveness, because the fish hold the lure longer and, thereby, allow more time for the angler to react.

The plastic worm was the progenitor of all types of soft lures, but even it has metamorphosed from its original configuration as a literal depiction of a common nightcrawler. It resembled little more than a stick in the water. The addition of a twisting tail breathed life into the hulk, vastly improving its appearance. Strangely, the worm inherited its life from its progeny, the plastic grub.

Whereas the worm imitated long, cylindrical life forms, a short, fat version was created to mimic more compact organisms. This "grub" was endowed with even less life than its forebear. Fortunately, a flat ribbon-like tail was added. Molded in a spiral coiled shape, this tail stretches out when drawn through the water. Seeking equilibrium, the tail undulates like a child's paper streamer in a strong breeze.

A third kind of lure is the swimming-tail shad. Its tail is constructed to vibrate rapidly, imitating the motions of small fish. The tail is molded on a small fish-like body. When retrieved, the similarity to a small swimming shad is striking.

These are the three basic weapons of the soft lure arsenal. As a licensed outfitter, guide and fishing instructor, I must be concerned with more than outward appearance. I judge all lures by six criteria and endorse wholeheartedly only those lures that fulfill all six requirements.

SIX LURE CRITERIA

First, the lure must be easy to rig. Plastics can be rigged for fishing in several different ways, but for 95 per cent of my fishing I utilize one of two simple methods.

Weed- and snag-filled conditions dictate the most foul-proof rig possible, the Texas-rigged plastic worm. This rig requires a plastic worm hook (Eagle Claw model 95JBL, size #2 to 1/0), a bullet-shaped plastic worm sinker (1/16, 1/8, 1/4 oz.) and a plastic worm (4 inches is probably the most effective size in Colorado waters).

Line (Berkley or Stren fluorescent) size should be determined by the density of the weeds/snags and the size of the fish anticipated. A 6- to 14-pound test line is adequate for most Colorado conditions.

To complete the rig: 1) pass the line through the worm sinker, bullet point toward the rod end of the line; 2) tie on worm hook using a reliable knot (Palomar, improved clinch); 3) insert the hook point in the tip of the worm head and pierce half inch longitudinally; 4) hook point exits the side of the worm head half inch below tip (hook should exit on same side as either edge of twister tail on worm); 5) slide worm up hook shank until hook eye with knot is inside the worm head; 6) turn hook so hook point can pierce worm body; and 7) pierce worm body and hide hook point and barb inside worm body.

This rig necessitates a needle-sharp hook and a vigorous hook-setting motion in order to drive the hook point through the plastic worm body and into the fish's jaw.

When retrieved, the sliding worm sinker sits on and protects the fragile tip of the worm head from abrasion while the only exposed portion of the hook is the smooth shank and bend. The Texas rig is practically weedless and snag-proof. The worm should lie straight when retrieved, as any bends will cause the rig to spin and be ineffective.

The jig is the rig to use when fishing clean bottoms (sand, clay, rock, gravel, rubble, etc.). A jig is a molded lead head on a specially bent jig hook. They are pre-made and may be purchased where worms, grubs and shad are sold. They are usually classified by the weight of the lead head. I use 1/16, 1/8 and 1/4 oz. sizes in most instances.

Worms, grubs and shad are all rigged on a jig in the same manner: 1) insert the hook point in the tip of the lure body; 2) thread the

Tom Lentz photo

body on the hook until the hook shank is nearly covered; 3) hook point exits side of lure (plane of hook shank and point and the plane of the twister or swimming tail must be the same); 4) body is pushed up over the collar of the lead head. Again, the worm, grub or shad body must be straight or the rig will not run true during the retrieve.

Second, the lure must be easy to fish. Much has been written about the plastic lures and how difficult they are to fish. Nothing could be further from the truth. As long as they are rigged to run straight and true, it is difficult to fish soft plastics without catching fish, where fish exist.

Using a pumping retrieve, a fish is hooked almost automatically by the rod's motion. With reeling and lifting retrieves, set the hook at *any* sensation that the lure has touched something. Often the strike is so light it is all but undetectable. Remember to hold the rod as lightly as possible. A light grip on the handle allows the rod to reveal the slightest impediment to the lure's progress. You will automatically grip the rod tightly during the hook set. In addition, a delicate touch is much less fatiguing. To avoid fatigue I use ultralight tackle for all my fishing—bluegills to pike.

Third, the lure must be fishable under a wide variety of conditions. I regularly catch the first fish of the spring and the last fish of the fall on 2-inch plastic grubs. During the warmer period, larger plastics are equally or more effective. Since the lures are both visually and audibly detectable, the low light levels of murky water or night pose little problem for the fish. The common thread woven through the fabric of obvious characteristics exhibited by fishes' food organisms is movement, and the swimming, twisting tails amply represent this trait.

Fourth, a lure is only practical if it is readily available. Today, plastic lures are widely distributed under such brand names as Mr. Twister and Tom Mann's Baits. My favorite plastic worm (and the fishes', so far as I can determine) is the four-inch Ribworm. This multiple segment worm is marketed under Dick Gasaway's FINMASTER label. (The High Country Bass Pro Shop in Denver and All Pro Fish 'N' Sport Shop in Littleton, Colo., are among sources for soft plastic lures and attendant materials.)

Fifth, the lures must be inexpensive. To catch fish, especially large fish, you must fish where they live. Unfortunately, big fish live in tangles, snags and next to the bottom.

Tom Lentz photo

To catch them, the lures must be fished in harm's way, both the fish and obstructions notwithstanding. In this era of five-dollar crankbaits, a lost lure or two puts a substantial hole in the fishing budget. Soft plastics cost only 10 to 35 cents, hook and sinker included. You can afford to fish them where the big fish live.

Sixth, the lure must be effective. Since 1977, when I began to fish with soft plastics, I have caught most species of game fish present in Colorado. These include species as diverse as bluegills, channel catfish, kokanee salmon, white bass and carp. All species and all sizes are susceptible. In addition to the aforementioned fish, I have also recorded: 4 lb. and 4 lb. 3.25 oz. smallmouth bass (Colorado state record, 1977-1979); brook, rainbow and brown trout from 12 inches to 6 pounds; pike over 15 pounds; 13-inch black crappie; dozens of walleyes from 7 inches to 7 pounds; and numerous largemouth bass, including a pair of 7½-pound fish. This partial list attests to the effectiveness of soft plastic lures.

COLORS

Soft plastic lures are sold in a range of colors that would make a rainbow green with envy. Some colors seem to consistently outperform others, and some also are more effective in one type of lure than others. The following is a list of lure type, size and colors that I have found to be consistently productive.

Ribworm: four to six inches; black, purple, motor oil glitter, smoke glitter (body)/chartreuse (tail).

Grubs: 1½ to 3 inches; smoke glitter, motor oil glitter, orange glitter, chartreuse glitter, silver gray, pearl, black, yellow, purple, avocado green.

Shad: 1½, 2 and 2½ inches; pearl, smoke glitter, orange glitter, clear glitter, chartreuse glitter. (The pearl shad is a killer for large trout if it is colored with felt-tip marking pens to resemble a small rainbow trout.)

Fish these lures in parts of the lake that are different from the immediately surrounding area. Examples: where the bottom changes from rock to sand; the deep water edge of weed beds; a point jutting out from a straight bank; just inside dirty water meeting clear water along a leeward shore.

Although these lures work in any water with game fish populations, I strongly advise concentrating efforts on densely populated impoundments. This is especially true if you are unfamiliar with plastic lures or the species of fish sought. Highly recommended waters are: Chatfield Res. for largemouth bass and crappies; Spinney Mountain Res. for cutthroat trout; Dillon Res. for rainbow and large brown trout; Elevenmile Canyon Res. for pike and trout; Horsetooth Res. for walleye and smallmouth bass; Pueblo Res. for trout, bass, walleye, pike and crappie.

Lastly, let the fish decide which lure color, size and type is most appealing in a given circumstance. Change the combinations until you find a producer. A good way is first to use small lures to establish a color preference, then to change types and sizes until the best color, type, size combination is found.

The first time you find the right combination, you will also find out why this potent Rx is just what the doctor ordered. □

Tom Lentz is a Denver-based licensed fishing instructor and guide.

Tom Lentz photo

Rio Grande
El Norte's best

Adjacent communities:
Creede, Del Norte, Monte Vista, Alamosa, Antonito.

Principal Highways:
U.S. 160, 285; Colo. 149, 374, 142, 17.

Some of the most rewarding angling in the Rockies is among the lakes and streams of the Rio Grande basin.

Fishing the Rio Grande has a mystique no other area of Colorado matches. The 14,000-foot peaks, gray granite palisades, aspen and coniferous forests, cottonwood streamsides, rustic cabins and old mine buildings—even the shimmering waters—all are enhanced with an intangible Spanish heritage.

The rainbow, brook and brown trout seem all the more tempting because they abound in a land where places like Rio Grande, Conejos, Canyon Diablo, La Manga and Monte Vista mingle with the names of the Old West—Shotgun Knob, Indian Ridge, Horse Thief Pasture, Wagon Wheel Gap, Deadman Creek. Among them is some of the best trout fishing anywhere.

Portions of the Rio Grande and some of its tributaries are Gold Medal trout streams—prime quality for big trout.

Rio Grande rises in Rio Grande National Forest west of Rio Grande Reservoir, flows east past Creede and out of the mountains. As the river dashes and surges southeast into New Mexico, the remarkable fishery of its upper reaches is characterized by clear water with long, deep pools and sprawling riffles broken by large boulders. Below Monte Vista, the river loses its sparkle. By the time it concludes its 100-mile journey through Colorado, it leaves the state silt-ladened and with some good size northern pike to be taken from its murky waters.

From the Rio Grande headwaters east to the town and stream of South Fork, the Rio Grande flows mostly through private land, but its tributaries and some stretches are on national forest lands. Its tributaries flow from the north from La Garita Mountains and La Garita Wilderness Area, and from the south of out the San Juan Mountains and the Weminuche Wilderness. Hwy 149 roughly parallels the Rio Grande from near Creede to the east, downstream through Del Norte. At Del Norte, the Rio Grande breaks out into the arid San Luis Valley, angles southeast through Monte Vista and, at Alamosa, the Rio Grande swerves south. Some of its western tributaries offer fine fishing in the Rio Grande National Forest and the South San Juan Wilderness before it leaves Colorado.

RIO GRANDE RESERVOIR

At the headwaters of the Rio Grande,

about 27 miles west of Creede, the **Rio Grande** or **Farmer's Union Reservoir** (9541 ft; 2000 ac minimum) is a 7-mile-long body of water. Its southern shore is the Weminuche Wilderness Area's northern border. The reservoir was drained in 1982 and restocked with a range of catchable size rainbow, cutthroat and brown. In the mid-1980s, it's a top notch fishery and as popular as ever. The stretch of river below the reservoir to Box Canyon has been subject to significant improvements designed to improve fish habitat and fishing.

To reach Rio Grande Reservoir, travel 25 miles southwest of Creede on Hwy 149. Just before Spring Creek Reservoir Campground, the road forks. Follow the western fork to Bristol View Ranger Station. From the ranger station, the road goes southwest past three campgrounds. At the eastern end of the reservoir is Thirtymile Campground. There are two other campgrounds on the reservoir also—Reservoir and Lost Trail. Just past Reservoir Campground in Horse Thief Pasture is a primitive gravel boat ramp. It is a very steep and rough ramp, not suitable for launching boats with cars or recreational vehicles.

Rio Grande Reservoir is fed by several tributaries, including the Rio Grande above the reservoir to the west. The river, which averages 15 feet wide, can be reached by a rough 4-wheel-drive road. It is open and offers fine fishing for cutthroat and rainbow to 10 inches. About 7 miles above the reservoir, to the west, Rio Grande forks. The northern fork is Quartzite Creek.

Quartzite Creek averages 6 to 8 feet wide and is rated good for cutthroat to 10 inches. The stream is about 5 miles long and is swift and open. A 4-wheel-drive road that follows the Rio Grande beyond the reservoir branches north and follows Quartzite Creek for a short section, and then runs over Stony Pass, just north of Quartzite Creek.

Where the road forks, the southwestern road follows Bear Creek. **Bear Creek** enters the Rio Grande River from the south about 8 miles above the reservoir. Its length can be paralleled in a 4-wheel-drive vehicle.

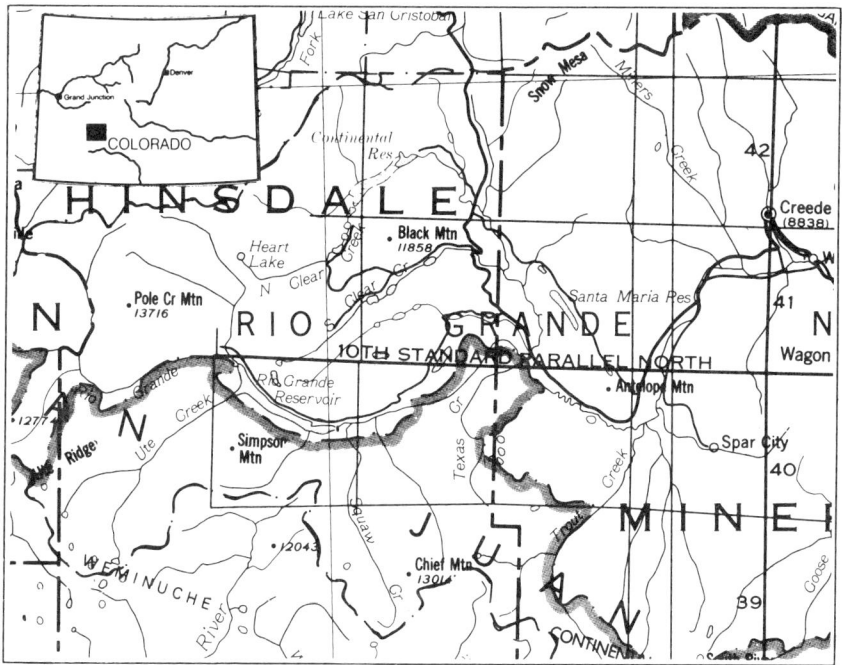

Upper Rio Grande

It averages 4 feet wide and is rated fair in the lower portions for small cutthroat. The upper stretch of the stream is fishless due to the acidity of the water from old mine drainage.

Pole Creek enters Bear Creek from the north near Bear Creek's confluence with the Rio Grande. With its tributaries, Pole Creek offers 20 miles of fishing in streams 8 to 20 feet wide. An easy trail follows Pole Creek from the fork in the road at Bear and Quartzite Creek to Pole headwaters. Pole is open water with good fishing for cutthroat to 12 inches.

Where the Rio Grande feeds into the reservoir from the west, **Lost Trail Creek** also enters the reservoir from the north. A trail less than 0.5 mile west of Lost Trail Campground on the reservoir follows Lost Trail Creek and its tributaries. Access is by trail bike, horse or foot. The western water network in the area offers more than 25 miles of streams averaging 8 feet wide. Both Lost Trail Creek and **West Lost Trail Creek** are small with beaver dams, and are typical high country streams with brook and cutthroat. The upper reaches are accessible by 4-wheel drive from Carson ghost townsite. Inquire at Creede for directions.

UTE CREEK

Ute Creek enters Rio Grande Reservoir from the south near the west end of the reservoir. The Ute Creek trailhead is near the Lost Trail Campground at the west end of the reservoir. Ute Creek has three main forks, all beautiful wilderness streams. Their headwater lakes are probably the most popular lakes in the Weminuche Wilderness.

Ute Creek forks upstream about 6 miles south of the reservoir. **West Ute Creek** offers 5 miles of brushy fishing for small cutthroat, and is rated good. Where the creek forks, the trail also forks, with the western trail following West Ute Creek. At the headwaters of West Ute Creek and southwest of Rio Grande Reservoir, **West Ute Lake** (11,801 ft; 16 ac) is reached by a marked trail from the West Ute Creek Trail. It is heavily fished but rated good for 10- to 16-inch cutthroat, and rainbow to 12 inches.

Upper West Ute Lake (12,000 ft; 4 ac) has bigger cutthroat averaging 14 to 18 inches. It lies less than 1.5 miles northwest of West Ute Lake.

West Ute Creek is also paralleled by a trail leading to its headwater lakes. It is overpopulated with brook. At its headwaters, **East Ute** or **Main Ute Lake** (11,847 ft; 32 ac) is the biggest and deepest headwater lake. It is 125 feet deep. East Ute is 10 miles southwest of Rio Grande Reservoir by trail. It is stocked with cutthroat, and has the biggest fish of all the Ute headwater lakes. Pack in dinner, because fishing can be slow. But if the fish are biting, prepare to catch some splendid large ones.

Just to the west of East Ute Lake by trail are the **Twin Lakes** (11,792 ft; 16 and 4.8 ac). The smaller lake has rainbow and the larger lake has brook 10 to 14 inches. An occasional cutthroat can be caught in either lake.

Northwest of Twin Lakes, less than 2 miles by trail, is **Middle Ute Lake** (11,949 ft; 11.5 ac). It is surrounded by willows and sometimes is called **Willow Lake.** Fishing in this lake is cyclical. One year the catches all will be small, but that indicates the following season will produce large catches. The lake occasionally winterkills; check locally. It is rated good for cutthroat 10 to 14 inches.

Weminuche Creek enters the Rio Grande Reservoir from the south just 4 miles east of Ute Creek, and is regarded as a basic brook trout stream. It too drains the high peaks of the Weminuche Wilderness and offers fishing from a trail paralleling the stream for about 5 miles. The trail leads over Weminuche Pass to the headwaters of the Los Pinos River which flows south to the New Mexico border and the Navajo Reservoir.

To the east of Weminuche Creek about 2.5 miles, **Big Squaw Creek** enters the Rio Grande River from the south, just east of the Rio Grande Reservoir. Big Squaw Creek stretches about 10 miles south to Continental Divide in the San Juan Mountains in the Weminuche Wilderness. A trail follows the stream from Thirtymile Campground, near the mouth of the reservoir, to its headwaters. The upper stretches of the stream have brook, and the lower stretches, near the reservoir, have brook and brown to 16 inches. At the headwaters of Big Squaw Creek, north of the Continental Divide, **Squaw Lake** (11,650 ft; 10 ac) has a naturally produced brook population. It is a fluctuating reservoir that predates the wilderness designation.

Little Squaw Creek, about 1.5 miles east of Big Squaw Creek and 2 miles east of Rio Grande Reservoir, also enters the Rio Grande River from the south. It enters at River Hill Campground on the road leading to the reservoir. It has tremendous food forage, promoting rapid fish growth; it is not uncommon for a fish to gain 2 pounds in 18 months. It is a cutthroat stream good for trout 10 to 14 inches. There is no trail to the lower portion of the stream, but the upper portion can be reached by the trail from Thirtymile Campground.

NORTHERN TRIBUTARIES

Crooked Creek flows from the northwest, and enters the Rio Grande near Spring Creek Reservoir Campground on Hwy 149, about 10 miles downriver from Rio Grande Reservoir. A road from Bristol View Ranger Station follows the creek about 3 miles to the foot of Crooked Canyon. Crooked Creek, **House Creek** immediately to the south and **Regan Lake** (10,100 ft; 90 ac) have stocked brook and rainbow, some to 14 and 16 inches..

Just south of Crooked Creek and southeast of Regan Lake, **Road Canyon Reservoir** (9725 ft; 100 ac) is located on the road leading to Rio Grande Reservoir. Road Canyon Reservoir has been a research site over the last 15 years, including research with aerator pumps. These electric pumps circulate the water, capturing oxygen and reducing winterkill that is common to shallow lakes. The reservoir offers good fishing for brook up to 2 pounds and rainbow up to 5 pounds. At the south end of Road Canyon Reservoir is Road Canyon Campground.

CLEAR CREEK AREA

Clear Creek enters the Rio Grande from the north just 3.5 miles southeast of Spring Creek Reservoir Campground on Hwy 149. About 3.25 miles upstream from its confluence with the Rio Grande River, Clear Creek forks to become North Clear Creek and South Clear Creek. At the fork is South Clear Creek Campground on Hwy 149, north of Spring Creek Reservoir Campground.

North Clear Creek is crossed by Hwy 149. It flows from the northwest and the northern San Juan Mountains. North Clear is the larger of the two forks. At its headwaters is **Heart Lake** (11,600 ft; 30 ac). Heart is a shallow lake, but it usually does not winterkill. Reach Heart Lake by turning west off of Hwy 149 at South Clear Creek Falls Campground. The road leads past Brown Lakes, then forks. Follow the northern road to Pearl and Castle Rock lakes. From there, travel is by 4-wheel drive for about 5 miles west. Heart has a naturally produced brook population, with brook up to 15 inches; most average 10 to 12 inches.

Pearl (10,350 ft) and **Castle Rock Lakes,** just to the east of Heart Lake, are private lakes.

Downstream about 2.5 miles from Castle Rock Lake, **Continental Reservoir** (10,300 ft; 50 ac) has been drained and restocked with catchable size and subcatchable Snake River cutthroat, rainbow and brook. Continental Reservoir can be reached by vehicle by turning west off Hwy 149 near the North Clear Creek Falls Campground. The road to Rito Hondo Reservoir has been improved and graveled. Continental has a new boat ramp and toilet facilities near it.

Buck, Deadman, Kitty and **Ruby Creeks** flow into North Clear Creek in the Continental Reservoir area. All of these streams are about 5 feet wide, have beaver ponds, and offer good fishing for 10-inch rainbow and cutthroat.

Rito Hondo Reservoir (10,240 ft; 40 ac), just to the east of Continental Reservoir about 2 miles, can be reached by the same road to Continental. Rito Hondo has been stocked with rainbow, but the bulk of the population is brook. An occasional lunker may be lured here, and DOW officials tell of 6-pound brook. No motor-propelled boats or rafts are permitted, but there is a boat ramp on its west shore.

Big Spring Creek enters North Clear Creek from the north at North Clear Creek Falls Overlook Campground, about 12 miles northeast of Rio Grande Reservoir. Big Spring Creek is about 5 miles long and 5 feet wide with some beaver ponds. It is rated fair for small brook, cutthroat and rainbow. One of its main tributaries from the east is **Mesa Creek.** Mesa has no access and is a rugged stream to follow. It has some beaver ponds and is rated fair for small brook, cutthroat and rainbow.

North Clear Creek below the North Clear Creek Falls Overlook Campground to its confluence with Clear Creek has cutthroat, brook and some rainbow. Portions of the stream flow through posted private property, and fishing is by permission only.

South Clear Creek feeds into Clear Creek from the west and is crossed by Hwy 149 at South Clear Creek Falls Campground. The upper reaches of South Clear Creek are private, including some of its headwater lakes lying less than 5 miles north of Rio Grande Reservoir. These lakes include **Lost Lakes** and **Hermit Lake.** Hermit Lake is a private fishing club and was the first U.S. Homestead Permit issued for the purpose of commercial fishing. Near Hwy 149 on South Clear Creek, **Brown Lakes** (9840 ft; 180 total ac) have rainbow and brook from 8 to 15 inches. Access to these lakes is gained by turning west at South Clear Creek Falls Campground. No camping is permitted at either lake. Both lakes are very shallow, the farthest west lake being about 9 feet deep and the eastern lake about 7 feet deep. These lakes sometimes winterkill, but aeration by electric pump has reduced winterkill. Brown Lakes are stocked with cutthroat, rainbow, brown and brook. Fishing is good for rainbow 12 to 14 inches.

TEXAS CREEK

Texas Creek enters the Rio Grande from the south at about the same point that Clear Creek enters from the north, 18 miles southwest of Creede. Texas Creek stretches more than 10 miles south in the Weminuche Wilderness. Access to its headwaters is by hiking the Fern Creek Trail off Hwy 149 about 16 miles southwest of Creede. The stream is rated good for small brook in the upper meadows, and brown and rainbow in the lower stretches of the stream.

Fern Creek is a very small, fishless tributary of the Rio Grande about 2 miles east of Texas Creek. The Fern Creek Trail leads about 3 miles to the Fern Creek headwater lakes. The first lake by trail is **Little Ruby Lake** (11,250 ft; 3 ac). Little Ruby Lake is about 19 feet deep and occasionally winterkills. It is stocked with rainbow and brook, and is rated good. South of Little Ruby Lake, **Ruby Lake** (11,290 ft; 30 ac) is 55 feet deep. It is the site of an old homestead, and cabins are available on a first-come first-served basis. It is rated good for rainbow and brook from 10 to 14 inches.

Trout Creek is the next major tributary downstream to the east. It enters the Rio Grande from the south. It stretches more than 13 miles along the Weminuche Wilderness northeast boundary. Its **West** and **East Forks** are the wilderness. Access to Trout Creek to where it enters the wilderness is over a rough road; from the wilderness boundary to its headwaters, travel is by foot or hoof only. Road access is about 6 miles southwest of Creede south to Spar City. Follow the road until it forks; stay with the western fork for access to Trout Creek. The creek averages 20 feet wide and is rated fair for cutthroat near the headwaters, and fair for 8- to 10-inch brown and rainbow in the lower reaches. At the headwaters of West Trout Creek, **Trout Lake** (11,685 ft; 24 ac) is in the Weminuche Wilderness. In the early 1900s, farmers and their draft horses dammed the east end of the lake for irrigation. The lake is still used for irrigation, but a conservation pool agreement maintains the lake at about 18-foot depth. It has cutthroat 10 to 18 inches.

Middle Creek enters the Rio Grande from the south less than 0.25 mile east of Trout Creek. It reaches south about 10 miles, and access is by a rough road that reaches its headwaters. Take the Spar City road where it leaves Hwy 149 about 6 miles southwest of Creede. When the road forks, follow the west fork.

About 5 miles upstream from Middle Creek's confluence with the Rio Grande, **Love Lake** (10,000 ft; 5 ac) lies on Middle Creek. It is a 9-foot-deep lake accessible by car and rated good for small brook and rainbow with an occasional lunker brown taken. There are campsites on the lake. No motor-propelled boats or rafts are permitted.

Red Mountain Creek is a major tributary of Middle Creek. It enters Middle Creek from the east and flows from the south. Follow the Spar City road, turn south just before reaching Spar City to the Ivy Creek Campground. A rough road follows Red Mountain Creek to its headwaters. Portions of the river are on private property. This stream is rated poor because a flood in the early 1970s damaged the canyon. Even thouth it has been restocked, it has never regained its reputation as a good fishing stream. **Ivy Creek** is a tributary of Red Mountain Creek entering from the east and flowing from the south. Its upper stretches are in the wilderness. It is about 6 feet wide, and rated fair to good for 8- to 10-inch cutthroat.

Lime Creek is to the east of Red Mountain and Ivy creeks. It enters the Rio Grande from the south about 9 miles southwest of Creede. Take the Spar City road south from Hwy 149 west of Creede. Lime Creek runs through Spar City. The stream contains small brook, but is rated poor for fishing.

CREEDE AREA

The next main stream entering the Rio Grande comes from the north to meet the Rio Grande near Rio Grande Campground, southwest of Creede about 8 miles. **Seepage Creek, Ghost Lake** and **Seepage Lakes** exist as long as the water level in **Santa Marie Reservoir** (9470 ft; 350 ac) is kept filled above the 8000-ft level. When the reservoir drops below this level, Seepage Creek and lakes dry up. The lakes have a geological foundation that will not hold water if they are not receiving as much water as is flowing out. Santa Marie Reservoir is a private trout club. And Seepage Lakes, Upper (30 ac when full), Lower (20 ac when full) and Ghost Lake (8 ac when full) have rainbow 8 to 16 inches. Inquire locally before planning to fish Seepage and Ghost lakes.

Miners Creek flows into the Rio Grande from the north, 3 miles west of Creede. It feeds from the northern San Juan Mountains. Access is by trail bike, foot or horse. The first 3 miles are accessible by a rough dirt road, the rest by trail. Turn north off Hwy 149 just west of Creede at the "Sunnyside" sign. The stream averages 6 feet wide, is open and has medium-swift waters rated fair for cutthroat in the upper headwater stretches, and fair to good for brook, rainbow and brown in the lower stretches.

Rat Creek is one of the main tributaries of Miners Creek entering from the northeast. It is a steep tumbling stream averaging 4 feet wide, with beaver ponds. Access is by driving northwest out of Creede on 4-wheel-drive road. The upper reaches of Rat Creek are good for brook. The lower stretches are on private land.

Deep Creek, about 8 miles long, enters the Rio Grande from the south, 2 miles due south of Creede. Access to the mouth of Deep Creek is by driving to the southeast corner of Creede airport. A trail from a parking area on the south side of the Rio Grande follows the stream from near the airport to the headwaters. Or the headwaters may be reached by driving to Spar City and from there to the end of the road. Deep Creek averages 3 feet wide; it is open and swift, offering good fishing for small brook.

Willow Creek enters the Rio Grande from the north. It flows through Creede and meets the Rio Grande about 2 miles south. About a mile north of Creede, Willow Creek forks. **West Willow Creek** begins at San Luis Pass in Gunnison National Forest. Access is by car on a rough road north out of Creede. **East Willow Creek** also feeds from the Continental Divide and access is easy by car; access to the upper half is by 4-wheel drive only. Fishing is good in the forks for brook. Willow Creek just south of the forks and through Creede has no fish. In the 1890s, zinc dumps precluded any fish life. The habitat is poor and the channel often changes direction, making it an undesirable stretch of river to rehabilitate.

BELLOWS CREEKS

Bellows Creek lies east of Willow Creek and Creede about 5.5 miles, and enters the Rio Grande from the north. For 5 miles upstream from the confluence with the Rio Grande, it is closed, private land. Bellows forks at this point, and **West Bellows Creek** offers 8 miles of excellent fishing in a 10-foot-wide stream for brook and brown to 12 inches. The water is open but not swift; some beaver ponds. West Bellows headwaters are in the Wheeler Geologic Area, a spectacular, colorful rock formation set aside to perpetuate the beauty and uniqueness of this area. Access to the headwaters of West Bellows and Wheeler Geologic Area is from Wagon Wheel Gap on Hwy 149. This 4-wheel-drive road is sometimes closed in the spring when the road becomes boggy; check locally.

East Bellows Creek flows just east of West Bellows. It is a swift, 5-foot-wide stream. It is a unique stream because it doesn't freeze over. It is fed by warm spring waters. Access to the upper reaches of East Bellows is by 4-wheel drive, north from Wagon Wheel Gap.

Goose Creek enters the Rio Grande from the south near Wagon Wheel Gap on Hwy 149. A rough road follows the stream south to its headwaters and lakes in the Weminuche Wilderness. Goose Creek is about 12 miles long and about 6 feet wide, and supports cutthroat and brook to 12 inches. The water is open with a few beaver dams. Campsites are plentiful and scenic, but in the lower stretches, from Lake Humphreys at the wilderness boundary downstream, are mostly private holdings.

Fisher Creek is a main tributary of Goose Creek about 2 miles above Humphreys. It heads near South River Peak on the Continental Divide. Both **Lake Humphreys** and **Hay Press Lake** are closed, private lakes. The state has an agreement with the holders of Lake Humphreys for cutthroat eggs, which are planted throughout southwestern Colorado. A trail from Lake Humphreys into the wilderness leads

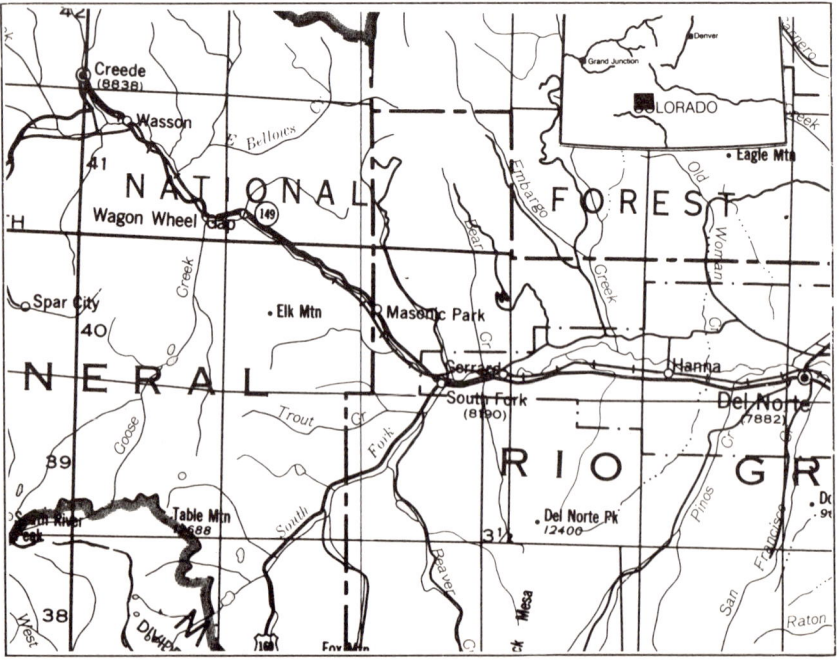

Rio Grande

up Fisher Creek to **Goose Lake** (11,600 ft; 25 ac). The lake is a fluctuating reservoir with a maximum depth of 20 feet. It is usually kept full. The lake is rated good for cutthroat 10 to 18 inches; camping on the lake.

SOUTH FORK

The **South Fork of the Rio Grande** enters the Rio Grande from the southwest at the town of South Fork, about 20 miles east of Creede. It offers 20 miles of fishing; the lower 10 miles are paralleled by US 160. The portion of the river upstream not paralleled by highway is accessible by a trail from Big Meadows Campground on Big Meadows Reservoir. South Fork averages 15 feet wide; it is easily fished and is rated only fair for 10-inch brown, rainbow and some brook up in the higher reaches. Portions of the river are fished with permission only. There are several campgrounds along the highway and stream, south from South Fork to Wolf Creek Pass on the Continental Divide.

Big Meadows Reservoir (9200 ft; 114 ac) is near the Twin Bridges off US 160, about 8 miles north of Wolf Creek Pass. The reservoir has brook to 8 inches and rainbow to 12 inches.

Archuleta Creek flows into Big Meadows Reservoir from the southwest. It is a small stream, about 4 feet wide, with small cutthroat. At its headwaters, **Archuleta Lake** (11,700 ft; 13 ac) in the Weminuche Wilderness Area is rated good for 10- to 16-inch cutthroat and brook.

Hope Creek enters the South Fork from the west about a mile downstream from Big Meadows Reservoir. A road going north from Big Meadows leads to Hope Creek. Reach the headwaters by foot or horse. Just north of Hope Creek, **Shaw Reservoir** (9850 ft; 20 ac) can be reached by road. Shaw suffers partial winterkill, but it has ample feed and offers good fishing for cutthroat and rainbow. Fishing is prohibited as posted from May 20 to June 20.

When the road leaves the South Fork, about 12 miles south of the town of South Fork, it follows **Pass Creek** over Wolf Creek Pass. Pass Creek enters the South Fork from the southeast. A rough road parts from US 160 to the east and runs past Tucker Ponds Campground to the headwaters of Pass Creek. The stream averages 6 to 10 feet wide and is partially brushy. Fishing is fair for rainbow, brook and cutthroat. Several small lakes are along the stream, including **Pass Creek Lake** (9500 ft; 1.5 ac), which lies on US 160 about 4.5 miles north of Wolf Creek Pass. The lake sometimes winterkills, but is rated fair for 6- to 10-inch rainbow. The two **Tucker Ponds** (9700 ft; 1.5 ac and 2.5 ac) lie off of US 160 to the east. Access to the ponds and the Tucker Ponds Campground is by taking the access road about 4.5 miles north of Wolf Creek Pass. These ponds are stocked with rainbow and some brook. **Alberta Park Reservoir** (10,200 ft; 30 ac) can be reached by turning east off US 160 about 1.5 miles north of Wolf Creek. This reservoir is near the headwaters of a Pass Creek tributary and is rated fair for 6- to 12-inch rainbow and brook.

Farther north, **Lake Creek** enters the South Fork from the west, about 10 miles south of the town of South Fork. The creek is good fishing for small brook. **Hunters Lake** (11,400 ft; 8 ac) is about 7 miles north of Big Meadows Reservoir. It is rated good for brook, but sometimes winterkills. Take the road north from Big Meadows Lake to reach Hunters Lake.

PARK CREEK

Park Creek enters the South Fork from the southeast about 7 miles south of the

---

Ramble House
Alton and Virginia Cole
P. O. Box 116
Creede, Colorado 81130
Phone (303) 658-2482

Fishing Tackle • Gifts
Cameras • Film • USGS Maps
Excellent Selection of
Productive Flies

town of South Fork. A road going southeast from Park Creek Campground on US 160 parallels the creek to its headwaters near Summit Pass. The creek averages 6 to 12 feet wide. A rough road parallels the stream to its headwaters then loops back to Monte Vista, a beautiful all-day drive. Park Creek is stocked with catchable rainbow, and offers good fishing for browns, cutthroat and brook. It receives a lot of fishing pressure.

Another major tributary of South Fork is **Beaver Creek,** which also enters from the east, about 4 miles south of South Fork at Highway Springs Campground. Access is by taking the secondary road a mile south of the town of South Fork. The road roughly parallels US 160 for about 3 miles, then follows Beaver Creek southeast to its headwaters. About 10 miles upstream at Beaver Creek headwaters is **Poage Lake** (11,100 ft; 12 ac). The lake produces huge cutthroat, though difficult to catch.

Race Creek is a tributary of Beaver Creek that enters Beaver from the east about 5 miles downstream from Poage Lake. It is rated fair to good for small cutthroat and brook. The stream is about 10 miles long, but has no access trail. The upper reaches are accessible by a rough road from Poage Lake, or by a 4-wheel-drive road from Cross Creek near Beaver Creek Reservoir. At the headwaters of Race Creek are **Crystal Lakes** (11,300 ft; 10 ac). Upper Crystal has brook, although it sometimes winter-kills, and Lower Crystal Lake is good fishing for brook to 12 inches.

Cross Creek is another tributary of Beaver Creek which enters from the east about a mile upstream of Beaver Creek Reservoir. Cross is a narrow 3-foot-wide stream that is a little brushy; poor fishing.

Beaver Creek Reservoir (8763 ft; 110 ac) is about 2 miles from the confluence of Beaver Creek and the South Fork. It is rated good for brook, rainbow, brown and some kokanee. A steep boat ramp is located at its southern end.

Millions Reservoir (8700 ft; 4 ac) is a small pond located less than a mile east of South Fork on the Beaver Creek Road. It is stocked with put-and-take rainbow.

North of the town of South Fork, **Alder Creek** enters the Rio Grande. Its lower 3 miles are on private land and posted. A road follows **West Alder Creek,** and then forks east to provide access to the upper reaches of all branches of Alder Creek. Alder and all its forks are rated fair for small rainbow, brook and brown.

GOLD MEDAL TROUT WATERS

The stretch of the Rio Grande from just above the town of South Fork, downstream 22.5 miles to Del Norte has been tagged gold medal trout waters. This honor brings some special restrictions. The portion of the river from Masonic Park, west of South Fork, to the Coller Bridge is restricted to the use of artificial flies and lures only, and daily bag and possession limits for trout are two fish. All brown taken under 16 inches in length must be returned to the water. This section of the river, about 2.5 miles, is heavily fished. Anglers are making off with the fastest growing, more aggressive brown. Downstream from South Fork, the Rio Grande flows mostly through private holdings, but several sections have been leased for public fishing. A total of 7.68 miles of the river between South Fork and Del Norte are open to public fishing. Check locally for exact locations. Look for signs indicating open fishing.

Willow Creek flows into the Rio Grande from the south about a mile east of the town of South Fork. Its upper reaches are accessible by a rough road south from Gerrard on US 160. Willow is a brushy stream with little or no fishing.

Embargo Creek enters the Rio Grande from the north about 5 miles east of the town of South Fork. A rough road from US 160 leads to the headwaters of this stream and Cathedral Campground. The lower portion of Embargo cuts through private land, and 5 miles of the headwater stream are open by trail only. On US 160, just east of Gerrard about 4 miles, turn north to cross the Granger Bridge. Drive 10 miles to Cathedral Campground. Road continues about 1 mile to the Embargo Creek trailhead. Embargo Creek is rated fair for cutthroat in the higher reaches, and browns in the lower reaches.

DEL NORTE AREA

Pinos Creek enters the Rio Grande from the south, 3 miles west of Del Norte. A paved road traveling southwest from Del Norte parallels Pinos to its highest reaches. Pinos is rated fair for brown and brook to 10 inches. **Burro Creek** enters Pinos Creek from the east about 10 miles upstream from the Pinos-Rio Grande confluence. It is rated fair for small brook. On the East Fork of Burro Creek, **Fuchs Reservoir** (9700 ft; 20 ac) can be reached by the road running parallel to Pinos. Fuchs is often drained very low causing some fish loss; but otherwise it can be good for rainbow.

The Rio Grande flows southeast into the San Luis Valley as it leaves Del Norte. The force of the river is greatly reduced from this point as irrigation drawdowns increase.

East of Monte Vista, **Home,** or **Sherman Lake** (7627 ft; 67 ac), is on the Soldiers Home Road. It is stocked with pike, channel catfish and rainbow. Usually the best fishing on Home Lake is in the spring or winter when pike up to 4 pounds are taken.

ALAMOSA RIVER

About 2 miles south of Alamosa and 25 miles southeast of Monte Vista, the **Alamosa River** enters the Rio Grande. It is a 25- to 30-foot-wide stream with poor fishing near its mouth. Pollution from old mines has ruined this stretch. Above the lower 3 miles, Alamosa River is rated poor to fair for 8- to 10-inch rainbow and a few small brook and cutthroat. The Alamosa River, Alamosa Campground and Terrace or Alamosa Reservoir can be reached by turning west off US 285 onto Hwy 15, about 12 miles south of Alamosa. **Alamosa Reservoir** (825 ft; 150 ac) is a greatly fluctuating water body that drains dry at times. Alamosa River above the reservoir offers no fishing. Alamosa River below the reservoir has some cutthroat and rainbow. The lower reaches of the river are on private land and are not stocked.

LA JARA CREEK

La Jara Creek flows from the west and enters the Rio Grande at the town of La Jara, 13 miles south of Alamosa on US 285. Hwy 15 west from La Jara provides access to La Jara and its headwaters. At the headwaters of La Jara Creek, **La Jara Reservoir** (9700 ft; 800 ac) is rated good for 10-inch brook. Boats and motors are allowed, but are not available to rent. There are primitive campsites on the reservoir. A spring at the upper end of the reservoir provides drinkable water. Several small streams feed into La Jara Reservoir including **Upper La Jara Creek,** which contains brook. **Torsido** and **Jim Creeks** are posted no fishing. The Rio Grande cutthroat, a protected species, has been introduced to these streams.

Jarosa Creek feeds into La Jara Creek from the west about 2.5 miles downstream from the reservoir. It is rated good for brown and brook. La Jara Creek below the reservoir is fair for brook.

About 30 miles southeast of Alamosa, **Sanchez Reservoir** (2000 ac) is at the headwaters of **Culebra Creek,** which enters the Rio Grande from the east. The reservoir is about 5 miles south of the of town San Luis. About 20 miles south of Alamosa on US 285, take Hwy 142 east about 30 miles to San Luis. The reservoir is about 5 miles south of town. Fishing at Sanchez has improved remarkably in recent years with yellow perch going to 14 inches, and 30- to 40-pound northern pike offering the best fishing. Some walleye are taken. There are no trout, bass or crappie. There is an improved boat ramp.

CONEJOS RIVER

The notable fishing in this area is on the beautiful **Conejos River,** which offers some of the better fishing in the state. The river starts from the north near the town of Platoro, about 25 miles southwest of Del Norte. From Platoro, the Conejos runs south through the Rio Grande National Forest, along the South San Juan Wilderness, then cuts east along Hwy 17 near the town of Antonito, where it crosses US 285. From there the river flows north to meet the Rio Grande River. In all, the river is more than 75 miles long. And the best fishing on thr Conejos is west of US 285 and Antonito.

Conejos, Spanish for rabbits, is the largest tributary of the Rio Grande. Portions of the stream have been designated wild trout waters and are subject to special fishing restrictions.

Most of the eastern portion of the Conejos flows through private land; however, the section of the river west of Mogote, on Hwy 17 about 5 miles west of Antonito, to the headwaters offers about 60 miles of fishing that is open to the public. Some 20 miles of the Conejos have received stream improvements to enhance fishing. Also, several new leases have been obtained and are indicated by signs. This is an exceptionally scenic valley with high cliffs and ramparts. The stream averages 60 feet wide through this section, and flows through a canyon. It is a beautiful mountain stream with abundant pools and riffles. The upper portion offers mostly brown, and the lower portion offers good fishing for brown and rainbow.

The Conejos is easily fished and wadable, except during spring high water. At Elk Creek Campground on Hwy 17, about 20 miles west of Antonito, a road parts north to the headwaters of the Conejos. East of this road junction, a portion of the river near Aspen Glade Campground on Hwy 17, has been designated wild trout waters and is restricted to artificial flies and lures.

Platoro Reservoir (9970 ft; 800 ac) is near the headwaters of Conejos, just west of the town of Platoro. It fluctuates greatly but offers very good fishing for rainbow and brown. Boat rentals are available.

Upstream from Platoro Reservoir, **North Fork, Middle Fork of Conejos** and **El Rito Azul** are locally known as the Three Forks. A road to Platoro Reservoir ends at the reservoir and a trail leads to the Three Forks which are in the South San Juan Wilderness. Another fork entering the Platoro Reservoir from the west, **Adams Fork,** also is accessible by trail only. These streams average 6 to 18 feet wide and, combined, offer about 25 miles of fishing. They contain cutthroat, brook and brown.

Mix Lake (9970 ft; 25 ac) lies at the east end of Platoro Reservoir, with Mix Lake Campground on its north shore. It is a put-and-take lake rated fair for rainbow. It sometimes winterkills. Northeast of Mix Lake is **Kerr Lake** (11,300 ft; 50 ac), which is rated excellent for cutthroat. It is restricted to artificial flies and lures only. Access is over a rough road leading from Mix Lake.

LAKE FORK

The **Lake Fork of Conejos** enters the Conejos from the west about 8 miles south of the town of Platoro. Portions of this stream have been designated wild trout waters. Since the Rio Grande cutthroat was introduced to the stream fishing is subject to special restrictions to help establish and maintain this species. A road south of Lake Fork Campground leads about 0.5 mile west to the trailhead for Lake Fork. Stay on the road for quicker access to the headwaters of Lake Fork and another trail leading to **Big Lake** (9800 ft; 15 ac) on the Lake Fork. Both Big Lake and **Rock Lake** (9650 ft; 5 ac) have been stocked with the Rio Grande cutthroat (a protected species) and offer only catch-and-release fishing. They have been designated wild trout waters, and are restricted to artificial lures and flies.

Saddle Creek enters the Conejos from the west just below Lake Fork. It forms the northern border of the South San Juan Wilderness. It is very swift, brushy and difficult to fish, but rated good for small cutthroat, rainbow and brook. A Forest Service road follows the creek for about 6 miles. Sign reads Conejos Peak and Tobacco Lake.

Tobacco Lake (12,250 ft; 20 ac) is at the headwaters of Saddle Creek, just inside the wilderness. A trail leads 2 miles to the lake. It and **Bear Lake** (11,500 ft; 25 ac), feeding Saddle Creek closer to its confluence with Conejos River, are very temperamental high mountain wilderness lakes. When the fishing is good, it is very good for rainbow and cutthroat.

SOUTH FORK

The **South Fork of Conejos** enters the main stream from the west 32 miles west of Antonito and about 6 miles downstream from Lake Fork Campground. It is about 12 feet wide, stretching 14 miles through the scenic country of the South San Juan Wilderness. A trail from the Conejos River follows the stream to its headwaters and several of its headwater lakes. The South Fork offers easy fishing for rainbow, brook, cutthroat and some brown to 11 inches. It is rated very good. **Blue Lake** (11,000 ft; 30 ac) is 12 miles up the South Fork. Access to it is good from Platoro Reservoir, following the Rito Azul drainage. Blue is rated good for brook and a few cutthroat.

Canyon Rincon is a tributary stream of the South Fork entering from the north 4 miles downstream from Blue Lake. It is a small and fast stream, supporting only a few small cutthroat.

At the headwaters of Canyon Rincon, **Twin Lakes** (11,700 ft; 2 ac each) are good for rainbow averaging 12 inches, with the western lake being the best. **Glacier Lake** (11,950 ft; 15 ac) at the head of the South Fork, and less than a mile from Twin Lakes, is rated fair for rainbow from 12 to 15 inches.

Timber Lake (11,300 ft; 12 ac), also feeding into Canyon Rincon, is rated fair to good for 12-inch cutthroat and rainbow. It lies 2 miles south of Twin Lakes, 12 miles from the Conejos.

Other lakes in this area include **Green Lake** (11,550 ft; 15 ac) at the head of Canyon Verde. **Canyon Verde** is rated very good for small cutthroat and rainbow. And Green Lake offers good fishing for rainbow and cutthroat averaging 12 inches. Follow the trail up the South Fork Conejos and head south up Canyon Verde drainage.

Trail Lake (12,000 ft; 20 ac) is a long, narrow temperamental lake at the top of the Continental Divide, 3 miles past Green Lake. It is rated fair for rainbow from 15 inches to 5 pounds.

Hansen Creek, a tributary of South Fork, feeding from the north just 3 miles above the mouth of South Creek, provides 4 miles of fishing in a 6-foot-wide stream. It is brushy at its lower end and rated good for 10- to 12-inch cutthroat and brook. No trails lead into this drainage.

No Name Lake (11,350 ft; 10 ac) is just south of the South Fork Conejos River. It can be reached by a 7-mile trail from near the Spectacle Lake Campground on the Conejos River Road. Though No Name sometimes winterkills, it can be excellent at times for cutthroat.

The same trail leading to No Name Lake also leads to **Ruybalid Lake** (11,150 ft; 12 ac). This lake gets heavy fishing pressure and is stocked with brook.

SPECTACLE LAKE

Spectacle Lake (9100 ft; 10 ac), near Spectacle Campground on the Conejos River Road, is strictly a put-and-take lake. It is stocked with 8- to 12-inch rainbow and receives heavy fishing.

Elk Creek enters the main Conejos from the south at Elk Creek Campground on Hwy

Waders/hip boots permit the fisherman to avoid catching shrubs and branches

17 where the Conejos River turns from the north and heads east. Elk Creek is about 25 miles west of Antonito. It is 12 feet wide and meanders through three fine meadows. It has brook and brown, mostly small. Elk Creek is excellent fly water, especially above the second meadow; accessible by trail from Elk Creek Campground. Several tributary lakes feed the Elk, including **Beaver Lake** (9600 ft; 4 ac), which is rated fair for 10- to 12-inch cutthroat, and **Rock Lake** (9900 ft; 10 ac), which is a temperamental lake harboring very large cutthroat to 11 pounds. Both of these lakes are about a 3-mile hike from Elk Creek Campground and lie just inside the wilderness boundary. In the same area, **Duck Lake** (10,000 ft; 15 ac) offers good fishing for brook.

South Elk Creek enters the main Elk at the first meadow. It is a 3-foot-wide stream offering fishing very similar to Elk Creek.

There is no trail up South Elk, but the trail leading to La Manga Creek's headwaters and Red Lake also provides access to the upper reaches of South Elk Creek.

BORDER STREAMS

La Manga Creek, an 8-foot-wide, open stream, offers 6 miles of fishing for brook and a few small cutthroat. It enters Elk Creek about 2 miles west of Elk Creek Campground. At its headwaters, **Red Lake** (11,550 ft; 15 ac) contains 12- to 16-inch cutthroat and rainbow, and is rated good. It is in the wilderness area and can be reached by a trail from Hwy 17 about 5.5 miles west of Elk Creek Campground.

Rio de Los Pinos meets the Conejos after dipping through northern New Mexico. It junctions with Conejos northeast of Antonito. It is 10 to 15 feet wide and about 8 miles west of Elk Creek Campground. Less than 15 miles of the stream's headwaters are in Colorado. **Trujillo Meadows Reservoir** (10,000 ft; 70 ac) is near the river's headwaters. It can be reached by a road going north past Neff Mountain near Cumbres Pass on Hwy 17. It is a temperamental body of water, but not as temperamental as the alpine lakes to the north. It has cutthroat and brown.

In this same area, the headwaters of the

KEITH'S TAXIDERMY STUDIO
Fish • Rugs • Wallheads
Life Size Mounts

Keith Daniel 303-852-5865/303-852-3025
9186 S. Rd. 4 E Monte Vista, CO 81144
10 miles S. of Monte Vista, Hwy 15 (gunbarrel) then 4 miles E. on 370, and 3/4 mile north on Rio Grande County 4E.
-OR-
3 miles S. of Alamosa on Hwy 285, 10 miles W. on 370, and 3/4 miles north on Rio Grande County 4E.

Chama River edge into Colorado from New Mexico. A Forest Service road from Lobo Lodge, 5 miles northeast of Chama, New Mexico, leads into the forest where the stream is open to public fishing. The Chama is about 10 feet wide, fairly open, and flows through meadows with pools and riffles. It is good for cutthroat and rainbow averaging 10 inches. The **Chama Lakes** (11,700 ft; 800 ac total) at the headwaters of the Chama river offer poor fishing. Periodically the lakes go dry due to drought. DOW has stopped stocking these lakes. □

U.S. FOREST SERVICE DISTRICT RANGER STATIONS

Creede Ranger District
Rio Grande National Forest
P.O. Box 270
Creede, CO 81130   303/658-2556

Del Norte Ranger District
Rio Grande National Forest
810 Grand Ave., P.O. Box 40
Del Norte, CO 81132   303/657-3321

Alamosa and Conejos Ranger Districts
Rio Grande National Forest
Hwy 285 North, P.O. Box 520 G
La Jara, CO 81140   303/274-5193

Rio Grande National Forest Headquarters
1803 W. Hwy 160
Monte Vista, CO 81144   303/852-5941

Saguache Ranger District
Rio Grande National Forest
626 Gunnison, P.O. Box 67
Saguache, CO 81149   303/655-2547

FISHING TIPS

Grasshoppers and crickets often tempt trout and bass. Hook them through the collar so they will move naturally in the water. Cast upstream and take in line as it floats back. Use a bubble with a spin cast outfit. In lakes, a split shot 1 to 3 feet up from the bait causes it to go down in the water.

Trout in a stream may lie below a log or rock, under an undercut bank, in the deep water of a bend, above a fallen log, in the mouth of a feeder stream, in deep water along a stone ledge or outcropping. Late evening fly fishing is often productive.

Be sure to use a swivel with spinners. They prevent line twisting and make changing lures or flies quick and easy.

U.S. Forest Service campgrounds

U.S. Forest Service compilation was current as of 1985.

Asterisks denote fee areas. Some campgrounds are open only Memorial Day weekend through Labor Day. Below freezing weather could mean no water supply.

RIO GRANDE RIVER DRAINAGE

RIO GRANDE NATIONAL FOREST
Headquarters: 1803 W. Hwy. 160, Monte Vista, CO 81144

Campground name	Elevation	No camp sites	Travel trailers	Drinking water	Length of stay (days)	Location and directions
Marshall Park*	8800	15	Yes	Yes	10	On Colo. 149, 6 mi SW of Creede
Road Canyon	9300	5	Yes	No	—	6 mi SW of Colo 149, 20.5 mi SW of Creede
River Hill*	9300	20	Yes	Yes	14	9.5 mi W of Colo. 149 20.5 mi W of Creede
Thirty Mile*	9300	33	Yes	Yes	14	11 mi SW of Colo. 149, 20.5 mi SW of Creede
North Clear Creek*	9800	25	Yes	Yes	14	2 mi N of Colo. 149, 23 mi W of Creede
Lost Trail	9500	7	Yes	Yes	14	16.5 mi SW of Colo. 149 20.5 mi SW of Creede
South Clear Creek Falls*	9700	11	Yes	Yes	14	On Colo. 149, 24.5 mi SW of Creede
Ivy Creek	9200	4	No	No	—	8.7 mi SW of Colo. 149 6.5 mi SW of Creede
Rio Grande	8900	4	Yes	Yes	—	10 mi SW of Creede on Colo. 149

RIO GRANDE

Name	Elevation					Location
Stormking	9200	11	Yes	Yes	14	14.5 mi NW of La Garita by forest road
Poso	9000	11	Yes	Yes	14	12 mi NW of La Garita by forest road
Palisade*	8300	13	Yes	Yes	10	On Colo. 149, 9.7 mi NW of South Fork
Cross Creek	8900	8	Yes	No	14	6 mi S of US 160, 2.4 mi SW of South Fork
Big Meadows*	9300	45	Yes	Yes	14	2 mi SW of US 160, 12.5 mi SW of South Fork
Upper Beaver*	8800	13	Yes	Yes	—	5.6 mi SW of South Fork on US 160 and forest roads
Beaver Creek*	8700	20	Yes	Yes	14	4.9 mi SW of South Fork on US 160 and forest roads
Park Creek*	8500	13	Yes	Yes	3	On US 160, 8.2 mi SW of South Fork
Tucker Ponds	9700	16	Yes	No	14	2.6 mi S of US 160, 14 mi SW of South Fork
Highway Springs	8400	11	Yes	No	3	On US 160, 5 mi SW of South Fork
Cathedral	9500	29	Yes	Yes	14	11.6 mi N of US 160, 9 mi W of Del Norte
Alamosa*	8600	10	Yes	Yes	—	17 mi W of Colo. 15, 12 mi S of Monte Vista
Stunner	9800	10	Yes	No	—	34 mi W of Colo. 15, 12 mi S of Monte Vista
Rock Creek	9400	13	Yes	Yes	—	13.5 mi SW of Colo. 15, 2 mi S of Monte Vista
Comstock	9500	8	Yes	Yes	—	16.5 mi SW of Colo. 15, 2 mi S of Monte Vista
Lake Fork*	9000	20	Yes	Yes	14	16 mi NW of Colo 17, 23 mi W of Antonito
Mix Lake	10,100	22	Yes	Yes	14	22 mi NW of Colo. 17, 23 mi W of Antonito
Aspen Glade*	8600	34	No	Yes	14	On Colo. 17, 17 mi W of Antonito
Spectacle Lake*	8700	24	No	Yes	14	5 mi NW of Colo. 17, 23 mi W of Antonito
Conejos*	8700	16	No	Yes	14	6 mi NW of Colo. 17, 23 mi W of Antonito
Trujillo Meadows*	10,000	21	No	Yes	14	Off Colo. 17, 40.8 mi W of Antonito
Elk Creek*	8700	31	No	Yes	14	On Colo. 17, 24 mi W of Antonito
Mogote	8400	22	No	Yes	—	15.4 mi W of Antonito on Colo. 17

San Luis Valley
best around the edges

Adjacent communities:
Del Norte, Center, Saguache, Alamosa.

Principal Highways:
U.S. 285, 160; Colo. 114, 17, 150, 15.

Not all of the San Luis Valley is tributary to the Rio Grande as it flows through the valley. There's rewarding fishing in numerous unheralded streams remote from the famed fishery. One of these is **Saguache Creek** in the northwest part of the San Luis Valley. It offers about 50 miles of fishing between its headwaters in Rio Grande National Forest and the water-absorbing valley floor at the charming and historical town of Saguache.

It is one of the longest and best fisheries in the valley. Other creeks coming out of the precipitous Sangre de Cristo Mountains that wall the east side of the valley are short, fast and difficult to reach. Little information about them is available to entice the adventurous fisherman.

Saguache Creek is reached from the north by driving west from Saguache on Highway 114 to North Pass, and about 5 additional miles down the west side; or by going 8 miles east of Gunnison on US 50, then south on Hwy 114. A sign along the highway 5 miles from the pass summit indicates a dirt road leading south to Stone Cellar Campground and Saguache Park. The campground is 15 miles from there, at the confluence of Middle and North Forks of Saguache Creek.

North Fork Saguache Creek is a 5-foot-wide stream with fair fishing for brook and cutthroat. A trail parallels 8 miles of it upstream from the campground.

The headwaters of the **Middle Fork Saguache Creek** are in La Garita Wilderness. The stream is stocked with rainbow and has naturally produced populations of cutthroat and brook. Fishing, from the campground upstream to the wilderness boundary, is with artificial flies and lures as posted. There are many beaver ponds.

At the headwaters of the Middle Fork, **Machin Lake** (pronounced "machine") (12,300 ft; 10 ac) is about 15 miles from the campground; the last 8 miles is by trail. The lake is stocked with cutthroat and a 5- to 6-pounder is not an uncommon catch. The lake occasionally winterkills.

The **South Fork Saguache Creek** also is accessible from the Stone Cellar Campground. A road roughly parallels the stream for 7 miles to the wilderness boundary. The South Fork is good fishing for cutthroat and brook. At the point where the South Fork flows from the wilderness, **Wannamaker Creek** enters from the southeast. Both streams are small and brushy. Wannamaker is rated good for brook and also has a small population of cutthroat.

Below the campground, a 4-wheel-drive road parallels Saguache Creek until it flows through a deep, rugged canyon (sometimes called Box Canyon) and is accessible only by trail. The creek and canyon mouth also are accessible by a road leading southwest from Hwy 114 about 21 miles west of Saguache. The road forks 1.5 miles from the highway, take the right (west) fork to the creek. The road crosses the creek and continues a mile, but leads away from the canyon and the creek. Tributary streams from the southeast include **California Gulch, Johns** and **Bear Creeks,** all with beaver ponds and good fishing for small brook.

As Saguache Creek turns east toward Saguache, it flows through private land for 21 miles. Some sections offer excellent fishing for brown; get permission to fish. Just west of Saguache, 3 miles of stream near Raby Ranch have been leased for public fishing. Inquire in Saguache for exact access.

Sheep Creek enters the Saguache from the north, 21 miles west of Saguache. A dirt road follows upstream about 2 miles to where the road forks. The west fork leads another 6 miles to the upper portion of the stream that has brook. **Spanish Creek,** a western tributary of Sheep, has no fish.

Baldy Lake (11,250 ft; 5 ac) is in the Gunnison National Forest. Access is best from the trail that heads above upper Saguache Forest Service Station. Follow the trail up Sheep Creek and over the Continental Divide. Baldy Lake is stocked and is rated good for 12- to 16-inch rainbow. It sometimes winterkills.

Middle Creek enters the Saguache from the north about 10 miles east of Sheep Creek, about 10 miles west of town. A good dirt road follows the creek 10 miles to the national forest. At the end of the road, continue another 5 miles by trail to the headwaters. Only the portions accessible by trail are open to good brook trout fishing.

The eastern tributaries of Middle Fork, including **East Middle Creek** and **Indian Creek,** offer the same type of fishing as the main stream.

Ford Creek enters the Saguache from the north 0.25 mile east of Middle Fork. Ford flows through private land, but its upper tributary, **Tuttle Creek,** is on Forest Service land. Tuttle is closed to fishing to augment populations of Rio Grande cutthroat which have been introduced.

By the time Saguache Creek reaches town, most of its water has been diverted and what's left is soon soaked into the porous ground of the valley floor.

LA GARITA CREEK

La Garita Creek flows east out of the La Garita Mountains. It is reached via US 285 17 miles north of Monte Vista. Turn west at the sign to the town of La Garita. From town, rough roads parallel the stream and its tributaries. The creek is a small, fairly brushy and ponded stream with small cutthroat, brown and some brook. It is rated fair.

Carnero Creek is a tributary of La Garita flowing from the northwest. Carnero is a small meadow stream with beaver ponds. It is rated fair for small brook and a few cutthroat. The lower 15 miles flow through private property. Tributaries of Carnero, including **South Fork, Cave Creek** and **Miners Creek,** are small with beaver ponds that offer good fishing for brook.

In the San Luis Valley northeast of La Garita and south of Saguache about 10 miles on US 285 is a conglomerate of lakes known as **Russel Lakes.** These lakes are a waterfowl habitat with virtually no fish.

East of the Russel Lakes are the **Mishak Lakes,** which often are dry.

SAN LUIS CREEK

At the north end of the valley, **San Luis Creek** heads near Poncha Pass on US 285. The stream flows through private property its entire length. Fishing is marginal and permission to fish seldom is granted.

South of Poncha Pass on the west side of the valley near the town of Alder, **Clover, Alder** and **Spring Creeks** are small streams with beaver ponds. They offer fishing for small brook. Access is by 4-wheel-drive roads.

About 10 miles south of Alder on US 285 at Villa Grove, **Kerber Creek** enters the San Luis from the west. A road west from Villa

Grove leads to Bonanza. At Bonanza, several tributaries enter Kerber. Its upper reaches and small tributaries include **Upper Kerber, Brewery, Slaughterhouse** and **Elkhorn Gulch Creeks,** and are rated good for small brook. A maze of roads provides access. Inquire at Bonanza. Kerber Creek, below the town of Bonanza, flows fishless through private land.

SANGRE DE CRISTOS

On the east side of the San Luis Valley, several streams flow from the Sangre de Cristo Mountains. Near the town of Mineral Hot Springs, about 5 miles south of Villa Grove, **Garner, Major** and **Black Canyon Creeks** provide fair fishing for small brook. Access is by driving west from Mineral Hot Springs to Valley View Hot Springs.

South of Valley View Hot Springs, several other streams drain the Sangre de Cristos. Access is limited, so chances are good for good fishing. Most of these small streams have a lake at their headwaters. Streams include **Cotton, Wild Cherry** (locally called **Short Creek**), **Rito Alto** and **San Isabel Creeks.** They are brushy and rated fair to good for rainbow and cutthroat; some have brook. Their headwater lakes include **Cotton Lake** (11,500 ft; 11 ac), **Cherry Lake** (11,800 ft; 8 ac), **Rito Alto Lake** (11,300 ft; 7 ac) and **San Isabel Lake** (11,650 ft; 5 ac), offering fair to good fishing for cutthroat. Catching an occasional lunker rainbow is possible from Cotton Lake. Inquire locally about access and fishing.

Farther south along the Sangre de Cristos, due east 12 miles from Moffat, **North** and **South Crestone Creeks** flow from the mountains. A road from the town of Crestone leads about 2 miles northeast of North Crestone Creek Campground. From there a trail leads up the stream to the **Lake Fork of Crestone Creek.** The trail to the north leads to San Isabel and Rito Alto lakes. There is about 5 miles of fishing along North Crestone for cutthroat, rainbow and brook to 10 inches. It is rated fair to good. **North Crestone Lake** (11,800 ft; 15 ac) is 5 miles from North Crestone Campground over a steep, marked trail.

South Crestone Creek flows south of the town of Crestone. Portions of the stream flow through private land. The upper stretches contain brook trout and can be reached by trail from about 1 mile southeast of town. **South Crestone Lake** (11,800 ft; 10 ac) and **Willow Creek Lake** (11,550 ft; 8 ac) are at the headwaters of South Crestone. They are reached by steep rough trails. South Crestone Lake sometimes winterkills, but it is rated fair to good for 10- to 12-inch rainbow and cutthroat. Willow Creek Lake is rated good for 12-inch cutthroat.

Southeast of Crestone in the Sangre de Cristos are **Cottonwood Creek** and **Cottonwood Lake, Deadman Creek, Deadman Lake, Sand Creek, Upper** and **Lower Sand Creek Lakes** and **Little Sand Creek Lake.** These streams and small lakes are difficult to reach because a private land grant blocks access. Generally they have brook and cutthroat.

MEDANO CREEK

Twenty miles west from the town of Mosca on Hwy 17 is **Medano Creek** in Great Sand Dunes National Monument. At the end of the road are Dunes and Pinyon Flats campgrounds. Medano Creek, a brushy, swift stream with small brook and brown, flows along the eastern edge of the monument. It is 12 miles to the headwaters of the stream from the campgrounds. **Medano Lake** (11,500 ft; 4 ac) is accessible by 10 miles of rough 4-wheel-drive road from the campground. The road leads to Medano Pass. A trail from the west side of the pass leads 3 miles to the lake and fair fishing for small brook.

Southeast of Alamosa about 30 miles are two reservoirs on **Trinchera Creek.** Trinchera Creek flows on private property from the east and feeds into the Rio Grande south of Alamosa. **Mountain Home Reservoir** (8145 ft; 639 ac) is 3 miles south of US 160 at Fort Garland. Take Hwy 159. The reservoir offers fishing for rainbow. **Smith Reservoir** (7721 ft; 500 ac) is 3 miles south of US 160 at Blanca and about 7 miles west of Mountain Home Reservoir. Smith offers very good fishing for rainbow averaging 2.5 pounds. ☐

That's where we're headed

DOW FISHING LEASES

COCHETOPA AND PAULINE CREEKS
Coleman easement and lease
Location: 25 miles southeast of Gunnison in Saguache County (20.6 mi of water)

SAGUACHE CREEK
Raby lease
Location: 5 miles northwest of Saguache on Hwy 114 (3.2 mi of Saguache Creek)

U.S. Forest Service campgrounds

U.S. Forest Service compilation was current as of 1985.

Asterisks denote fee areas. Some campgrounds are open only Memorial Day weekend through Labor Day. Below freezing weather could mean no water supply.

NORTHERN SAN LUIS VALLEY

RIO GRANDE NATIONAL FOREST
Headquarters: 1803 W. Hwy. 160, Monte Vista, CO 81144

Campground name	Elevation	No camp sites	Travel trailers	Drinking water	Length of stay (days)	Location and directions
Luders Creek	10,000	6	Yes	Yes	—	11 mi NW of Colo. 114 22 mi NW of Saguache
Stone Cellar	9500	3	Yes	Yes	—	30 mi SW of Saguache off Colo. 114
Buffalo Pass	9100	30	Yes	Yes	—	.2 mi S of Colo. 114, 27.6 mi NW of Saguache
North Crestone Creek*	8300	14	Yes	Yes	—	1 mi S of Crestone by forest road

Southwest rivers opportunities bypassed

Adjacent communities:
Pagosa Springs, Arboles, Bayfield, Durango, Ignacio, Mancos, Cortez.

Principal Highways:
U.S. 160, 550; Colo. 151, 172, 140.

In south-southwest Colorado, 10 south-flowing streams rise clear and cold in the mountains, then cascade into some of the least-frequented terrain in the state, much of it a part of the Southern Ute Indian Reservation.

These streams are the Navajo and San Juan rivers, the Rio Blanco, the Piedra and Los Pinos rivers, Vallecito Creek and the Florida, Animas, La Plata and Mancos rivers. They flow out of the pine and aspen of San Juan National Forest into the vast arid pinon-juniper country and, as they do, the fishing goes from delightful to scant.

Three major bodies of water provide fishing and other recreation in this area between Pagosa Springs, Durango and Mancos. They are Navajo Reservoir on the Colorado-New Mexico state line, and Vallecito and Lemon reservoirs northeast of Durango. Echo Canyon and Pastorious reservoirs and Capote Lake also offer convenient angling and other water recreation.

Logging and Forest Service roads web the area, but in the Weminuche Wilderness Area, north of US 160, access is by foot or hoof only. The Weminuche Wilderness Area is in the San Juan and Rio Grande National forests along the Continental Divide.

The Southern Ute Tribe has developed an extensive tourism program and stocks some of the better angling waters and manages campgrounds and other facilities. A tribal fishing permit is required. See special insert elsewhere in this chapter for particulars.

NAVAJO RIVER

The San Juan River drainage is spread throughout the San Juan National Forest just west of the Divide. Its far eastern fork is the **Navajo River.** There are several small streams feeding the Navajo that offer good angling. Some of the higher streams are seldom fished. Much of the river flows on private lands which are stocked in exchange for public access. Check before casting.

The western forks of the Navajo River offer marginal fishing. Where the Navajo River meets the San Juan River on the Southern Ute Indian Reservation, there is good catfishing. The Navajo River intersects US 84 about 3 miles northwest of Chromo.

Navajo Reservoir (6085 ft; 3000 ac on the Colorado side of the Colorado-New

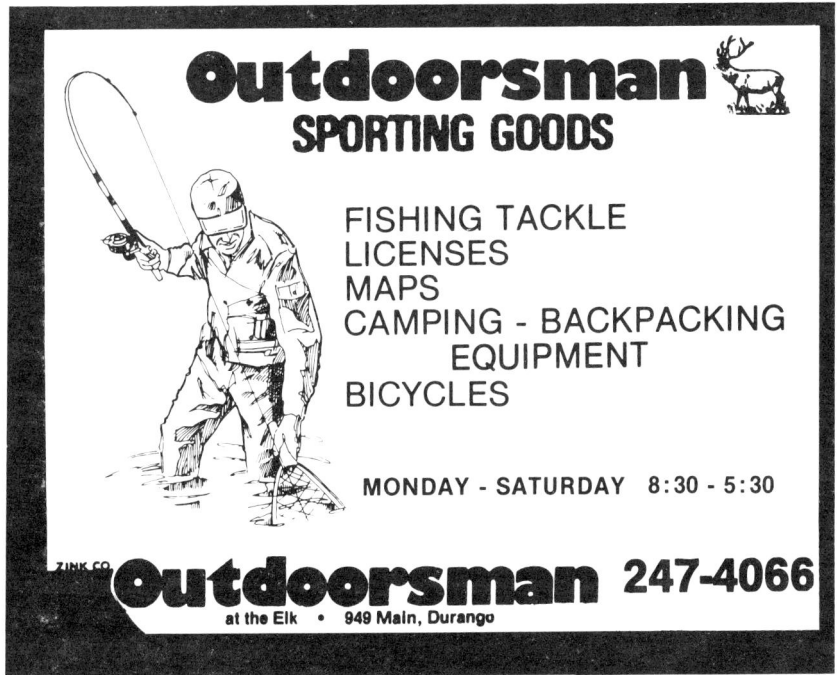

Mexico state line) is a fluctuating water body formed behind Navajo Dam. The reservoir is fed by the Piedra, Los Pinos and San Juan rivers. A Ute Indian fishing permit is required.

The New Mexico side of the 35-mile-long reservoir has some 12,600 surface acres. A New Mexico fishing license is required of anglers in that part of the reservoir.

The reservoir has large- and smallmouth bass, rainbow and brown trout, bluegill, northern pike and crappie. Boat registration and inspection stickers from either state are valid on the reservoir. The boat ramp at Arboles is huge and there is a visitor center and camping with showers and flush toilets as well as RV dump facilities.

May and June is a good time for crappie near Arboles Marina. The Piedra and San Juan arms of the reservoir offer large catfish. Spring and fall on the Piedra arm are good for trout, and the small, brushy coves on the north side of the reservoir offer good bass fishing.

Located on pinon-juniper land, the reservoir fluctuates a lot. The area is very hot and dry in summer. Service facilities are available at Arboles, just west of the reservoir.

Accessibility is from Pagosa Springs by a 40-mile gravel road west and north of the San Juan River. From Chimney Rock, access is 7 miles east on US 160 and then south on Hwy 151. From Durango, take Hwy 172 southeast via Ignacio about 35 miles.

SAN JUAN RIVER

The **San Juan River** has widely dispersed tributaries. The East and West Forks join at Saddle Back Ranch, 13 miles north of Pagosa Springs. The river then flows southward and, at the New Mexico state line, meanders west in and out of the two states and finally enters the Navajo Reservoir in Colorado near Arboles. Not real swift, rather shallow and rocky bottomed, it is easily worked and usually wadable except in early season. The San Juan offers 40 miles of fishing for rainbow, brown, a few brook and cutthroat averaging 10 inches; some larger have been taken below Pagosa Springs. US 160 parallels the river upstream nine miles from Pagosa Springs toward Wolf Creek Pass. About 20 per cent of the river above Pagosa to the Forest Service boundary is tightly posted; the rest is open by permission.

Northeast of Pagosa Springs, the **East Fork of San Juan** is about 10 miles long and unwadable until mid-July. It muddies rapidly after rainfall. This fly fishing stream contains rainbow, cutthroat, and brook to 13 inches, and an occasional brown. Turn east off US 160 about 11 miles northeast of Pagosa Springs to East Fork Campground. **Crater Lake** (11,000 ft; 22 ac), at the head of East Fork, is stocked and rated good for cutthroat to 12 inches. Access is by 4-mile hike from Elwood Pass. **Quartz Creek** enters the East Fork of San Juan about 8 miles upstream from East Fork Campground. It is a 5-mile creek paralleled by a good trail. Quartz Creek is a heavy, canyon stream, offering cutthroat to 15 inches on flies. Rated good. **Quartz Lake** (11,500 ft; 3 ac) is reached by a good but steep trail 5 miles from the junction of Quartz Creek and East Fork. It is a timberline lake with cutthroat to 13 inches. Rated fair to good. Best access is by trail at the end of Mill Creek Road. This gravel road junctions with US 84 about 0.25 mile south of US 160 at Pagosa Springs. Road runs 12 miles, then a 4.5-mile hike on trail to lake—first 2 miles steep. **Sand Creek** enters the East Fork from the south 3 miles upstream from East Fork Campground. A small mountain stream 3- to 5-feet wide, it offers 6 miles of trail fishing for

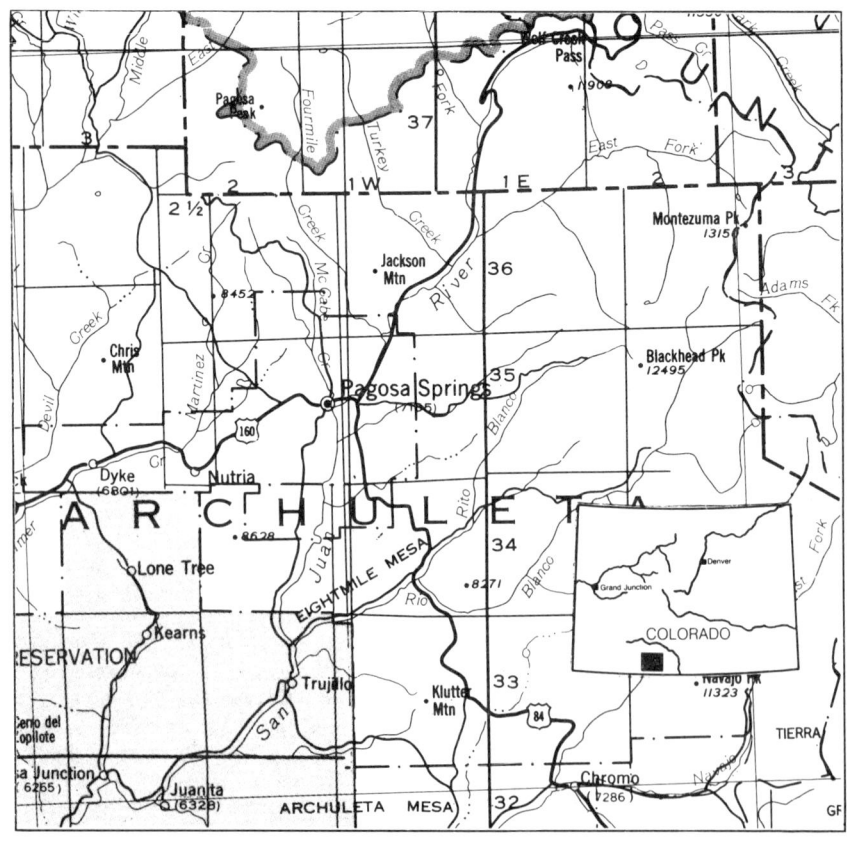

San Juan River

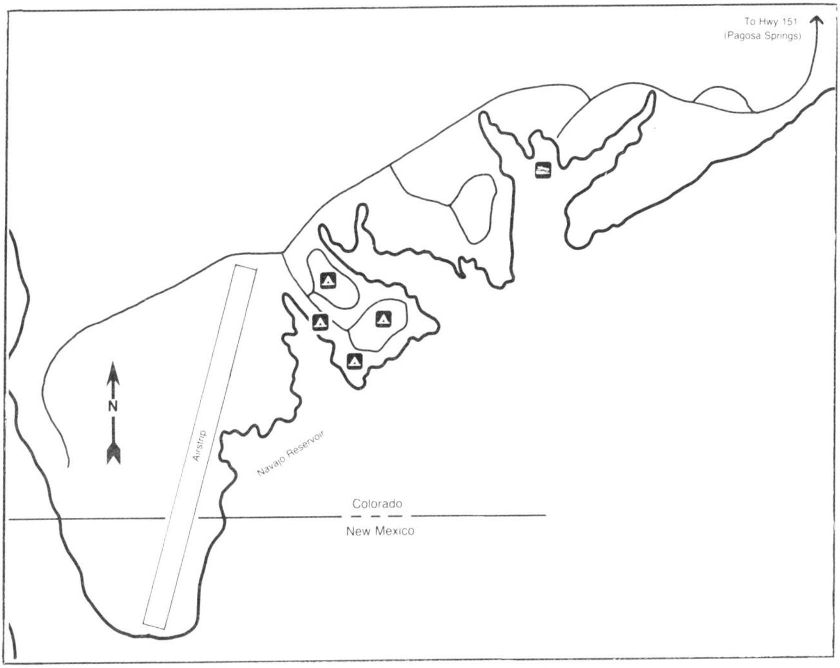

SOUTHWEST RIVERS   47

Navajo State Recreation Area

small cutthroat. Rated fair to good.

The **West Fork of the San Juan** joins the East Fork at the Saddle Back Ranch on US 160, 11 miles north of Pagosa Springs. It has 12 miles of good fishing through canyon country with fine pools and sharp drops. Accessible by rugged trail. Wadable only during low water. Good for rainbow and cutthroat averaging 10 inches; through the canyon they are slightly larger. Reached by turning west off US 160, 6 mi south of Wolf Creek Pass summit, at West Fork Campground. Rough road continues beyond campground about 1 mile to Borns Lake. The lower 4 miles of the West Fork, from its junction with the East Fork to the campground, is tightly posted private lands. **Beaver Creek** enters the West Fork from the east, 4 miles above the end of road at Borns Lake. It offers 6 miles of trail fishing in very rough country with numerous waterfalls. Stream is 4 to 6 feet wide and rated good for cutthroat to 10 inches. **Cimarron Creek** enters the West Fork from the west 5 miles above the end of road at Borns Lake. This 3-foot-wide stream offers good fishing on flies for small cutthroat. **Borns Lake** (8371 ft; 10 ac) is poor fishing because of winter kill. There is a parking lot here to allow access by foot to the upper reaches of the West Fork. Below Borns Lake at the West Fork Campground are the small **Hatcher Lakes** (8050 ft; 3 ac). These lakes have been stocked with rainbow. There may be a few browns from earlier stocking.

Turkey Creek enters the San Juan River about 2 miles downstream from the East and West Fork branches, about 8 miles north of

---

Pagosa Sports

Fishing Tackle • Hunting & Camping Supplies • Licenses

"Call us for information on hunting & fishing conditions."

432 Pagosa St.
(P.O. Box 1387)
Pagosa Springs
Colorado 81147
(303) 264-5811

Pagosa Springs on US 160. The highway crosses a bridge marked Turkey Creek. The creek contains small brook and some brown, cutthroat and rainbow. This 12-foot stream flows through a mountain canyon and offers good fly fishing. Good trail follows the creek upstream beginning at a sign 0.25 mile north of Turkey Creek bridge. Trail continues northwest 16 miles to Turkey Creek Lake. First few miles can be traveled by 4-wheel drive. **Turkey Creek Lake** (11,135 ft; 23 ac) is a crater lake at timberline. It produces fine catches of small brook trout and a few mackinaws. Campsites near by. Lake seems to be overpopulated and could use fishing pressure.

Fourmile Creek is very similar in character to Turkey Creek. It enters the San Juan about 4 miles south of Turkey Creek and about 4 miles north of Pagosa Springs. Access to creek by rugged road at north end of Pagosa Springs. At the Fourmile Creek headwaters, **Lower Fourmile Lake** (11,400 ft; 12 ac) is fair for cutthroat, and **Upper Fourmile Lake** (11,700 ft; 12 ac) is good for cutthroat up to 14 inches, but they are difficult to catch. Both lakes are stocked and are reached by a paved road leaving north edge of Pagosa Springs through unusually scenic country. Creek has numerous waterfalls. Five miles by trail from end of road to headwaters. **Snowball Creek** enters Fourmile Creek from the north about 5 miles above the Fourmile Creek mouth. Access by 4-wheel-drive road for 4 miles to headwaters.

South of Pagosa Springs (1.5 miles) **Mill Creek** flows into the San Juan River. Access is by dirt road from the Pagosa Springs rodeo grounds. Marginal fishing.

On the west side of US 84 about 3 miles south of Pagosa Springs is **Echo Canyon Reservoir** (7200 ft; 118 ac). It offers excellent early spring fishing for cutthroat to 14 inches. It is becoming a warm water fishery with bass, perch, crappie and carp competing with trout. Two-pound bass are taken frequently. Catfish up to 18 pounds. Stocked with rainbow. Boats allowed.

RIO BLANCO

The **Rio Blanco** has terrible fishing because the San Juan-Navajo diversion tunnel takes most of the water. Higher elevations have beaver dams. The Rio Blanco meets the San Juan River at the northeast corner of the Southern Ute Indian Reservation. The **Rito Blanco,** a tributary of the Rio Blanco, can be reached by taking US 84 at Pagosa Springs by turning east at the rodeo grounds to follow Mill Creek road about 5 miles. Turn south of Forest Service road and follow road about 5 miles to upper part of Rito Blanco where the stream is 5- to 6-feet wide. Poor for small cutthroat in lower part due to irrigation diversions, but fair in upper reaches. Lower section of the Rito Blanco is tightly posted.

Fish Creek enters the Rio Blanco near the end of the Blanco Basin Road. This road can be reached by turning northeast off US 84 at Rito Blanco Creek on 657. Fish Creek has two main forks. The main stream is very small and fishable for 6 miles by trail for small cutthroat and brook. Rated fair. The **North Fork of Fish Creek** is paralleled by Fish Lake Pack Trail about 7 miles. At its headwaters is **Fish Lake** (11,800 ft; 9 ac).

TROPHY TAXIDERMY
National Award Winner Annually Since 1978

S.W. Colorado's Premier Fish Taxidermist

"We ship anywhere in the U.S."
- Don Tomberlin, Wildlife Artist

**65 County Road 207
Durango, CO 81301**

(303) 247-2201

SOUTHWEST RIVERS 49

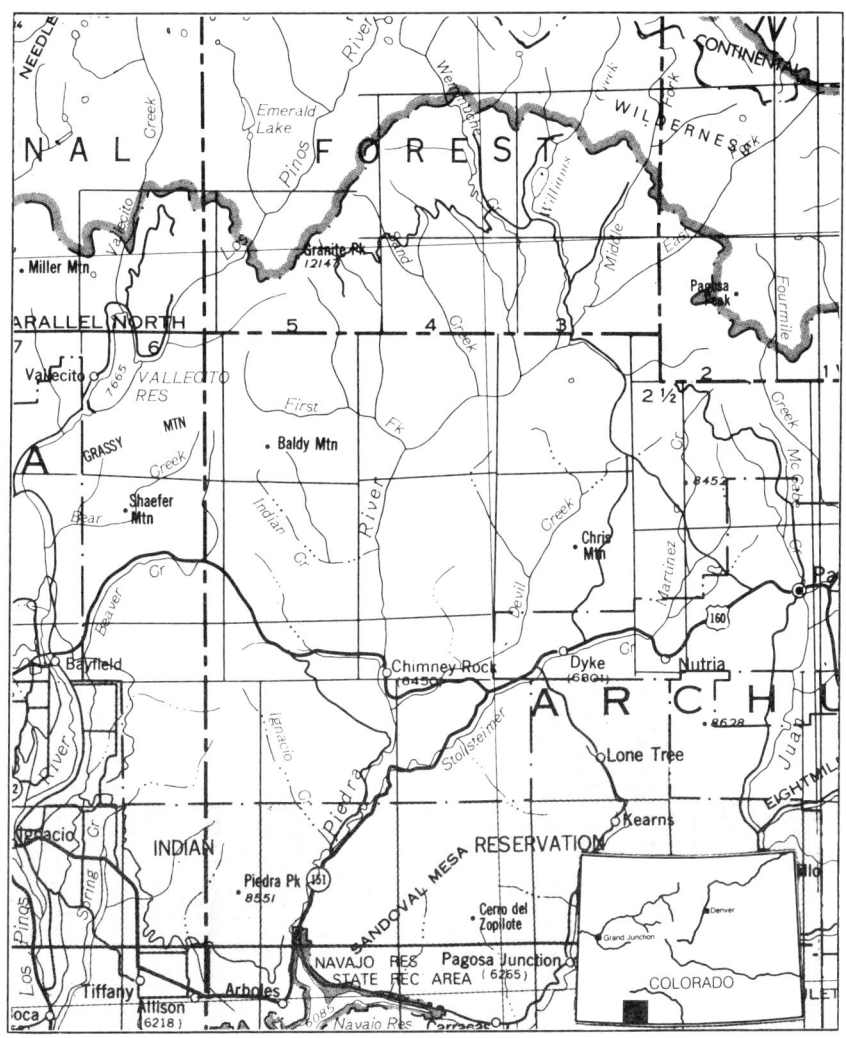

Piedra River, Navajo Reservoir

Rated good for cutthroat trout to 18 inches. Campsite below lake. **White Creek** enters the Rio Blanco at the Hamlin Ranch, reached by the Blanco Basin Road. Watch for turnoff to Crescent Lake. White Creek offers 2 miles of small stream fishing for small cutthroat and brook. Extensive network of beaver ponds. **Opal Lake** (9250 ft; 1 ac) is at the headwaters of White Creek, and is reached by 2 miles of unmarked trail. Rated good for brook and rainbow to 11 inches. The **Big Branch** of the Rio Blanco is fed by **Buckles Reservoir** (9350 ft; 10 ac) and **Harris Reservoir** (9450 ft; 37 ac). They are reached by a Forest Service road that junctures with US 84 about 22 miles south of Pagosa Springs; marked with sign. Buckles is fair to good for rainbow and cutthroat; a few brook to 20 inches. Although Harris fluctuates greatly, it has been a good producer of cutthroat, rainbow and brook to 13 inches, some larger. Harris often is choked with weeds by August. Fair campsites.

PIEDRA RIVER

West of the San Juan River about 15 miles, the **Piedra River** is a 40-mile stretch that has trout fishing its entire length. The headwater tributaries are in the Weminuche Wilderness, and the lower river is on reservation lands. Portions of the Piedra have been identified as suitable for Wild and Scenic River protection. US 160 crosses the Piedra River 22 miles west of Pagosa Springs at Chimney Rock. The section of the Piedra River below US 160 is noted for large browns taken on bait and lures. Rainbow to 10 inches also are caught using bait and flies. The river averages 30 feet wide and is rather slow moving with alternate pools and rocky riffles. A good road follows the east side of the river north for 12 miles to First Fork of the Piedra River and Piedra Hunter Campground. A good time to fish the tributaries is immediately after summer showers.

The headwaters of the **East Fork of the Piedra River** are near the northeast boundary of the Weminuche Wilderness Area. They are fed by several mountain streams running from alpine lakes barren of trout. The East Fork is 9 feet wide and about 10 miles long. The upper reaches are accessible by trail that follows the Divide from the Middle Fork. Wadable and fine for flies. Cutthroat to 10 inches. Rated excellent. There are several back country streams, including **Deadman, Pagosa** and **Plumtaw Creeks** that offer good fishing for cutthroat and brook.

The **Middle Fork of Piedra River** can be reached from the Piedra Road which goes north from US 84 about one mile west of Pagosa Springs. Road follows stream for about 6 miles. No trail to upper 6 miles of stream; very rough country.

Williams Creek enters the Piedra River about 1 mile downriver from the Middle and East Forks. A 16 mile, 10-foot-wide stream rated fair to good for rainbow and cutthroat to 10 inches. Fishing is excellent below Williams Creek Reservoir during rainbow spawning period in May. Road follows stream to Cimarrona Campground. Three other campgrounds are along stream. **Williams Fork Lake** (11,500 ft; 3 ac) at timberline is 12 miles north from the end of the road at Cimarrona Campground. Good trail parallels Williams Creek to lake. This lake is not stocked, but has a very good, self-sustaining cutthroat population. **Indian Creek** joins Williams Creek about 4 miles above the end of the road. Good for small cutthroat in lower end. **Williams Creek Reservoir** (8242 ft; 343 ac) is rated excellent for 9- to 14-inch rainbow and brook. Boats and motors are allowed. Rental boats at store 1 mile below reservoir.

Weminuche Creek forks north from the Piedra River about 2 miles downstream of Williams Creek Fork. Access is by following Forest Service north road to Williams Creek Reservoir and cutting west before reaching reservoir. Upper part is stocked with cutthroat and rainbow. Lower part, in Weminuche Valley, is on private lands.

The lower country streams and creeks feeding the Piedra River, including **Stollsteimer, Martinez, Heflin** and **Sullenburger Reservoir,** probably are not worth fishing. Most of the streams flow through private lands and are not stocked.

LOS PINOS RIVER

Midway between the Piedra River and Durango, **Los Pinos River** intersects US 160 at Bayfield. The 25 miles of public fishing water above Vallecito Reservoir to the north averages 20 feet wide with pools, riffles and rapids. Rated good for brown, rainbow and cutthroat to 14 inches. Horses are available for upper reaches. Below the Vallecito Reservoir to Bayfield, Los Pinos meanders through private lands. This 12-mile stretch holds rainbow to 16 inches and some big brown. Wadable except in spring. It averages about 30 feet wide with fine riffles and pools. From Bayfield south, Los Pinos enters the Southern Ute Indian Reservation. It is heavily stocked by the federal government, and fishing requires Ute Indian tribe permit. County Primary Road 511 south of Bayfield to Ignacio roughly parallels the river. Because of ideal fish habitat—suitable spawning sites and plenty of food—fish populations are virtually self-sustaining. This makes Los Pinos a likely candidate for wild trout water designation.

> *A single hook usually penetrates faster and holds more securely than double or treble hooks.*

Near the northern boundary of the Weminuche Wilderness, **Snowslide, Rincon La Vaca, North Fork, Rincon La Osa, Canon Paso** and **Sierra Vandera** are small tributaries at the headwaters of Los Pinos. These streams are rated fair for small cutthroat. They are located in the Weminuche Wilderness Area and are accessible by long trail from the Pine River Campground northeast of Vallecito Reservoir. Several small lakes, including **Granite Lake** (10,400 ft; 35 ac), **Elk Lake** (11,550 ft; 6 ac) and **Divide Lake** (10,000 ft; 3 ac) are stocked by aircraft and rated fair to good for cutthroat and a few rainbow. All three lakes are in exceptionally beautiful settings.

Flint Creek enters Los Pinos about 12 miles north from the end of the road at Pine River Campground. This typical, fine mountain stream, 6 to 8 feet wide with deep pools and fast riffles, offers good cutthroat fishing. It is fed by **Big Flint Lake** (11,650 ft; 38 ac), which is reached by a steep 8-mile trail up Flint Creek. Excellent for 10- to 14-inch cutthroat. Not open before middle of June. **Little Flint Lake** (11,870 ft; 10 ac) is across the canyon from Big Flint Lake. Trail connects. Fair for 10- to 12-inch cutthroat. Camping is best below lake along trail; however, there are ample sites on lake.

Lake Creek enters Los Pinos from the north about 6 miles above the end of the road at Pine River Campground. It is a 5-mile stream with many large pools. Good for small natives and rainbow. Several lakes, including **Moon Lake** (11,700 ft; 12 ac) and **Half Moon Lake** (12,200 ft; 2 ac), are at the headwaters of Lake Creek. They have small rainbow and cutthroat and stunted brook. Three miles downstream, **Big Emerald Lake** (10,033 ft; 280 ac) has a good reproducing cutthroat-rainbow hybrid population. Big Emerald Lake is 242 feet deep, the second deepest natural lake in the state. **Little Emerald Lake** (10,000 ft; 15 ac) is south of Big Emerald Lake only a few hundred yards. **Dollar Lake** (11,550 ft; 10 ac) drains into Big Emerald Lake from the west. Dollar is being stocked with the Emerald Lake strain of cutthroat-rainbow. All three lakes offer good fishing but are restricted to artificial flies or artificial lures only, and all sport fish more than 12 inches must be returned to the water. Check Colorado Division of Wildlife Fishing Regulations.

VALLECITO CREEK

Vallecito Creek enters Los Pinos at Vallecito Reservoir and stretches north to the Divide offering 22 miles of fishing, 19 miles by trail. Vallecito is fast, heavily fished, wadable in shallows, and averages about 15 feet wide with plenty of pools and riffles. It contains rainbow, brook and cutthroat to 10 inches and is rated as a good fly stream. **Irving, Johnson, Sunlight, Leviathan, Rock** and **Storm King Creeks** are the principal fishing tributaries. Each offers about 4 miles of small-stream fishing and some beaver ponds. Fine fly fishing for small cutthroat and few rainbow. There are a number of good lakes in the upper reaches

---

Overlooking Vallecito Lake   **Near Durango**

Relaxing Atmosphere In A Beautiful Setting
OPEN ALL YEAR
22 Cabins • Large Playground • Some Fireplaces
Rt. 1 Bayfield, Colorado 81122 • (303) 884-2563

> **BEAR PAW LODGE**
> Vallecito Lake, Colorado
> Fishing • Boating
> Hunting • Hiking • Horses
> *Modern & Spacious*
> *1, 2, & 3 Bedroom Cabins*
> **"In the Woods"**
> OPEN YEAR ROUND
> **(303) 884-2508**
> 18011 County Rd. 501
> Bayfield, Colorado 81122

of these creeks. Many are accessible by horse from the Vallecito Campground at the north end of Vallecito Reservoir. Most of the alpine lakes, including **Storm King Lake** (12,300 ft; 13 ac), **Silex Lake** (12,400 ft; 4 ac), **Mystery Lake** (12,600 ft; 5 ac), **South Leviathan Lake** (12,100 ft; 8 ac), **North Leviathan** (12,400 ft; 6 ac), **Sunlight Lakes** (11,650 ft; 12 ac combined), **Hazel Lake** (12,650 ft; 10 ac), **Columbine Lake** (12,400 ft; 4 ac) and **Irving Lake** (11,650 ft; 7 ac) are nestled in the rugged Needle Mountains. Most are stocked with cutthroat by aircraft. Trails connecting lakes are steep. On the east side of Vallecito Creek, **Hidden Lake** (12,000 ft; 15 ac) and **Lost Lake** (11,800 ft; 10 ac) are rated good for cutthroat and rainbow. These lakes are two of the most popular fishing holes in the Needle Mountains.

At the mouth of Vallecito Creek, about 19 miles north of Bayfield, is **Vallecito Reservoir** (7500 ft; 1720 ac when full).

Vallecito Reservoir has the state record for two big fish. The state champion brown trout, a 24-pound, 10-ounce lunker 27.6 inches long, was pulled out in 1972. The year before, a monster northern pike a shade over 4 feet long was landed and tipped the scales at an official 30 pounds, 1 ounce.

The reservoir can be reached by turning north off US 160 in Bayfield. Follow this secondary road up Los Pinos River to the Vallecito dam. The reservoir is fished principally by trolling, but fishing from rocky points on shore is excellent at times. Rainbow are stocked. Currently, the Division of Wildlife is trying to increase the kokanee salmon population. Pike were stocked in the early 1960s and now are self-sustaining. There are a few walleye, last stocked in 1962, and an occasional brown. Boats and motors available. Cabins, resort and three campgrounds on east side. Spring and fall are the best seasons in this popular area.

UTES HAVE GOOD FISHING

The Piedra, Los Pinos and the Animas rivers flow through the Southern Ute Indian Reservation. These waters can be fished, but in addition to a Colorado fishing license, a tribal permit is required. Permits are $7 for 5 days and $13 for the season. A permit also allows some camping along the water ways. Some streams and reservoirs have specific regulations and fishermen should contact the Wildlife Conservation Office, Southern Ute Tribal Affairs Building (on Hwy 172, downtown Ignacio), P.O. Box 737, Ignacio, CO 81137, 303/563-4525 for information.

Fishing on reservation lands without a state license is punishable by state law. Persons fishing on the reservation without a tribal permit are subject to federal court fines.

Capote Lake (6600 ft; 34 ac), at the intersection of US 160 and Hwy 151, is managed by the Southern Utes and is stocked with catchable rainbow and cutthroat, mostly in the 14- to 16-inch range, but some larger. Fishing at Capote is $3.50 per day for adults; $1.75 per day for children under 15. Permits can be bought at the lake. Capote Campground is near the lake. Camping is $6 a night.

On the New Mexico-Colorado border, Navajo Reservoir requires only a state license.

Ignacio is tribal headquarters. The Sky Ute Lodge in the center of town has information on summer pow-wows, rodeos, Friday night bingo and other activities held at the community center and rodeo grounds. There is also a small arts and crafts museum at the lodge. For lodge reservations and activities information, write one month in advance to Sky Ute Lodge, Box 277, Ignacio, CO 81137 or call 303/563-4531.

FLORIDA RIVER

The **Florida River** originates more than 20 miles north of Durango and enters the Animas below Durango from the northeast. It is a typical mountain stream about 10 feet wide. At its headwaters, **City Reservoir** (10,960 ft; 100 ac) is rated excellent for small brook and a few cutthroat. Logging roads along the ridges on both sides of the Florida river offer access. Other lakes in the area, **Castilleja Lake** (12,050 ft; 3 ac), **Stump Lakes** and **Lost Lake,** do not offer good fishing due to winter kill.

Lemon Reservoir (8150 ft; 400 ac when full) has good rainbow and kokanee to 15 inches. The reservoir can be reached by following a good paved road northeast out of Durango. Three campgrounds, Transfer Park, Florida and Miller, are located near or on the reservoir. Florida River below the reservoir flows through private land.

ANIMAS RIVER

To the west of Los Pinos River and flowing through Durango, the **Animas River** has about 75 miles of fishable water. Heading near Silverton, the river is east of Hwy 550 and flows south through Durango and leaves Colorado below Bondad. Up to 100 feet wide in places, it can be waded at some riffles when the water is low. The river is stocked downstream from Elk Creek drainage, south of Silverton about 4 miles. Near Silverton the river runs deep into the West Needle Mountains and then joins with US 550 again at Rockwood. The narrow gauge railroad parallels the Animas through the Needle Mountains. This 100-year-old route provides fishermen novel access to some of the Animas drainages nestled in the mountains. In June through August, the train runs four times a day. Reservations should be made 4 to 6 weeks in advance. This stretch of the Animas, winding through scenic canyons, contains rainbow and cutthroat 8 to 14 inches, and some brown, and is rated good. Water is fast with pools and riffles abundant. From Trimble, on US 550, south 9 miles to Durango, the Animas is slow, meandering and deep with 6- to 11-inch rainbow. Mosquitoes are thick from late spring until September. This stretch is fair for 10- to 12-inch rainbow. Below Durango the river is less polluted than it was a few years ago. Excellent brown fishing from Durango to the Southern Ute Indian Reservation border. A former record brown was caught within the Durango city limits.

NORTH OF SILVERTON

At the Animas headwaters north of Silverton, there are several small lakes, including **Denver Lake** (12,000 ft; 0.2 ac), but because of heavily mineralized water, fish populations do not do well; consequently, this area is not stocked.

Cunningham Creek enters the Animas from the southeast at Howardsville, about 7 miles northeast of Silverton. It is reached by Hwy 110, then a dirt road southeast along the creek for 3 miles. Cunningham is a 5-mile creek averaging 6 feet wide. Fair for small rainbow. At the end of the road, a steep marked trail leads south 3 miles to **Highland Mary Lakes** (12,000 ft; 47 and 11 ac). These lakes are rated excellent for brook, cutthroat and rainbow from 10 to 18 inches. Poor campsites. One mile farther south of the Highland Mary Lakes over a grassy ridge are the **Verde Lakes** (12,000 ft; 15 and 13 ac). There is no defined trail connecting the lakes. Excellent for small brook and a few 8- to 10-inch cutthroat and rainbow.

SOUTH OF SILVERTON

Mineral Creek enters the Animas from the west just below Silverton. Accessible by US 550. Highway follows creek north to Red Mountain Pass. **Columbine Lake** (12,700 ft; 22 ac) lies at the head of **Mill Creek,** a fork of Mineral Creek, southwest of Chattanooga. The lake is near the Divide. It is not stocked because a brook population has become self-sustaining. Southwest of Columbine is **Crystal Lake** (12,300 ft; 1 ac), near Ophir Pass. It is accessible by a dirt road from US 550 at **Middle Fork.** At the headwaters of the **South Fork of Mineral Creek** are several alpine lakes. A good road west off US 550 follows the South Fork to South Mineral Campground. From there a good trail continues up South Fork Mineral Creek to **Ice Lake** (12,300 ft;

15 ac), **Little Ice Lake** (11,400 ft; 2 ac), **Island Lake** (12,400 ft; 5 ac) and **Fuller Lake** (12,600 ft; 12.5 ac). North of the South Mineral Campground a 4-wheel-drive road leads to **Clear Lake** (12,000 ft; 30 ac), which is being stocked with brook. All of these lakes are good for cutthroat fishing.

Elk Creek enters the Animas from the east about 7 miles south of Silverton. It can be reached by narrow-gauge railroad or by a Forest Service trail from Molas Lake on Molas Pass, located on US 550 about 3 miles south of Silverton. The hike is about 4 miles south to the mouth of the creek. The creek varies from 8 to 10 feet wide and is easily fished. The lower part is good for cutthroat, brook and rainbow to 10 inches; upper reaches are too mineralized.

Molas Lake (10,600 ft; 20 ac), **Little Molas Lake** (10,900 ft; 7 ac) and **Andrews Lake** (10,800 ft; 10 ac) feed into the Animas about 3 miles south of Silverton. All three are easily reached from US 550. They are good for rainbow and brook. City campground is usually open in early June on Molas Lake. Heavily fished.

Tenmile Creek enters the Animas from the east about 3 miles downstream of Elk Creek. It is about 4 miles long and averages 4 feet wide. Lower end is fast water and is rated fair; upper stretches meander with some beaver ponds and are rated excellent. Rainbow from 6 to 14 inches. At its headwaters is cobalt blue **Balsam Lake** (11,435 ft; 100 ac), which has no fish due to the high mineral content of water. Good camping.

Noname Creek flows into the Animas about 2 miles south of Tenmile Creek and about 13 miles north of Tacoma. The creek runs 6 miles, and water is similar to Tenmile Creek. To the south of Noname Creek, **Ruby Lake** (10,850 ft; 8 ac) is at the headwaters of **Ruby Creek** (no fish), but can be reached from Noname Creek. The lake is good for 1- to 2-pound rainbow. Access is by railroad from Durango.

Needle Creek enters the Animas river from the east 15 miles upstream from Rockwood just south of Needleton. Access by railroad; leave train at Needleton. Creek is rated fair for rainbow and cutthroat to 10 inches; about 10 feet wide and wadable except in the spring. The **Needle Creek Lakes**, 4 in number, are located in this drainage. **Webb Lake** (10,960 ft; 10 ac), **Jewell Lake** (12,000 ft; 10 ac), **Pearl Lake** (11,575 ft; 14 ac) and **Little Emerald Lake** (11,270 ft; 14 ac) are accessible by following a good trail up the north side of Needle Creek. About 2 miles upcreek, ford the stream at the old water wheel. Take steep Lime Mesa Trail along tributary. About an hour's hike from the ford, lakes are rated good for rainbow to 13 inches. Camping is best at Webb Lake.

Cascade Creek forks north from the Animas about 3 miles above Electra Lake. US 550 crosses this tributary. Take FS 785 road north to Cascade Summer Group Home, a couple miles north of Purgatory Ski Area. Access road off US 550 follows the creek for about 2 miles; from there take 4-wheel-drive road. Creek is about 5 miles long, averaging 6 feet wide. Fair for small cutthroat, rainbow and brook. **Lime Creek** enters Cascade Creek near Purgatory Campground at Purgatory Ski Area. Creek is about 5 feet wide and more than 12 miles long. Numerous pools in rugged canyon. Some beaver ponds. Rated fair for small rainbow and some brook. **Potato Lake** (9800 ft; 9 ac) feeds into Lime as well as other small lakes, including **Twilight Peaks Lake**. Lakes are rated fair for rainbow and brook to 15 inches, but some involve difficult climbs.

Canyon Creek flows into the Animas from the east just below Tacoma. About 4 miles south of Tacoma, turn east off US 550 at Trimble Springs, cross the Animas and drive north on Missionary Ridge Road about 4 miles. Stream is marked by sign. Stream is narrow, 3 feet wide, but good for small brook. **Henderson Lake** (10,000 ft; 5 ac) a tributary of Canyon Creek, is good in early spring for fat 10- to 12-inch rainbow and brook. Poor to fair in late season; suffers some winter kill.

Beautiful **Electra Lake** parallels US 550, but is 99 per cent private. Some fishing is allowed. Gatekeeper at south end of lake will allow public parking lot to fill then closes gate. Stocked with some cutthroat.

Also a few brook.

South of Electra, **Haviland Lake** (8150 ft; 4 ac) is owned and developed by the Division of Wildlife. It is 1 mile east of US 550 and 21 miles north of Durango, marked by sign. The lake has undergone extensive reconstruction, consequently fishing is rated good for rainbow to 12 inches. Motors are not allowed, and rental boats are not available. Campground is located on the southeast shore. Haviland is located at the headwaters of **Elbert Creek.** Elbert is a small, brushy and ponded creek good for brook and brown to 14 inches. It junctions with the Animas about 6 miles below Canyon Creek.

Hermosa Creek enters the Animas from the northwest at Hermosa on US 550, about 10 miles north of Durango. The stream originates more than 20 miles north. Upper reaches are accessed by turning west near Purgatory Campground on US 550. Follow road about 5 miles to Sig Creek Campground. Can fish headwaters from here, which rate poor to fair for small cutthroat and rainbows. Road follows the **East Fork of Hermosa Creek.** Lower part of Hermosa Creek can be reached from US 550 at Hermosa. Follow Forest Service road about 4 miles to where fishing is fair for small rainbow. Trail follows upstream about 15 miles to Sig Creek Campground; Hermosa Creek varies from 4 to 12 feet wide. **Dutch Creek,** about 5 miles from the Hermosa-Animas fork, enters Hermosa Creek from the north. It is a small tributary fair for cutthroat and a few rainbow to 12 inches.

Junction Creek enters the Animas at the northwest edge of Durango. A good road opposite the fairgrounds proceeds west 4 miles to Junction Creek Campground and Recreation Area. From Junction Creek Campground, the road does not follow the stream but runs northeast of the river about 8 miles and meets the Junction Creek headwaters at Neglected Mine. There is no trail along the stream. It's rocky and clear, rated fair for small cutthroat and rainbow.

South of Durango, **Pastorius Reservoir** (6850 ft; 38 ac) is on reservation land but a tribal permit is not necessary. Turn south off US 160 about 5 miles east of Durango at Loma Linda. Proceed south about 2 miles; Pastorius is to the west about 0.75 mile. First stocked in 1966, Pastorius has nice northern pike, some bluegill, yellow perch and is being stocked with rainbow and bass. Limited number of channel catfish.

LA PLATA/MANCOS RIVERS

West of the Animas River, the La Plata and Mancos rivers offer marginal fishing. **La Plata** intersects US 160 about 12 miles west of Durango at Hesperus. Graded dirt road goes north at Hesperus along La Plata's west bank for about 8 miles. Kroeger Campground is about 6 miles up. From Hesperus it is about 12 miles to La Plata's headwaters. Water is posted from Hesperus 3 miles north to Mayday mine and is rated poor. From Mayday north, river offers fair fishing for small rainbow and a few brook.

The **Mancos River** forks just above the old sawmill in the town of Mancos at the intersection of US 160 and Hwy 184. Two forks, the west and the middle, afford fair results. The **West Mancos River,** the longest fork, accessible by about 40 miles of logging roads, is fair in the upper reaches for rainbow, cutthroat and brook. The **Middle Mancos River** in Echo Basin has many small ponded tributaries that offer fair fishing for small rainbow and cutthroat. Gravel roads parallel lower 15 miles.

Several reservoirs dot the Mancos River drainage. **Jackson Gulch Reservoir** (7825 ft; 70 ac) has gained in popularity recently. At one point it was drained to clear out the pike population and then stocked with rainbow and catfish. Catches of 5- to 6-pound rainbow are reported. **Joe Moore Reservoir** (7680 ft; 35 ac), north of Hwy 184, is good for rainbow, brown and bass; some up to 6 pounds. Other reservoirs include **Summit Reservoir** (7388 ft; 300 ac) and **Puett Reservoir** (7261 ft; 150 ac), which have heavy pike populations. Most of these reservoirs are fished by New Mexico fishermen during long holiday weekends. Weekday fishing offers quiet, serene settings. Local fishermen have taken an interest in bass.

South of Hwy 160, the La Plata and Mancos are marginal fisheries at best. ☐

WILDERNESS FISHING

The Weminuche and South San Juan wilderness areas offer anglers not only fishing but immersion in some of the wildest terrain remaining in Colorado, complete with spectacular views and denizens of mountain and forest. The Weminuche is north and west of Pagosa Springs; the South San Juan to the southeast.

Access is by foot and horseback. Visitors can hope to see bear, elk, deer, porcupine, beaver, coyotes, bighorn sheep as they keep an eye peeled for hawks and eagles soaring over an extravanganza of wildflowers. Lakes with no names and not on maps can teem with cutthroat trout in the 2-pound category. Likewise crystaline lakes and streams may also be barren.

U.S. Forest Service campgrounds

U.S. Forest Service compilation was current as of 1985.

Asterisks denote fee areas. Some campgrounds are open only Memorial Day weekend through Labor Day. Below freezing weather could mean no water supply.

ANIMAS, LOS PINOS AND SAN JUAN RIVER DRAINAGES

SAN JUAN NATIONAL FOREST
Headquarters: Federal Bldg., 701 Camina del Rio, Durango, CO 81301

Campground name	Elevation	No camp sites	Travel trailers	Drinking water	Length of stay (days)	Location and directions
Cimarrona*	8400	21	Yes	Yes	14	28 mi NW of Pagosa Springs on county hwy and forest road
Bridge*	7800	19	Yes	Yes	14	17.8 mi NW of Pagosa Springs on county hwy
Williams Creek*	8200	69	Yes	Yes	14	19.5 mi NW of Pagosa Springs on county hwy
Teal*	8300	15	Yes	Yes	14	21 mi NW of Pagosa Springs on county hwy
Blanco River*	7200	16	Yes	No	14	15 mi SE of Pagosa Springs on Colo. 160
Middle Fork Hunter Camp	8500	10	Yes	No	14	18 mi NW of Pagosa Srings on county hwy and forest road
Mesa Spring Hunter Camp	9700	3	Yes	No	14	14 mi W of Pagosa Springs on US 160 and forest road
Turkey Springs Hunter Camp	8200	11	Yes	No	14	8.5 mi W of Pagosa Springs on US 160, county hwy and forest road

SOUTHWEST RIVERS

East Fork*	7600	26	Yes	Yes	14	On US 160, 10 mi NE of Pagosa Springs
Wolf Creek*	8000	26	Yes	Yes	14	On US 160, 14 mi NE of Pagosa Springs
Old Timers*	7900	11	Yes	Yes	14	11 mi N of Bayfield on county hwy 501
Graham Creek*	7900	26	Yes	Yes	14	12.6 mi N of Bayfield on county hwy 501
North Canyon*	7900	22	Yes	Yes	14	12.6 mi N of Bayfield on county hwy 501
Pine Point*	7900	30	Yes	Yes	14	18 mi N of Bayfield on county hwy 501
Middle Mountain*	7900	24	Yes	Yes	14	13 mi N of Bayfield on county hwy 501
Pine River	8100	9	Yes	Yes	14	16 mi N of Bayfield on county hwy 501
Miller Creek*	8000	11	Yes	Yes	14	11 mi NW of Bayfield on county hwy 501
Vallecito*	8000	80	Yes	Yes	14	18.4 mi N of Bayfield on county hwy 501
Transfer Park*	8600	25	Yes	Yes	14	17 mi NW of Bayfield on county highway
Florida*	8500	20	Yes	Yes	14	17 mi NW of Bayfield on county highway
First Fork Hunter Camp	7100	10	Yes	No	14	9 mi N of Chimney Rock by forest road, off US 160
Lower Piedra	6600	17	Yes	Yes	14	1 mi N of Chimney Rock on forest road
Ute	6900	32	Yes	Yes	14	4.2 mi SE of Chimney Rock on US 160
Junction Creek*	7,300	34	Yes	Yes	14	5 mi NW of Durango by county highway and forest road
Purgatory*	8800	14	Yes	Yes	14	On US 550, 14 mi SW of Silverton
Sig Creek	9400	9	Yes	Yes	14	17 mi SW of Silverton on US 550 and forest road
South Mineral*	9800	23	Yes	Yes	14	6.6 mi W of Silverton on US 550 and forest road
Haviland Lake*	8100	45	Yes	Yes	14	On US 550, 17.5 mi N of Durango
Kroeger*	9000	11	Yes	Yes	—	6.5 mi N of Hesperus on county highway
Transfer	8500	13	Yes	Yes	—	12 mi NE of Mancos on county highway
Thompson Park*	7800	51	Yes	Yes	14	On US 160, 5.5 mi E of Mancos

Dolores River in the midst of change

Adjacent communities:
Dolores, Cortez, Pleasant View, Dove Creek, Uravan, Gateway.

Principal Highways:
U.S. 666; Colo. 184, 141.

The **Dolores River** starts at Lizard Head Pass (elevation 10,000 ft) beside Hwy 145 at the Dolores-San Miguel county line. It gathers waters from the south sides of Wilson Mountain, Dolores Peaks and Sheep Mountain, and from the west side of Hermosa Peak, and flows southwest in two forks, which join below the village of Stoner. The Dolores then flows southwest through the town of Dolores and then northwest through cedar breaks and desert to join the Colorado River in Utah. Confined to Dolores and Montezuma counties, the main Dolores, its West Fork, and Ground Hog Reservoir are the main fishing waters of the drainage.

Dolores River offers 35 miles of fishing in Montezuma County. It has been rated fair in spring for rainbow and brown to 1.5 pounds, though occasionally fish up to 5 pounds are taken. Forest Road 504 follows the west side of the river downstream from Dolores. It averages 40 feet wide and is wadable except in spring. It has brown and rainbow from 6 to 14 inches. Much land is posted, but permission often is granted upon request.

MCPHEE RESERVOIR

The bright spot in Dolores River fishing is McPhee Reservoir, which in 1985 was nearing completion northwest of the town of Dolores. It's only on the most current maps.

The Bureau of Reclamation has erected the 270-foot high, 1100-foot long McPhee Dam 10 miles downstream from town. When full, the reservoir, 2.4 miles across at maximum width, will back up to the Fourth Street Bridge in Dolores. In its coves and niches, black bass, crappie, catfish, Lake McConaughy rainbow trout and other species are thriving. In July 1984, 500,000 of the prolific, fast-growing rainbow fingerlings were stocked, and by spring were nine inches long. By the time the reservoir opens to public fishing in 1986, the angling should be superb.

The Forest Service will manage the McPhee Recreation Area that includes a 6-lane boat ramp, 114-car parking lot, 20 picnic tables, 80 individual camping units and four group camping areas.

Another center, at House Creek, offers a 4-lane boat ramp, 75-car parking lot, 56 campsites and two group camping areas plus picnic areas and shower/bath houses.

In the spring of 1985 the runoff was above normal and the minimum pool of water was achieved, and additional filling was scheduled. Inquiries about fishing and the availability of the facilities may be made to the U.S. Forest Service Dolores Ranger Station. Phone 303/882-7296 or write P.O. Box 210, Dolores, CO 81322.

Downstream from the dam to Bradford Bridge, the road was scheduled for rebuilding in the summer of 1985. Bradford Bridge, about 10 miles down from the dam, is where many float trips begin.

The Dolores River is easy to fish and rated good to excellent on flies; in the past it has been one of the state's best late season streams.

Hwy 145 from Dolores to Lizard Head Pass (54 mi) parallels main Dolores. There are Forest Service camping facilities at Forks Campground, Priest Gulch Campground (22 mi north of Dolores) and Cayton Campground is at Barlow Creek near Lizard Head Pass.

The upper Dolores has rainbow and natives to 12 inches. Several small streams enter the river from the east above the old mining town of Rico. **Barlow** and **McJunkin Creeks** from the south; **Lizard Head, Snow Spur, Slate, Coke Oven** and **Coal Creeks** from the north are small creeks with natives and brook. Barlow Creek is rated good—the others fair.

Some sections of the river are polluted below the town of Rico.

Scotch Creek enters the Dolores from the east 3 miles below Rico. It offers 4 miles of fishing in a 3-foot-wide stream for small

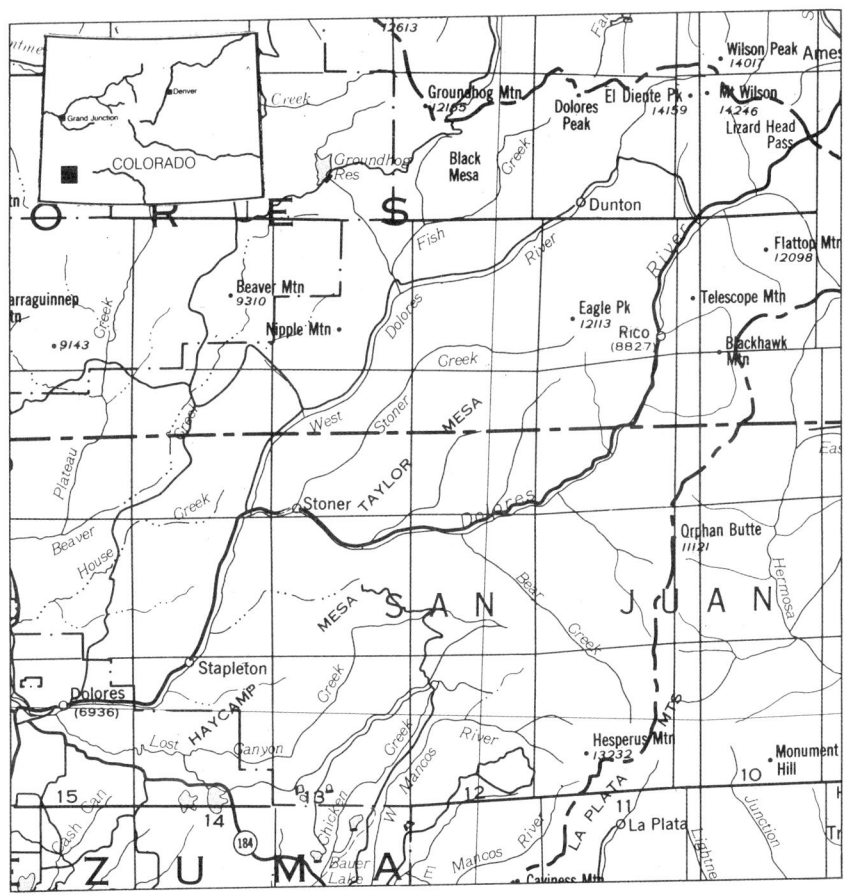

Upper Dolores River

brook and natives. Rated fair.

Ryman Creek enters the Dolores from the southeast. It offers 4 miles of small stream fishing for natives, and brook up to 6 and 7 inches. Rated fair. **Roaring Fork Creek** joins the river above the Priest Gulch Campground. A new USFS timber road makes 10 miles of stream accessible. Fair for 7- to 12-inch native and brook.

Priest Gulch Creek enters the Dolores 10 miles above Stoner from the north at Priest Gulch Campground. It offers 5 miles of trail fishing for small natives on flies and bait. Rated fair.

Bear Creek enters the river from the east 8 miles above Stoner. Offers 25 miles of small stream fishing for small rainbow, natives and brook. Restricted to fly fishing. Rated fair.

Taylor Creek enters Dolores River from the north 4 miles above Stoner. Can drive 4 miles upstream. A small stream with small natives and brook, it is rated fair.

Stoner Creek enters Dolores from the north near Stoner Guard Station, 17 miles north of Dolores on Hwy 145. Ten miles of fishing in a stream up to 6 feet wide for small natives. Trail is blocked by private landowner. Taylor Creek timber sales road is within 2 miles of the upper end. Rated fair.

About 1.5 miles below Stoner, the West Fork of the Dolores joins the mainstream.

WEST FORK

The **West Fork of the Dolores** is accessible from Hwy 145, 13 miles northeast of Dolores. Turn off on marked Dunton Road, which parallels West Fork for 28 miles. Fishing in the stream (averaging 15 ft wide) for small rainbow, cutthroat and brown, with a larger fish on occasion, is rated good. There are about 8 miles of posted water. Restricted to flies from Burro Bridge above Dunton upstream to Navajo Lake. **Cold, Kilpacker** and **Meadow Creeks** enter West Fork above Dunton, 35 miles upstream from turnoff at Hwy 145. Eleven miles of trail fishing for natives and rainbow to 10 inches. Rated fair. **Navajo Lake** (11,150 ft; 10 ac) is at the foot of 14,159-foot El Diente Peak. In a spectacular setting, it is reached by a steep, 5-mile trail beginning at Burro Bridge Forest Service Campground 2.5 miles northeast of Dunton. Usually ice covered until July 1. Stocked with brook. Restricted to flies and lures. Fishing below the lake is poor. **Ground Hog, Little Fish** and **Willow Creeks** enter West Fork about 12 miles up Dunton Road from the turnoff at Hwy 145. About 30 miles of trail fishing in streams 3 to 4 feet wide with beaver dams. Rated fair. **Fish Creek,** which offers some 14 miles of water, can be reached by a road that turns off at the mouth of Ground Hog Creek to go up Fish Creek for 4.5 miles, ending at the campground. The upper end is reached by a forest road that turns west at Dunton to cross the upper creek. A pretty mountain stream about 15 feet wide with many beaver ponds, it is good for rainbow and cutthroat to 12 inches.

GROUND HOG ANGLING

Ground Hog Reservoir (8,720 ft; 600 ac when full) is looking up as a good fishing spot. The fluctuating reservoir was drained a few years ago for maintenance and repairs. Restocked with rainbow, cutthroat, brown and brook, fishing has been very good. Once subject to heavy fishing pressure, it recently has received relatively scant attention. Camping and boat ramps are available.

Below the confluence of the West Fork and the Dolores itself, the Dolores River flows through private land where permission to fish is necessary. **Lost Canyon Creek** flows into the Dolores just south of the town of Dolores. This often brushy, 4- to 5-foot-wide creek is fair for cutthroat; it is mostly on private land and fishing is diminished by irrigation fluctuations. Upper reaches in national forest are okay for small trout.

Eight miles west of Dolores, **Narraguinnep Reservoir** (7,050 ft; 386 ac) is an irrigation reservoir reached by Hwy 147. It offers rainbow, perch, crappie, northern pike, bluegill, channel catfish and some walleye. There is no camping. There is a boat ramp.

Disappointment Creek (which joins the river in the high country northeast of the River below Dolores) is just that.

To the Utah state line, the winding river is scenic, but silt-laden, often slow-moving and with banks, cliff clefts and canyon rims crawling with rattlesnakes in spring, summer and fall.

South of the town of Dolores on Hwy 145 is the city of Cortez in the heart of the Montezuma Valley. **Totten, Summit** and **Puett** (irrigation) **Reservoirs** east of the community are promising fisheries. Totten has good size panfish, some northern and walleye pike as well as channel catfish. Puett has some walleye, bass and catfish. Summit may be poisoned in 1983 and a fresh start made to upgrade the fishing there. Boating is allowed. Areas tend to be victimized by vandals and litterers.

Denny Lake (6,085 ft; 11 ac) in the city of Cortez has bass, crappie, catfish, bluegill and some rainbow. It is heavily stocked; trout and other species fishing is good in the spring. Nonpowered boats are permitted. ☐

U.S. Forest Service campgrounds

U.S. Forest Service compilation was current as of 1985.

Asterisks denote fee areas. Some campgrounds are open only Memorial Day weekend through Labor Day. Below freezing weather could mean no water supply.

DOLORES RIVER DRAINAGE

SAN JUAN NATIONAL FOREST
Headquarters: Federal Bldg., 701 Camina del Rio, Durango, CO 81301

Campground name	Elevation	No camp sites	Travel trailers	Drinking water	Length of stay (days)	Location and directions
Priest Gulch*	8000	13	Yes	Yes	14	On Colo. 145, 24 mi NE of Dolores or 10.5 mi NE of Rico via Colo. 145
Burro Bridge*	9000	15	Yes	Yes	14	24 mi NE of Colo. 145, 13 mi NE of Dolores
Cayton*	9400	27	Yes	Yes	14	On Colo. 145, 44 mi NE of Dolores or 6 mi NE of Rico
Forks*	7200	6	Yes	Yes	14	On Colo. 145, 11 mi NE of Dolores
Mavreeso*	7600	14	Yes	Yes	14	16.5 mi NE of Dolores on Colo. 145 and county hwy
West Dolores*	7800	13	Yes	Yes	14	17.5 mi NE of Dolores off Colo. 145
Hay Press	9300	11	No	No	—	8 mi S of Glade Park
McPhee	7000	136	Yes	Yes	14	NW of Dolores

San Miguel River scenic angling

Adjacent communities: Telluride, Nucla, Naturita, Uravan.

Principal Highways: Colo. 145, 141.

The **San Miguel River** rises in several high basins beneath 12,000- and 13,000-foot peaks above the town of Telluride in some of the most scenic country in Colorado. The mountains are steep, the valleys narrow and winding.

The area is heavily mineralized, as is evident from present and past mining operations with their workings, tailings ponds, aerial tramway lines, picturesque settings and ghost towns.

At higher elevations, sedimentary rock formations contribute considerable sediment to the streams, especially after heavy summer rains and during spring snowmelt. So the San Miguel and the **South Fork** of the San Miguel, which originates just below the town of Ophir, are clear, beautiful streams one day, muddy torrents another.

These natural conditions don't offer the prime trout fishing such beautiful terrain would seem to produce. The river is stocked with catchable size rainbow trout up to 12 inches.

LAKE FORK

The **Lake Fork** of the San Miguel parallels Hwy 145 as it rises in the vicinity of Lizard Head Pass. It is small and brushy with small brook and rainbow. **Trout Lake** (9,750 ft; 200 ac) is beside the highway and offers 8- to 12-inch rainbows, some brook and an occasional cutthroat. This is a pretty site. Boats and camping are available, and fishing can be good.

The **Howard Fork** of the river comes down through Ophir to merge with **East Fork** and form the South Fork. Fishing is poor. Above Ophir at timberline are the **Alta Lakes** (11,250 ft; 11-15 ac). These are shallow lakes with rainbow. They are reached by driving 1.5 miles east from town on the only road, then north 3 miles. A 6-mile-long road off Hwy 145 near Telluride goes to Alta Lakes; it is usually open early in July.

TRIBUTARIES

Numerous creeks feed down steep slopes into the San Miguel. Many of them, such as **Bilk Creek,** (which enters the river just below the confluence of the South Fork), **Deep Creek, Bear Creek** and **Fall Creek** are 4-6 feet wide, fast, brushy, and contain small brook and rainbow. Dirt roads from Hwy 145 provide access in good weather. The Fall Creek Road provides about 12 miles of access into rugged terrain beneath Mt. Wilson (14,017 ft).

Woods Lake (9,400 ft; 30 ac), with its rainbow, brook and occasional cutthroat and brown, is a stocked lake of the Colorado Department of Natural Resources. It is reached by a 9-mile-long dirt road that leaves Hwy 145 about 3 miles above Placerville. Camping is available off state property below the lake. Fishing is good in late summer; artificial flies and lures only.

About 7 miles below Telluride at Placerville, **Leopard Creek** enters the San Miguel. Although readily accessible by Hwy 62, which parallels it, Leopard Creek offers only fair to poor fishing. Some portions of the river are privately stocked, and summer-fall fishing is good where stream improvements have been made.

Saltada and **Beaver Creeks** enter the San Miguel 5 and 2 miles, respectively, above Norwood. These are small, brushy streams with small fish.

Gurley Reservoir (8,264 ft; 400 ac when full) has stocked rainbow and brook and northern pike. Northern pike less than 24 inches long must be returned to the water immediately. It's a fluctuating irrigation reservoir, where boats are allowed and fishing can be good. The reservoir is reached by driving south on the Norwood-Dolores Road, which goes south from Hwy 145 about 0.5 mile east of Norwood. There is camping.

MIRAMONTE

Miramonte Reservoir (7,755 ft; 420 ac) is a state recreation area and probably offers the best fishing in the San Miguel River area. It has good size rainbow, although most are in the 10- to 14-inch range. There is a good boat ramp. Fishing is prohibited in the inlet areas and streams (W. Naturita Creek) and the canal from Middle Naturita Creek from March 1 to June 1. It is 18 miles south of Norwood via the Norwood-Dolores Road. Camping is allowed. This is a fee area.

The San Miguel River below Norwood offers generally poor fishing, although some channel catfish are taken. Mineralization and siltation drastically diminish the stream well before its juncture with the Dolores River below the uranium mining town of Uravan. ☐

FLOAT FISHING

An inflatable rubber raft, paddle frame and two long wooden oars are not standard equipment in the fisherman's outfit. Yet, a growing number of the more than 300,000 people who float Colorado Rivers are fishermen exploring new waters.

Colorado, with its rugged terrain and deep canyons, can be a difficult place to fish. The advent of the float-fishing industry has opened up some of the state's hottest fishing.

Fishing while floating can offer access to those deep, impenetrable canyons and trailless stretches of creek, and does away with battling the brush and hanging up on streamside trees and bushes. Many of the best float-fishing streams add surges of excitement to the trip on whitewater stretches. The Roaring Fork, the Upper Colorado, the Gunnison, the Arkansas, the North Platte, all offer the combination of good fishing and exciting rapids. And, these rivers require no permits for river running.

Hiring commercial outfitters and guides for float fishing is a good idea for those unfamiliar with the river or handling a boat in white water. Trips from a half-day to a week can be arranged through commercial outfitters, and range in price from $25 to $300. More than a dozen outfitters across the state currently offer fishing packages with their float trips. For information on outfitters, contact the Western River Guides Association, 7600 E. Arapahoe, Suite 114, Englewood, CO 80112; phone 303/771-0389.

DOW FISHING LEASE
Applebaugh easement
Location: 13 miles west of Telluride along Hwy 145 (1.02 mi of river)

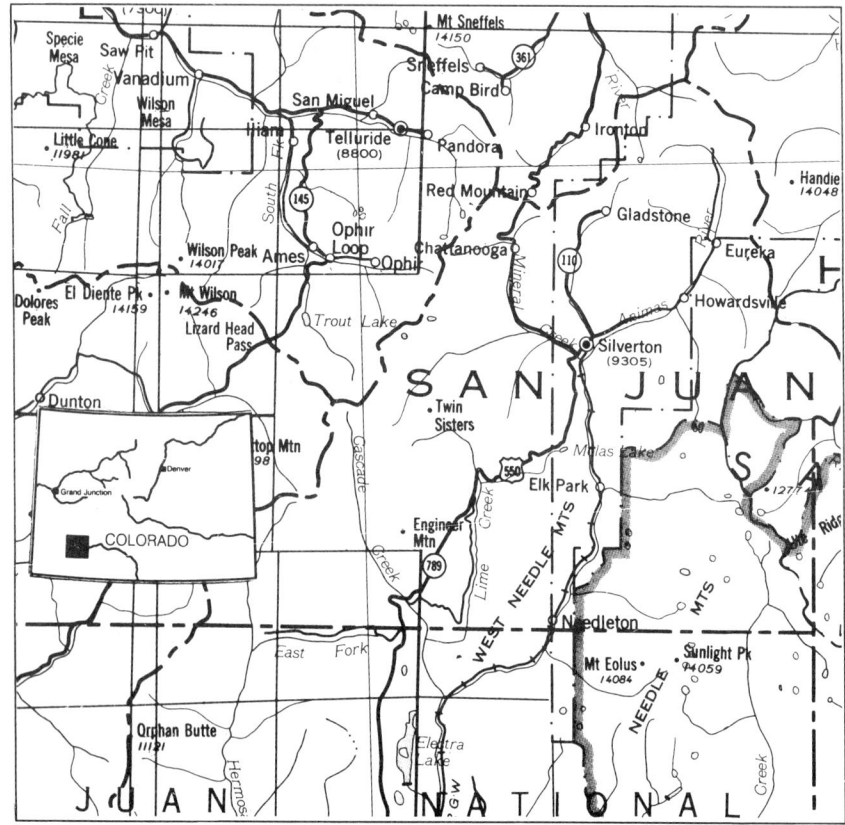
Animas and San Miguel Rivers

U.S. Forest Service campgrounds

U.S. Forest Service compilation was current as of 1985.

Asterisks denote fee areas. Some campgrounds are open only Memorial Day weekend through Labor Day. Below freezing weather could mean no water supply.

SAN MIGUEL RIVER DRAINAGE

SAN JUAN NATIONAL FOREST
Headquarters: Federal Bldg., 701 Camina del Rio, Durango, CO 81301

Campground name	Elevation	No camp sites	Travel trailers	Drinking water	Length of stay (days)	Location and directions
Sunshine*	9500	15	Yes	Yes	14	On Colo. 145, 8 mi SW of Telluride
Matterhorn*	9500	23	Yes	Yes	14	On colo. 145, 10 mi SW of Telluride

Early autumn snows herald fine fishing beneath golden aspen in southwest Colorado.

Gunnison River angler's playground

Adjacent communities:
Gunnison, Crested Butte, Lake City, Montrose, Delta.

Principal Highways:
U.S. 50; Colo. 135, 92, 133.

The Gunnison River basin has the best the Rocky Mountain region has to offer in fishing, scenic beauty and western hospitality. Blue Mesa Reservoir, the state's largest body of water, Taylor Reservoir and hundreds of miles of sparkling clear, trout streams help make it one of the most popular outdoor recreation lands in the West.

There are northern pike, mackinaw, cutthroat, rainbow, brook and brown trout, as well as kokanee salmon to tempt the angler whether he or she prefers remote high country lakes or the readily accessible roadside lakes, streams and reservoirs. The fishing is there.

The City of Gunnison is the bull's eye for information and supplies as well as a change of pace from mountain camping.

The description of the Gunnison begins just west of Monarch Pass with mention of tributary streams, their lakes and creeks.

Tomichi Creek heads above the town of White Pine, 11 miles north of US 50 on a dirt road at the western foot of Monarch Pass. You can drive 5 miles past White Pine to a Forest Service campground. The creek is about 5 feet wide, brushy, swift and rocky. It offers small brook and rainbow along the road and brown 6 to 10 inches long. Good fly stream downstream from Sargents. Below White Pine, permission is necessary from landowners. From the foot of west Monarch Pass, Tomichi parallels US 50. It offers about 30 miles of fishing for brook and brown, and there are lots of suckers. This is private land with some posting. Permission from all landowners is advised. Mosquitoes can be overwhelming, even after using skeeter dope, nets and gloves. Tomichi averages 12 to 15 feet wide, as it meanders through meadows. It enters the Gunnison 1 mile southwest of the town of Gunnison. It is wadable and easily fished. Tomichi offers mostly brown and some rainbow averaging 11 inches; some large brown are taken from under banks. Bait can be used early and flies when water clears; excellent fly stream. Rated good; best in early spring, late summer and autumn.

Canyon Creek enters upper Tomichi Creek from the north 3 miles below White Pine and offers 5 miles of fishing for brook to 10 inches. Rated fair to good; brushy and difficult to work; beaver dams.

Marshall Creek enters Tomichi Creek from the southeast about 1 mile west of Sargents along US 50. Follow the road that turns south at Sargents, which goes over

Marshall Pass for 40 miles to Poncha Pass and Salida. It follows the creek for 10 miles. There's good fly water in the lower sections for 12-inch brown; very few brook. Lower 6 to 7 miles are on private land, where permission is necessary. Upper reaches are good for brown, rainbow and brook to 10 inches. Good campsites.

Needle Creek enters Tomichi Creek from the south 4 miles above Doyleville along US 50, and about 23 miles east of Gunnison. The lower stream is brushy and has some small brook and a few rainbow. Turning off US 50 south onto a dirt road, travel 5 miles to **Needle Creek Reservoir** (8800 ft; 6 ac). Route is very confusing; inquire locally. Although this deep reservoir fluctuates greatly, it has some rainbow and brook. Creek is accessible another 5 miles for small brook.

Razor Creek merges with Tomichi about a mile below Doyleville. A good all-weather road south from Doyleville provides good access to fair fishing for small rainbow and brook. Road meets Cochetopa Creek Road about 16 miles southwest of Doyleville.

COCHETOPA CREEK

Cochetopa Creek rises along the Continental Divide about 30 miles south of Tomichi Creek and flows north. Hwy 114 from US 50 parallels Cochetopa for about 18 miles before turning east. Good road continues south to **Lower** and **Upper Cochetopa Dome Reservoirs** state recreation area, at about 9000 feet elevation. The Division of Wildlife has leased 6 miles of Cochetopa and **Pauline Creeks.** Some good browns can be taken here.

Los Pinos Creek, which enters the Cochetopa about 4.5 miles downstream from this reservoir, is fair for brook and, at higher elevations, some cutthroat. A good road to Old Agency follows Los Pinos. This is a wild trout water and is strictly catch-and-release fishing. The reservoirs are stocked with rainbow, brook and some cutthroat.

Quartz Creek enters Tomichi from the north at Parlin, 12 miles east of Gunnison on US 50. Hwy 162, which goes over Cumberland Pass into Taylor Park, parallels Quartz Creek for 18 miles to Pitkin. The road is narrow in places over the pass, but the scenery is beautiful. Around 10 feet wide, Quartz Creek offers rainbow, brook and a few brown to 12 inches on bait early and flies later. Rated good. Forest Service and DOW teamwork has improved 1.3 miles of the creek, and fishing has improved.

Lower section is posted but permission often is granted. Very bushy from Ohio City to Roosevelt Mine, 4.5 miles upstream. Cabins are available in Ohio City and Pitkin, with camping facilities at Forest Serice camps at Pitkin (16 mi north of Parlin) and Quartz Creek (7 mi north of Ohio City), both on Hwy 162.

Two mile above Pitkin, the road forks. The east fork leads 2 miles to a campground at **Middle Quartz Creek** . The creek is good for small rainbow and brook. To get to **South Quartz Creek,** which is good for small brook, drive another 0.5 mile. Both streams are 3 to 4 feet wide, with beaver ponds.

CAMPER COURT

See and Fish the More Than 200 Lakes On the Grand Mesa

Featuring one of the state's largest campground laundry facilities, swimming pool, showers, full hookups, and over 130 spaces.
Expanded facilities will include: new waterpark with water slide and wave pool; ice skating rink.

(303) 242-2527
2819 Hiway 50 • Grand Junction, CO 81503

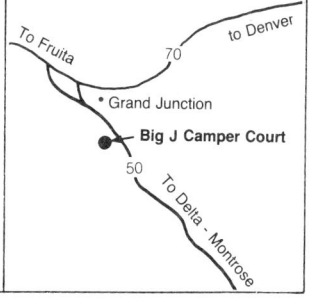

> **WESTERN SLOPE HOMES**
> **ALL PARTS & SUPPLIES**
> **FOR R.V.'s**
> Open May - September
> 912 W. Gunnison Ave., Gunnison CO
> (across Hwy. 50 from A&W Drive-In)
> **(303) 641-2430**
> *"We cater to fishermen
> and love fish stories."*
> -Carol Uelmen, Proprietor

Quartz Creek above Pitkin is known as **North Quartz Creek**. It is paralleled by the Cumberland Pass Road, and can be good for small brook, rainbow and brown. Four miles of the creek have been improved, fisherman parking has been provided and fishing is reported good. It has many ponds. **Gold Creek** enters Quartz from the north at Ohio City. Accessible by about 8 miles of rough, dirt road that ends at the campground. Stream is about 4 feet wide, brushy; contains small rainbow and brook.

A drive north from the Gold Creek Campground on a poor 4-wheel-drive road leads 3 miles to **Upper Lamphier Lake** (11,700 ft; 4 ac). Good for small cutthroat. **Lower Lamphier Lake** (11,250 ft; 3 ac) is about 0.25 mile down the drainage. Fair for 8- to 12-inch cutthroat. From Upper Lamphier the visible notch that is seen in the ridge to the north is Gunsight Pass.

Hike 3 miles through the pass over a rough, steep trail to **Henry Lake** (11,700 ft), a deep 13-acre lake. Fair for 8- to 12-inch cutthroat and some large rainbow. It can also be reached from Lottis Creek Campground on the Taylor River, 7 miles by good horse trail.

Boulder Lake (11,100 ft; 20 ac) is reached by 2.5 miles of well-marked trail from Gold Creek Campground. The lake is overstocked with naturally produced small brook. **Mill Lake** (11,500 ft; 2 ac) is reached from Boulder Lake Trail just before crossing Fossil Ridge. (North about 1 mile along Lamphier Creek drainage.)

Crystal Lake (11,250 ft; 3 ac) is reached from Willow Creek, which enters Quartz from the northwest about 0.5 mile below Ohio City. Use 4-wheel drive to go 5 miles upcreek to old Carbonate King Mine, and then hike 5 more miles by marked trail over and down Fossil Ridge. South of the ridge, Boulder Lake can be seen. Crystal Lake is opposite Boulder Lake on the north side of the ridge. Crystal is fair for 8- to 12-inch cutthroat, some rainbow.

To the north and northwest of Fossil Ridge are stream drainages that create the Gunnison River itself at the village of Almont. The foremost of these is the Taylor River and Taylor Reservoir set in the great basin of Taylor Park, about 25 miles northeast of the city of Gunnison.

TAYLOR RESERVOIR

An irrigation reservoir with a fluctuating water level, the **Taylor Reservoir** (9330 ft) is about 4 miles long and 2 miles wide when full. It contains rainbow and brown, averaging 11 inches, and many larger fish. Stocked with kokanee, northern pike and mackinaw. Mackinaw under 20 inches and northern pike under 24 inches must be returned to the water immediately. Only one mac over 20 inches may be kept. Boats are available; motors are allowed. Fishing is very good in May, early June and late fall. Trolling is good most of the summer. There is a Forest Service campground. The reservoir also is accessible from Buena Vista by traveling west on the Cottonwood Pass Road. Good gravel roads in the area are maintained by the county and the Forest Service.

From the head of Taylor Reservoir to its source above Bowman, the river is followed by a dirt road for 22 miles. The river is 15 to 20 feet wide, rather slow and shallow, and is especially fine for fly fishing for rainbow, brown and brook to 10 inches. The river above the reservoir is good in early season for German brown, Loch Leven and mackinaws that come up from the reservoir. Wadable except in spring; there are several camping areas.

Taylor forks at Bowman at the end of the road. Use Jeep or pickup for 5 miles along main Taylor to the west for small cutthroat on flies.

The Forest Service has constructed two reservoirs of 3 and 5 acres, the **Pot Hole Lakes** (9724 ft), located 5 miles above Taylor Reservoir off the road to Dorchester. Heavily stocked, they are good for rainbow to 12 inches.

Bowman Creek, entering Taylor at Bowman, is small and swift. It is rated fair for small brown, rainbow and cutthroat. A trail follows the creek.

Taylor Lake (12,400 ft; 30 ac) is 4 miles from Bowman by 4-wheel-drive road. No buildings are left at this old ghost town site, just good campsites. Bowman is located at the confluence of Bowman Creek and Taylor. Taylor is rated good for rainbow and brook to 13 inches. Campsites are located below and around lake. No boats or rafts allowed. Heavily fished.

Pine Creek enters Taylor from the north, 0.5 mile below the ranger station at Dorchester. It is a 4- to 6-foot-wide stream with beaver ponds, and offers 4 miles of fair fishing for small cutthroat and brook. Trail is only fair.

Tellurium Creek joins the Taylor 1 mile below the ranger station. About 6 feet wide with ponds. Eight miles of fishing can be reached by 4-wheel-drive trail. The creek is fair to good for cutthroat in the upper stretches and small brown in lower. **Tellurium Lake** (12,300 ft; 6 ac) is a deep lake above timberline on the west fork of the creek. It is reached by a rough road, steep hike, but it's beautiful. Good (but temperamental) for medium-size cutthroat. Sometimes called **Ptarmigan Lake.** Campsites below lake.

Italian Creek junctions from the west with Taylor below Bowman at the Dorchester Ranger Station. Five miles of fishing in a 4-foot-wide stream for brown and brook to 12 inches, and some cutthroat; rated good; campsites.

Red Mountain Creek enters Taylor River from the northeast about 3 miles above Pie Plant Cow Camp. Drive 1.5 miles up marked dirt road. This 3-foot-wide stream is fishable for another 3 miles by trail. Beaver ponds. Fair for small brook.

Illinois Creek enters Taylor River from the east, 2 miles above the upper end of the reservoir. Rough road up 3 miles of creek offers 6 miles of fishing for small brook and browns in a stream 4 feet wide. Rated fair. Campsites. **Illinois Lake** (10,720 ft; 2 ac) is 1.5 miles by trail from the end of the road. (Consult map.) Good for cutthroat to 12 inches. Lake has heavy fishing pressure.

TEXAS CREEK

Texas Creek flows into Taylor Reservoir from the east. Can drive 12 miles upcreek with Jeep or pickup, 6 miles by car. There are 16 miles of fishing in a stream about 10 feet wide. Good for rainbow, brook and cutthroat to 10 inches. Very good for browns in the fall.

Texas Creek Lakes (10,500 ft) lie hidden in timber 8 miles upcreek on the south

Lake trout or mackinaw

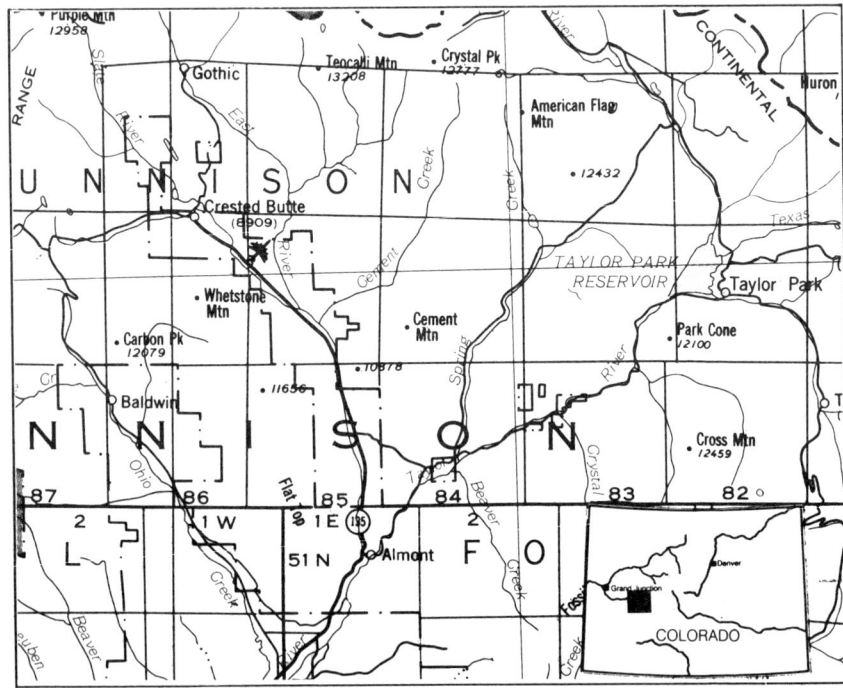

Taylor Reservoir, Taylor River

side, across the stream from the road. There are 3 small lakes, but only the two easternmost have fish. No boats or rafts allowed. Rated fair for brook to 10 inches with some bigger trout possible, especially in the center lake. They are shallow; good fly lakes, though temperamental.

Willow Creek enters the Taylor Reservoir from the east. It has 3.5 miles of water open only to fly fishing from the bridge near the Trading Post upstream to Kentucky Gulch. Very good for brooks and browns 6 to 12 inches. Good for spawning browns in the fall when they swim up from the reservoir. The creek is paralleled by a good gravel road that follows **West Willow Creek** to Cumberland Pass. Stream forks at the town of Tincup. At the church in Tincup, a good gravel road follows **East Willow Creek** for 3.5 miles to **Mirror Lake** (11,000 ft; 27 ac) sign. The lake is fair for small brook and browns, averaging 10 inches; few rainbow; early season best. Campground. No motor boats. A pickup road east from Tincup follows **Middle Willow Creek.** All are small streams up to 10 feet wide, with much willow meadow and pond fishing for good brook and trout populations. Contain small cutthroat in upper ends with rainbow and brown in lower stretches. These are all good streams from midsummer on.

Pass Creek and **Cow Creek** enter Willow Creek from the north about 3 miles above Taylor Reservoir. Creeks are reached by short rough road from Hwy 162. They are small streams with beaver dams offering small brook trout. Rated fair. Pass crossed by Cottonwood Pass Road 3 miles above Taylor Park Trading Post. **Cow Lake** (11,400 ft; 6 ac) is at the head of Cow Creek. Take Timberline Trail from the top of Cottonwood Pass south for 3 miles; sign. Good for 10-inch cutthroat and a few small brook.

TAYLOR RIVER

Averaging 40 to 50 feet wide, the **Taylor**

GUNNISON RIVER

River below the dam is deep and runs fairly fast with deep pools and riffles. Wading is difficult to dangerous. It offers rainbow and brown 10 to 14 inches; many larger fish have been taken. Flies are usually best after mid-July. Heavily fished after July 1. There are a number of Forest Service campgrounds and several posted properties. Taylor is considered one of the best streams in the state. Excellent fishing with good populations of caddis, stone and mayflies. Some big trout flourish here. The river water comes from the bottom of the Taylor Reservoir and is especially cold. There are deep holes; can be dangerous to fish.

Lottis Creek enters Taylor River from the east, 4 miles below the reservoir dam at the Forest Service campground. Fishable up from the mouth by trail or via Union Park on **North Lottis Creek** for upper section. Fun fishing, except for the times it is so windy it knots not only the leader but the flyline as well. **South Lottis Creek** on Gunsight Pass Trail, has cutthroat trout from 3 miles above campground. Another 6.5 miles drivable on dirt road to Union Park Road from Willow Creek bridge near Trading Post. It is 4-wheel drive from there. Cow Camp is located where Lottis Creek leaves the park and flows into the canyon. **Cameron, Cross Mountain** and **Lottis Creeks** are small streams with beaver dams containing brook, cutthroat, rainbow and brown to 10 inches. Rated excellent both in the park and below it. Lottis has brown to 12 inches in the lower part and small brook with some lunkers in the upper section. Campsites.

Crystal Creek enters Taylor near Almont. Six-mile stream, 4 feet wide, contains small cutthroat. Rated fair with flies; fast water.

Spring Creek enters Taylor River from the north, 7 miles above Almont on Hwy 306 at Harmel Resort. Good for browns. Can drive upcreek on a good Forest Service road. Road continues down **Rocky Brook Creek** another 12 miles to Taylor Park. This 48-mile loop through beautiful country is highly recommended. Stream averages 10 feet wide with rainbow to 10 inches. Open, easy fishing; rated good early and fair later. Cabins are available at the lower end of Spring Creek and there are ample campsites upstream.

Rocky Brook and **Bear Creek** in Deadman's Gulch are tributaries of Spring Creek, entering it about 7 miles above its mouth. Small streams with beaver dams offer fair fishing for small cutthroats and brook. The Division of Wildlife has built an 82-acre lake 12 miles up Spring Creek. Known as **Spring Creek Reservoir** (9900 ft), it is fair to good for 12-inch browns and rainbow. The rainbow trout stamp is good here for a double limit. There are some Yellowstone cutthroat and some big trout. The trick is to catch them. Boats are not available, although allowed. Motors are prohibited. Forest Service campground. Beautiful setting. Good fishing for brook in

Boating along the northern shore of Blue Mesa Reservoir.

beaver ponds above the reservoir.

East Beaver Creek enters Taylor River from the south, opposite Spring Creek. It is 10 miles long, 3 feet wide. Lower reaches are brushy; parks and beaver dams upstream offer small brook and brown. Can be very good fishing. Accessible from One Mile Campground on Taylor Road. A 4-wheel-drive road crosses the creek to continue south for 4 to 5 miles. Rated fair.

EAST RIVER FISHING

The **East River** joins the Taylor at the village of Almont 10 miles northeast of Gunnison on Hwy 135 to form the Gunnison River. The East River offers 35 miles of fishing up to the community of Gothic. From Almont to the Glacier Schoolhouse, a mile of the river is paralleled by Hwy 135. Along this stretch there are good pools and riffles. The river swings east of the road for about 9 miles before nearing it again about 1.5 miles below Gothic. Much of the stream bank is lined with willows, so wading is a necessity. Lower half below Crested Butte is heavily posted; fishing only with permission. Contains rainbow, brook and brown trout to 10 inches, with larger fish common, especially browns. Rated good after June. Open to flies only from the confluence with the Taylor River upstream to the bridge at Roaring Judy State Hatchery. One and a half miles of stream are open to fishing, although fish over 12 inches must be returned to the water.

The East River runs on the east side of Crested Butte Mountain. Accessible by a road heading northeast leaving Hwy 135 about 2 miles south of the town of Crested Butte. It's 5 miles to the mouth of Brush Creek. Above Brush Creek, the East River is posted.

Fishermen "lost" about 6 miles of DOW-leased wild trout waters of the East River in 1984 because of bad manners. Disturbing lifestock, trampling hay, interfering with haying and not using turnstiles and paths resulted in the access across private land being posted and closed to public fishing. It is now leased to a more considerate private group.

Brush Creek enters East River from the east opposite Crested Butte Mountain. Reached by dirt road leaving Hwy 135, 2 miles south of the town of Crested Butte. Turn east, travel 5 miles. Rought dirt road drivable from the mouth of creek for 3 miles up **West Brush Creek.** Brush Creek, recently reclaimed and lower reaches restored by AMAX Mining Co., shows promise; upper portion is stocked. Can be Jeeped within 3 miles of Twin Lakes at the head of **Middle Brush Creek** . Four-wheel-drive roads go up both Middle and East Brush. West Brush Creek averages 6 feet wide. Good results are reported as far up as the falls for small rainbow, brook and cutthroat. Middle Brush Creek is fair to good for small brook, cutthroat and rainbow. **Twin Lakes** (11,800 ft; lower 3 ac, upper 7 ac) is reached by 3 miles of trail from Middle Brush Creek Road at the foot of Pearl Pass Road to Aspen. Lies at the foot Teocali Peak, the highest in the area. Heavily stocked with rainbow to 10 inches; some large rainbow in upper section. Campsites below lakes; beautiful lakes nestled in alpine country.

Spencer Lake (10,000 ft; 3 ac) is located in timber. It is situated up Middle Brush Creek and is difficult to find. Faint trail leaves Middle Brush Road 0.5 mile west of where Twin Lakes Trail leaves the road. Rated fair to good for small brook.

East Brush Creek enters Middle Brush 5 miles from the mouth of Brush Creek. It has 6 miles of fishing in a 4-foot stream with a few beaver ponds and much brush. East Brush is hard to fish, but is rated good for cutthroat to 11 inches.

Farris Creek joins East River from the north about 4 miles above Cement Creek on private land. Accessible by rough dirt road; 4-wheel drive or pickup from Brush Creek Road recommended. Turn right 0.75 mile above Veltrie Ranch; then it is 3 miles to the creek at the Forest Service boundary. There is private posted land downstream, where permission to fish generally is not granted. Farris is about 3 feet wide with large beaver ponds and deep pools. Good for small brook.

Cement Creek enters East River from the east at Glacier Spur, 11 miles above Almont on Hwy 135. Accessible its entire

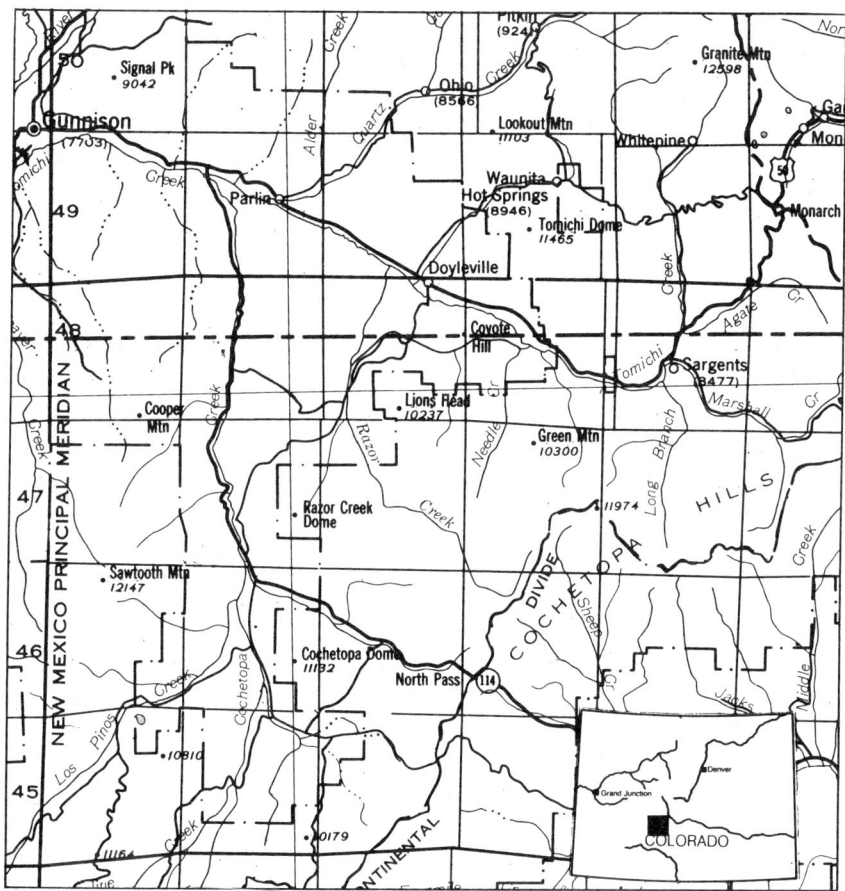

Tomichi and Cochetopa Creeks

length (12 miles) over good dirt road. Turn east from Hwy 135 at sign. One resort on the creek allows fishing by permission; many campsites. Forest Service Cement Creek Campground is 4 miles off Hwy 135. Brushy in lower part, Cement Creek meanders through a park higher up. Rated fair to good for rainbow, brown, cutthroat and a few brook to 10 inches

The road from Crested Butte to Gothic (8 miles) has the **East River** on the east side when traveling north 4 miles to Gothic. Gothic is the site of the Rocky Mountain Biological Research Station. Several long-term research projects are being conducted in the vicinity. The area downstream is known as "meanders" and it requires walking 1 to 2 miles down a very steep hill. Fishing is in slow water for rainbow, brook and brown to 10 inches. Rated good at times, especially fine for flies. Road crosses East River at Gothic and follows the stream 4.5 miles to its source near Schofield Pass. Small, 4 feet wide, it is fair for small brook and rainbow.

Emerald Lake (10,500 ft; 12 ac) is on Schofield Pass about 4.5 miles above Gothic in Gothic Natural Area, along a rough road that often is snowbound. Rated fair for catchable rainbow and brook, with a few large ones taken. Ponds in the area are research sites and closed to fishing. Beautiful lake and country; campsites. Takes 4-wheel drive over the pass to headwaters of the Crystal River in Pitkin County.

Copper Creek enters East River at Gothic from the east. It is small and swift, offers poor to fair fishing for small cutthroat and rainbow. **Copper Lake** (11,450 ft) is up Copper Creek, 6 miles from Gothic by 4-wheel drive. It contains cutthroat up to 12 inches; is rated fair. Forest Service campground at lake. **East Maroon Lake** (12,500 ft; 5 ac) is located 2 miles north of Copper Lake on good marked trail; has cutthroat averaging 12 inches. Rated good. No campsites of any value. Often iced over into midsummer.

CRESTED BUTTE AREA

Slate River enters the East River 6 miles below Crested Butte and is accessible by good dirt road north from town. Road crosses the creek just east of town and then parallels Slate River northwest for 9 miles to Pittsburg and 2 miles beyond. Eight feet wide, the stream is open above, brushy near mouth. Contains brook, brown and rainbow to 10 inches. Some Snake River cutthroat and small brook in uper reaches. Rated fair to good. Campsites. **Nicholson Lake** (8900 ft), a small lake, is located about 3 miles north of Crested Butte on the Slate River Road to Pittsburg, which goes right around it. Has brook to 10 inches. Rated fair; many rough fish.

Oh Be Joyful Creek enters Slate River about 6 miles north of Crested Butte; accessible by dirt road north of town. (Inquire in Crested Butte.) By 4-wheel drive it's 7 miles upstream, but not far with car. Beautiful small stream, 6 to 8 feet wide, offers small cutthroat and brook. Rated fair.

Blue Lake (11,100 ft; 5 ac) is reached by a good 2-mile trail from the end of the road up the South Fork of Oh Be Joyful Creek. Stocked with small rainbow and cutthroat. Rated fair. No campsites at lake. Ice is late to leave—usually July.

Peeler Creek joins Oh Be Joyful Creek from the west, 2 miles above the mouth. Small and seldom fished. **Peeler Lake** (10,800 ft; 5 ac) is located up Peeler Creek by a good steep trail 4 miles from the end of the road. Lake is off the main trail to the left, or south 0.5 mile in timber; very difficult to find. Contains brook from 8 to 10 inches, with some fish to 16 inches. Rated good but very temperamental.

Washington Gulch Creek enters Slate River east of Crested Butte; accessible from marked dirt road 2 miles north of town. Offers 2 miles of fishing in a stream 4 feet wide; brushy at mouth; open upstream. Fair for small brook.

Meridan Lake (9700 ft; 40 ac) is reached by traveling a dirt road up Washington Gulch north of Crested Butte. The road forks 2 miles from town; take the left fork 2 more miles to where a trail can be seen across the creek. It leads 0.25 mile to the lake. Steep hike. Fishing for rainbow from 10 to 12 inches.

Lake Irwin (10,350 ft; 30 ac) is sometimes called Lake Brennand. It is reached by Hwy 135, 8 miles northwest of Crested Butte on the Kebler Pass Road. A closed-off dirt road from the highway leads north about a mile to a Forest Service campground and the lake. It's a well-worn track, so it's easy to follow. Fishing for rainbow and brook to 10 inches is good. Particularly pretty site.

Green Lake (10,560 ft; 5 ac) at the headwaters of **Wildcat Creek** is good for small cutthroat. It is reached by trail from Kebler Pass Road about 3 miles west of Crested Butte. Most of Wildcat Creek is on private land. It provides fair fishing for small brook and cutthroat in the national forest area.

Coal Creek, which parallels Hwy 135 for several miles, has 6- to 10-inch brook and some good brown trout. It appears to be recovering from acid mine drainage pollution. It is often overlooked as a fishery, even in the town of Crested Butte, where it flows into Slate River.

Between Almont and Gunnison, **Ohio Creek** enters the Gunnison River at the north edge of the city of Gunnison after flowing 15 miles southeast through private meadowland (where permission to fish is necessary). Extreme upper reaches are in national forest and are accessible via the Ohio Pass Road leading from Gunnison to the summit of Kebler Pass. The creek contains rainbow, brown and brook, with some cutthroat in the upper area. Usually good in

GUNNISON RIVER

spring; fair later.

Tributaries to Ohio Creek include **Pass, Castle** and **Carbon Creeks,** all with access across private property to national forest. There are intermittent brushy stretches and many beaver ponds for brook, cutthroat and rainbow that are found in these 4- to 5-foot-wide creeks. There is camping at Cow Camp on Castle Creek. About 2.5 miles by trail from the end of the road at Cow Camp is **Costo Lake** (10,000 ft; 15 ac). It is inside the West Elk Wilderness Area and is a good fishery with 12- to 14-inch brook and some cutthroat.

Mill Creek flows into Ohio Creek from the west. Walk past a posted 3-mile section to the national forest. Some brook and rainbow.

West of the city of Gunnison, about 5 miles along Hwy 50, **Beaver Creek** enters the Gunnison River from the north, and **South Beaver Creek** comes in from the south. Both are on private property; permission is needed; brushy, and fair for brook and rainbow.

BLUE MESA RESERVOIR

With 73 miles of shoreline, **Blue Mesa Reservoir** (7519 ft; 9000 ac when full) is Colorado's largest body of water and a favorite fishing hole. It is part of the Curecanti National Recreation Area.

Beginning 9 miles west of Gunnison, the reservoir is 23 miles long and it receives tremendous fishing pressure for brown, rainbow, kokanee salmon and mackinaw

---

SUNNYSIDE CAMPGROUND
Only Full-Service
RV Park on Blue Mesa
OUTBOARD MOTOR RENTALS
SMALL ENGINE REPAIR & SERVICE
MARINE ENGINE REPAIR
DRY STORAGE
12 Mi. West of Gunnison
on Blue Mesa Reservoir
DICK & JEAN OSWALD, Owner, Mgr.
P.O. Box 808, Gunnison, CO 81230
(303) 641-0477

---

from both bank and boat anglers. More than 30 streams flow into it, providing food and spawning habitat. State and federal fish hatcheries annually stock hundreds of thousands of trout and salmon, many 8 inches and up.

The reservoir is divided into three large basins. From the east (the upstream end) they are: **Iola, Cebolla** and **Sapinero Basins.** Most of the shoreline is open and without cover, even in picnic and camping areas, although manmade screens provide some shielding. At that altitude, hats and sunscreen lotions are essential, even on cloudy days.

At the extreme east end of the reservoir, Hwy 149 moves south from Hwy 50, across a bridge to skirt the south shore for about 2 miles to Iola Campground before turning south to Powderhorn, Lake City and high country fishing in their respective vicinities. Several miles of the southern shoreline are accessible only by water or foot.

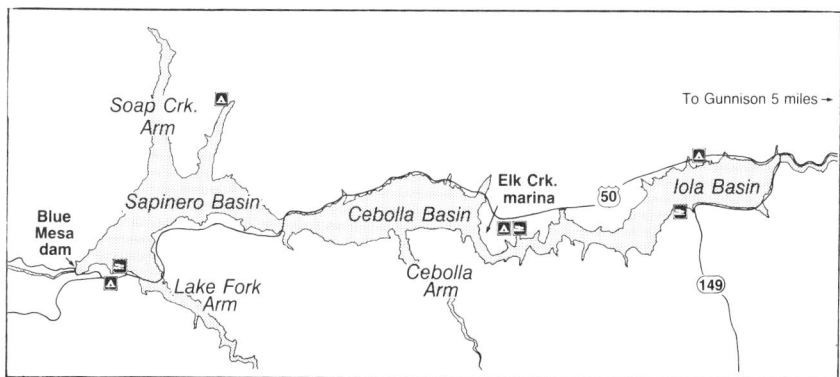

Blue Mesa Reservoir

MARINA

Hwy 50 follows the north shore, and near its midpoint a service road leads to Elk Creek Marina, which has boat and tackle rentals, boat slips, guide service and supplies. A public boat launch is free. There also is a campground, RV dump station, picnic ground and first aid station.

Cleo Loken, marina operator, opened a second, smaller marina in 1984 near the boat ramp on the Lake Fork Arm of the reservoir. It has gas, boats and tackle rental, bait and a small convenience store. The marinas are open from 7:30 a.m. to 6:30 p.m. during the tourist season. (Tackle rental does not include flies, lures, bubbles, sinkers, etc., just rod, line and reel.)

The Hwy 50 bridge spans the reservoir at the narrows between Cebolla and the most westerly basin, Sapinero, and continues west across the Lake Fork Arm and past the dam. Just past the bridge, on the south side of the reservoir, a good all-weather road goes southeast to provide access to fishing in the Lake Fork of the Gunnison River and Cebolla Creek drainages. (These will be discussed later.) Just west of the dam, another road leads southeast to the same areas. Boat fishermen tend to troll along the submerged river channel and up and down the major arms of the reservoir. Casting from boats and bait fishing are popular around the island in Cebolla Basin, around bridge pilings and in creek inlets. Fishing deep for big browns and rainbows causes clusters of fishermen near the dam.

Shore anglers tend to like the east end and the creek inlets where the incoming streams merge with impounded water. In winter, auger-bearing ice anglers concentrate their chipping in Iola Basin, where fishing often is good.

Winter anglers use boat ramps to drive out on the ice. Other winter fishing spots include areas off Stevens Creek, the Elk Creek boat ramp, Middle Bridge and Lake Fork—if it's frozen over. Ice fishing tends to taper off in March.

Fishing in early spring for rainbow can be excellent, whereas browns near the tributaries are sought in the fall.

Boaters should realize that strong winds rake the reservoir into white caps early in the afternoon on most midsummer days, but abate by late afternoon, allowing evening fishing. The water level can fluctuate as much as 100 feet over a season, but doesn't appear to affect long-term fishing.

The setting for Blue Mesa Reservoir is one of western beauty with cliffs, stone outcroppings and escarpments crowning the northern shore. The south shore is austere, featuring rolling hills of sagebrush and scrub oak.

Less than a dozen of the more than 30 streams that flow into Blue Mesa Reservoir have much fishing. Two, **Lake Fork of the Gunnison** and **Cebolla Creek,** drain vast areas south of the reservoir that offer superb angling opportunities in the streams and lakes among 13,000- and 14,000-foot peaks of the Continental Divide.

LAKE FORK ANGLING

The Lake Fork of the Gunnison River heads in the old mining area of American Basin 20 miles southwest of Lake City in high, very precipitous and rugged country. **Sloan Lake** (12,080 ft; 10 ac) is the source of the stream; although stocked with brook and cutthroat trout, they tend to winterkill. Local inquiry is suggested to acertain the situation. Sloan is reached by 4-wheel drive by taking an old mining road southwest from Whitecross townsite about 4 miles below the lake. Last mile is often too steep to be negotiated by vehicle.

Cooper Lake (12,700 ft; 5 ac) and **Cooper Creek,** which flows south into the Lake Fork just above Whitecross, have brook and cutthroat to 10 inches. Although deep, the lake tends to winterkill. Fishing above Whitecross is in the stream and some ponds for brook, cutthroat and some rainbow.

Below Whitecross, the Lake Fork is in a

Fishermen spent more than half of the $1 billion spent for all hunting and fishing in Colorado in 1981, according to the Colorado Division of Wildlife.

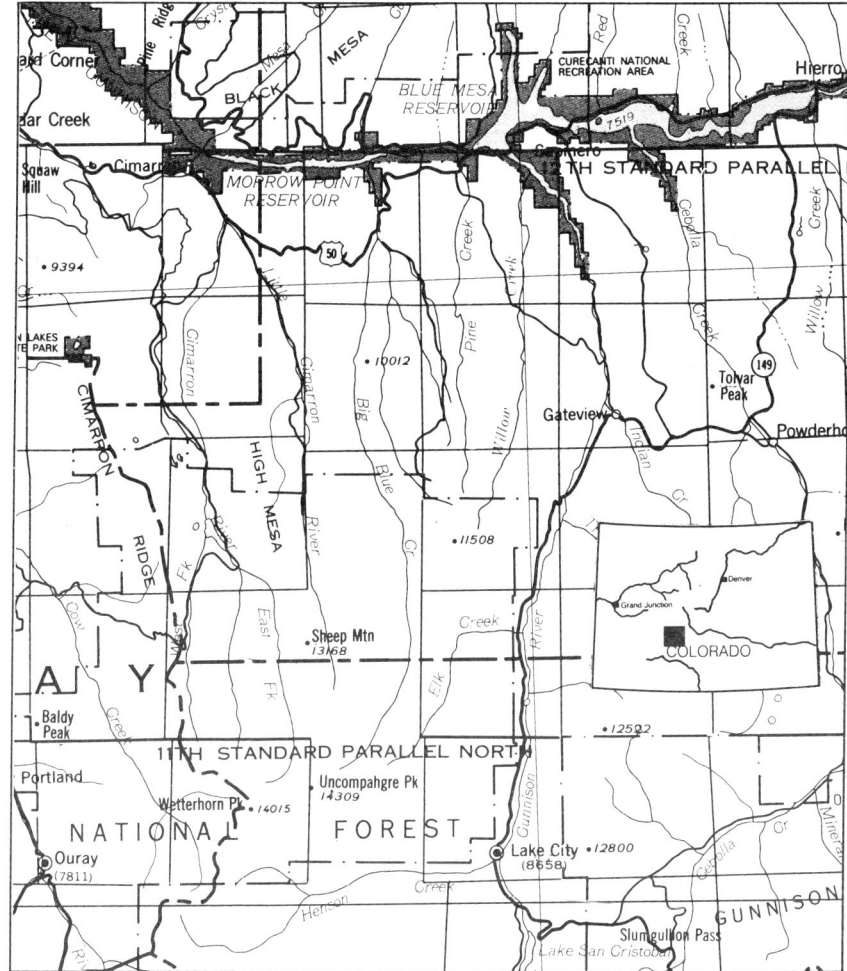

Blue Mesa Reservoir, Lake Fork of the Gunnison River

steep canyon for more than 2 miles and is very difficult to reach above the confluence with Cottonwood Creek. **Cottonwood Creek** has about 6 miles of good fishing above its confluence with the Lake Fork. It is brushy and hard to fish on the lower reaches, but open meadow and beaver ponds in the upper reaches and tributaries offer cutthroat and brook.

Cataract Creek flows into Cottonwood Creek near its confluence with the Lake Fork at the ghost townsite of Sherman. About 2 miles upstream are beaver ponds, usually good for small brook and some cutthroat. **Cataract Lake** (11,800 ft; 15 ac) is 5 miles upstream by trail. The first mile is steep, then it's relatively easy walking. Ice covered until July, it contains brook trout, including some 14 to 15 inches. Several small ponds to the west may be worth checking out.

Downstream from Sherman to Mill Creek Campground, the Castle Lakes and Williams Creek Campground, the Lake Fork is heavily fished and stocked with rainbow. There also are brook and brown. Brushy stretches alternate with some ponds and pools. Spectacular country.

LAKE CRISTOBAL

Lake Cristobal (9000 ft; 2.5 mi long) is a large, natural lake offering good fishing for rainbow, brown, brook, cutthroat and some mackinaw. It is heavily fished and stocked. Mossy area on the upper end is good for flies. Boats are available. Just below the outlet is Argenta Falls. Good road circles the lake. Fly fishing only from the bridge above the lake down the stream to the lake.

Just above Cooke Falls, a bridge spans the Lake Fork and connects with the Park Creek Road to provide access to **Waterdog Lake** (11,100 ft; 11 ac). The 5-mile road begins at T Mountain Resort and heads northeast. Fishing is for 10-to 12-inch brook and rainbow.

At Lake City, **Henson Creek** races into the Lake Fork from the west. A well-marked road leads 16 miles up the historic mining valley past many abandoned mines and townsites. The lower reaches of the creek are in canyon and are difficult to reach below Treasure Falls. Above, it contains rainbow, brook and some cutthroat from 11 to 13 inches, although most are smaller. Much of the stream is posted for fly fishing only. Narrow valley; camping limited. Eight miles upstream, **North Henson Creek** joins the stream at Capitol City townsite. Fair fishing for small brook and cutthroat. The whole area is a 4-wheel-drive mecca and is heavily traveled, since the Henson Creek Road goes over Engineer Pass (about 13,000 ft) to Ouray. Most tributary streams are small, swift and too vertical to offer much fishing.

Crystal Lake (11,700 ft; 12 ac) and **Larson Lakes** (11,000 ft; 8 ac) are reached by trail heading west from Hwy 149 about 2 miles north of Lake City. Fair to good fishing for rainbow, brook and some cutthroat. Good trail. Crystal Lake, which is about 2 miles south of Larson Lakes, also can be reached by Cemetery Road just south of Lake City. Good campground. **Hay Lake** (10,100 ft; 1 ac) is a small pond with lively brook trout fishing.

About 10 miles north of Lake City, a marked dirt road leads west about 9 miles up and out of the Lake Fork drainage to Soldier Creek and Big Blue Campground. First part of route is rough. (This is discussed under the Cimarron River section of the Gunnison River.)

Below Lake City, the Lake Fork is a substantial stream for more than 25 miles to the Lake Fork Arm of Blue Mesa Reservoir. The river meanders through meadows and brushy sections, and much of it is posted as private property as far as the village of Gateview. From Gateview to the reservoir, the river is in deep canyon. Rainbow and brown trout are sought with lures and bait, and some good-size fish are taken from deep holes and stretches of fast water. Most of this section is public land, and a dirt road north from Gateview on the east side of the river provides access to the reservoir. A good road continues northwest from Gateview to join Hwy 50 just west of the Blue Mesa Dam.

The terrain south of the reservoir has numerous dirt trails and roads. A good map and local inquiry are strongly recommended, even though major routes are marked.

Boaters coming up the Lake Fork Arm will find a put-in campground on the west bank that's sheltered from reservoir winds.

CEBOLLA CREEK

Cebolla Creek rises east of Lake City and is reached via Hwy 149 over Slumgullion Pass; by going south, traversing Spring Creek Pass on Hwy 149, the headwaters can be reached from Creede when winter snows have receded.

The creek flows for more than 40 miles to join Blue Mesa Reservoir at its midsection.

The Forest Service has 5 campgrounds in the upper reaches of Cebolla Creek between Slumgullion Pass and Cathedral townsite. The terrain ranges from rolling timber to steep rock cliffs and outcrops. There are numerous small creeks. **Deer Creek Lakes** (10,500 ft; 6 lakes of 3 to 4 ac each) are stocked and easily fished for 9- to 13-inch rainbow and an occasional cutthroat. Campground. **Mill Creek** and **Brush Creek** as well as Cebolla have small brook and cutthroat in this area. Streams often are brushy, but fishing can be good. Try beaver ponds.

Rough and **Mineral Creeks** are difficult

to reach and hard to fish in some sections, yet can be rewarding for cutthroat and brook. Both are accessible; but only by horse or foot traffic. Sections of the trail are very rough and steep.

Spring Creek merges with Cebolla at Cathedral. Up to the falls on **Cascade Creek** about 6 miles, stream and beaver pond fishing can be good for cutthroat and brook. Some posted sections. Again, beautiful country. Ask permission to cross private land.

There is roadside fishing along the creek in the **Cebolla Creek State Wildlife Area** just north of Cathedral for brook and rainbow.

Downstream to Powderhorn, Cebolla Creek is followed by the road, and much of the creek is posted. There are many ponds. Seek permission to fish on private land.

POWDERHORN

From Hwy 149, 2 miles northwest of Powderhorn, a dirt road heads north up the **Powderhorn Creek drainage.** The road becomes a trail before entering the Powderhorn Primitive Area. The **East, Middle** and **West Forks of Powderhorn Creek** are good for small brook, and the upper portions contain some cutthroat. Many beaver ponds. **Powderhorn Lakes** (11,859 ft; 6 and 8 ac) can be excellent for cutthroat and brook from 12 to 13 inches. Sometimes winterkill occurs and the lakes often are frozen over until midsummer. Local inquiry is a good idea, as some areas are bog and swamp.

Below Powderhorn, Cebolla Creek flows through sagebrush country and offers some rainbow and brown trout fishing. No highway. Access is difficult and stream side is a patchwork of public and private property. Ask for information in Powderhorn.

A put-in campground on the west side of Cebolla Arm is accessible by boat.

NORTH SIDE

On the north side of Blue Mesa Reservoir, **Beaver, Steuben, Willow, East Elk, Red, West Elk, Coal** and **Soap Creeks** enter the reservoir from what is some of the best big game hunting country in the state.

These streams tend to be small and brushy, with willow growth and only fair fishing for brook and some small rainbow and, occasionally, beaver pond fishing for brook. Access is generally steep and rough by 4-wheel road or trail.

Deadend roads up Red and East Elk creeks are not maintained and are better considered for hiking. The Dry Creek Road is a good 13 miles to **Rainbow Lake** (10,847 ft; 10 ac when full). Creek often is dry, lake is fair for brook and rainbow when there's sufficient water. Nice campground.

There is a put-in campground on West Elk Arm that's reachable only by boat. There is private property upstream and permission to cross it should be sought.

Soap Creek (Sapinero Creek on old maps) has a good gravel road north along its west side to Soap Creek and Commissary Gulch campgrounds. Turn off Hwy 50, cross Blue Mesa Dam on Hwy 92 and go up canyon a few hundred yards to sign, turn back east and road follows above the reservoir about 7 miles before a turnoff to a road that descends to the reservoir at Soap Creek inlet. Main road continues on, following the creek for 8 more miles to Big Soap Park. Trail continues 2 miles to West Elk Wilderness Area boundary.

Soap Creek is about 10 feet wide and is fair to good for brook and rainbow, especially early in the season. Generally, ample campsites are available in addition to campgrounds.

The Bureau of Reclamation and the National Park Service have made many improvements since 1979 by adding campgrounds, picnic areas and other facilities for visitors.

For 50 miles below Blue Mesa Dam, the Gunnison River is at the bottom of precipitous canyons where access is infrequent, difficult and sometimes dangerous. Howev-

---

In 1981 fishermen spent $598 million of more than $1 billion spent for hunting and fishing in Colorado, according to the Colorado Division of Wildlife.

er, the fishing for brown and rainbow can be superb, as indicated by gold medal status of a major portion of the stream.

Though dammed in two locations, creating long reservoirs that lap at canyon walls, this is not an area for spur-of-the-moment or casual fishing. Angling these waters must be a well-planned endeavor warranting investigation beyond the parameters of this fishing guide. Employment of a professional guide is worth considering, especially for trips into the canyon below Crystal Dam.

Morrow Point Dam arcs across the Gunnison River 12 miles below Blue Mesa Dam and backs the river up about 11 miles to create **Morrow Point Reservoir** (7200 ft; 820 ac). A landslide closed the road to Morrow Point Dam in 1985, blocking access to the upper end of Crystal Reservoir and Morrow Point Dam. The reservoir is up to 400 feet deep and has mackinaw, kokanee, rainbow and some brown trout. Ice is usually off by Memorial Day. The best access is down Pine Creek on the south side of the reservoir just below Blue Mesa Dam. Only small boats can be managed down—and back up—the stairs. Improved boat launching facilities are being planned. There is no fishing 200 yards below Blue Mesa Dam as posted.

Canyon walls along Morrow Point Reservoir are so steep that there are few opportunities to fish without a boat. The reservoir has fish weighing several pounds. Bait, lures, streamers and flies can be used. Boaters should be aware of spastic winds and having to go against the current to return to the launching site.

Streams entering Morrow Point Reservoir include Curecanti and Blue Creeks. **Curecanti Creek** flows in from the north and is accessible by walking or 4-wheel drive from Hwy 92 about 10 miles west of Blue Mesa Dam. The highway goes up Soap and Black mesas, and access to the reservoir from the very, very steep north side requires a treacherous, arduous effort down and up again. Although from a road map it looks short, it is not worth the effort. Where the highway heads north up Curecanti, 4 miles west of Blue Mesa Dam, the reservoir is 500 feet below. Curecanti offers fair fishing in the stream and its many beaver ponds for brook trout 7 to 11 inches long. It extends several miles to the north.

Blue Creek enters the reservoir from the south across from the Curecanti Creek inlet. About 9 miles east of Blue Mesa Dam on US 50, a Forest Service road goes off to the south for some 30 miles providing access to rainbow, brook and cutthroat fishing in **Big Blue Creek, Soldier Creek** and many beaver ponds in Uncompahgre National Forest. At the confluence of Big Blue and Soldier creeks is the Big Blue Campground. This is high country, around 9800 feet elevation, where meadow fishing is rated fair. A trail goes up Big Blue Creek a dozen miles to its headwaters at the foot of 14,309-foot-high Uncompahgre Peak.

CIMARRON RIVER

West of Big Blue Creek is the Cimarron River drainage.

The **Cimarron River** flows into the Gunnison just below Morrow Point Dam and power plant. Four miles east of the Cimarron Store on US 50, a good road goes south up the river almost 20 miles providing access to **Little Cimarron River** and **Fall Creek,** which have some brook and cutthroat trout fishing.

About 2.5 miles south from US 50, a road goes off to the southwest 18 miles to Silver Jack Reservoir, Big Cimarron and Beaver Lake campgrounds and numerous small lakes.

Silver Jack Reservoir (8800 ft; 250 ac) is at the juncture of the **West, Middle** and **East Forks of the Cimarron River.** Fishing is good for rainbow spring and fall. Streams in the area, accessible by trail, have brook, rainbow and cutthroat. The road goes up West Fork about 8 miles, paralleling the stream, to its headwaters near Owl Creek Pass. No boats are allowed on Silver Jack. A landslide and washout has closed the Owl Creek Pass road on the Ridgway side. From the Cimarron side, it is still negotiable for getting to high lakes and streams.

Beaver Lake (8750 ft; 5 ac) is an old lake 3 miles below Silver Jack on the river. It is fair fishing for rainbow. No boats allowed;

there is a campground.

To the west of the river, less than 2 miles, in the same area as Beaver Lake, are **Hampton Lake** (9650 ft; 10 ac), which is good for rainbow, brook and cutthroat to 12 inches, and **Fish Creek Reservoirs No. 1 and No. 2** (9350 ft; 15 and 25 ac). The two reservoirs are less than 0.25 mile apart and are good fishing for 10- to 12-inch rainbow in early summer. A fish die-off was reported at Hampton in early 1985. No reports on its extent. Inquire locally. The reservoirs are reached by 4-wheel-drive road heading west below Big Cimarron Campground.

Three miles of the Cimarron River are open to public fishing above its confluence with the Gunnison River. The lower Cimarron was stocked with some 200,000 kokanee salmon fry in 1985 in hopes of building a population of the fish. It'll be 1988 or so before snagging can take place, if the experiment works. Water is clearest late summer and fall, and fly fishing is good, according to Bill Newberry of Newberry's Store at Cimarron. He's knowledgeable about Crystal Reservoir fishing, too. At Cimarron, a paved road winds down the canyon to the Gunnison and provides access to **Crystal Reservoir** (6759 ft), created by Crystal Dam some 3 miles downstream. Small boats may be carried down to the water from a parking lot 100 yards away. **Warning:** *reservoir fluctuates a lot—from 4 to 10 feet some days—making it very difficult to get back out of the river to the parking area if the water level has dropped. It takes a 7.5 hp motor to come back upstream. Some boaters end up hiking the shoreline pulling their boats against the current to return to the launching area.*

BLACK CANYON OF THE GUNNISON

Fishing in Crystal Reservoir can be excellent; 2- to 5-pound rainbow and brown are not uncommon. Lures, nightcrawlers, plugs, streamers and trolling all seem to work at one time or another.

The reservoir is in the Black Canyon of the Gunnison, where for 53 miles the canyon rim is 1730 to 2700 feet above the river. Half of this distance, the lower 26 miles from the eastern boundary of Black Canyon of the Gunnison National Monument downstream to the confluence of the river with the North Fork of the Gunnison, is gold medal trout fishing water. The trick is to get to it. Recent stream surveys, which required use of a helicopter, revealed that fishermen consistently hook 18-inch rainbow and brown, and that the fish are in prime condition.

High volumes of water through the canyon in 1983, 1984 and 1985 indicate that fishing could be superb, if water levels drop. Some outfitters float the canyon, which is great, if one can hang on and fish simultaneously.

Fishing pressure between the confluence of Smith Fork and North Fork on the west end of the gold medal waters is very heavy because this is the most accessible portion of the stream. In the gold-medal-water stretch, fishing is with artificial flies and lures only; all trout between 12 and 16 inches long must be returned to the water immediately. Daily possession limit is 4 trout, only one of which may be over 16 inches.

Just beginning

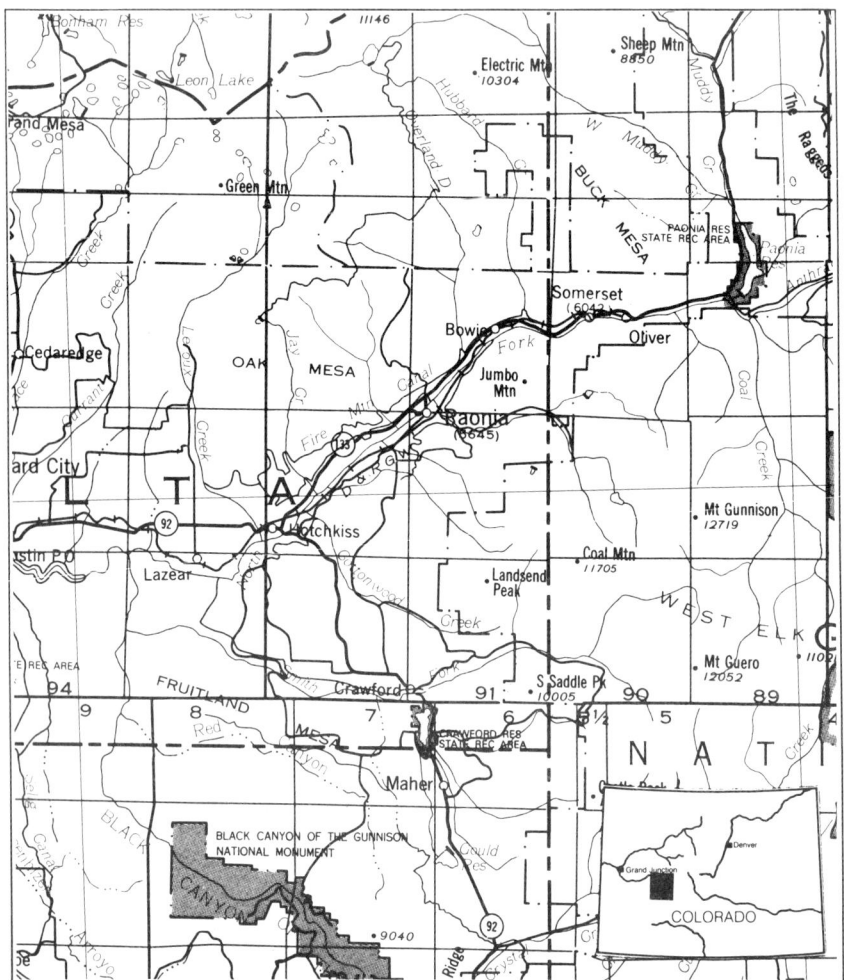

North Fork Gunnison River

Black Canyon of the Gunnison National Monument is a fascinating diversion for the angler and companions, although it offers little fishing access, unless one is an accomplished technical mountain climber. Check with monument personnel about access. The monument is 6 miles east of Montrose via US 50, then 5 miles to the south rim. The north rim is accessible via a 14-mile dirt road from Crawford.

Smith Fork Creek enters the Gunnison in Black Canyon about 11 miles downstream from the monument boundary. It drains the west side of the West Elk Mountains and just isn't much of a fishing stream, although there are some rainbow and brook. The upper reaches and Smith Fork Campground are on a good road 7 miles east of Crawford. From Crawford west, access is on private, posted land where permission to fish is unlikely.

Little Coal Creek, which feeds the Smith Fork just inside the national forest 6 miles east of Crawford, is good fly fishing, but tends to get fished heavily for brook and rainbow. **Crawford Reservoir** (6550 ft;

340 ac when full) is a mile south of Crawford along Hwy 92. Good fishing for rainbow 8 to 12 inches and some good catfish, with 12- and 15-pounders caught nearly every year that run 20 to 24 inches long. Other warm water fish are taken on bait. The lake is a state park with camping, trailer facilities and boat ramps; some ice fishing. It is a fee area.

Gould Reservoir, just south of Crawford Reservoir, is private, often dry late in the year and is not stocked. It may have some rainbow and perch. Permission is needed to fish.

Four miles downstream from Smith Fork Creek, the Gunnison leaves its canyon and is joined from the east by North Fork of the Gunnison. The 4 miles between Smith Fork and North Fork are heavily fished, being accessible by boat coming upstream from North Fork confluence, and by trail and 4-wheel-drive roads over BLM land. Inquire at BLM office in Montrose for access routes and maps. The fishing pressure is heavy for brown and rainbow. There also are flannelmouth suckers, roundtail chub and the protected Colorado squawfish.

NORTH FORK GUNNISON RIVER

The **North Fork** and its tributaries drain a vast area to the east and north. It and many of its tributaries are tapped for irrigation water and, since the terrain is readily eroded, the streams often are muddy after summer showers and spring runoff. Late in the year, there is some good fishing.

The headwaters of the North Fork comprise East and West Muddy Creeks and Anthracite Creek, which merge just below Paonia Reservoir.

Muddy Creek rises 18 miles north of the reservoir in a host of small streams with brook and cutthroat. **Clear Fork Creek, Jones Creek, East Fork Muddy Creek** and **West Muddy Creek** join East Muddy Creek from the west and north. **Lee Creek** follows Hwy 133 down from McClure Pass, and **Spring** and **Dugout Creeks** flow in from the east. These streams have small brook, sometimes rainbow and cutthroat. There are many beaver ponds and, usually, open meadow as well as brushy segments.

Paonia Reservoir (6450 ft; 300 ac when full) is fair fishing spring and fall for rainbow, but poor in summer. Usually lots of suckers and some good size northern pike, which respond best in summer. Northerns under 24 inches must be returned to the water immediately.

GRAND MESA

Anthracite Creek joins the North Fork from the east. Its headwaters are in several tributaries high in rugged mountains. The creek is fair for rainbow, brook and some brown to 12 inches. The upper reaches primarily contain cutthroat and brook, and there are plenty of beaver ponds.

Tributaries include **North Anthracite Creek, East Anthracite Creek, Ruby Anthracite Creek** and **Middle Anthracite Creek.** Access is by the Kebler Pass Road

---

BETTER FISHING

Better fishing in Colorado can result from catch-and-release angling. Fish returned to the water have a chance of surviving—to grow, propagate and be caught again.

Returning fish to the water isn't as simple as it sounds. Fish are easily subject to being fatally injured. Following the steps below can help a fish survive to be caught again.

—Do not play the fish to total exhaustion before landing it.

—Keep the fish in the water as much as possible while removing the hook and preparing to release it.

—When removing the hook, do not squeeze the fish or put your fingers in its gills.

—If the fish has swallowed the hook, do not pull the hook out. Instead, cut the line as close to the hook as possible leaving the hook inside the fish.

—When releasing the fish, hold it gently in the water, head facing upstream until it has become reacclimated. Move it slowly back and forth to help it regain its equilibrium.

Colorado DOW

> *A fish's range of vision is proportional to its depth—the deeper the fish, the greater the area it can see.*

between Crested Butte and the North Fork, where it comes in at Paonia Reservoir. The road often is closed by snow until late June. Foot trails lead up most creeks from Erickson Springs Campground, which is 5 miles by road east of the reservoir.

Dollar Lake (10,050 ft; 2 ac) is poor fishing for stocked brook to 10 inches. It sometimes winterkills. Northwest from Dollar, **Lost Lake** (9870 ft; 8 ac) is 1 mile from the Lost Lake Campground on Lost Lake Slough. Lost Lake is good for 8- to 10-inch brook. **Lost Lake Slough** (9625 ft; 53 ac) is a fluctuating reservoir. It has fair to good fishing for stocked rainbow and natural brook to 10 inches. Best results are early in the season. A campground is located on its north shore and is accessible by a rough road 2.5 miles from the Anthracite Creek Road and 8 miles southeast of Erickson Springs.

Coal Creek enters the North Fork Gunnison River from the south just below Paonia Reservoir. It is rated fair to good for rainbow and brook to 12 inches. A dirt road follows the stream to its headwaters. Flowing into Coal Creek from the east, **Cliff Creek** provides small stream fishing for cutthroat, rainbow and brook to 10 inches. At its headwaters, **Sheep Lake** (10,505 ft; 10 ac) is just inside the West Elk Wilderness. It is reached by 8 miles of trail from the end of the road on Coal Creek. It offers fair fishing for rainbow and cutthroat to 16 inches. It is a good fly fishing lake.

Little Gunnison, Cascade, Robinson and **Willow Creeks** also feed into Coal Creek and offer similar fishing.

About 2 miles west of Somerset, **Hubbard Creek** enters the North Fork from the north. A rough road leading to the east end of Grand Mesa follows the creek for several miles. Hubbard is fair for brook trout on its upper reaches. The road, like others in the area, is slippery and treacherous during and immediately after rain.

At the headwaters of Hubbard Creek is **Overland Reservoir** (10,800 ft; 170 ac), which is good for 10-inch rainbow, cutthroat and brook. Two miles southwest by trail from Overland is **Crater Lake** (10,000 ft; 6 ac). It is rated poor as few fish survive winterkills, but those that do may be 18 to 20 inches long. Nearby streams are rated good to excellent fishing for brook, cutthroat and rainbow to 12 inches.

On the west side of the town of Hotchkiss, **Leroux Creek** enters the North Fork from the north. It stretches 22 miles to the south end of Grand Mesa. The creek is good for small rainbow at the lower end and cutthroat at the upper. At its headwaters are several reservoirs that are rated poor with the exception of **Goodenough Reservoir** (10,400 ft; 25 ac), which is accessible by road. It is rated fair to good for 10- to 12-inch cutthroat and rainbow. Some large brown are taken. Less than a few hundred yards west, **Dogfish Reservoir,** about the same size as Goodenough, is rated fair for the same type of fishing.

West of Hotchkiss, the North Fork flows through mostly private land and permission to fish is a good idea. Some good rainbow and brown are in the stream. As the Gunnison flows toward Delta and then Grand Junction, increased in size by North Fork waters, there is good brown and rainbow fishing all the way to the town of Austin, about 8 river miles downstream. This is a popular floating area. There are many suckers, chubs and other trash fish in the river, and streams that flow into it usually are muddy, silt-laden and fishless, except at their highest elevations.

UNCOMPAHGRE RIVER

The **Uncompahgre River** joins the Gunnison at Delta after a long, winding trip from the mountains near Ouray, some 60 miles to the south. Initially clear and fast as it runs from the San Juan Mountains, it provides good fishing for rainbow and brown between Ouray and Montrose, although public access is difficult because much of the valley is in private ownership.

Canyon Creek flows into the river in Ouray and offers rainbow and brook trout fishing. Take the Camp Bird Mine Road southwest from town. Most streams in the immediate Ouray area are too steep and fast for fish.

Dallas Creek joins the Uncompahgre from the southwest about 3 miles downstream from Ridgway. Its upper portions and tributaries are reached by driving west from Ridgway on Hwy 62 for 5 miles and then south 2 miles to where the road forks. Take the west fork of the road 7 more miles to the Uncompahgre Wilderness boundary. Two miles farther south are the **Blue Lakes** (11,000 to 12,000 ft; 3 to 5 ac), with fair fishing for rainbow and cutthroat. **East Fork of Dallas Creek** has fair fishing for cutthroat and rainbow inside the wilderness. **West Fork of Dallas Creek** has similar fishing via a private road that turns off Hwy 62 about 6 miles west of Ridgway; a rough road for about 8 miles, then trail.

Coming into the Uncompahgre from the southwest, 8 miles north of Ridgway, is **Cow Creek.** It rises 18 miles to the southwest and its upper 10 miles are in national forest and open to public fishing for small rainbow and cutthroat. Several roads west from Hwy 550 lead to the creek at its intersection with the Owl Creek Pass Road. The Owl Creek Pass road is blocked by a landslide and washout on the west side of the summit. Upper reaches are across 4 miles of private land by 4-wheel-drive road; then trail. Many small streams in this area and beaver ponds have small cutthroat and good dry fly fishing for them. Inquire in Ridgway about permission to cross private land.

Downstream from Ridgway to Montrose and Delta, the river is essentially part of the valley's irrigation system. **Fairview Reservoir** (6270 ft; 20 ac) is just off US 50 about 5 miles east of Montrose. It is fair to good for rainbow. Turn off US 550 at Fairview and go southeast 1.5 miles; or south off the highway a half-mile east of the Black Canyon of the Gunnison National Monument Road.

Sweitzer Lake (5100 ft; 127 ac), in the Sweitzer Lake State Recreation Area, is a warm water fishery stocked with channel catfish and other warm water fish. It is 1.5 miles south of Delta on US 50, then east a mile.

From Delta to Grand Junction, the Gunnison River is muddy and often shallow with mostly rough fish. □

U.S. FOREST SERVICE DISTRICT RANGER STATIONS

Grand Mesa, Uncompahgre and Gunnison
 National Forest Headquarters
1603 Main St., P.O. Box 138
Delta, CO 81416   303/874-7691

Paonia Ranger District
Gunnison National Forest
North Rio Grande St.
Paonia, CO 81428

Ouray Ranger District
Uncompahgre National Forest
101 N. Uncompahgre Ave., P.O. Box 1047
Montrose, CO 81401   303/249-3711

Cebolla and Taylor Ranger Districts
Gunnison National Forest
216 N. Colorado
Gunnison, CO 81230   303/641-0471

RIVERWOOD

Hwy 50, just north of Delta Bridge   on the Gunnison River
Grand Mesa, Black Canyon nearby

**Pond or River Fishing on Premises
Riverwood RV Park-All New
Tent Sites Available
Free Mini-Golf
Bed & Breakfast at adjoining Riverwood Inn**

677-1575 Road, Delta, CO 81416   (303) 874-3854

RESERVATIONS ACCEPTED

U.S. Forest Service campgrounds

U.S. Forest Service compilation was current as of 1985.

Asterisks denote fee areas. Some campgrounds are open only Memorial Day weekend through Labor Day. Below freezing weather could mean no water supply.

GUNNISON RIVER DRAINAGE

GUNNISON NATIONAL FOREST
Headquarters: 11th and Main St., Box 138, Delta, CO 81416

Campground name	Elevation	No camp sites	Travel trailers	Drinking water	Length of stay (days)	Location and directions
Gold Creek	10,000	6	Yes	Yes	14	1.3 mi NE of Ohio City by forest road
Comanche	9100	4	No	No	14	2 mi N of Ohio City by forest road
Middle Quartz	10,200	7	Yes	No	14	7 mi NE of Pitkin by forest roads
Pitkin*	9400	22	Yes	Yes	14	1 mi E of Pitkin by forest road
Quartz*	9800	10	Yes	Yes	14	4 mi N of Pitkin by forest road
Snowblind	9800	23	Yes	Yes	14	8 mi N of US 50 and Sargents
Almont*	8000	10	Yes	Yes	3	On Colo. 135, 1 mi N of Almont
Cement Creek*	9000	13	Yes	Yes	14	4 mi NE of Colo 135, 7.5 mi SE of Crested Butte
Lost Lake	9600	10	Yes	No	14	18 mi W of Crested Butte off Colo 135
Lake Irwin	10,200	31	Yes	No	14	2 mi N of County Hwy 2, 7 mi W of Crested Butte
Avery Peak	9600	10	Yes	No	14	7.4 mi N of Crested Butte by County Hwy 3 and forest road
Gothic	9600	4	No	No	14	7.8 mi N of Crested Butte on forest road
Mosca	10,000	16	Yes	No	14	15.1 mi NE of Almont by forest road
North Bank*	8600	17	Yes	Yes	14	6.5 mi NE of Almont by forest road
Cold Spring	9000	6	No	No	14	12.9 mi NE of Almont by forest road
Dinner Station*	9600	22	Yes	Yes	14	32.5 mi NE of Almont by forest road

GUNNISON RIVER

Campground name	Elevation	No camp sites	Travel trailers	Drinking water	Length of stay (days)	Location and directions
Dorchester	9800	13	Yes	Yes	14	21.6 mi NE of Almont by forest road
Lakeview*	9400	35	Yes	Yes	14	17.9 mi NE of Almont by forest road
Lodgepole*	8800	16	Yes	Yes	14	11.7 mi NE of Almont by forest road
Lottis Creek*	9000	23	Yes	Yes	14	13.8 mi NE of Almont by forest road
Mirror Lake	11,000	10	Yes	No	14	22.3 mi NE of Almont by forest road
One Mile*	8600	26	Yes	Yes	14	6.2 mi NE of Almont by forest road
Rivers End*	9400	15	Yes	Yes	14	19.9 mi NE of Almont by forest road
Rosy Lane	8600	17	Yes	No	14	6.9 mi NE of Almont by forest road
Spring Creek	8600	11	Yes	No	14	7.2 mi Ne of Almont by forest road
Commisary	7900	7	Yes	No	14	22 mi NW of Gunnison off US 50 by forest road
Soap Creek	7700	13	Yes	No	14	21 mi NW of Gunnison off US 50 by forest road
Spruce*	9500	10	Yes	Yes	—	8 mi NE of Colo. 149, 9 mi SE of Lake City
Cebolla*	9500	5	Yes	Yes	—	9 mi NE of Colo. 149, 9 mi SE of Lake City
Slumgullion*	11,500	21	Yes	Yes	14	On Colo. 149, 6.4 mi SE of Lake City
Deer Lakes*	10,900	4	Yes	Yes	14	2.5 mi, NE of Colo. 149, 9 mi SE of Lake City
Williams Creek*	9200	20	Yes	Yes	14	On county road 6 mi off Colo. 149, 2 mi SW of Lake City
Erikson Springs	7800	5	No	Yes	14	12 mi E of Somerset off Colo. 133
Mesa	9000	5	Yes	No	14	18 mi SE of Crawford on Colo. 92
McClure	9100	19	Yes	No	14	5 mi SW of Redstone on Colo. 133

GUNNISON AND UNCOMPAHGRE RIVER DRAINAGES
GRAND MESA—UNCOMPAHGRE NATIONAL FORESTS
Headquarters: 11th and Main Streets, Box 138, Delta, CO 81416

Campground name	Elevation	No camp sites	Travel trailers	Drinking water	Length of stay (days)	Location and directions
Antone Spring	9700	7	Yes	Yes	—	1 mi W of Colo. 90, 24 mi SE of Montrose

Name	Elevation	Sites	Toilets	Water	Fee	Location
Iron Spring	9500	7	Yes	No	—	1 mi W of Colo. 90, 24 mi SW of Montrose
Beaver Lake	8800	11	Yes	Yes	14	20 mi S of US 50, 20 mi E of Montrose
Big Blue	9800	11	Yes	No	14	9 mi NW of Colo. 149, 10 mi N of Lake City
Big Cimarron	8600	16	Yes	Yes	14	20 mi S of US 50, 20 mi E of Montrose
Columbine	8700	4	No	No	—	11 mi NW of Colo. 90, 24 mi SW of Montrose
Amphitheater*	8400	31	Yes	Yes	7	½ mi E of US 550, 1 mi S of Ouray
Divide Fork	9200	9	Yes	Yes	—	15 mi SW of Colo. 141, 13 mi SW of Whitewater
Carson Hole	8400	5	No	No	—	7 mi SW of Colo. 141, 13 mi Sw of Whitewater

There's a big brown here someplace!

White River
marvelous to muddy

Adjacent communities:
Meeker, Rangely.

Principal Highways:
Colo. 64, 789, Rio Blanco County Rd. 132.

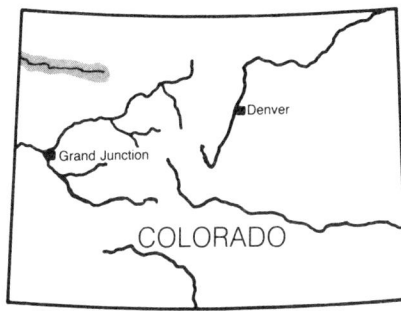

The **White River** originates in one of the best year-after-year trout fisheries to be found anywhere—Trappers Lake on the edge of the Flat Tops Wilderness. While the river is predominately a whitefish water from Meeker downstream, the upper stretches are the home of brook, rainbow, cutthroat and some brown trout. The river is stocked with rainbow and cutthroat near Meeker.

It flows west through beautiful valley pastureland before reaching the town of Meeker. West of the junction of Hwys 13 and 64 south of Meeker, fishing quality declines. As the river moves through sagebrush country (the bottomlands often are irrigated pasture) to Rangely and then into Utah, the once clear, swift waters become silt-laden and slow moving.

The Flat Tops Wilderness offers some of the finest fishing in Colorado. (See the separate chapter on the Flat Tops Wilderness, which discusses lakes and streams not tributary to the White River.) There are scores of lakes, beaver ponds and streams. Although some of them are barren, many (including unnamed waters) have superb cutthroat, brook and rainbow trout fishing, especially in late summer and early fall. Much of the area is soggy from melted snow and water, and the mosquitoes sometimes are intolerable.

Trappers Lake (9627 ft; 320 ac) is accessible by driving up the White River Road from Meeker, taking the Elk Creek Road north from New Castle (W. of Glenwood Springs) or driving south from Steamboat Springs or Hayden.

Fishing at Trappers has improved in recent years and 14- to 15-inch cutthroat are common, thanks to restrictions on size and catch. Be certain to check current regulations. The Trappers Lake Lodge has a marina where small boats and canoes can be rented. Also, one can pack a canoe or boat to the Forest Service campground where there is a launching area. (See the Flat Tops Wilderness chapter.) The lake is one of the most scenic and productive fisheries anywhere.

The White River, its tributaries downstream from Trappers Lake including Marvine Creek and the South Fork of the White River will be discussed first; then fishing in the Flat Tops proper. Streams with lakes outside the wilderness are described along with the river system itself.

Skinny Fish Creek and **Lynx Creek** enter the river from the northeast—1.5 and 2.5 miles, respectively, below Trappers Lake.

They are fair for small rainbow and cutthroat. About 3 miles from the road and just before crossing the last stream below Skinny Fish Lake, turn left and go up the hill. Follow along the creek for 0.75 mile to **Elk Lake** (4 ac). It no longer has big rainbow, and recently has been poor for 10- to 12-inch cutthroat. **McGinnis Lake** (9,500 ft; 10 ac), about 0.75 mile southeast of Skinny Fish Lake on the same trail, is good for cutthroat and rainbow from 10 to 14 inches. The lakes are stocked with rainbow.

Big Fish Creek, which enters the river from the south near Himes Peak campground, is good for 10-inch rainbow.

Ripple Creek, where County Road 132 forks 11 miles above Sizemore Resort, is small, fast and brushy. Poor for small rainbow and cutthroat though over a mile of water is stocked periodically. Trails lead to numerous lakes.

Snell Creek enters White River from the north 1 mile below Ripple Creek. A steep trail leads up this small fast creek. The first 1.5 miles are very brushy. First mile above the road is stocked. Fishing is poor in lower part; rated fair in upper for small brook and cutthroat. **Pagoda Lake** (10,000 ft; 55 ac) is a shallow lake in the bottom of a pine timbered mountain park. Trail leaves road just above Snell Creek; sign, 6 miles to lake. Lies about 0.75 mile southeast of the junction of Snell and Ripple Creek trails. No motorized vehicles are allowed—only hiking or horseback. An easier trail takes off from the summit of Ripple Creek Pass 4 miles above Ripple Creek lodge. Trail is marked. It leaves west of the road opposite the sheep corrals. It's about 4 miles to lake. Pagoda is good for 10- to 14-inch brook and some cutthroat.

MARVINE CREEKS

Marvine Creek enters the White River from the southeast at Sizemore Resort, 8 miles above the town of Buford. Marked road follows creek for 6 miles to Forest Service campground. Fishing is open to the public for 0.25 mile after crossing first bridge. Then private land to campground where stream forks. State stocks 2 miles. **West Fork** of **Marvine Creek** is 5- to 6-feet wide, brushy and meandering. This water and setting is as beautiful as an angler could ask for. Fair for small brook and cutthroat. One of the best and easiest trails in the region follows the **Middle Fork of Marvine Creek,** which is about 10 feet wide and rated fair to good for 10-inch brook and cutthroat.

East Marvine Creek is fast and very brushy. It is rated poor to good for cutthroat in early season.

SOUTH FORK

The **South Fork** of White River is followed by a marked road that leaves the Newcastle-Buford Road 1 mile southwest of Buford. The road follows the stream much of the way for 11 miles to a Forest Service campground at the wilderness boundary. The river is posted for 9 miles from the turnoff to the forest boundary—it's all open inside the wilderness. There are 16 miles of good trail to the headwaters. The river is 20 to 30 feet wide and fast, with many deep pools. Much of the stream flows through wide, deep canyons; brushy much of the way

---

ADAMS'
Fishing and Hunting Lodge
Hilkey & Spriggs, Owners
"Your Gateway to the Marvine"

- Trout Fishing
- Horse Rentals
- Wilderness Pack Trips
- Hiking
- Elk & Deer Hunting
- Bowhunting
- Lodge & Cabins
- Family Vacations

Located adjacent to the White River National Forest on Marvine Creek, 32 miles east of Meeker, Colorado.

ADAMS' LODGE 2400 RBC #12
Meeker, CO 81641

Lodge Phone	303-878-4412
Winter Home Phone	303-878-4440
	303-878-4338

Write or Phone For Reservations

Trappers Lake

to headwaters from the campground. Good to excellent for brook, cutthroat and rainbow to 14 inches, and whitefish to 11 inches. The upper end, which has beautiful fly water, is very good for cutthroat and rainbow to 1 pound. There are 6 miles of quality water where only flies are allowed. The South Fork Canyon also is accessible by trail from Deep Lake and Trappers Lake.

Bailey Lake (8,800 ft; 5 ac) is reached via trail south from an old schoolhouse in Buford that now is a community center. It is a steep 4 miles to lake, a half-mile more to **Swede Lake** (8,850 ft; 4 ac). Both are good for brook and rainbow to 12 inches.

Peltier Lake (9,000 ft; 13 ac) is about 8 miles up South Fork from the junction with Newcastle-Buford Road. You can drive about 1.25 miles above the first Stillwater bridge, and then hit the trail up Hill Creek campground for 3 miles to sign: "Peltier Lake Trail." Good trail but very steep. Lake is shallow with open shoreline. Rated good for brook, 10 to 12 inches, best early and late season.

LAKE AVERY

Lake Avery (6,985 ft; 264 ac) is rated good for 10- to 15-inch rainbow with some taken to 5.5 pounds. Some bank fishing, but trolling from boat gives best results. Boat ramp, campground, tables and dumping station are available, but no drinking water. Excellent fishing from when the ice goes out until mid-June. Summer weed growth hampers bank fishing. Lake Avery is just north of the confluence of the White River and the South Fork a mile below Buford. Good road to the north between confluence and Buford leads to lake, which is hidden by hills from the highway. (Each spring DOW nets more than $1,000 in fines from successful fishermen at Lake Avery. Most violations are for possessing too many fish and fishing without a license.) It would be unsportsmanlike not to advise you that, while you're in the valley, Sleepy Cat Dude Ranch serves superb steaks.

The Bel-Aire fish hatchery a mile below Buford has been closed for years, but the Division of Wildlife ponds and frontage on both the White River and South Fork are stocked with rainbow. Fishing is fair to good; some brown trout may be in the lower South Fork on DOW land.

North Elk Creek, about 10 feet wide, offers about 8 miles of fair to good fishing for 8- to 12-inch cutthroat and brook; a few larger cutthroat are possible. Trail takes off from the highway about 3.5 miles below Buford. Hike 5 miles to best fishing. Creek has some ponds. Lower end posted and permission is required.

Miller Creek is reached from County Road 132 about 15 miles east of Meeker on road to the south off highway. Posted water from turnoff to Forest boundary. Road forks after 4 miles. Right fork continues 2 miles; the one to left for 1 mile. Campsites at both. Both the **East Fork** and **Middle Fork** are fair for small rainbow, brook and cutthroat. The creeks are about 6 feet wide, fast and a little brushy. There are a few ponds about halfway up. Good in early season with both bait and flies. Very clear water after July 1. Access to the upper reaches of East, Middle and West forks is possible in dry weather with 4-wheel drive.

Downstream from Buford, much of the stream is on private land—often pasture with cattle. Scenic area, but permission to fish is required. Stream is still clear with good riffles and is good for rainbow, brook and some cutthroat and whitefish. The whitefish near Meeker are in the 15- to 16-inch range and there seem to be plenty of 'em. Rainbow and brook are stocked in the Meeker area.

RIO BLANCO RESERVOIR

Downstream from Meeker, fishing generally is poor. About 20 miles west of town, just above the junction with Piceance Creek and Hwy 64, is the 120-acre **Rio Blanco Reservoir.** It has spring rainbow stockers, then large and smallmouth bass, crappie, perch, northern pike, channel catfish and bullheads. Fishing is generally slow, but some good bass are reported to 4 pounds along the dike. Bass catch is restricted to 15-inch minimum size to help increase the populations. □

U.S. FOREST SERVICE DISTRICT RANGER STATIONS

White River National Forest Headquarters
Old Federal Bldg.
P.O. Box 948
Glenwood Springs, CO 81602   303/945-2521

Blanco Ranger District
White River National Forest
361-7th St., P.O. Box 358
Meeker, CO 81641   303/878-4039

DOUBLE LIMITS ON RAINBOWS AT 13 LAKES/RESERVOIRS

Beginning with the 1985 season, fishermen could be seeing double rainbows. A special Rainbow Trout Stamp is available for $11 which permits the angler to take a double limit—16 instead of 8—of the scrappy fish from 13 designated lakes and reservoirs.

The stamps are available where fishing licenses are sold and are attached to the fishing license.

The 13 waters with double limits allowed with a signed stamp in possession are:

Big Eggleston Lake on Grand Mesa in Delta County
Carter Lake in Larimer County
Chatfield Reservoir on the Jefferson/Douglas county line
Green Mountain Reservoir in Summit County
Home Lake (Sherman Lake on some maps) in Rio Grande County
Horsetooth Reservoir in Larimer County
Jackson Gulch in Montezuma County
Ruedi Reservoir on the Eagle/Pitkin county line
Spring Creek Reservoir in Gunnison County
Trinidad Reservoir in Las Animas County
Twin Lakes in Lake County
Williams Fork Reservoir in Grand County
Willow Creek Reservoir in Grand County.

The double limit rainbow stamp program is experimental for 1985 only and may or may not be extended pending a review of the results. See the current fishing regulations.

TROUT AND SKIING

Skiing is beginning to interfere with fishing in the high Colorado Rockies.

In an effort to extend their ski seasons, some ski area operators are making artificial snow in November and December. Water for the man-made snow is taken from high streams at a time of year when the creeks have barely enough water to sustain fish naturally.

This further, rapid reduction in water supply traps trout in shallow water where they become prey to predators or freeze solid. The only new moisture is snow, little of which replenishes the streams before spring snowmelt.

The impact in some areas—almost all of them above 10,000 feet—is severe. Some ski area operators volunteer to restock the stream with small trout, but their life expectancy is predictable.

The resulting put-and-take fishery is viewed by some fishermen as a poor substitute for a wild trout stream that's made it on its own. ☐

U.S. Forest Service campgrounds

U.S. Forest Service compilation was current as of 1985.
Asterisks denote fee areas. Some campgrounds are open only Memorial Day weekend through Labor Day. Below freezing weather could mean no water supply.

WHITE RIVER DRAINAGE

WHITE RIVER NATIONAL FOREST
Headquarters: Old Federal Bldg., Box 948, Glenwood Springs, CO 81601

Campground name	Elevation	No camp sites	Travel trailers	Drinking water	Length of stay (days)	Location and directions
North Fork*	8000	47	Yes	Yes	14	25.4 mi E of Meeker on Colo. 132 and County Hwy 8
Trappers Lake*	9800	57	Yes	Yes	5	35.6 mi E of Meeker by Colo. 132 and forest roads
East Marvine*	8200	7	Yes	Yes	10	25.6 mi E of Meeker by Colo. 132 and forest roads
Marvine*	8200	18	Yes	Yes	10	25.6 mi E of Meeker by Colo. 132 and forest roads
Meadow Lake	9600	5	Yes	Yes	14	34.8 mi N of Newcastle off County Road 245
South Fork	8000	17	Yes	No	10	23.2 mi SE of Meeker by Colo. 132 and County Hwy 8
Himes Peak	9500	9	Yes	No	10	48 mi E of Meeker on Colo. 132 and county and forest roads

Flat Tops Wilderness remote, wild & superb

Adjacent communities:
Meeker, Steamboat Springs, Eagle, Kremmling, New Castle.

Principal Highways:
No roads in wilderness.

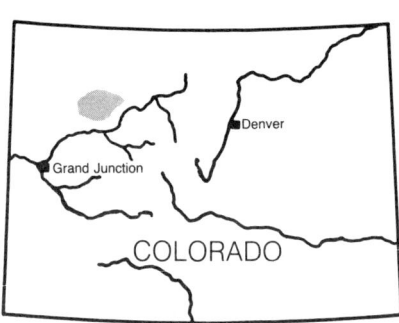

Some of the finest fishing in Colorado is in the Flat Tops Wilderness, a 196,000-acre "high island" between Steamboat Springs and Glenwood Springs.

Many of the streams and lakes are natural fish habitat, and the trout are fat and well nourished on bumper crops of insects and aquatic feed. A lot of the angling is hard to get to, since access is either by horseback or on foot. If there's an area that warrants an outfitter or guide to make the most of it, the Flat Tops is it.

The "Tops" is a maze of pathways, soggy bogs, timbered ridges, hidden ponds and brushy marshes...it's anything but flat once you're on the ground. It's easy to get lost on this 9600-foot-high plateau with dense timber, 11,000-foot flat-topped mountains and rocky ridges.

The Flat Tops receives enormous amounts of snow in average years and is one of the most water-productive areas in the Rocky Mountains. The early-season traveler will find snowbanks embroidering lakeshores and reposing in sheltered areas.

While the "growing season" for rainbow, cutthroat and brook trout and mackinaw is short, many lakes are rich in natural foods, and fish weighing several pounds often are caught. Not all lakes have fish, and several are so temperamental that one wonders if they do. The Flat Tops has several lakes more than 150 feet deep that are splendid fisheries. Trapper's Lake is famed as a cutthroat fishery—a reputation it perpetuates despite being fished heavily.

Veteran outfitters and guides have been known to stock cutthroat in nameless waters for their guests' benefit. Over the years, some substantial fisheries have materialized in out-of-the-way places in terrain that lends itself well to lost and hidden lakes. Backpacking anglers have been known to find a cutthroat paradise one summer only to search fruitlessly in subsequent years to find it again.

The Colorado Division of Wildlife regularly stocks several waters, especially those most accessible. Some lakes, great fisheries in the past, no longer are stocked, usually because of natural factors.

With all the water, there are lots of bugs. Bumper crops of mosquitoes and flies can be expected spring through fall. Insect repellents simply aren't enough. Leather gloves and mosquito net helmets are recommended. Take skeeter juice for the dog.

Very deep and steep canyons lead off the

wilderness on the east, south and west sides, and provide good fishing for hikers in good physical condition.

The wilderness is reached by taking good roads east up the White River from Meeker, southwest from Steamboat Springs, northwest from Dotsero near the junction of the Colorado and Eagle rivers and west from Yampa.

The northeast portion of the Flat Tops in the Routt National Forest drains to the north and east into the Yampa River.

TRAPPERS LAKE

The discussion of fishing in the Flat Tops begins with the headwaters of the White River. The **North Fork White River** flows mostly outside the wilderness, and discussion of that stream appears in the White River chapter. Its headwaters are at **Trappers Lake** (9627 ft; 320 ac), near the northeast wilderness boundary. Trappers is one of the

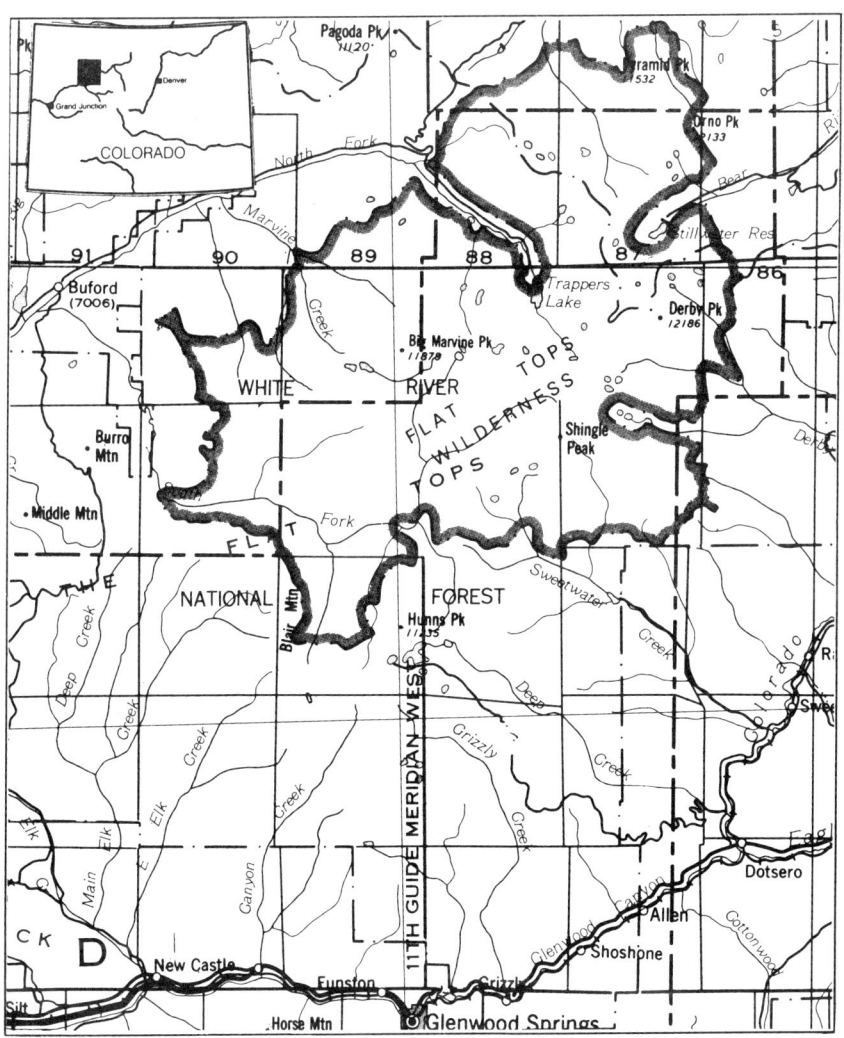

Flat Tops Wilderness

most picturesque lakes with really good fishing in the state. It is very accessible. Take a good county road east from Meeker 50 miles (through Buford) until the road deadends at the Trappers Lake campgrounds. Because of the heavy fishing pressure it receives, fishing is restricted to artificial flies and lures having no more than one hook attached. Only the northwest shore is not in the wilderness. Trappers has a reputation of quality fishing for naturally produced 11- to 13-inch cutthroat. It is a wild trout water. Fishing is prohibited in all inlets and upstream for one-half mile. Fishing is prohibited from January 1 through July 31 in the outlet, downstream 0.25 mile and within 100 yards of each inlet and outlet stream. All trout taken between 11 and 16 inches must be returned to the water immediately. There, a small launching area for carry-in boats is available a few yards from the parking area. Rental boats are available, but no motors are allowed. Fishing from a boat is an excellent way to enjoy Trappers.

East of Trappers Lake about a mile up a trail, **Little Trappers Lake** (9941 ft; 30 ac) can be reached by an easy 1.5-mile trail. Follow **Little Trappers Creek,** which is moderately fast and brushy. Best fishing is in the upper part just below **Little Trappers Lake.** The shallow lake and stream are rated fair for 10- to 12-inch cutthroat and rainbow, with a few larger ones taken.

En route to Little Trappers Lake, **Coffin Lake** is on the north side of the stream about 0.5 mile east of Trappers Lake. Coffin Lake (9700 ft; 10 ac) is full of natural feed and has cutthroat to 5 pounds, though the average is about 16 inches.

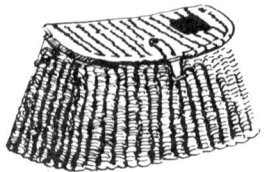

Surprise Lake (11,200 ft; 9 ac) is about 2 miles southeast of Little Trappers Lake. Take trail southwesterly to top of the rim where the trail turns south. The lake lies in timber just below the rim. It is rated good for rainbow to 12 inches.

Due west of Trappers Lake is **Anderson Lake** (9400 ft; 4 ac). A mile hike on a well-defined trail from Trapline Campground, it is poor for brook and occasional rainbow.

South of Trappers Lake about 2 miles up the North Fork is **Wall Lake** (10,980 ft; 12 ac). It is a very deep lake that is rated good for 14- to 16-inch cutthroat; many are taken weighing up to 3 pounds. A steep 5-mile trail from Trapline Campground accesses Wall Lake.

North and west of Trappers Lake about 2 miles is **Lake of The Woods** (9000 ft; 10 ac), a small and shallow water, which is rated good for brook and cutthroat, although it is heavily fished. There are some rainbow, with reports of an occasional trout up to 4 pounds. Access is from the county road, where a sign indicates the lake is a quarter-mile hike.

WHITE RIVER TRIBUTARIES

Big Fish Creek flows into the North Fork White River from the south about 1.5 miles downstream from Lake of the Woods. The creek is good fishing for 10- to 12-inch rainbow. At its headwaters, **Gwendolyn Lake** (9750 ft; 2 ac) is a deep lake with shallow areas. It is rated poor for 10- to 16-inch cutthroat. There is no trail and the lake is difficult to find. About 3 miles upstream from the Big Fish-North Fork confluence, Big Fish Creek flows through **Big Fish Lake** (9400 ft; 20 ac), which is rated fair for rainbow that average 10 inches, though lunkers to 8 pounds are occasionally taken.

Boulder Creek, a small tributary of Big Fish Creek, enters from the north. At its headwaters is **Boulder Lake** (9750 ft; 2 ac), rated good for 10- to 12-inch rainbow.

Downstream from Big Fish Creek about 3 miles, **Mirror Creek** enters the North Fork from the south. At the headwaters of the 3-mile-long stream is **Mirror Lake** (10,000

ft; 12 ac), a deep, beautiful crater lake that is rated excellent for small brook. Downstream from Mirror Lake less than a half-mile, **Shamrock Lake** (9900 ft; 2 ac) is a good fly fishing lake for fat brookies averaging 10 inches.

From here the wilderness boundary cuts southwest across the forks of Marvine Creek. Marvine Creek enters the North Fork from the south about 8 miles east of Buford. At the wilderness boundary, the creek branches in three directions.

MARVINE CREEKS/LAKES

The middle fork of **Marvine Creek** averages about 10 feet wide and is rated fair to good for 10-inch brook, cutthroat, rainbow and some whitefish. Near its headwaters are the Marvine Lakes. **Upper Marvine Lake** (9325 ft; 65 ac) to the east is good for brook averaging 14 inches. **Lower Marvine Lake** (9325 ft; 88 ac), 6 miles from the Marvine Campground on the wilderness boundary and less than a quarter-mile from Upper Marvine, is rated excellent for brook and cutthroat averaging 10 to 14 inches, though many larger ones are taken. Downstream about a mile, **Isle of the Pine Lake** (9200 ft; 7 ac) and **Ruby Lake** (9100 ft; 1 ac) are east of the stream. Ruby is a crater lake located in lava rock; rated fair for 10-inch cutthroat and rainbow. Pine is rated fair to good for 12-inch rainbow-cutthroat hybrids. Downstream another mile, **Slide Lake** (8650 ft; 12 ac) sits in a swamp. Marvine Creek flows through this lake. Slide is heavily fished for 10- to 15-inch cutthroat and rainbow.

Northeast of Marvine is **East Marvine Creek,** stretching about 8 miles from the Marvine Campground. It is a very fast and brushy stream generally rated poor, though it can be good in early season. At its headwaters are several lakes. **Mary Loch Lake** (9800 ft; 3 ac) is surrounded by heavy timber with a steep ridge wrapping around it high above. It is a good fly fishing lake for rainbow averaging 10 inches and cutthroat to 14 inches. Downstream about a mile, **Shallow Lake** (9950: ft; 1 ac) lies east of the stream and is rated fair for cutthroat and rainbow to 11 inches. Just northwest of Shallow is **Rainbow Lake** (9950 ft; 10 ac), rated good for 10- to 12-inch cutthroat. **Guthrie Lake** (9270 ft; 13 ac) is shallow and rated good for 10-inch brook. About a mile northwest of Guthrie, **Johnson Lake** (9000 ft; 9 ac) is a murky lake with difficult fishing for small rainbow; occasionally a lunker is pulled from it.

Southwest of East Marvine and the middle fork of Marvine Creek, **West Marvine Creek** is about 6 feet wide, brushy and meandering. It is rated fair for small brook and cutthroat.

The next stream west is **Ute Creek**, which flows out of the wilderness and meets the North Fork about a mile west of Marvine Creek. A trail from the North Fork road leads up the stream to its headwaters in the wilderness. Ute is a small, brushy stream with a few small headwater ponds and is fair fishing for brook and cutthroat.

SOUTH FORK

The wilderness boundary drops south at this point. And the next major stream flowing from the wilderness to the west is the **South Fork White River.** The South Fork is reached by a good road that leaves the Newcastle-Buford Road about a mile southeast of Buford. The road follows the stream much of the way for 11 miles to South Fork Campground on the wilderness boundary. There's a trail from that point for 16 miles to the South Fork headwaters near the eastern boundary of the wilderness. Much of the stream is in wide, deep and brushy canyons. There are some good pools. The South Fork is rated very good for brook, cutthroat, rainbow and whitefish to 11 inches. The upper end, which has some beautiful fly waters, is good for cutthroat and rainbow to 1 pound. There is a 6-mile stretch of quality water where only artificial flies are allowed.

Patterson Creek enters the South Fork from the south about 8 miles east of the South Fork Campground. At its headwaters are the **Elk Lakes** (10,400 ft; about 5 ac each). Only one has fish, and it is rated fair for 10- to 12-inch rainbow. Downstream on Patterson, **Jet Lake** (10,450 ft; 7 ac) lies to the west of the creek. It is rated fair for 12-inch rainbow and brook.

North of Jet and west of Patterson Creek are: **Shadow Lake** (10,450 ft; 14 ac), which is deep and lightly fished, rated poor for small rainbow; **Blair Lake** (10,640 ft; 28 ac) fair for 12-inch rainbow, brook and cutthroat; and **Crater Lake** (11,146 ft; 30 ac) rated fair for brook with some mackinaw taken to 15 pounds. These lakes rest on the southwest boundary of the wilderness and can be approached by a 4-wheel-drive road from Buford. The last mile or two must be hiked, as they are in the wilderness.

Entering the South Fork from the north, **Lost Solar Creek** is only 5 miles east of South Fork Campground. A trail follows Solar Creek to its headwaters. The creek has very few fish.

EAST RIM WATERS

The southeast portion of the Flat Tops Wilderness is drained by **Sweetwater Creek.** It flows southeast, entering the Colorado River 7 miles north of Dotsero. Take the second road to the east off Hwy 301 coming north from Dotsero. Drive 12 miles to Sweetwater Lake and Campground. Rough road continues up 3 more miles toward wilderness boundary. The creek is ponded and rated good for small rainbow and brook. At the headwaters of Sweetwater Creek are several lakes, including **Rim Lake** (10,824 ft; 14 ac), a deep crater lake on the rim of a cliff, about 8 miles upstream from Sweetwater Lake. (Sweetwater Lake is outside the wilderness. It is discussed in the Colorado River chapter.)

Turret Creek is the only fishable tributary of Sweetwater. It enters Sweetwater from the north about 1.5 miles above the lake. Turret is small and brushy with fast waters and beaver ponds. It is rated good for small cutthroat, brook and rainbow.

North of Sweetwater, the headwaters of the **Derby Creeks** feed from the wilderness and meet the Colorado River near Burns on the road north from Dotsero, or west from McCoy on Hwy 131. Only the **North** and **Middle Forks Derby Creek** are in the wilderness. These streams are loaded with brook, some to 2 pounds, and could use some fishing pressure. Besides, they are excellent eating. Keep an eye open for bighorn sheep in the area. At the headwaters of the North Fork, **Hooper Lake** (10,900 ft; 16 ac), **Keener Lake** (10,900 ft; 12 ac), **Edge Lake** (11,050 ft; 7 ac) and **Bail Lakes** (10,800 ft; 1 to 4 ac) are all good fishing for rainbow. These lakes may be reached by trail from the Stillwater Reservoir, due north on the Yampa-Bear River, which is accessible by car; or from the south by driving a 4-wheel-drive road from Burns northeast 18 miles to the wilderness boundary and then hiking about 3 miles along the stream.

The **Middle Fork Derby Creek** is the westernmost branch of Derby Creek. A trail follows the stream to its headwater lakes. They include **Deer Lake** (11,100 ft; 4 ac), a headwater lake on the rim of the Flat Top that is good in late season for 11-inch cutthroat. **Lower Island Lake** (10,800 ft; 19 ac) and **Upper Island Lake** (10,900 ft; 26 ac), are best in late season after spawning. Lower Island has cutthroat 9 to 10 inches. And Upper Island is rated good for 11-inch cutthroat. Downstream about 3 miles, **Lower** and **Upper Muskrat Lakes** (10,300 ft; both 1 ac) are shallow lakes good for rainbow to 2 pounds. □

Yampa River
a range of angling

Adjacent communities:
Phippsburg, Oak Creek, Steamboat Springs, Hayden, Craig, Maybell.

Principal Highways:
U.S. 40; Colo. 131.

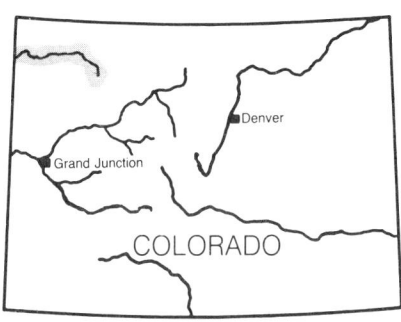

Flowing out of the east side of the Flat Tops Wilderness, the Yampa River (known locally as Bear River) races northward to Steamboat Springs in one of the more scenic valleys in Colorado. West of "Steamboat," it picks up the waters of the Elk River before flowing on past the city of Craig. From Craig it rolls and winds through dry, brushy hills into Dinosaur National Monument on the Colorado-Utah state line. There the clearer flow of the Green River absorbs the Yampa's murky waters.

The Yampa offers more than 100 miles of fishing—from mountain trout to sizable catfish in murky western waters.

The Yampa is brimming with whitefish. They are an overlooked resource and run to two pounds in many stretches of the river. Smoked, they are delicious. They go for small flies and are fun to catch. There is no limit on whitefish.

The Yampa headwaters in the Routt National Forest average 50 feet wide and tease fishermen with challenging fly fishing from midsummer on. Rainbow, brook and brown to 10 inches are there for the taking. For the most part, lakes and some reservoirs offer bigger trout than the river itself.

When the Yampa swings west at Steamboat Springs, it averages 100 feet wide with deep holes. Spinning is grand; and worms,

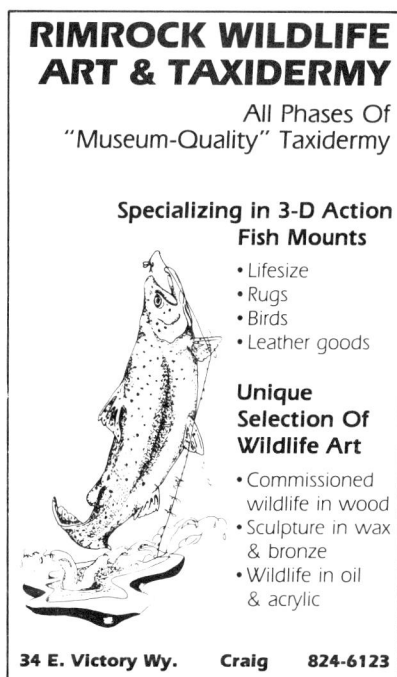

RIMROCK WILDLIFE ART & TAXIDERMY

All Phases Of "Museum-Quality" Taxidermy

Specializing in 3-D Action Fish Mounts

- Lifesize
- Rugs
- Birds
- Leather goods

Unique Selection Of Wildlife Art

- Commissioned wildlife in wood
- Sculpture in wax & bronze
- Wildlife in oil & acrylic

34 E. Victory Wy.   Craig   824-6123

102 YAMPA RIVER

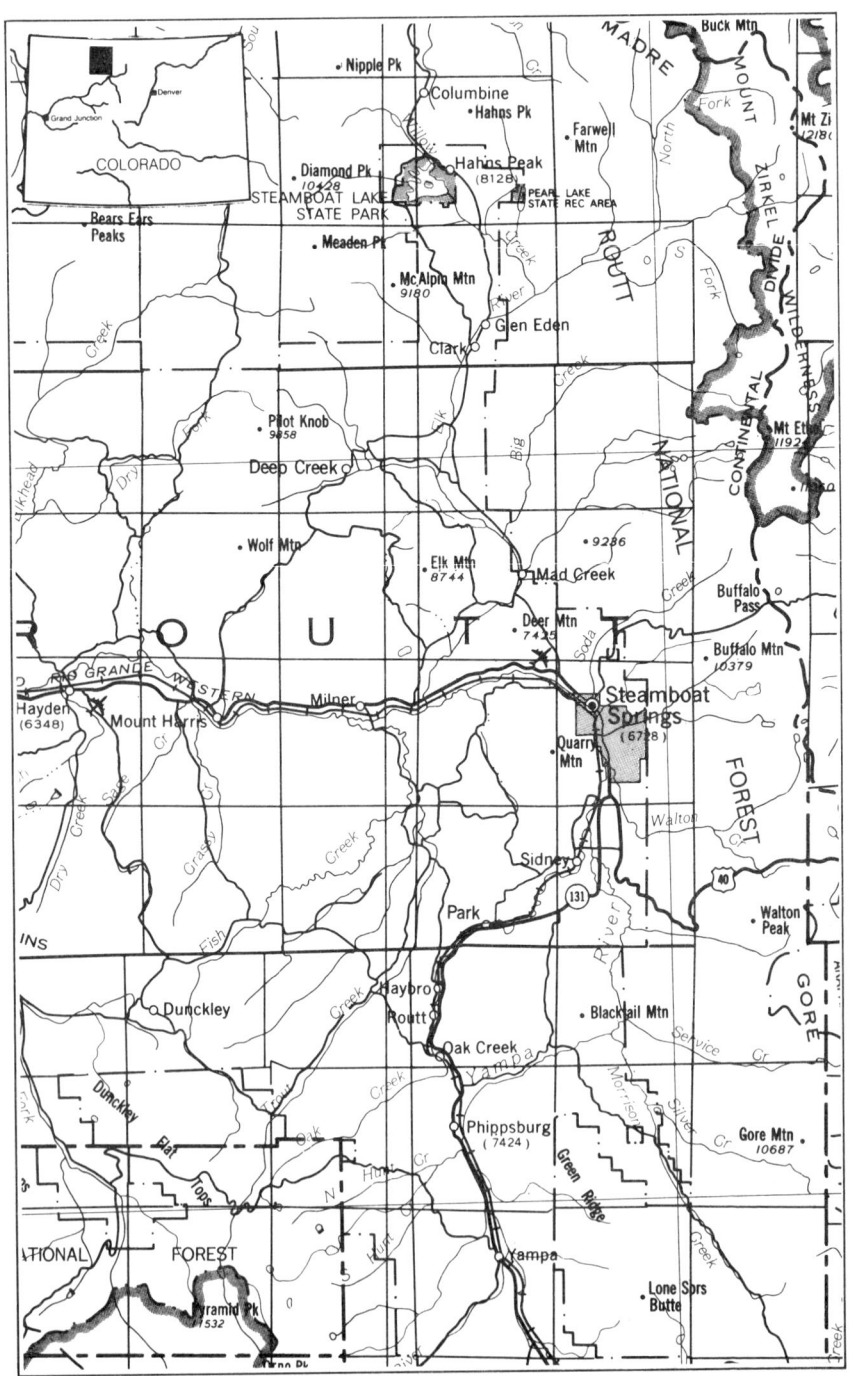

Yampa and Elk Rivers

grasshoppers, fly larvae and minnows are favorite trout cuisine.

The Yampa is paralleled by a good road that runs to its headwaters. The river is about 30 feet wide with much slow water; some shallow canyons. Good fishing for trout averaging 9 inches. At its headwaters are a few reservoirs and several lakes. Two marked trails leave from the dike at Stillwater Reservoir. These trails lead to numerous lakes and to lakes at the headwaters of the North Fork of Derby Creek on the Colorado River. Yampa headwaters lakes include: **Mosquito Lake** (10.600 ft; 13 ac), which is fair for brook to 13 inches. **Skillet Lake** (10,700 ft; 7 ac) lies to the north of Mosquito about 0.5 mile and is rated fair for brook from 10 to 12 inches. **Little Skillet Lake** (10,800 ft; 2 ac) lies 0.5 mile west of Skillet. No trail, and rough terrain. Little Skillet is deep and rated good for brook to 12 inches. **Rainbow Lake** (10,800 ft; 2 ac) is a small pond nestled against a ridge. Good for rainbow to 14 inches.

STILLWATER RESERVOIR

Stillwater Reservoir (9700 ft; 165 ac when full) is nearly surrounded by the Flat Tops Wilderness. It is 18 miles southwest of Yampa, accessible by a good road and is rated good for brook and cutthroat from 10 to 12 inches. There is a Forest Service campground and boat ramp at the reservoir; only electric motors on boats. It is heavily fished. The area is a jumping-off point for trips into the wilderness.

A 1.5-mile trail north from Stillwater Reservoir leads to **Little Causeway Lake** (10,750 ft; 5 ac). Little Causeway is rated fair for brook averaging 10 inches. It sometimes winterkills.

Just below Stillwater Reservoir and Little Causeway Lake, **Smith Creek** feeds into the Bear River from the north. At Smith Creek headwaters, **Smith Lake** (10,355 ft; 11 ac) is rated very good fly fishing for small cutthroat and brook to 16 inches. Below Smith Lake, **Lower Smith Lake** is a beaver pond with a few cutthroat to 12 inches.

Down the Bear River from Stillwater Reservoir about 2.5 miles, is **Upper Stillwater Reservoir** (9700 ft; 47 ac), which sometimes is referred to as the **Yampa Reservoir,** and more recently as Bear Reservoir. It has a concrete platform, which provides access to a portion of the shoreline for handicapped people. Both Bellaire and Tasmanian rainbow were stocked there in 1984 to ascertain which might be the better fish for the reservoir. It is called the upper even though it is the lower of the two reservoirs. It is rated fair fishing for rainbow averaging 9 inches, a few brook and cutthroat, and a large population of whitefish to 14 inches. Stillwater Campground is there.

MANDALL CREEK AND LAKES

Mandall Creek feeds into the Yampa Reservoir from the north. At its headwaters are seven **Mandall Lakes** (10,500 to 10,800 ft; totaling 29 ac), but all do not have fish. A trail from Stillwater Campground leads to the lakes. At the highest reaches, **Black Mandall Lake** is good for rainbow to 16 inches. Southwest of Black, **Slide Man-**

We Are A Full Service Fishing & Outdoor Shop
(303) 879-7568

• Guide Services
• Fishing Schools
• Rod & Reel Repair
• Bamboo Rod Reconstruction Specialists

744 Lincoln Avenue
Steamboat Springs, CO 80477

Map and License Headquarters for N.W. Colorado

dall has been rehabilitated and restocked with cutthroat averaging 10 inches. Below Slide, **Upper** and **Lower Twin Mandall Lakes** have brook, and fishing is rated fair. **Beaver** and **Mud Mandall Lakes** are rated fair for brook.

A new reservoir was completed in the fall of 1980. Just downstream from the Yampa Reservoir is **Yamcollo Reservoir** (9700 ft; 168 ac). It offers fishing for whitefish, rainbow, a few brown and brook and a few large mackinaws. Both Bellaire and Tasmanian rainbow were stocked in Yamcollo in 1984 to ascertain if one might be the better fish for the reservoir.

Just below the Yamcollo, **Rams Horn Lake** (9700 ft; 4 ac) can be reached over a rough road of less than a mile from the Bear River Road. Rainbow fishing can be good. Ice fishing often is good for rainbow and brook.

Below Rams Horn, **Gardner Park Reservoir** (9630 ft; 65 ac) is also accessible by a good road. Occasionally it winterkills, but plenty of feed promotes fast fish growth.

Several county roads, forest service roads, and a major highway provide good access to the river and many of its tributaries. At the town of Yampa, **Phillips Creek** joins the river. It is a small stream flowing mostly through private land so fishing is by permission only. Fair for 10- to 11-inch rainbow and brown with some large brown taken.

North of the town of Yampa, **Watson Creek** enters the Yampa River from the southwest. It is 10 to 20 feet wide, but irrigation draws leave it muddy and dry; consequently, there's not much fishing. But at the Watson Creek headwaters, **Heart Lake** (9900 ft; 24 ac) offers challenging fishing for trophy size rainbow. On its northeast shore is Heart Lake Campground. This 18-foot-deep lake has plenty of food, so trout thrive. There are some big fish here. The trick is to get 'em.

A southern tributary of Watson is **Moody Creek,** and at its headwaters is **Blue Lake.** Neither Moody or Blue has fish.

HUNT CREEK

Downstream of the Watson confluence and north of the town of Yampa about 5 miles, **Hunt Creek** enters the Yampa River from the southwest. Hunt has three forks that are all rated good, but they are tightly posted. The road from Phippsburg on Hwy 131 reaches the forks, and secondary roads to the west follow **North** and **Middle Hunt Creek Forks.** At the headwaters of North Hunt Creek, **Crosho Lake** (8900 ft; 50 ac) offers good ice fishing; campsites below the lake. Some grayling may remain here, but it's mostly rainbow water. The land behind the locked gate and over the cattle guard is private posted land. About 200 yards west of the gate, a trail leads 0.75 mile to **Allen Basin Reservoir** (8700 ft; 87 ac), which lies on the Middle Hunt Creek. It is a fluctuating irrigation reservoir and is rated very good for cutthroat, brook and rainbow averaging 13 inches; good fly water; restricted to artificial flies and lures. This doesn't look like much of a fishery, but it could be the best accessible fishing in the drainage. The walk up is easy.

Near the headwaters of the South Hunt Creek, **Chatfield Reservoir** (10,500 ft; 12 ac) pools below a towering cliff. It occasionally winterkills, but has a few cutthroat to 14 inches.

North of Phippsburg, the Yampa River angles northeasterly. Yellow Jacket Pass Road from the east intersects Hwy 131 about 2 miles north of Phippsburg and runs alongside the river, eventually rejoining Hwy 131 south of Steamboat Springs. About 5.5 miles east on Yellow Jacket Pass Road, **Little Morrison Creek** enters the Yampa from the south. Small and brushy, it is rated good for brook to 10 inches in the early spring, and poor to fair for the rest of the year. Access is on a good road to the southeast up the creek for 18 miles or so to Lynx Pass and the Lynx Pass Campground.

About a mile east of Yellow Jacket Pass Road, a rough road turns north off the Lynx Pass Road to provide access to Service Creek.

Service Creek flows into the Yampa about 3 miles downstream from Little Morrison Creek near Blacktail Mountain. Service is rated excellent for small brook in the upper stretches in Routt National Forest. It is about 15 feet wide and has some beaver ponds. The lower portion is heavily fished. A Forest Service trail follows the creek for 15 miles. Upper part is easily fished; lower part features good, fast water.

Green Creek enters the Yampa River south of US 40 and north of Service Creek. Its lower portions are too fast for fish, though a few ponds harbor trout. The upper stretches are excellent for small brook. Green Creek is about 15 feet wide.

Harrison Creek enters the Yampa about 2 miles downstream of Green Creek. Its lower parts are swift, too fast to fish. The creek is rated fair to good for small brook with some cutthroat in the upper reaches. Best fishing is late season. Access to Harrison and Green creeks is easiest from the big bend of US 40, 6 miles west of the summit of Rabbit Ears Pass at the Harrison Creek Campground.

CHAPMAN RESERVOIR

Oak Creek enters the Yampa from the southwest 19 miles north of the town of Oak Creek. This small stream, 10 to 15 feet wide, has a plethora of ponds. It is rated fair for small cutthroat, rainbow and brook. About 14 miles southwest of the mining town of Oak Creek, at the headwaters of Oak Creek, are **Sheriff Reservoir** (9700 ft; 25 ac), which is rated fair to good for rainbow to 10 inches; **Oat Lake** (10,100 ft; 3 ac), which is also good for rainbow and cutthroat to 14 inches; and **Chapman Reservoir** (9100 ft; 25 ac), which can be reached by a rough road. Chapman is heavily fished, but rated fair to good for rainbow to 12 inches; best for larger fish in the early spring and especially late fall. Boats are allowed on Chapman, but not available to rent; only electric motors are allowed. All of these headwater lakes are located in the Routt National Forest just outside the Flat Tops Wilderness Area.

Walton Creek enters the Yampa River from the east 2 miles south of Steamboat Spring. Its upper tributary is **Fishhook Creek.** The upper reaches northwest of the Rabbit Ears Pass summit are accessible by a rough road from Rabbit Ears Pass. Drive north to Dumont Lakes, follow the road north from there. The last mile or two must be hiked. Walton Creek averages 15 to 30 feet wide, meandering through many meadows. Its midsection cuts through a rough canyon. Walton has many small forks and its tributaries all are rated good for small brook in the upper parts, and rainbow and brook in the lower reaches. The lower reaches are on private land; request permission to fish.

At the headwaters of Fishhook Creek is **Lake Elmo** (10,000 ft; 14 ac). It is good for 8- to 12-inch brook, with some weighing 2 pounds. Other headwater lakes include **Fishhook Lake** (9900 ft; 16 ac) and **Lost Lake** (9900 ft; 20 ac). Both are good for brook to 11 inches. Fishhook is shallow, 5 feet deep, and may experience winterkill.

Fish Creek feeds into the Yampa from the south just downstream of Walton Creek and a mile south of Steamboat Springs. A road east at the eastern edge of Steamboat Springs is marked "Fish Creek Falls." Fish Creek is easily fished, good for small brook above the falls, but is usually poor in the lower stretches due to low water. The creek forks just above Fish Creek Falls Campground. A trail follows the south fork, the main creek, for 7 miles to **Long Lake** (9900 ft; 40 ac), which can be good to excellent for small brook. Long Lake is restricted to hand propelled and electric motor-powered boats. In the same area are several other small lakes (many with rainbow or brook) that drain to the east into the North Platte River.

On the **Middle Fork of Fish Creek, Fish Creek Reservoir** (9900 ft; 40 ac)is a fluctuating water body owned by the city of Steamboat Springs. Drive north from Steamboat to the reservoir by the Buffalo Pass Road. Drive past Dry Lake Campground, about 7 miles, to Buffalo Pass. From the pass, drive about 6 miles south past the Dinosaur Lake trailhead to Granite Campground, located on the east side of the reservoir. Fish Creek Reservoir is stocked with creel-size rainbow. **Lake Dinosaur** (10,150 ft; 20 ac) is at the headwaters of the **North Fork of Fish Creek** and is rated fair for 9-inch cutthroat and brook. The North Fork enters Fish Creek near Fish Creek Falls

Campground. It is fast and rough to fish, but excellent for small brook. The North Fork's upper reaches and Dinosaur Lake are reached by the same roads taken to Fish Creek Reservoir. A map is recommended for even short crosscountry hikes in this area.

Spring Creek and **Butcherknife Creeks** enter the Yampa River at the town of Steamboat Springs. They are both very small, deep streams producing rainbow and brook to 7 inches.

Soda Creek enters the Yampa at the north edge of Steamboat. Its headwaters are north of Buffalo Pass about 2.5 miles. Access to the headwaters is by taking the trail north from Buffalo Pass. The North Fork has small cutthroat, the South Fork has small brook. Both are rated good. The main creek averages 20 feet wide and has several ponds.

Northwest of Steamboat Springs are two major fishing waters. One is Steamboat Lake on County Road 129 about 25 miles north. The other is the Elk River and its tributary streams and associated lakes. Main access to both areas is via County Road 129 north from US 40 (about 1.5 miles west of Steamboat Springs). It is well marked.

At Glen Eden, about 18 miles northwest of Steamboat, the road forks and the easterly bearing highway follows the Elk River toward the stream's headwaters. The west and northerly fork leads to Steamboat Lake, Hahns Peak Lake and the headwaters of the Little Snake River. These are described farther on.

ELK RIVER

Bulldozing and channeling have pretty well ruined nearly 20 miles of the Elk River between Glen Eden and the Yampa. What is available is posted against fishing anyway. Upstream, the river drains the northwest side of the Mount Zirkel Wilderness Area and tends to offer the best fishing after August 1. It varies from 50 to 100 feet wide. It has unusually slippery footing and sports a great range of water from fast and turbulent to deep and quiet. The upper Elk is rated good for 10-inch rainbow, a few brook and cutthroat. It is also good for whitefish averaging 11 inches. Some large brown and rainbow are taken in the early season. The best fishing on the Elk probably is in the vicinity of Hinman Campground, 5 miles east of Glen Eden, and upstream for 4.5 miles to Seedhouse Campground. The river is mossy in the late season.

The **North Fork of Elk River** enters the Elk at Seedhouse Campground. It is about 30 feet wide, a partially brushy stream that flows through mountain parks and small canyons. The lower part is rated fair to good and the upper is excellent for 8-inch brook and rainbow. Late season fishing is best. Access is by turning north at Seedhouse Campground onto a dirt road that parallels the stream to the Mount Zirkel Wilderness Area boundary. Tributaries of the North Fork include **English, Lost Dog** and **Trail Creeks.** All are small with some beaver ponds. Fishing is good for small brook and a few cutthroat. Trail Creek is rated best. At the headwaters of Trail Creek, **Sanchez**

All the necessities for the fisherman, including good old hospitality.
Stop by and tell some tales. **(303) 879-3849**

Creek flows west from **Sanchez Lakes** (10,500 ft; 4 ac total) in the Mount Zirkel Wilderness. The two Sanchez lakes are about 0.25 mile apart and are reached by driving north along the North Fork to Diamond Park at the wilderness boundary. From there, hike north on a trail about 3.5 miles along the Continental Divide. The lakes lies just under the west side of the Continental Divide. The upper lake is good for 12-inch cutthroat while the lower lake has cutthroat and rainbow averaging 9 inches.

The **South Fork of Elk River** enters the Elk about 0.25 mile southeast of Hinman Campground. The South Fork is fed by several tributaries. At its headwaters, to the southeast, there are several small lakes in the wilderness area about 5 miles southeast of Box Canyon Campground. **Ptarmigan Lake** (10,700 ft; 5 ac) is rated fair for small cutthroat. In the same locale, **Dome Lake** (10,080 ft; 17 ac) is 12 feet deep and rated fair for cutthroat to 11 inches. Due to good growing conditions, it has some large fish; occasionally 5- to 10-pound fish are taken. **Wolverine Creek** flows into the South Fork from **Wolverine Basin** and **Wolverine Lake** (10,240 ft; 7.3 ac). This 25-foot-deep lake is rated good for 12-inch rainbow and is stocked with cutthroat. Southeast of Wolverine, **Pristine Lake** (11,040 ft; 9.7 ac) is rated good for small brook. This is a self-sustaining lake and is not stocked. Northernmost of this group of lakes is **North Lake** (10,300 ft; 6 ac), rated excellent for small brook. Access to these headwater lakes is by driving east from Box Canyon Campground about 3 miles to trailhead; signs specify main trails.

Three Island Creek feeds from the east into the South Fork near Box Canyon Campground, just south of Seedhouse Campground. At its headwaters, **Three Island Lake** (10,000 ft; 35 ac) is rated excellent for 9-inch brook. Fish the east side of the lake, where it is wadable. The creek below the lake is good for small brook. Follow the trail marked "Divide" southeast from Three Island Lake to reach **Beaver Lake** (10,400 ft; 6 ac). It is good for 12-inch brook.

Burn Creek enters the South Fork from the southeast about 2 miles from the South Fork's confluence with Elk River. Burn is a small and brushy stream rated good for small cutthroat and brook.

Hinman Creek enters the Elk River from the north about 2 miles downstream from the South Fork at Hinman Campground. It has several tributaries including **Scott Run.** Hinman and its tributaries are small and brushy; rated good for small cutthroat and brook.

Southwest of Hinman, the largest tributary of the Elk River, **Willow Creek,** is also the best fishing tributary. Draining Steamboat Lake, it is 25 to 30 feet wide with many ponds. Willow is a good early season and summer stream. It is rated good for 9-inch rainbow, brook and cutthroat. Two roads provide access. About 2 miles northeast of Glen Eden, Willow Creek is the first stream crossed by the road at its juncture with Elk River. It is also reached by traveling north from Glen Eden on County Road 129. Above Steamboat Lake, **Hahns Peak Lake**

(8200 ft; 38 ac) has been developed by the Colorado Division of Wildlife. The lake has a brushy bottom and offers easy bank fishing; rated fair with flies. Hahns Peak is stocked with creel-size rainbow. Fish show little growth. Motor-propelled boats and rafts are prohibited.

STEAMBOAT LAKE STATE PARK

Steamboat Lake (8000 ft; 1053 ac) is 0.75 mile south of Hahns Peak Lake. It is fed by several small streams that offer little fishing. Steamboat Lake is stocked with rainbow and offers good sport the entire summer for 8- to 17-inch rainbow, 11- to 17-inch brown, brook to 17 inches and a few cutthroat averaging 10 inches. Both boat and shore angling have resulted in good fishing. Supplies and a 240-site campground are found at the northeast end of the lake at the village of Hahns Peak. Because it is a state park, a parks pass or daily fee is required, which also is valid for Pearl Lake. It is a popular boating and water skiing area. There is a marina.

Several streams flow into Steamboat Lake, including **Floyd, Mill, Dutch** and **Larson Creeks.** These streams are rated poor and offer no fishing—at best a few brook and cutthroat in the upper reaches.

Lester Creek Reservoir or **Pearl Lake** (8000 ft; 190 ac) is 3 miles east of Steamboat Lake. The access road is well marked. The reservoir has plenty of feed and has a good population of fat cutthroat that is supplemented through stocking. Lester is 80 feet deep. Sometimes it is difficult to entice the fish because the food supply is so ample in the reservoir. Cutthroat from Lester weigh from 1.5 to 6 pounds, with a few large rainbow taken. It's a good and pretty place to fish.

Farther south, **Big Creek** enters the Elk River from the north and east, about 9 miles north of Steamboat Springs. The lower end of Big Creek is mostly posted, but the upper 6 miles are on public land with the exception of a 1-mile stretch. Big Creek is rated excellent for small brook with some cutthroat in the upper reaches.

About 6 miles northwest of Steamboat Springs, **Mad Creek** enters the Elk River. It flows from the east from the Mount Zirkel Wilderness Area. The lower 3 miles of the Mad are tightly posted. A road follows the Mad for about 2 miles and from there a trail follows the stream along its North Fork into the wilderness area. Fishing is excellent for brook on both the **North Fork** and **South Fork of Mad Creek.** No groomed trail follows the South Fork. You're on your own. At the headwaters of both forks lie several

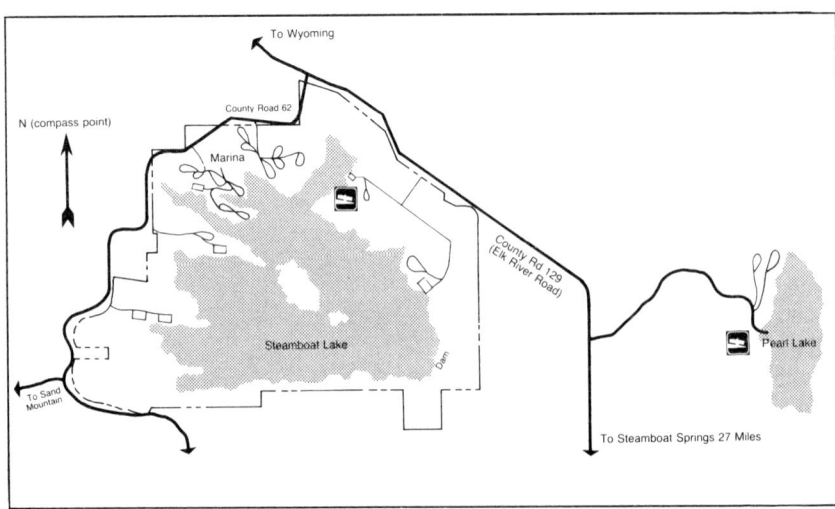

Steamboat Lake State Park

lakes including **Big Creek Lakes** (10,600 ft; 8 ac), **Lake of the Crags** (10,900 ft; 6 ac), **Luna Lake** (10,500 ft; 38 ac), **Lake Elbert** (10,800 ft; 19 ac), **Rosa Lake** (10,000 ft; 5 ac), **Mirror Lake** (10,000 ft; 12 ac), **Lake Margaret** (10,000 ft; 40 ac), **Lake Edward** (10:,000 ft; 10 ac) and **Fish Hawk Lake** (10,000 ft; 9 ac). These lakes are interconnected by trails. Margaret and Edward lakes are good for small cutthroat. Luna Lake is good for small cutthroat also and is perhaps the most scenic lake in the area. Mirror Lake has a few cutthroat. Big Lake is excellent for small cutthroat to 12 inches. Lake of the Crags often winterkills. Elbert Lake is good for small cutthroat. Fish Hawk Lake is good for small brook and cutthroat. And Rosa Lake is good for 12-inch brook and cutthroat.

West of Steamboat Springs about 10 miles along US 40, **Trout Creek** enters the Yampa from southwest of Milner. Its upper reaches stretch to Oak Creek and can be reached by a good-weather road. Road network is very confusing, inquire locally. All 18 miles of Trout Creek are fishable; the upper parts are the best. Good fly water in the national forest area. The lower stretches have smaller volume and murky water, with brushy banks. Trout Creek is rated fair for 8- to 12-inch rainbow. From the west, **Fish Creek** is the largest tributary of Trout Creek and is rated fair for small rainbow and cutthroat. Its headwaters can be reached from Milner or Hayden by driving south on county roads. Good fishing north of the Yampa River ends about here.

The next incoming stream, **Elkhead Creek,** along with the rest of the north-feeding streams to the west, is silt-laden and spasmodic in flow. Elkhead Creek is a small 12-foot-wide stream that can be fished easily. Its upper reaches are inhabited by a few rainbow and cutthroat; lower reaches are rated poor for cutthroat and brook. The beaver ponds are the upper end's salvation. Elkhead enters the Yampa about 35 miles west of Steamboat Springs and 10 miles west of Hayden. Tributaries include **First, Armstrong, Knowles, Stukey, Circle, Torso** and **Hole-in-the-Wall Creeks.** The tributaries are near the headwaters. Road access to the lower reaches is by turning northeast off US 40 about 9 miles west of Hayden, or 6 miles east of Craig.

Elkhead Reservoir (6300 ft; 440 ac) is about 3.5 miles up the Elkhead Reservoir Road. It is a turbid, nonfluctuating lake offering unpredictable fishing for a few spring-planted rainbow and a few catfish, but more often chub and suckers. Some decent largemouth bass and some small-mouth bass have been tempting anglers, some of whom have done well. Elkhead Reservoir serves primarily as a water skiing resort. Plans are on the drawing board to build another reservoir above the Elkhead that would serve as a silt trap, perhaps resulting in improved fishing in Elkhead Reservoir.

The **North Fork of Elkhead Creek** is rated fair for cutthroat. Access to the headwaters in the Elkhead Mountains is by driving north out of Hayden. Road forks after 0.75 mile. Follow the right fork, County Road 80, and continue 17 miles to California Park Campground. This road continues for access to Slate Creek and other tributaries of the Little Snake River.

Fortification Creek is a small brushy stream that flows through Craig and into the Yampa from the north. It is rated fair to poor for small cutthroat. Hwys 13 and 789 follow the creek north from Craig. **Cottonwood Creek** and **Little Cottonwood Creek** enter Fortification about 15 miles north of Craig. They offer little or no fishing. At the headwaters of Little Cottonwood, **Freeman Reservoir** (8750 ft; 14 ac) is stocked with cutthroat and sometimes offers good fishing for 10- to 12-inch cutthroat.

Little Bear Creek flows out of the Elkhead Mountains north of Craig and into **Ralph White Lake** (6300 ft; 90 ac). Ralph White Lake is rated fair to good for rainbow to 12 inches. The stream is of little fishing value.

WILLIAMS FORK RIVER

South of the Yampa, the west-flowing **Williams Fork River** originates from tributaries flowing northward out of the high country just north of the Flat Tops Wilderness. The best fishing is in the upper reaches

Lower Yampa River

of the East Fork of the Williams Fork, the South Fork of the Williams Fork and some of the smaller associated streams and lakes.

The river flows westward through Hamilton and then north to merge with the Yampa River about 10 miles southwest of Craig. The Williams Fork upstream from Hamilton is 20 to 30 feet wide and is good fishing for rainbow and cutthroat. Almost all but the uppermost reaches are on private or leased land.

The river is reached by driving north on the Poose Creek-Vaughn Lake Road from the White River or south on Highways 13-789 between Meeker and Craig. At Hamilton turn east for ready access to the river and its major tributaries. From Oak Creek, it is reached by going west over Dunckley Pass.

The **East Fork of the Williams Fork** is over a steep wall northwest of Stillwater Reservoir and flows northwesterly out of the Flat Tops Wilderness. There are several deep lakes that offer good fishing for brook, rainbow and cutthroat.

The East Fork of the Williams Fork is about 24 miles east up the Williams Fork from Hamilton. It is 13 more miles on a good road to Pyramid Ranger Station and public fishing in Routt National Forest. The lakes are another 7 to 10 miles by trail to the south and are, perhaps, more readily reached from the White River access near Trappers Lake. From Pyramid hike up the stream for fair fishing for 9- to 12-inch brook, cutthroat and rainbow. Marked trail leads to the headwater lakes. Lakes include **West Lost Lakes** (8500 ft; 17 and 20 ac), the five **East Lost Lakes** (8700 ft; 30 to 50 ac), **Round Lake** (8100 ft; 7 ac) and **Causeway Lake** (9000 ft; 20 ac). West Lost Lake is the closest and best fishing. A good but steep trail leads to the lakes, and forks just before West and East Lakes. East Fork trail leads 3 miles to Round Lake. Causeway Lake is 1 mile farther. The trail makes a loop to hit all lakes. West Lake has brook and cutthroat; East Lake has rainbow; and the others are stocked with cutthroat.

Poose Creek enters the East Fork of Williams downstream about 6 miles from Pyramid Ranger Station on the Vaughn Lake Road. Poose is a small, brushy and fast stream, and is rated good for small cutthroat and rainbow. Poose is paralleled by a road to its headwaters and to **Vaughn Lake** (9500 ft; 36 ac). Vaughn Lake is stocked with creel-size rainbow. The lake is 24 feet deep.

A mile south of Pagoda, the **East Fork** and the **South Fork** converge to form the

Williams Fork River. Good roads go up each fork. The south road follows the South Fork of the Williams Fork about 10 miles through private land to where a lower quality road goes off to the southeast following the mainstream. After a mile, the road forks again. Take the west fork, still following the stream, about 2 miles into the national forest. Trails then provide access to small streams with cutthroat, brook and rainbow. Fishing is usually good.

South Fork tributaries include **Beaver, Indian Run** and **Pine Creeks.** The tributaries and South Fork are brushy, small often fast water and some ponds. Fish mostly are small, but some make it to 10 inches. Best fishing is early spring; poor thereafter.

Seeking current information at the Hamilton store is recommended. Ask about whom to contact for fishing from private property. To fish on the Williams Fork from Hamilton downstream to the Yampa, permission is necessary. Some scrappy 15-pound-category northern pike have been caught in the backwaters and oxbows of the Yampa both east and west of Craig. Late evening fishing is recommended.

West from Craig, the Yampa River is heavy, wide and somewhat turbulent, taking on the appearance of coffee with cream. Fishing is spotty, but there are plenty of whitefish and catfish, and an occasional squawfish, a protected species, may be landed.

LITTLE SNAKE RIVER

About 2 miles east of Maybell, US 40 crosses the Yampa as the stream and highway wind through high, arid desert. About 15 miles west, the **Little Snake River** joins the Yampa from the north in very eroded, desolate country.

This long river reaches into Wyoming and its tributaries spread back into Colorado in the Routt National Forest. Its upper reaches in Colorado are accessible by State Hwy 13 north from Craig, or a secondary road northwest from Steamboat Springs. The Little Snake varies from 50 to 100 feet wide with many types of water. It offers marginal fishing due to tremendous fluctuations from irrigation draws. As the water returns from irrigation use, it is warm and murky, hardly a suitable home for a feisty trout. There are several tributaries of the Little Snake, including **Slater, Willow, Fourmile Creeks** and the **South** and **Middle Forks.** Slater is stocked with creel-size rainbow but offers poor to fair fishing. The lucky fisherman might find a brook in the Middle or South Forks. Little fishing is to be found in Fourmile Creek. Tributaries of the Middle Fork are **King Solomon, Box, Summit, Smith, Independence, Little Red Park, Silver City** and **Whiskey Creeks.** All of these tributaries are rated good for 7- to 9-inch brook and cutthroat, especially in their upper courses. County Road 129 north from Steamboat Springs crosses several of these creeks.

GREEN RIVER

West of the Little Snake River confluence, the Yampa River flows into **Dinosaur National Monument,** which is named for remarkable deposits of fossil bones. The petrified remains of crocodiles, turtles and 14 species of dinosaurs have been excavated from the 140-million-year-old Morrison Formation.

Midway in the Monument, the muddy Yampa is met from the north by the clearer Green River. The **Green River** enters Colorado from the extreme northwest corner of the state and flows south to meet the Yampa at Echo Park. Reach Echo Park by turning north at the Dinosaur National Monument Headquarters on US 40 about 5 miles east of the Utah state line. Where the Yampa meets the Green at Echo Park, the two rivers converge and become the Green river as it flows back into Utah.

Access to the Yampa as it enters the monument is by driving northwest 11 miles from US 40 about 15 miles west of Maybell. From the point that the Yampa enters the Monument, it wanders about 40 miles west before meeting Green River. This stretch of the Yampa is home to channel catfish and northern pike as well as a few Colorado protected species. Fishing is marginal until reaching the confluence of the Green and Yampa, where the fishing is good for catfish. The Yampa is dotted with campgrounds on its banks as it winds through the rough, dry canyon. It is a floaters favorite.

The **Green River** is a much clearer, cooler and faster river. Its flow is determined by the Flaming Gorge Reservoir Dam in the southwest corner of Wyoming and the northeast corner of Utah. The Green River used to be a very cold river because its flow was drawn from the bottom of the reservoir. During this time the trout sought the lower and somewhat warmer waters of the Green, below the Yampa-Green confluence. In recent years, that has changed. The Green is much warmer now; the water from Flaming Gorge comes out from near the top of the reservoir, resulting in trout migrating toward the reservoir. The Bureau of Reclamation is working with Utah fish managers to improve angling below the dam by mixing warmer and cooler waters. What impact this will have on the Colorado portion of the Green isn't known.

Where the Green enters Colorado it flows through Browns Park National Wildlife Refuge, which is accessible via Hwy 318 northwest of Maybell. Fishing for rainbow, a few brown and, in summer, catfish is poor to fair, although the rainbow are 12 to 15 inches. The river fluctuates almost daily because its flow is determined by computers at Flaming Gorge Dam where electric power is generated. The fluctuations aggravate erosion and the stream is often silty. There are two primitive campgrounds (no water) in the refuge, each about 2 miles from the highway. Several roads lead to the river.

After passing through the refuge, the Green enters the Dinosaur National Monument. It immediately cuts through the famous Gates of Lodore where the river canyon walls become nearly vertical and there is no landing. Inside the Monument, the Green can only be reached by boat. To float this river requires a boating permit issued to floating guides and individuals who apply each winter. This stretch of the Green may have a few trout, but it gets very little fishing. The fast waters lure mostly whitewater boaters.

The favored fishing in this area is just over the Colorado-Utah state line and requires a Utah fishing license. It can be worth the price. The stream is **Jones Hole Creek.** It enters the Green below the Yampa-Green confluence in Utah from the east. Its headwaters run along the state line. This stream is a favorite of anglers who claim catching 15-inch brown and rainbow on a regular basis. Access is limited to hiking in. Inquire at Jensen, Utah, on US 40.

The Yampa is a popular floaters' stream, especially west of Craig. The Cross Mountain stretch northwest of Maybell and US 40 is perilous and access is limited. Local inquiry is recommended. Several companies offer 1- to 4-day float trips on the Yampa and Green rivers in Colorado. The "floating segments" of the lower river are primarily for sport, not fishing.

U.S. FOREST SERVICE DISTRICT RANGER STATIONS

Routt National Forest Headquarters
Hunt Bldg.
137-10th St., P.O. Box 771198
Steamboat Springs, CO 80477   303/879-1722

Hahns Peak Ranger District
Routt National Forest
57-10th St., P.O. Box 1212
Steamboat Springs, CO 80477   303/879-1970

Bear Ears Ranger District
Routt National Forest
356 Ranney St., Craig, CO 81625

Yampa Ranger District
Routt National Forest
300 Roselawn, P.O. Box 7
Yampa, CO 80483   303/638-4516

U.S. Forest Service campgrounds

U.S. Forest Service compilation was current as of 1985.

Asterisks denote fee areas. Some campgrounds are open only Memorial Day weekend through Labor Day. Below freezing weather could mean no water supply.

YAMPA RIVER DRAINAGE

ROUTT NATIONAL FOREST
Headquarters: Hunt Bldg., 137 10th St., Box 1198, Steamboat Springs, CO

Campground name	Elevation	No camp sites	Travel trailers	Drinking water	Length of stay (days)	Location and directions
Lynx Pass*	9080	11	Yes	Yes	14	2.5 mi N of Colo. 131, 9.5 mi E of Toponas
Toponas Creek*	9000	8	Yes	Yes	14	On Colo. 131, 5.8 mi E of Toponas
Blacktail Creek*	9000	8	Yes	Yes	14	On Colo. 131, 12.1 mi E of Toponas
Gore Pass	9500	12	Yes	Yes	14	On Colo. 131, 13.3 mi E of Toponas
Horseshoe	10,200	7	Yes	Yes	14	13.6 mi SW of Yampa by forest roads
Stillwater*	9800	29	Yes	Yes	14	12.7 mi SW of Yampa by forest roads
Cold Springs*	10,200	5	Yes	Yes	14	14 mi SW of Yampa by forest roads
Vaughn Lake	9500	8	Yes	No	14	32 mi W of Colo. 131, .3 mi S of Phippsburg
Summit Lake	10,300	17	Yes	No	14	8.8 mi NE of Steamboat Springs by forest roads
Dry Lake	8000	8	Yes	No	14	4.2 mi NE of Steamboat Springs by forest roads
Meadows*	9300	32	Yes	Yes	14	On US 40, 9.6 mi SE of Steamboat Springs
Walton Creek	9400	14	Yes	No	14	On US 40, 17 mi E of Steamboat Springs
Dumont Lake*	9500	12	Yes	No	14	24.3 mi SE of Steamboat Springs off US 40
Hahns Peak Lake*	8500	26	Yes	Yes	14	2.5 mi W of County Hwy 129, 11 mi N of Clark
Box Canyon	7900	11	Yes	No	14	8.1 mi NE of Clark on forest roads
Hinman*	7600	13	Yes	Yes	14	4.3 mi NE of Clark on forest roads
Seed House*	8000	23	Yes	Yes	14	8.9 mi NE of Clark on forest roads
Granite	9900	6	No	No	14	16.5 mi SE of County Hwy 36, 4 mi N of Steamboat Springs
Freeman	8800	12	Yes	No	14	17.5 mi NE of Craig off Colo. 13

Hooked on Fishing?

Get all the angles on your sport by subscribing to **COLORADO OUTDOORS,** the Colorado Division of Wildlife's bimonthly magazine. It's the only magazine devoted to the state's wildlife. Not only will you get articles on Colorado fishing, but also on hunting, camping, boating, history, and a variety of other subjects. Use the coupon below to subscribe for one, two, or three years.

Fill out and mail the coupon below — today!

Mail to: COLORADO OUTDOORS, 6060 Broadway, Denver, CO 80216

ORDER FORM Please send COLORADO OUTDOORS magazine to the address listed below for
☐ 1 year $ 5.00
☐ 2 years $ 9.00
☐ 3 years $12.00

Name _____

Street Address _____

City _____ State _____ Zip _____

☐ New   ☐ Renewal

Audit Validation:

North Platte River bountiful beginnings

ADJACENT COMMUNITIES:
Walden

PRINCIPAL HIGHWAYS:
Colo. 14 and 125

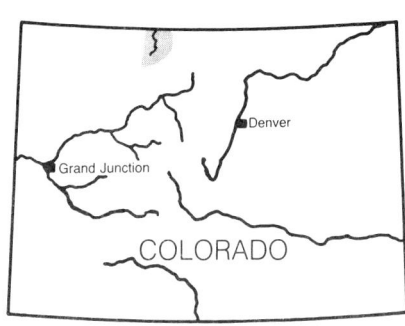

The North Platte River runs through Colorado as Colorado was before the development boom of the past 25 years. There's the vivid blue sky and lush, green meadows and willow-fringed streams wih rainbow, brown, brook and cutthroat trout.

The nearest superhighway is more than 100 miles away. The chains of standardized restaurants and motels, the billboards and trappings of exploitive commercialism are elsewhere. It's a treat just to be in the North Park, let alone fish its ample waters.

The North Platte River rises in the Sierra Madre Mountains on the west side of the park, a 50-square-mile open region just south of the Wyoming state line in northwest central Colorado. The river and its tributary streams, rising out of a U of ragged mountains that rim the park, offer remote and often good fishing. Much of the ranch land in the park is posted and the area is laced with small streams and irrigation ditches. Flood hayfield irrigation is common, so waders are a must for most stream fishing. So is mosquito dope.

In Colorado, the North Platte is a deep and wide river, with portions designated wild trout waters. Many deepholes and riffles afford excellent fishing with spinners and bait in the early season, and bait and flies after midsummer. Muddy waters from spring runoff hamper good fishing in the spring and early summer. Most of the trout are brown with some rainbow averaging 12 inches, though lunkers to 28 inches have been taken.

Access to the North Platte in Colorado is by Hwy 125 north from Granby to Walden and north to Hwy 312 west from Cowdrey, and Hwy 14 from its junction with US 40 on the east side of Rabbit Ears Pass north to Walden.

Most of the North Platte in Colorado is heavily posted, but the headwaters in the Mount Zirkel Wilderness Area, portions of the waterway near the Wyoming border and sections that have been leased are open to the public and offer challenging, remote fishing. A Routt National Forest map is helpful in tracing the streams. It is available at the Forest Service Ranger Station in Walden for a buck.

SW PARK FISHING

In the southwest corner of North Park, **Grizzly Creek** and **Little Grizzly Creek** help form the river's headwaters. Grizzly is a meandering, often brushy stream up to 25

feet wide and often roily. Several ponds characterize its upper reaches in Routt National Forest. It surges north through private lands, but some generous property owners grant permission to fish. Public access is off Hwy 14 southwest of Walden. Fair to good for 10- to 16-inch brown, rainbow and brook. Upper reaches are paralleled by Hwy 14 for 10 miles from Spicer to the junction with US 40 at Muddy Pass.

Muddy Pass Lake (8800 ft; 10.5 ac) is a small lake at the head of Grizzly Creek. It is located on US 40 about 1 mile west of the Hwy 14 junction, just east of Rabbit Ears Pass. Stocked with catchable rainbow to 12 inches, this lake is under Division of Wildlife observation to determine the extent of winterkill.

Colorado Creek enters the Grizzly from the west about midway between Spicer on Hwy 14 and Muddy Pass. Access is by following a dirt road that parallels the stream. Take the first lefthand turn, head northwest; road ends at headwaters. There are several small lakes near the headwaters, including **Lost Lake** (10,000 ft; 15 ac), which is fair to good for 8- to 15-inch rainbow and brook; **Round Lake** (10,060 ft; 16 ac), good for 8- to 14-inch brook; and **Percy Lake** (10,035 ft; 17 ac), which is good for 10- to 12-inch brook.

Arapaho Creek merges with Grizzly Creek at Spicer. The lower reaches of the Arapaho to the forest boundary are closed to the public. Above the forest boundary, in the Rabbit Ears Mountains 30 miles south of Walden, this slender, brushy, ponded stream is good to excellent for small, wild brook. There are three forks at the headwaters, with **Middle** and **West Forks of Arapaho Creek** the best.

Access to upper forks is by good improved road leaving Hwy 14 about 5.5 miles north of Spicer. This road winds through the minute Arapaho Lakes. Perhaps better called ponds, they are shallow with good feed, and rated fair for 8- to 14-inch rainbow and brown. Best fishing is in early season before most fishermen begin to muster.

The lakes include **Bundy Lake** (10,100 ft; 2 ac), which is very good for small brook and some rainbow; **Willow Lake** (9100 ft; 3 ac) also has small brook; and **Long, Alder, Round, Cliff** and **Disappointment Lakes,** all about 2 to 3 acres at about 9000 feet altitude. Long and Alder are fair for rainbow. Disappointment is fair to good for rainbow and brown. And Round has rainbow and brook.

East of Spicer, **Seymour Reservoir** (8300 ft; 35 ac) is a fairly new lake with good food conditions for fish. Turn east 1.5 miles north of Spicer, follow the road 2.5 miles to the north end of the reservoir.

This stretch of stream from Spicer north to the confluence of Little Grizzly meanders tightly through hayfields and private land.

At the junction of Grizzly and Little Grizzly creeks, near Hwy 14 about 9.5 miles south of Walden, a small northern portion of the North Platte and a portion of the Grizzly and Little Grizzly are leased properties for public fishing. This is posted as the Peterson Lease by DOW and allows good fishing along more than 6 miles of stream.

LITTLE GRIZZLY

Little Grizzly Creek enters the North Platte where Hwy 14 heads northeast to Walden. It gushes out of the Park Range Mountains lacing several alpine lakes at its headwaters. The lower stretches, from its junction with Grizzly Creek to Grizzly Creek Campground at the forest boundary, are tightly posted. Little Grizzly averages about 20 feet wide, and is rated fair to good for 10- to 12-inch brown, rainbow and brook. The headwaters are rated fair for brook and rainbow. Access to its upper reaches and campground is by turning west at Hebron and driving about 11 miles. From there, several roads lead to the high country lakes along the Continental Divide.

Crosby Creek feeds into the Little Grizzly from the south. From Grizzly Creek Campground, drive south to Hidden Lakes Campground. Hidden Lakes Campground is surrounded by small lakes and reservoirs. **Stambaugh Reservoir** (8800 ft; 11 ac) is about 300 yards off the road and stocked with rainbow. Fishing is rated poor for rainbow 8 to 10 inches. North of Stambaugh, **Sawmill Lake** (8700 ft; 15 ac) is poor fishing—shallow with winterkill. **Hidden Lakes** (8900 ft; 11 and 4 ac) offer poor fishing.

Pole Mountain Reservoir (8240 ft; 4 ac) is only 1.5 miles west of Coalmont near Hwy 14. It is on private land and is difficult to get permission to fish. The reservoir is 6 feet deep, full of weeds and is poor fishing.

Paralleling Little Grizzly Creek on the north is **Chedsey Creek.** It enters the Little Grizzly about 5 miles from the Little Grizzly-Grizzly confluence. It is one of the best tributaries of the North Platte for prime fishing. The lower reaches are on private land, but the upper reaches skirt around the peaks south of Mount Zirkel Wilderness Area. Its headwaters are fed by **Albert Lake** (10,177 ft; 11 ac), **Round Mountain Lake** (9880 ft; 10 ac), **Whale Lake** (10,050 ft; 11 ac), **Martha Lake** (10,303 ft; 10 ac), **Summit Lake** (10,000 ft; 7 ac) and **Jonah Lake** (10,164 ft; 9 ac), which are accessible from the Grizzly Creek Campground about 8 miles west of Coalmont new Hwy 14; or from the west at Steamboat Springs via the Buffalo Pass Road. Lakes are near the pass or within 2 to 3 miles by trail. Farther down Chedsey Creek, **Tiago Lake** (8850 ft; 8 ac), **Teal Lake** (8800 ft; 16 ac) and **Burns Reservoir** (8600 ft; 9 ac) can be reached by driving from Grizzly Creek. Teal and Tiago can be good for 10-inch rainbow. Boats allowed with electric motors only. Burns is fair to good for 9- to 10-inch rainbow.

Whalen and **Newcomb Creeks** are small tributaries that feed into Chedsey Creek from the north and are accessible by the same road to Teal and Tiago lakes. Lower portions are on private lands and posted. Upper parts are open and fair to good for small brook, cutthroat and rainbow.

ROARING FORK

Roaring Fork of North Platte feeds into the North Platte about 10 miles west of Walden. Lower reaches are on private land, but higher portions are on Routt National Forest land and fed by alpine lakes in the Mount Zirkel Wilderness. The Roaring Fork provides fair fishing for brown, rainbow and occasional brook. Good fishing often is on private lands, but get permission first.

There are portions of the Roaring Fork that have been leased by the Colorado Division of Wildlife. Just west of the Roaring Fork and **Raspberry Creek** confluences, about 3 miles west of the Roaring Fork and North Platte confluence, portions of the stream are open. Inquire locally about regulations, boundaries and access. Area is signed for public access. Also, about 1.5 miles east of the Raspberry Creek-Roaring Fork confluence, parts of the North Platte and Roaring Fork are open to public fishing.

NORTH PARK LEASES
MICHIGAN RIVER
Brownlee easement
Location: the area east of Hwy 125 between Walden and Jackson County Airport and extending one mile east (3.36 mi of river)
Brownlee lease
Location: 2 miles north of Walden on Hwy 125 (4.12 mi of river)
Murphy lease
Location: 0.75 mile east of Walden (6.32 mi of river)
ROARING FORK RIVER; RASPBERRY CREEK
Butte Land & Cattle Co. lease
Location: 14 miles west of Walden, southwest of Delaney Butte (5.5 mi of water)
NORTH PLATTE AND ROARING FORK RIVERS
Manville lease
Location: 9.2 miles west of Walden, south of Delaney Lakes (7.6 mi of river)
North Park Angus lease
Location: 10 miles north of Walden, west of Hwy 125 (2.12 mi of river) Note: access only along river
Peterson lease
Location: 9.6 miles south of Walden on Hwy 14 (6.35 mi of water)
Verner and Brownlee easement
Location: 6 miles west of Walden, on the road to Delaney Lakes (2.25 mi of water)
Willford lease
Location: access to area same as to North Park Angus lease (1.02 mi of river)

At the headwaters of the Roaring Fork, the alpine lakes include: the three **Rainbow Lakes** (9800 ft; 127 ac total), **Slide Lakes** (10,500 ft; 6 ac and 7.3 ac), **Roxy Ann Lakes** (10,220 ft; 65 and 5 ac) and **Ceanothuse Lake** (10,420 ft; 8 ac), which are reached from County Road 18, the Delaney Butte Lakes Road. Rainbow lakes are fair to good for 8- to 16-inch rainbow and cutthroat. Marked trails lead to other lakes. Lower Slide is fair for rainbow and cutthroat. Upper Slide is fair for rainbow, brown and cutthroat. The Roxy Ann Lakes are located about 1 mile north of Slide Lakes. Lower Roxy Ann Lake (65 ac) has cutthroat, rainbow and perhaps a golden or two. Upper Roxy Ann, or Spike Lake, has fair fishing for cutthroat. Ceanothuse lies about 2 miles past Upper Slide Lake and is well hidden. It is fair for 10- to 18-inch cutthroat.

DELANEY BUTTE LAKES
North of the Roaring Fork at its confluence with the North Platte, the **Delaney Butte Lakes** (8100 ft; 67, 150 and 163 ac) have ample feed and give rapid growth to the brown trout that inhabit them. The lakes are about 9 miles west of Walden. Fish average 10 to 14 inches, with many large ones taken. Rated fair with best results in early spring and the late season. Subject to heavy fishing pressure, the lakes are mostly mossy at midsummer, and difficult to fish from shore.

Though not available for rent, boats with motors are allowed; campsites at lakes. Take Hwy 125 west from Walden, and continue west past Walden Reservoir; cross the North Platte. Road comes to a T intersection; head north to South Delaney Lake. Route is well marked.

NORTH FORK'S TOPS
The **North Fork of North Platte River** is one of the best trout streams in the state; it enters the Platte from the north, due west of Walden. Leave Walden driving west on Hwy 125, continue west about 5.5 miles; turn north, cross the Platte; road intersects North Fork and offers several dirt roads to higher reaches. The North Fork is about 20 feet wide with many deep holes, riffles, and plenty of food. It meanders with a regular flow of clear water through brushy banks, with beaver ponds near the forest boundary. It is mostly posted in the lower parts where it is fair to good for 12-inch rainbow, brown and brook. Inside the National Forest, it is fair to good for small brook. Tributaries include **Bear, Ute, Shafer, Goose, Lake, Hill, Lone Pine** and **Forester Creeks.** All are small, brushy and ponded. This is prime fly fishing. Fair to good for small brook and cutthroat. At the headwaters of these tributary streams, in the Mount Zirkel Wilder-

ness Area, **Peggy Lake** (11,165 ft; 8 ac), **Blue Lake** (10,000 ft; 29 ac), the two **Twin Lakes** (9800 ft; 8 and 37 ac) and **Ute Lake** (9750 ft; 6 ac) are good for some brook and large mackinaws. Best access is from the Monahan Mine up the North Fork of North Platte.

Bear Lakes (10,000 ft; 20 and 13 ac) at the head of Bear Creek on the North Fork is rated poor for 8- to 16-inch cutthroat because of lack of food. There are some brown.

At the headwaters of Lone Pine Creek, downstream from Bear Creek on the North Fork, are **Big Horn Lake** (10,100 ft; 16 ac) and **Katherine Lake** (9860 ft; 22 ac). Both lakes are in the Mount Zirkel Wilderness Area and difficult to find as there is no marked trail. Rated good for 8- to 12-inch brook with an occasional mackinaw in Katherine.

FABULOUS LAKE JOHN

On the east side of the North Fork, **Lake John** (8050 ft; 556 ac) averages about 14 to 15 feet deep, but has areas to 22 feet deep. It abounds with 14- to 16-inch Snake River cutthroat and rainbow common in this excellent natural fishery. Abundant food has produced many large rainbow, brown and brook averaging 15 inches. Be prepared for hordes of eager anglers, especially on weekends and holidays. This is a good night-fishing lake, especially with a floating donut outfit. Best fishing is with baits and lures, though fly fishing can be good after midsummer from a boat anchored off the moss beds. Campsites are available, but there is no fuel or potable water. Boats and motors are allowed. Accessible by two well-marked routes. Take the Delaney Butte Road northwest; turn north after 5.5 miles; follow road across the North Platte for 6 miles, turn north just before the high school. Another route leaves west from Cowdrey for 8 miles, then turn south for about 5.5 miles.

Cowdrey Lake (7940 ft; 80 ac) is accessible from Hwy 125 about 1 mile south of Cowdrey and is well marked. A boat is needed to fish, but none is locally available; motors are allowed at wakeless speeds only.

> *In 1981 sportsmen spent $598 million on fishing and fishing-related items, according to the Colorado Division of Wildlife. Resident expenditures topped $565 million, while nonresident sportsmen paid nearly $33 million.*

Once a good fishery for rainbow and brown, it is coming back from killoff. It's been stocked with catchable-size trout and should be good year-round fishing again by 1986 or 1987. It tends to be very mossy in late summer.

There are several leases on the North Platte and its tributaries in the Walden-Cowdrey area. Due east of Walden, 6.3 miles of the Michigan River upstream has been leased. North of Walden and south of the county airport, 3.3 miles of the Michigan River has been leased. At Brownlee, north of Walden, a 4-mile stretch of the Michigan has been leased. And west of Cowdrey, north of the road, about 2 miles of the North Platte (beginning at the road downstream) has been leased also. Leased waters are signed for public fishing and are subject to restrictions. Check locally for exact locations and regulations.

In the east-southeast part of the North Park, the **Michigan River** enters the North Platte about 1 mile west of Cowdrey. This 25-foot-wide stream meanders through meadows, has many holes and can be waded. Good feed conditions make it possible for rainbow, brown and brook to grow from 8 to 24 inches long in the lower parts of the stream. At the forest boundary, the Michigan forks into three branches.

The **North Fork of Michigan River** is about 10 to 15 feet wide, brushy, with ponds. It is rated fair for cutthroat above the lake, and rainbow, brook, brown and some cutthroat below. An improved road to the east leaves Hwy 14 about 2 miles north of Gould. This road runs past Michigan Lake to the headwaters of the North Fork.

North Michigan Lake (8920 ft; 66 ac) is good for brook averaging 12 inches, and a few rainbow and cutthroat; flies and lures only.

AGNES LAKES

The **Middle Fork of Michigan River** flows along the shoulder of Hwy 14 southeast of Walden. It heads near Cameron Pass. The 12-mile stretch of water averages 15 feet wide and is rated fair to good for small cutthroat, brook and rainbow. At its headwaters, Agnes Lakes offer remote and scenic fishing. **Lower Lake Agnes** (10,660 ft; 22 ac) is reached by a dirt road that leaves Hwy 14 near the foot of the west side of Cameron Pass. It is a deep, cold, treacherous, rocky glacial lake with cutthroat, rainbow, brown and an occasional large brown. Best in July. **Upper Lake Agnes** (11,200 ft; 4.2 ac) is reached by a difficult trail from Lower Agnes. Upper Agnes is rated fair for cutthroat. Both lakes may have ice until early July. Downstream on the Middle Fork, **Ranger Lakes** (9200 ft; from 1 to 5 ac) are along Hwy 14 about 5.5 miles west of Cameron Pass. Stocked with put-and-take rainbow 9 to 11 inches. The Middle Fork along this stretch is rated fair for small rainbow and brook.

The **South Fork of Michigan River** enters the Michigan about 0.25 mile below Gould on Hwy 14. It is one of the most heavily fished streams in this region, but holds up well. It is not stocked and offers fair to good fishing for small cutthroat, brook and rainbow. Near the confluence, it is heavily posted. Accessible by a secondary road that leaves Gould at Aspen Campground. Road follows stream for about 2 miles to Pines Campground. From there the road travels about another 4 miles to the trailhead, which reaches the headwaters near Baker Pass.

From Gould down the Michigan, the stream flows through private lands. North of Walden about 1.5 miles, the **Illinois River** enters the Michigan River. The Illinois originates more than 20 miles to the south, above Rand. It is about 20 feet wide and edges through willows and meadows on private lands. Good holes and feed. Portions of the river are in a State Wildlife Area and have special restrictions. Best fishing is early season. Fair fishing at headwaters in the Never Summer Mountains. Access is from Rand on Hwy 125. Road runs south to the Illinois River headwaters, and to the headwaters of the tributary stream, **Jack Creek.** It is the principal tributary of the Illinois River and it is good for small brook.

Willow Creek enters the Illinois near Rand. Mostly posted from Rand to the forest boundary. Its upper part, in the forest, is small, brushy and ponded. Good for small brook and rainbow. Reached by a road that turns west from Hwy 125 about 0.25 mile inside the forest boundary; it is 5 miles to the headwaters. Or follow the road at Rand south along the creek. The road goes to the headwaters, where **Longs Lakes** (9860 ft and 10,000 ft; a total of 2 ac) are rated fair for 10- to 12-inch cutthroat and some brook. The lakes often suffer winterkill.

CANADIAN RIVER

Back on the North Platte River, just north of Cowdrey and the Michigan Fork of the North Platte on Hwy 12, the **Canadian River** enters the North Platte. The Canadian River rises in Colorado State Forest and flows northwest. Despite its promise, it is not an outstanding fishery and only the higher, hard-to-reach portions of it merit investigation. The private section is poor due to lack of feed and cover. This 20- to 25-foot-wide stream has a shifting sand bottom. Fair for small brook near the forest boundary; cutthroat can be caught near the headwaters.

Ruby Jewel Lake (11,240 ft; 4 ac) is at the headwaters of the Canadian River. Reached by 3 miles of steep trail from the junction of Jewel Lake Road and State Forest Road. Turn east at the North Fork of the Michigan River to the North Michigan Reservoir and follow the road north for about 1 mile. Turn east and follow the road northeast. Deep timberline lake is rated poor for 10- to 12-inch cutthroat. Waters are restricted to artificial flies and lures.

The best tributaries on the Canadian are **Clear** and **Kelly Creeks.** These streams are small and brushy with beaver ponds. Rated fair to good for small brook, and some cutthroat are found in the upper parts. Reach these tributaries by taking Hwy 14 south from Walden. At Michigan Hill, turn east. Road eventually crosses the Canadian River, then Kelly and Clear creeks. A better

---

SPORTSMAN'S SUPPLY

For your quality fishing and hunting supplies

Fishing & Hunting Licenses

Russ Bybee-your source for fishing information.
Call early mornings for update on regional conditions.

Box 246   **Walden, CO 80480**   **(303) 723-4343**

---

route might be to drive east from Walden about 4 miles; the road then angles south, then north. Stay on the road, cross the Canadian River, then cross the tributaries feeding from the east.

At the headwaters of Clear Creek, **Clear Lake** (10,580 ft; 9 ac) is rated good for cutthroat from 10 to 16 inches. Artificial flies and lures only. About 2 miles south is **Kelly Lake** (10,800 ft; 25 ac). To hike from Clear to Kelly means some steep climbing. Better access is to take an old road that goes to the headwaters and the trailhead to the lake.

North of the confluences of Michigan and Canadian rivers in the northeast corner of North Park, **Pinkham Creek** enters from the east, paralleling Hwy 127. Pinkham flows through Kings Canyon and is fed from the Medicine Bow Mountains. Lower portion is on private land and is posted; the upper part is small and brushy, and is rated fair for small brook. Access to the headwaters is by dirt roads from Kings Canyon.

North of the Pinkham confluence, and about 8 miles north of Cowdrey, **Camp Creek** enters the North Fork near Hwy 125. This 11-mile stream is mostly in Routt National Forest. It is small and brushy and difficult to fish. Rated fair to good for small brook.

BIG CREEK ANGLING

The headwaters of several North Platte tributaries poke into Colorado from Wyoming. The **South Fork of Big Creek** enters Colorado near Pearl, 20 miles northwest of Cowdrey. Reach Pearl by traveling northwest from Cowdrey. Big Creek, deceptively deep on the flat stretches, is often good spring and fall fishing for 5 miles below the lakes. Narrow, fast waters, except in the beaver ponds 2 miles below the lakes. Rainbow, brook and brown 8 to 12 inches. The **Big Creek Lakes** are accessible from Pearl or from the road leading from the North Fork of the North Platte. **Lower Big Creek Lake** (9000 ft; 350 ac) has a good campground at its north end. **Upper Big Creek Lake** (9010 ft; 113 ac) is a deep and timbered lake stocked with put-and-take rainbow. Both lakes lack natural feed for fish to do well. Upper Lake is fair to good for rainbow, small kokanee, brown and small brook. Boats are allowed. Some boating restrictions as posted. Upstream at the headwaters of Big Creek, **Seven Lakes** (10,700 ft; 14 ac) can be reached by trails from Lower Big Creek Lakes. Though there are 7 lakes, 6 are too shallow to support fish. The one lake is rated fair for 8- to 12-inch cutthroat.

North of Big Creek, **Beaver Creek** and **Davis Creek** also flow from the northwest to join the North Platte in Wyoming. Both creeks are good for small brook; many ponds. Accessible from Big Creek Road. Be certain to get permission to cross and fish from private land. Don't hesitate to leave your business card with obliging ranchers to support your affirmation as a responsible sportsman.

ENCAMPMENT RIVER

Encampment River can be reached from Big Creek Road. This tributary is beautiful water in beautiful country as it stretches into Wyoming to join the North Platte River at Encampment. The road from Pearl leads to Big Creek Lakes, then on northwest to the

Encampment and its tributaries. The headwaters of the tributaries can be reached by trails. The **South Fork of Hog Park Creek** is the farthest west and is rated excellent for 8- to 9-inch cutthroat and brook. The **West Fork of Encampment** joins the river about 0.75 mile south of where the road crosses the main stem of Encampment. From the confluence, it is 7 miles upstream to the headwaters of the West Fork. **West Fork Lake** (9400 ft; 20 ac) is located at the headwaters just east of the Continental Divide. West Fork Lake is rated excellent for small brook. Downstream from the West Fork Lake, **Manazares Lake** (9240 ft; 4 ac) is about 0.5 mile west of the main trail, but good trail provides access. Good fishing for brook and cutthroat. On the main stem of Encampment, fishermen will find good fishing from the trail along this 25-foot-wide waterway. Waters are rated excellent for small brook and some big brown. At its headwater, **Gem Lake** (10,160 ft; 7 ac) is excellent for brook averaging 11 inches. Trail is steep to this lake. Access is from Seven Lakes on the South Fork of Big Creek or by trail up the main fork of the Encampment River.

The North Platte is a 75-foot-wide, clear, tumbling river as it races into Wyoming, where its waters provide some of the finest fishing imaginable. After a run of more than 200 miles, it sweeps deep and roily in a grand arc to the southeast to join the South Platte River at North Platte, Nebraska. (See the North Platte River chapter in the Wyoming section of this book.) □

U.S. FOREST SERVICE DISTRICT RANGER STATIONS

North Park Ranger District
Routt National Forest
612 Fifth St., P.O. Box 158
Walden, CO 80480   303/723-4707

U.S. Forest Service campgrounds

U.S. Forest Service compilation was current as of 1985.

Asterisks denote fee areas. Some campgrounds are open only Memorial Day weekend through Labor Day. Below freezing weather could mean no water supply.

NORTH PLATTE RIVER DRAINAGE

ROUTT NATIONAL FOREST
Headquarters: 137 10th St., Box 771198, Steamboat Springs, CO 80477

Campground name	Elevation	No camp sites	Travel trailers	Drinking water	Length of stay (days)	Location and directions
Big Creek Lake*	9000	36	Yes	Yes	14	16.6 mi NW of Cowdrey by forest roads
Grizzly Creek*	8500	12	Yes	Yes	14	24 mi SW of Walden off Colo. 14
Hidden Lakes*	8900	9	Yes	Yes	14	28.6 mi SW of Walden off Colo. 14
Aspen*	9900	12	Yes	Yes	10	1 mi SW of Gould by forest road
Pines*	9200	11	Yes	Yes	14	3 mi SE of Gould by forest road

Laramie River
small but good

Adjacent communities:
Fort Collins; Woods Landing, Wyo.

Principal Highways:
Colo. 14; the Laramie Road; Wyo. 10.

The **Laramie River** is ideal for early-season fly fishing and remains a top-notch fishery much of the year. It and the nearby lakes and beaver ponds are prime brook trout waters, though some rainbow, brown and cutthroat also are available.

Most of its 27 miles in Colorado is paralleled by the Laramie Road that goes north from Hwy 14 just east of Chambers Lake. About half the river is in Roosevelt National Forest and the rest flows through private ranchlands where permission to fish is absolutely necessary. The stream is well posted, but it is not stocked. Some of the lakes and tributary streams are stocked. The Hohnholz Wildlife Area offers good fishing.

Don't hesitate to try a small fly on even the most inauspicious beaver pond. Many ponds are teaming with brookies, some to 14 inches or so.

CHAMBERS LAKE

The Laramie River heads at **Chambers Lake** (9164 ft; 350 ac when full), a crater lake used as a diversion basin to send water down the Cache la Poudre River for irrigation. Chambers' water level fluctuates greatly. Hwy 14, 52 miles west of US 287 at Fort Collins, skips past Chambers' south-east shore. From Hwy 14, the Laramie Road heads north along Chambers' flat east shore. Trolling and bait fishing from the banks give best results for rainbow averaging 8 to 10 inches, kokanee to 10 inches and occasional brown and cutthroat. There are a few lake trout. Flies are often successfully used at the mouth of **Fall, Joe Wright** and **Trap Creeks,** which enter the lake's southern and eastern shores. Chambers is rated fair, with best results in October when the water is low. No boats are available to rent, and boats and motors are allowed at wakeless speeds only. A campground on Chambers' southern end has trails up western drainages to the Rawah Wilderness Area and alpine lakes.

Laramie Lake (9300 ft; 36 ac) is about 1 mile northeast of Chambers Lake by trail. Rated fair for rainbow to 1 pound with occasional lunkers. Fish are there, but hard to catch.

Lost Lake (9290 ft; 25 ac) lies between Chambers Lake and Laramie Lake about 1 mile north of Hwy 14 on the Laramie Road. It is shallow, and often winterkills. Good for rainbow to 12 inches.

On the west side of Chambers Lake, **Fall Creek** carries water from several alpine lakes in the Rawah Wilderness Area. Fall Creek is rated poor for small fish, but at its headwaters Blue and Hang lakes offer challenging fishing for cutthroat. Access to the lakes is by pack trail from the campground on Chambers' southern shore. **Blue Lake** (10,720 ft; 16 ac) is fair for cutthroat and rainbow to 14 inches, some smaller brook. **Hang Lake** (11,160 ft; 4 ac) is 0.75 mile above Blue to the southwest by a marked trail. Good for large cutthroat, though they are difficult to entice.

West Branch Creek, downstream on Chambers Lake about 5 miles, meets the Laramie River at Tunnel Campground on the Laramie Road. A trail from the campground follows the West Branch into the Rawah Wilderness and forks with the river. The northwestern trail follows the **North Fork of the West Branch** for good brook fishing to its headwater lakes. The southwestern trail stays with the West Branch to its tributary lakes.

At the head of the North Fork, **Bench Lake** (10,950 ft; 6 ac) is about 8 miles from Tunnel Campground. Two miles after fork, trail makes several switchbacks. Bench is very good for 10- to 12-inch brook. **Rock Hole Lake** (11,200 ft; 6 ac) is difficult to find, but lies over the ridge south of Bench Lake. There is no direct trail to the lake, but it can be reached by bushwacking from Bench Lake or by taking the trail that breaks south from the North Fork trail about 2.5 miles after the fork. This same trail leads to the **Twin Crater Lakes** (11,045 ft; 7 and 17 ac). They are good for 10- to 12-inch cutthroat.

WILDERNESS

The West Branch of the Laramie reaches high into the Rawah Wilderness Area to **Carey Lake** (11,044 ft; 5.7 ac), **Island Lake** (10,900 ft; 15 ac) and **Timber Lake** (10,900 ft; 10 ac). They are about 8 miles southwest of Tunnel campground. The trail forks just before reaching Carey Lake and goes south to Blue Lake and Hang Lake in the Fall Creek drainage. This trail leads all the way to Chambers Lake and is a shorter route to the headwaters of West Branch Creek. The lakes at the West Branch

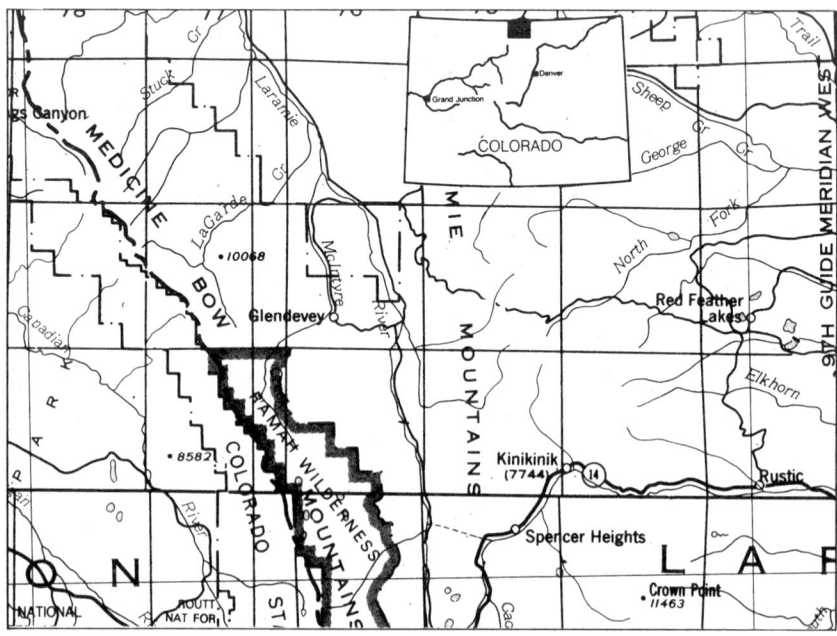

Laramie River

headwaters are about 0.5 mile apart. Carey Lake is fair for brook and cutthroat to 12 inches, and Timber Lake is good for rainbow and cutthroat to 10 inches.

The West Branch lakes, along with the lakes at the headwaters of Rawah Creek, are located in the Rawah Wilderness Area. The Rawah is steep mountainous country dotted with more than 35 bodies of water. The Rawah Wilderness is very popular and the fishing pressure is heavy. Many of its waters are stocked.

Rawah Creek feeds into the Laramie River from the southwest about 7 miles downstream from Tunnel Campground. At its headwaters in the Rawah Wilderness are several alpine lakes. A trail from Rawah Ranch, 1 mile south of the Laramie-Rawah confluence, roughly follows the Rawah to its headwaters. Follow the trail to the headwaters for good, small brook fishing. The lower reaches are fair to good for small rainbow. At the headwaters of the Rawah, the stream forks as does the trail. Take the trail to the right (heading west) about 0.75 mile to **Little Rainbow Lake** (10,838 ft; 6 ac), a shallow cirque lake which is rated fair for small brook and rainbow. The Little Rainbow is also accessible from McIntyre Lake to the north. A pack trail from Glendevey heading south to the headwaters of the McIntyre Creek goes along the east shore of the McIntyre Lake to Little Rainbow Lake and on to the Rawah Lakes.

The **Rawah Lakes** lie east of Little Rainbow at the headwaters of Rawah Creek. These lakes are known by several names, but on U.S. Geological maps they are numbered. Take the trail to Little Rainbow Lake. **Lake No. 1** (10,700 ft; 8 ac) is a shallow, heavily fished lake on the trail. It is rated good for small brook. Good campsites. South of Lake No. 1 less than 0.5 mile by trail, is **Lake No. 2** (10,750 ft; 8 ac), which also is shallow, but rated very good for small brook and an occasional rainbow. **Lake No. 3** (10,850 ft) is a deep 25-acre lake about 0.75 mile up creek from No. 2. It has brook and rainbow up to 13 inches that are difficult to catch. Good fly lake. Easiest fishing is with spinning gear. Rated fair to good most of the summer. Good campsites.

Lake No. 4 (11,400 ft; 31 ac) lies farthest south and is set far from the main trail. The trail to the lake is not well marked. Follow trail from other Rawah Lakes to the ridge top and then hike west along the ridge. Trail is steep in places. Lake No. 4 is a deep lake with sheer sides and is difficult to fish. Cutthroat 11 to 17 inches.

Over the ridge to the east from Rawah Lakes is the **Upper Sandbar Lake** (10,690 ft; 9 ac). Hike 0.25 mile south of Rawah Lake No. 2 to trail junction, turn east. Follow trail about 0.5 mile to **Middle Sandbar Lake** (10,600 ft; 1 ac) and **Lower Sandbar Lake** (10,600 ft; 4 ac). The Sandbar lakes are very shallow and rated good for brook 9 to 10 inches. They are heavily fished; waders are helpful.

Follow the trail from the Rawah Lakes beyond Upper Sandbar Lake to **Big Rainbow Lake** (10,720 ft; 6 ac). This lake suffers winterkill; fishing is doubtful, but there are a few brook and rainbow.

CAMP LAKES

To the southeast of Big Rainbow Lake, **Upper Camp Lake** (10,720 ft; 41 ac) can be reached from Rainbow by following the ridge. Upper Camp is good for brook, cutthroat and a few rainbow averaging 11 inches. It is easy to fish but waders are desirable. Downstream of Upper Camp Lake is **Lower Camp Lake** (10,510 ft; 13 ac). Lower Camp Lake can be reached from Lower Sandbar Trail or from a horse trail that follows the ridges from Tunnel Campground on the Laramie River Road. It is rated very good for brook to 14 inches. Good fly lake; heavily fished. Good campsites.

Several tributaries flow into the Laramie below Rawah Creek. From the west, these include **Drink, Stub** and **Link Creeks,** and, from the east, **Nunn** and **Deadman Creeks.** Most of the streams are small, brushy, fast and wadable, and offer good brook fishing.

Farther downstream, **McIntyre Creek** enters the Laramie River from the southwest about 4 miles north of Four Corners. At Four Corners, a road going west parallels the stream south to Glendevey and then loops back to the Laramie River Road south of Four Corners (about 7 miles). West of Glendevey about 0.5 mile is the Hooligan Roost Campground. A trail from the campground follows the stream about 5 miles. Stream continues another 5 miles to headwaters. McIntyre is primarily a brown trout stream. The lakes at the headwaters can be reached by Rawah Creek Trail or a pack trail heading south of the Browns Park Campground outside of Glendevey.

McIntyre Lake (10,200 ft; 14 ac) is shallow and rated fair for brook from 9 to 11 inches; an occasional large brown is taken. Easy to fish; good campsites. To the west, **Sugar Bowl Lake** (10,790 ft; 8 ac) is a moderately deep lake and tends to be overpopulated with small brook; needs more fishing. Good for small brook and some mackinaw. **Iceberg Lake** (11,100 ft; 6 ac) lies farther west. There is no trail. Best access is by hiking up the farthest west fork of McIntyre in the lakes area. **Upper Twin Lake** (10,600 ft; 9 ac) is fairly deep. It and Lower Twin Lake are on the middle fork in the lake area. Both are good for small brook with a few larger brown taken occasionally. **Lower Twin Lake** (10,500 ft; 5 ac) is very shallow and lies 0.5 miles north of Upper Twin Lake. These lakes do not get much fishing pressure. Good for small brook and some brown.

Downstream, heading north from Four Corners to the Colorado-Wyoming border, the Laramie River flows through private land. There are several streams feeding into the Laramie along this stretch. Tributaries include **La Garde, Forrester** and **Grace Creeks,** which are good fishing for brook in the upper reaches and browns near the confluences. Grace Creek access road is closed, as posted.

HOHNHOLZ LAKES

On either side of Grace Creek, the **Hohnholz Lakes** offer excellent feeding conditions as they are full of shrimp. These lakes are on the **Hohnholz State Wildlife Area.** The Laramie River in this stretch has been designated wild trout waters. Fishing regulations are posted. The river is fished with artificial flies and lures only. There are some nice brown here, with a limit of two fish of any kind. The Laramie River Road loops in this area for easy access to the three lakes. **Eastern Hohnholz Lake No. 1** (7900 ft; 8 ac) is about 16 feet deep and stocked with catchable trout. **Little Hohnholz Lake No. 2** (7900 ft; 37 ac), located between the two lakes, is also stocked with catchable trout. The western and largest lake is **Hohnholz Lake No. 3**(7900 ft; 40 ac). It is about 30 feet deep and contains the largest fish. Brown trout fingerlings stocked several years ago have thrived and offer some good action to the 12- to 14-inch size. All three lakes are rated good for rainbow averaging 11 inches.

There is no overnight camping in the wildlife area, except at the designated Laramie River camping area. Only handpaddled boats are allowed.

North of the Hohnholz Wildlife Area, near the Colorado state line, four other main tributaries of the Laramie River, **Stuck, Johnson, Pole** and **Fish Creeks,** offer good brown fishing in the lower reaches and good brook fishing near the headwaters. Several dirt roads web the area.

On the east side of the Laramie River, the upper reaches of **Sand Creek** stretch into Colorado from its confluence with the Laramie River east of Woods Landing, Wyoming. Sand Creek offers about 10 miles of water with small brushy ponds that are difficult to work. Best access is by turning east at Four Corners on the Laramie River Road to Sand Creek Pass. Road roughly parallels the stream from the pass north. Sand Creek is heavily fished in the early season when rated fair for small brook and brown to 14 inches. The creek has several beaver ponds near Sand Creek Pass that are stocked with brown.

See Wyoming Section for additional discussion of the Laramie River. □

The Colorado Division of Wildlife owns or leases from private owners 66,000 surface acres of water and 93 miles of stream open to public fishing.

Cache la Poudre River last of the untamed

Adjacent communities:
Fort Collins.

Principal Highways:
Colo. 14.

The **Cache la Poudre River** rises in the northwest section of Rocky Mountain National Park and flows northerly out of the park before looping east towards the city of Fort Collins.

Hwy 14, the Cameron Pass road, parallels the river for most of its mountainous 47 miles. The river has some fine fly fishing and a variety of water to tempt anglers in pursuit of its rainbow, brown and brook trout. Be assured there are trophy-caliber trout in the Poudre.

La Poudre is the last major Front Range stream that has not had a major dam and reservoir constructed on it, although some of its waters are diverted for irrigation. Portions of the stream are private and closed to public fishing. Where Hwy 14 follows the stream, there are many cabins as well as stores, cafes and tackle/bait shops. The lower reaches of the river above Teds Place may have a few cutthroat and whitefish.

The headwaters of the Poudre River in Rocky Mountain National Park can be reached by following the pack trail south along the Poudre River from Big South Campground on Hwy 14 near Chambers Lake. The trail follows the river more than 20 miles to its headwaters on US 34, Trail Ridge Road, in the park. This section of river offers some of the Poudre's best fishing. It averages 20 to 30 feet wide with all types of water. A rough road leaving Hwy 14 where the bridge crosses Joe Wright Creek also reaches the high branches of the Poudre. Sign reads "Long Draw Reservoir." The headwaters of the Poudre are good for cutthroat, brown and a few rainbow averaging 10 inches, though larger fish are taken.

At the Poudre's headwaters, **Poudre Lake** (10,700 ft; 14 ac) at Milner Pass just off the Trail Ridge Road in the park offers lots of feed for brook. Downstream 7 to 10 miles, follow the pack trail to where **Chapin, Hague** and **Cascade Creeks** feed into the Poudre. These tributaries offer good brook fishing in the lower reaches. Obey park regulations when fishing in the park. There is no park fishing permit.

At the headwaters of Cascade Creek, **Mirror Lake** (11,000 ft; 19 ac) lies outside the park boundary in the Roosevelt National Forest. It can be reached from the trail at the headwaters of the South Fork Cache la Poudre or by a trail that forks from the Poudre River near Hague Creek. Mirror is fair for small brook, though some 14-inch

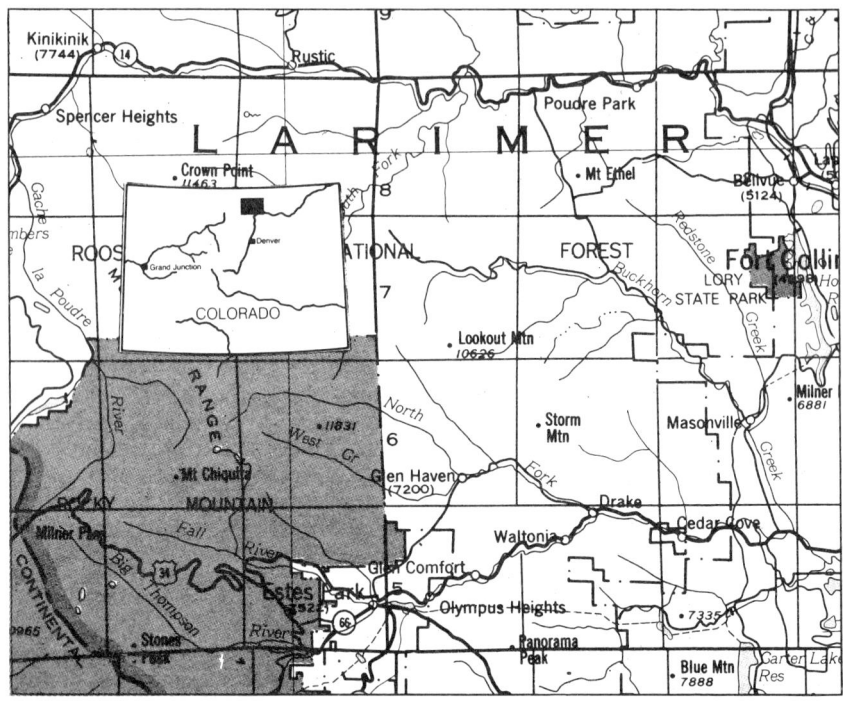
Rocky Mountain National Park, Cache la Poudre

brook have been taken. It's a long trip in, so plan to stay overnight.

LONG DRAW

Long Draw Reservoir (10,100 ft; 160 ac) is on the west side of the Poudre, set in bighorn sheep country just outside the park. This reservoir fluctuates greatly, so fishing is rated poor; however, a few large cutthroat are taken. Access to Long Draw Reservoir is by turning south from Hwy 14 at Chambers Lake along Trap Creek. Turn right just after Trap Lake; sign reads "Long Draw Reservoir." **Long Draw Creek** has fishing with flies and lures only from the reservoir to the park boundary.

Corral Creek intersects the access road to Long Draw Reservoir about 1 mile before the reservoir. Corral is a small brushy stream with small cutthroat. It enters the Poudre from the west.

Joe Wright Creek enters the Poudre from the southwest. Its headwaters are at Cameron Pass on Hwy 14. The creek itself does not offer a great deal of fishing and is subject to special restrictions, but **Zimmerman Lake** (10,495 ft; 11 ac) near its headwaters produced the state record grayling. The 1-pound, 7-ounce grayling was caught in 1974 and was 15 inches long. Zimmerman is a glacial lake reached by a trail which junctures with Hwy 14 at the west end of Joe Wright Reservoir; 1 mile to Zimmerman. At the outlet of the lake, a small falls cascades down the mountainside. It can be seen from Hwy 14. This record-producing lake is restricted to artificial flies and lures only, and fishing is prohibited in the inlet area, as posted. Rated fair for 8- to 12-inch cutthroat and some grayling. This lake is stocked, but has strong natural reproduction.

Joe Wright Reservoir (10,184 ft; 163 ac when full) is on Hwy 14 just 3 miles upstream from Chambers Lake. This elongated body of water is a new home for the Emerald Lake cutthroat from the Weminuche Wilderness Area, northeast of Durango. Because of stocking the Emerald Lake species to establish good fishing in Joe Wright, artificial flies and lures only may be used. All trout under 16 inches must be returned. There are lots of fish, just not many big enough to keep...yet. Also, fishing is prohibited from the Hwy 14 bridge to the reservoir inlet from January 1 to July 31 as posted. Only electric motors may be used on boats.

Trap Creek, a southern tributary of Chambers Lake, is paralleled by a dirt road leading to **Trap Lake** (9960 ft; 13 ac). This shallow put-and-take lake is fair for rainbow, brook, cutthroat and kokanee. At Trap Lake the road forks; on the east fork, **Peterson Lake** (9300 ft; 41 ac) offers difficult fishing for cutthroat to 14 inches, some larger. This lake is a part of the city of Greeley's water supply. Boats are not allowed. Follow the trail along the east shore 0.5 mile east to Cache la Poudre River.

Joe Wright Creek enters the south end of Chambers Lake (see Laramie River) and picks up again off its eastern shore. Just off Hwy 14 near Chambers' eastern shore, **Barnes Meadow Reservoir** (9153 ft; 113 ac when full) is stocked with fingerling rainbow.

As the Poudre weaves its way through the steep canyons in the Roosevelt National Forest, several tributary streams cut in from the steep ridges to feed the main stream.

Midway between the Joe Wright Creek fork and the village of Kinikinik, **Sheep Creek** flows into the Poudre from the south. The lakes at its headwaters were once an old reservoir site. What remains are a few beaver ponds that have had all fish removed for the introduction of the greenback cutthroat, a protected species in Colorado. No fishing is allowed in the ponds.

At Kinikinik, about 8 miles downstream from the Joe Wright Creek fork, **Roaring Creek** enters the Poudre from the north. The 5-mile-long stream is 5 to 8 feet wide and is rated fair for small brook and cutthroat. It is open to the public and accessible by pack trail from Kinikinik.

Downstream from Kinikinik to Rustic, three fine stretches of the river have been designated wild trout waters. There are many signs with current regulations.

WILD TROUT WATERS

Wild trout waters with naturally reproducing trout on the Poudre testify to its quality fishing. While only the middle section, from Grandpa's Bridge to Hombre Ranch, has a 16-inch minimum on keepers in 1985, all three special areas probably will have that restriction in 1986.

Evidence to date shows that significantly improved fishing results from allowing the fish to grow large enough to reproduce naturally. Consequently, most angling is catch and release.

Boundaries:

From the Poudre River Fish Hatchery intake structure at mile post 83.3 to the confluence with Black Hollow Creek at mile post 87.2;

From Hombre Ranch west boundary at mile post 91.2 to Grandpa's Bridge at mile post 94.8; and

From the dam and intake structure of the irrigation canal at mile post 115.7 to the dam and intake structure of the Poudre Valley canal at mile post 119.3.

Only manmade flies and lures may be used.

SOUTH FORK

The **South Fork Cache la Poudre** enters the main Poudre about 1 mile west of Narrows Campground just east of Indian Meadows, about 28 miles west of Fort Collins on Hwy 14. A secondary road at Egger, about 5 miles west of Narrows Campground on Hwy 14, heads south about 4 miles and then parallels the South Fork for a few miles. Follow this road to Tom Bennett

All it takes is concentration!

Campground to reach alpine lakes and the headwaters of the South Fork. The stream above the headwaters at the Rocky Mountain Park boundary and 1 mile downstream are closed to fishing.

Emmaline Lake (11,000 ft; 4 ac) and **Cirque Lake** (11,000 ft; 2 ac) are above timberline on Fall Creek, which feeds into the South Fork from the west. **Fall Creek** is rated poor for small fish. Both lakes are near the park border. Take the road from Tom Bennett Campground to Fall Creek; hike about 3 miles to the lakes. Trail forks on Fall Creek. The trail to the south leads into the park to Mummy Pass. It can be followed to Mirror Lake and the main fork of the Poudre.

Above Bennett Campground near the Lazy D Ranch, **Beaver Creek** enters the South Fork. This 7-mile stream is 6 to 8 feet wide with several ponds. It is rated fair to good fishing for small brook and cutthroat. From Bennett Campground, drive west to Sky Ranch. From there the road goes another 2.5 miles to Comanche Reservoir. At Comanche Reservoir, a foot trail leads to Beaver Creek's headwater lakes, including **Browns Lake** (10,520 ft; 20 ac). The last part of this 4-mile hike is steep but easy. Browns Lake is good for brook that average 12 inches. To the southeast of Browns, less than a 0.25 mile, is **Timberline Lake** (10,500 ft; 4 ac), a shallow lake with small brook.

Comanche Reservoir (9400 ft; 20 ac) is downstream from Browns and Timberline lakes. It can be reached by vehicle. A trail leading to the upper lakes follows the north shore. Comanche is rated fair for brown and cutthroat to 10 inches. Downstream from Comanche on Beaver Creek, **Hourglass Reservoir** (9200 ft; 20 ac) is located on the south side of the road. It is private.

Elkhorn Creek enters the Cache la Poudre from the north near Narrows Campground at Hwy 14. It is rated only fair, and the lower end is entirely posted; but, permission sometimes is granted. Open waters in the upper stretches can be reached by two dirt roads. Travel north out of Fort Collins on US 287, make a west turn at Livermore. Follow the road to Red Feathers Lakes. A paved road south of the Red Feathers Lake Road leads to the upper Elkhorn and Bellaire Lake campgrounds. Another route is to turn north off Hwy 14 at Glen Echo. Follow this road to Goodell Corner and turn west up Manhattan Creek. Follow the road about 4 miles to upper Elkhorn Creek and then on to the Red Feather Lakes. On the same road, north of Elkhorn Creek, **Bellaire Lake** (8600 ft; 11 ac) is good fishing for 9- to 11-inch rainbow. It is a put-and-take lake with a campground at its south end. There are accommodations also at Red Feather Lakes.

NORTH FORK

The **North Fork Cache la Poudre River** is a narrow, fast mountain stream rated fair for small rainbow and brook. It enters the main Poudre about 5 miles north of Teds Place on US 287. Much of the upper part is tightly posted. Some tributaries near the headwaters are open to the public. These include **Sheep, Beaver, Cornelius, Panhandle** and **George Creeks.** These are small streams with beaver ponds, rated fair to good for small brook (larger ones are taken occasionally) and some browns. These streams are accessible from a road that goes west from US 287 about 3 miles north of Livermore. This road leads to Four Corners on the Laramie River Road.

On Panhandle Creek, **Panhandle Reservoir** is private. But below the Panhandle Creek confluence with the North Fork, **Creedmore Lakes** (8300 ft; all three less than 10 ac) lie about 12 miles north of the Red Feathers Lakes. Only one lake, where the campground is located, has fish, and it is rated good for 10- to 12-inch rainbow. It is accessible from Red Feathers village. Follow the paved road north from town. It parallels Columbine Creek for a short stretch, then follows North Lone Pine Creek east to a left turn marked by sign, "Creedmore Lakes."

Farther downstream on the North Fork, **Halligan Reservoir** is closed to the public.

Rabbit Creek enters the North Fork just 5 miles northwest of Livermore on US 287. Below this confluence, **Lone Pine Creek** enters the North Fork from the west. Several roads lead from Red Feather Lakes and head west to the headwaters of Lone Pine Creek. This small, brushy, ponded stream is fair to good for brook to 9 inches. East and downstream of Lone Pine headwaters are the **Red Feather Lakes** (8365 ft). They are reached from US 287 about 21 miles north of Fort Collins. Turn west at Livermore at the sign. Travel 24 miles to lakes over good road. The largest of the group, **Dowdy Lake** (8133 ft; 115 ac), is the only lake where motors are allowed. It is rated good for rainbow averaging 12 to 13 inches, with a few to 5 pounds taken; Dowdy also has brown and brook. Trolling gives best results. On the west and south sides of the lake are several campgrounds with facilities for trailers. **Parvin Lake** (8130 ft; 63 ac) is fenced as a Wildlife Commission research area. Fishing by regulations as posted.

There's a creel clerk on duty much of the time who will explain the experimental work with Colorado cutthroat, greenback cutthroat and the Pike's Peak cutthroat trout. They are marked by having some fins clipped off. Information sought includes comparable rates of growth, catchability and other factors to be considered in managing fishing statewide.

The walk from parking area to lake is about 100 yards. There is no shoreline parking, overnight camping or fishing. The lake is closed November 1 to April 30. Daily possession and size limits may vary. The lake is open from 10 a.m. to 10 p.m. No boating or inflatable devices. Rated good with flies for rainbow and brown averaging 11 inches.

The next lake to the west is West (Twin) Lake (8200 ft; 25 ac). It is a very temperamental lake, but rated fair to good for 11-inch rainbow. Campground on south shore; boats without motors are allowed.

Seaman Reservoir, (5748 ft; 150 ac) at the confluence of the North Fork and the Cache la Poudre River, is owned by the city of Greeley. It is not stocked. Those wishing to fish there must be willing to tackle a ferocious hike from the west side because other banks are private. Inquire at the local Forest Service for trail information. Fishing is for brown and some migrant rainbow.

Photo by Bob Saile

Below the North Fork confluence just south of Teds Place to the Valley Canal, a section of the Cache la Poudre is the third portion of the Poudre River that has been designated wild trout waters. Inquire at Teds Place for specifics and restrictions.

Below the North Fork confluence near Bellvue, **Watson Lake** (5120 ft; 49 ac) is 10 to 12 feet deep. Take US 287 north from Fort Collins to Bellvue junction. Follow road west about 1 mile until the road crosses the Poudre. Take the first road to the right. Watson is rated fair to good for 8- to 10-inch rainbow, brown and small brook. It is easy to fish, but no boats are allowed. Camping is prohibited except at designated sites. Live bait and ice fishing also are prohibited. The west side is closed to the public.

HORSETOOTH RESERVOIR

South of Watson Lake and southwest of the Poudre River, **Horsetooth Reservoir** (5430 ft; 1875 ac) is part of the Colorado-Big Thompson reclamation project. About 7 miles long, the Horsetooth averages about 0.75 mile when full and has many deep coves. Access is a few miles south of Fort Collins at Cunningham Corner on US 287. Sign indicates 4 miles to dam and 2 miles more to boat dock; surfaced. Fair to good for 12-inch rainbow, bass to 4 pounds, crappie, 10-inch kokanee, 2- to 3-pound walleye, some mackinaw up to 30 pounds and ring perch to 11 inches. Boats are available at the concession; motors are allowed. Holders of a rainbow trout stamp make take a total of 16 rainbow trout. Limits have been set on spearfishing; check regulations. ☐

U.S. Forest Service campgrounds

U.S. Forest Service compilation was current as of 1985.

Asterisks denote fee areas. Some campgrounds are open only Memorial Day weekend through Labor Day. Below freezing weather could mean no water supply.

CACHE LA POUDRE RIVER DRAINAGE

ROOSEVELT NATIONAL FOREST
Headquarters: Federal Bldg., 301 S. Howes, Box 1366, Fort Collins, CO 80521

Campground name	Elevation	No camp sites	Travel trailers	Drinking water	Length of stay (days)	Location and directions
Big South	8400	3	Yes	No	14	On Colo. 14, 55 mi W of La Porte
Chambers Lake*	9200	53	Yes	Yes	14	On Colo. 14, 60 mi W of La Porte
Browns Park	8400	28	Yes	No	14	21 mi N of Colo. 14, 59 mi W of La Porte
Skyline	8600	8	Yes	No	14	4 mi N of Colo. 14, 59 mi W of La Porte
Tunnel	7900	2	Yes	No	14	34.8 mi W of La Porte
Tunnel	8600	49	Yes	No	14	6 mi N of Colo. 14, 59 mi W of La Porte
Mountain Park*	6700	45	Yes	Yes	14	On Colo. 14, 17.6 mi W of La Porte
Ansel Watrous*	5800	19	Yes	Yes	14	On Colo. 14, 11.8 mi W of La Porte
Sleeping Elephant*	7900	15	Yes	Yes	14	On Colo. 14, 33 mi W of La Porte
Tom Bennett	9000	12	Yes	No	14	16 mi S of Colo. 14, 22.3 mi W of La Porte
Kelly Flats*	6800	23	Yes	Yes	14	On Colo. 14, 18 mi W of La Porte
Dowdy Lake South Shore*	8100	31	Yes	Yes	14	1 mi E of County Hwy 4, 1 mi E of Redfeather
West Lake*	8200	29	Yes	Yes	14	1 mi E of County Hwy 4, 1 mi E of Redfeather
Bellaire Lake*	8600	13	Yes	Yes	14	4 mi S of County Hwy 4, 1 mi S of Redfeather
Creedmore Lake	8300	10	No	No	14	18 mi N of Redfeather on forest roads
North Fork Poudre	9200	9	Yes	No	14	8 mi W of Redfeather on Hwy 4 and forest road
Dowdy Lake West Shore*	8100	24	Yes	Yes	14	1.5 mi E of Redfeather on County Hwy 4

Rocky Mountain National Park

Adjacent communities:
Estes Park, Grand Lake, Granby.

Principal Highways:
U.S. 34; Colo. 7, 66, 278.

Few settings have the grandeur for fishing of Rocky Mountain National Park, refuge of the rare greenback cutthroat trout. Only a few of the 3.5 million annual visitors even wet a line, and then with sporadic success, even in waters with good trout populations. It's tempermental angling, but there are brown, brook, rainbow, Colorado River cutthroat, Yellowstone cutthroat—and hybrids thereof—to tempt any fisherman.

The repopulating of park streams with the greenback cutthroat has been a success and many stretches are open to catch-and-release fishing.

Fishermen need only a Colorado fishing license. No park fishing permit exists. It's a good idea to get a copy of park fishing rules. Handpowered boats are allowed on all lakes except Bear Lake.

The setting of high altitude, heavy snowfall, short summers—as exemplified by the Never Summer Mountain Range—don't lend themselves to big fish. But there always are exceptions.

Rocky Mountain National Park spans the Continental Divide in northcentral Colorado, 76 miles northwest of Denver. While no major fishing waters are among the exceptionally rugged 13,000- and 14,000-foot peaks, there are some sections of streams and remote lakes that challenge the angler who is willing to hike or ride horseback to reach them.

The National Park Service now stocks only cutthroat species. Populations of rainbow, brook and brown are reproducing naturally since they were introduced in streams years ago. Fishing, except for children 12 years old and under, is with flies and artificial lures only. Only children may use bait (worms, preserved fish eggs, insects only), and even possession of bait by adults is illegal. Children may not use bait in catch-and-release waters.

PROTECTED WATERS

Waters closed to fishing to protect the greenback cutthroat are: Bear Lake; Lake Nanita outlet for 100 yards on North Inlet Creek; Ouzel Lake and Ouzel Creek in the North St. Vrain Creek drainage; Lake Odessa, Fern Lake and Fern Creek in the Big Thompson River drainage; West Creek above West Creek Falls in the North Fork of Big Thompson River drainage; and North Fork of Big Thompson above Lost Falls.

The Big Thompson River in Forest Can-

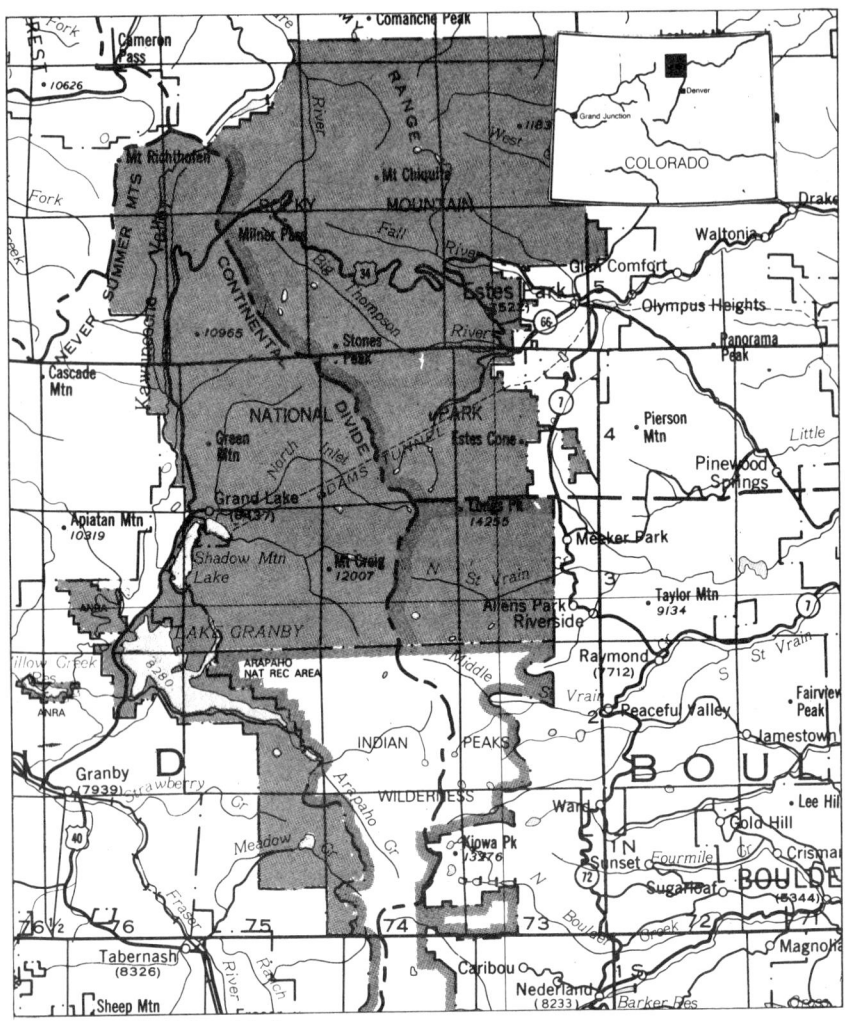

Rocky Mountain National Park

yon, previously closed, is now open to catch-and-release fishing for the greenback, as is the Fay Lakes drainage tributary to Roaring River.

Other lakes and streams in the park are open to fishing year-round. Ice fishing in the deeper lakes—Black Lake, Sprague Lake and the Glacier Gorge lakes area—can be very productive. If you don't know, check out which lakes have fish and which don't before going to all that work augering through the ice.

After August 1, the beaver ponds on Hidden Valley Creek are open for brook trout fishing with barbless hooks only. Any greenback cutthroat caught are to be returned to the water immediately.

Park rules provide for possession of 8 trout over 8 inches long of any species (with the exception of greenback cutthroat) and 10 brook trout.

Rocky Mountain National Park is reached from the east via Hwy 34 west from Loveland, or northwest on Hwy 36 from

Lyons. From the southeast, Hwy 72 joins Hwy 7 near Raymond; Hwy 7 enters the park. From the west and southwest, Hwy 34 (Trail Ridge Road) north from Granby provides the only road access. There is no road entering from the north.

Description of some of the more likely fishing waters in the park begins in the park's southeast corner as accessible by Hwy 7 at Allenspark. It goes north, then west across the top of the park, south along the west boundary, and then to the southern streams and lakes.

SOUTHEAST

North St. Vrain Creek, slightly north and east of Allenspark, is fair fishing for brook and brown to 10 inches, and rainbow and cutthroat, mostly small. Access is via the Wild Basin Campground and Ranger Station. **Sandbeach Lake** (10,300 ft; 17 ac) is 6 miles west of Copeland Lake on the park boundary. The trail between the lakes is rough and steep. Sandbeach is deep when full, with a sloping, sandy shoreline. It is fair for rainbow and cutthroat from 6 to 14 inches.

Thunder Lake (10,600 ft; 17 ac) is 7.5 miles west of Wild Basin Campground on a good trail, Allenspark-Wild Basin Trail. Fishing is only fair, but there are some good-size rainbow. **Box Lake** (10,700 ft; 6 ac) is about 1.5 miles south of Thunder, crosscountry (no trail); it is deep and at timberline. Can be fair to good for brook to 12 inches. A half-mile farther south is **Eagle Lake** (10,800 ft; 12 ac), which probably is barren.

To the southeast is **Ouzel Lake** and **Ouzel Creek,** both closed to fishing in 1985. The park plans to open them in 1986 for catch-and-release fishing with flies and lures only. These are greenback cutthroat waters. **Bluebird Lake,** above Ouzel Lake, is barren. South and east is **Cony Creek,** a pretty stream with good fishing for rainbow and cutthroat as it drains the southeastern part of the park. Near its head is **Pear Reservoir** (10,582 ft; 7 ac). It is deep, with a rocky shoreline and is fair for cutthroat to 12 inches. South of it and just outside the park are the **Hutcheson Lakes** (10,200 ft; 0.5 to 3 ac). They and the creek are good for cutthroat. To the west, **Cony Lake** (11,440 ft; 2 ac) may be barren. Access as far as Pear Reservoir is on the Finch Lake-Pear Reservoir Trail, which heads out of both Allenspark and the Olive Ridge Campground on Hwy 7. It is about a 10-mile hike. From Wild Basin Ranger Station, it is about 7 miles by walking up North St. Vrain Creek and, at the Calypso Cascades sign, heading south up Cony Creek. Beyond the cascades, the trail is poor and the going rough. Pretty country.

North of Allenspark about 7 miles, a well-marked road leads west to Longs Peak Ranger Station, the trailhead and campground. Southwest of the station is **Peacock Pool** (11,360 ft; 4 ac) and **Chasm Lake** (11,800 ft; 19 ac), both on **Roaring Fork of Cabin Creek.** Take the Longs Peak Trail to a fork in the trail about 2.5 miles below the boulder field. A sign indicates the Chasm Lake Trail to the west, directly toward the diamond (east face) of Longs Peak. It is 0.75 mile to Peacock to fish for brook and cutthroat to 9 inches. Another 1.5 miles, mostly westerly, is Chasm, very deep and rocky, and hard to fish for cutthroat. There are some large ones, but they are very temperamental. Chasm is about 4.5 miles from the campground. Roaring Fork has some cutthroat and brook. Pools are best, but access often is difficult.

BIG THOMPSON

Farther north, the **Big Thompson River** flows northeastward out of the heart of the park into the town of Estes Park and Lake Estes. Its lower reaches provide meadow fishing, although, from a mile west of the Moraine Park bridge, it is brushy upstream. Fishing is fair to good for 10-inch brown, rainbow and some brook. Access to it and several high lakes is from the Beaver Meadows entrance, west of Estes.

Going west into the park, turn south at the first junction to Moraine Park. After a mile turn west onto the dirt road along the Big Thompson River to Fern Lake trailhead parking area and picnic ground. To the west, up **Spruce Creek,** are **Spruce Lake** (9640 ft; 4 ac) and **Loomis Lake** (10,200 ft;

3 ac), which are open to fishing for rainbow and brook, respectively. Rough country although the trail is obvious; fishing is poor to fair. **Fern Lake** and **Fern Creek** are closed to fishing in 1985, as is **Odessa Lake.** The park expects to open Fern Lake and Fern Creek to catch-and-release fishing in 1986. It's a beautiful place to fish. To the northwest, Forest Canyon on the "Big T" is open to catch-and-release fishing.

Southwest and above Forest Canyon of the Big Thompson River are the **Gorge Lakes,** a half-dozen lakes above timberline which are very difficult to reach and are recommended only to seasoned hikers in excellent physical condition. Access is cross country from the Milner Pass parking area on Trail Ridge Road, at the Continental Divide. **Rock Lake** and **Little Rock Lake** (10,300 ft; 1 ac), **Arrowhead Lake** (11,200 ft; 43 ac) and **Donut Lake** (11,520 ft; 5 ac) have cutthroat. Access via Forest Canyon is extremely difficult; inquiry is advised. High lakes like these provide unpredictable fishing.

Going back to the Bear Lake Road south of Moraine Park and the Big Thompson River, several lakes are fishable and many of them are heavily fished. One mile west and south of Bear Lake is **Dream Lake** (9840 ft; 6 ac) with small cutthroat and brook; a mile more along the trail is **Emerald Lake** (10,200 ft; 7 ac) with cutthroat; and to the south, **Lake Haiyaha** (10,200 ft; 6 ac), a deep lake, also provides cutthroat fishing. However, all are rated poor.

From the Glacier Gorge parking area on the Bear Lake road, several lakes are accessible up a steep, well-marked trail to the southwest. A mile above Alberta Falls, **Brook Creek** joins **Glacier Creek** from the southwest. Up Brook Creek 3.5 miles from the trailhead is **The Loch** (10,200 ft; 15 ac). **Glass Lake** (10,900 ft; 5 ac) and **Sky Pond** (11,000 ft; 11 ac) are 0.5 mile apart and 2 miles farther up Loch Vale. Each is fair to good for brook and cutthroat. The Loch has some rainbow and is rated fair.

Five miles south up Glacier Creek is **Black Lake** (11,000 ft; 9 ac) with fair to good fishing for brook and cutthroat. It is a tough, rocky trail for horse and man. Downstream, the creek between Black and **Mills Lake** (10,000 ft; 16 ac) is poor, though the fish are there. Mills has rainbow, and its companion, **Jewel Lake** (10,230 ft; 3 ac), has cutthroat. Both lakes are less than a mile upstream from Glacier Falls. Glacier Creek has good populations of cutthroat and some rainbow.

About halfway between Jewel and Black lakes up the ridge west of Glacier Creek are **Lake Solitude** and **Shelf Lake,** both believed to be barren.

Sprague Lake (8720 ft; 3 ac) is a shallow roadside lake midway between Glacier Junction and Moraine Park. It is good for brook to 10 inches.

NORTH CENTRAL

From Estes Park west, Hwy 34 parallels **Fall River** for 6 miles until the highway crosses the stream at Horseshoe Park and proceeds up Trail Ridge. Fishing in the Fall River below its confluence with Roaring River, a stretch of more than 8 miles, was destroyed in 1982. It's still poor angling despite stocking as the sand and rocky bottom have yet to stabilize and there is little food. **Lawn Lake** (10,987 ft; 20 ac), near the head of Roaring River, was good fishing and heavily fished until the Lawn Lake Dam broke, flooding the downstream rivers and streams, and reducing the size of the man-made reservoir from its original 40 acres. Although smaller, it is still a good fishery. The trail to the lake has been rebuilt, but the dam hasn't. Debris from the flood created a dam, impounding 11 acres of water named **Godbolt Lake,** locally also known as **Flood Lake.** It offers excellent fishing for brown and brook trout.

Fishing on the upper reaches of Fall and Roaring rivers is poor. It will probably take several years before Fall River again becomes the fine fishery it once was.

Above Lawn Lake a mile by trail, are **Crystal Lake** (11,480 ft; 25 ac) and **Little Crystal Lake** (11,560 ft; 4 ac.) Crystal is poor to good for cutthroat. Little Crystal appears to be fished out.

Moving downstream, a mile above the Fall River-Roaring River confluence on the old Lawn Lake Trail, and above Horseshoe

Falls, the Ypsilon Lake Trail crosses Roaring River and heads northwest to **Ypsilon Lake** (10,520 ft; 7 ac) and **Chiquita Lake** (11,360 ft; 4 ac). This is a rough 3-mile hike for fair fishing for good populations of cutthroat in Ypsilon. Chiquita is virtually barren. Due north of Ypsilon are three **Fay Lakes** (11,000 ft; 1 to 5 ac). No trail, but it is a 1.5 mile hike for cutthroat. Greenback cutthroat are catch and release fishing only. The lower lake is best.

In the northeast corner of the park, the **North Fork of Big Thompson River** flows east from the 13,000-foot peaks of the Mummy Range. There are several high lakes including **Lost Lake** (10,500 ft; 9 ac) and **Lake Husted** (11,000 ft; 1 ac). Lost is fair for brook and cutthroat; Husted, a mile west of Lost and above timberline, has many brook trout.

Inside the park, the North Fork is fast, with beaver ponds, and supports some brook and cutthroat trout. Access is by the Dunraven Road, 1.75 miles northeast of Glen Haven, which follows the stream. From the parking area at the end of Dunraven Road, it is 2.5 miles to the park boundary and another 4.5 miles to Lost Lake. The river above Lost Falls may be closed in 1983 or 1984. Inquire locally.

The principal fishing on the north and northwest sides of the park is in the **Cache la Poudre River** and its tributaries. The river originates at brook trout-filled **Poudre Lake** (10,700 ft; 14 ac) at Milner Pass on Trail Ridge Road (Hwy 34). The river can be seen in the canyon north of the road. Park car along the road and hike down to the stream for good fishing for small brook trout, especially late in the season. It is a rough hike back up to the road. Poudre River Trail runs along the west side of the river. Tributary streams—**Chapin Creek, Hague Creek, Willow Creek** and **Cascade Creek**—are all good brook trout streams for a mile or so up from the river. Hague has some cutthroat.

WEST SIDE FISHING

On the far west side of the park, the **North Fork of Colorado River** flows south more than 13 miles in the park and 5 miles on private land before entering Shadow Mountain Reservoir. It is a medium-size, often brushy stream with rainbow, browns and lots of brook trout, especially above Lulu City trailhead at the northern end of the river. There are many beaver ponds. Several small streams enter the river from the west, but generally they are poor fishing for small fish. Moving south, **Lake of the Clouds** (11,400 ft; 3 ac), above timberline at the headwaters of Hitchens Gulch on **Big Dutch Creek,** has cutthroat. It is a 6.5-mile hike northwest from the western foot of Milner Pass.

Farther south, **Timber Creek** and **Timber Lake** (10,900 ft; 10 ac) on the east side of the river are closed to fishing after being rehabilitated and stocked with fingerling Colorado River cutthroat. **Julian Lake** (11,080 ft; 6 ac), at the headwaters of **Onahu Creek,** is virtually barren but might have a cutthroat or two. The creek has some brook trout to 10 inches. It is reached by a difficult walk from the signed trailhead above Green Mountain Ranch on Hwy 34, 6 miles north of Grand Lake.

Also reached from the Green Mountain Trail, **Tonahutu Creek** fishing is the best in the meadows. It is reached by walking east 2 miles up the Green Mountain Trail from the trailhead on Hwy 34, 5 miles north of Grand Lake. Fishing is good for small brook and, higher up above Granite Falls, for cutthroat to 10 inches. It is a great open-meadow fishing stream for children.

The last 5 miles of the Colorado River above Shadow Mountain Reservoir are on private property. The area tends to be brushy except where improvements have been made.

Several small streams flow out of the park from the east and into Grand Lake, Shadow Mountain Lake or the Colorado River downstream from Shadow Mountain Lake. Foremost of these is **North Inlet Creek** which flows through the town of Grand Lake and into the lake. North Inlet has brook in the 3 miles below Cascade Falls, and cutthroat above the falls. It is heavily fished and fishing is fair to good.

Three miles above the falls, the trail forks. The west fork goes 9 miles to **Lake Nokoni** (10,800 ft; 25 ac) and another half mile to **Lake Nanita** (10,800 ft; 34 ac). Both are very deep and are heavily fished for cutthroat. The outlet of Nanita is closed to fishing for 100 yards downstream.

Flowing into North Inlet from the east about 5 miles from Grand Lake is **Ptarmigan Creek.** It drains **Ptarmigan, Snowdrift** and **Bench Lakes,** of which only the latter has fish; cutthroat trout, very temperamental. It is about a mile by steep trail from North Inlet.

East Inlet Creek flows into the southeast shore of Grand Lake. The lower 5.5 miles below Lone Pine Lake have brook trout. **Lone Pine Lake** (9840 ft; 13 ac) is shallow, usually loaded with small brook and heavily fished. Upstream 1.5 miles is long, narrow **Lake Verna** (10,200 ft; 33 ac). It too has plenty of brook. **Spirit Lake** (10,240 ft; 8 ac) and **Fourth Lake** (10,400 ft; 7 ac) both have brook and are a short walk upstream from Spirit. At timberline at 11,020 feet is 7-acre **Fifth Lake** with cutthroat to 12 inches.

Paradise Creek, which flows from the south into East Inlet between the falls and Lone Pine Lake, has good fishing for cutthroat, especially in the upper reaches, but it takes a very strenuous effort to get there. At the headwaters of the first sizable tributary to Paradise Creek, an arduous 7 miles from East Inlet, is **Lake Adams** (11,200 ft; 5 ac) with cutthroat. □

PARK CAMPGROUNDS

There are five campgrounds in the park. All have water in above-freezing weather. None have hookups of any kind for RVs or trailers. All individual sites are $6 per night.

The campgrounds and number of sites: **Long's Peak,** 30—tents only. No pickup campers, RVs, trailers or motorhomes. **Moraine Park,** 250; **Glacier Basin,** 152 plus 18 group sites; **Timber Creek,** 100; **Aspen Glen,** 20 (to reopen July 1985).

An underhand or sidearm cast will keep a bubble lower so there's less noise as it enters the water.

Arapaho National Recreation Area

Adjacent communities:
Granby, Grand Lake.

Principal Highways:
U.S. 34, 40; Colo. 278.

Fishermen can find most of what high-country lake fishing is all about in the big "lakes" of the 36,000-acre Arapaho National Recreation Area.

Among them, Shadow Mountain Lake, Lake Granby and Willow Creek Reservoir have mackinaw, brown, cutthroat, rainbow and brook trout as well as some of the best kokanee salmon action anywhere.

A smaller water, Monarch Lake, has brook, rainbow and some brown. All of the waters are at elevations around 8300 feet. While bank fishing is common, the best results come from fishing from boats. Wil-

---

GRAND LAKE OFFERS NONFISHING DELIGHTS

One of the features of fishing the Grand Lake-Shadow Mountain Reservoir-Lake Granby complex is the advantage to nonfishing members of a family or group.

While some are out after a mackinaw like the 31-pound, 47-inch caught in Grand Lake in June 1985, the nonanglers have a great selection of activities to choose from.

The No. 1 enterprise is gawking at fellow visitors; after that, shopping in quaint stores and observing demonstrations of skills and crafts. Available are horseback riding, nature hikes, picnicking, water skiing, canoeing, sailing and just lying back under a fragrant pine to read or listen to the mountain wind.

It doesn't have to be a holiday weekend for the village of Grand Lake to be jammed with tourists, and the festive atmosphere is contagious. The historic John Holzworth Ranch, just inside nearby Rocky Mountain National Park, is a living museum of frontier life on an early-day Colorado ranch. Demonstrations of several domestic and farm skills are conducted daily during the summer.

The Grand Lake Marina rents a variety of power and sail boats as well as canoes. It also features a dinner tour boat on the lake. It is operated by Kevin Cox and Tom Phillips. A licensed fishing guide is available along with rental tackle.

ARAPAHO NATIONAL RECREATION AREA

SUPER HOOKS

GRAND LAKE TACKLE COMPANY
P.O. Box 185 • Grand Lake, Colorado 80447

low Creek Reservoir allows only hand-powered craft, and Monarch Lake is strictly a shallow, carry-in pond.

Grand Lake, adjacent to Shadow Mountain Reservoir, is the largest natural lake in Colorado. It is just outside the recreation area.

The lakes are all linked together by channels, as part of the Big Thompson Water Diversion Project, which divert water from the upper Colorado River Valley on the west side of the Continental Divide through the Adams Tunnel to the Big Thompson River on the eastern slope.

NRA recreation facilities include four developed campgrounds with 340 overnight camping spaces, six public boat launching ramps (boating regulations are posted), eight picnic areas and 14 miles of hiking trails.

Lake Granby

Also open to the public are 11 marinas.

The NRA headquarters is located at Shadow Mountain Village, about 11 miles north of Granby on US 34.

Arapaho National Recreation Area
Shadow Mountain Village
Grand Lake, CO 80447
303/627-3551

The communities of Granby and Grand Lake are the principal supply centers.

Located just southwest of Rocky Mountain Park, the area is reached by taking Trail Ridge Road through the park or turning north from US 40 just west of Granby. The area is a favorite of boaters, wet-suited water skiers, sailors and visitors who enjoy the beautiful location, clear air and pine forests. □

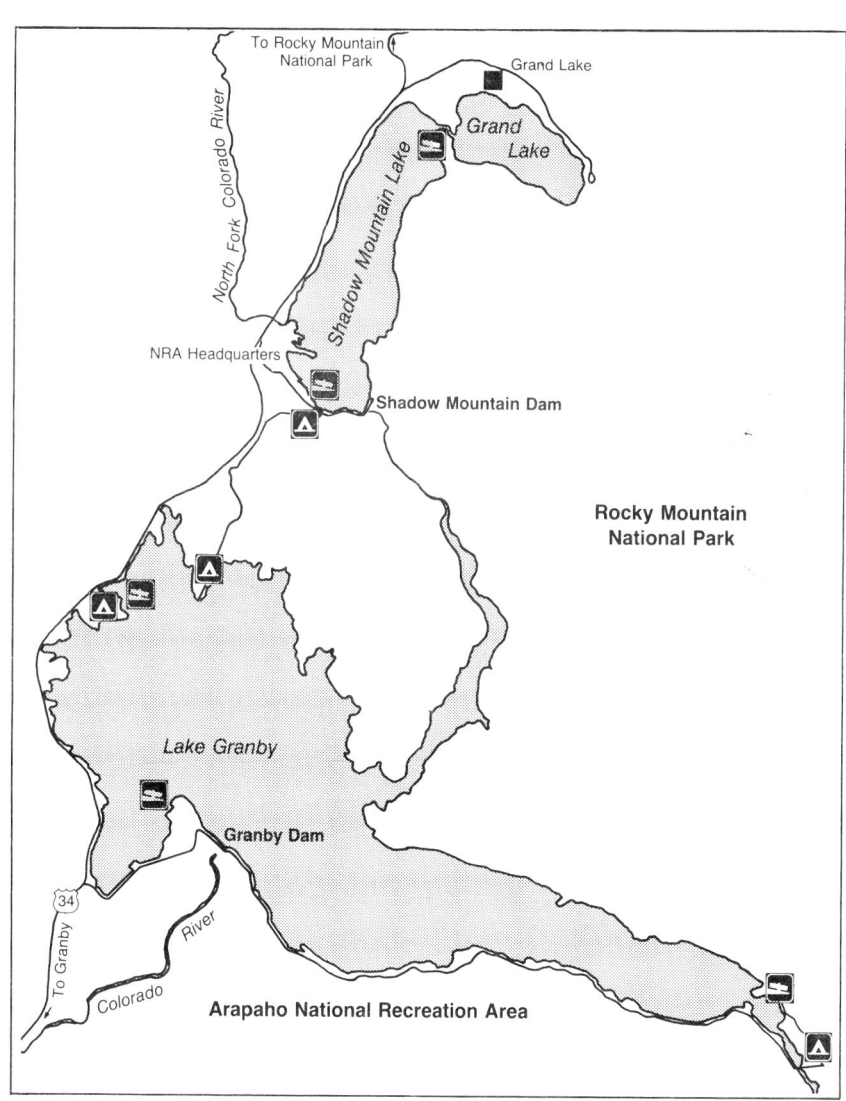

Arapaho National Recreation Area

Colorado River can be grand

Adjacent communities:
Grand Lake, Granby, Hot Sulphur Springs, Kremmling, Glenwood Springs, Silt, Rifle, Parachute, DeBeque, Palisade, Grand Junction, Fruita.

Principal Highways:
U.S. 34, 40, 6, I-70; Colo. 131, 340.

Some of the best fishing in the West is found in the Colorado River, its tributaries and nearby lakes. No angler could ask for more challenging and beautiful terrain in which to fish for more than a dozen different species of game fish.

The angling ranges from roadside fishing for whopper trout and trolling for 30-pound mackinaw to packing into the back country for cutthroat and golden trout in snow-fringed lakes above timberline.

The Colorado originates as a virgin stream high in the snowy mountains of northwest Rocky Mountain National Park. First south and then westerly, it finds its way across the Colorado Plateau en route to the Grand Canyon and then to the salty Sea of Cortez in Mexico.

Inside the park, its headwaters offer little fishing as it heads down the Kawaneechee Valley toward the town of Grand Lake.

Flowing into the Colorado River from the west out of Never Summer Mountains, **Baker Creek** has fair to poor brook trout fishing, but there are some cutthroat in the upper end. At the headwaters in Routt National Forest, **Parika Lake** (11,450 ft; 3 ac) is fair for cutthroat. It's a 5- to 6-mile hike from trailhead in Rocky Mountain National Park. A dirt road runs a mile west from Hwy 34 to access Baker Gulch, about 8 miles north of Grand Lake. Seek permission to cross a short stretch of private land. To the south, **Bowen Creek,** like Baker, is small and brushy and has some brook and maybe brown in the lower end, cutthroat higher up. Upstream, **Bowen Lake** (11,000 ft; 10 ac) and to the northeast **Blue Lake,** (10,650 ft; 5 ac) have some cutthroat. Access is via the Kawaneechee Road, which goes west off Hwy 34 a mile north of Grand Lake. It's a 12-mile trip to Bowen Lake; a

---

WINDING RIVER CAMPGROUND
GRAND LAKE, CO
Ranch Camping Vacation
Ideal for Fishing

- Tent & R.V. Sites
- Horseback Riding
- Tackle Shop
- Ice Cream Socials

1½ miles north of Grand Lake on U.S. Hwy. 34 - turn left on Rd. 491- 1½ miles.

Box 629, Grand Lake, CO 80447
(303) 627-3215 • (303) 466-1930

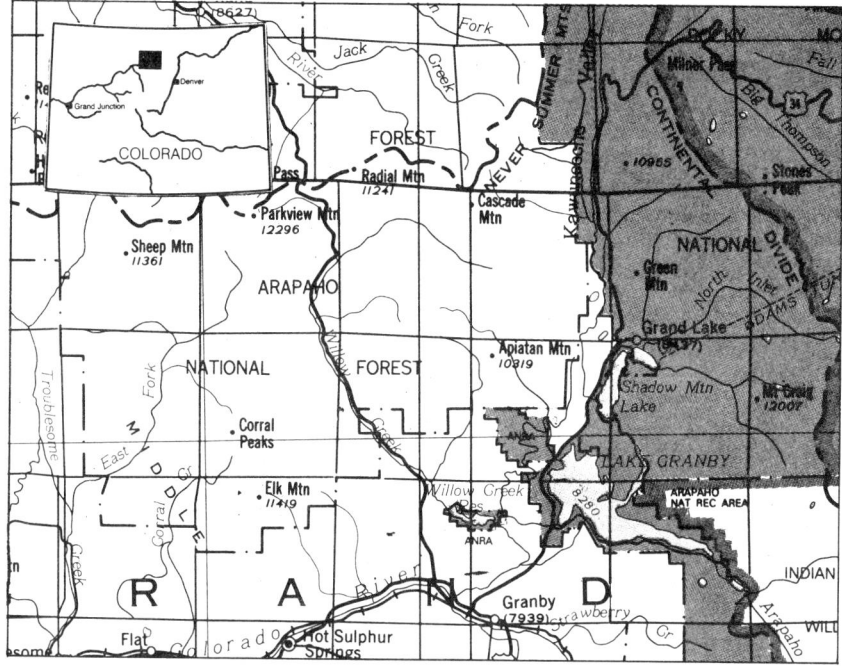

Grand Lake, Upper Colorado River

northwesterly hike to Blue Lake is 4 miles by trail off the east side of Bowen Lake. Beautiful country.

En route to Bowen, the road crosses three branches of **Supply Creek,** which is fair to poor for brook and maybe a rainbow or two. Farther south, **Stillwater Creek** is fair for cutthroat higher up; brook on lower reaches. Like Supply Creek, it is small and brushy.

The North Fork of the Colorado flows into Shadow Mountain Lake, a principal reservoir of the Colorado-Big Thompson Project. Connected to it by channel is **Grand Lake** (8376 ft; 500 ac), a beautiful blue-water natural lake in an idylic mountain setting. Just outside Rocky Mountain National Park, it has long been a tourist haven and summer home center. Nearly 300 feet deep, it has rainbow, kokanee salmon and is one of the best mackinaw (lake trout) fisheries in the state, with fish to 20 pounds and more caught nearly every year. Some enormous macs are believed to be in the lake. Shoreline access is limited by private property, but there is a marina with boat rental. Rainbow fishing is best in spring. The channel usually is good fishing, but there are some suckers. Trolling and inlet fishing usually produce best, but in general, fishing is best early in the spring through June to mid-July. Wet flies and lures are good for brown and rainbow. Sucker meat tempts mackinaw. Ice fishing is popular, as is some spear fishing by scuba divers in summer.

SHADOW MOUNTAIN

Shadow Mountain Lake (8367 ft; 1800 ac) is a fluctuating reservoir with rainbow, kokanee, brown and some mackinaw, but not as many macs as in Grand Lake, because Shadow Mountain is only about 20 feet deep. It is often choked with weeds in late summer, but the fish are there. Best for rainbow and browns through July; later, kokanee is better. Two marinas with boat rentals. Popular for fishing is the submerged Colorado River channel and shoreline. Some boating areas are restricted. Ice fishing often is good, but only portable shelters are allowed. They must be removed at the end of each day.

Lake Granby (8280 ft; some 4000 ac) has 41 miles of shoreline when full. Fishing is mostly for rainbow, kokanee and mackinaw, although there are some big brown trout. Mackinaw fishing has picked up in recent years with 30-pounders and up being caught by trollers. The bag and possession limit is one mac. All mackinaw 20 inches or smaller are to be returned to the water immediately. Five marinas with rentals. Fishing is similar to Shadow Mountain, although Lake Granby fluctuates, most from water project withdrawals. Fishing is prohibited at Columbine Bay and Twin Creek inlets from October 1 through December 31. Some boating restrictions. Snagging season is January and February.

Fishing below Granby dam in the Colorado River to its juncture with the Fraser River is good for brown and rainbow with some big browns to 12 to 15 pounds taken. Get permission to fish from private property.

At the southeast tip of Lake Granby, **Roaring Fork, Grouse** and **Irving Hale Creeks** enter the reservoir. The lower reaches of each are too fast for fish, and fishing at the upper ends is limited mostly to cutthroat. **Watanga Creek,** a tributary to Roaring Fork Creek, and **Watanga Lake** (10,800 ft; 3 ac) have cutthroat, but access is over a steep, very rough trail that follows Roaring Fork Creek to Watanga Creek confluence. They are reached by hiking upstream from the lakes.

A mile southeast of the southeast tip of Lake Granby is **Monarch Lake** (8300 ft; 130 ac) and the west trailhead to the Indian Peaks Wilderness to the east and southeast. A few hundred yards of stream between Monarch Lake Dam and Lake Granby are all that remain of the **South Fork of the Colorado River.**

The rest is inundated by Lake Granby. Monarch is a pretty, quiet water littered with downed timber on the south and west ends, and it offers good fly fishing for brook 6 to 15 inches. People fish from the dam with bait, but results often are poor. Flies are better.

BUCHANAN CREEK

Flowing into Monarch Lake are **Buchanan Creek** (from the northeast) and **Arapaho Creek** (from the southeast). Buchanan has brook in its lower reaches, some rainbow and cutthroat at the higher elevations. It is heavily fished despite steep sections of trail leading to the Continental Divide and Indian Peaks Wilderness Area.

Two miles upstream from Monarch Lake, **Hell Canyon Creek** flows from the north into Buchanan. A very steep, rocky trail roughly parallels the creek 3 miles to **Long Lake** (9920 ft; 6 ac), which is fair for rainbow and cutthroat, as is **Crawford Lake** (10,110 ft; 3 ac), another half-mile upstream. About 2 miles farther upstream, and a little easier going than the very arduous stretch to Long Lake, is **Stone Lake** (10,683 ft; 7 ac), and a few hundred yards farther, **Upper Lake** (10,730 ft; 8 ac). They have somewhat better cutthroat fishing than the two lower lakes. Very scenic country and the creek itself above Crawford Lake offers some fishing for cutthroat.

About a mile east of Hell Canyon Creek

A WORLD OF ACTIVITIES FOR THE ENTIRE FAMILY

Located 3 miles south of Grand Lake on U.S. 34, overlooking **Shadow Mountain Lake**

Open All Year • Call For Reservations or Information
Paul & Lois Linton
P.O. Box 609, Grand Lake, CO 80447, (303) 627-3654

on Buchanan Creek, **Cascade Creek** gushes in from the southeast. Five miles up at its headwaters are **Mirror Lake** (10,350 ft; 1 ac) and **Crater Lake** (10,400 ft; 10 ac). Mirror has small brook; Crater has brook, rainbow and small mackinaw. Fishing pressure is periodically heavy from backpackers and a few horsemen. A mile below Mirror, a trail heads up a small tributary 1.5 miles to **Pawnee Lake** (11,000 ft; 12 ac), which is only fair fishing for brook. There is a campground. Streams in the area are not stocked.

Back at the Buchanan Creek-Cascade Creek confluence, Buchanan continues northeast toward the Continental Divide. About 2 miles upstream, a sign indicates the Gourd Lake Trail, a very steep, rough hike 2 miles up to **Gourd Lake** (10,850 ft; 15 ac). A deep lake surrounded by timber and giant rocks, it has big cutthroat, if they can be tempted. Difficult to fish. Limited camping sites. A trail leads north to **Island Lake** (11,500 ft; 16 ac) for small cutthroat. Spectacular terrain.

At Monarch Lake, **Arapaho Creek** comes from the southeast through timber at Arapaho Pass. It is shallow and has poor fishing for brook. It and tributary streams are not stocked.

To reach Roaring Fork Creek, Monarch Lake and the Buchanan Creek trailhead, turn east off Hwy 34 at the sign about 5 miles north of Granby and follow the southshore road along Lake Granby to its end. There are two campgrounds. Bring mosquito repellent.

A mile south of Lake Granby in Arapaho National Forest is **Strawberry Lake** on **Strawberry Creek.** The lake is private, winterkills, and probably has no fish. The creek has small brook.

About 3.5 miles due south of Monarch Lake is **Meadow Creek Reservoir** (9990 ft; 140 ac), a developing fishery for brook and rainbow to 12 inches, with best fishing early summer. Below the dam, the creek is good for brook for about a mile. Thereafter it is dewatered by irrigation diversions. Upstream 3 miles at timberline is **Columbine Lake** (11,100 ft; 8 ac), which gets a lot of fishing for 12-inch cutthroat. The stream also has some cutthroat.

Access to Meadow Creek is by taking a dirt road north from US 40 about 0.75 mile east of Tabernash. Go through Meadow Creek Campground to end of road above the reservoir. It's an easy hike for a mile or so to Columbine.

FRASER RIVER

The **Fraser River** originates at the northwest side of Berthoud Pass and flows past winter Park ski area to join the Colorado River just west of Granby. The upper reaches are stocked with catchable brook and rainbow. Brushy with willows and some trees, but mostly delightful fishing, although close to US 40 for about half of its 7 miles above Idlewild. Below, the river is on mostly private property and permission to fish is needed.

The best fishing is in Fraser Canyon downstream from Tabernash, where rainbow and brown await the angler. There is some private land posted against fishing. Access is by walking the Denver and Rio Grande Railroad grade. A train wreck in the spring of 1985 dumped several railroad cars into the river. The impact on fishing of the wreck and of salvage operations hasn't been ascertained. From a mile below Tabernash to a mile above Granby, about 5 miles of stream, the river is classified as a wild trout water. The river is often low after midsummer because of water diversions.

Several small creeks enter the Fraser from the east, mostly via Ranch Creek. They include the **South, Middle** and **North Forks of Ranch Creek, Little Cabin, Cabin, Hamilton,** and **Hurd** and **Trail**

Fletcher's Gun Repair & Sporting Goods

Firearms & Ammunition
Hunting & Fishing
Licenses & Supplies

**217 W. Agate Ave.
Granby • 887-3747**

Photo by Bob Saile

Creeks. They are small, brushy and with small trout, if any. Tributary streams on upper reaches are too steep and swift for fish.

East of Winter Park via the Rollins Pass road are **Deadman, Pumphouse** and **Corona Lakes,** all above 11,000 feet elevation. Deadman, closest to the road, has cutthroat, but tends to winterkill. Pumphouse has cutthroat and Corona rainbow. The lakes are visible from the pass and are readily reached by hiking old roads or trails. Snow usually keeps the road closed until July. The road is blocked to vehicles on the east side, so access from South Boulder creek on the east side of the Continental Divide is by foot.

On the west and south sides of the Fraser River there are numerous streams including **Vasquez, Elk, St. Louis,** and **Crooked** and **Pole Creeks.** All but St. Louis Creek are dewatered and offer little fishing.

St. Louis Creek is a beautiful forest stream with brook, cutthroat and rainbow. It is the only one stocked. It is reached by a good road from Fraser that runs a dozen miles into the National Forest. There are two campgrounds. **St. Louis Lake** (11,400 ft; 4 ac) at the head of the creek is reached by steep, 3-mile-long trail from the end of road. Fair for cutthroat. Lower reaches of St. Louis Creek are on private land, are brushy and hard to fish for brown and rainbow. Permission is needed.

North of Granby, **Willow Creek** flows into the Colorado River from the northwest. It is stocked with rainbow and brook and has some brown trout on the lower reaches. It has several small, brushy tributaries. **Pass Creek** and **Cabin Creek** are the best of these and are fair for small brook. Access is via Hwy 125, Willow Creek Pass Road, which leaves US 40 about 2 miles west of Granby and follows the stream most of the way to the top of Willow Creek Pass, about 20 miles. Cabin Creek Road goes off to the west about 8 miles north from US 40. Pass Creek parallels the road for about 4 miles until its juncture with Willow Creek about 16 miles from US 40.

Willow Creek Reservoir (8130 ft; 260 ac) is a private open-irrigation reservoir that fluctuates in summer. It has a zone around most of it that is open to the public so fishermen can cast for rainbow and brook. Holders of the rainbow trout stamp may take a double limit. Motor-powered boats are prohibited. Campground on lake shore. Turn off Willow Creek Road to the east about 3.5 miles north of US 40 to reach the reservoir.

GOLD MEDAL

From the confluence of the Fraser River downstream more than 20 miles to Troublesome Creek, the Colorado River is classified as a gold medal trout stream with large rainbow and browns. The designation is possibly the result of modest fishing pressure, because most of the land is posted against trespassing and fishing without permission. Fishing has been largely catch and release. Landowners are very alert to their rights and don't hesitate to have intruders prosecuted.

Several small streams enter the river above Hot Sulphur Springs, but none has much fishing. West of Hot Sulphur Springs fishing for rainbow and brown in cold, dreary **Byers Canyon** along the highway and railroad is popular. But far more pleasant and productive waters are just downstream.

Beaver Creek comes into the Colorado at the west end of Byers Canyon. A road follows the creek upstream for 12 miles. Fishing is fair for brook. Downriver a mile, **Little Muddy Creek** is small and brushy on lower levels, but in the forest, it has brook and rainbow. Access is by Williams Fork River Road and Keyser Creek Road to Church Park. Many beaver ponds.

WILLIAMS FORK RIVER

The **Williams Fork River** flows north to enter the Colorado River at the village of Parshall, about 2.5 miles below **Williams Fork Reservoir.** The headwaters for this 25-mile-long stream are among the 12,000- and 13,000-ft peaks of the Williams Fork and Vasquez mountains. (There is another Williams Fork River in Colorado—a tributary to the Yampa River, south of Craig.)

The Williams Fork is a clear, sparkling stream with good riffles and some holes. It remains one of the better insect-producing waters because of environmental safeguards that were put in place during the 1960s and 1970s when AMAX Henderson Mine facilities were under construction.

The headwaters have been diverted in several places by the Denver Water Department. Above the diversions, fishing for cutthroat can be good in **McQueary, Bobtail, Steelman Creeks** and the **Middle** and **South Forks** of the Williams Fork itself. **McQueary Lake** (10,960 ft; 3 ac) can be excellent for cutthroat to 14 inches. The trail to the lake is steep and the ice leaves late.

The lower reaches of these creeks have some brook, rainbow and brown. Although the water department voluntarily maintains minimum stream flows, about 200 yards of **Bobtail Creek** are dry. Steelman has a reproducing brook population below the diversion.

The higher tributaries join the river near the Sugarloaf and South Fork campgrounds (8,990 ft), which are about as far as a passenger car can readily go.

The river downstream to the reservoir generally has good access, although there is some posted land.

The **Kinney Creek** drainage is heavily fished for brook, rainbow and some cutthroat. **Horseshoe Lake** (11,250 ft; 5 ac) and **Evelyn Lake** (11,200 ft; 4 ac) are good for natives to 14 inches. Evelyn is accessible from **Keyser Creek** Road. Keyser is fair for trout.

Below the mine mill tailings pond beside **Ute Creek** are several small streams flowing into the river from the west: **Lost, Mule, Skylark, Battle, Bull Run** and **Copper Creeks** tend to be brushy with some ponds and small brook trout.

RESERVOIR FISHING

Williams Fork Reservoir (7,800 ft; 690 ac when full) is a fluctuating reservoir of the Denver water department. Nonetheless, it has rainbow and brown trout, northern and walleye pike and kokanee. Fishing rates fair to good; occasionally, it's outstanding. Boat ramp, camping and state recreation areas are on the west side.

Private land on both sides of the river below the dam to the Colorado River provides good fishing. Permission is required and access is limited.

You can reach the river, reservoir and creeks from the north on good roads that branch off US 40 about 0.75 mile east of Parshall and 6 miles west of Parshall at Troublesome Creek. Also there is access by Road 132 east from Hwy 9 about 5 miles south of Green Mountain Reservoir (on the Blue River). The road crosses the Williams Fork Mountains and intercepts the stream at midcourse near the mine mill.

Sometimes the headwaters can be reached from the east by 4-wheel drive over Jones Pass. Take the Henderson Mine road off Hwy 40 near Berthoud Falls on the east side of the Continental Divide. Local in-

---

Complete Service of Mercury Outboard Motors

Boat Rentals
Fishing & Boating Equipment
Mooring and Dock Slips
Gas Pumps
627-3605

LAKE KOVE MARINA

Box 469, Grand Lake, CO 80447
(Located north end of Shadow Mountain Lake,
¼ mile from the town of Grand Lake)

COLORADO RIVER-BLUE RIVER

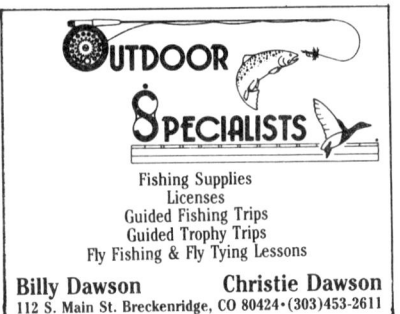

Outdoor Specialists

Fishing Supplies
Licenses
Guided Fishing Trips
Guided Trophy Trips
Fly Fishing & Fly Tying Lessons

Billy Dawson   Christie Dawson
112 S. Main St. Breckenridge, CO 80424 • (303)453-2611

quiry is advised as the road can be impassable on the west side of the divide, even in midsummer, because of snow drifts and flooding. Even 4-wheelers get stranded.

Troublesome Creek enters the Colorado from the north, midway between Parshall and Kremmling. It, and a host of tributary streams, are brushy and often difficult to fish, but they have lots of small brook trout. A road going north from US 40 about 6 miles west of Parshall provides access. Most of the stream is on private property and permission to fish is necessary. At Kremmling, Hwy 9 provides access to the Blue River flowing into the Colorado from the south.

BLUE RIVER

The Blue River flows north from Hoosier Pass into Dillon Reservoir and down through the Green Mountain Reservoir to join the Colorado River about 2 miles south of Kremmling. Its 60 miles of fishing are closely regulated in an effort to restore it to the superb fishery it once was. Hwy 9 generally follows the stream except below Green Mountain Reservoir.

Only an hour and a half drive from Denver via I-70, the Blue River Valley, its tributary streams and adjacent lakes receive some of the heaviest fishing in the state. Including the two reservoirs, the area offers rainbow, brown, kokanee salmon, brook, cutthroat, mackinaw and a hybrid brook-cutthroat.

The Blue is essentially a limited kill stream, meaning the size and number of trout that may be kept is restricted to two trout. Angling is with artificial lures and flies. From Breckenridge to Dillon Reservoir the two trout must be over 16 inches; from Dillon Reservoir to Green Mountain Reservoir, all brown trout under 16 inches must be returned to the water immediately. From Green Mountain Dam to the Colorado River, trout must be over 16 inches. Smaller trout must be released. The river is wild trout water from the dam 2.5 miles downstream and gold medal water all the way to the Colorado River.

The Blue River begins on the north side of Hoosier Pass (11,539 ft) with the merging of several small streams. The most important ones flow out of the Ten Mile Range on the west side of the valley. Dotted among the 14,000- and 13,000-foot peaks are several small, high lakes.

Above the picturesque mining-camp-turned-ski-town of Breckenridge, the river flows through timber and brush on private land; most property is posted. Fishing for brook, rainbow and brown in the town itself

can yield pleasant surprises, especially in spring and fall.

Blue Lakes (11,500 ft; 50 ac, 6 ac) are located in the Monte Cristo Creek drainage. You can drive the 2 miles to the dam at the upper lake from a marked junction on Hwy 9 about 7 miles south of Breckenridge at the foot of the north side of Hoosier Pass. The upper lake is stocked with rainbow and cutthroat and offers somewhat better fishing than the lower lake; both are rated fair.

McCullough Gulch, to the north between the Blue and Mohawk lakes, has several unnamed lakes at 12,000 feet and higher, up to 20 acres in size, some of which are good for cutthroat.

A good road leads to 1 mile below the lowest lake, which is a dud. Upstream are many small ponds. Over a ridge to the north are **Mohawk Lakes** (11,700 ft). These deep lakes are reached by trail from the junction of Spruce Creek Road and the Blue River about 5 miles south of Breckenridge on Hwy 9. Only the three larger lakes have fish. Drive 3 miles and then walk 1 mile to first lake (12 ac in size); 1 mile farther to second lake (10 ac), and 440 yards more to the third, also 10 acres. The three lakes are fair for cutthroat to 12-13 inches. **Crystal Lake** (11,991 ft; 5 ac) is reached from the Mohawk Road off Spruce Creek. Go about 5 miles and then 4-wheel drive 3 more to lake. **Upper Crystal** (12,750 ft) is 1 mile above the lower lake by old wagon road. Once stocked with golden fingerlings, fishing has been poor, as fish often do not survive the severe winters at that altitude. Fair to good for cutthroat. All of these lakes are high and subject to winter kill. They are heavily fished for stockers.

Rainbow Lake (9100 ft; 3 ac) lies south of the town of Frisco on Miners Creek. Signed road leaves Hwy 9 one mile south of Frisco; 1.5 miles to lake. Good for 8- to 12-inch stocked rainbow.

Downstream from Breckenridge, the river is channeled through old gold dredge tailings for much of its length and offers good potential for spring rainbows and fall browns and brooks.

The **Swan River** flows into the Blue from the southeast about 2 miles upstream from the Blue River arm of Dillon Reservoir in a brushy, hard-to-get-to, hard-to-fish area just east of Hwy 9. The stream also is lined by dredge tailings for most of its length. On the lower 3 miles the Division of Wildlife has reconstructed the river to improve spawning habitat and reproduction potential of kokanee salmon, brown and rainbow trout on the gravelly bottom. Fishing is only with flies and lures for three miles upstream on the Swan from its confluence with the Blue River. The same stretch is closed to fishing from October 1 through January 31.

Access is off Swan Mountain Road, which crosses the river just to the south, where the river enters the reservoir, or by turning east on a good dirt road from Hwy 9 about 2.3 miles south of the Swan Mountain Road. The dirt road passes a subdivision before heading south up the west side of the creek. The North Fork of the Swan is on public land. It and some ponds are fair for small cutthroat. Middle Fork and mainstream are fair for brook and cutthroat. Fishing pressure tends to be heavy.

The Swan is also a limited kill stream with the possession limit being two different species of trout over 16 inches.

DILLON RESERVOIR

Dillon Reservoir (9000 ft; 2033 ac when full) was built in the 1960s by the Denver Water Department. It is a fluctuating reservoir that changes from a beautiful, large mountain lake rimmed by snowy peaks when it is full, to an ugly, mud-rimmed pond when volume is down because of drought or heavy drawdown.

Nonetheless, it can provide very good

fishing from boat and shore. It is heavily fished and heavily stocked. No fishing is allowed from the dam. The 24.5 miles of shoreline have numerous access points for fishermen; there are boat launching ramps at Frisco Bay, Frisco Marina, Blue River Inlet and Peak 1 Campground. The marina rents boats and tackle.

Fishing for large rainbow in the spring just after the ice has broken up is often excellent; some have been caught weighing 4 and 5 pounds. Dillon has brown trout to 20 pounds, but they're hard to catch. Night fishing often is good for bigger browns. The reservoir has small kokanee and some brook trout to 14 inches; cutthroat to 20 inches. The reservoir is one of the better fish egg generating bodies of water in the state.

The U.S. Forest Service (Arapaho National Forest) operates 7 campgrounds around the lake on the east, south and west sides. They all are easily reached by either Hwy 9, US 6 or the Swan Mountain Road, which connects the other two highways on the south and east sides of the reservoir.

Dillon Reservoir can be reached from the east by exiting I-70 at the Silverthorne exit or via Hwy 6 over Loveland Pass. From the west, access is via either of two Frisco exits. The Silverthorne-Dillon exit also connects with Hwy 9 to the north, which follows the Blue River downstream from the dam. The Frisco exits link up with Hwy 9 southbound to Breckenridge. Dave Luke at Frisco Sporting Goods is knowledgeable about local conditions.

Several streams enter the reservoir, but only one, Tenmile Creek, offers very good fishing.

TENMILE

Tenmile Creek, tributary to the Blue, enters Dillon Reservoir from the southwest near Frisco. Paralleled by I-70 in Tenmile Canyon west of Frisco, the lower portion has been successfully rehabilitated into a decent fishery, especially for 15- to 20-inch browns in the fall spawning season. Good also for rainbow and brook. Easy access from the highway or bicycle path on east side from Frisco to Wheeler Junction. Ponds at Wheeler Junction are stocked. There are some big trout here, but most anglers don't fish for them. Fishing above Wheeler Junction (Copper Mountain Ski Area) is poor.

Clinton Reservoir (10,900 ft; 13 ac) is alongside Hwy 91, a mile north of the summit of Fremont Pass. It's got to have some lunker cutthroat in addition to the 8- to 10-inch variety. It opened to public fishing in 1984, and is for artificial flies and lures only. The limit is two trout over 16 inches, with any smaller returned to the water. No boating allowed.

West Tenmile Creek flows down from the east side of Vail Pass to Wheeler Junction. Easy access, but fishing for small brook is fair at best.

Copper Mountain village has done some good stream improvement and hopes to establish some quality waters. But, it will be private. They operate a kids' pond, open to the public, that's got some good trout in it.

North Tenmile Creek comes into the main creek from the west at Frisco. Fast and

WildernesSportS

Summit Place Shopping Center
Dillon-Silverthorne Interchange
303/468-5687

Fishing & hunting licenses

Fishing equipment to rent

Backpacking equipment & apparel

USGS Maps

Hand-tied flies

brushy with some ponds, it is fair to good for brook and rainbow to 10 inches. **Officer's Gulch Pond** is 4 miles west of Frisco on the north side of I-70. It is stocked with rainbow and brook.

Lost and Wheeler Lakes are in the Gore Eagles Nest Wilderness. **Lost Lake** (11,600 ft; 2 ac) at the head of Officer's Gulch Trail is 3 miles upcreek from Officer's Gulch Pond via a steep, rough trail. It has cutthroat to 12 inches and brook and rainbow.

The two **Wheeler Lakes** (11,000 ft; 7 ac) arc up the Wheeler stock trail, about 4 miles from I-70 at Wheeler Junction. The lakes are 0.25 mile from the main trail by a marked side trail. They are about a quarter-mile apart by connecting trail. The first lake is weedy, shallow and has no fish. The other has plenty of 15-inch cutthroat, but they are difficult to catch. Lost Lake (10 ac) is 1.5 miles farther along the main trail and is stocked with cutthroat. Parking is along I-70 just north of the I-70 and Hwy 91 junction at Copper Mountain ski area. The climb is steep and arduous from a marked trailhead.

SNAKE RIVER

The **Snake River,** one of the prettier tributaries of the Blue, enters Dillon Reservoir on the east side. Because of development and pollution, fishing is poor. US 6 generally follows the **North Fork** from the east arm of Dillon Reservoir to the foot of Loveland Pass. From 15 to 20 feet wide, it is in timber or brush; it runs fast and has some holes and beaver ponds. Stream and road part 6.5 miles east of Dillon. Good gravel road to the right goes 6 miles to Montezuma, generally following the main stream. The whole lower valley, about 4 miles, is developed by Keystone ski area and associated building activity. The South Fork is not stocked because of mine pollution. Beaver ponds on upper reaches have small brook.

Among the tributaries to the **South Fork** of the Snake are **Deer Creek,** which comes in from the south about 2 miles above Montezuma townsite, and **Peru Creek,** which is about 5 miles from Hwy 6. Both are affected by mine drainage, and fishing for small brook is poor. **Chihuahua Creek** flows into Peru Creek about 2 miles upstream from the turnoff. Just past the creek is a rough, steep, 4-wheel-drive trail 4 miles up to **Chihuahua Lake** (12,200 ft; 10 ac). Need to walk the last 2 miles. Stream is steep and fast and there is fair fishing for cutthroat. Lake is fair for 9- to 12-inch cutthroat.

Up a fairly good dirt road 6 miles along Peru Creek is **Gray's Lake** (12,500 ft; 1.5 ac). It snuggles right up against the Continental Divide at the base of 14,270-foot-high Gray's Peak. Small and overfished, it has been stocked with brook and rainbow.

Keystone Creek comes into the Snake River in the midst of a condominium development about a mile west of the ski area. It is brushy with some ponds, especially at high elevations. It is reached via an old road up Keystone gulch. Fair for small brook.

Soda Creek and **Reynolds Reservoir** are on private land. The creek flows into the Snake River arm of the reservoir. The higher reaches in Arapaho National Forest have rainbow, brook and some cutthroat. Fishing is only fair. Access is by dirt road to the south about 300 yards east of the Swan Mountain Road turnoff from Hwy 6 at the east end of the reservoir. Don't be surprised if roads once open are now posted against trespass, even if they are in the national forest.

LEASED WATERS

Downstream from Dillon Dam the Blue River meanders through developed property and ranchlands, and often is posted. The Division of Wildlife has leased 3/4-mile of river adjoining the Forest Service Boulder Creek Campground on the north. So there is more than a mile of open fishing from Blue River Campground downstream past the Boulder Creek Campground. Regulations limit possession to 2 trout over 16 inches. Rainbow, brook and some hybrid cutthroat-natives are found. The river is a stone's throw from Hwy 9 and the avid fisherman-motorist has trouble keeping his eye on the road instead of the river.

A second DOW lease opens up about 2 miles of the east bank of the river between Brush Creek and Green Mountain Reser-

voir. The lease boundaries are signed and fenced.

In the stretch between Dillon Dam and Green Mountain Reservoir 18 miles downstream, the Gore Mountain Range and its Gore-Eagles Nest Wilderness Area dominate the landscape to the west. On the east are the Williams Fork Mountains. A mile or more of ranchland separates the river from the national forests and public access to several small streams and lakes. The creeks coming in from the west are better fishing; creeks from the east side probably are not worth fishing.

WILDERNESS FISHING

The Gore-Eagles Nest Wilderness is a very rough, harsh area. Access into the often rocky barrens with few trees is across open terrain with some aspen and coniferous forest. Hiking in summer can be hot and tiring. The lower reaches of the creeks usually are brushy and difficult to fish. Water quality tends to be high, however. The higher elevations are austere.

Because it is so close to Denver, the area,

especially the north end, is heavily used. Trails are good. There is much opportunity for cross-country hiking; use of topographic maps is recommended.

South, Middle and **North Willow Creeks,** the four **Willow Lakes** and **Salmon Lake** are in the wilderness. The creeks are good for 8-inch brook at the lower elevations, brook-cutthroat hybrids at the higher reaches, and, in the lakes, cutthroat to 10-12 inches. Access is via the Dillon-Wheeler and Gore Range trails that begin as a dirt road on the west side of Silverthorne. After 1.8 miles to the wilderness boundary, the trail crosses South Willow Creek where the Dillon-Wheeler trail goes upstream to the west to Buffalo Pass. The Gore Range trail continues northerly, crossing Middle and North Willow creeks. The trail leaves North Willow for about 2 miles and loops back south to **Salmon Lake** (11,200 ft). It skirts the east side of the lake to continue upstream to the **Willow Lakes** (11,480 ft) in a basin between two 13,000-foot peaks. It's about a 5-mile hike and a 2200-foot elevation rise.

Access to the Gore Range Trail also is possible a little north of the Silverthorne town limit just before Hwy 9 crosses Willow Creek. A dirt road heads west for less than a mile.

About 6 miles north of Silverthorne on Hwy 9, a dirt road across from the Blue River campground traverses west for about 2.7 miles to the wilderness boundary. This provides access to **South** and **North Rock Creeks** and **Pebble Creek,** all of which have small ponds with brook and, usually, cutthroat in their upper reaches.

A mile farther south on the highway, another dirt road across from Boulder Campground goes west up **Boulder Creek.** A mile or so of private property is posted. It is about 2.3 miles to the wilderness boundary and about 2 more miles by trail to **Boulder Lake** (10,160 ft). The trail continues on a mile or so to a waterfall in the creek. Some small ponds in the higher reaches have cutthroat. Like other areas in the wilderness, this drainage is heavily fished for small brooks, cutthroats and hybrids.

Slate Creek and the Slate lakes are reached by taking the Boulder Creek Road to the wilderness boundary and hiking north on the Gore Range Trail for about 3 miles to Slate Creek. A trail up the stream leads to the lakes at the foot of steep, rocky mountainsides. The trail to the upper lake is very steep and rough. **Slate Lake** (9800 ft; 20 ac) has good size rainbow and brook, and a few mackinaw may lurk in the depths. **Upper Slate Lake** (11,000 ft; 15 ac) has brook and cutthroat, which also may be found in the creek above the lake.

A paved road exits Hwy 9 about 13 miles north of Silverthorne to Green Mountain Reservoir. The road also provides access to Black, Cataract, Elliott and Martin creeks that flow into the reservoir from the west.

GORE RANGE LAKES

Black Lake (8891 ft; about 60 ac) is 4.5 miles up **Black Creek** by road. It and Blue Lake are outside the wilderness and are stocked with brook, cutthroat, hybrids. A few brown trout may be present. Upstream into the wilderness are several tributary streams and ponds that reportedly have small cutthroat. **Cliff Lake** (10,740 ft; 3 ac) and its cutthroat are reached by a very strenuous cross-country trek west from Dora Lake or northwesterly from a tributary of Black Creek.

Otter Creek is another fast tributary (with brook, cutthroat, hybrids and possibly browns) that drains **Surprise Lake** (10,000 ft; 8 ac) and **Dora Lake** (12,225 ft; 12 ac). Both are most easily (and it isn't that easy) reached by Gore Range Trail going south from Cataract Creek Trail. Dora is good for cutthroat to 15 inches. Surprise has some brook and cutthroat.

Cataract Creek is a good-sized, fast flowing stream that provides access to the very popular north end of the wilderness. A 1.8-mile road leads up from the reservoir road just north of the bridge over the creek to **Lower Cataract Lake** (8630 ft; about 60 ac). There is a 4-unit campground at the creek. The creek and lake have brook, brown, cutthroat and hybrid trout and kokanee in the lower reaches of the stream in the fall.

The lake is a main jumping off place for hiking into the Eaglesmere lakes, Tipperary Lake, Upper Cataract Lake, Mirror Lake and, just outside the wilderness, Mahan

Lake—all in especially scenic, rugged terrain. Good sign at trailhead, if vandals haven't destroyed it.

Upper Cataract Lake (10,700 ft; 40 ac) is a deep lake that can be very good for brook and good size cutthroat when the trout are striking. It and **Tipperary Lake** (9750 ft; 10 ac), which also has some rainbow, are 4 and 2 miles, respectively, above Lower Cataract Lake by steep trail up the tributary to the mainstem of the creek. Upper stretches of the creek itself are fair to good for small cutthroat. **Mirror Lake** (10,550 ft; 5 ac) is shallow, but sometimes good for cutthroat.

The **Eaglesmere Lakes** are a 4-mile hike with one good, steep section. **Upper Eaglesmere** (10,950 ft; 20 ac) and **Lower Eaglesmere** (10,250 ft; 12 ac) are heavily fished for cutthroat, rainbow and brook.

Mahan Lake, which also can be readily reached by the Spring Creek Road going west from the north end of Green Mountain Reservoir, is shallow, flat, weedy and tends to winterkill. Possibly some brook there.

Green Mountain Reservoir (7950 ft) is a popular fishing spot. It is a fluctuating reservoir and varies from 2100 acres when full to 224 acres in drought years. It usually is full in summer, and drawn down to varying degrees by autumn. It is a shadeless setting for the most part. Fishing for kokanee salmon is excellent and the fall spawning season snagging is a major attraction. Kokanee here are among the largest in the state at around 2 pounds and up and there are a lot of them. Snagging salmon is permitted only from September 1 to December 31.

The reservoir, which may be fished by boat, has some big browns, rainbow, cutthroat and hybrid brook-cutthroat, a few mackinaw and a lot of suckers. A double limit of rainbow may be taken by holders of the rainbow trout stamp. The reservoir is popular with ice fishermen in winter because it is so easy to reach. The reservoir is well stocked and fishing at inlets of tributary streams is usually good, especially when the ice recedes in the spring. It is heavily fished. There is a campground, resort accommodations, boat ramps, boat rental and picnic ground.

Below Green Mountain Dam the Blue River is good for rainbow and brown trout with some big browns. This is gold meda water with catch-and-release fishing encouraged. The first 2.5 miles below the dam is also classified as wild trout water, so that only trout over 16 inches may be kept and only two of them in possession. Releases of water from the reservoir make fishing unpredictable. **Elliott, Martin, Deep, Spring** and **Spruce Creeks** offer some brook, rainbow and hybrid cutthroat fishing. Much of the fishing is on private land and some of it is posted. Permission to fish is necessary since public and private land boundaries are not always signed. The river is west of Hwy 9. The highway to State Bridge crosses the river about a mile above the Blue's confluence with the Colorado River.

GORE CANYON

Coming into the Colorado, opposite the Blue River confluence, is **Muddy Creek.** Its lower reaches are fair for rainbow and brown, but it is brushy and hard to work, and mostly on private land where permission to fish is necessary. On the upper reaches there are many small streams and ponds with brook and rainbow, but again, often brushy and hard to fish for small trout. US 40 roughly parallels the stream for nearly 30 miles through sagebrush and some timber to Muddy Pass.

Inquire locally for precise directions to those areas where the highway comes close to the Colorado. There is at least one turnout near Parshall, and another downstream, where state and federal land adjoin the river and public fishing is possible for very brief stretches. Fishing in the Colorado is good in this vicinity, so it's worth the effort to get permission to fish from private property.

West of Kremmling, the Colorado River enters **Gore Canyon** where it offers excellent fishing water for good size rainbow and brown. Access is via a dirt road west from town off US 40. Drive 2 miles on the west side of the river heading toward the canyon. Then hike the railroad grade for 5 miles for fishing downstream. From the upper end of Gore Canyon downstream to State Bridge is wild trout fishing, and it's often very good. Check posted regulations.

RANCHO DEL RIO
White Water Guide and Fishing Service
"Where Every Season Has Its Place"

Fish & Float Trips on the Colorado River

Guided Trout Fishing and Float Trip: Full day and half day trips on the Upper Colorado River fishing for Rainbow, German Brown, and Native Cutthroat trout from the BLM Pumphouse put-in to Rancho Del Rio, State Bridge, and Alkali Creek.

We Include In Fishing Float Trip Price: Raft with swivel seats or dory, life jackets, cooler, transportation from Rancho Del Rio to put-in point and back to Rancho Del Rio from take-out point and a professional, licensed guide.

Cabins and Camping — Beautiful rustic cabins to sleep as many as 42 guests. Camp on 41 acres of river front property. Tents, R.V.'s, trailers all welcomed.

Raft Trip — Twelve miles on the Upper Colorado River that will take you through exciting stretches of rapids through the Lower Gore and Red Gorge Canyons.

For Reservations and Information:

Rancho Del Rio
4199 Trough Road
Bond, Colorado 80423
Phone (303) 653-4431

Your hosts:
Mark and Mary Bernhardt

Sportsman Quik Stop
West end of Kremmling
on Hwy. 40

Rods • Reels • Flies • Bait
Licenses • Ice • Groceries • Gas

Ask us about fishing conditions

**Kremmling CO
(303) 724-9523**

Gore Canyon also can be reached by driving south of Kremmling about a mile on Hwy 9 and turning west on the Trough Road. At 8.5 miles, a sign indicates the Bureau of Land Management Pumphouse Recreation Area, where many floaters put into the river. Road goes to river for fishing either upstream or downstream. Streamers, nightcrawlers and big flies are all worth a try.

Canyon Creek and **Blacktail Creek** enter the river from the northwest, but offer only fair fishing for brook. Blacktail is accessible from Gore Pass on Hwy 134 at the campground west of the summit about 0.75 mile. It is brushy and fishing is difficult.

Sheephorn Creek enters the Colorado less than a mile above Radium. A dirt road leads some 20 miles southeast up the creek to the edge of the Gore Eagles Nest Wilderness. Most of it is private land where permission to fish for brook and rainbow is needed. **Gutzler Lakes** are not fishable. Upper reaches have numerous beaver ponds and small lakes such as **Walters Lake**, **Lone Lick Lakes** and some small streams. Fishing is mostly for small brook and some cutthroat.

South of Sheephorn is **Piney River**, which flows from the southeast into the Colorado just above State Bridge. It drains Piney Lake, which is most easily reached from Vail. Piney is a decent stream with brown, rainbow, brook and, on the upper reaches, cutthroat. Three miles south of State Bridge on Hwy 131, a dirt road leads east; after about a mile it crosses the river. Private land, so ask permission to fish. Also ask directions to reach Piney's headwaters, some 15 miles distant. Or take the shorter route, the Piney Lake-East Meadow Creek Road heading north from Vail. **Meadow Creek, East Meadow Creek, North Fork Piney River, East Fork Piney River, Horseshoe Creek** all have trout, but fishing is fair and most likely places are heavily fished by hikers, since the area, except for Piney Lake, is in the wilderness.

Piney Lake (9295 ft; 35 ac) is about 15 miles north from the north I-70 service road at Vail. Keep to the left on the main road for 9 miles, then, when road forks, take the right-hand fork to the lake. The southwest part is private, but the rest is forest, and fishing for brook trout is fair. Upstream on the river there are many pools, but they are heavily fished for cutthroat.

DERBY CREEKS

Between State Bridge and Burns, several small, muddy creeks enter the Colorado. They have small brook and some rainbow in brushy, hard-to-fish waters. Access is via private land. About 0.75 mile downstream from Burns, **Derby Creek** enters the Colorado after draining a southeast portion of the Flat Tops Wilderness. The only dirt road out of Derby Junction village at the mouth of the creek eventually leads 9 miles to Derby Guard Station and the creek. From here, access to its upper reaches is by 4-wheel drive to wilderness boundary and then by trail. This is very rugged country with some excellent fishing. It's also scenic.

South Fork Derby Creek heads at

Mackinaw Lake (10,780 ft; 5 ac) and **Crescent Lake** (10,750 ft; 14 ac) more than 10 miles by rough road into a cul de sac in the wilderness. Both lakes have cutthroat and mackinaw, with macs to 22 inches being taken from the namesake lake. Three miles down the creek, **Emerald Lake** (9600 ft; 2 ac) has small brook. The creek itself has brook and cutthroat. This is bighorn sheep country, so a glimpse of Colorado's state animal is possible.

From the guard station, a rough road goes up **Middle Fork Derby Creek** 5 miles to the juncture with North Fork Derby Creek. A trail goes 5 miles up Middle Fork providing access to several lakes, including barren **McMillan Lake** and several others with no fish. Some of these, including **Muskrat Lake** (10,240 ft; 1 ac) and **Mud Lake** (10,320 ft; 1 ac), are stocked, but winterkill. These are accessible 0.75 mile off the main trail by an old road to the north. **Deer Lake** (11,150 ft; 4 ac) is a beautiful lake with good cutthroat. It is about 4 miles up from Muskrat Lake turnoff. South of Deer Lake are **Upper Island Lake** (11,250 ft; 26 ac) and **Lower Island Lake** (10,800 ft; 19 ac). Upper has cutthroat to 20 inches or so; the lower offers rainbow and cutthroat. Best fishing is late in the season. The Island Lakes are about 3 miles from the Muskrat Lake cutoff over a good trail, though on the final leg to Upper Island it is steep. Middle Fork itself offers good angling for cutthroat, especially in hard-to-reach sections of deep canyons. **North Fork Derby Creek** is through canyon for much of the 5 miles to **Hooper Lake** (11,100 ft; 18 ac), which is barren, and **Keener Lake** (10,740 ft; 30 ac), which has rainbow; some good ones to 5 pounds—if you can get them. About 1.5 miles east of these lakes is **Edge Lake** (10,960 ft; 7 ac), which also has large rainbow, and the **Bailey Lakes** (10,760 ft; 1 to 4 ac), which have small brook and rainbow.

Access to North Fork Derby Creek is over a very rough 4-wheel-drive road from about 5 miles north of the Derby Guard Station to Stump Park and the wilderness boundary. From there it is a strenuous 6-mile hike to the lakes. About 2 miles up from Stump Park and to the west is **Solitary Lake** (10,640 ft; 2 ac), which has brook and rainbow. Roads built before the area was designated a wilderness provide relatively good direction, and trails off them to lakes are easily located.

For 7 miles downstream from Derby Junction, the Colorado River is in a narrow canyon. There is fishing for rainbow and brown from either side, but the stream is not wadable. Eastside access is at Burns and via the railroad grade. A good road follows the stream on the west side.

SWEETWATER

Sweetwater Creek enters the Colorado from the west 7 miles north of Dotsero. A good road leads up 12 miles through private land to **Sweetwater Lake** (7711 ft; 80 ac), a very pretty lake in an idyllic geologic setting. The lake is deep and has fishing for brook and rainbow, some sizable. A resort offers a cafe, boats (no motors) and horseback riding. There is a campground. From Sweetwater, trails lead up the creek into the wilderness. About 8 miles up, **Indian Lake** (10,560 ft; 7 ac) is barren; **Rim Lake** (10,824 ft; 14 ac) is deep and, although stocked, just doesn't sustain fish. Fishing for rainbow is poor. **Shepherd Lake** (10,750 ft; 20 ac), a mile west of Rim Lake, is good for natives and mackinaw. Trails to these lakes are rough and steep.

Turret Creek, a mile above Sweetwater Lake, is brushy and has some rainbow,

Colorado River

brook and cutthroat; mostly small.

Deep Creek flows into the Colorado River 1.75 miles above Dotsero and I-70. A good road parallels it for about a mile and a half before swinging around to the south and west, to eventually reach **Deep Lake** and **Heart Lake** after some 30 miles. The creek runs north of the road in a deep, wild canyon that has few visitors. It is reported to produce brook and rainbow. West of the road are many small lakes and beaver ponds, many of which are barren.

White Owl Lake (10,650 ft; 12 ac) is fair to good for rainbow. It is stocked, but often winterkills. It is less than a mile off the Heart Lake-Deep Lake Road about 3 miles south of Deep Lake. **Kline's Folly Lake** (10,650 ft; 4 ac) is alongside the road about a quarter-mile from Heart Lake. It has rainbow. It often winterkills, but is stocked early in the season. **Supply Basin Lake** (10,750 ft; 5 ac) is similar to Kline's Folly, and is reached by easy 1-mile trail south from Heart Lake. **Bison Lake** (10,780 ft; 20 ac) is due west of Heart Lake and is fair for stocked rainbow. **Heart Lake** (10,700 ft; 122 ac) is poor fishing for brook and is not regularly stocked.

Deep Lake (10,450 ft; 45 ac) has big mackinaw, and each spring ardent fishermen wade through snowdrifts to get there soon after ice is out. That's when fishing is best. Macs, or lake trout, to 20 pounds and larger, are there along with catchable-size rainbow and some brook. The state record mac was caught here in 1949. It was 42 inches long and weighed 36 pounds.

There are campgrounds at Kline's Folly, Supply Basin, Deep Lake and Bison Lake.

By 4-wheel-drive road south from the Heart Lake Road at Heart Lake is **Grizzly Lake** (10,550 ft; 6 ac), and a mile farther, **Monument Lake** (10,746 ft; 13 ac); both tend to winterkill, but there may be some brook trout. To the southeast 3 miles by 4-wheel drive is **Palmer Lake** (10,650 ft; 8 ac), which has some cutthroat and good campsites. To the east, **Grizzly Creek** and **South Grizzly Creek** area accessible by 4-wheel drive by taking a road west from the Heart Lake Road 2 miles above Crane Park, about 6 miles southeast of Heart Lake. The stream is hard to get to, even on foot, because of deep canyons, but it has brook and rainbow.

Below Dotsero, the river is heavy and unwadable but with plenty of rainbow and brown trout (including big ones) and lots of suckers. Bait and spinners are effective but fishing can be tedious.

A mile below Dotsero, the smaller, clearer Eagle River sweeps in from the east.

EAGLE RIVER

The Eagle River has been one of Colorado's classic trout streams. But it is being dewatered and polluted to the point that its future as a fishery is questionable. In 1985, mine drainage from recently closed workings is beginning to affect the river below the village of Gilman. Orange gunk is being deposited on rocks and at the water's edge, and it is expected to worsen. It destroys the food supply and viability of fish reproduction.

Already 24,000-acre-feet of water are being diverted from headwater tributaries to the eastern slope, and another 20,000-acre-foot diversion is planned.

Extensive real estate development and other water withdrawals are also diminishing the size and nature of the river, while increasing siltation. It is a complex picture, with fishing one of the most readily evident indicators of change.

The Eagle River rises in heavy timber on the north side of Tennessee Pass, about 11 miles north of Leadville. Its two principal tributaries here are the South Fork of the Eagle River and Homestake Creek. To the northeast, on the northwest side of Vail Pass, Gore Creek, the river's other principal headwaters stream, originates. These streams merge just west of Vail near Minturn.

Brush and Gypsum creeks are major tributaries on the lower stretches. I-70 and US 6 & 24 flank the river west of Minturn as it flows through open pasture and ranchland.

The **South Fork Eagle River** flows as a small forest creek 5 miles north from Tennessee Pass, often through heavy brush with beaver ponds. At Camp Hale, at the foot of the pass, it is joined by **East Fork Eagle**

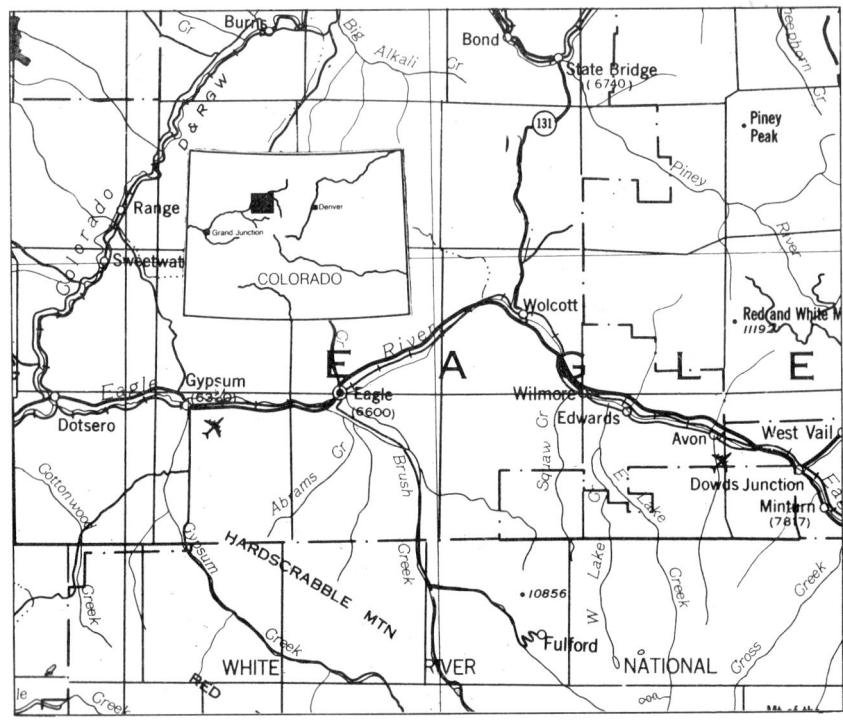

Eagle-Colorado Rivers confluence

River coming down from the Robinson tailings pond of AMAX Climax molybdenum mine. For 3 miles it is channeled along the airstrip at Camp Hale, training center for the 10th Mountain Division in World War II. Fishing is for small brook and rainbow. The river is rated poor on the upper reaches, but fair near Camp Hale, because the river is stocked and the Forest Service has made stream improvements. Stocked fishing ponds at Camp Hale are just off Hwy 24 and easy to fish for rainbow and brook.

HOMESTAKE CREEK

Just below Redcliff, the clear waters of **Homestake Creek** enter the Eagle. About 3 miles south of Redcliff, a good road leaves Hwy 24 to the west at Blodgett Campground and goes southwest 11 miles up the creek to **Homestake Reservoir** (10,260 ft; 300 ac) in a 3-mile-long cul de sac in the Holy Cross Wilderness Area. The reservoir has rainbow, brook and cutthroat, and is heavily fished—although fishing is difficult because of steep rock banks.

At the southwest corner of the reservoir, a small creek comes down from **Paradise Lakes** (11,200 ft; 2 to 20 ac). A very steep, 2-mile hike to these 5 above-timberline lakes can provide fair fishing for brook and cutthroat. There is heavy fishing pressure from hikers.

Three miles above the reservoir is **Upper Homestake Reservoir** (10,500 ft; 17 ac). Follow the creek-side trail for cutthroat fishing. This is very rugged and scenic country.

A quarter-mile below Homestake Reservoir, a trail parallels the **East Fork of Homestake Creek** for 5 miles. After about 3 miles, a trail breaks off to the east along a small stream. It's a mile along the east branch to **Isolation Lakes** (11,600 ft; 2 and 3 ac). Although above timberline, the lakes offer good cutthroat fishing. Two miles farther, at the headwaters of East Fork, is **Lonesome Lake** (11,520 ft 10 ac) which also has cutthroat.

GOLD PARK

Downstream about 3 miles is Gold Park and Gold Park Campground. It is a major trailhead for hiking into the Holy Cross Wilderness and scores of lakes to the west and north. On a summer weekend, 100 cars may be parked here, for the 122,600-acre wilderness is one of the most heavily used areas in Colorado. Fishing pressure is very heavy summer and fall, largely because 19th century mining roads and trails provide ready, if strenuous, access to spectacular mountain country.

From Gold Camp, a vehicle-bustin' road goes 3.5 miles southwest up Missouri Creek to provide access to the Brady Lakes, Sopris Lake, Lake Esther, the four Missouri Lakes, Fancy Lake and the two Mulhall Lakes. Missouri Creek, Sopris Creek, Fancy Creek and French Creek contribute their waters to the Homestake Water Collection system. Most of their headwaters lakes are fishable.

Proceed up **Sopris Creek** from the end of the Missouri Creek Road at the wilderness boundary. Follow the old road about a mile; then a faint trail accesses **Brady Lake** (10,890 ft; 8 ac). To the north a quarter-mile is **Sopris Lake** (10,890 ft; 5 ac), which sometimes is referred to as a Brady Lake. Both have cutthroat. **Esther Lake** (11,280 ft; 4 ac) lies to the southwest a mile by cross-country trek. Follow the stream up to the lake for good brook fishing.

The **Missouri Lakes** (11,400 ft; 4 to 13 ac) are about 4 miles by trail from the end of the road. The lowest lake is barren; the other three have brook and cutthroat trout. A quarter-mile below the Homestake Water System intake tunnel on Homestake Creek, and above Gold Park a mile, **Fancy Creek** merges with Homestake. At its headwaters is **Fancy Lake** (11,500 ft; 4 ac). It can be reached by a trail up the creek or by an old road from Hunky Dory Lake and Holy Cross City to the north. Fancy Lake has brook. The **Mulhall Lakes** (11,920 ft; 2 and 4 ac) can be reached by going north on a trail a hundred yards north of Fancy Lake to a stream, then upstream a total distance of about 0.75 mile. Mulhalls have rainbow and cutthroat. They can also be reached via Holy Cross City.

French Creek dribbles (most of its water having been diverted) into Homestake at Gold Park after draining Cleveland Lake, Hunky Dory Lake and the Seven Sisters Lakes. An old road to Holy Cross City provides access via 4-wheel drive to **Hunky Dory** (11,600 ft; 6 ac) and **Cleveland Lakes** (11,920 ft; 20 ac), which have brook and cutthroat. Cleveland, the better of the two, also has some rainbow. Both are on the edge of the wilderness. The road is easier to walk than drive, although a 4-wheel drive can make it from midsummer on.

Seven Sisters Lakes (12,700-11,840 ft; 6 to 12 ac) are on **French Creek** to the north of Hunky Dory. A trail follows the stream. Fishing at the three lowest lakes is for brook and some cutthroat. The fourth lake has brook and cutthroat; higher ones are barren. The lakes are heavily fished, since they are only a mile or so into the wilderness; all are above timberline.

About 4 miles south of Gold Park are the **Lost Lakes,** also known as **Chain of Lakes** (10,500 ft; 4 to 15 ac). From the northeast corner of Gold Park by the old bridge abutments, cross Homestake Creek and go upstream to a steep trail heading south into the timber. Lakes are very clear and trout are wary, but there is good fishing for cutthroat; uppermost lake is possibly the best of the three.

About 4 miles up the road from Hwy 24, a trail (watch for the sign) goes off to the north to the **Whitney Lakes** (10,600 ft; 15 and 5 ac), a steep 3-mile hike. The lower lake has brook and rainbow; the upper, smaller lake has cutthroat.

Other tributary streams to Homestake Creek tend to be too steep and fast for fish except at the higher elevations where some small cutthroat and a brook may be found in pools and ponds. The same conditions prevail on the east tributaries to the Eagle River between its east fork and Gore Creek at the junction of Hwy 24 and I-70.

EAGLE RIVER CANYON

Four miles downstream from Redcliff Bridge, the Eagle River is in a deep, narrow canyon. Access is only along the railroad track beside the river. At the north end of the canyon, as Hwy 24 crosses the river, a dirt road goes west to provide access to the Fall and Cross Creek drainages on a terrible dirt road that takes an hour to travel 8 to 10 miles.

About 4 miles into the forest is Tigiwon Campground and a good place to leave the car, although the road goes on another 4 miles to Half Moon Campground and the wilderness boundary. From Half Moon, trails go north to Cross Creek and the summit of Mount of the Holy Cross (14,005 ft), and south above Fall Creek to Lake Constantine. This area receives very heavy traffic and heavy fishing pressure, and most lakes are stocked.

Lake Constantine (11,400 ft; 13 ac) is a 5-mile hike from Half Moon. It is fair for cutthroat, rainbow and brook, but some big ones lurk there, also. **Fall Creek,** downstream from the lake to the river, is in a deep canyon; often brushy and very difficult to reach and fish, but it and the beaver ponds are loaded with brook trout.

Above Constantine by steep streamside trail are the **Tuhare Lakes** (12,300 ft; 12 ac). The lower and, a short distance beyond, the upper (12,400 ft; 43 ac) are good for cutthroat, but are heavily fished by iron-legged, leather-lunged fishermen. It helps to have both hands free on the climb up from Constantine.

The Seven Sisters Lakes are accessible by taking a southeast trail about a half-mile above Constantine. Tricky creek crossing.

Hagerman Peak and Snowmass Lake

CROSS CREEK

Cross Creek is a productive rainbow, brook, brown and—at the upper levels—cutthroat fishery, but it has been getting heavy fishing pressure.

Tentatively slated for construction in 1986 is a portion of the Homestake II water project. It would take most of the water from Cross and West Cross creeks and seriously diminish downstream water flows and, undoubtedly, the fishing in this beautiful country.

Access is from Tigiwon Campground upstream, or from Half Moon Campground by a 3-mile hike to **East Cross Creek** and another 2 miles to the mainstream by a well-marked and well-trod trail.

Cross Creek offers a variety of fishing: fast canyon water, open and brushy streams, beaver ponds and high mountain lakes. At the headwaters of East Cross Creek is **Lake Patricia** (12,500 ft; 10 ac) with cutthroat. It is about 5 miles from Half Moon Campground. Farther up is **Bowl of Tears,** a large shallow pond with no fish.

A steep, rugged trail goes 2 miles down the west side of East Cross Creek to the main stream trail. About 4 miles upstream, **West Cross Creek** enters the main stream above Reeds Meadows. Strictly a no-trail situation upstream to four **West Cross Creek Lakes** (12,240 ft to 11,680 ft; averaging 12 ac). Best route is probably to continue up Cross Creek 5 miles to Blodgett Lake and then head north-northwest along the ridge to West Cross Creek. The four lakes then lie about a quarter-mile apart—all easy walking from Blodgett—for good fishing for cutthroat.

Harvey Lake (11,000 ft; 20 ac) is about 3 miles upstream from West Cross Creek juncture. It is good for brook and cutthroat, including some big ones. Harvey is just off the mainstream 1.5 miles up a small creek.

Another 2 miles upstream, beyond the old mill site, the creek forks. The left, or east fork, leads 0.25 mile to **Treasure Vault Lake** (11,600 ft; 23 ac) and some good cutthroat. The right fork leads a similar distance to **Blodgett Lake** (11,650 ft; 25 ac) for similar angling.

These lakes also are accessible by a 4-mile hike on established trails from Holy Cross City via Fancy Pass or by a 6-mile hike from Missouri Lakes.

Just north of Minturn, **Grouse Creek** joins the Eagle. A Forest Service trail leads up **West Grouse Creek** 6 miles to **Olsen Lake** (11,200 ft; 10 ac), 0.25 mile off the trail in timber. Trail goes past Olsen to the two Turquoise Lakes at the head of Beaver Creek. Olsen is hard to find, but has cutthroat. **Turquoise Lakes** (11,000 ft; 6 ac each) are 4.5 miles from Olsen and have cutthroat. Higher lake is deeper, better fishing.

Grouse Lake (10,700 ft; 5 ac) is 5 miles up Grouse Creek by a good trail from where the trail forks, a mile from Hwy 24. Good fishing for small brook.

VAIL VICINITY

Gore Creek joins the Eagle River 2 miles downstream from Minturn. The Gore is an astonishing stream, since the town of Vail and construction associated with the Vail ski area have surrounded much of it with development. Still, it has brown, rainbow, cutthroat and brook trout. On its lower reaches in the town of Vail, it has been designated a gold medal water for quality fishing from the confluence of Red Sandstone Creek downstream and is open to fishing with flies and lures only. Catch and release is encouraged. Portions of the stream are posted. Fishing is possible in town and along the golf course. Only one rainbow and one brown trout may be kept. Check current regulations.

Gore Creek originates in the southern end of the Gore-Eagles Nest Wilderness north of I-70 in the vicinity of Red Buffalo Pass. North of the creek, **Gore Lake** (11,400 ft; 5 ac) has cutthroat and is among several smaller unnamed lakes with uncertain fishing status. Five miles down through brush and timber, **Black Gore Creek** joins Gore Creek from the south after a 10-mile run from near the summit of Vail Pass. Near the summit, the two **Black Lakes** can be seen at 10,400 feet elevation. They are heavily stocked with rainbow and heavily fished. They tend to be temperamental, but often are good fishing. Easy access from I-70.

Downstream, **Bighorn**, **Pitkin** and **Booth Creeks** plunge down steep valleys to Gore Creek. They are too fast to fish at lower reaches, but in higher terrain have small cutthroat and some brook. Get off I-70 and use the north service road to find parking. **Pitkin Lake** (11,400 ft; 8 ac) is at timberline and requires a strenuous 8-mile hike. It and **Booth Lake** (11,500 ft; 5 ac) both are heavily fished for cutthroat. Booth Creek Trail provides access; roadside signs note creeks.

Lost Lake (10,300 ft; 18 ac) is a deep lake at the headwaters of **Red Sandstone Creek** that flows into the Gore west of Vail. It is a deep, beautiful lake reached by taking the Red Sandstone Creek Road out of Vail, 9 miles to the end of the road; then it's an easy 1-mile trail to the lake. Heavily fished.

From the confluence of Gore Creek downstream 14 miles to Wolcott, the Eagle River is fair to good fishing for 10- to 14-inch rainbow and brown; many larger fish are taken. Some posted access, so ask permission to cross private land. Best access is to take US 6, which generally follows the river down the valley, instead of I-70. A mile of the river runs through state land just below the confluence of Gore Creek and the river. Slow down by the bridge for a sharp turn onto Hwy 24 and a service road by the river.

DOWNSTREAM

Beaver Creek enters the Eagle from the south at Avon. Development of a ski area and related projects have left its lower reaches off limits to public fishing. Upper reaches have cutthroat and brook. **Beaver Lake** (9750 ft; 5 ac), a half-mile inside the Holy Cross Wilderness, has good brook and cutthroat fishing. An old road leads to the boundary, then it's an easy hike. Upstream from Beaver Lake 6 miles are the **Turquoise Lakes** (11,000 ft; 6 ac each) with cutthroat.

Lake Creek flows into the Eagle from the south below Edwards. Two miles south from Edwards and US 6, it forks into **East Lake Creek** and **West Lake Creek.** A road goes 3.5 miles up East Lake Creek to the wilderness boundary, but it is often blocked by a private gate. Seek permission to cross and assurance that you can get back out again. Then there is a trail for 8 more miles through a steep, rough canyon that has a propensity for rain and high humidity. Trail is poorly marked; a good topographic map, compass and the ability to use them are highly recommended. Lake Creek has brown, rainbow and cutthroat.

At upper elevations, the **Gold Dust Lakes** (11,400 ft; 15 to 20 ac total) require a 2-mile climb to the west up a small creek to a bench; follow stream south past the first two lakes to three larger ones that produce cutthroat to 15 inches. Don't count on a trail. To the north a half-mile is **Big Pine Lake** (11,280 ft; 5 ac) and over a steep, 12,000-foot ridge is **Lake Thomas** (11,600 ft; 15 ac), which also has cutthroat and big rainbow. This is hiking country; horses are not advised.

Three good cutthroat lakes lie about 2 miles south of Gold Dust Lakes on the other side of an unnamed 12,730-foot mountain. **Big Spruce Lake** (12,000 ft; 15 ac), **Horseshoe Lake** (11,600 ft; 8 ac) and **Big Lake** (11,600 ft; 11 ac) are reached by hiking cross country from Gold Dust Lakes or up the unnamed creek that drains them from East Lake Creek.

West Lake Creek provides access to East Lake Creek by a recently constructed Forest Service trail. Signs provide directions. The road goes 6 miles up from the confluence of East and West Lake creeks. Before crossing the bridge above the confluence, stop and hike up a third of a mile and see that the shelf road hasn't been washed out. Remainder of the road is good. West Lake Creek is fair for brown at lower levels; cutthroat higher. At its headwaters is **New York Lake** (11,300 ft; 40 ac) which is good for cutthroat. To get there, go up West Lake Creek on the old road to old Polar Star Mine. Just below the mine, the road forks. Take the east road up 1.5 miles to timberline and continue east around a hill into a saddle from which New York Lake can be seen below. A vertical difference of 700-800 feet makes it a rough hike down and back up again.

Middle Lake (11,200 ft; 18 ac) is between West and East Lake creeks and is best reached from the west by driving the road to its end and then hiking southeast over slide rock to the lake to fish for cutthroat.

BRUSH CREEK

Brush Creek, which flows from the south into the Eagle River just west of Eagle, has brook, rainbow and, at lower levels, brown. The lower dozen miles where the stream flows through meadows are on private property and often is brushy. Permission to fish is necessary. The stream forks 2 miles into the forest, as does the road. **East Brush Creek** continues southeast another 12 miles past beautiful Yeoman Park and Fulford Cave campgrounds. At the headwaters is **Mystic Island Lake** (11,300 ft; 30 ac) and **Lake Charles** (11,000 ft; 16 ac), both in the wilderness. Both are fair to good for cutthroat and brook. The stream itself has brook and cutthroat. The area is heavily fished; many beaver ponds.

Three miles up East Brush Creek, **Nolan Creek** comes in from the east. It has about 3 miles of fishing in stream and ponds for brook and rainbow. Nolan is paralleled by an old mining road to Fulford. A 3-mile trail from Fulford to the southwest leads to **Nolan Lake** (10,800 ft; 7 ac) at the headwaters of the creek. It is deep and has good brook trout fishing.

Nolan Creek also provides access to New York Lake to the east via old mining roads. Fulford is outside the wilderness; Nolan Lake is just inside.

SOUTH OF EAGLE

The road up **West Brush Creek** leads 4 miles to **Sylvan Lake** (8510 ft; 42 ac) and a state campground. Lake is stocked with rainbow and brook. Sylvan Lake is good ice fishing, and rainbows to 5 pounds sometimes are caught. Brook trout in the lake are prolific. Road continues above the lake following the creek to Crooked Pass and the Fryingpan River Valley. The pass is dangerously slippery when it rains. West Brush Creek is fair for brook and rainbow; it tends to be brushy—hence its name. Many beaver ponds.

Antone's Cabin Creek enters West Brush Creek just below Sylvan Lake. **Antone's Cabin Lakes** have no fish.

GYPSUM CREEK

Seven miles down the Eagle, **Gypsum Creek** flows in from the south. The lower 6 miles are poor fishing, the next three have small brook. A road leads from the town of Gypsum 18 miles to **Lede Reservoir** (9500 ft; 28 ac). It is stocked with catchable rainbow, but is usually dry by the end of summer. To the west, coming off Red Table Mountain, are many small, brushy streams that are mostly irrigation and stockwatering channels, which have no fish. The ponds at their heads are little more than watering holes. There are fish in three of the lakes, if you can find them in the timber: **Lost Lake** (10,900 ft; 5 ac) is stocked with brook. It is reached by hiking west from Lede Reservoir to **Ragged Lakes** and then up the creek flowing into the southwest corner of Ragged Lakes (not the creek coming in from the south).

Red Lake (10,800 ft; 2 ac) has brook, but often winterkills. A 4-wheel-drive road up **Red Creek** goes within 100 yards of the lake. To the west, **Rim Lake** (10,700 ft; 8 ac), **Sugarloaf Lake** (10,710 ft; 7 ac) and **Shingle Lake** (10,500 ft; 4 ac) lie below the rim of the mountain and offer brook, cutthroat and rainbow. With no trails, they lie 3 to 5 miles from Gypsum Creek Road through timber. Inquire locally for these and **Borah, Sourdough** and **Muckie's Lakes,** all with small brook or rainbow.

Eagle River downstream from Wolcott to Eagle has good fishing for rainbow and brown to 14 inches; many larger. Rainbow fishing is best in fall and spring, but the river in this stretch becomes muddy from tribu-

---

Interstate 70 construction has virtually ended fishing in Glenwood Canyon and blocked access to Grizzly Creek. There's no parking unless construction has been suspended.

taries after rain. Some of the best water has been leased by the state. It begins a mile east of Eagle and extends 6.3 miles as posted, on the north side of the river only. From the south bank, 2 to 3 miles are open. Signs indicate public waters. Inquire in Eagle. Other stretches are open by permission. Below Eagle and past Gypsum to the Colorado, fishing can be good, but permission is needed.

From Gypsum to the Colorado River, 6 miles, the Bureau of Land Management owns the south bank and has a campground and 1 mile of public fishing on both sides of the river, a mile west of Gypsum. The stream contains rainbow, brown and suckers. Brushy; waders needed.

Downstream from the confluence of the two rivers, access is across private land for 2 miles to Glenwood Canyon. There, behind Shoshone Dam, the river becomes broad and quiet. Fishing is from the roadside in murky water for rainbow, brown and suckers. Fishing is fair to poor through most of the canyon, although some whitefish start to show up about 3 miles below the dam at Grizzly Creek. A beautiful stream, **Grizzly Creek** has rainbow, and access is easy from the highway through the canyon.

At Glenwood Springs, the Roaring Fork River, a gold medal trout stream, enters the Colorado.

ROARING FORK RIVER

For more than half its 59 miles, the **Roaring Fork River** is a premium trout fishing water in one of the most scenic valleys in Colorado. Brown and rainbow trout to 20 inches are common in its riffles and pools,

```
┌─────────────────────────────────────┐
│ ROARING FORK ANGLERS                │
│ Call for current river conditions—  │
│ (303) 945-0180                      │
│ • Guide Service                     │
│ • Complete Angling Necessities      │
│ • Licenses                          │
│ • Personalized Assistance           │
│ • Flies & Fly Tying Materials       │
│ 2114 Grand Avenue                   │
│ Glenwood Springs, CO                │
└─────────────────────────────────────┘
```

even though it is very heavily fished. There is a substantial population of good-size whitefish in the river. They are good eating and there is no limit on them.

The Colorado Division of Wildlife has classified the 8-mile stretch between Aspen's Hollum Lake and the Woody Creek Bridge as wild trout water, and restricted anglers to artificial flies and lures only. All trout caught are to be returned to the river immediately.

The Roaring Fork between Crystal River confluence and the Colorado River, 14 miles, is gold medal trout water with a limit of two trout, one each of brown and rainbow caught on artificial flies or lures. Bait fishing is permitted only from November 1 through March 31.

The limit in prime water between Woody Creek Bridge and the Crystal River (nearly 22 miles) is two fish.

There also are many suckers in the lower 20 miles of the river, and fishermen are encouraged to keep them to make room for more trout.

The river rises at Independence Pass near Hwy 82 on the Continental Divide, races through forest and surges through meadows to Aspen and then into its canyon before picking up the waters of the fabled Fryingpan River, also a gold medal stream, and the Crystal River on its way to the Colorado.

From the headwaters downstream 15 miles, the river roars and tumbles through rocks and timber with good pools and some riffles that are fair to good for small brook trout and a few rainbow. A few cutthroat are found near the juncture with Lincoln Creek.

Below the pass 1.5 miles there is a parking place on a curve and a trailhead to **Linkins Lake** (12,008 ft; 11 ac), 0.75 mile by steep trail. Follow a sign up to the left. Fishing for brook and stocked rainbow is best on the deeper side. From the same trailhead, 2 miles up the river, **Independence Lake** (12,490 ft; 9 ac) has brook trout to 16 inches if not winterkilled. A half-mile north by easy trail, **Lost Man Lake** (12,450 ft; 10 ac) also has rainbow. **Lost Man Creek** has small rainbow, brook and cutthroat downstream to **Lost Man Reservoir** (10,590 ft; 6 ac), which is heavily fished for rainbow and brook. North of the reservoir,

Scott Lake (12,020 ft; 5 ac) is up on a bench above the creek to the west about midway between the lake and reservoir; a steep 0.5-mile climb for good, small brook fishing. Lost Man Creek is accessible downstream from the lake or by going upstream across Hwy 82 from where it enters the Roaring Fork at Lost Man Campground. Off Hwy 82 to the south, 10 miles below Independence Pass at the Lincoln Gulch Campground, a 4-wheel-drive road crosses the river and follows **Lincoln Creek** 6 miles to **Grizzly Reservoir** (10,560 ft; 28 ac) and Portal Campground. Best fishing is early summer for rainbow. South above the reservoir a mile by road, **Truro Creek** joins Lincoln Creek with **Truro Lake** (12,300 ft; 7 ac). The lake is good for cutthroat, as is **Jack**

ASPEN BASALT
CERAMIC BATHROOMS
HEATED POOL
HOT TUB
GASOLINE, PROPANE
**Fishing • Hunting • Rafting
Skiing & Snowmobiling Nearby
Open All Year
Grocery Store • Gift Shop
Box 880, Basalt, Co. 81621
(303) 927-3532**

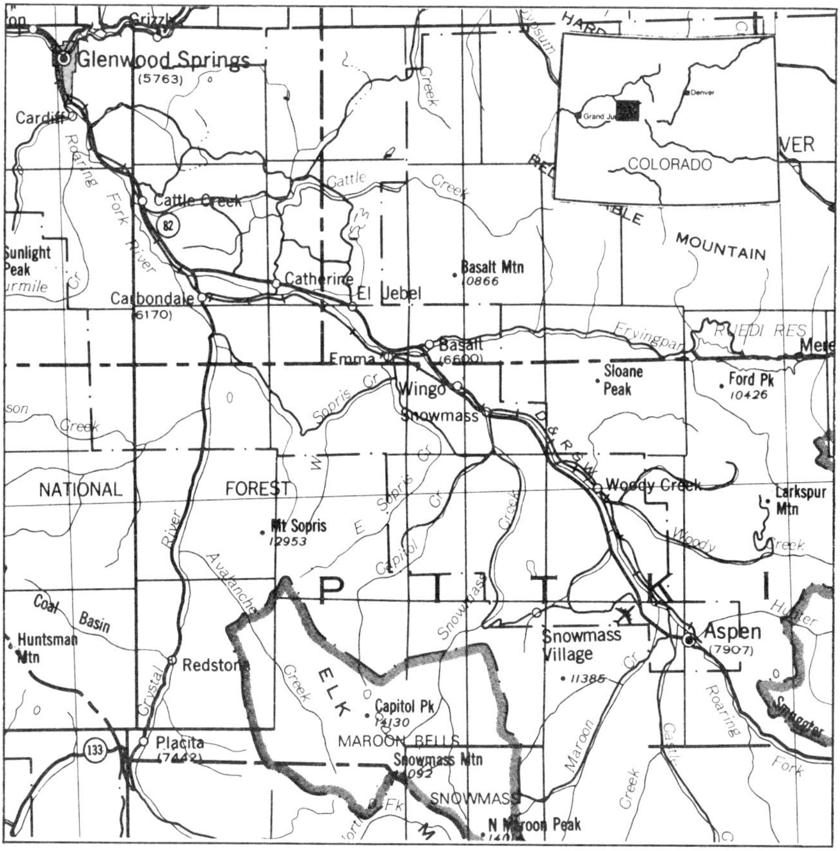

Lake (12,150 ft; 3 ac). Both lakes are to the west and up a steep slope. Directly across the valley to the east is **Grizzly Lake** (12,560 ft; 8 ac), producing rainbow. Ac-

Roaring Fork, Fryingpan, Crystal Rivers

cess to Grizzly Lake is a circuitous trail up Grizzly Creek from the east side of Grizzly Reservoir.

Farther up Lincoln Creek, a mile along the old road, a trail leads up a creek to the west to two lakes. At the fork in the creek, about a mile up, the south fork goes to **Anderson Lake** (12,840 ft; 9 ac), which is fair for small rainbow. The north fork leads a mile to **Petroleum Lake** (12,300 ft; 12 ac) and good rainbow fishing. The area is rarely open until mid-July, when the ice goes out and snowdrifts melt. **Ruby Lakes** at the top of the drainage are barren.

Two miles downstream from Grizzly Reservoir, **Tabor Creek** flows into Lincoln Creek from the south. Three miles by trail up the creek, a smaller creek comes in from the west out of **Tabor Lake** (12,320 ft; 6 ac). The lake has cutthroat.

Down the Roaring Fork 1.75 miles from Lincoln Gulch is Weller Campground and a trail leading south a half-mile to **Weller Lake** (9520 ft; 5 ac), which is fair for rainbow. The river is in a deep canyon and hard to fish for its small cutthroat and rainbow.

ASPEN ANGLING

Above Aspen the river meanders through meadows, and there are a few ponds. There also is a mix of public and private land. Public fishing is allowed along much of the river on the north edge of town. Observe signs. Evening fly fishing for brown and rainbow can be delightful.

Fishing for brown and rainbow in the town of Aspen itself can be good, depending on the volume of stream flow.

Castle Creek enters the Roaring Fork from the south on Aspen's northwest side after a 15-mile dash out of the 12,000- and 13,000-foot peaks of the Elk Mountains above Ashcroft. A winding, paved road from Hwy 82 follows the creek a dozen miles. The stream is fair to good for cutthroat, rainbow and small brook. Brushy in places, with some beaver ponds and private land. Above Ashcroft 3.5 miles, **Pine Creek** flows in from **Cathedral Lake** (11,855 ft; 17 ac). A steep 1-mile road leads to the lake where fishing for rainbow, brook and cutthroat has been increasing in recent years. There is a campground there and at the confluence of Pine and Castle creeks.

American Lake (11,365 ft; 8 ac) is due west of Ashcroft, but is most readily reached by a 3-mile trail from Elk Mountain Lodge downstream from Ashcroft about a mile. American has rainbow and surprisingly little fishing pressure.

Conundrum Creek is a substantial stream, less dewatered by irrigation than Castle Creek, but offers only fair to poor fishing for most of its 10 miles.

From the northeast, **Hunter Creek** enters the river on Aspen's north edge. It offers fair fishing for cutthroat and brown on lower reaches and cutthroat higher up in the Hunter-Fryingpan Wilderness Area. A fair road leads 6 miles to the wilderness boundary from town.

Maroon Creek, East Maroon Creek and **Maroon Lake** (9580 ft; 15 ac) have mostly rainbow and a few brook. Unless you're camping with a permit at Maroon Lake Campground, access is by shuttle bus to the lake. Not as heavily fished as in the past, and fishing is often good. The creek and lake are stocked.

West Maroon Creek and **Crater Lake** have few if any fish. Shuttle bus operates from Aspen Highlands ski area parking area near junction of Hwy 82 and the paved road to Maroon Lake from 8 a.m. to 6 p.m., July 1 through Labor Day, and then weekends until early October. The 1985 fare was $2.50 for adults; $1 for children. Daytime access is by permit only. Inquire at Forest Service Aspen District Ranger's Office, 303/925-3445. No camping reservations. The campground is on a first-come-first-served basis, and is usually full every summer night. One-day camping limit at Maroon Lake. Three other campgrounds along road.

WILDERNESS

Maroon Lake is a principal access to the Maroon Bells-Snowmass Wilderness and receives heavy backpacker, but not necessarily fisherman, traffic.

Willow Creek joins Maroon Creek a mile up the road from Aspen Highlands parking lot. Good horse trail follows it 9 miles to **Willow Lake** (11,705 ft; 18 ac) and good fishing for brook and cutthroat; some large ones are in this alpine meadow lake.

Access to fishing on the Roaring Fork downstream from Aspen is good because of agreements and leases negotiated by the Colorado Division of Wildlife with sportsmen-minded landowners.

Brush Creek flows into the Roaring Fork from the west and **Woody Creek** from the east downstream from Aspen. Both are poor fishing for small trout.

On downstream, **East Snowmass Creek** is poor fishing. **Snowmass Creek** and **Snowmass Lake** (10,980 ft; 84 ac) are good fishing. The creek has many beaver ponds and excellent brook trout, though it is brushy. The lake, deep and in a glaciated pocket of mountains, has rainbow to 20 inches and larger and some smaller cutthroat. It is 7 miles into the wilderness from the end of the road, 11 miles south from the Snowmass store on Hwy 82 where the creek enters the river. There is a campground at the wilderness boundary.

At the creek's headwaters, the **Pierre Lakes** (12,300 ft; 18, 27 and 15 ac) have cutthroat. Access is rugged. It entails walking an old, closed-off road 1.5 miles up Snowmass Creek from the wilderness boundary to the third stream coming in from the west. Leave the main trail to Snowmass Lake and go up the north side of **Bear Creek** by very steep trail to the lakes—about 4.5 miles. The largest and highest lake tends to have the best fishing, though all three are good.

West Snowmass Creek is the first creek inside the wilderness, and drains **Moon Lake** (11,720 ft; 9 ac), which has cutthroat. Ignore streamside trail and go on up the main Snowmass Creek Trail to the second creek, **Copper Creek,** and follow the trail up it to timberline—about 3 miles. Take the draw to the right and, at the end of a break in the top of the ridge to the northwest, Moon Lake is visible to the north, a half-mile away across slide rock.

Directly west of Moon Lake over a steep ridge is **Capitol Lake** (11,600 ft), a deep lake with good size cutthroat. Access is up Capitol Creek Road, which follows Capitol Creek from its juncture with Snowmass Creek about 2 miles above Hwy 82. Four miles up, at the monastery, take the northwest fork in the road 3 more miles to Cow Camp. Then hike into the wilderness up Capitol Creek, 5 miles to the lake.

Four miles by trail to the south from Capitol Lakes, over a 12,000-foot ridge, is **Avalanche Lake** (10,900 ft; 29 ac). It has fair to good fishing for cutthroat, some of them large. Capitol Creek has small brook and is brushy at lower elevations.

Hardscrabble Lake (10,150 ft; 4 ac) and its poor fishing for cutthroat is a 0.75 mile walk from the wilderness boundary at Capitol Creek. Sign indicates trail.

Williams Lake (10,800 ft; 7 ac) is a mile southwest of Hardscrabble by trail from the inlet. It has brook and a few cutthroat.

Two miles west of Basalt, **Sopris Creek** joins the Roaring Fork. About 8 miles up **West Sopris Creek** is **Dinkle Lake** (8400 ft; 6 ac), a pothole irrigation reservoir with rainbow and brown. Best fishing is early in the year. Creek is private below lake, but fair fishing above for cutthroat, brook and some rainbow.

Christine Lake (6725 ft; 3 ac) is on the west edge of Basalt town limit just off Hwy 82 on the blacktop road to the east just west of the Chevron station. Stocked with rainbow and brown. Campground.

FRYINGPAN RIVER

At Basalt, the **Fryingpan River** enters the Roaring Fork. The Fryingpan is a gold medal trout stream from Basalt upriver 13 miles to the Ruedi Reservoir dam. It is exceptional water, most of it open to public fishing for brown and rainbow averaging 12 to 14 inches with many larger ones. Fishing is with artificial flies and lures only. From the dam downstream 2 miles to the White River National Forest boundary, all trout must be returned to the river immediately. Below the boundary to the Roaring Fork River, children 15 years old and younger may use bait; adults must use artificial lures and flies. Possession limit is one brown and one rainbow, but not two of either species. No limit on suckers and whitefish. There are

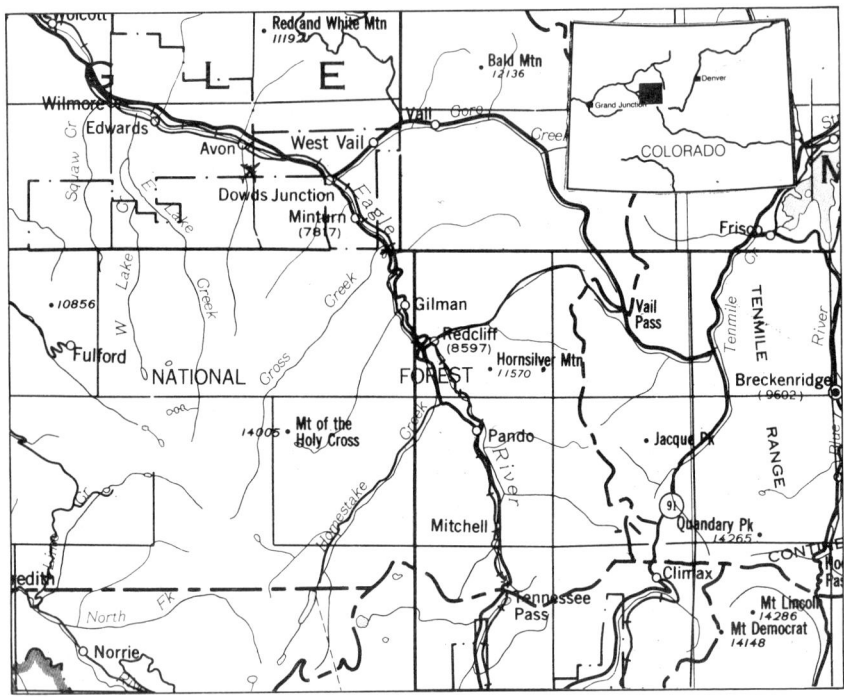

Upper Eagle and Fryingpan Rivers

some brook and cutthroat in the waters below the dam that run to 18 inches. This is a catch-and-release section and no fish may be kept.

According to Bob Jackson of the Taylor River tackle shop in Basalt, the green drake fly hatch in late summer and early fall often results in spectacular angling for the accomplished fly fisherman.

As might be imagined, this section of the river is heavily fished most of the year. Until the restrictions on possession and catch and release fishing were implemented, this stretch of the Fryingpan was in danger of being fished out except for put-and-take "fishing."

Ruedi Reservoir (7750 ft; 1000 ac when full) is just the opposite. It is a slow to poor fishery for rainbow and brown. Since it was filled in 1969 with water from one of the best trout fisheries in the world, it has been a disappointment to anglers despite heavy stocking. It has rainbow and kokanee salmon; two boat ramps, one of them paved; a marina and three campgrounds on or near the water. Fishing is from both shore and boats. With a rainbow trout stamp, a double limit may be taken.

Upstream from the reservoir the river fluctuates in volume because of diversions of water through tunnels to Turquoise Lake on the east side of the Continental Divide. Minimum stream flows are maintained greatly to the benefit of the fishery. Stocking of rainbow and cutthroat in the upper reaches has been resumed below the diversions. Cutthroat, brook and rainbow are found in streams above diversions of the river and its tributaries.

Two miles above the reservoir, **Lime Creek** enters the Fryingpan. It rises 10 miles to the northeast in the Holy Cross Wilderness at the **Strawberry Lakes** (11,200 ft; 4 ac total) where there are brook. To the west at the base of Avalanche Peak is **Sherry Lake** (11,800 ft; 7 ac) with brook. Downstream from Strawberry are **Fairview** (10,640 ft; 10 ac), **Halfmoon** (10,300 ft; 3

ac), **Eagle** (10,060 ft; 12 ac) and **Woods Lakes.** Woods Lake is private. The others, all in wilderness, have brook. Stream between them tends to be brushy with small brook trout.

Below Woods Lake, which is on a dirt road, Lime Creek runs through a deep canyon and is difficult to reach. The road from Eagle winds down west of the creek below Woods Lakes to the river. It is perilously slippery when wet.

Two miles above the reservoir, both the road and the Fryingpan River fork. Brushy **Last Chance Creek** joins the North Fork Fryingpan River here, from the north. It has brook. Eight miles upstream by trail is **Lake Josephine** (11,420 ft; 2 ac) with brook. To the northwest 2 miles, **Tellurium Lake** is barren.

LOVELY COUNTRY

The **North Fork Fryingpan River** flows 10 miles from above the **Savage Lakes** (11,300 ft; 15 and 25 ac). The smaller upper lake and the larger lower lake have brook trout. Earlier populations of mackinaw apparently are gone. **Carter Lake** (10,300 ft; 3 ac) has brook and cutthroat. Brook and cutthroat are found upstream in the canyon as well as in a series of high lakes some 3 miles above Carter Lake. It is hard hiking from the river.

From the south, **Mormon Creek** drains **Mormon Lake** (11,400 ft; 14 ac), 4 miles upstream to the southeast. It has brook, but is rough hiking through brush. Savage, Carter and Mormon lakes are all just inside the wilderness.

Two miles downstream on the North Fork, **Cunningham Creek** flows in from the southeast a mile above Elk Wallow Campground. It has fair fishing for brook. Much of its water is diverted to the Eastern Slope. A mile by trail above the campground is **Diemer Lake** (9900 ft; 12 ac), a weedy pond stocked with brook. Fishing should be better since weed control efforts began in 1982.

Sellar Lake (10,170 ft; 7 ac) is shallow and rated fair for rainbow. It is southwest of Diemer Lake, a mile by old road.

From 2 miles above Ruedi Reservoir, the

ASPENALT LODGE
on the Frying Pan River
Moderate Rates Include
Deluxe Continental Breakfast
• Riverfront Rooms Available
• Fishing Guides & Lessons Available
Call for Reservations (303) 927-3191
Write For Brochure Box 428, Basalt CO 81621

Fryingpan flows some 17 miles down from its origins along the Continental Divide in the Hunter-Fryingpan Wilderness. A good road follows upstream nearly 12 miles to the wilderness boundary. The **Fryingpan Lakes** (11,000 ft; 2 ac total) are teeming with small brook and an occasional cutthroat. They are about 5 miles by trail from the Boustead Tunnel West Portal and the end of the road.

Tributary streams from the south, **Martin Creek** and **Granite Creek,** and the two **Granite Lakes** (11,700 ft; 3 and 5 ac) have small brook in the 6- to 7-inch range. Access is by wilderness trail.

Ivanhoe Creek flows into the river from the east. A bumpy dirt road generally follows the creek 5 miles to its headwaters at **Ivanhoe Lake** (10,900 ft; 30 ac) on the way to Hagerman Pass. The lake has rainbow and receives moderate fishing pressure. It lies along the old Colorado Midland Railroad grade. History buffs may be advised that the locomotive that went off the track and down into Hell Gate Canyon (3 miles downstream) has been salvaged despite legends to the contrary. The creek is fair to good fishing for rainbow and brook.

Lyle Creek flows into Ivanhoe Creek 2 miles below the lake. Up Lyle Creek 1.5 miles in the Holy Cross Wilderness is **Lyle Lake** (11,600 ft; 10 ac). It and the stream are fair to good for brook. The lake also has mackinaw.

The South Fork of the Fryingpan River rises 12 miles southeast in the Hunter-Fryingpan Wilderness 12 miles southeast of the village site of Nast. Much of the river is good fly fishing with riffles, pools, rapids and quiet stretches with rainbow and cutthroat. The river canyon is steep, deep and rough going in many sections. A road follows the river on the canyon rim for 6 miles into the wilderness. Access is by forest road west from Norrie, 6 miles down the Fryingpan from Nast. Five miles above Norrie, the road forks. The East Fork passes **Chapman Lake** (9200 ft; 15 ac), which should not be confused with Chapman Dam and Campground 2 miles away on the main river. The lake is fair to good for brook and cutthroat. A clear trail to it is evident 2 miles up from the fork in the road. Good road continues on 4 more miles, then a trail to upper reaches. All of it offers good fishing.

At the fork in the road, the West Fork goes 2.75 miles up **Chapman Creek,** a fast stream with some cutthroat. In the wilderness 2 miles southwest of the end of the road, where there are water diversion structures, is **Sawyer Lake** (11,050 ft; 12 ac). It has cutthroat. It is a rough hike up Sawyer Creek from this point. An easier trail goes southwest 7 miles from Chapman Campground, through the timber and across Twin Meadows to Sawyer.

Chapman Dam and Campground has a 15-acre pond which is good for rainbow and brook. Stocked and heavily fished.

CRYSTAL RIVER

The **Crystal River** flows more than 35 miles through some of the most scenic terrain in Colorado to join the Roaring Fork River from the south 2 miles below Carbondale. It and its tributaries and lakes have rainbow, brook and cutthroat trout. Browns may be found close to the Roaring Fork. The Crystal is a swift stream and its valley is very popular with tourists and fishermen. It is heavily stocked, and it is seldom that trout over 13 inches are caught except in the most out-of-the-way places.

Hwy 133 leaves Hwy 82 about 10 miles south of Glenwood Springs, 12 miles north of Basalt near Carbondale. It follows the river and is paved 20 miles to Bogan Flats at the foot of McClure Pass. A poorly paved road continues 5 miles upriver to Marble and 5 more to Crystal. After that it is strictly 4-wheel drive up the river's south fork to Schofield Pass. Sections of road above Marble are one-way traffic.

At the ghost town of Crystal, the north and south forks merge. The **North Fork of the Crystal River** flows 7 miles from its origins to join the South Fork at Crystal. The North Fork has many beaver ponds and open, but difficult, fishing in a canyon for cutthroat. It is heavily fished. A dangerous 4-wheel-drive road above the river is often blocked by snow until midsummer. **Geneva Lake** (10,950 ft; 33 ac) is reached by driving 2.5 miles up the north fork from Crystal to Lead King Basin. Leave vehicle and hike north up a steep switchback trail to the lake. A deep lake with shallow shoreline, it has brook to 12 inches. From the inlet to Geneva Lake it is 2 miles upstream to **Little Gem** (or **Upper Geneva) Lake** (11,700 ft; 3 ac) with some cutthroat, but fishing usually is poor. Over a ridge a half-mile northwest of Geneva Lake is **Snowfield Lake** (11,600 ft; 1 ac) with brook. No trail.

The **South Fork of the Crystal River** is paralleled by a very dangerous road that often is snowfilled and impassable until late July. Fishing in the fast water of Crystal Canyon is for brook and cutthroat. **Galena Lake** (12,100 ft; 12 ac) is temperamental for cutthroat. Above timberline, it is reached by a trail going over a ridge to the northwest at Elko Park near the summit of Schofield Pass. It is about 2 miles. Be prepared for cold weather.

In view just off the road between Marble and Crystal is **Lizard Lake** (10,000 ft; 3 ac). Stocked and usually well fished, it is changing from a rainbow to a brook trout fishery.

Beaver Lake (7950 ft; 30 ac) is a state fishing area at Marble that is stocked with brook and rainbow. It is heavily fished. Boats are allowed, but no motors; also no camping.

Yule Creek is good fishing for cutthroat to 12 inches. It races into the Crystal River from the south at Marble. Walk 4 miles up an old road past the marble quarries and 4 miles more in rough terrain. Four miles past the quarries and off the trail to the northeast, are the **Yule Lakes** (12,000 ft; 3 to 8 ac)

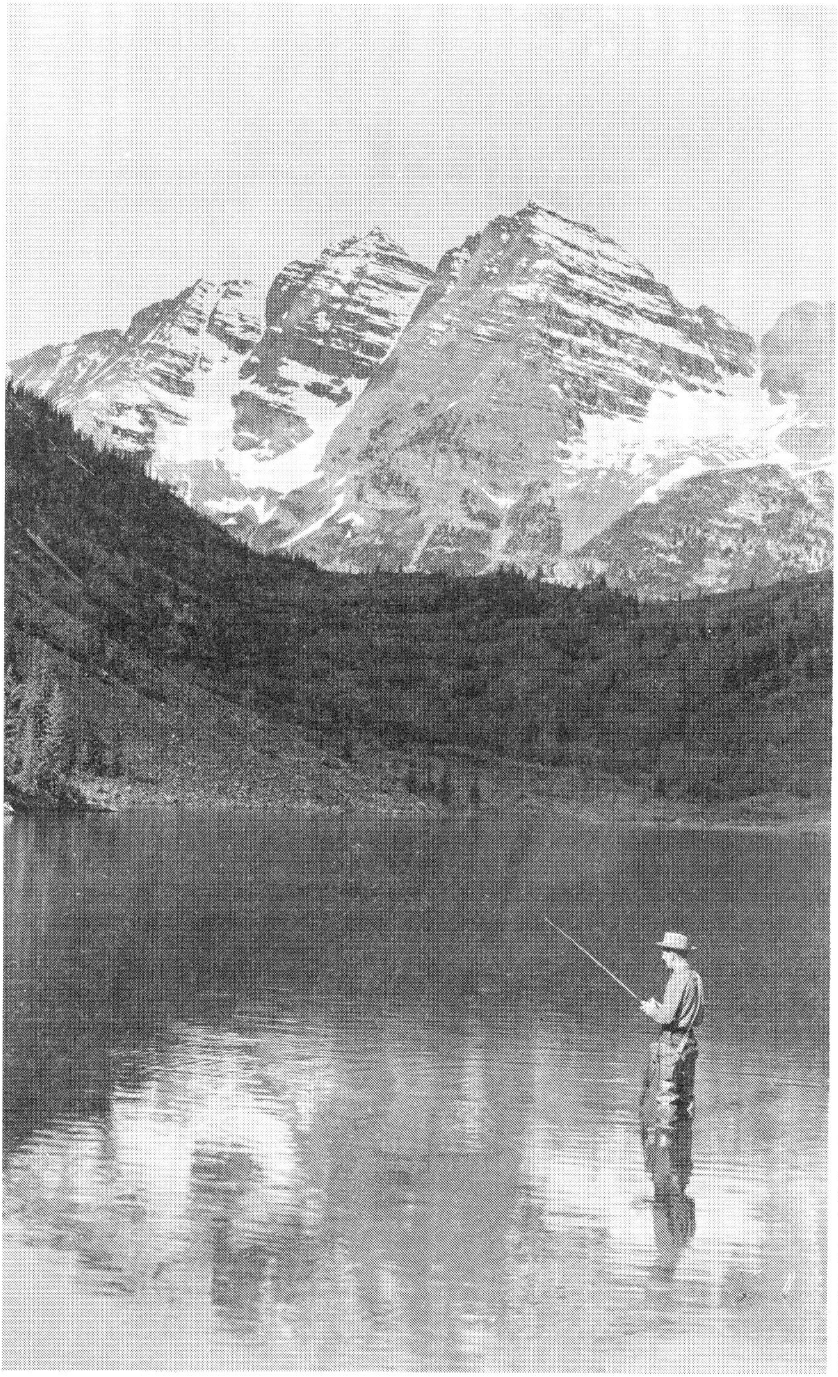

Photo courtesy Colorado Visitors Bureau

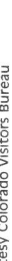

with cutthroat. Fishing is poor, but there may be some fair size trout. Take a dim trail up the second creek coming into Yule Creek above Thompson Flat. The northernmost lake has no fish.

Just below Marble is **McKee Pond,** a 2-acre, put-and-take rainbow fishing hole with rainbow and brook. Heavily fished; stocked by Division of Wildlife.

Along the road about 1.75 miles downstream from Marble, **Island Lake** (7800 ft; 3 ac) is stocked and trout seem to respond best to bait. On down the river to Redstone, there are beaver ponds and some posted stretches. The Forest Service and Division of Wildlife have cooperated on stream improvements to improve fishing.

Lily Lake, a mile below Marble Cemetery, is private and usually winterkills. **Hawk, Big Kline** and **East Creeks** are too precipitous to fish. **Coal Creek** is sterile and a source of pollution to the river.

Avalanche Creek flows into the Crystal north of Redstone. It has two campgrounds a half-mile off Hwy 133. Fishing in it and **Avalanche Lake** (10,700 ft; 6 ac) at its headwaters is poor. The lake usually winterkills. There is a trail up the creek.

The best fishing in the Crystal River drainage is probably in the **Thompson Creeks,** which flow into the river from the west 4.5 miles south of Carbondale. Angling is for rainbow and cutthroat in small streams, reached by taking County Road 108 from the only traffic light in Carbondale on Hwy 133. After a couple of turns, the road veers west to Jerome Park and then south to Thompson Creek, a total distance of about 12 miles. A good map is handy here. A dirt road goes west up the creek into the forest and to **North Thompson Creek.** Back at Jerome Park, going south about 1.5 miles south of the Cemetery Road to the west, a dirt road goes off to the southeast. After 2 miles it comes to the creek and, after another mile, swings west toward **Middle Thompson Creek.** Observe posted signs and gates. Good, clear, swift water for mostly rainbow, but also cutthroat.

Lake Ridge Lakes have no fish.
Prince Creek enters the Crystal just below the fish hatchery south of Carbondale. A road from Hwy 133 to the east parallels it through private land toward Dinkle Lake. The creek, as does **Sopris Creek,** has cutthroat in the upper reaches; brook in the lower. The **Thomas Lakes** (10,200 ft; 13 ac each) at the headwaters of Prince Creek are good for cutthroat. Take 2.5-mile trail south from Dinkle Lake; or 0.25 mile east of the lake a 4-wheel-drive road goes southwest, then south. About a mile up, watch for the trail to Thomas Lakes angling to the west. It's a 1.5-mile walk to access trails between the lakes which are a quarter-mile apart.

Downstream from the hatchery, the Crystal River is on private property to its junction with the Roaring Fork. Fishing in the Roaring Fork, a gold medal stream in this stretch, is with flies and lures only except as noted previously. Most access is through private land and permission to cross it is necessary. Many landowners are accommodating, but a fisherman's poor manners can keep the gates closed and locked. Take the county road from the stoplight in Carbondale north; it follows the river north on the west side of the Roaring Fork to Glenwood Springs. Hwy 82 runs along the east side of the river, but access is by private road.

COLORADO RIVER WEST

West of Glenwood Springs the Colorado River flows past rouge-red cliffs on the south side of the river that give way to dry and irrigated pasture west of New Castle. On the north bank, fruit orchards characterize small acreages. Fishing in the river is surprisingly good; fishermen should use US 6 and the old road on the south side to access the stream. The river has good, long riffles, some boulders and deep pools, and bait fishing or fishing with bait and lures; spoons and spinners can pull in some good size brown, rainbow, round-tailed chub and carp. The river also is home to whitefish. The river is too deep to wade, but there are sandbars and shale-rock stretches that provide some variation to straight bank fishing. An 18-pound brown was landed near Rifle in 1982.

West of Silt the river becomes increasingly muddy and fishing is generally poor except in some isolated stretches. Tributary streams are fair fishing at best except several miles upstream. Land ownership is a mixture of private and Bureau of Land Management, so inquiry for information and permission is prudent.

CANYON CREEK

About 6.5 miles west of Glenwood Springs on I-70, **Canyon Creek** enters the Colorado River from the north. Canyon Creek is a small, brushy creek rated fair for small brook and cutthroat. About 4 miles north of the highway, Canyon Creek forks in several directions with its tributaries spreading near the boundary of the Flat Tops Wilderness. Reach the headwaters and the wilderness boundary by taking a dirt road north from 5 miles east of the town of New Castle at Interchange 109 on I-70.

East Canyon Creek is an 8-mile-long tributary feeding into Canyon Creek from the northeast. It offers the same type of fishing as the main stream. At its headwaters is **Blue Lake** (10,406 ft; 9 ac) which is rated fair to good for brook to 15 inches. Access is by hiking 5 miles from the road that follows the main stream; or by driving on a 4-wheel-drive road from Glenwood Springs. Inquire locally.

To the northwest, **Adams Lake** (10,804 ft; 40 ac) feeds the west fork of Canyon Creek. The lake is rated fair for 12-inch brook, cutthroat and rainbow, with some lunkers taken occasionally. Access is 6 miles by 4-wheel-drive road from the sign at Heart Lake, near the headwaters of Deep Creek. Heart Lake is accessed via the Deep Creek Road 2 miles north of Dotsero, east at Glenwood Springs.

Possum Creek is another tributary of Canyon Creek and lies farther east than East Canyon Creek. Possum offers fair angling for small brook and some cutthroat. It flows through some posted private land.

ELK CREEK

At New Castle, about 13 miles east of Rifle and 13 miles west of Glenwood Springs, **Elk Creek** enters the Colorado from the northwest. The Buford Road goes northwest another 2.5 miles to **Main Elk Creek** coming in from the north. The road that follows it winds 5 miles to the national forest, then 15 miles more before becoming 4-wheel drive. Access to Main Elk Creek is cross country 3 miles northwest for good fishing for small rainbow.

The Buford Road forks 2.5 miles west of Main Elk Creek. The west fork leads 4 miles to Harvey Gap Reservoir and on to Rifle Creek. The north fork winds 22 miles before intersecting with a road from the east. Cliff Lakes and Meadow Creek Lake are 2.5 and 5 miles, respectively, to the east.

Cliff Lakes (9650 ft; 6 ac) are shallow; easy fishing for 11-inch rainbow and brook. Fishing pressure is heavy. **Meadow Creek Lake** (9550 ft; 55 ac) is rated good for rainbow and brook to 16 inches. There is a campground. Downstream from the reservoir, **Meadow Creek** offers fair to good fishing for 3 miles for small brook, rainbow and a few cutthroat.

Harvey Gap Reservoir (6402 ft; 380 ac) is one of the most promising fisheries in western Colorado. It has rainbow, brown, largemouth and smallmouth bass, channel catfish, crappie and green sunfish. There are brown to 8 pounds and likely larger. Excellent bass fishing. Boats are limited to 20 hp motors. Five-day camping limit. Live bait is permitted. The reservoir can be reached from the Buford-New Castle Road or by good road north from US 6 about 1.5 miles west of Silt and 3 miles east of Rifle. The reservoir is 7 miles north.

RIFLE CREEK

Rifle Creek enters the Colorado River from the north at the town of Rifle. Hwy 325 goes north about 17 miles to Rifle Gap Reservoir and State Recreation Area. It is a fee area. At the reservoir, the road forks, with the west road leading north to Hwy 13, and to the Rio Blanco Store and Meeker. The road east follows East Rifle Creek past Rifle Falls.

Rifle Gap Reservoir (5960 ft; 600 ac) is a clear water reservoir favored by scuba divers. The reservoir is framed in sandstone and shale cliffs; a small herd of buffalo grazes near its west end. On the north shore area are several campsites as well as a boat

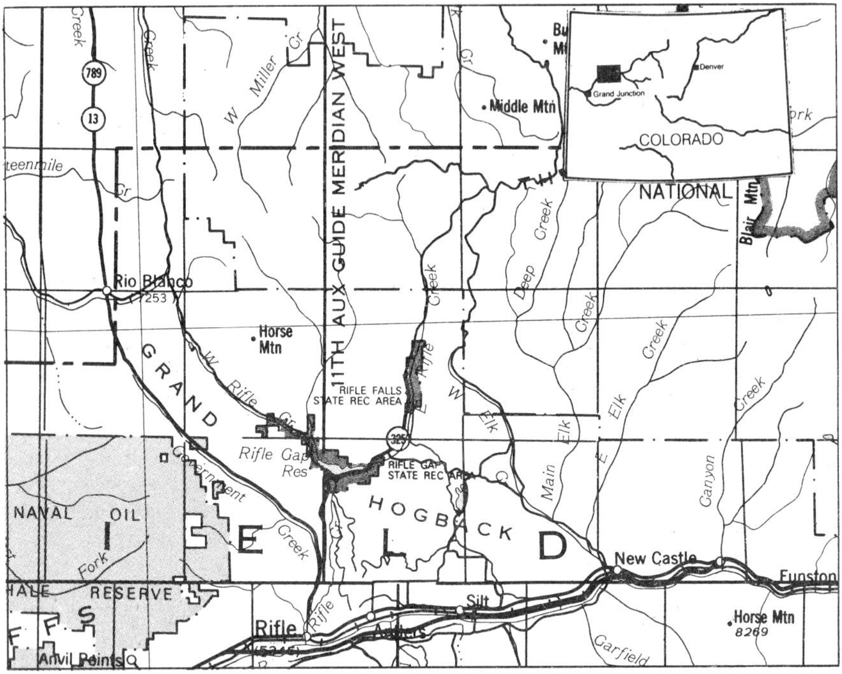

Rifle Creek, Colorado River

ramp and public swimming. Auger-bearing fishermen flock to Rifle Gap Reservoir for ice fishing. Fishing in the reservoir is for German brown and rainbow trout, walleye and bass. (Special restrictions: Daily bag and possession limits for taking of game fish by underwater spearfishing is 2 fish and is permitted from July 16 through March 14 of the following year.) Use of live fish for bait is legal.

Below the reservoir, Rifle Creek flows through private land. Above the reservoir there are about 2 miles of public access to fishing along **Middle** and **West Rifle Creeks.** Fishing pressure is heavy. **East Rifle Creek** enters the reservoir from the northeast through private land for 5 miles up from the reservoir to Rifle Falls State Recreation Area and Fish Hatchery, where fishing on public land is for rainbow and cutthroat. The falls spill in three segments and cloak mysterious caves and rock formations. There is a campground. Four miles north of the falls, the road enters the national forest and 2 miles farther are three campgrounds. The road continues north to intersect at Triangle Park with the Buford-New Castle Road. Meadow Creek Lake is 12 miles northeast off a road that junctions to the east at Hiner Springs. Fishing pressure is heavy.

PARACHUTE CREEK

Parachute Creek joins the Colorado at the town of Parachute (formerly Grand Val-

ley). It comes from a deep canyon to the northwest. A good road provides access to fishing from private land on the lower 7 to 8 miles. Permission to angle for rainbow and brook is needed.

From Parachute, the Colorado River moves south, swinging west past the Roan Cliffs and the town of DeBeque.

Roan Creek enters the Colorado from the northwest at DeBeque. Take a secondary road north from DeBeque. Keep left at the second fork. This road parallels the stream for about 15 miles. Roan offers poor fishing.

West of DeBeque the river enters DeBeque Canyon and some attractive water with mostly rough fish. Fishing pressure is very light. Just below the confluence with Plateau Creek is Island Acres Recreation Area between I-70 and the river. A pond is stocked with rainbow. Handpropelled and sail boats are okay.

PLATEAU CREEK

Plateau Creek is a major tributary feeding into the Colorado from the south. It flows from the east and stretches 25 miles along the valley north of the Grand Mesa. Plateau Creek is 20 to 25 feet wide and is paralleled by the Plateau Valley Road for most of its distance. Plateau offers fishing for rainbow 10 to 11 inches. Below the town of Collbran, it flows through private lands. Above the town of Collbran, access to those areas open to public fishing can be a problem. Inquire locally.

A surfaced road, not the Collbran Road, leaves the north end of Collbran and heads east up a hill. After 7 miles, the road forks; the right fork leads to **Vega Reservoir** (8100 ft; 900 ac). Vega is rated good for rainbow averaging 12-16 inches with some to 3 pounds. Trolling and shore fishing both give good results. It is heavily fished and a popular family outing site.

Entering the Grand Valley east of Grand Junction, the Colorado is tapped severely for irrigation water. Fishing below Roller Dam at Palisade begins to improve in the 2 miles above the confluence with the Gunnison River; fishing is excellent for catfish averaging 1.5 to 2 pounds with some as

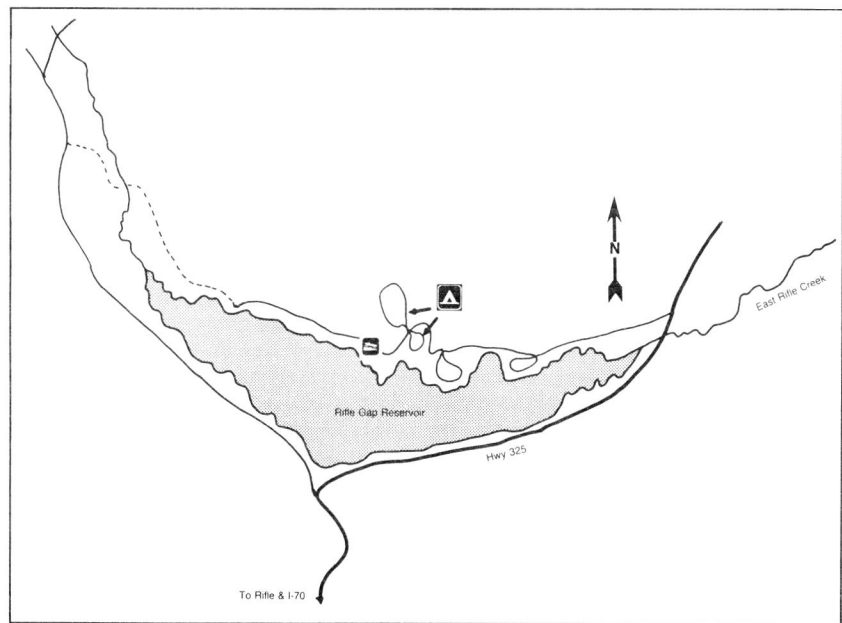

Rifle Gap & Falls State Recreation Area

Colorado River, Grand Mesa

large as 6 pounds. There are also some rainbow, brown, whitefish, razorback suckers, carp and the protected Colorado River squawfish. West of Grand Junction, Highline State Recreation Area offers fishing in **Highline** and **Mack Mesa Lakes** for rainbow, bass, crappie, catfish and walleye. There is a boat ramp, 25-site campground and plenty of welcome shade. Entry fee is $2 per car; campsite is $4 per night. This true oasis is reached by taking Hwy 139 north from Loma for 6 miles. West to the Colorado-Utah state line there are more than 30 miles of river with fishing for the same species. Local inquiry on fishing and access is recommended, but fishing usually is poor to fair, unless you find the "right" spot.

GRAND MESA

Grand Mesa is one of the largest and most scenic flat top mountains in the West. Rising 5000 feet above the Gunnison and Colorado Rivers, its 34,200 acres encompass hundreds of lakes and ponds sprinkled through alpine meadows and pine forests.

The fishing for rainbow, brook, brown and splake can be outstanding. So is the competition for them, unless the angler with topographic map, compass, insect repellent and net hat and gloves is willing to venture off the beaten path.

Portions of "The Mesa" near the roads are almost park-like with paths, horseback riding trails, picnic areas, campgrounds, resorts and summer homes. As one gets into the denser forests of Engelmann and blue spruce, alpine and Douglas fir, aspen and ponderosa pine, amid bogs and brush and rocky ridges, however, the terrain becomes more primitive. Elk, deer, bear, more than 200 species of birds and many smaller creatures may be the angler's companions. But there is no companion as affectionate as the mosquito. Come well prepared.

The two-mile-high oasis rising from the surrounding Colorado Plateau desert attracts thousands of visitors. In winter, the mesa is literally buried in snow—5 and 10 feet and more.

In spring, the melting snow becomes the lifeblood of abundant apple, pear, cherry, peach and apricot orchards, vineyards, and produce fields near Cedaredge, Delta, Palisade, Grand Junction and other communities at the foot of the mesa. Consequently many lakes actually are reservoirs that collect, store and release water through the growing season. Late summer fishermen should inquire locally about water levels in lakes and reservoirs they aim to fish.

There are many campgrounds, which are often full on summer weekends and holidays. Those pulling trailers are advised to inquire locally about the long haul to the mesa top, for many roads are narrow and steep, and overheating of vehicles is common. At campground/trailer park entrances, it's a good idea to stop, park and scout an area on foot just to see whether a trailer, especially a large one, can negotiate the service road.

Grand Mesa is easily reached from the north by turning east off I-70 about 20 miles east of Grand Junction (or about 26 miles west of DeBeque) in DeBeque Canyon. From the south, turn east from US 50 at Delta onto Hwy 92. After 4 miles, turn north at the intersection of Hwy 65.

Most lakes on Grand Mesa are clustered and have similar fishing conditions. Frequent drawdowns of water during the irrigation season causes fishing to vary greatly. Inquire in the town of Mesa and pick up a U.S. Forest Service map of Grand Mesa National Forest. Most of the waters are accessible from Hwy 65 which cuts 25 miles across Grand Mesa, north and south. This description begins at the northwestern edge of the plateau and follows Hwy 65 to the village of Grand Mesa.

Mesa Creek, which flows through Sunset Lake, offers some beaver pond fishing below the lakes. It flows north to enter Plateau Creek. Mesa Creek is brushy and difficult to fish. It is rated fair for 8- to 10-inch rainbow and a few brook.

MESA LAKES

At the top of a hill on the north side of the plateau, **Mesa Lakes,** at the headwaters of Mesa Creek, lie along Hwy 65 about 12 miles south of the town of Mesa. The Mesa Lakes are at an elevation of about 9900 feet and are on both sides of the highway. The

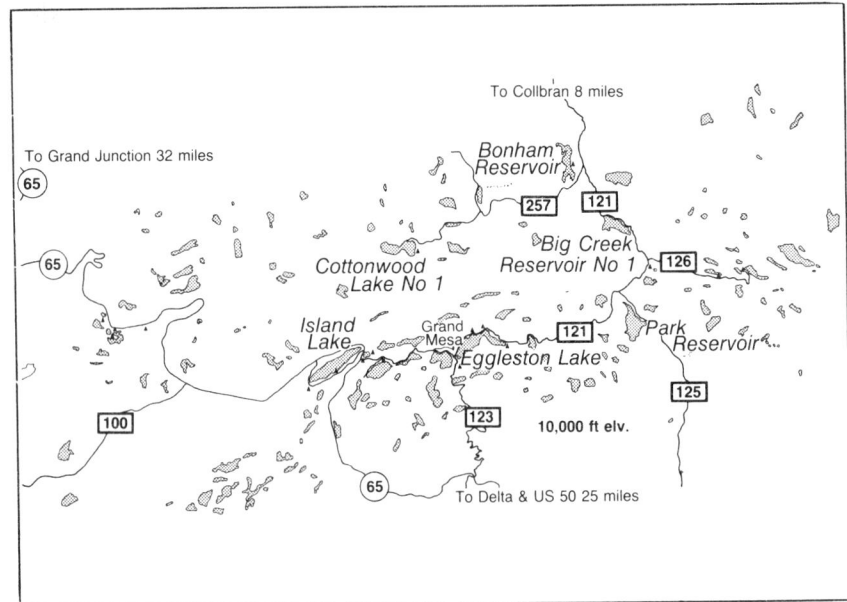

Grand Mesa National Forest

lakes, in light timber, are only a short distance apart. **Mesa Lake** (22 ac), the largest, and **Beaver Lake** (8 ac), near the village of Skyway, receive the greatest fishing pressure, yet still offer the promise of large fish. South of Mesa Lake, **South Mesa Lake** (11 ac) and **Lost Lake** (3 ac) are stocked with catchable rainbow and fingerling brook. Both of these lakes are natural lakes accessible by marked trails from Glacier Springs Picnic Grounds on Mesa Lake; it's a mile to South Mesa Lake and another 0.5 mile to Lost Lake. **Sunset Lake** (15 ac), **Glacier Springs Pond** (2 ac), **Jumbo Lake** (6 ac) and **Water Dog Lake** (20 ac) also are grouped near Skyway. Jumbo and Beaver maintain constant water levels; Sunset, Mesa and Water Dog fluctuate with irrigation demands. With the exception of Lost Lake, boats are available on all lakes.

On Hwy 65 south about 2 miles east from Mesa Lakes, a sign marks the Griffith Lakes to the north. The Griffith Lakes are at about 10,000 feet elevation. A 0.25-mile trail leads to **Griffith Lake** (37 ac), the closest lake. **Middle Griffith Lake** (25 ac), the only other fishery of the group, is located about 100 yards below the dam of Griffith. Both lakes are rated fair, especially in the early season for 9- to 13-inch rainbow, but they are best known for the big browns taken on large wet flies at night. They are reached by trail from Water Dog Reservoir. **West Griffith Lake** and **Monroe and Barnes Reservoirs** usually are drained each year.

Northeast of Griffith Lakes about a mile, the Bull Creek Reservoirs can be reached by trail leaving from the big bend in Hwy 65 about 2 miles east of Mesa Lakes. There are 12 reservoirs in this group, but only five have fish. **Bull Creek Reservoir No. 1** has rainbow to 2 pounds; **No. 2** is stocked with rainbow; and **No. 3** which is drained each year, has no fish. Nos. 1 and 2 are restricted to artificial flies and lures only, and fish less than 12 inches must be returned to the water. **Bull Creek Reservoirs Nos. 4 and 5** and **Bull Basin Reservoir** are east of Bull Creek Reservoirs Nos. 3 and 4, and are rated poor due to low waters.

About 2.25 miles south of the Bull Creek Reservoirs trailhead on Hwy 65, Lands End Road comes from the west to junction with Hwy 65. Turn west on this road for access to some of the western plateau lakes. Most of the lakes run dry at times, but **Carson Lake** (10,000 ft), in a steep-sided bowl at the headwaters of the westerly flowing Kannah Creek, has been a good producer of brook to 12 inches, a few rainbow and 12-inch cutthroat. No boats are allowed. **Kannah Creek** flows about 9 miles west off the mesa and eventually empties into the Gunnison River. It has a series of beaver ponds below the Carson dam and is rated good for naturally produced cutthroat and some rainbow. Turn south off the Lands End Road onto the Carson Road to reach the lake.

ISLAND LAKE

Back on Hwy 65 traveling east from the Lands End Road, the highway skirts the largest lake on the Mesa. **Island Lake** (10,250 ft; 199 ac) is a good trolling and fly lake for 10-inch rainbow (though sometimes they are taken up to 18 inches) and brook. A few large splake (cross between mackinaw and brook) are taken. Grand Mesa Lodge has resort accommodations including several campgrounds. Rental boats are available. Electric motor, sail or hand-powered boats are permitted. No outboards. **Little Gem Reservoir** (10,000 ft; 9 ac) lies southwest of Island Lake less than 0.25 mile, and is accessible by the road that encircles Island Lake. It is rated poor for 9- to 11-inch rainbow. **Rim Rock Lake** (10,100 ft; 12 ac), southwest of Little Gem, is often dry.

Beyond Rim Rock Lake about 2 miles southwest on the forest road from Island Lake, the Granby Reservoirs at 10,300 feet are spread through a wide valley. The lakes and reservoirs are identified by numbers, which appear on the dams. Several of the dozen lakes are nearly dry during the late summer months. However, **Granby Reservoir No. 5** is rated good for big brown and rainbow from 8 inches to 6 pounds. **Nos. 6 and 7,** which are combined, are rated poor for small rainbow, though there are large ones to 6 pounds reported. **No. 9** is not stocked. **No. 12** is rated good for rainbow from 12 inches to 3 pounds. Fishing after dark with big flies has resulted in catches of two pounders. No boats are available.

At the southwest end of the Granby Reservoirs, the four Battlement Lakes are at about 10,000 feet elevation. Only **Big Battlement Lake** (12 ac) and **Little Battlement** (11 ac) have fish. Signs on the dams distinguish the lakes. Both of these lakes are rated fair to good for brook and rainbow.

ACCOMMODATIONS

At the northern end of Island Lake, Hwy 65 turns south and parallels the eastern shore for a short distance. After about 0.25 mile, it is intersected by a good paved road to the east which leads to the village of Grand Mesa and the eastern end of the mesa itself.

Carp Lake (10,250 ft; 10 ac) lies northeast of Hwy 65 at the road junction to Grand Mesa village. It is rated fair to good for 10-inch rainbow; best results are with bait. No motor-propelled boats or rafts are permitted. Less than a mile northeast, **Mosquito Lake** (15 ac) is rated good for 8- to 10-inch rainbow. South of Carp Lake about 2 miles, east of Hwy 65, **Ward Creek Reservoir** (30 ac) is rated fair for brook and rainbow averaging 10 inches.

Southeast of Carp Lake about 0.25 mile is deep **Ward Lake** (10,300 ft; 55 ac). Ward is rated good for 8- to 16-inch rainbow. A rough Forest Service road leads around the west side to the south about 0.25 mile to **Deep Slough Reservoir** (10,000 ft; 27 ac).

Next to Ward Lake to the east is **Alexander Lake** (10,300 ft; 35 ac), rated fair for 12-inch rainbow. North of Alexander and north of the road is **Hotel Twin Lake** (10,350 ft; 25 ac). The name Twin Lake derives from the fact that at low water this lake becomes two. It is heavily fished and rated fair to good for rainbow and brook to 14 inches. A rough road goes around the north side of the lake to the west to **Matt Arch Slough** or **Arch Lake.** A trail from the parking lot at the east end of Twin Lake leads 0.25 mile northeast to **Forrest Lake,** sometimes called **Upper Hotel Lake** (10,300 ft; 25 ac). It is rated fair for brook to 10 inches. No boats are available on this lake. A 1.5-mile trail northeast from Forrest Lake leads to **Butts Lake** (10,500 ft; 18 ac), one of the prettiest lakes on Grand Mesa. It offers lots of sport for 10- to 12-inch cutthroat. No motor-propelled boats or rafts are permitted.

> *Low light conditions offer the best cover for fish and the best fishing for man. Twilight, clouds, and wind all disturb the water surface and scatter light rays. Fish stay under cover to protect themselves and to ambush others. Drop your line for trout in the shadows of undercut banks, fallen trees and large boulders.*

West of the village of Grand Mesa on the south side of the highway is **Baron,** or **Barren, Lake** (10,200 ft; 30 ac), rated good for rainbow and brook from 10 to 12 inches.

At Baron Lake, a road goes south to Hwy 65 and off the mesa. A northeast road leads to more lakes and eventually to the town of Collbran in the valley north of the Grand Mesa.

On the road south from Grand Mesa village to Cedaredge and Delta, the first lake encountered is **Reed Reservoir** (10,000 ft; 15 ac). Reed is rated good for 8- to 10-inch rainbow; however, it often is dry by late summer.

Kiser Creek drains Reed and other lakes near the village of Grand Mesa. **Kiser Slough Reservoir** (10,000 ft; 18 ac) is about 0.5 mile south of Reed. It is fair to good fishing for rainbow to 15 inches. Boats are allowed on this lake, but it, too, is often drained by irrigation draws.

Across the road to the east from Baron Lake is **Eggleston Lake,** an elongated lake stretching along the south side of the Collbran Road. Eggleston (10,200 ft; 130 ac) is rated good for rainbow from 10 to 12 inches, but some to 3 pounds. The double limit rainbow trout stamp is applicable here. Boats are available, and campsites are nearby. On the north side of the road, a trail leads about 0.25 mile from Crag Crest Campground to **Upper Eggleston Lake** (10,400 ft; 25 ac), which is good fishing for cutthroat and brook to 16 inches and 12- to 13-inch rainbow. No boats are available.

A half mile east of Eggleston, **Youngs Creek Reservoir** is at the head of Youngs Creek on the south side of the road. The reservoir (10,300 ft; 25 ac) is along the road and can be good for rainbow. Best fishing is before July 4.

TRICKLE PARK RESERVOIR

As the Collbran (or Trickle Park Road) continues east and begins to cut north, it passes **Trickle Park Reservoir** (9950 ft; 80 ac). The reservoir is 0.5 mile from the road to the southeast, but can be seen from the road. It is good fishing for rainbow averaging 12 inches. About a half-mile north, **Vela Reservoir** (10,150 ft; 25 ac) lies just south of Trickle Park Campground. It is a put-and-take lake, rated good for 8- to 11-inch rainbow.

Near Trickle Park Campground, a good dead-end road travels east to the Twin Lakes and Weir and Johnson Reservoir. **Twin Lakes** (10,400 ft; 18 ac) are good fishing for small rainbow. They lie on the north side of the road, about 2 miles east of Trickle Creek Campground. Beyond the Twin Lakes, **Weir and Johnson Reservoir** (10,250 ft; 60 ac) is rated good to excellent for small brook.

South of Twin Lakes and Weir and Johnson Reservoir, and accessible only by foot from these lakes or from the Trickle Park Reservoir, is **Bonita Reservoir** (10,000 ft; 64 ac), which has fair fishing for cutthroat to 15 inches; motor-propelled boats and rafts are not permitted. Southeast of Bonita 0.25 mile is **Cedar Mesa Reservoir** (9950 ft; 35 ac) offering the same type of fishing; and farther to the northeast about a mile over a hill, **Cole Reservoir No. 1** (10,400 ft; 25 ac) is rated good for cutthroat and rainbow averaging 10-12 inches.

About 0.75 mile northeast off Weir and Johnson Reservoir, accessible by trail, is **Leon Lake** (10,500 ft; 85 ac), a long and narrow lake that is one of the most consistent trout producers on the Mesa. The upper end, where Leon Creek enters, usually offers the best fishing. Trolling usually is successful. No boats are available. It receives heavy fishing pressure, yet remains rated good for brook to 14 inches. Two small lakes about a mile west of Leon, **Finney Cuts Lakes** (10,500 ft; 6 ac) are rated fair for 10- to 12-inch cutthroat. To the northeast of Leon Lake about a mile is **Colby Horse Park Reservoir** (10,150 ft; 12 ac) which is accessible by the same trail from Weir and Johnson Reservoir. Colby is fair to good fishing for cutthroat averaging 10 inches. Boats are not allowed. Both Leon and Colby Horse Park Reservoir can be reached by a rough 4-wheel-drive road south of Trickle Park Reservoir about 4 miles; or from Vega Reservoir north of the Grand Mesa.

Northeast of Colby about 3 miles are the **Monument Creek Reservoir,** and north of Colby about 2 to 4 miles are **Kenny Creek Reservoir** (9900 ft; 18 ac) and **Youngs Lake** (10,200 ft; 8 ac). These lakes and reservoirs are connected by a network of 4-wheel-drive roads. They are rated fair for rainbow, brook and a few cutthroat. The best access to these lakes is by the 4-wheel-drive road east off of the Collbran Road, about a mile north of Bonham Reservoir. This road swings to the east along Kelly Reservoir and on to Leon Creek. Monument Reservoirs are accessible by trail from Leon Creek.

North of Trickle Park Campground on the Collbran Road, **Big Creek Reservoir No. 1** (10,100 ft; 50 ac) is on the west shoulder of the road. It is rated fair in the summer for 10-inch rainbow; good in the fall.

North of Big Creek Reservoir about 1.5 miles, **Bonham Reservoir** (9850 ft; 64 ac) is rated fair to good for 10- to 14-inch rainbow and cutthroat, with best fishing results in early season. A good road follows around the reservoir's north end about 5 miles to Cottonwood Lakes, which are less than a mile east of the Griffith, Bull and Mesa lakes discussed earlier.

COTTONWOOD LAKES

Silver Lake (10,150 ft; 11 ac), to the far southeast of the Cottonwood group, is good fishing for 12-inch cutthroat. This lake can be reached from the Bonham Reservoir by trail, or by taking County Road 257 from the Bonham Lake Campground. **Neversweat Reservoir** (10,050 ft; 17 ac), to the northwest of Silver Lake about a mile, is fair fishing for rainbow and brook averaging 14 inches. Other lakes within a 2-mile radius

are: **Kitson Reservoir** (10,050 ft; 28 ac), rated fair for brook and rainbow averaging 10 inches; **Cottonwood No. 5** (10,000 ft; 20 ac), which offers slow fishing for 16- to 19-inch brook and cutthroat; **Cottonwood No. 4** (10,240 ft; 28 ac), rated fair, especially late season, for 10- to 12-inch rainbow; **Lily Lake** (10,250 ft; 6 ac) is rated fair for 14-inch rainbow and brook, and reportedly is best in late season with flies; **Cottonwood Lake No. 1** (10,150 ft; 85 ac) is rated fair for rainbow and brook averaging 12 inches; **Cottonwood Lake No. 2** (10,050 ft; 18 ac) has no fish; and **Currier** (9900 ft; 15 ac) and **Blackman** (9600 ft; 15 ac) **Reservoirs** at the north of the Cottonwoods have some rainbow, but are rated poor.

All of these lakes and reservoirs are at the headwaters of Cottonwood Creek which flows north into Plateau Valley. Cottonwood Creek has some beaver ponds below the reservoirs. Access to the lower reaches of the stream is from Molina. □

U.S. FOREST SERVICE DISTRICT RANGER STATIONS

Arapaho National Recreation Area
Shadow Mountain Village
US Hwy 34
Grand Lake, CO 80447   303/627-3451

Dillon Ranger District
Arapaho National Forest
Dillon Visitor Information Center
101 W. Main, Drwr. Q
Frisco, CO 80443   303/668-5404
                              303/668-3314

Middle Park Ranger District
Arapaho National Forest
210 South 6th, P.O. Box 278
Kremmling, CO 80459   303/724-3244

Holy Cross Ranger District
White River National Forest
401 Main, P.O. Box 190
Minturn, CO 81645   303/827-5715

Eagle Ranger District
White River National Forest
Fifth & Walls Sts., P.O. Box 720
Eagle, CO 81631   303/328-6388

Sopris Ranger District
White River National Forest
620 Main, P.O. Box 248
Carbondale, CO 81623   303/963-2266

Aspen Ranger District
White River National Forest
806 W. Hallam
Aspen, CO 81611   303/925-3445

Rifle Ranger District
White River National Forest
1400 Access Rd.
Rifle, CO 81650   303/625-2371

Collbran Ranger District
Grand Mesa National Forest
P.O. Box 338
Collbran, CO 81624   303/487-3249

Grand Junction Ranger District
Grand Mesa-Uncompahgre National Forests
Federal Bldg., 4th and Rood Ave.
P.O. Box 1150
Grand Junction, CO 81501   303/242-8211

DOW FISHING LEASES

BLUE RIVER
Borysow lease
Location: 7 miles north of Silverthorne (0.75 mi of river)

BLUE RIVER
Division of Wildlife-owned
Location: at inlet to Green Mountain Reservoir (2.4 mi of river)

EAGLE RIVER
Horn lease
Location: Beginning 1 mile east of Eagle, then east 6.33 miles (3.5 mi of river north side only, 2.33 mi of river both sides)

U.S. Forest Service campgrounds

U.S. Forest Service compilation was current as of 1985.

Asterisks denote fee areas. Some campgrounds are open only Memorial Day weekend through Labor Day. Below freezing weather could mean no water supply.

COLORADO RIVER

ARAPAHO NATIONAL FOREST
Headquarters: Federal Bldg., 301 S. Howes, Box 1366, Fort Collins, CO 80521

Campground name	Elevation	No camp sites	Travel trailers	Drinking water	Length of stay (days)	Location and directions
Idlewild*	9000	24	Yes	Yes	14	1 mi NW of Winter Park on US 40
Robbers Roost	9700	9	Yes	No	14	4.5 mi S of Winter Park on US 40
Byers Creek	9400	6	Yes	No	14	6.5 mi SW of Fraser on St. Louis Creek road
St. Louis Creek	9000	18	Yes	Yes	14	2.8 mi SW of Fraser on St. Louis Creek road
Meadow Creek	8500	5	Yes	No	14	3.5 mi NE of Tabernash on forest road

Tabernash	8600	20	Yes	No	14	3.5 mi NW of Tabernash on US 40
Denver Creek	8600	22	Yes	No	14	11 mi NW of US 40, 3 mi NW of Granby
Sawmill Gulch	8500	5	Yes	Yes	14	8.8 mi NW of US 40, 3 mi NW of Granby
South Fork*	9000	28	Yes	Yes	14	19.6 mi SW of Parshall on county highway and forest road
Horseshoe*	8700	7	Yes	Yes	14	17 mi SE of Parshall on county highway
Sugar Loaf*	9000	17	Yes	Yes	14	20.3 mi SE of Parshall on county highway and forest road
Peak One*	9100	79	Yes	Yes	10	1.5 mi SE of Frisco on Colo. 9
Prospector*	9100	108	Yes	Yes	10	3.5 mi S of Dillon on county highway
Blue River	8400	20	Yes	No	10	9 mi NW of Dillon on Colo. 9
Heaton Bay*	9100	76	Yes	Yes	10	2.5 mi NE of Frisco on US 6 and county hwy
Rainbow Lake	9100	5	Yes	No	10	Off Colo. 9, 2 mi E of Frisco
Frisco Marina	9000	55	Yes	No	10	On Colo. 9, 1 mi E of Frisco
Sentinel Island	9000	13	No	No	10	2 mi NE of US 6 by boat, .5 mi E of Frisco
Snake River	9000	65	Yes	No	10	On US 6, 3 mi E of Dillon
Frisco Bay	9000	55	Yes	No	10	On Colo. 9, 1 mi E of Frisco
Blue River Inlet	9000	48	Yes	No	10	On Colo. 9, 3 mi E of Frisco
Giberson Bay	9000	48	Yes	Yes	10	On US 6, 2 mi N of Frisco
Windy Point	9100	61	Yes	No	10	6 mi E of Dillon off US 6
Cataract Creek	8600	4	Yes	No	10	15.4 mi S of Kremmling on Colo. 9 and county highway

WHITE RIVER NATIONAL FOREST
Headquarters: Old Federal Bldg., Box 948, Glenwood Springs, CO 81601

Sweetwater Lake	7700	9	Yes	Yes	14	15.3 mi W of Burns on county highway
Blodgett*	8900	6	Yes	Yes	10	On US 24, 3.6 mi S Redcliff
Gore Creek*	8700	17	Yes	Yes	10	On US 170, 5.6 mi E of Vail

COLORADO RIVER

Campground name	Elevation	No camp sites	Travel trailers	Drinking water	Length of stay (days)	Location and directions
Half Moon	10,000	7	Yes	Yes	10	On US 24, 6 mi S of Minturn
Homestake	8800	6	Yes	No	10	On US 24, 2 mi S of Redcliff
Hornsilver*	8800	12	Yes	Yes	10	On US 24, 1.5 mi S of Redcliff
Tigiwon*	9900	6	Yes	Yes	10	4.5 mi S of Minturn by forest road
Black Lakes	10,500	6	Yes	Yes	10	On US 6 and I-70 10.7 mi SE of Vail
Fulford Cave	9600	6	Yes	Yes	14	14.1 mi SE of Eagle by county highway and forest road
Yeoman Park	9000	15	Yes	Yes	14	13 mi SE of Eagle by county highway and forest road
Deep Lake	10,500	21	Yes	No	14	47.2 mi NE of Glenwood Springs by US 6 and 24, county highway and forest road
Klines Folly	10,200	4	Yes	No	14	14.8 mi N of Glenwood Springs on US 6 and 24, county and forest roads
Supply Basin	10,200	6	Yes	No	14	14.7 mi N of Glenwood Springs off US 6 and 24
Avalanche	7400	10	Yes	No	14	13 mi S of Carbondale by Colo. 133 and forest road
Bogan Flats*	7600	37	Yes	Yes	14	22 mi S of Carbondale by Colo. 133 and forest road
Janeway	6800	9	Yes	No	14	11 mi S of Carbondale by Colo. 133
Redstone*	7200	24	Yes	Yes	14	14 mi S of Carbondale by Colo. 133
Chapman*	8800	85	Yes	Yes	14	21.3 mi E of Basalt by county highway
Elk Wallow	9000	8	Yes	No	14	22.5 mi E of Basalt by county highway
Mollie B*	7800	26	Yes	Yes	14	On Ruedi Reservoir, 15.5 mi E of Basalt by Hwy 104
Little Maud*	7800	22	Yes	Yes	14	On Ruedi Reservoir, 15.5 mi E of Basalt by Hwy 104
Little Mattie*	7800	20	Yes	Yes	14	On Ruedi Reservoir, 15.5 mi E of Basalt by Hwy 104
Difficult*	8000	47	Yes	Yes	5	On Colo. 72, 4.9 mi SE of Aspen
Lincoln Gulch	9700	7	Yes	No	5	On Colo. 82, 9 mi SE of Aspen

Campground name	Elevation	No camp sites	Travel trailers	Drinking water	Length of stay (days)	Location and directions
Lost Man	10,700	9	Yes	No	10	On Colo. 82, 14.2 mi SE of Aspen
Silver Bar	8300	4	No	Yes	1	3.6 mi SW of Aspen of forest road
Silver Bell	8400	4	Yes	No	3	6.2 mi SW of Aspen on forest road
Silver Queen	9100	6	Yes	Yes	3	7.3 mi SW of Aspen on forest road
Maroon Lake*	9600	43	Yes	Yes	3	9.2 mi SW of Aspen on forest road
Weller	9200	11	Yes	No	5	On Colo. 82, 11.5 mi SE of Aspen
Portal	10,700	7	Yes	No	10	17 mi SE of Aspen on Colo. 82 and forest roads
Little Box Canyon	7600	4	Yes	Yes	14	18.9 mi N of Rifle by Colo. 325 and forest road
Three Forks	7600	4	Yes	Yes	14	18.4 mi N of Rifle by Colo. 325 and forest road

GRAND MESA NATIONAL FOREST
Headquarters: 11th and Main Streets, Box 138, Delta, CO 81416

Campground name	Elevation	No camp sites	Travel trailers	Drinking water	Length of stay (days)	Location and directions
Weir and Johnson	10,500	12	Yes	No	14	11 mi E of Colo. 65, 16 mi N of Cedaredge
Fish Hawk	10,200	5	Yes	Yes	14	6 mi E of Colo. 65 & 12 mi N of Cedaredge
Carp Lake*	10,300	20	Yes	Yes	14	On Colo. 65, 16 mi N of Cedaredge
Cottonwood Lake*	10,100	42	Yes	Yes	14	15 mi SW of Collbran by forest road
Valley View*	10,200	8	Yes	Yes	14	On Colo. 65, 16 mi N of Cedaredge
Twin lake	10,300	13	Yes	No	14	10 mi E of Colo. 65, 16 mi N of Cedaredge
Crag Crest*	10,100	11	Yes	Yes	14	3.5 mi E of Colo. 65, 16 mi N of Cedaredge
Eggleston Lake*	10,100	6	Yes	Yes	14	3.5 mi E of Colo. 65, 16 mi N of Cedaredge
Island Lake*	10,300	42	Yes	Yes	14	On Colo. 65, 18 mi N of Cedaredge
Kiser Creek	10,100	12	Yes	No	14	3 mi E of Colo. 65, 16 mi N of Cedaredge
Little Bear*	10,200	40	Yes	Yes	14	On Colo. 65, 17 mi N of Cedaredge
Trickle Park	10,100	6	Yes	No	14	8 mi E of Colo. 65, 17 mi N of Cedaredge
Ward Lake*	10,200	27	Yes	Yes	14	1 mi E of Colo. 65, 16 mi N of Cedaredge

Arkansas River brown trout haven

Adjacent communities:
Leadville, Buena Vista, Salida, Canon City, Florence, Pueblo.

Principal Highways:
U.S. 24, 50; Colo. 306, 162, 69, 96, 165.

Fishing the Arkansas River is undergoing change, and some of the change seems to be for the worse. It's hoped that other changes are for better fishing. Fortunately, the scores of adjacent lakes and streams continue to be the mainstay of superb angling in the midst of spectacular Rocky Mountain scenery.

The extent of harm to fishing from polluted water that drains from abandoned mines is still being determined. The large volumes of water that have diluted the drainage for the past 15 years are being diverted through different channels, leaving about 16 miles of the river with diminished fish populations, as will be described.

More cheering are the stream improvements to boost brown trout angling, efforts to increase the wild rainbow trout populations and annual instead of biannual stocking of lakes and streams with rainbow and Pike's Peak cutthroat trout. Also, the gold medal ranking of stretches of the river for premium trophy-size trout fishing continues.

Turquoise Lake, Twin Lakes, Clear Creek Reservoir and Pueblo Reservoir are heavily fished as they offer marvelous angling from boat and shore.

The Arkansas begins its way to the Mississippi as a group of small, brush-lined creeks along the Continental Divide near Leadville. West of the river, snow-crowned 14,000-foot peaks spawn scores of clear streams, many of which offer excellent cutthroat and rainbow trout fishing.

LEADVILLE VICINITY

The mountains have scores of lakes, mostly with brook and cutthroat trout, spectacular scenery, and the physical challenge of getting to where the fish are.

Twin Lakes, Turquoise Lake and Pueblo Reservoir offer fine trolling and boat fishing, and the Royal Gorge has brown trout fishing for the sure-footed.

Releases of water from Turquoise Lake as part of the Fryingpan-Arkansas Project, the Homestake Water Project and others, make the flow of water in the Arkansas unpredictable, especially in spring and summer. One morning it will be running bank full and by midafternoon it will be down a foot or more; and vice versa. While the trout manage this (especially the fall-spawning brown), the caddis fly hatch and other key elements in the food chain have been damaged. The situation is being watched closely

ARKANSAS RIVER

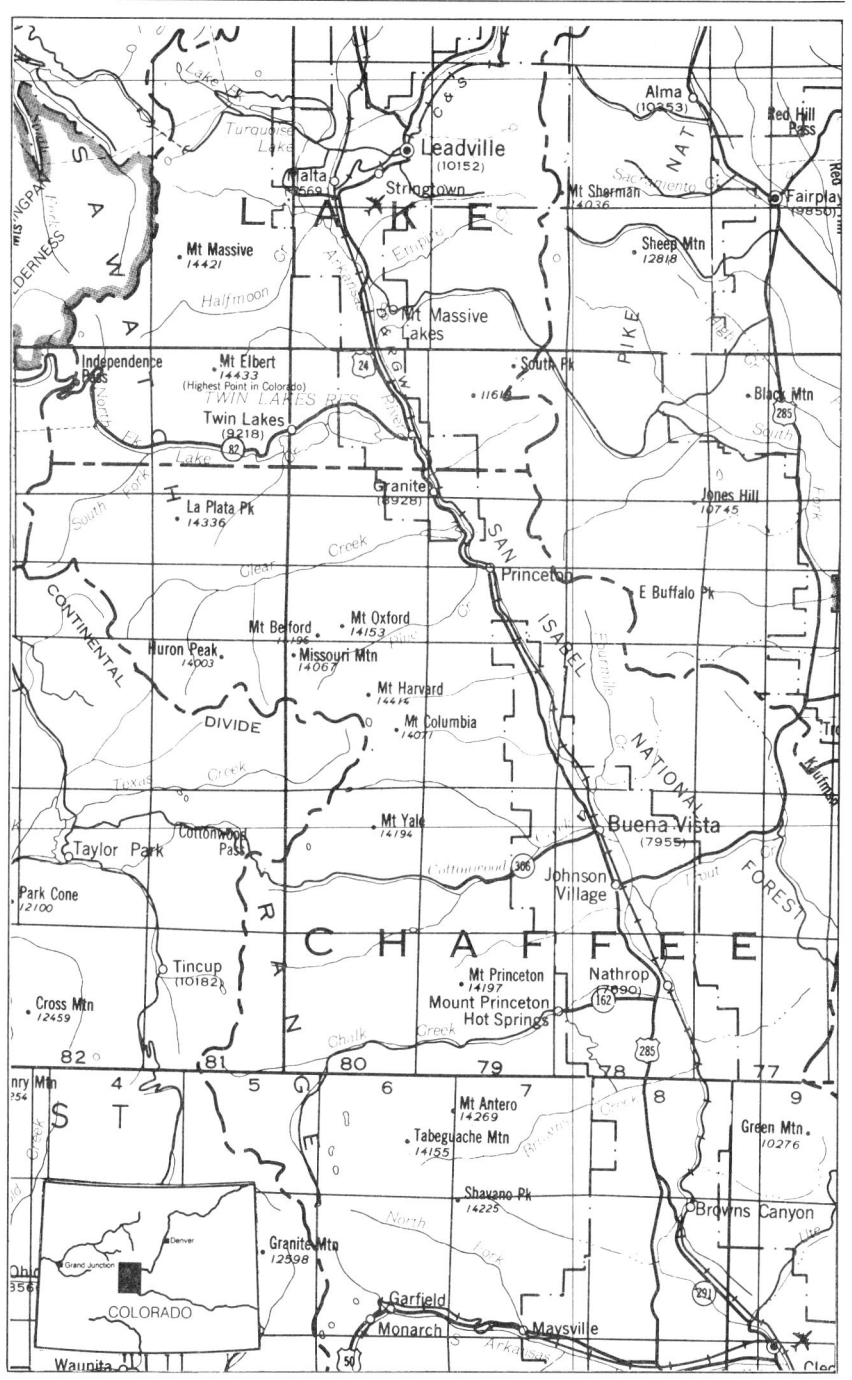

Upper Arkansas River

by biologists.

Along US 50 from the stockyard bridge at Salida downstream 28 miles to Fernleaf Gulch, the Arkansas is full pools, riffles and boulders, and is classified as a gold medal trout water. DOW shocking revealed the deep holes to be without brown trout. Instead they were found in aquatic cover elsewhere in the river. Upstream from Salida, the river from Gas Creek to Fourmile Creek and downstream from Salida from Texas Creek to 1.5 miles above Parkdale are wild trout waters. The river is not stocked above Canon City.

East-flowing streams from the Sangre de Cristo Mountains are described in this chapter.

East Fork of the Arkansas rises on the southside of Fremont Pass and, for 10 miles, runs along Hwy 91 to Leadville. It is a small brushy stream with brook trout. About 4.5 miles from the pass, a dirt road leaves the highway going west up a rough 4-wheel-drive road 2.5 miles to **Buckeye Lake** (11,900 ft; 2 ac), where there is fair fishing for cutthroat. Two miles northwest of Leadville, the East Fork merges with south-flowing **Tennessee Creek** to form the Arkansas River. **West Tennessee Creek** flows east out of the Holy Cross Wilderness to join Tennessee Creek coming south from Tennessee Pass along US 24, about 7 miles northwest of Leadville. A road through some private land roughly follows the stream to the wilderness boundary. Both creeks have brook and rainbow. The old road in the wilderness may be hiked 0.75 mile to the first of the **West Tennessee Lakes** (11,800 ft; 15 ac) and, a half-mile farther, a 15-acre lake. Fishing in both is for cutthroat and brook.

In that vicinity, **Deckers Lake** (11,350 ft; 14 ac) is reached by turning west from US 24 about 6 miles north of Leadville at Homestake Trout Club-Sylvan Lakes signs. A dirt road, sometimes closed off and padlocked, goes southwest up Longs Gulch to the wilderness boundary. Hike from the end of the road 0.5 mile upcreek on trail to the lake to fish for cutthroat. Lakes and ponds by the road are private, as are **Sylvan Lakes** to the north.

Northeast of Homestake Peak, **Slide Lake** (11,725 ft; 35 ac) is a deep lake sometimes called **Homestake Lake.** It is on the wilderness boundary. A rough road leads to it from Hwy 24, turning west at the south foot of Tennessee Pass. Take the first right-hand gravel road up through timber almost a mile, then left at the big green garage. Lake is about 5 miles from the highway. **East Tennessee Creek** joins the mainstream from the northeast. Very brushy in its lower reaches; pretty water, but only small fish. **Tennessee Creek** flows south on private land through open meadow with some brush, and is fair for brown and brook. Ask ranchers' permission to fish for brook and brown.

TURQUOISE LAKE

The best fishing in the Leadville area is at **Turquoise Lake,** a giant gem at 9869 feet elevation. It is 1650 acres when full. Stocked with rainbow, kokanee and cutthroat, it is heavily fished from boats and from the shore.

There are mackinaw in Turquoise, but they don't reach the size of the 30-plus-pounders at Twin Lakes Reservoir 12 miles to the south. Snake River cutthroat and some brown trout have been planted in the lake with expectations they will thrive. A good paved road leads west 4.5 miles from Leadville to the dam and a paved road circles Turquoise Lake. There are three campgrounds and boat ramps. It is a very popular area year-round, and provides outstanding ice fishing in winter.

Lake Fork Creek feeds into the reservoir from **Timberline Lake** (10,950 ft; 26 ac), 2.5 miles upstream, which has cutthroat and is surrounded by timber. It is in the Holy Cross Wilderness, but take the 4-wheel-drive road from Turquoise Lake's west end to within a mile of Timberline. The creek has brook, and closer to Turquoise Lake, rainbow and brown.

It is a tough cross country hike through timber and swamp for 2 miles to the southwest of Timberline to **Virginia Lake** (11,500 ft; 7 ac). Up against the Continental Divide, the lake has cutthroat and lots of mosquitoes. It also can be reached by easy walk across 1.5 miles of tundra from Hagerman Pass and then down 800 nearly-vertical feet to the lake.

Also just inside the wilderness a mile north of Turquoise, are **Galena Lake** (11,050 ft; 2 ac), a shallow pond, and **Bear Lake** (11,000 ft; 12 ac), both with cutthroat. A 5-mile-long 4-wheel-drive road leads to within a half-mile of Bear; then hike across the wilderness boundary. The road is off the north side of the Turquoise Lake loop and often is barricaded. **St. Kevin Lake** (11,850 ft; 5 ac) is up the ridge to the northwest of Bear. Follow along the old road to the end and keep on the ridge, up a mile from Bear. St. Kevin has cutthroat.

Along the south side of the reservoir, the old Colorado-Midland railroad grade continues a bumpy 6 miles to the abandoned Busk-Ivanhoe Tunnel and the trailhead to **Native Lake** (11,250 ft; 5 ac), **Windsor Lake** (11,650 ft; 50 ac), **Upper Notch Lake** (12,200 ft; 5 ac) and **Lower Notch Lake** (11,950 ft; 7 ac), sometimes called **Rainbow Lake.** All have cutthroat and are heavily fished. There are some brook, especially in Windsor and in many of the unnamed ponds in the vicinity. A well-marked trail leads from the tunnel parking area. Wildflowers are in abundance here as are wild strawberries. **Hagerman Lake** (11,400 ft; 5 ac) is along an old railroad grade 1.5 miles to the west and appears to be barren. It is very shallow and probably winterkills. **Lake Fork Creek** flows southwest from Turquoise Lake to join the Arkansas on ranch land about 4 miles southwest of Leadville. Lake Fork has fair fishing; some kokanee, brook, rainbow and brown on the lower reaches. The creek has carried heavy volumes of water to the Arkansas as part of the Homestake and Frying Pan-Arkansas water projects for the past 15 years or so. Now these waters brought by tunnel under the Continental Divide to Turquoise Lake are channeled to a man-made forebay at the hydro-electric plant north of Twin Lakes 11 miles to the south.

But the power plant doesn't operate continuously, and one doesn't know when there will be extra water in Lake Fork Creek and the river or when there won't. Fishing for brook and rainbow is unpredictable and usually fair at best.

This same water dilutes poisonous mine drainage water from **California Gulch** south of Leadville near the point where it enters the Arkansas from the east. Without the dilution factor, insects and other food sources for trout, and often fish themselves, perish. The river downstream a dozen miles to Lake Creek, where the Independence Pass road to Aspen (Hwy 82) junctions with Hwy 24, is affected by fluctuating water volumes and erratic changes in its quality.

This same stretch is some of the most accessible and attractive river, because US 24 parallels it. What it offers the fisherman is difficult to say. The four miles of the river between Lake Creek and the Otero intake plant, for water pumped to Colorado Springs, is also to be affected when water from Twin Lakes is released through a channel and conduit instead of down Lake Creek and into the Arkansas.

Division of Wildlife efforts to get California Gulch on the Environmental Protection Agency list of priority cleanup sites has been unsuccessful.

Beautiful, clear **Halfmoon Creek** flows in from behind Mt. Elbert and Mt. Massive. It has many pools and riffles and is stocked with rainbow. A few brook may be found on the upper reaches and a few brown may come up a way from the Arkansas. **Emerald Lake** (10,000 ft; 10 ac) is a put-and-take pond with rainbow.

Emerald and Halfmoon are reached by a good but bumpy gravel road, through private property, that turns south from the westerly Fish Hatchery Road (paved) a half-mile west of US 24 at Malta, 2 miles west of Leadville. Beyond the trailhead for Mt. Massive and Mt. Elbert, the road heading

---

SUGAR LOAFIN'
Destination Campground

- **Good Trout Fishing**
- **Full Hook-up Drive Thrus**
- **Tent Sites in the Pines**

Off US-24 at Mile Post 177 on Rd. 4,
then 4 mi NW

303 Colorado 300 Leadville, CO 80461
(303) 486-1031   Winter (303) 486-1613

upcreek narrows to 4-wheel drive, and then it's hiking. Upper reaches of both branches of the creek are mostly brook-trout fishing. Two miles up **North Halfmoon Creek** are **North Halfmoon Lakes** (12,000 ft; about 5 ac each). They are easy to find to the east on the side of Mt. Massive. The lakes have fair fishing for cutthroat; other lakes in the area are barren. The Halfmoon area is heavily fished, but it is stocked only from Emerald Lake down; the upper reaches generally are poor.

Alongside US 24 about 3.5 miles south of Leadville is **Crystal Lake** (9350 ft; 10 ac). A nice and very popular fishing pond between the highway and railroad track, it is stocked with brook, cutthroat and rainbow, and is heavily fished by both bait and hardware casters. Boats are not allowed.

About three miles farther south on US 24 and to the east are **Big Union Creek,** which parallels the Weston Pass road and is poor fishing, and **Mt. Massive Lakes,** which are private subdivision ponds and not open to public fishing.

TWIN LAKES, LAKE CREEK

At Balltown, southwest of Leadville, Hwy 82 from Aspen and US 24 intersect. Turn west 3 miles to **Twin Lakes Reservoir** (9200 ft; 1700 ac) and **Lake Creek,** which are skirted by Hwy 82. A dam has made the two lakes one, and the fishing is for brown, rainbow, mackinaw, kokanee salmon and an occasional brook. There are boat ramps, picnic grounds and camping on the bench to the north of the lakes, and to the west along Lake Creek. This is a very popular fishery because the mackinaw are in the 30-pound range. All mackinaw less than 20 inches must be returned to the water immediately. The possession limit is one mackinaw. Rainbow trout stamp holders may take two limits. Ice fishing in recent years has been outstanding.

Lake Creek is a fast, full stream through rough country. It is considered dangerous to wade and is a menace to small children, except in its shallower upper reaches. It has stocked rainbow and brook with a few cutthroat near Independence Pass. There are two campgrounds. The creek is heavily fished and fishing is fair to good, especially

Twin Lakes trophy

from midsummer on. The portion of the creek between Twin Lakes and the river is virtually a spillway, though there are some rainbow and brown in the quieter sections of it. The **South Fork of Lake Creek** is polluted and reported poor fishing for brook.

Blue Lake (12,495 ft; 23 ac) is up a rough 4-wheel-drive road north off Hwy 82 that follows on upcreek as the highway switchbacks up the mountain for the final two miles to the summit. Follow the dirt road to the end, then take the trail west a mile to a little stream; follow it to Blue for good cutthroat fishing. **Crystal Lake** (12,475 ft; 8 ac) is south up **Crystal Lake Creek,** about 3 miles south from Lake Creek. Across from Monitor Rock and Twin Peaks Campground, a very steep trail follows the creek on Hwy 82. The creek is reported good fishing for cutthroat.

Willis Gulch is a small creek, brushy on lower levels, that feeds into Lake Creek from the south at the west end of Twin Lakes. At the headwaters of the West Fork is **Willis Lake** (11,800 ft; 22 ac) with cutthroat. It is a steep 5-mile hike along lakeside trail or from the Parry Peak Campground. From the trailhead, keep to the west up the larger stream. Try for rainbow and brown in the creek's lower portions; it's difficult fishing.

CLEAR CREEK RESERVOIR

About 5 miles south of Balltown and 14 miles north of Buena Vista, County Road 120 heads west past Clear Creek Reservoir and up Clear Creek for 18 miles before becoming 4-wheel drive and then trail. It provides access to some spectacular country and fair fishing in the Collegiate Peaks Wilderness to the south for persons willing to hike or ride horseback to it. Not all the streams and lakes have fish.

Clear Creek Reservoir (8875 ft; 170 ac) is a very popular, heavily stocked fishery for boat and shore fishermen. It offers good fishing for rainbow to 14 inches, brown and kokanee; good fishing with lures and bait and trolling. Pike's Peak cutthroat are being put into the reservoir to ascertain their suitability for it. There is a boat ramp, but no overnight camping or open fires in this state wildlife area. There is a campground along the creek immediately above the reservoir.

Clear Creek is a fabulous stream, but offers only fair fishing for rainbow, brook and brown trout and, in the upper reaches, small cutthroat. The lower part meanders through brushy flats; along the lower 5 miles there is some private property where permission to fish should be asked. Then there is forest and open fishing in fast waters, and some canyon sections. The village of Vicksburg is a trailhead for backpacking into the wilderness. Streams feeding into Clear Creek are too steep to fish except at highest elevations. There are several waterfalls. No fishing is allowed in the creek below the reservoir.

North Fork of Clear Creek is reached by trail from the end of the road near Winfield. It has fair angling for brook and small cutthroat. **Alan Lake** (12,100 ft; 2 ac) is 3.5 miles by trail up the North Fork at the headwaters of a small tributary stream coming in from the northwest. The creek enters North Fork just below the beaver ponds. There's no clear trail, and it's a steep hike for cutthroat.

South Fork of Clear Creek offers 5 to 6 miles of similar fishing (and some beaver ponds) along a rough road for 3 miles to the wilderness boundary. At its headwaters are: **Lake Ann** (11,800 ft; 18 ac), 3 miles up a well-defined trail from the end of the road, where fishing is for cutthroat; **Harrison Flat Lake** (12,155 ft; 10 ac); and another small lake a mile northwest of Lake Ann. On the creek a mile below Lake Ann, a stream comes in from the west. It can be followed up to Harrison, which also has cutthroat. Other ponds in the area are shallow and fishless.

To the northeast, **Cloyses Lake** (11,000 ft; 18 ac) is mostly on private land, but a small part of the shoreline is public. There is some rainbow, cutthroat and brook trout fishing. A caretaker usually stays at the lake in summer. The lake is on **Lake Fork Creek,** from where a steep 4-wheel-drive road provides access into the wilderness. The creek has brook and cutthroat in the upper portions.

Two miles south of Clear Creek on US 24, a dirt road goes west to provide access to **Pine Creek,** which has brook in its lower reaches and cutthroat at higher elevations in the Collegiate Peaks Wilderness. A well-defined trail goes 8 miles to **Silver King Lake** (12,600 ft; 16 ac), where there is fishing for temperamental cutthroat. The trail up Pine Creek intersects the north-south Main Range Trail about 3.5 miles up. **Rainbow Lake** (11,650 ft; 5 ac) is about 2 miles to the south. It has cutthroat.

BUENA VISTA AREA

On the east side of the Arkansas, **Fourmile Creek** has rainbow and brown trout in the stream and in beaver ponds at its headwaters, about 8 miles east of US 24. Access is on a dirt road east from the highway 2 miles north of Buena Vista, or from the heart of town. Inquire locally. Road provides access to the Buffalo Peaks area.

North Cottonwood Creek joins the Middle Cottonwood Creek from the northwest 2 miles west of Buena Vista along Hwy 306. Inquire in Buena Vista about road access across private property. The creek has stocked rainbow and brook, and fishing can be good. A rough road goes 10 miles to the wilderness boundary. Three miles inside the wilderness, **Horn Fork Creek** races in from the north. It has cutthroat.

Bear Lake (12,377 ft; 18 ac) is 3 miles up Horn Fork Creek by trail. It has cutthroat. **Anglemeyer Lake** (11,338 ft; 1 ac) has small cutthroat. There's no trail; it's hard to find, even with maps. It is about 1.5 miles down Horn Fork Creek from Bear Lake and 0.25 mile upslope through timber to the west. A small stream flows out of it and joins Horn Fork Creek just above **Kroenke Creek** confluence. **Kroenke Lake** (11,500 ft; 14 ac) has cutthroat. Follow an old trail 2 miles upcreek to the west.

Middle Cottonwood Creek has about 15 miles of fishing for brown, rainbow, brook and, at higher elevations, cutthroat. Hwy 303 to Taylor Park on the west side of the Continental Divide in the Gunnison River drainage parallels the creek most of the way. About 9.5 miles west of Buena Vista, beginning across from **Rainbow Lake,** which is private, the wilderness boundary is just north of the highway. The creek is heavily fished and is stocked. The lower 7 miles or so are on private land, so seek permission to fish for rainbow and brown coming up from the river.

South of Kroenke Lake in the wilderness north of Middle Cottonwood Creek is **Hartenstein Lake** (11,430 ft; 16 ac). The first mile of a 3-mile hike is along an old road along **Denny Creek.** Keep to the west on a good trail. There is fair to good fishing for good size cutthroat. A sign 12 miles west of Buena Vista indicates access a half-mile above Collegiate Peaks Campground.

South off Middle Cottonwood up **Ptarmigan Creek** 4 miles is **Ptarmigan Lake** (12,147 ft; 28 ac). Access is from the highway 2 miles west of Denny Creek along an old logging road and then trail. The lake offers cutthroat fishing.

South Cottonwood Creek joins Cottonwood about 8 miles west of town. A good road parallels it to **Cottonwood Lake** (9500 ft; 43 ac), a state recreation area and campground. The road continues several miles more. The lake has rainbow, cutthroat and brook; the stream has brook, rainbow and cutthroat at higher elevations. It is stocked to within 5 miles of origin and heavily fished. Many small ponds with brook and cutthroat are at higher elevations.

Two miles south of Buena Vista, US 24-285 comes into the Arkansas River Valley from the east. It follows **Trout Creek** for more than 5 miles. The stream, brushy for more than half its length, is stocked with Snake River cutthroat, rainbow, brown and brook and is very heavily fished. Some private land is posted. Access is from US 24-285, 10 miles east of Buena Vista.

Fishing in the Arkansas River south of Buena Vista along US 285 is along meadow and pasture, and permission is needed to cross private property to fish to 2.5 miles below Nathrop, where the river is on BLM land as it enters Browns Canyon. Access is along a road paralleling a railroad track southeast of Nathrop. At the end of the road, walk the railroad right-of-way and the trail beside it for fine fishing for brown trout, especially in autumn. Fishing may be difficult, but some large fish are in the river. Also, the canyon is reached from Hwy 291 where it crosses the river near Salida. This stretch is often loaded with kayaks, inner tubes, rubber boats and other craft used by river runners. Fishermen can be dismayed by the number of them, and most have learned to fish late evening or early morning. Local inquiry is suggested to learn about river races and other water events, especially in spring and early summer when the river runs full.

MT. PRINCETON AREA

Chalk Creek flows into the Arkansas from the west at Nathrop. Just south of town, Hwy 162 proceeds west to Mt. Princeton Hot Springs, Alpine, the upper reaches of the stream, and a passel of high lakes with cutthroat trout fishing. The road goes some 20 miles along old railroad and mining road rights-of-way. Private and forest land is interspersed, and some sections are posted against fishing. Chalk Creek is heavily fished and is stocked with cutthroat, rainbow and brook from St. Elmo down. The lower stretches contain brown. Get permission to fish on private land in the valley. Brushy in many sections, the stream has a good volume of water most of the year. Just east of Alpine, **Baldwin Creek** flows in from the south from **Baldwin Lake**

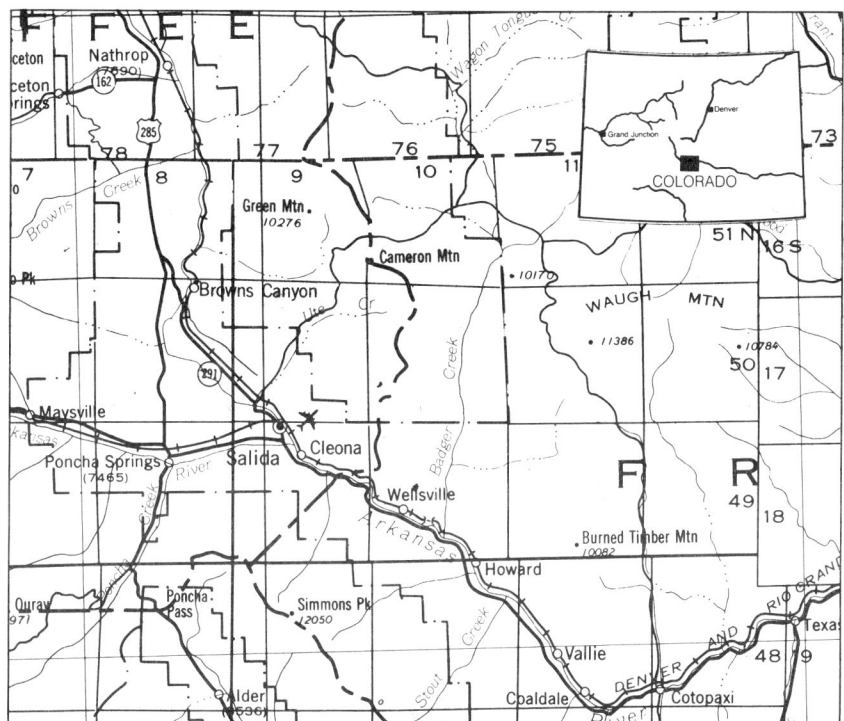

Arkansas River, Texas Creek

(12,000 ft; 21 ac). An old road, unsafe to drive, goes upstream 3 miles. The lake has cutthroat; the stream some brook—maybe. **Fehling's Reservoir** at Alpine is private.

Just east of St. Elmo, **Grizzly Creek** joins Chalk Creek. Upstream 2.5 miles by abandoned mining road is **Grizzly Lake** (11,202 ft; 14 ac) and fishing for some good brook trout to 14 inches, as well as a few cutthroat. There is camping by the lake. The creek's beaver ponds can be lively with brook. **Rosedale Lake** (12,100 ft; 3 ac) is 2 miles south of Grizzly Lake by faint trail up a ridge to the west at the head of the drainage. Rosedale has cutthroat.

At St. Elmo, Chalk Creek comes in from the south and **North Fork Chalk Creek** from the west. Fishing is only fair on North Fork. A road along Chalk Creek leads to **Hancock Lake** (11,500 ft; 53 ac) and **Upper Hancock Lake** (11,580 ft; 7 ac). May have to walk 3 miles along an old road bed due south from the townsite of Hancock for

cutthroat. The upper lake often winterkills, so fishing potential is uncertain. A new outlet for the lake has been built and a spawning bed constructed for emerald lake rainbow, which have been stocked there. Trail goes on over Chalk Pass to the Middle Fork of the South Arkansas River along Hwy 50 east of Monarch Pass.

Pomeroy Lakes are up the ridge to the east of Chalk Creek about 3 miles from Romley Mill site by 4-wheel drive. **Pomeroy Lake** (12,035 ft; 36 ac) and **Upper Pomeroy Lake** (12,250 ft; 38 ac) have cutthroat, with the upper lake producing some trout over 15 inches. The lakes are about a half-mile apart.

Tunnel Lake (12,000 ft; 6 ac) has no fish.

Three miles south of Chalk Creek on US 285 is **Browns Creek.** It has some brook and brown, but fishing is best in the canyon in the national forest west of the highway. Access is south of Mt. Princeton Hot

Springs, or take a graded road west from US 285 a mile south of Centerville (Gas Creek). Go west about 4 miles until road forks; take the south fork about 1.5 miles to creek. The river between **Gas Creek,** a mile south of Nathrop, and **Fourmile Creek,** 5 miles down river, is gold medal trout waer.

MONARCH PASS AREA

At Salida the **South Arkansas River** flows east from Monarch Pass to join the Arkansas. US 50 generally follows the stream for 25 miles. It is stocked with rainbow and brook from Monarch Park down. Brown trout are in the lower reaches below Fooses Creek. Fishing is fair to good, but often difficult because of brush and timber.

West of US 50 at altitudes of 11,000 to 12,000 feet are several lakes with cutthroat trout. They are reached by marked trails from Garfield. The three **Waterdog Lakes** also have brook. **Monarch** and **Grass Lake** have grayling as well as cutthroat. **Hunt Lake** has small cutthroat and **Boss Lake Reservoir** also has a few rainbow. Monarch Lake is in timber a third of a mile north and at a lower elevation than Grassy Lake. It is very difficult to find and it's easy to get lost.

The **Middle Fork South Arkansas River** flows into the mainstream from the north at Garfield. A road parallels it for about 3 miles. It has many cutthroat, especially in beaver ponds. The **North Fork South Arkansas River** is reached via dirt road north from US 50 at Maysville. It has rainbow and brown. Upstream, **Hunkydory Lake** (11,750 ft; 5 ac) has cutthroat. It is 2 miles southwest of Shavano townsite, up a small creek. **North Fork Lake** (11,440 ft; 20 ac) is a reservoir at the end of the road, about 9.5 miles from Maysville. It has cutthroat. **Island Lake** (11,750 ft; 8 ac), west up the feeder creek to the reservoir, has cutthroat. It sometimes winterkills.

Entering the South Arkansas from the south are **Fooses Creek,** which is between Garfield and Maysville, and downstream **Green Creek, Pass Creek, Little Cochetopa Creek** and **Poncha Creek.** Fooses has the runt brook and lots of them. Green has lots of brook above the Cinderella Mine, and brown below and in Willow Creek. It is good fishing, although the trout aren't much more than 10 inches. Pass has brown, cutthroat and brook, and good beaver pond fly fishing. **Pass Creek Lake** (11,300 ft; 5 ac) at the head of Pass Creek has cutthroat and grayling. Little Cochetopa Creek has similar fishing. The creeks are reached by dirt roads and then trails from US 50 west of Poncha Springs.

US 285 south of Poncha Springs to Poncha Pass parallels Poncha Creek for 5 miles, then leaves the stream. The Marshall Pass road follows the creek to its headwaters. The creek has brown and stocked rainbow on its lower reaches, brook and cutthroat at higher elevations. There are some brushy sections, but they are easy to fish. **O'Haver Lake** (9600 ft; 15 ac) is heavily fished for stocked rainbow. Some brook and brown are caught occasionally. There is a campground. **Beaver Creek** is virtually fishless. **Silver Creek** joins Poncha Creek near O'Haver Lake. It has some brook and rainbow. The **Silver Creek Lakes** and stretches of the stream are private property. Foot or horseback traffic only are allowed at the end of the county road. **Starvation Creek,** also a tributary of Poncha, has mainly brook trout.

East of Marshall Pass (10,842 ft) there is access to the north to **Ouray Creek,** with brook trout, and **Grays Creek,** with cutthroat. Trails to them are marked.

BELOW SALIDA

Below Salida for 28 miles to Fernleaf Gulch, the Arkansas River is gold medal trout water that produces big brown trout, as mentioned earlier. Waters are posted with

LAZY J RESORT & RAFTING CO., INC.
Log cabins and motel • float fishing & whitewater rafting • RV & tent campground • swimming pool • cafe • fishing supplies • outfitter services for hunting

An ideal destination resort for sportsmen and their families. Fish from our riverbanks or our rafts. Between Salida & Canon City on U.S. Hwy 50—on the Arkansas river.
P.O. Box 85-F   Coaldale, CO 81222
Dale and Linda Jeffries   303-942-4274

regulations. Artificial flies and lures only for 1.75 miles downstream from Salida. Even experienced fishermen are challenged in this stretch. It is heavily fished, but not stocked. There are some rainbow and brook hooked occasionally. Most fishing is from the highway side of the river. It is not wadable. In the 7.5 miles between Stockyard Bridge and Badger Creek, fishing is limited to artificial flies and lures. Two brown trout over 16 inches may be kept. Smaller browns and all rainbow trout are to be returned to the water immediately.

The rainbows are wild, and DOW is endeavoring to establish a good population of them. Fishing has improved since the restrictive regulations were imposed a few years ago.

Howard Creek enters the Arkansas from the west just east of the village of Howard. A road from US 50 goes up the stream, but it is all private property and permission to fish is necessary. Access to **Hunts Lake** (11,300 ft; 4 ac), at the headwaters of **Spring Creek,** also requires the property owners' okay.

Hayden Creek enters the Arkansas at Coaldale. A dirt road goes 6 miles up the creek through much posted land to national forest campgrounds and to access to the **Bushnell Lakes** (12,000 ft; 4 and 8 ac) and the **Stout Creek Lakes;** both are to the north by trail in rugged terrain. Rainbow are stocked near the campground. Brook trout are found upstream; brown downstream. From Hayden Creek Campground, the Rainbow Trail goes northwest up **North Prong Creek** 3 miles to where the trail forks. The left (west) fork goes to Bushnell Lakes, a tough hike 3 more miles in very rugged country. Lake fishing is for rainbow and cutthroat 12 inches and longer. The next northwest drainage holds the Stout Creek Lakes at about the same elevation. From Bushnell Lakes, it's strictly cross country 2 miles around the mountain to the northwest.

Just downstream on the Arkansas from Hayden Creek is a 1.25-mile stretch of river restricted to artificial flies and lures only, as posted. **Big Cottonwood Creek** enters the river from the south. It has brown and brook.

SANGRE DE CRISTOS

Texas Creek enters the Arkansas from the south at Texas Creek, 26 miles west of Canon City. Hwy 69 goes up the creek to provide access to lakes and streams on the east side of the Sangre de Cristo Mountains in San Isabel National Forest. Texas Creek has some brown trout.

For the most part, streams flowing east out of the Sangre de Cristos are in very rugged country. They have fast, clear water and many offer superb beaver-pond fishing. Most have a lot of willow and brush, and the trails to, along and above them are steep. The Rainbow Trail in the national forest runs along north and south at about the 9000- to 10,000-foot elevation. Signed trails go up most creeks that have any fishing to offer. Lakes are at timberline or above. Portions of the Sangre de Cristos are very popular with backpackers, many of whom don't fish.

About 14 miles south of the Arkansas River, a quarter-mile south of Hillside, a road leaves west off Hwy 69 and turns northwest 5 miles to **Lake Creek,** Lake Creek Campground and the trailhead to **Rainbow Lake** (10,400 ft; 20 ac). Above the campground, the road is 4-wheel drive. Rainbow Lake fluctuates and is fair fishing for stocked trout, mostly rainbow. **Silver Lake** (12,000 ft; 5 ac) is three miles up **North Lake Creek** by 4-wheel-drive road, but 2 miles of the road above Cloverdale Mine is closed. The lake is shallow; poor fishing for cutthroat.

Downstream from Rainbow Lake, **Balman Reservoir** (9400 ft; 5 ac) is heavily fished for stocked rainbow. There are a few brook. Lake Creek in the forest is fair for brook.

About 2 miles west of Hillside, take the Rainbow Lake Road and turn southwest up Spruce Creek Road to a Forest Service woodcutting area near the Peerless Mine. A trail (closed to vehicles) goes southwest to connect with Brush Creek Trail. It's about 5 miles of walking. **Spruce Creek** has little fishing.

Southeast of North Lake Creek, **North Brush Creek** receives only light fishing

ARKANSAS RIVER

COME TO THE LARGEST RAFTING RANCH ON THE ARKANSAS RIVER!

Family fun adventures with horseback riding, wagon rides along a portion of old Canon City-Leadville stagecoach road, scenic and historic Ghost Town Tours. Oar or paddle-powered ARKANSAS RIVER trips from 1/3 day to 3-day trips, including the ROYAL GORGE. ARKANSAS ADVENTURES is based 27 miles west of Canon City at Texas Creek on U.S. 50. ROYAL GORGE RIVER ADVENTURES is located 8 miles west of Canon City at Junction U.S. 50 & Royal Gorge bridge turn-off.

ARKANSAS ADVENTURES RECREATION RANCH

- ★ 1,000 acre ranch
- ★ Chuckwagon cookouts
- ★ 250' swinging bridge
- ★ Riverside camping
- ★ Horseback rides
- ★ Gold panning
- ★ Floating trips
- ★ Rock climbing
- ★ Brown trout fishing
- ★ 3 miles private river front
- ★ Ghost Town tours

TOLL FREE IN COLORADO 1-800-892-8929 (Seasonal)

MAIN OFFICE	TEXAS CREEK RIVER	ROYAL GORGE RIVER
(303) 936-1005 (Year 'round)	(303) 275-3229	(303) 269-3700
910 S. Eliot, Denver, CO 80219	(Seasonal)	(Seasonal)

---

pressure for small but plentiful brook. At the headwaters, **Upper Brush Creek Lake** (11,635 ft; 44 ac) and **Lower Brush Creek Lake** (11,500 ft; 45 ac) are good fishing for cutthroat and brook. The upper lake also has some rainbow and other trout to 16 inches.

South Branch Lake (11,500 ft; 3 ac) is shallow and reached by hiking cross-country. No recent report on fishing.

At the headwaters of **Middle Brush Creek**, at the foot of Electric Peak, **Banjo Lake** (12,320 ft; 2 ac) is shallow and winterkills. Fishing situation is not known. Access is by an above-timberline trail. Fishing downstream on Middle Brush Creek is fair for brook. **South Brush Creek** is poor fishing.

Swift Creek, west of DeWeese Reservoir in the national forest, is heavily fished. A road goes to the campground by the beaver ponds where fishing is usually good for brook and cutthroat.

A road open to 4-wheel drives and trail bikes continues up Swift Creek to **Lake of the Clouds**—9 to 11 acres at about 11,200 feet elevation. The upper lake is good for rainbow and cutthroat, the lower for cutthroat. The middle lake is shallow and fishing is poor. Easy access means the lakes are heavily fished, and stocking is done several times a season. Take the first county road west from Hwy 69 north of Westcliffe. After 6 miles, the road forks; take the south fork to the campground. Signs provide direction to this very popular area.

DEWEESE RESERVOIR

DeWeese Reservoir (7665 ft; 240 ac) is privately owned, but the Colorado Division of Wildlife manages it for fishing. It is heavily stocked with rainbow; occasionally some brown and cutthroat are caught as well as blue gill. Kokanee died off when the water got too warm. There is an unimproved boat ramp—and camping. Fishing is fair to good. Downstream from the dam on **Grape Creek** there is some good stream fishing for rainbow and brown on state and BLM land. Access across private land, where the gate is locked, is usually tolerated without permission as long as livestock is not disturbed. Some difficult fishing in the canyon.

To the southwest, **North Taylor Creek** and a small lake are poor fishing. **Middle Taylor Creek** is heavily fished, since there is good road access. The stocked beaver ponds and campground are 9 miles due west of Westcliffe. A road continues upcreek to within 400 yards of **Hermit Lake** (11,300 ft; 20 ac), which has brook and cutthroat. **Eureka Lake** (12,000 ft; 10 ac) has good size cutthroat. It is reached by hiking a trail south a mile from **Horseshoe Lake** (12,000 ft; 10 ac), which has a 4-wheel-drive road to within a quarter-mile of its shores. Horseshoe has rainbow.

NEAR WESTCLIFFE

Goodwin Creek and **Goodwin Lakes** are reached via a good road from the Tanglewood subdivision west of Westcliffe about 10 miles. Signs indicate the way. The creek is fairly good fishing for rainbow and brook. It has beaver ponds and some fast water. Seven miles of trail up the creek are closed to trail bikes. Goodwin Lake (11,600 ft; 7 ac) has good cutthroat angling. The pond below it is shallow and has only stray fish. Campsites are available.

At the head of **Venable Creek, Venable Lakes** (12,000 ft; 6 and 9 ac) and the beaver ponds below them have good cutthroat fishing. The trail from Alvarado Campground upstream to the lakes is open to trail bikes for 7 miles. Signs mark trails. Venable Creek fishing is best in beaver ponds. The trail above Venable Lakes is closed to bikes.

Going south 2 miles is **Comanche Lake** (11,680 ft; 20 ac). A trail across Phantom Terrace has several hundred feet of 4-foot-wide trail with a 1000-foot drop on either side. Horsemen walk it in cowboy boots leading their mounts. The lake has good rainbow and cutthroat fishing, although it is temperamental. A trail from Alvarado Campground also leads 5 miles up the creek to Comanche.

Cottonwood Creek has a few fish and is being considered for a plant of the protected greenback cutthroat trout.

At the head of **Dry Creek,** the **Dry Lakes** (12,000 ft; 14 ac) have little fishing pressure on their cutthroat populations, because the lakes are tough to reach. Access is on Schoolfield Road west from Hwy 69 about 2.5 miles south of Westcliffe; then 2 miles west on Schoolfield to Macey Lane and south 2 more miles to Horn Road; then west 3 miles past Horn Creek Ranch to Rainbow Trail. Then hike north a mile to Dry Creek, the first one, and up the creek about 4.5 miles.

Horn Road also leads to **Horn Creek**, which is only fair for cutthroat. Horn Lakes, 4 miles up from the end of the road, and the beaver ponds are stocked and are fair to good for cutthroat. Trail is closed to bikes. **Main Horn Lake** (11,800 ft; 24 ac) at the headwaters offers good cutthroat fishing when they're willing. To the north 1.5 miles is **Little Horn Lake** (11,680 ft; 3 ac), a pond among beaver ponds, with cutthroat. There is considerable horseback traffic in this drainage.

Macey Creek has three lakes at its headwaters between 11,500 and 12,000 feet elevation. The creek and the lakes have fair fishing for cutthroat on the upper reaches above the waterfall, brook and some cutthroat below. Access is from the Rainbow Trail south from Horn Creek, then up Macey Creek 4 miles to lakes.

COLONY LAKES

North Colony Lakes are between 11,500 and 12,500 feet on **North Colony Creek** in hard-to-reach country. Three of the lakes offer good fishing for rainbow and cutthroat; no recent reports on others. Access is up a faint trail from Rainbow Trail. The bench lake, northernmost up a short tributary, is stocked. Backpackers like this valley.

South Colony Lakes are a mile from the end of a 4-wheel-drive road up the **South Colony Creek.** The upper lake at 12,000 feet has 16 acres with cutthroat, and some good size ones. It is heavily fished. The lower lake is shallow, with fair to poor fishing. The stream has brook, rainbow and cutthroat, and is heavily stocked and sometimes nearly fished out in peak season. Take Hwy 69 south from Westcliffe about 3.5 miles to sign and Colfax Lane. Continue south on Colfax Lane to the end, about 5 miles, then turn west about 7 miles to the end. Hike Rainbow Trail north for North Colony Creek. The road continues upstream on South Colony Creek. Private land blocks shorter access to North Colony Creek and North Colony Lakes.

A 4-wheel-drive road goes up **Grape Creek** to wind back north toward **Music Pass Creek** and over Music Pass to provide access to **Sand Creek Lakes** on the west side of the Sangre de Cristos. Sand Creek Lakes are not readily reached from the west. **Upper Sand Creek Lake** (11,745 ft; 42 ac) and **Lower Sand Creek Lake** (11,450 ft; 62 ac) are heavily fished for cutthroat. They are stocked.

Sand Creek has some fine fishing for cutthroat and brook, and is followed intermittently by a pack trail. Very rough country after the creek swings west into the canyon. **Little Sand Creek Lakes** are at the headwaters of **Little Sand Creek,** which joins Sand Creek from the north. Don't expect to take horses all the way to the lake, but leave them at north end of the valley.

Access to the Sand Creek Lakes area is from Colfax Lane south from Hwy 69 south of Westcliffe as noted in Colony descrip-

tion. Turn east at the end of Colfax Lane, then south on a 4-wheel-drive road, keeping south and not turning west on side roads. Once over Music Pass, go down a half-mile to the north-south trail. Continue north a half-mile or so to where the trail goes through timber to Lower Sand Creek Lake. No vehicles are allowed. Upper Sand Creek Lake is on the north at the end of the trail. Must hike the last half-mile to the lake. While this area is only 15 miles from Hwy 69, it is wild country. Roads and trails are often in snow and blocked by snowdrifts until mid-July. Inquiring of Forest Service and Wildlife personnel in Westcliffe before going into the area is strongly encouraged to get precise and up-to-date information as conditions change. Topographic maps are essential and, since they contain more detailed information, can save time and frustration, and maximize enjoyment of the area and its fishing.

To the south of Music Pass, most of the land on the east side of the mountains is private and there is little public fishing. Some reservoirs and lakes have fishing, and those that are open to the public are described in the chapter on Eastern Colorado.

ARKANSAS RIVER

Downstream from Texas Creek, the Arkansas River is contained in the Arkansas River Canyon, which has room for the river, the highway and a railroad. This is wild trout water and is not stocked, but it still offers fishing for brown to the east end of the canyon, 1.5 miles west of Parkdale on US 50. The Bureau of Land Management and DOW have made stream improvements between Parkdale and Cotopaxi to enhance fishing. At Parkdale, the Arkansas winds southeast through Royal Gorge as the highway continues east. Access to the gorge is along the railroad right-of-way. Fishing is for brown trout in heavy, turbulent water. Downstream from the gorge is Canon City, after which the river flows through private land. Permission to fish is required.

A mile east of Canon City, turn south from US 50 on Fourmile Road to where it junctures with Hwy 115. Turn east to Florence to the intersection of Hwy 67 in town. (Continuing east on US 50 will provide access to Pueblo Reservoir.)

WET MOUNTAINS

From Florence, Hwy 67 leads south to fishing in the Wet Mountains between Wetmore and Rye, which is 26 miles west of Pueblo on Hwy 165. **South Hardscrabble Creek** has 4.25 miles of fishing in the national forest, 25 miles south of the Arkansas River. The best fishing is in the spring as runoff subsides. Fishing in beaver ponds for rainbow and brook shouldn't be overlooked. There are some brown in the creek. By late summer the water level drops, but it's a fun stream to fish. The creek flows east past Florence Picnic Ground, then north, and is paralleled by a forest road.

South on Hwy 165 is **Ophir Creek,** which has lively fishing for small brook upstream from the campground. Burns Meadow Road provides access.

Ten miles northwest of Rye, **Lake Isabel** (8475 ft; 20 ac) is along the highway. It contains mostly rainbow, a few brook and some brown in the 15-pound-and-up class. Best fishing is after ice-off from April to mid-June. Boats are allowed; no motors. It is heavily stocked and very heavily fished.

St. Charles River feeds into Lake Isabel and is heavily stocked and rapidly fished out. The upper stretches have small brook. Below the lake are brown trout, but it is very difficult to hike downstream to where the good fishing is (and back again). It's good fly fishing water. The **Little St. Charles River,** just south of Lake Isabel, received stream and trout habitat improvement work in 1983; no recent report on fishing.

While there are numerous little creeks and tiny streams in the area, few have decent fishing. One that does is **Greenhorn Creek.** It is stocked with rainbow and is adjacent to Hwy 165. Hiking upstream a mile or so provides good fly fishing for brook and rainbow.

The Arkansas River is on private land from Florence downstream about 15 miles to the Pueblo Reservoir State Wildlife Area. It is stocked with put-and-take rainbow and landowners usually grant permission to fish. A few warm water fish from the reservoir migrate up this far.

The **Pueblo Reservoir State Wildlife Area** is an 8-mile stretch of the Arkansas River upstream from Pueblo Reservoir. The upper end of the reservoir rests in the wildlife area, and, when the reservoir is high, it spreads into the wildlife area. Fishing in the wildlife area is going through some changes. The Lake McConaughy rainbow trout was introduced to the stream in 1982. This Nebraska rainbow is more tolerant of warmer water temperatures than its cold water cousins. Since the wildlife area stream gets very warm during the summer months, it has not been a favored home of trout. In summer 1982, boulders that had been moved aside to aid in filling the reservoir were moved back into the stream to improve fish habitat.

Restrictions in the wildlife area include: all black bass less than 15 inches must be returned to the water immediately; boating is prohibited during the waterfowl season, November 1 to mid-January; overnight camping and fires are prohibited; and the daily bag and possession limit for underwater spear fishing is 2 fish and is permitted from July 16 though March 14 of the following year; open 5 a.m. to 10 p.m.

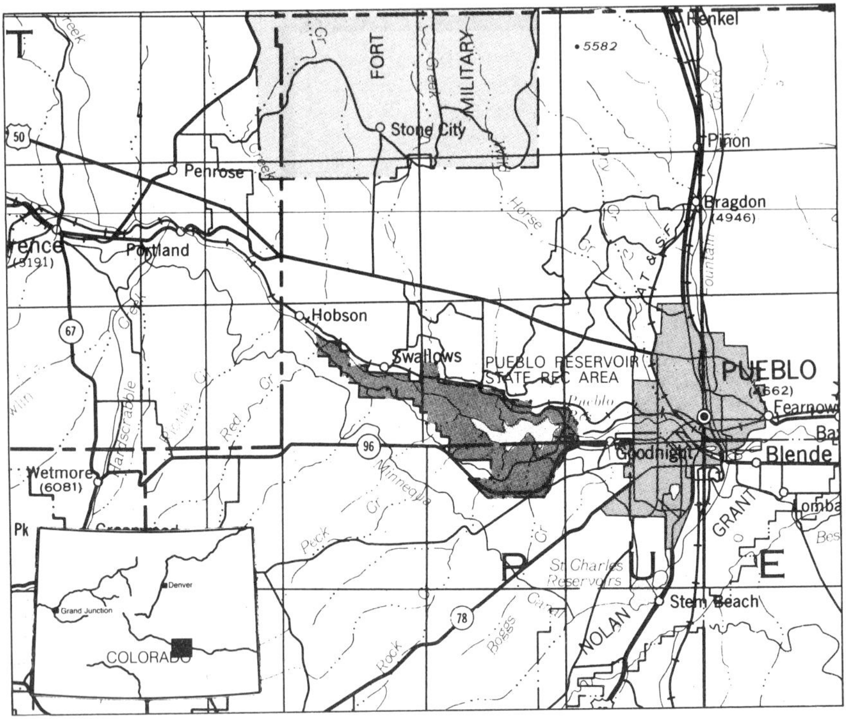

202 ARKANSAS RIVER

Arkansas River, Pueblo Reservoir

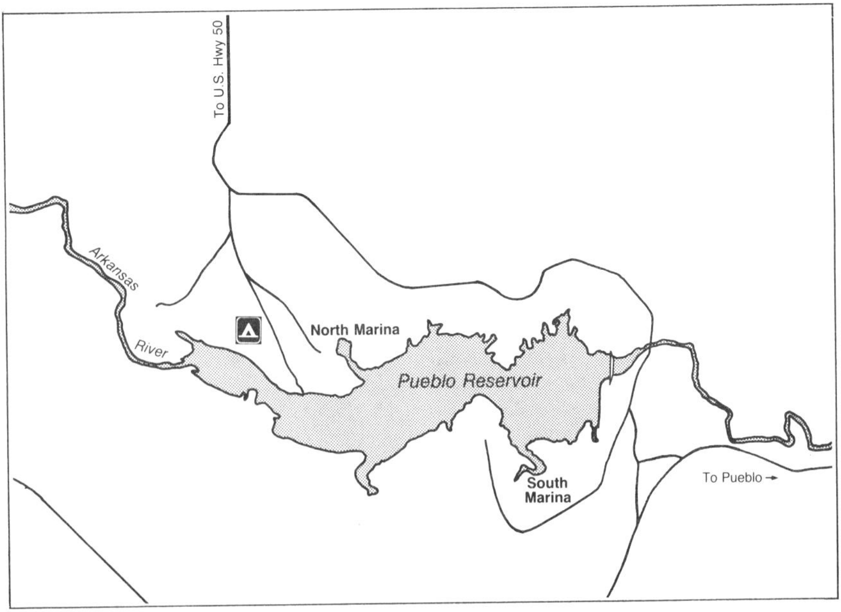

Pueblo Reservoir

PUEBLO RESERVOIR

Pueblo Reservoir (4900 ft; 1300 to 3000 ac) is in the Pueblo State Recreation Area. Open 5 a.m. to 10 p.m. When the reservoir is near capacity, its upstream end spreads into the Pueblo Reservoir State Wildlife Area. Pueblo Reservoir offers fishing for walleye, largemouth and smallmouth bass, crappie, bluegill, rainbow, perch and some brown trout. Along with fishing, water skiing and swimming are popular sports on the reservoir. Camping facilities include showers, electricity and laundry. The camping fee is $5 per night in addition to the recreation area entrance fee, which is $2 a day or $20 a year per vehicle. Restrictions include: public access is permitted between the hours of 5 a.m. and 10 p.m.; fishing is prohibited in those areas by the dam and outlet structures as posted; boating is prohibited during the waterfowl season, November 1 to mid-January, as posted; and all black bass taken less than 15 inches in length must be returned to the water immediately. North access to the recreation area is by turning west on US 50 just north of Pueblo. From US 50, turn south on McCullough Blvd. to the reservoir. The route is well marked. From the south, a park entrance on Hwy 96 also is well marked.

East of Pueblo, the river offers limited fishing, mostly for suckers, carp and other rough fish. Several reservoirs do provide enjoyable fishing for warm water species such as bass, perch, catfish and crappie. They are described in the chapter on Eastern Colorado. □

U.S. FOREST SERVICE DISTRICT RANGER STATIONS

Leadville Ranger District
San Isabel National Forest
Post Office Bldg., P.O. Box 970
Leadville, CO 80461   303/486-0749

Salida Ranger District
San Isabel National Forest
230 W. 16th
Salida, CO 81201   303/539-3591

San Carlos Ranger District
San Isabel National Forest
248 Dozier St.
Canon City, CO 81212   303/275-1626

Pike and San Isabel National Forest Headquarters
910 Hwy 50 West
Pueblo, CO 81008   303/544-5277 Ext. 321

Timpas Unit-Carrizo District
San Isabel National Forest
East Hwy 50, P.O. Box 817
La Junta, CO 81050   303/384-2181

Pikes Peak Ranger District
Pike National Forest
320 West Fillmore
Colorado Springs, CO 80907   303/636-1602

U.S. Forest Service campgrounds

U.S. Forest Service compilation was current as of 1985.

Asterisks denote fee areas. Some campgrounds are open only Memorial Day weekend through Labor Day. Below freezing weather could mean no water supply.

ARKANSAS RIVER DRAINAGE

SAN ISABEL NATIONAL FOREST
Headquarters: 910 Hwy 50 West, Box 5808, Pueblo, CO 81002

Campground name	Elevation	No camp sites	Travel trailers	Drinking water	Length of stay (days)	Location and directions
Half Moon	9900	24	Yes	Yes	14	8.4 mi SW of Leadville by US 24 and forest roads

ARKANSAS RIVER

Campground name	Elevation	No camp sites	Travel trailers	Drinking water	Length of stay (days)	Location and directions
Molly Brown*	9900	49	Yes	Yes	10	3.8 mi W of Leadville by forest roads
Parry Peak*	9500	26	Yes	Yes	14	1.8 mi SW of Twin Lakes via Colo. 82
Collegiate Peaks*	9800	29	Yes	Yes	7	9.8 mi W of Buena Vista by Colo. 306 and forest roads
Cottonwood Lake*	9600	28	Yes	Yes	10	10.5 mi SW of Buena Vista by Colo. 306 and forest roads
Cascade*	9700	19	Yes	Yes	10	9.3 mi SW of Nathrop by Colo. 162 and forest roads
Mt. Princeton #2*	8900	13	Yes	Yes	10	7.8 mi W of Nathrop off US 285
Monarch Park*	10,500	37	Yes	Yes	10	On US 50, 13.3 mi W of Poncha Springs
O'Haver Lake*	9200	24	Yes	Yes	7	6.4 mi SW of Poncha Springs, off US 285
Garfield*	10,000	11	Yes	Yes	10	On US 50, 13 mi W of Poncha Springs
North Fork Reservoir	11,000	8	Yes	Yes	10	13 mi NW of Poncha Springs off US 50 and forest roads
Hayden Creek #1	8000	11	Yes	Yes	7	4.6 mi SW of Coaldale by forest road
Lake Creek	8300	11	Yes	Yes	10	2.8 mi W of Hillside on forest road
Alvarado*	9000	44	Yes	Yes	10	10 mi SW of Westcliffe by Colo. 69 and forest roads
Blue Lake*	10,500	15	Yes	Yes	7	4.9 mi SW of Cuchara by Colo. 12 and forest road
Bear Lake*	10,700	15	Yes	Yes	7	4.5 mi SW of Cuchara off Colo. 12
Cuchara*	9500	25	Yes	Yes	7	On Colo. 12, 3.5 mi S of Cuchara
Lake Isabel*	8800	48	Yes	Yes	10	8 mi NW of Rye off Colo. 165
Ophir*	8900	27	No	Yes	10	7 mi W of Beulah off Colo. 76
Oak Creek	7600	17	No	Yes	10	12.3 mi SW of Canon City on county road

South Platte River from great to gone

Adjacent communities:
Fairplay, Lake George, Littleton, Denver, Brighton, Greeley, Fort Morgan, Brush, Sterling, Julesburg.

Principal Highways:
Upper Reaches—U.S. 24; Colo. 9, 67; Denver to Greeley—U.S. 85, I-25; Colo. 75; Denver to Nebraska state line—U.S. 34, 6, I-76; Colo. 144, 138.

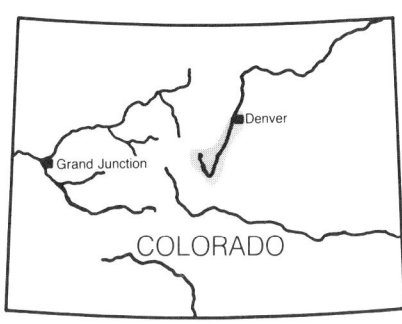

The South Platte River has long been a trout angler's dream. Generations ago, railroad excursions from Denver hauled picnickers and fishermen to its fabled clear waters southwest of Denver. Amazingly, much of the very popular river is still open to public fishing, though the railroad no longer runs up Waterton Canyon and the North Fork. Good roads make much of the river accessible, even the wild trout and gold medal waters, where the rainbow and brown provide some of the best year-round angling anywhere.

Near its headwaters close to Fairplay in South Park are three marvelous fisheries—Antero, Spinney Mountain and Elevenmile reservoirs—where the river has been dammed to provide water to city dwellers a 100 miles away. In the mountains, Cheesman Reservoir is now open. All offer big fish.

Now is the time to fish the South Platte near Deckers and upstream of the private Wigwam Club section. Plans for Two Forks Dam and Reservoir at the juncture of the river and its North Fork, 34 miles southwest of Denver, call for inundating much of this naturally productive, exceptional fishery. It may be crowded, but the early riser and the fading-light fisherman will have fished a legendary water before it is no more.

HEADWATERS

The Middle Fork of the South Platte River heads north of Alma on Hoosier Pass, flows south through Fairplay into Spinney Mountain, and then into Elevenmile reservoir about 24 miles southeast of Fairplay. The South Fork of the South Platte rises west of Fairplay at Weston Pass. It flows southeasterly, in and out of Antero Reservoir, to merge with the Middle Fork near Hartsel and form the South Platte River northwest of Spinney Mountain.

The North Fork of the South Platte heads on the east side of Kenosha Pass, 22 miles east of Fairplay, in an entirely different drainage. It flows southeast to merge with the South Platte River about 34 miles southwest of Denver.

From Elevenmile Canyon Reservoir, the river changes direction. It flows northeast through Elevenmile Canyon to Cheesman Lake, then on to its confluence with the North Fork of the South Platte at the head of South Platte Canyon, 34 miles southwest of Denver. Much of the length of the North Fork flows along US 285.

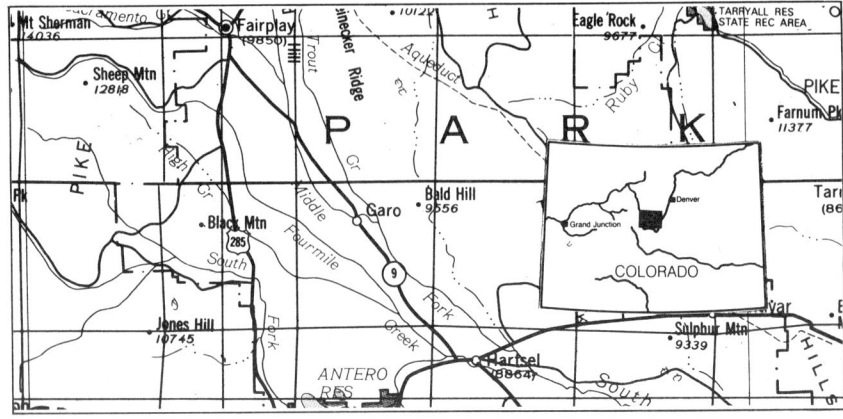

South Platte River Headwaters, Antero Reservoir

The South Platte Canyon was dammed by the Denver Water Department in 1982 at Strontia Springs. Once through the canyon, the river enters Chatfield Reservoir and the metropolitan Denver area. From Denver it flows northeasterly across the plains and into Nebraska.

MIDDLE FORK

The **Middle Fork of the South Platte River** rises on the northern flanks of 14,000-foot Mt. Democrat and Mt. Lincoln. The **Wheeler Lakes** (12,500 ft and 12,180 ft; 4 ac and 28 ac, respectively) offer fair to good fishing for cutthroat trout to 10 inches, with the lower, larger lake being more productive. The lakes are 3.5 miles northwest over rough 4-wheel road from **Montgomery Reservoir** (10,820 ft; 80 ac when full). Montgomery is stocked with rainbow and some native, with fish to 15 inches. Algae bloom in summer hampers angling; drawdown prevents ice fishing. Best in spring and fall. Montgomery and the lakes are reached by dirt road west from Hwy 9 just south of the summit of Hoosier Pass.

The Middle Fork south to Fairplay shows the impact of gold mining and dredging, but flows clear with many riffles. It is fair fishing for rainbow and some brown. At Alma, 6 miles north of Fairplay, **Buckskin Creek** joins the river. Six miles up the creek by good road are **Kite Lake** (12,000 ft; 6 ac) and **Lake Emma** (12,620 ft; 9 ac). Both are fair for rainbow to 12 inches. Kite is uphill from the road to the north and right on an easy trail much used by mountain climbers. There is a campground at Kite.

Lake Emma is out of view to the west, up a brushy, grassy slope. Emma contains some small cutthroat to 10 inches. The creek itself is only fair for small brook, rainbow and cutthroat.

Two miles south of Alma, well named **Mosquito Creek** is fair for small cutthroat and some rainbow. Three fishable lakes are among the many ponds and lakes along the stream and at the headwaters.

Oliver Twist Lake (12,250 ft; 6 ac) is reached by taking the Mosquito Pass Road (about 4.3 miles west from Hwy 9) to where the road forks. Take the north fork (the poorer, less traveled road) about 2 miles more to where a road rambles off to the south to the London Mine buildings. The lake is about a half-mile northwest. From the London Mine turnoff, the valley road continues on about 2 more miles to **Cooney Lake** (12,600 ft; 8 ac). There's a bad bog that may not be negotiable. Fishing at both lakes is for cutthroat to 10-12 inches. There is much 4-wheel and trailbike activity in this area, since Mosquito Pass provides 4-wheel access to Leadville when snow drifts have melted.

West of Hwy 9, **Pennsylvania** and **Sacramento Creeks** and, across Hwy 9 to the east, **Beaver Creek,** are small, clear streams with small cutthroat and rainbow.

Old mining roads make them easily accessible, but some areas are private property and are posted. Willows and bog and some ponds in the lower reaches.

FOURMILE CREEK

Fourmile Creek rises in Horseshoe Basin west of Fairplay and flows east and then south. To reach Fourmile, a good gravel road turns west off US 285 a mile south of Fairplay and crosses private land for 3 miles before entering Pike National Forest. There is some posted land. Fourmile Creek is 6 to 8 feet wide and is fair for rainbow and brook in stream and ponds. Buildings from the ghost town of Leavick have been moved to Fairplay for preservation as South Park City. Two small lakes are located at Fourmile Creek's headwaters. Fishing is reported only fair.

Twelvemile Creek is just over a low divide south of Fourmile Creek, and flows into the South Fork of the South Platte River above Antero Reservoir. It and the **Twelvemile Lakes** (11,580 ft; 3 ac, upper; 11,180 ft; 8 ac, lower) have cutthroat and small brook trout. Campsites are dotted along the creek, and there are some beaver ponds for small brook. The area is reached by taking a good gravel road west from US 285 about 4.5 miles south of Fairplay. After 4 miles, a dirt road goes off to the right and ends within a mile of the lower lake. A 4-wheel-drive vehicle can make it to the lower lake.

SOUTH FORK

Southwest of Twelvemile Lake, the **South Fork of the South Platte River** doesn't look like much at its headwaters at Weston Pass. At the pass, **Ruby Lake** (11,850 ft; 2 ac) is a rock-rimmed pond with small rainbow and cutthroat. The river flows south for 10 miles through mostly private land to US 285. In this section are some small brook and rainbow. Tributary creeks from the south, **Rich, Rough and Tumbling, Lynch** and **Willow** are small, hard-to-fish creeks with small trout, mostly brook.

From US 285 downstream 2.5 miles,

BAIT 'N' BULLET SHOP
Buy, Sell & Trade Guns

Complete Fishing Supplies • Licenses-Bait-Tackle • Camping Outfitters

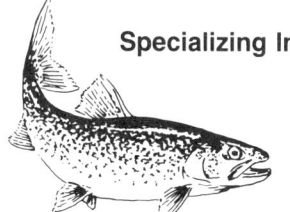

Specializing In:
- Fire Arms
- Big Game Hunting Supplies
- Water Fowl Hunting Supplies
- Fishing Tackle

Compare our low prices.

RELOADING SUPPLIES
659-3286 SPORTSMAN'S GIFTS

59 So. 1st Ave., Brighton, CO 80601
1 block E. & ½ block S. of US Hwy 85 & Colo. Hwy 7

DOW has leased access to what is called the Knight-Imler State Wildlife Area, where fishing is only with flies and lures; trout 16 inches or less must be returned to the water immediately, and only two over 16 inches may be kept. The public is welcome on the lease for only 25 feet on each side of the stream itself, as posted.

(Editor's note: Here's a great fishing challenge that can be lost if fishermen litter, have poor manners and no respect for private property. It's happened so often.)

From its appearance, **Antero Reservoir** (8000 ft; 1000 ac when full) gives no hint that it is one of the easiest to reach and best fishing places in Colorado. On a high, windswept park without trees or shrubs, it's a giant pothole containing rainbow, brown and a few brook. Northern pike planted several years ago have thrived, somewhat to the detriment of less voracious trout. Grayling planted several years ago didn't take.

The best fishing is from boats. It's hard to fish from shore since it is shallow—waders are essential. It's a good spincaster's lake when the wind isn't blowing. Brown and rainbow to 10 pounds are not uncommon; the pike are even larger. As a state recreation area, it has a campground, boat ramps and picnic area.

Fishing is prohibited from the dam and the south and west shores, as posted. The islands are off limits. Ice fishing often is excellent. (Portable shelters only.)

Antero is a state wildlife area, and there are a host of rules—no boating from 9 p.m. to 4 a.m. and boat mooring in designated areas only. Antero is reached via US 24 or US 285 on several access roads. It is 6 miles west of Hartsel and about 20 miles south of Fairplay.

Leaving the reservoir, the South Fork flows easterly to join the Middle Fork east of Hartsel and become the South Platte Riv-

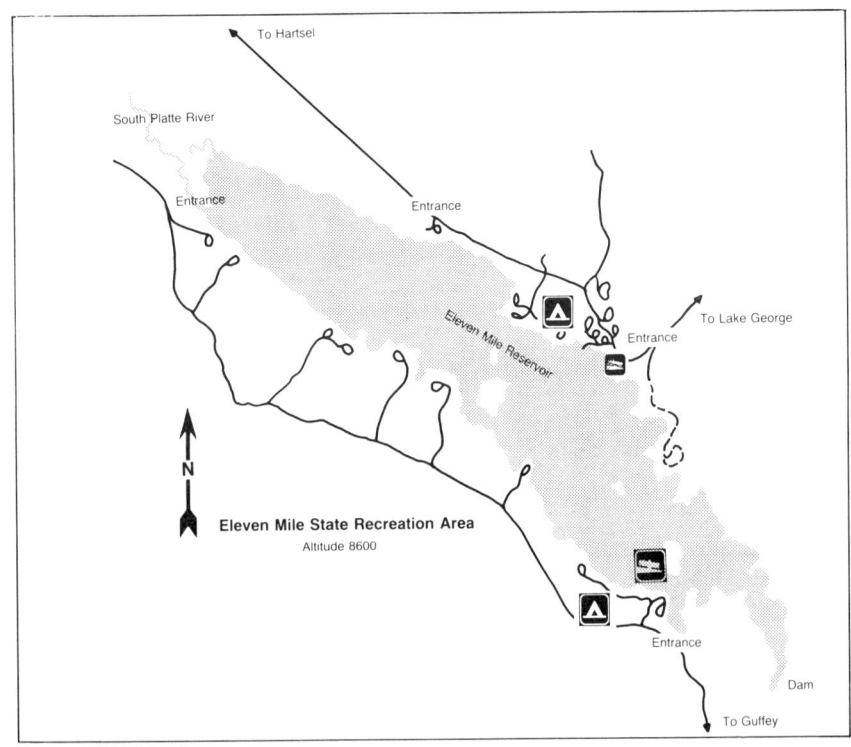

Eleven Mile Reservoir

er. Just above Hartsel, **Trout Creek** joins the Middle Fork. Trout Creek begins near Palmer Peak north of Fairplay and flows south through private ranchland, where permission to trespass and fish is necessary. A sometimes passable dirt road parallels the creek much of the way. There's fair fishing for brook and rainbow. The Colorado Division of Wildlife has leased several miles of fishing along the stream.

At the juncture of Trout Creek and Middle Fork is the Tomahawk State Wildlife Area. Some stretches of both streams are posted for fishing only with flies and lures. While 8 trout may be taken, only 2 may be more than 16 inches long; others that large or larger must be returned to the water immediately. No camping or fires are allowed.

From the lower area boundary to the bridge below the U.S.G.S. water gauging station, it is wild trout water.

SPINNEY MOUNTAIN

Spinney Mountain Reservoir (8700 ft; 2500 ac when full) was constructed in the late 1970s and early 1980s as part of the city of Aurora water system. In 1982 it was stocked with 500,000 Yellowstone cutthroat trout and some large rainbow and brown after the reservoir and several miles of upstream river had been treated to kill rough fish.

Opened to public fishing in the spring of 1983, it was an immediate hit for outstanding fishing. There is plenty of natural food for fish. There has been considerable migration upstream on the South Fork from the reservoir, which is bounded by private land, although the City of Aurora, which owns Spinney Mountain, tried to claim it. There's a four-fish limit. Cutthroat to 18 inches have been common.

Among the rules are: no fishing from 10 p.m. to 4 a.m., no overnight camping and no overnight stays. There is a boat ramp, but no marina. There is no ice fishing. The reservoir is operated by the Aurora Department of Utilities. There is a $2 per vehicle daily fee or a $10 annual permit. The permits may be obtained from the ranger at the reservoir.

Marked access is 8 miles south from US

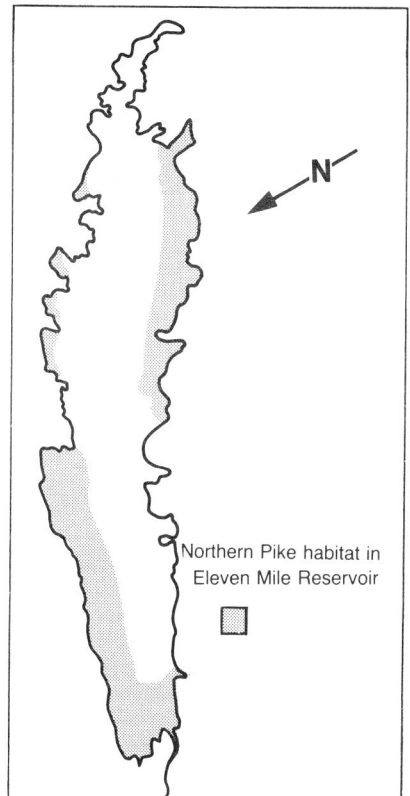

Northern pike habitat

24 and 6 miles east of Hwy 9 on good county roads. From US 285 at Fairplay, the reservoir is 23 miles south via Hwy 9. A boat ramp and picnic area are located on the north shore. There's no fishing downstream from the dam for 1 mile from September 1 through December 1.

ELEVENMILE RESERVOIR

A good road leads east and south from Hartsel to **Elevenmile Reservoir,** a state recreation area. Elevenmile is also reached from US 24 from Lake George by Elevenmile Canyon and Arkansas Gulch roads. The Guffey Road off Hwy 9 south of the reservoir also offers good access.

Elevenmile provides good fishing; it is, therefore, heavily fished from boats and from shore. Rated good for rainbow,

Good enough; not big enough

brown, mackinaw, northern pike. It often produces the largest kokanee salmon in the state. The record kokanee for both snagging and angling in the reservoir are in the 6-pound range and more than 24 inches long. Browns and rainbows to 20 pounds are possible, and 2 and 6 pounders are commonly caught. Big streamers are a favorite lure. The northerns are in the trophy-size range, and some fishermen are more intent on catching them than hooking trout. See map.

Boat ramps and campgrounds on both north and south shores. Taking carp with bow and arrow is encouraged. Like Antero Reservoir, Elevenmile is owned by the Denver Water Department. In drought years, it is drawn down substantially. Ice fishing is often excellent. Only portable shelters may be used.

Elevenmile Canyon, just below the dam, runs northeast nearly to Lake George and has a half-dozen Forest Service campgrounds in a 10-mile stretch. The canyon is open to fishing for rainbow and browns.

Lake George is a private lake just west of Hwy 24. From a mile below the Lake George Dam the river is open to Cheesman Reservoir and is accessible by foot trail most of the dozen miles. Happy Meadows Campground, just east of Lake George, has a dirt road leading from it about 2.5 miles downstream. Fishing in this stretch is for brook, brown and rainbow.

The South Platte from Beaver Creek (which enters the river 5 miles north of Lake George) to The Wigwams property line is wild trout water. That means fishing with artificial flies and lures only, possession of two trout, and all trout less than 16 inches must be returned to the water immediately. Note posted regulations at streamside. Just keep the ones too big for the frying pan.

Between Lake George and Cheesman Reservoir, **Tarryall Creek** joins the South Platte. Tarryall rises northwest of Como and winds across South Park to Tarryall Reservoir, then through the Tarryall Mountains to join the South Platte River. Three miles of the creek above the confluence are wild trout waters.

Above Como, north of US 285 east of Fairplay, the creek has several beaver ponds; some of it is posted, although access from Boreas Pass Road is on foot. Small brook and occasional rainbow. South from Como, Tarryall Creek winds through private land for more than 14 miles before entering Tarryall Reservoir. In this section, it is joined by **Michigan, Jefferson** and **Snyder Creeks.** All of these small streams contain small brook and range from open land to willowbrush fishing. Local inquiry and permission to fish is recommended.

JEFFERSON LAKE

A little north and west of Kenosha Pass, **Jefferson lake** (10,687 ft; 125 ac) is situated at the headwaters of Jefferson Creek. It is a very popular fishery, with brook, mackinaw and rainbow. Jefferson Lake is heavily stocked and fished. Boats are allowed. It is low in late fall, exposing a sandy area on the northeast side from which fly fishing for brook and rainbow can be good both morning and evening. The lake (and Michigan Lakes to the southwest) is reached by a good road north from US 285 in the village of Jefferson. Two miles north of the village, the road to Jefferson Lakes goes off to the right. A mile farther is the road to Michigan Lakes and upper Michigan Creek. The upper lake is barren. **Lower Michigan Lake** (11,222 ft; 4 ac) is fair for small brook and some cutthroat. The lake is on private property; permission to enter should be requested.

Tarryall Reservoir (9500 ft; 175 ac) is a state recreation area that has camping, a boat ramp and a picnic ground. Fishing is prohibited from the dam. Fishing is for kokanee, rainbow and brown with some 2 to 3 pounders and up possible. It is heavily fished from boats, and is open for ice fishing. Downstream, some stretches of the creek are restricted to fly and lure fishing only—as posted. The three miles above the creek's confluence with the South Platte River is wild trout water with catch-and-release fishing.

CHEESMAN RESERVOIR

Cheesman Reservoir (6842 ft; 18 miles of shoreline) is owned by the Denver Water Department. Until 1982 it was closed to fishing. Fishing is managed by DOW, but vandalism, littering, trespassing and other misbehavior could close it at any time. It's artificial flies and lures only, and the daily limits in the reservoir and Goose Creek is two brown trout over 16 inches, with smaller trout, including all rainbows of any size, to be returned to the water immediately.

The reservoir offers some good fishing for good size brown and rainbow. Shore fishing only; no boats. Angling is prohibited from a half-hour after sunset to a half-hour before sunrise. There's no overnight camping, no fires, no firearms, no dogs and no fishing from November 1 through April 30. Access is by foot up the river from The Wigwams at Hwy 67 just west of Deckers or by the forest and maintenance road west from the Wigwam Picnic Ground at Wigwam Creek.

From Cheesman Dam downstream to the upper Wigwam Club boundary, it's only fly- and lure-fishing and catch-and-release fishing. The Wigwam Club property is private, posted and patrolled for trespassers. From the club's lower boundary, 6 miles downstream to Scraggy View picnic ground, 2 brown trout over 16 inches may be taken; it's fly and lure angling. All rainbow trout must be returned to the water. This is very popular fishing year-round. Its proximity to Denver and Colorado Springs, the quality water and angling make it a favorite.

From Cheesman Dam to the Wigwam Club property, the trout are shy and selective; the persistent, cautious fisherman may have an edge on the crowd. Deliberate presentation of very small dry flies is suggested, with patterns being rotated to find one that works. Fluctuating water levels have affected success in the past.

At the resort and community of Deckers, the river is joined from the south by **Horse**

Rainbow Falls Park

Colorado's Finest—Year 'Round
Fishing, Camping, Stables
No Fishing License Needed
Fish Where the Fish Are
Family & All
Adults—$7 per day   Kids—$3.50 per day
$6 for Wilderness Camping per Vehicle
Hwy 67—10 Miles N. of Woodland Park
303/687-9074

Creek. It is best in spring and fall when trout swim up from the South Platte, but has mostly small rainbow and brook. **West Creek,** which flows northerly into Horsecreek, is paralleled for 10 miles of its length by Hwy 67 from Woodland Park (12 miles south). West Creek contains small brook and rainbow. **Manitou Lake** (7700 ft; 10 ac) is about 6 miles south of the village of Westcreek along Hwy 67. It is stocked with rainbow; some brook are caught occasionally. The lake is on **Trout Creek,** which flows into **Rainbow Falls,** a series of private ponds. We've had some good reports on Rainbow Falls Park, a private fishery open to the public for a fee. It's mostly rainbow fishing. Trout Creek is poor to fair for brook and rainbow.

At Deckers, the South Platte is up to 100 feet wide; it has many boulders, fast water sections and deep holes. Prime fishing.

From Deckers north to the village site of South Platte, where the North Fork of the South Platte joins the mainstream, the stream and beautiful valley attract hundreds of thousands of visitors annually, most of them on weekends and holidays. On midsummer days, the fisherman can expect swimmers (despite posting against swimming), rock throwers and people floating the stream in inner tubes.

The quiet hours of early morning are a particularly good time to try these waters, for 14- to 19-inch rainbow and brown are still there. Lake autumn and early spring are good fishing times, but you're bound to have company.

THE NORTH FORK

The **North Fork of the South Platte** is a stream of an entirely different character. It originates on the northeast side of Kenosha Pass where US 285 crosses into the South Park. The upper reaches of the North Fork and its tributaries, **Beaver Creek, Handcart Gulch** and **Kenosha Creek,** are small, with clusters of willows and some ponds. Fishing is poor for small brook. **Gibson Lake** (11,500 ft; 4 ac) is reached from the east foot of Kenosha Pass by driving north on the Hall Valley Road toward Webster Pass.

Travel 9 miles and leave car near old mining road at Handcart Gulch. Hike 3 miles northwest on old Missouri Mine road; where it deteriorates, take trail to the west up Lake Fork Creek. It's a 3,000-foot elevation rise to fishing for good size brook trout at the base of Whale Peak at the Continental Divide. There's camping at the Hall Valley Campground. The area is popular with 4-wheel drivers and trail bikers.

Downstream, a half-mile above Grant, the Roberts Tunnel of the Denver Water Department brings water from Dillon Reservoir on the Blue River. The 23-mile-long tunnel can contribute either a trickle of water or a whole new stream, four or five times the flow of the natural North Fork at that point.

As a result, the river has been rebuilt downstream to its confluence with the South Platte River at the site of South Platte village so it can handle the additional water. In the stretch paralleling US 285, the river can be dangerous, because it is deceptively swift, deep and powerful.

Much of the river in this area is private property and posted. Permission to fish is necessary. Reconstruction of the river included many measures to promote fishing. Boulders, small dams, riffles, gravel areas for spawning and willow plantings to minimize erosion were among the measures taken in both fast and quiet water sections. Fishing is for brook, rainbow and some brown in the lower reaches. Ask permission to fish private land.

GENEVA CREEK

Geneva Creek, which enters the North Fork at Grant, is barren above the falls because of natural conditions. For the 4.5 miles north from the South Platte to the falls, the stream is alternately public and posted private land. The waters are stocked with rainbow. **Threemile Creek** (entering Geneva from the northeast) offers some rainbow to 10 inches. Farther north, **Scott Gomer Creek** appears to be nearly fished out, as is **Burning Bear Creek** and other creeks in the area.

A good trail up Scott Gomer Creek, from Geneva Creek just above the falls, leads 6

Father and son

miles to **Abyss Lake** (12,640 ft; 20 ac). Sandwiched between the 14,000-foot peaks of Mt. Evans and Mt. Bierstadt, it has rainbows, some up to 18 inches. It's a temperamental lake, and fishing is either good or bad. Scott Gomer Creek downstream to Geneva Creek has some brook in beaver ponds. Tends to be fished heavily.

Continuing north, **Duck Lake** (11,100 ft; 42 ac), up Duck Creek on the south side of Guanella Pass, is a fair fishery. Private property owners intimidate users of the public shore area of the lake on the west side, so lake is lightly fished. Some 400 to 500 feet of the west shoreline is in the national forest. Access without trespassing is steep and difficult, and is from the high terrain. It can become a nasty situation with criminal trespass charges.

Northwest above Duck Lake in the forest are the two **Square Top Lakes** (12,240 ft; 1 ac each). They are most easily reached by trail or cross country from the top of Guanella Pass, about a 2-mile hike west from the pass. Fair to good for cutthroat.

West of Square Top Lakes is **Shelf Lake** (12,000 ft; 9 ac), at the headwaters of Geneva creek by a fair road up the valley. Park car at ruins of old mill and hike 3 miles on good trail. Fair to good for cutthroat and rainbow to 12 inches. There are two FS campgrounds in the valley, at Burning Bear Creek and Geneva Creek above the Guanella Pass turnoff. Many campsites; pretty country; zero stream fishing.

From Grant downstream past Bailey and to the village of South Platte, the North Fork races through mostly private land that's posted, developed for resorts or mountain ranches. **Deer Creek** flows south off the slopes of Mt. Evans to enter the North Fork a few miles east of Bailey.

The upper reaches of Deer Creek are in national forest and are accessible by turning off Hwy 285 to the north 3 miles northeast of Bailey. Good road goes about 9 miles to Deer Creek and Meridian campgrounds, where trails head up into forest. Fair for

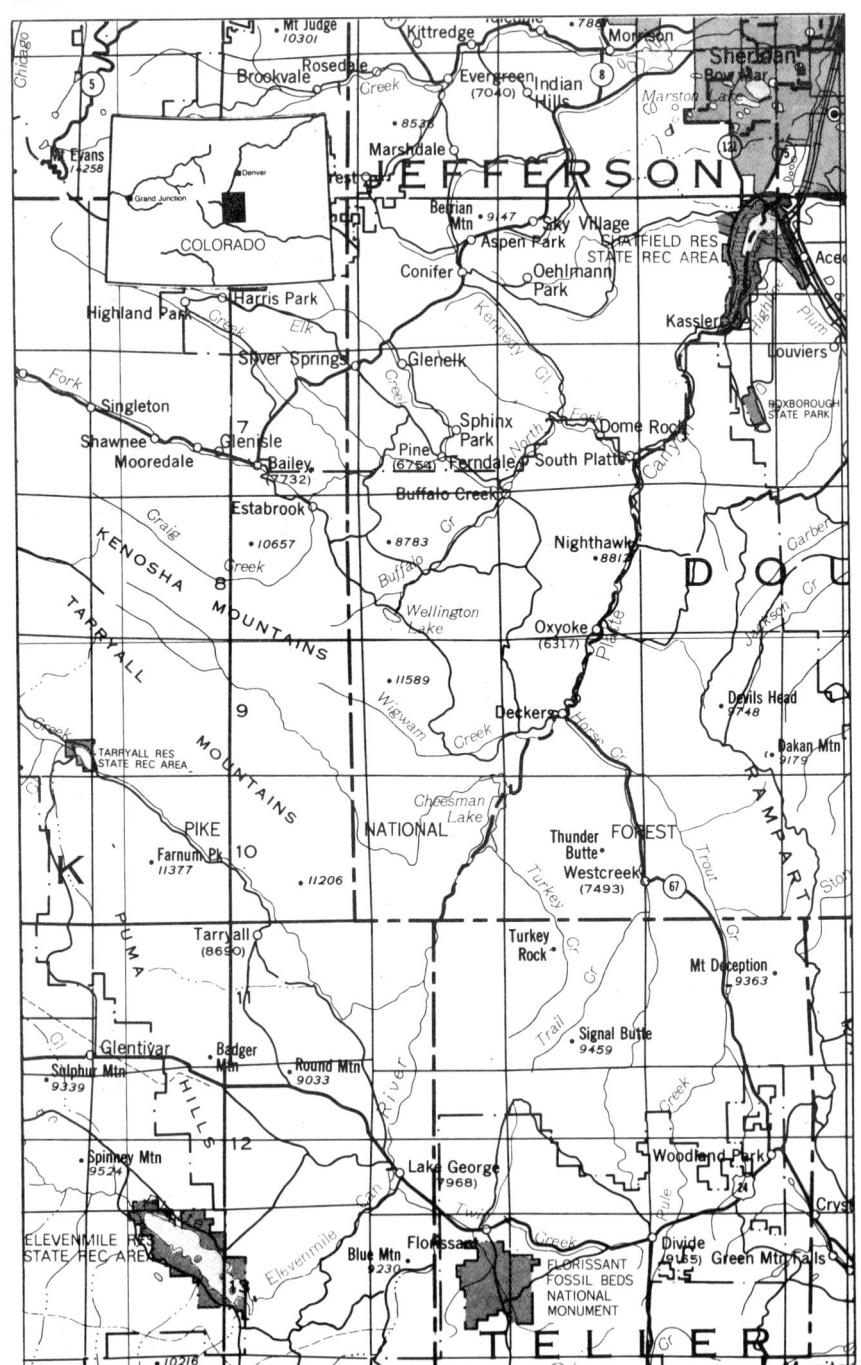

South Platte River

rainbow. A popular area, the lower reaches and hillsides are heavily developed with cabins and summer homes.

Elk Creek, which intersects US 285 at Shaffer's crossing, is poor for brook. Mostly private; access difficult.

Heading northeast out of Bailey on US 285 and southwest on 126, **Buffalo Creek** is small and bushy with some rainbow and brook. It flows from the west into the North Fork at the community of Buffalo Creek. At its headwaters to the southwest is popular **Wellington Lake** (8015 ft; 480 ac). Heavily stocked with rainbow, the lake has boating and a campground about 2 miles away. There is a picnic ground at the lake. Fishing pressure is heavy, especially in spring.

The North Fork joins the South Platte at the entrance to South Platte River Canyon, also called Waterton Canyon. The 8-mile-long canyon was blocked in 1982 with the completion of the Strontia Springs Dam of the Denver Water Department. Water in the reservoir behind the dam will fluctuate a lot. In the deeper sections there is limited natural habitat for trout. Fishing is anticipated to be poor because of the very restricted natural food-producing nature of the area.

From the dam downstream to a point 300 yards upstream from the Denver Water Department's Marston diversion structure, there is fly and lure fishing. All trout over 12 inches are to be released. Stream improvements have been made and the water is being managed to improve fishing. Naturally occurring insects and larvae may be used as bait—(worms are not insects and are not permitted).

CHATFIELD RESERVOIR

Chatfield Reservoir (5426 ft; 1150 ac when full) is a state recreation area on the south side of the metropolitan Denver area. More than 2 million visitors a year visit the 5600-acre park to enjoy a wide range of outdoor activity. It has become one of the best and most popular year-round fisheries. Bass fishing is beginning to be significant.

The reservoir is stocked with trout, bass, catfish, perch, bluegill and crappie. It is heavily fished from shore and boats. Boat ramps are located on the south and northwest shores. Camping is permitted in late spring, summer and early fall and there are solar-heated shower and laundry facilities. Chatfield is reached by driving south to the end of Wadsworth Blvd. (Hwy 121), or via Hwy 470 west from US 85, about 3 miles south of Littleton. US 85 is also known as South Santa Fe Drive. From the south the recreation area may be reached by taking Titan Road west from US 85 about 5.7 miles north of Sedalia. The reservoir is 2 miles west; 1.5 miles north. The area is open 24 hours, and holders of the rainbow trout stamp may take a double limit. Black bass must be over 15 inches or returned to the water immediately. There is a pier near the marina for handicapped anglers. Ice fishing has been excellent.

There are 5 walk-in ponds south of the reservoir, with warm water fishing for crappie, sunfish, blue gill, bullhead, largemouth bass, yellow perch and suckers. Belly boats are permitted.

Downstream from Chatfield Dam, the South Platte River flows through a gravel mining area that is to be a city of Littleton wild area park when mineral extraction ends about 1994. Gravel pits and stream contours are being sculpted to provide good fish habitat. Access is restricted.

Quality of the river water deteriorates rapidly through the metropolitan area; however, there is angling for catfish, carp and suckers. There are some big fish here and anglers go after them with cheese and bread balls, liver chicken parts and similar gourmet fare. (See article on urban fishing and list of metro area fishing sites.)

Besides Chatfield there are 6 other good fishing reservoirs in the metropolitan area. Bear Creek Reservoir is in the southwest quadrant of the area; Cherry Creek and Quincy reservoirs in the southeast; Barr Lake in the northeast; Standley Lake in the northwest and Evergreen Lake in the foothills to the west.

BEAR CREEK RESERVOIR

Bear Creek Reservoir (5700 ft; 1205 ac) has stocked rainbow, which have grown nicely. Also suckers, black bass, bluegill, green sunfish, smallmouth bass, tiger muskie, yellow perch, and bullheads. No boats

SOUTH PLATTE

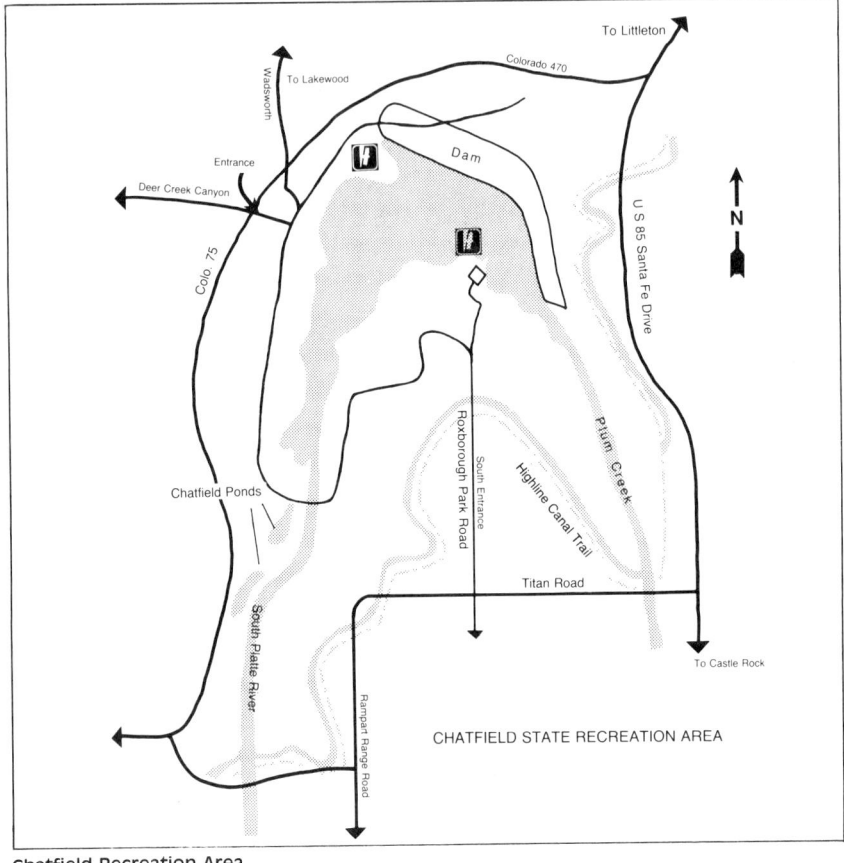

Chatfield Recreation Area

are allowed. Reservoir is lightly fished. A Lakewood parking pass is $2 for persons under 50 years; $1 for people over 50. Walk-in access is free. There is a marina with boat rental near the boat ramp. Hours are 6 a.m. to 10 p.m. from May through September; 6 a.m. to 8 p.m. winter hours. Boat horsepower is limited to 5 hp. Fishing, including ice fishing, has been only fair. Access is by walking from access road off Morrison Road 0.75 mile west of S. Kipling Street or south from a signed area about 1.75 miles farther west on Morrison Road.

The area also may be reached by traveling north from West Hampden Avenue (US 285) on the Soda Lakes Road, about 8.5 miles west of South Santa Fe Drive in Englewood.

Upstream on Bear Creek there is some fishing for rainbow, but they are small and the stream tends to be fished out. At Evergreen, west on Hwy 74 from Morrison is **Evergreen Lake** (7072 ft; 55 ac). In a pretty setting, it is stocked with and heavily fished for rainbow, brown and brook. It is reached by Hwy 74 west from Morrison or by taking the El Rancho exit from I-70 in the foothills west of Denver and going south through Bergen Park and Hiwan to Evergreen.

Upper Bear Creek, above the lake, is heavily developed and mostly posted to the Mount Evans State Wildlife Area in Arapaho National Forest. Several small creeks with small trout. Area is popular with hikers. **Bear Track Lakes** (11,100 ft; 1 and 2 ac) are poor to fair for rainbow. Reached by hiking about 6 miles southwest from Camp Rock Campground. **Summit Lake** (12,830 ft; 33 ac) and **Lincoln Lake** (11,620 ft; 13 ac) may be reached by the Bear Creek Trail by walking west from Camp Rock Campground. Campground is reached by driving up Bear Creek Road to its end. Summit Lake is adjacent to the Mt. Evans Road, and Lincoln Lake is a steep descent of some 1200 vertical feet down and a mile from the road. Great view to east from road, the highest in the U.S. at 14,000 feet elevation. Summit is barren; Lincoln tends to be fished out, but some rainbow or cutthroat may be taken.

CHERRY CREEK RESERVOIR

Cherry Creek Reservoir (5548 ft; 800 ac) is a state recreation area visited by more than 2 million people annually. The reservoir is good fishing for trout, black bass, walleye, northern pike, crappie, yellow perch, sunfish, bluegill, channel catfish, bullheads, suckers, carp and other rough fish. A 16-pound walleye and a 22-pound carp from Cherry Creek hold the state records for their species.

A 2-pound tench from the reservoir is also a record. The area has large brown, rainbow and northern as well as big catfish. There are boat ramps on the east and west sides. In good weather the water teems with sailboats and other watercraft. The reservoir is heavily stocked and fished. It is usually

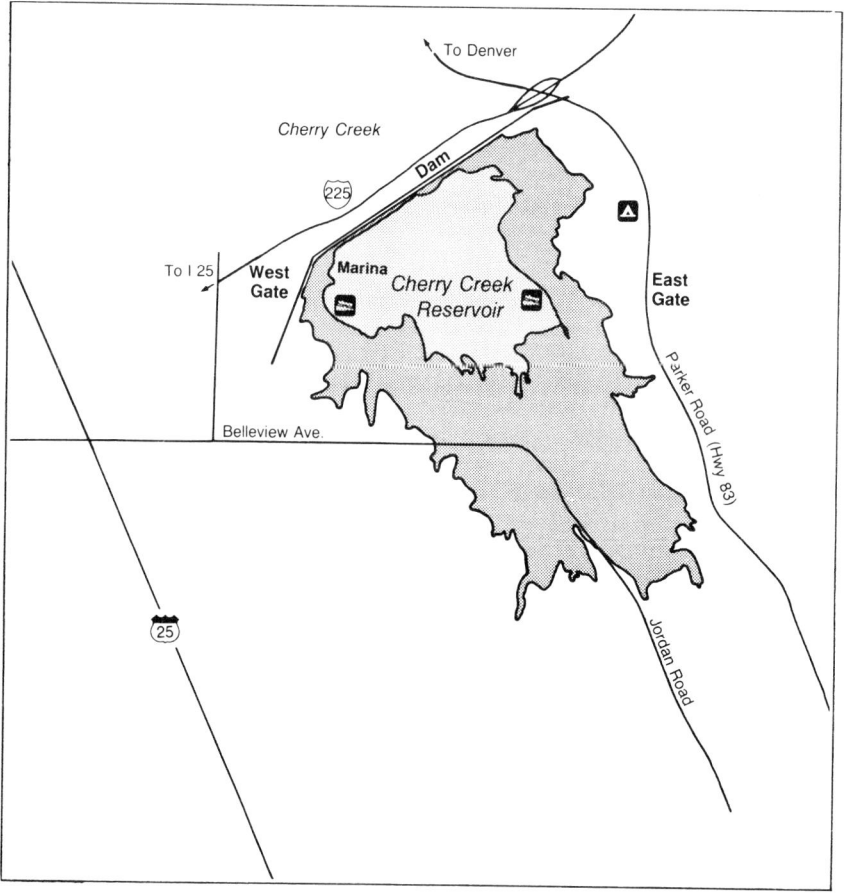

Cherry Creek Reservoir

best after the ice is out or late in the fall when the weather diminishes the number of boaters.

Northern pike and walleye fishing is good to excellent. Ice fishing is popular and often superb. The reservoir is rapidly approaching a critical stage for oxygen content in the water—especially in hot weather—so that its status as a fishery could decline. The area is closed to additional people when a rated capacity of visitors is reached, usually on holidays and summer weekends.

Cherry Creek Reservoir is accessible from the east by Hwy 83 (Parker Road). I-270 crosses the dam, and access via Parker Road and Yosemite Street is signed from the interstate. It is also reached by taking the Belleview Exit east from I-25 to Yosemite Street and then north to access road. Jordan Road, which goes north from County Line Road (between Arapahoe and Douglas counties) just west of Cherry Creek, reaches the area from the south.

QUINCY RESERVOIR

Quincy Reservoir (5,544 ft; 160 ac) is open to public fishing from 2 p.m. to 1 hour after sunset on weekdays, and sunrise to an hour after sunset on weekends and holidays by the City of Aurora. Only artificial flies and lures are permitted when fishing for rainbow and brown trout, largemouth bass, suckers and yellow perch. Aurora Park Permit ($2 per visit or $10 per year) is required.

All trout under 16 inches and black bass under 15 inches must be returned to the water immediately. The limit is 2 fish. Fishing is rated good to excellent. The reservoir is closed from November 1 through April 30. Ice fishing is forbidden. This is an exceptionally good metro area fishery. Access is off of East Quincy Avenue 3 miles east of Parker Road in the southeast metro area.

STANDLEY LAKE

Like other Denver area recreation spots, **Standley Lake** (5506 ft; 1200 ac) gets lots of attention from boaters, waterskiers and fishermen. Operated by the City of Westminster, it is basically a waterskiing lake. Boating is allowed, but limited to those with one of 350 permits that sell for $100 to $200. Reservoir can fluctuate significantly, putting boat ramps out of the water by 100 feet or more. Fishing is for stocked walleye, black bass, catfish, green sunfish, smallmouth bass, yellow perch and some rough fish. No fishing from dam. Hours for vehicular access are limited as posted. Walk-in fishing access anytime. Parking fee at 88th Avenue entrance. The only public access is by taking West 88th Avenue west from Wadsworth Blvd. to the Kipling Street parking area. Jefferson County Open Space owns most of the south shore, but fishing from it is difficult and usually poor.

BARR LAKE

Barr Lake (5210 ft; 1660 ac) in Barr Lake State Park northeast of Denver has largemouth bass, smallmouth bass, crappie, carp, channel catfish, Sacramento perch, suckers and yellow perch. It is recognized as a good catfish and carp lake as well as a popular birdwatching area. It is open from 5 a.m. to 10 p.m. A state parks pass is required. It's a popular fishery, especially for bass and crappie from handpowered boats. No motorboats permitted. Free walk-in access.

It is just east of I-76 and west of Picadilly Road. North boundary is Bromley Lane; southern, 128th Avenue. Park entrance, parking and boat ramp are off Picadilly Road. □

U.S. FOREST SERVICE DISTRICT RANGER STATIONS

South Park Ranger District
Pike National Forest
Located NW of the junction of Hwys 9 & 285
P.O. Box 218
Fairplay, CO 80440   303/836-2404

South Platte Ranger District
Pike National Forest
Ste. 107, 393 S. Harlan
Lakewood, CO 80226   303/234-5707
           Recording: 303/234-5706

Clear Creek Ranger District
Arapaho National Forest
101 Chicago Creek, P.O. Box 730
Idaho Springs, CO 80452   303/567-2901
       Denver Metro Phone: 303/893-1474

DOW FISHING LEASES

SOUTH FORK
SOUTH PLATTE RIVER
Imler-Knight Wildlife Area
Location: 10.5 miles south of Fairplay on Hwy 285, east of highway (2.19 mi of river)

MIDDLE FORK
SOUTH PLATTE RIVER
Tomahawk Ranch-DOW-owned
Location: 5 miles northwest of Hartsel on Hwy 9 (3.81 mi of river)

MIDDLE FORK SOUTH PLATTE RIVER; TROUT CREEK
Buffalo Peaks Ranch lease
Location: 7 miles northwest of Hartsel on Hwy 9 (6 mi of river)

TARRYALL CREEK
Location: 20 miles south of Jefferson in Park County (1 mile of stream below Tarryall Dam)

Fishing license receipts are the major source of funding for fish management and research activities.

Fishing on ice

U.S. Forest Service campgrounds

U.S. Forest Service compilation was current as of 1985.
Asterisks denote fee areas. Some campgrounds are open only Memorial Day weekend through Labor Day. Below freezing weather could mean no water supply.

SOUTH PLATTE RIVER DRAINAGE
PIKE NATIONAL FOREST
Headquarters: 910 Hwy 50 West, Box 5808, Pueblo, CO 81002

Campground name	Elevation	No camp sites	Travel trailers	Drinking water	Length of stay (days)	Location and directions
Jefferson Creek*	10,100	17	Yes	Yes	10	4.9 mi NW of Jefferson by county and forest roads
Lodgepole*	9900	35	Yes	Yes	10	3.8 mi NW of Jefferson by county and forest roads
Aspen*	9900	12	Yes	Yes	10	4 mi NW of Jefferson by forest roads
Buffalo Springs	9000	17	Yes	No	10	.5 mi W off US 285, 13.6 mi S of Fairplay
Michigan Creek	10,000	13	Yes	No	10	5.1 mi NW of Jefferson by forest roads
Selkirk	10,500	15	Yes	No	10	4.3 mi NW of Como by forest roads
Fourmile	10,500	14	Yes	Yes	10	5.7 mi W of Fairplay off US 285
Weston Pass	10,200	14	Yes	No	10	11 mi W of US 285, 5 mi S of Fairplay
Kenosha Pass	10,000	25	Yes	Yes	14	On US 285, 3.1 mi NE of Jefferson
Lost Park	10,000	10	Yes	No	10	17 mi SE of US 285 at Jefferson
The Crags	10,100	18	Yes	Yes	14	5.5 mi SE of Divide off Colo. 67
Blue Mountain*	8200	21	Yes	Yes	14	2 mi S of Lake George on forest roads
Cove*	8400	5	Yes	Yes	7	9 mi SW of Lake George by forest roads
Reservoir*	8500	24	Yes	Yes	7	9.6 mi SW of Lake George by forest roads
Spruce Grove*	8600	28	Yes	Yes	14	On County Road 77, 12.2 mi NW of Lake George
Round Mountain*	8500	16	Yes	Yes	14	On US 24, 5.2 mi NW of Lake George

Springer Gulch*	8300	15	Yes	Yes	7	5.2 mi SW of Lake George by forest roads
Clyde*	9500	10	Yes	Yes	14	7 mi E of Victor off Colo. 67
Wye*	9800	21	Yes	Yes	14	9 mi SW of Colorado Springs off US 24
Springdale	9100	11	Yes	No	14	1.7 mi E of Woodland Park by forest roads
South Meadows*	8000	57	Yes	Yes	14	On Colo. 67, 5.5 mi N of Woodland Park
Colorado*	7800	63	Yes	Yes	14	7.8 mi N of Florissant via Colo. Hwy 1
Wildhorn	9100	10	Yes	Yes	14	20 mi N of Woodland Park off US 24
Riverside*	8000	12	Yes	No	10	2 mi SW of Lake George on forest road
Goose Creek	8100	10	Yes	Yes	14	15 mi SW of Colo. 67, 17.6 mi NW of Woodland Park
Big Turkey	8000	10	Yes	Yes	14	5 mi SW off Colo. 67, 11.2 mi NW of Woodland Park
Molly Gulch	7500	15	Yes	Yes	14	12 mi SW of Colo. 67, 18.4 mi NW of Woodland Park
Painted Rocks*	7800	15	Yes	Yes	14	8.5 mi NW of Woodland Park off Colo. 67
Jackson Creek	8100	9	Yes	Yes	14	15.4 mi S off Colo. 67, 10 mi W of Sedalia
Indian Creek*	7500	10	Yes	Yes	14	8 mi W of Sedalia off Colo. 67
Top of the World	7500	7	Yes	No	14	1.8 mi SE of Buffalo Creek by forest road
Lone Rock*	6400	18	Yes	Yes	14	8.4 mi SE of Buffalo Creek on County Hwy 126
Kelsey*	8000	17	Yes	Yes	14	5.2 mi S of Buffalo Creek on Colo. 126
Buffalo*	7400	41	Yes	Yes	14	4 mi SW of Buffalo Creek by forest roads
Hall Valley	9900	9	Yes	Yes	14	5 mi off forest road NW off US 285, 3 mi W of Grant
Deer Creek	9000	12	Yes	Yes	14	8 mi NW of US 285, 2.4 mi N of Bailey
Meridian	9000	18	Yes	Yes	14	8 mi N of US 285, 2.4 mi NW of Bailey
Burning Bear	9500	13	Yes	Yes	14	5 mi NW of Grant on forest roads
Flat Rocks*	8200	20	Yes	Yes	14	5 mi S of Colo. 67, 10 mi SW of Sedalia

Metro Denver offers improved angling

Adjacent communities:
Denver, Aurora, Englewood, Littleton, Lakewood, Edgewater, Golden, Arvada, Broomfield.

Close-to-home fishing is getting better and better. That's because the Colorado Division of Wildlife is putting more emphasis on warm water angling, and angling in and around communities with suitable fishing water open to the public.

Lunch-hour bass — Charles A. Walker photo

In the Denver metropolitan area, some 1.79 million fish were to be stocked in 1985 in the lakes listed in this article. Not all of them are of catchable size and some are food fish to help the lakes and ponds meet game fish appetites. And 100,000 of those stockers are catchable size crappie, bass, channel catfish and other species.

For thousands of youngsters, this means fishing without an adult having to drive them to and from their favorite fishing hole. Many fishing spots can be reached by RTD as well as bicycle or hoofing it.

Urban fishing is more than stocking. It's sampling water and keeping track of its quality and the organisms that nourish fish as well as the suitability for fish reproduction. It means notching or tagging fish to keep track of their growth and rate of growth and determining which fish provide the best fishing in any one pond, lake or reservoir.

The Denver area isn't the only place "backyard" angling is encouraged. It's also on the rise in Colorado Springs, Pueblo, Walsenburg, Trinidad, Fort Collins, Vail, Alamosa, Glenwood Springs, Loveland and many other Colorado communities.

And don't look down your nose at this sort of fishing. Trophy bass, walleye, crappie, tench and other species abound in the better waters. Cherry Creek Reservoir, Chatfield Reservoir, Kendrick Lake, Trinidad Reservoir and those ponds and reservoirs along the Arkansas River produced record caliber specimens. So, it's not just for kids.

ADAMS COUNTY FAIRGROUNDS LAKE
Adams County
West of US Hwy 85 and north of E. 124th Ave.

METRO DENVER 223

9 ac; max. depth is 22 ft
No boats. Open 7 a.m. to 11 p.m. Restrooms, playground.
Fish present: channel catfish, largemouth bass, crappie, bluegill, bullhead, carp, green sunfish, sunfish.

BALSAM PARK POND
Jefferson County, Lakewood
W. 1st Ave. and Balsam St.
1.5 ac; max. depth is 6 ft
No boats. Open dawn to 10:30 p.m. No facilities.
Fish present: carp, goldfish, bluegill, bullhead, crappie, green sunfish, suckers.

BARNUM PARK LAKE
Denver County
W. 6th Ave. and Federal Blvd.; Hooker St. and W. 3rd Ave.
9 ac; max depth is 5 ft
No boats. Open 5 a.m. to 11 p.m. Playground, restrooms.
Fish present: carp, channel catfish, bluegill, goldfish, suckers.

BARR LAKE STATE PARK
Adams County, I-76 and Bromley Ln., east to Picadilly Rd.
1,660 ac; max depth is 42 ft (full pool)
Extreme water level fluctuation.
Nongasoline-powered boats only, no boating in wildlife refuge. No fishing from dam. Parks pass required. Picnic facilities, restrooms and boatramp.
Fish present: channel catfish, smallmouth and largemouth bass, carp, yellow perch, Sacramento perch, sucker. Premier carp and channel catfish fishery. More details available in Parks brochure. Fee area; free walk-in fisherman access.

BASS LAKE
Prospect Park
Jefferson County, Wheat Ridge
South of W. 44th Ave. at Robb St.; also access from Youngfield St. east along Clear Creek.
3 ac; max. depth is 13 ft
No boats. Open dawn to 11 p.m. Restrooms at nearby Prospect Lake. Picnic facilities, flies and lures only. No bait.
Fish present: largemouth bass, bluegill, crappie, green sunfish, suckers. Minimum 15-inch size on bass.

BEAR CREEK PONDS
Jefferson County, Lakewood
W. Yale Ave. and S. Estes St.
10 ac total; max. depth is 12 ft
No boats. Open dawn to 10:30 p.m. No facilities.
Fish present: channel catfish, largemouth bass, bullhead, crappie, bluegill, green sunfish.

BEAR CREEK RESERVOIR
Jefferson County, Lakewood, S. Kipling St. and Morrison Rd. Walk-in access from Soda Lakes Rd. on west side of reservoir; north of US 285 (Hampden Ave.) at Soda Lakes Rd.
205 ac; max. depth is 45 ft
Boats to 5 hp; open 6 a.m.-10 p.m. May/Sept.; 6 a.m.-8 p.m. Oct/April. Lakewood Parks pass required for boats.
Fish present: rainbow trout, sucker, bullhead, bluegill, green sunfish, largemouth bass, smallmouth bass, tiger muskie, yellow perch. Minimum size bass 15 inches; tiger muskie, 36 inches.

BELL ROTH PARK POND
Adams County, Federal Heights
W. 86th Ave. and Pecos St.
3 ac; max. depth is 8 ft
No boats. Open dawn to 10 p.m. No restrooms.
Fish present: channel catfish, bluegill, yellow perch, crappie, green sunfish, carp, goldfish, bullhead, suckers.

BERKELEY HILLS POND
(Bryant kids' pond)
Adams County, W. 54 Ave. and Rosemary Ln.
0.5 ac; max. depth is 6 ft
Very small kids' pond. No boats. Open dawn to 10 p.m.
Fish present: largemouth bass, goldfish, bluegill, green sunfish.

BERKELEY LAKE
Denver County
Tennyson St. and W. 46th Ave.
40 ac; max depth is 12 ft
No boats. Open 5 a.m. to 11 p.m.
Fish present: channel catfish, crappie, largemouth bass, carp, sucker, green sunfish, bullhead, golden shiner, orange-spotted sunfish.

BIRDLAND LAKE
Jefferson County, Arvada
W. 51st Ave. and Garrison St.

3 ac; max. depth is 10 ft
Nonmotorized boats only. No ice fishing. Open dawn to 11 p.m.
Fish present: channel catfish, bluegill, largemouth bass, yellow perch, pumpkinseed, green sunfish.

BOWLES GROVE POND
Arapahoe County, Littleton
W. Bowles Ave. and S. Federal Blvd.
2 ac; max. depth is 6 ft
No boats. Open 6 a.m. to 10 p.m.
Fish present: carp, crappie, bluegill, bullhead, green sunfish, largemouth bass, orange-spotted bass, suckers, yellow perch.

BROOMFIELD COMMUNITY PARK PONDS
(Broomfield kids' ponds)
Boulder County, Broomfield
One pond at Main St. and Comm. Park Dr., another near W. Midway Blvd. and Kohl Blvd. Playground and restrooms at Community Park site.
3 ac total; max. depth is 6 ft
Very small. Kids' ponds.
No boats. Open 5 a.m. to 11 p.m.
Fish present: largemouth bass, bluegill, channel catfish, crappie, yellow perch, sunfish, bullhead.

BUTTS PARK POND
(Carroll Butts pond)
Adams County, Westminster
W. 94th Ave. and Perry St.
3 ac; max. depth is 5 ft
No boats. Open daylight hours.
Fish present: channel catfish, bluegill, crappie, yellow perch, bullhead, green sunfish, suckers, goldfish.

CAMENISCH PARK POND
Adams County, Westminster
W. 90th Ave. and Fontaine St.
3 ac; max. depth is 10 ft
No boats. Open dawn to 10 p.m.
Fish present: channel catfish, crappie, bluegill, largemouth bass, bullhead, green sunfish, pumpkinseed, suckers.

CARL PARK POND
Adams County
W. 54th Ave. and Meade St.
4 ac; max. depth is 8 ft
No boats. Open dawn to 10 p.m.
Fish present: largemouth bass, bluegill, sunfish, goldfish.

CARMODY PARK POND
Jefferson County, Lakewood
S. Kipling St. and W. Evans Ave.
3 ac; max depth is 4 ft
Very small. Kids' pond.
No boats. Open dawn to dusk.
Fish present: bullhead, sunfish, largemouth bass.

CENTENNIAL PARK LAKE
Arapahoe County, Englewood
Northeast of W. Union Ave. and S. Federal Blvd.
15 ac; max. depth is 27 ft
No boats. Open dawn to 11 p.m. Fishing pier.
Fish present: stocked rainbow trout, smallmouth bass, largemouth bass, bluegill, channel catfish, crappie, golden shiner, goldfish, green sunfish, pumpkinseed, suckers, yellow perch.

CHATFIELD PONDS
Jefferson and Douglas counties, south of Chatfield Reservoir and within Chatfield Reservoir State Recreation Area.
5 ponds totalling 140 ac; maximum depth 34 ft
Walk-in fishing only via trails from Chatfield Reservoir Rd; or east cross country from Hwy 75 (see map). Belly boats only. Parks pass required. No bridge over South Platte River between ponds 1, 2 & 3 and ponds 4 & 5. Open 24 hours (subject to change as posted).
Fish present: bullhead, channel catfish (No. 1 pond only), crappie, green sunfish, largemouth bass, suckers, yellow perch, bluegill.

CHATFIELD RESERVOIR
Jefferson and Douglas counties
US 85 (S. Santa Fe Dr.) and Hwy 470
1,100 ac; max. depth is 50 ft
Possible extremes in water fluctuation.
Various boating allowed. No boating in heron rookery. See brochure for details. Parks pass required. May close when rated park capacity is reached. Ice fishing ok. Marina, 3 boat-ramps, 300-ft fishing pier for handicapped.
Special 12- to 15-in. slot length limit on bass.
Fish present: stocked rainbow trout, crappie, yellow perch, largemouth bass, channel catfish, bluegill, green sunfish, sunfish, carp, bullhead, sucker. Ice fishing, camping.

CHERRY CREEK RESERVOIR
Arapahoe County, I-225 and Hwy 83; entrances

Cherry Creek Reservoir

off S. Parker Rd. and S. Yosemite St.
800 ac; max. depth is 30 ft
Various boating allowed. See Parks brochure for details. Parks pass required. Open 24 hours but may close when rated park capacity is reached. Ice fishing ok. Marina, 2 boatramps. Ice fishing, camping.
Fish present: stocked rainbow trout, largemouth bass, walleye, northern pike, crappie, yellow perch, bluegill, channel catfish, green sunfish, golden shiner, shad, carp, sucker, bullhead, tench.
State record walleye and carp caught here. Large northern pike and walleye, also.

CITY PARK LAKE
Denver County, Denver
E. 17th Ave. and Colorado Blvd.
25 ac; max. depth is 8 ft
No fishing from rental boats. Open 5 a.m. to 11 p.m. No private boats.
Fish present: carp, crappie, bluegill, bullhead, yellow perch, channel catfish, shad, green sunfish, largemouth bass.

CLEAR CREEK POND
Adams County, Hwy 224 along Clear Creek at Lafayette St.
3 ac; max. depth is 9 ft
No boats. Open 7 a.m. to 11 p.m.
Fish present: channel catfish, crappie, bullhead, green sunfish, largemouth bass, yellow perch, bluegill, pumpkinseed.

COLUMBINE POND
Jefferson County, Arvada
W. 52nd Ave. and Nolan St.
0.5 ac; max. depth is 4 ft
Extreme water level fluctuation.
Very small kids' pond. No boats. Open dawn to 11 p.m.
Fish present: bullhead, sunfish.

COTTONWOOD PARK LAKE
(Kendrick Lake No. 1)
Jefferson County, Lakewood
S. Oak St. and W. Evans Ave.
8 ac; max. depth is 7 ft
Nonmotorized boats only. Open dawn to 10 p.m.
Fish present: bluegill, largemouth bass, channel catfish, pumpkinseed.

CROWN HILL LAKE
Jefferson County, Wheat Ridge
W. 26th Ave. and Kipling St.
53 ac; max. depth is 13 ft
No boats. Open 5 a.m. to 11 p.m. No wading or tube fishing. Restrooms.
Special 12- to 15-in. slot length limit on largemouth bass.
Fish present: largemouth bass, bluegill, yellow perch, green sunfish, crappie, channel catfish, carp, sucker.

CUSHING PARK POND
Arapahoe County, Englewood
W. Dartmouth Ave. east of S. Santa Fe Dr.; W. Eastman St. and S. Huron St.
Open dawn to 11 p.m.
0.5 ac; max. depth is 7 ft
Very small kids' pond, playground, picnic area, restrooms.
Fish present: carp, goldfish, yellow perch.

EAST RESERVOIR
(in Kendrick Lake Chain)
Jefferson County, Lakewood
W. Florida Ave. and S. Kipling St.
21 ac; max. depth is 5 ft
Extreme water level fluctuation.
Nonmotorized boats only. Open dawn to 10:30 p.m.
Fish present: largemouth bass, carp, goldfish, yellow perch, pumpkinseed, bullhead, green sunfish.

ENGINEERS LAKE
Adams County
E. of I-76 on Hwy 224 at S. Platte River
11 ac; max. depth is 25 ft
Steep banked shoreline; walk-in only; picnicking.
Fish present: bullhead.

EXPOSITION PARK POND
Arapahoe County, Aurora
S. Havana St. (285) and E. Exposition Ave.
5 ac; max. depth is 5 ft
Extreme water level fluctuation.
No boats. Open dawn to dusk.
Fish present: carp, bluegill, bullheads, suckers, goldfish.
Good bullhead pond.

GARFIELD PARK LAKE
Denver County
S. Newton St. and W. Mississippi Ave. and W. Arizona Ave.
10 ac; max. depth is 4 ft
No boats. Open 5 a.m. to 11 p.m.
Fish present: crappie, bluegill, bullhead, largemouth bass, channel catfish, carp, green sunfish.

GARLAND PARK LAKE
(Lollypop Lake)
Denver County
Cherry Creek N. Dr. and S. Holly St.
4 ac; max. depth is 8 ft
No boats. Open 5 a.m. to 11 p.m.
Fish present: channel catfish, bluegill, largemouth bass, yellow perch, goldfish, green sunfish, bullhead, crappie, orange-spotted sunfish, golden shiner, suckers.

GREEN GABLES PARK POND
Jefferson County, Lakewood
S. Garrison St. and W. Florida Ave.
0.5 ac; max. depth is 6 ft
Very small kids' pond. No boats. Open dawn to 10:30 p.m. Playground.
Fish present: bluegill, crappie, largemouth bass, pumpkinseed, green sunfish.

HARVEY PARK LAKE
Denver County
W. Evans Ave. and S. Newton St.
8.5 ac; max. depth is 8 ft
No boats. Open 5 a.m. to 11 p.m. Playground.
Fish present: channel catfish, bluegill, crappie, largemouth bass, bullhead, yellow perch, carp, green sunfish, golden shiner, goldfish, pumpkinseed.

HOLBROOK PARK POND
Jefferson County, Lakewood
W. 8th Ave. and Garrison St.
0.5 ac; max. depth is 6 ft (full)
Extreme water level fluctuation.
Very small kids' pond. No boats. Open dawn to 10:30 p.m.
Fish present: occasionally bullheads, sunfish.

HUSTON PARK LAKE
Denver County
W. Kentucky Ave. and S. Clay St.
13 ac; max. depth is 6 ft
No boats. Open 5 a.m. to 11 p.m. Playground.
Fish present: largemouth bass, bluegill, bullhead, green sunfish, sucker, carp, channel catfish, crappie, yellow perch, golden shiner, sunfish, goldfish.

JEWELL PARK POND
Jefferson County, Lakewood
W. Jewell Ave. and Garrison St.
2 ac; max. depth is 5 ft
Nonmotorized boats only. Open dawn to 10:30 p.m. Fishing pier. Set up for waterfowl, fishing discouraged.
Fish present: channel catfish, bullheads, carp,

Your first cast for successful fishing is

TIM KELLEY'S FISHING GUIDE
to Colorado & Wyoming

Is the Best Yet*

Is a practical, sturdy paperback book that:

- Describes the fishing in 3,000 lakes & streams, and
- Gives directions to them—even the back-country anglers' paradises
- Features more than 60 maps
- Lists Forest Service campgrounds
- Offers a special new section on bass & warm water fishing
- Compiles a descriptive index to useful, publicly available maps
- Notes tackle shops especially helpful to the visiting angler
- Comprises more than 380 pages of useful information.

*Since Tim Kelley's first guide was published in 1954.

Hart Publications, Inc. 303/837-1917
P.O. Box 1917
Denver, CO 80201

TIM KELLEY'S FISHING GUIDE

The Official
Colorado-Wyoming
Fishing Guide

Send me _____ copies of the 17th edition @ $9.95 each plus $1.50 for postage and handling.

Name_____

Address_____ Phone_____

City_____ State_____ Zip_____

Payment Enclosed ☐   Make checks payable to:
Bill Me ☐   Hart Publications, Inc.
                            P.O. Box 1917, Denver, CO 80201
                            303/837-1917

The 17th edition is $9.95
plus $1.50 for postage and handling

TIM KELLY'S FISHING GUIDE

Tim Kelley's Fishing Guide is used by the Colorado Division of Wildlife, Wyoming Game & Fish Department, U.S. Forest Service and Chambers of Commerce as the basic reference to public fishing.

The 17th edition is available from leading sporting goods stores and fishing tackle shops, book stores and by mail from **Hart Publications, Inc.**, P.O. Box 1917, Denver, CO 80201 for $9.95 plus $1.50 for postage and handling.

(Colorado residents add 3% sales tax; Denver residents 6.6% and Denver suburban area 3.6% tax)

NO POSTAGE
NECESSARY
IF MAILED
IN THE
UNITED STATES

BUSINESS REPLY CARD
FIRST CLASS PERMIT NO. 3961 DENVER, COLORADO

POSTAGE WILL BE PAID BY ADDRESSEE

TIM KELLEY'S FISHING GUIDE
Hart Publications, Inc.

P. O. Box 1917
Denver, CO 80201

METRO DENVER 227

SMOOTH CURRENT. FROM HONDA.

We've got the full line of unbeatable Honda 4-cycle outboards and portable AC/DC generators at hard to beat prices! See us first—for "watt-ever" you need!

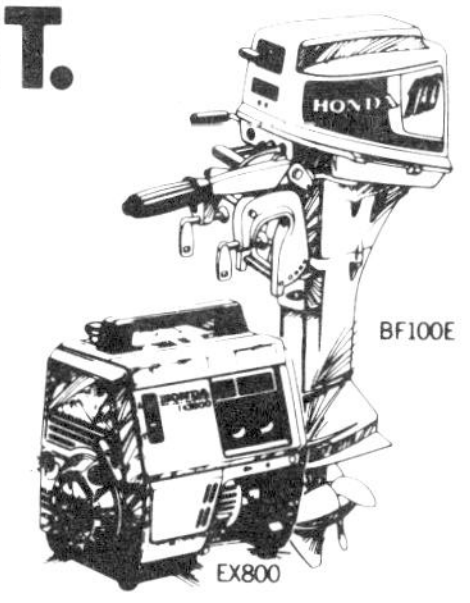

SALES • SERVICE • RENTALS • PARTS

Generator City
Your power products supercenter!

1700 N. Federal Blvd.
Denver, Colorado 80204
Next to Mile High Stadium

9625 E. Arapahoe Rd.
Englewood, Colorado 80112
Arapahoe at Dayton

Monday-Friday 8-5, Saturday 9-4

455-2800 790-4900
TOLL FREE IN COLORADO 1-800-521-1511

Photo courtesy Scott Roederer

crappie, bluegill, pumpkinseed, green sunfish, golden shiner.

JOHNSON POND
Jefferson County, Wheat Ridge
Southbound Wadsworth Blvd. and I-70
0.5 ac; max. depth is 4 ft
Very small kids' pond. No boats. Open dawn to dusk.
Fish present: green sunfish, crappie, bullhead, carp, pumpkinseed.

KENDRICK LAKE
Jefferson County, Lakewood
W. Jewell Ave. and S. Hoyt St.
33 ac; max. depth is 8 ft
Nonmotorized boats only. Open dawn to 10:30 p.m. Playground, fishing pier.
Fish present: largemouth bass, channel catfish, pumpkinseed, bullhead, bluegill, crappie, carp, golden shiner, green sunfish. Old state record crappie caught here.

KETTERING PARK LAKE
(Gallup Lake)
Arapahoe County, Littleton
S. Gallup St. and W. Lake Ave.
15 ac; max. depth is 9 ft
No boats. Open 6 a.m. to 10 p.m.
Fish present: largemouth bass, crappie, bluegill, channel catfish, green sunfish, carp.

KIWANIS PARK POND
Adams County
W. 80th Ave. and Valley View, E. of Zuni St.
3 ac; max. depth is 2 ft
Very small kids' pond. No boats. Open dawn to a half-hour after sunset.
Fish present: bullhead, green sunfish, carp, crappie, pumpkinseed.

LAKE ARBOR
Jefferson County, Arvada
Pomona Dr. and Lamar St. north of W. 80th Ave.
37 ac; max. depth is 19 ft
Nonmotorized boats only. Open dawn to 11 p.m. Fishing piers, playground.
Fish present: channel catfish, bullhead, largemouth bass, bluegill, green sunfish, sunfish, golden shiner, carp, crappie, pumpkinseed.

LAKE GENEVA
Arapahoe County, Littleton
S. Prince St. and Crestline Dr.
1 ac; max. depth is 6 ft
Handicapped and senior citizens only.
No boats. Open 7 a.m. to sunset.
Fish present: crappie, sunfish, bluegill, carp, channel catfish, largemouth bass, suckers.

LITTLE'S CREEK POND
Arapahoe County, Littleton
S. Broadway and Sterne Pkwy.
1 ac; max. depth is 5 ft
Very small kids' pond. No boats. Open 6 a.m. to 10 p.m. Playground.
Fish present: channel catfish, bluegill, green sunfish, sunfish, bullhead, carp, goldfish, suckers, largemouth bass, crappie.

MAIN RESERVOIR
(Osner Reservoir)
Jefferson County, Lakewood
W. Florida Ave. and S. Kipling St.; also access from S. Kipling St. and W. Mississippi Ave.
45 ac; max. depth is 19 ft
Extreme water level fluctuation.
Nonmotorized boats only. Open dawn to 10:30 p.m.
Fish present: stocked rainbow trout, small- and largemouth bass, bluegill, yellow perch, channel catfish, carp, green sunfish, sucker, pumpkinseed, crappie.

NORTH PROSPECT LAKE
(Tabor Lake)
Jefferson County, Wheat Ridge
Clear Creek (Youngfield St. or Prospect Park Access) off W. 44th Ave. at Robb St.
16 ac; max. depth is 26 ft
Nonmotorized boats with Wheat Ridge Parks permit. Restrooms.
Open dawn to dusk.
Fish present: largemouth bass, crappie, bluegill, channel catfish, green sunfish.

OVERLAND POND
Denver County
W. Florida Ave. and S. Santa Fe Drive
1 ac; max. depth is 7 ft
No boats. Fly casting practice pad. Open 5 a.m. to 11 p.m.
Fish present: crappie, bluegill, largemouth bass, carp.

POMONA LAKE
Jefferson County, Arvada
W. 80th Ave. and Estes St., west of Wadsworth
31 ac; max. depth 8 ft
Open dawn to 11 p.m.
Fish present: bullhead, channel catfish, green sunfish, crappie, largemouth bass, yellow perch.

PROSPECT PARK LAKE
(See also Bass Lake, North Prospect Lake & West Lake—all part of Prospect Park lakes)
Jefferson County, Wheat Ridge
W. 44th Ave. and Robb St.
7 ac; max. depth is 22 ft
Nonmotorized boats with Wheat Ridge Parks permit.
No fishing from boat. Open dawn to 11 p.m. Restrooms, picnic area.
Fish present: largemouth bass, bluegill, sunfish, crappie, channel catfish. Good bass fishing.

QUINCY RESERVOIR
Arapahoe County, Aurora
3 mi. east of Parker Road on E. Quincy Ave.
160 ac; max. depth is 58 ft
Open 2 p.m. to 1 hour after sunset weekdays; sunrise to 1 hour after sunset holidays and weekends.
Aurora park permit required; flies and lures only; 16-inch min. on trout; two fish limit. Good rainbow fishing.
Fish present: brown & rainbow trout, largemouth bass, smelt, suckers, yellow perch.

RIDGEVIEW PARK POND
Arapahoe County, Littleton
S. Prince St. and W. Rowland Ave.
1.5 ac; max. depth is 6 ft
Open 6 a.m. to 10 p.m. Picnic facilities. Very small kids' pond.
Fish present: bluegill, bullhead, carp, green sunfish, largemouth bass.

ROCKY MOUNTAIN LAKE
Denver County
W. 46th Ave. between Lowell & Federal Blvds.
29 ac; max. depth is 14 ft
No boats. Open 5 a.m. to 11 p.m.
Fish present: carp, bluegill, crappie, channel catfish, green sunfish, goldfish, sunfish, bullhead, pumpkinseed, largemouth bass, suckers.

ROTARY PARK POND
Adams County
W. 84th Ave. and Wagner Dr.
1 ac; max. depth is 4 ft
Very small kids' pond. No boats. Open dawn to 10 p.m. Playground.
Fish present: bullhead, carp, goldfish, suckers, sunfish.

ROTELLA PARK POND
Adams County
South of S. Coronado Parkway east of York St.
3 ac; max. depth is 10 ft
Extreme water level fluctuation.
Small kids' pond. No boats. Open 7 a.m. to 11 p.m. Restrooms, playground.
Fish present: channel catfish, largemouth bass, bluegill, pumpkinseed, bullhead.

SLOANS LAKE
Denver County
W. 23rd Ave. and W. 17th Ave. and Sheridan Blvd.
174 ac; max. depth is 9 ft
Boating with Denver Parks and Recreation permit. No fishing from boats.
Open 5 a.m. to 11 p.m.
Fish present: stocked rainbow trout, bullhead, carp, crappie, green sunfish, goldfish, yellow perch, channel catfish, bluegill, suckers, orange-spotted sunfish. Premier carp fishing.

SMITH RESERVOIR
(In Kendrick Lake Chain)
Jefferson County, Lakewood
W. Jewell Ave. and S. Moore Ct.
44 ac; max. depth is 17 ft
Extreme water level fluctuation.
Nonmotorized boats only. Open dawn to 10:30 p.m. Restrooms.
Fish present: smallmouth bass, largemouth bass, bluegill, carp, sucker, pumpkinseed, green sunfish, yellow perch. Previous state record smallmouth bass caught here.

STANDLEY LAKE
Jefferson County, Westminster
W. 88th Ave. and Kipling St.; Foot access only

off Alkire St. at W. 86th/87th Aves.
1210 ac; max depth 80 ft
Extreme water level fluctuation.
Various boating with Westminster city permit.
Westminster brochure has further details.
Walk-in fishing free. Fee for cars. Overnight access in Westminster areas. No fishing from dam. Boat ramps.
Fish present: walleye, channel catfish, largemouth bass, smallmouth bass, bluegill, yellow perch, carp, sunfish, sucker.

STERNE POND
Arapahoe County, Littleton
W. Aberdeen Ave. and S. Spotswood St.
3 ac; max. depth is 3 ft
Small kids' pond. No boats. Open 6 a.m. to 10 p.m. Playground; restrooms.
For children under 15 years old only.
Fish present: bluegill, crappie, yellow perch, largemouth bass.

TWIN LAKES PARK PONDS
Adams County
W. 76th Ave. near Broadway
7 ac; max. depth is 16 ft
No boats. Open 7 a.m. to 11 p.m.
Only north lake open to fishing.
Fish present: bullhead, sucker, carp, yellow perch, green sunfish, sunfish.

UNION SQUARE PONDS
Jefferson County, Lakewood
N. of Union Blvd. along W. 2nd Pl.
5 ponds with 8 total ac; max. depth is 8 ft
Open 24 hrs.
Fish present: bluegill, carp, channel catfish, green sunfish, largemouth bass.

VANDERBILT PARK POND
City and County of Denver
W. Tennessee Ave. west of S. Santa Fe Dr.
6 ac; max. depth is 15 ft
Open 5 a.m. to 11 p.m. Restrooms.
Fish present: green sunfish.

WARD ROAD POND
Jefferson County, Arvada
W. 48th Ave. and Ward Rd.
7 ac; depth is 30 ft
Open: 24 hrs.

No motorized boats, walk-in access only, flies and lures only, catch and release all fish. Good bass fishing.
Fish present: bullhead, bluegill, crappie, green sunfish, largemouth bass, pumpkinseed.

WASHINGTON PARK LAKES
Denver County
S. Downing St. and E. Louisiana Ave.
N. Lake: (Smith Lake)
10 ac; max. depth is 12 ft
S. Lake: (Grasmere Lake)
19 ac; max. depth is 6 ft
Restrooms, playground, fishing pier.
Fish present: largemouth bass, carp, bluegill, goldfish, green sunfish, sunfish, channel catfish, bullhead, yellow perch, grizzard shad; stocked rainbow in N. Lake.

WATSON LAKE
Arapahoe County, Littleton
W. Bowles Ave. and west of S. Platte River
7 ac; max. depth is 8 ft
No boats. Open 6 a.m. to 10 p.m.
Fish present: largemouth bass, smallmouth bass, bullhead, yellow perch, sucker, bluegill, crappie, channel catfish, carp.

WEBSTER LAKE
Adams County, Northglenn
E. 117th Ave. and Washington St.
13 ac; max. depth is 12 ft
Extreme water level fluctuation.
No boats. Open dawn to dusk. Fishing pier, restrooms, playground. Extreme water-level fluctuation.
Fish present: crappie, bluegill, largemouth bass, bullhead, yellow perch, channel catfish.

WEST PROSPECT LAKE
Jefferson County, Wheat Ridge
I-70 & Youngfield St. at Clear Creek
46 ac; max. depth is 15 ft
Nonmotorized boats with Wheat Ridge Parks permit.
Open dawn to dusk.
Fish present: bullhead, pumpkinseed, suckers green sunfish, largemouth bass, crappie bluegill. Good bass fishing.

Front Range streams challenge galore

Adjacent communities:
Evergreen, Georgetown, Idaho Springs, Rollinsville, Nederland, Ward, Estes Park, Lyons.

Principal Highways:
Colo. 74; U.S. 6; Colo. 119, 72, 7, 66; U.S. 34.

Numerous streams flow east out of the Front Range of the Rockies from the Denver area north to the Cache la Poudre River at Fort Collins. This is the "home" of the native greenback cutthroat trout, found in only a few streams, although successful reestablishment efforts have placed it in additional waters than those where it survived just a few years ago.

Stream improvement work, often the cooperative ventures of the Forest Service, Trout Unlimited, the Division of Wildlife and a few utilities, has enhanced fishing in several places. This has helped offset some of the alterations made for mining, irrigation, flood control and municipal use.

Close to the 13,000- and 14,000-foot peaks that crest this portion of the Rockies are scores of lakes, many with good, if somewhat sporadic, angling. Because it is close to some 2 million residents, this segment of Colorado often abounds with people, including determined fishermen.

Still, for the keen-eyed fisherman, there are pools and riffles with good trout fishing, even within city limits, where 1- and 2-pound trout somehow put up with fluctuating water levels.

CLEAR CREEK

Clear Creek is one of these. It rises near Loveland Pass some 40 miles west of Denver near the Eisenhower Tunnel on I-70. It follows I-70 to 6.5 miles below Idaho Springs, where Hwys 6 and 40 emerge from Clear Creek Canyon. I-70 turns south and the stream follows the smaller highways until it emerges from the canyon at Golden. It offers some decent fishing above Idaho Springs.

Atop Loveland Pass is **Loveland Lake** (11,800 ft; 4 ac). It is shallow and fair for stocked rainbow. It is just west of the sum-

---

Paneled & Insulated
Wood Framed
Aluminum & Fiberglass

Will Build to Suit You

TOPPER MFG., INC.
1986 South Cherokee
Denver, Colorado 80223
Roland Watkins, Pres.
Merle Watkins, Sec., Treas.
778-6723

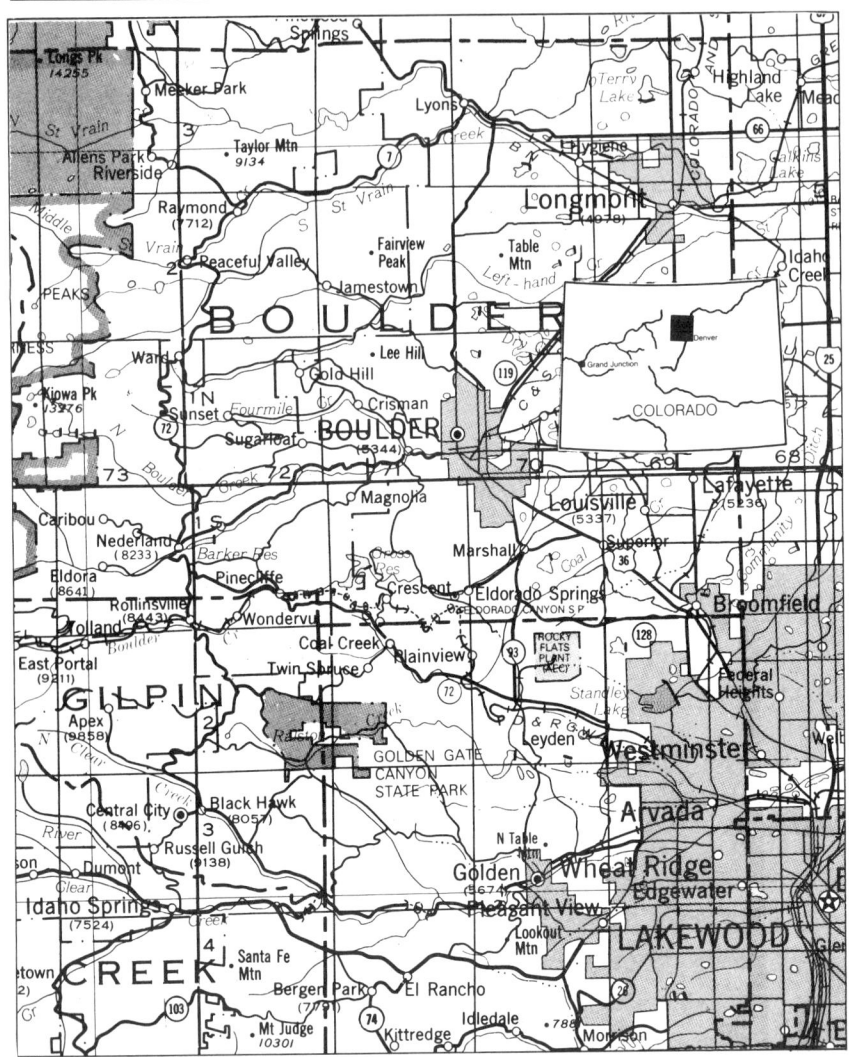

Front Range Streams

mit of the pass, but it is best to walk. Visible from Hwy 6.

From the headwaters east to Bakerville, the stream is brushy and hard to fish for small rainbow. Below Bakerville to the cascades below Empire, highway construction and mining have altered the stream, but some stretches may have trout.

About 2 miles east of the Eisenhower tunnel on the north side of the interstate is **Herman Lake** (12,000 ft; 7 ac). It no longer has fish.

At Georgetown, the creek has been dammed. Moderate size, shallow **Georgetown Lake** is stocked with brook, brown and rainbow; many fishermen and boats. In winter, good ice fishing, but watch out for iceboats, Jeeps and ice skaters. Windy.

SOUTH FORK CLEAR CREEK

The **South Fork of Clear Creek** enters at Georgetown. A road (paved most of the way) goes upstream to Guanella Pass. Green (Georgetown) Reservoir, 1 mile, is closed to the public. **Clear Creek Reservoir** (9900 ft; 45 ac) is stocked with rainbow, but fishing usually is poor. Lower Cabin Creek Reservoir of Colorado Public Service is a fluctuating waterbody and dangerous; fenced off and closed to fishing. Above the reservoir, the South Fork is brushy, has several beaver ponds, and attracts fishermen for small brook and rainbow. Several campsites and one campground.

Above the campground a road goes off to the west to **Naylor Lake,** which is private and posted. Trails from Naylor Lake go west 1 mile to **Silver Dollar Lake** (11,950 ft; 18 ac) and **Murray Lake** (12,080 ft; 11 ac). Both are above timberline and can be good for 12-inch cutthroat. Temperamental. Murray Lake is 0.5 mile northwest of Silver Dollar.

Below Georgetown, there is some private property to confluence with the **West Fork of Clear Creek,** which comes down from Jones Pass through the village of Berthoud Falls and the town of Empire. Rainbow and brook exist in this stretch, but fishing is poor to fair as it is also on most of the West Fork.

The West Fork flows past the Henderson and Urad molybdenum mines, which are near the Jones Pass road about 1.5 miles west of Hwy 40 at the east side of Berthoud Pass. Stream is often brushy, in light timber; difficult to fish for small rainbow. Woods Lake is up Woods Creek from the juncture of the Jones Pass Road and Hwy 40. Dirt road crosses West Fork about a quarter-mile from junction, goes up past Urad Mine to Woods and Hassell lakes. **Woods Lake** (10,700 ft; 31 ac) and **Hassell Lake** (11,400 ft; 9 ac), are fair for brook and rainbow. May need to walk in one mile from foot of dam. **Urad Reservoir** (10,560 ft; 30 ac) has brown and brook trout. No fish in section of creek in lower woods.

Bard Creek flows into the West Fork of Clear Creek from the west at the town of Empire. Small, many ponds, brushy, and good to fair for small brook and rainbow. Road travels upstream about 1.5 miles, then 4-wheel drive 2 more miles, then trail the rest of the way.

From the confluence of the West Fork and Clear Creek at the junction of Hwys 6,

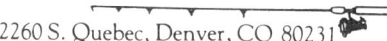

The Trout Fisher

Fine Tackle and Associated Merchandise
Friendly, Knowledgeable Service

Len Sanders
Proprietor
(303) 369-7970

2260 S. Quebec, Denver, CO 80231

40 and I-70, fishing for rainbow can be good as far as the east side of Idaho Springs. Paved service road provides best access. It's heavily fished, as stream is stocked. Downstream, water quality deteriorates rapidly.

At the headwaters of **Mill Creek,** which flows into Clear Creek at the truck stop and weigh station village of Dumont, are **Lake Ethel** (12,560 ft; 6 ac), **Byron Lake** (12,100 ft; 3 ac) and **Bill Moore Lake** (11,300 ft; 7 ac). Best access is from the town of Empire, going up North Empire Creek to ridgetop, then keep north across relatively level land to the creek. Hike upstream 1.5 miles to Bill Moore Lake. This is 4-wheel or horse country: no cars. A winding 4-wheel-drive road winds about 3 miles along the ridge to Bill Moore Lake. Use topographic map and take bearings from Breckinridge Peak (12,889 ft) on the south and Witter Peak (12,884 ft) on the north. The lakes are in the valley between. Lake fishing for 12-inch cutthroat is fair. The creek is fair to poor for small cutthroat. The lakes also may be reached by taking a dirt road just south of the summit of Berthoud Pass (US 40) to where the dirt road ends at a radio relay shack; then walk cross country along the Continental Divide to the northeast for about 2 miles.

Cone Lake (11,600 ft; 3 ac) is off the above-mentioned dirt road and below it, about a mile east of US 40. It's a steep descent and climb out. Fair to good for 9- to 10-inch cutthroat.

FALL RIVER

Fall River flows into Clear Creek a mile west of Idaho Springs. Access to its upper reaches and several small lakes and reservoirs is from an I-70 interchange marked Fall River Road/St. Mary's Glacier a mile west of Idaho Springs, or from the interstate service road. Lower portions of the road are paved through posted, fenced, private property. Just below St. Mary's Glacier is **St. Mary's Lake** (10,710 ft; 7 ac), with brook trout. It is on Silver Creek, just upstream from **Lake Quivira**, which is private and fished by guests of St. Mary's Lodge. It is about 8.5 miles from the interstate.

Through Arapaho National Forest, Fall River is only fair for small brook and rainbow. There is much posting and fishing is difficult because of brush and streamside timber.

From the paved road, about 6.5 miles from the interstate, turn west on a good dirt road at the old mining town site of Alice, now a mountain subdivision. Can drive about 1.5 miles before road becomes too rough and narrow to negotiate without 4-wheel drive. Road continues on to provide access to **Ice, Ohman, Reynolds** and **Steuart Lakes, Loch Lomond** and **Lake Caroline,** all high, above timberline waters at 11,200 to more than 12,000 ft. Ohman has no fish.

Loch Lomond (11,200 ft; 23 ac) is a manmade lake reachable by 4-wheel drive. The others are difficult, steep trail hikes by the waterfall at the west end of Loch Lomond. Lake Caroline (23 ac), with cutthroat, is to the south, around a rocky point. The others are upstream in the basin between James Peak on the north, and Mount Bancroft, on the south. Fishing for rainbow and cutthroat is fair to good, but temperamental. Loch Lomond is heavily fished for brook, brown and lake trout.

About 5.5 miles up Fall River Road from I-70 at the foot of a steep switchback, a dirt road goes off to the west along the river to **Chinns Lake** (11,000 ft; 10 ac), **Sherwin Lake** (11,090 ft; 7 ac) and **Slater Lake** (11,460 ft; 3 ac) and **Fall River Reservoir** (10,880 ft; 24 ac). They offer either brook, brown or cutthroat, or a combination of the three. After about 2 miles at a prominent fork in the road, take the south fork to Chinns and Sherwin lakes. Clear Creek Reservoir is on the north fork, about a mile.

All are fair to good for rainbow and cutthroat, but heavily fished. Slater Lake is a short hike northeast from Sherwin by easy trail along the stream. Camping sites.

At Idaho Springs, **Chicago Creek** bubbles into the Clear Creek from the southwest. Hwy 103 loops up from Bergen Park off Hwy 74 to Echo Lake and parallels Chicago Creek to Idaho Springs. The creek rises in the Chicago Lakes in a deep valley beneath 13,307-foot-high Mt. Warren. **Upper Chicago Lake** (11,700 ft; 10 ac) and **Lower Chicago Lake** (11,400 ft; 26 ac) are in spectacular settings, but heavily fished for cutthroat, and visited by campers, picnickers and hikers who walk in from Echo Lake on the Mt. Evans Road or up the creek on an old road past **Idaho Springs Reservoir** (10,600 ft; 16 ac). The reservoir has artificial fly and lure fishing for brook, cutthroat and suckers.

North Clear Creek rises northwest of Central City in Arapaho National Forest and flows southeasterly through Blackhawk to join Clear Creek in Clear Creek Canyon. Reaches below Apex on **Pine Creek** may have a few brook, but it is mostly private land. Otherwise polluted and puny with

Steve Reed photo

COLORADO SCHOOL OF FLY FISHING

AN ENJOYABLE LEARNING EXPERIENCE FLY FISHING THE ROCKIES

Estes Park

Call or Write: Scott Roederer
P.O. Box 1848
Estes Park, CO 80517
(303) 586-8812, 586-8843

In Estes Park contact The Fisherman's Fly.

only imaginary trout.

Golden Gate Canyon State Park has fishing for stocked rainbow and brook trout in small streams and ponds. The park is reached by taking the Golden Gate Canyon Road 0.5 mile north of Golden on Hwy 93 and winding 14 miles west. A parks pass or day permit is required. It also is accessible from the west via Hwy 119 north of Blackhawk.

Clear Creek is mostly channeled to its confluence with the South Platte River north of Denver. It fluctuates widely in water volume and degree of pollution; dewatered by domestic and industrial use. Rough fish, maybe some rainbow in pools. See urban fishing chapter.

SOUTH BOULDER CREEK

South Boulder Creek is a beautiful stream that arises along the Continental Divide west of Rollinsville in Gilpin County. The headwaters and several lakes are easily reached by driving west on a good gravel road to Moffat Tunnel—the Rollins Pass Road. Rollins Pass, also known as Corona Pass, is closed on the east side of the summit by a cave-in at Needle's Eye Tunnel.

From the parking area by the Moffat Tunnel more than a dozen lakes are accessible by trail, although the old Rogers Pass Road goes on up the main stream. The first creek coming in from the northwest of East Portal is **Arapaho Creek.** The trail up the creek to **Forest Lakes** (10,680 ft; both 5 ac) is beyond the creek about a third of a mile and cuts back and up about 2 miles to the lakes. Several small ponds in the area. The lakes have brook, rainbow, Loch Leven browns and cutthroat. Fishing is fair as fish are small in the two largest lakes. About 1.5 miles up a poorly defined trail from South Boulder Creek, a small stream comes in from the 4 **Arapaho Lakes** (10,165 ft; 10 ac for the largest). These lakes are fair to good for cutthroat. **Arapaho Creek** is fair for small cutthroat, as is the South Boulder Creek itself.

South of the Arapaho lakes over a ridge are 4 **Crater Lakes** (10,480-11,000 ft). They are 2.8 miles west of East Portal and upstream from the second stream coming into South Boulder Creek from the northwest. Ranging in size from 5 to 14 acres, all are fair to good for cutthroat. There are also some brook, rainbow trout and brown.

At the headwaters of South Boulder Creek lie **Clayton Lake** (11,000 ft; 6 ac) and, upstream against the Continental Divide, the **Iceberg Lakes** (11,640 ft; 10 and 6 ac). Clayton is just south of Crater Lakes and also is fair to good for cutthroat up to 12 inches. The Iceberg Lakes are fair for cutthroat.

Still to the south just off the main forest trail up South Boulder Creek about a mile from Clayton Lake is **Heart Lake** (11,320 ft; 17 ac), which is heavily fished for rainbow and cutthroat. Just south of Heart Lake are the **Rogers Pass Lakes,** both of which have cutthroat trout. They are at 11,000 ft and 3 and 6 acres in size.

Jenny Lake (10,920 ft; 5 ac) and **Yankee Doodle Lake** (10,710 ft; 6 ac) are northwest of South Boulder Creek and are most easily reached from East Portal by the narrow gauge railroad grade road over Rollins Pass. Yankee Doodle is lower and deeper, and fair for rainbow and brook. Both are heavily fished, often with bait, and are about 11 miles from East Portal by road.

Downstream from the village of East Portal, the stream is channeled and mostly private property. At the western edge of the railroad village of Tolland, a rough road goes south up a steep hill. Nearly at the top, a fork goes southwest to Mammoth Gulch, Mammoth Reservoir, Teller Lake, James Peak Lake and Echo Lake.

Teller Lake (9600 ft; 8 ac) is only fair for rainbow and brook. It is visible to the north from Mammoth Gulch Road. **Mammoth Reservoir** with brook, cutthroat and rainbow is private. The road goes another 2.5 miles to old mine and mill sites. From there a trail goes up a brushy stream to **Little Echo Lake** (11,184 ft; 14 ac) just off the trail to the north. It is deep with a brushy shoreline, but can be good for rainbow, cutthroat and possibly mackinaw. **James Peak Lake** (11,200 ft; 10 ac) is a few hundred yards west from Little Echo. It has mackinaw and cutthroat, but is above timberline and very temperamental.

Both of these lakes also can be reached over a 4-wheel-drive road on the ridge just south of Mammoth Creek. It follows the old Ute Trail to within a mile of James Peak Lake. The lakes are easy to see from the road. The Ute Pass Road goes west from the top of the hill south of Tolland. It is open, cutover country with a great view. The area is a maze of old roads and trails, and topographic maps are helpful.

GROSS RESERVOIR

East of Tolland, South Boulder Creek races clear past Rollinsville and Pinecliff through mostly private property and into its steep, rugged and narrow canyon to **Gross Reservoir** (7287 ft; 440 ac). There is bank fishing only at this fluctuating reservoir operated by the Denver Water Department. Access from the south is from Hwy 72 in Coal Creek Canyon. A dirt road turns off to the north about 1.25 miles east of Wondervu and winds down to the east end of reservoir.

From Boulder, the Flagstaff Mountain Road leads to Gross, about 12 miles southwest. Follow signs. Rainbow, mackinaw, brook, kokanee and some brown are in the reservoir. Fishing is best in the spring when reservoir is full. Because no boats are allowed, it's hard to get the bigger fish and most of the bank fishing is difficult. Some good sized fish—4-5 pounders and up. Fishing is not allowed from 9 p.m to 4 a.m. No camping; fires only in firepits on the north side; and no ice fishing.

Downstream from the dam, angling for brook and brown can be excellent, but tough to get to in the narrow canyon. The portion above Eldorado Springs is posted; from there downstream to juncture with Boulder Creek northwest of Valmont Reservoir, east of Boulder, the stream is on private land. There are isolated pools and places where fishing can be good. Permission to fish is recommended (and required by law). No fishing at Valmont.

MIDDLE BOULDER CREEK

West of Nederland, **Middle Boulder Creek** rises along the Continental Divide between Arapaho Pass on the north and Rollins (Corona) Pass on the south. If flows eastward and merges with North Boulder Creek in Boulder Canyon.

The headwaters of Middle Boulder Creek are reached by driving west from Hwy 119 on the south edge of Nederland on the road to Eldora. After 1.5 miles, the road forks; follow the stream on north fork 1.5 miles to Eldora and another 2.5 miles to Hessie, where the **North Fork of Middle Boulder Creek** enters from the north. There's a good road through private land to this point. Five miles above Hessie is Fourth of July Campground, 20 acres with no designated campsites, a few picnic tables and fire rings. The area serves mostly as a trailhead for south entry into the Indian Peaks Wilderness to the north at Arapaho Pass. The road was improved in 1982, but is still slow and rough. Stream is small, brushy and has some rainbow, especially between the falls 2 miles up from Hessie, and the campground. Road above the campground is closed. The area is heavily used with as many as 100 cars there on a summer or autumn weekend. From the campground, the trail to **Lake Dorothy** (12,100 ft; 16 ac) is an old mining road for most of the 2.5 miles. The lake is above timberline and is usually iced over until July; but, there is good fishing in late afternoon-evening for cutthroat in late summer. The lake is heavily fished.

Banana Lake (11,320 ft; 2 ac) is about a mile south of Lake Dorothy in high, rough country. It is fair for cutthroat and brown. It can be reached over a faint trail leading northwest 0.75 miles off the Diamond Lakes Trail, just west of the Fourth of July Campground.

West of the campground 1.5 miles is **Diamond Lake** (10,920 ft; 14 ac) and a mile farther west, **Upper Diamond Lake** (11,720 ft; 6 ac). Both are good for rainbow, cutthroat and some brook. Heavily fished. Campsites. Above timberline. Walk up Middle Boulder Creek from the parking area about a half-mile, take the well defined trail to the west that crosses the creek, and climb steeply. Upper Diamond Lake is in a cirque of rocks reachable by cross-country hike from the lower lake.

The **Neva Lakes** at the base of Mt. Neva are barren.

Up the **South Fork of Middle Boulder**

I catch 'em; the rest is up to you

Creek from Hessie about a mile, a trail from the south intercepts the main trail. A quarter-mile south through the woods is **Lost Lake** (9780 ft; 7 ac), which can be good for small rainbow and brook.

Six miles upstream on South Fork is **King Lake** (11,431 ft; 11 ac). It is above timberline and is fair for cutthroat and rainbow trout. It also can be reached from the summit of Rollins Pass by going north on the Corona Trail and dropping steeply down to the lake from the top of the divide after about a half-mile.

North from the east side of King Lake about 1.75 miles are **Betty Lake** (11,400 ft; 8 ac) and, 0.25 mile farther, **Bob Lake** (11,600 ft; 8 ac). Both are above timberline and fair for cutthroat. These two lakes are readily reached by walking along the top of the ridge north from Rollins Pass.

About a mile west of Hessie, a trail goes northwest up **Jasper Creek** to Jasper Lake, Devil's Thumb Lake, Storm Lake and Upper Storm Lake, Woodland Lake and Skyscraper Reservoir. Jasper Creek is fair for small rainbow and some brook.

A half-mile up Jasper Creek, a southwest trail leads about 2 miles to **Woodland Lake** (10,972 ft; 7 ac). **Skyscraper Reservoir** (11,221 ft; 11 ac) is situated a quarter-mile farther. Both are fair for rainbow; the larger water is deeper and has better fishing.

Following Jasper Creek north, **Jasper (Reservoir) Lake** (10,814 ft; 21 ac) is fair to good for brook and cutthroat. Due west about 2 miles, **Devil's Thumb Lake** (11,160 ft; 12 ac) is easily reached by trail from the south end of Jasper Lake. Devil's Thumb Peak is just to the northwest. The lake is fair to good for brook and cutthroat. This is above timberline fishing.

Northwest from the north end of Jasper Lake is **Storm Lake** (11,660 ft; 10 ac), which is fair for cutthroat but takes a steep climb. It may winterkill and be fishless.

Glacier Lake (9100 ft; 24 ac) is on the east side of Hwy 72, six miles north of Nederland. It is a private, posted manmade lake. It drains into **Fourmile Creek,** which flows easterly through Fourmile Canyon to enter Boulder Creek just east of Boulder in Boulder Canyon. The stream is stocked in some stretches and offers little public fishing for small rainbow.

BARKER RESERVOIR

Immediately east of Nederland along Hwy 119 is **Barker Reservoir** (8183 ft; 420 ac), a fluctuating reservoir that is one of the most heavily fished waters in the state. It is heavily stocked in summer with rainbow, and is largely a put-and-take operation. Good fishing for rainbow to 12 inches; some brown 12 inches or more and occasional brook. Boating and ice fishing are prohibited.

On downstream in Boulder Canyon, the highway follows Middle Boulder Creek. About 8 miles below Nederland, North Boulder Creek sweeps over Boulder Falls and merges with Middle Boulder Creek to form Boulder Creek, which sweeps through beautifully sculpted rock to Boulder and then northeasterly to join the St. Vrain Creek just east of Interstate 70 in Weld County.

NORTH BOULDER CREEK

North of Nederland about 3 miles, **North Boulder Creek** is crossed by Hwy 72. Its headwaters are to the west and northwest along the Continental Divide on the east side of the Indian Peaks Wilderness.

About 8 miles north of Nederland, a dirt road to the west leads 6 miles to seven ponds called **Rainbow Lakes** (10,120 ft; 1 to 4 ac) and the Rainbow Lakes Campground. This is the takeoff point for the Arapaho Glacier hiking trail.

The upper reaches of North Boulder Creek are in a privately owned valley south of Niwot Ridge and north of the Caribou Mining District. There are several lakes and ponds, including the four **Green Lakes** (11,680 to 10,960 ft; 11 to 34 ac), **Triple Lakes, Goose Lake, Island Lake, Silver Lake** and **Lake Albion,** all at 10,000- to 11,000-foot elevations and from 2 to 40 acres in size. These properties are posted and permission to fish is unlikely. Access is via private road. Downstream from Hwy 72, North Boulder Creek is on mostly private land.

West of Hwy 72 and west of Ward, **Left Hand Creek** rises in a basin that contains **Left Hand Park Reservoir** (10,600 ft; 100 ac when full). The reservoir fluctuates, is often windy and difficult to fish for stocked rainbow. The creek is brushy and in peat bog, and only fair for rainbow, brook and brown. East of Hwy 72, Left Hand Creek is brushy and fast, and flows alternately in and out of national forest and posted land. Two miles above the confluence with Little James Creek (Jim Creek), Left Hand Creek is fair for small rainbow and some brook. The stream is dewatered for irrigation as it works its way east of Jamestown and out of the mountains. **James Creek** is poor fishing. County roads in the Gold Hill and Jamestown areas provide access.

SOUTH ST. VRAIN CREEK

The Brainard Lake road goes west from Ward to provide access to Left Hand Park Reservoir, Brainard Lake and several other lakes in the **South St. Vrain Creek** drainage. This is a good road, heavily used and there are several picnic grounds and a campground at Brainard Lake. The creek is fair for small rainbow and some brook.

Brainard Lake (10,350 ft; 15 ac) is a beautiful, shallow lake with rainbow, brook and brown trout. It is in a very popular area and is heavily fished. En route to Brainard from Ward is **Red Rock Lake** (10,300 ft; 6 ac) on the south side of road. It is a pond with grass and lily pads, and is hard to fish for the decent size rainbow (to 12 inches) to be found there.

Moraine Lake (10,150 ft; 2 ac) is another pond with good feed like Red Rock Lake and, while it is difficult to fish (waders recommended), it produces some good rainbow despite its unimposing appearance. It is just south of Red Rock Lake, over a small hill.

Just upstream 0.5 mile from Brainard Lake is **Long Lake** (10,500 ft; 45 ac), with rainbow and cutthroat. Fishing is only with flies and lures. Only 2 fish over 12 inches may be kept. **Lake Isabelle** (10,852 ft; 30 ac) is 2.5 miles above Long Lake via a well-trod trail. Lake Isabelle, like its companions, is very heavily fished for rainbow and cutthroat. This is also fly and lure fishing with a two fish limit, one of which must be over 12 inches. A short distance northwest of Brainard Lake is a parking area and a trailhead to Mitchell Lakes 1.5 miles beyond. **Lower Mitchell Lake** (10,700 ft; 4 ac) and **Upper Mitchell Lake** (10,700 ft; 14 ac) have brook and cutthroat, and fishing can be good. Another 1.75 miles west up the stream is **Blue Lake** (11,320 ft; 16 ac), fair for cutthroat. Due west up a slope at about 11,410 ft is a 2-acre pond with cutthroat. Blue Lake also has brook.

MIDDLE ST. VRAIN

South St. Vrain Creek flows northeast and converges with **Middle St. Vrain Creek** 2.5 miles east of Riverside. Middle St. Vrain Creek's headwaters also are very scenic and popular and have many small streams and lakes west of Hwy 72. Two campgrounds are Peaceful Valley and Camp Dick, each just west of the highway a few hundred yards on a good Forest Service road.

The Middle St. Vrain is a fast, full stream that parallels the road for more than 8 miles. It tends to be brushy and difficult to cross, but with good rainbow fishing. It is joined by **Coney Creek,** flowing in from the southwest. A trail leads upward 3 miles to **Lower Coney Lake** (10,600 ft; 9 ac) and another mile to **Upper Coney Lake** (10,940 ft; 10 ac), where there is good fishing for cutthroat from 12 to 14 inches. The upper lake is the deeper of the two.

The trail up the Middle St. Vrain goes to Buchanan Pass. A trail about 6 miles up from Peaceful Valley Campground goes northwesterly a mile to **Red Deer Lake** (10,700 ft; 16 ac). Deep and easily fished for brook and rainbow and some cutthroat. **Pika Lake** (11,140 ft; 2 ac) is 1.8 miles by trail from end of the road along Middle St. Vrain Creek. It has cutthroat as do **Envy Lake** and **Gibralter Lake.** Gibralter is 2 miles northwest from the old sawmill site along the creek. Envy is 2 miles cross country and hard to find. The drainage (streams and lakes) receives heavy fishing pressure and is stocked heavily. Several lakes in the area are private, including **Stapp Lakes** and **Beaver Reservoir,** and usually are posted.

Below the confluence of the Middle and South St. Vrain Creeks there is good fishing, although much of the stream is posted. For 2 miles of the creek through Lyons, there is catch-and-release fishing in an improved stretch of the stream. Some good brown trout to 2 pounds are here. Access is along Hwy 7 south of Lyons.

North St. Vrain Creek rises in the southeastern portion of Rocky Mountain National Park and also is discussed in that chapter. Downstream from Hwy 7 and the park, the creek tends to be brushy and difficult to fish for browns and some rainbow. Several stretches are posted against fishing without permission.

Ralph Price Reservoir, formerly **Button Rock Reservoir,** is owned by the City of Longmont and remains closed to fishing. But upstream from the reservoir to Horse Creek is wild trout water; fishing is with artificial flies and lures only. Possession is two fish. Catch-and-release fishing is encouraged. Access is from Hwy 36 about 5 miles northeast of Lyons where the highway leaves creek. Turn left across bridge onto dirt road.

BIG THOMPSON RIVER

The Big Thompson River rises in Rocky Mountain National Park and flows east through Estes Park and down Big Thompson Canyon to Loveland. Just outside the park and south of the river is **Mary's Lake** (8050 ft; 42 ac), a fluctuating reservoir on the east end of the Alva B. Adams diversion tunnel of the U.S. Bureau of Reclamation's Big Thompson power and irrigation project. It is along Hwy 7 south of Estes Park about 2 miles and is fair to good for rainbow. It is heavily stocked as part of a put-and-take operation. Some big trout dwell at the intake of the lake, feeding on nutrients brought

---

THE FISHERMAN'S FLY
Downtown Estes Park
We Carry Fly Fishing
Equipment & Materials
Friendly advice on where to
fish always given
Call Chuck or Steve Christensen
303/586-8843
161 Virginia Drive • Estes Park, CO • 80517

through the tunnel from Grand Lake. See the Rocky Mountain National Park chapter for headwaters information on the Big Thompson.

Lake Estes (7475 ft; 185 ac) at Estes Park is stocked with rainbow and brown trout. Although most fish average 8 to 12 inches, some bigger ones are there. Boats and boating permits are available at the boathouse. Bait, flies and lures allowed. Heavily fished.

Downstream from the Lake Estes Dam, fishing for rainbow and brown is fair to good, especially in pools. The river is recovering well from the 1976 flood and fishing in the mid-1980s is better than forecast a decade ago. Lower sections are posted. Hwy 34 follows the river.

At Drake, the **North Fork of the Big Thompson River** enters the main stream. The North Fork rises in northeast Rocky Mountain Park. There are 6 miles of stream northwest of Glen Haven that are in national forest and accessible by road, although some sections of the stream are on private land. Above that, access for a dozen miles is by trail. Stream is fast and tends to have 8- to 12-inch rainbow and some brown, especially in pools.

Access to North Fork is easy from paved county road that makes a loop off Hwy 34 between Estes Park and Loveland. □

U.S. Forest Service campgrounds

U.S. Forest Service compilation was current as of 1985.
Asterisks denote fee areas. Some campgrounds are open only Memorial Day weekend through Labor Day. Below freezing weather could mean no water supply.

FRONT RANGE AREA
SOUTH PLATTE RIVER DRAINAGE

ARAPAHO NATIONAL FOREST
Headquarters: Federal Bldg., 301 S. Howes, Box 1366, Fort Collins, CO 80521

Campground name	Elevation	No camp sites	Travel trailers	Drinking water	Length of stay (days)	Location and directions
Mizpah	9600	11	Yes	Yes	14	On US 40, 6 mi W of Empire
West Chicago Creek	9600	20	Yes	Yes	14	10 mi S of Idaho Springs, on Colo. 103
Echo Lake*	10,600	17	Yes	Yes	14	14 mi SW of Idaho Springs by Colo. 103
Cold Springs*	9200	47	Yes	Yes	14	4.5 mi N of Blackhawk on Colo. 119
Pickle Gulch*	9100	30	No	Yes	14	1 mi off Colo. 119, 3 mi NW of Blackhawk
Columbine*	8900	24	Yes	Yes	14	2 mi NW of Central City by county road
Clear Lake	10,000	8	Yes	No	14	4 mi S of Georgetown on steep county road
Guanella Pass	10,900	9	Yes	No	14	8 mi S of Georgetown on county road

ROOSEVELT NATIONAL FOREST
Headquarters: Federal Bldg., 301 S. Howes, Box 1366, Fort Collins, CO 80522

Campground name	Elevation	No camp sites	Travel trailers	Drinking water	Length of stay (days)	Location and directions
Pawnee*	10,400	55	Yes	Yes	3	5 mi W of Ward via F.S. Rd 112
Rainbow Lakes	10,000	18	Yes	No	7	5 mi W of Colo. 72, 6.5 mi N of Nederland
Kelly Dahl*	8600	46	Yes	Yes	14	On Colo. 119, 3 mi S of Nederland
Camp Dick	8500	34	Yes	Yes	6.3	On Colo. 72, 7 mi S of Colo. 7, 15 mi W of Lyons
Peaceful Valley	8500	15	Yes	Yes	3	On Colo. 72, 15 mi SW of Lyons
Olive Ridge*	8400	56	Yes	Yes	3	On Colo. 7, 15 mi S of Estes Park

Eastern Colorado's warm water fishing: action at its best

Principal Highways:
Too numerous to mention.

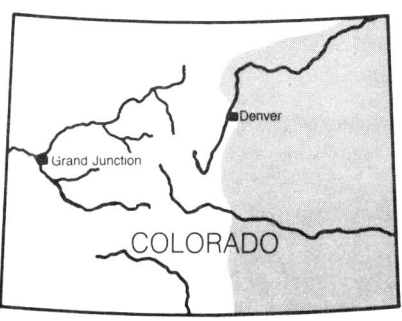

Eastern Colorado has hundreds of prairie ponds, lakes and man-made reservoirs, many of them open to fishing for bass, perch, walleye, catfish, crappie, bluegill and other warm water species. The Colorado Division of Wildlife stocks several varieties of fish and considers warm water fishing the fastest growing segment of Colorado angling.

For sheer action and the number and size of fish caught, it's hard to beat, though it is far from the traditional mountain lake and stream sport that comes to mind when Colorado fishing is mentioned.

For two-thirds of Colorado's population, "flatland fishing" is closer to home, quicker to get to and more family oriented than

Bass fishing

pursuing the elusive mountain trout. While anglers fish, there may be swimming beaches, sailing, crayfish and frog hunting and other activities nearby for the non-angler. Even in winter, ice skating is more warming than sitting by a hole in the ice.

Some very nonfish-oriented activities, including speedboat running and water skiing on the larger lakes, are sometimes frustrating to the serious fisherman. However, he soon learns when and where his efforts are most productive and least likely to be interrupted.

BASS FISHING

Bass fishing is getting some serious attention, and there are several bass clubs whose members not only often practice catch-and-release fishing—even of good-size catches—but also work on improving bass habitat and teaching youngsters to fish.

Eastern Colorado waters offer largemouth, smallmouth, rock, white, striped and wiper bass. The largest recorded of these species—a 10-pounder from Stalker Lake in Yuma County—is a record destined to fall soon. One can remember that the voracious bass tend to grow faster and get bigger sooner, so the flatland angler's chances of catching 4-, 5-, and 6-pounders are far greater than those of the trout fisherman hooking a similar size smoothie.

Bass are feisty and very good eating. There's no second-rate sport here, as they rival the wily trout for challenging angling.

Many eastern plains fishing waters are stopover places for migratory waterfowl in spring and fall. Ducks, geese, swans and cranes rely on the waters for rest stops. Consequently, during the migratory waterfowl hunting season beginning November 1 many of the lakes and reservoirs are closed to fishing and boating.

Some of the top bass waters in eastern Colorado are Cherry Creek Reservoir, Chatfield Reservoir, Bonny Reservoir, John Martin Reservoir, Nee Noshe Reservoir, Pueblo Reservoir, Brush Hollow Reservoir and Trinidad Lake.

Many fisheries have 15-inch minimum-size limits on bass in an effort to get natural

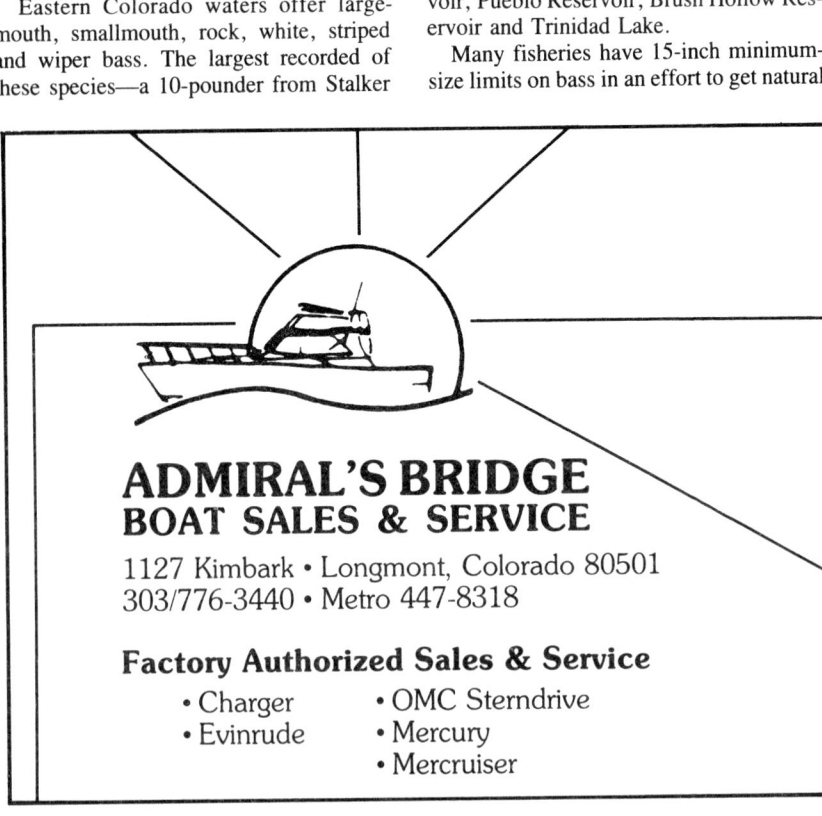

ADMIRAL'S BRIDGE
BOAT SALES & SERVICE

1127 Kimbark • Longmont, Colorado 80501
303/776-3440 • Metro 447-8318

Factory Authorized Sales & Service
- Charger
- Evinrude
- OMC Sterndrive
- Mercury
- Mercruiser

reproduction which should result in more and larger bass for the catching. The bass fishing clubs mentioned earlier are in Denver, Longmont, Colorado Springs, Pueblo and Fort Collins. Your local tackle shop can put you in touch with these sportsmen.

The eastern ponds, lakes, reservoirs and gravel pits are too numerous to mention. The major and most popular warm water fisheries are noted. The lakes and reservoirs in the Denver metropolitan area are described in the Metro Denver fishing chapter. And several reservoirs and lakes that feed into main streams are discussed with that stream. Discussion of the eastern fisheries begins north of Denver.

The 16 **Sawhill Ponds** (100 ac total) offer good fishing for crappie, bluegill, yellow perch, bullhead, channel catfish, largemouth bass and suckers. Some of the ponds have good size, scrappy bass in the 5-pound category. One pond has rainbow trout. This popular area is west off 75th Street between Jay Road and Valmont Drive, Boulder. It's about 2 miles north of Arapahoe Avenue.

Valmont Reservoir is closed to fishing.

BOULDER RESERVOIR

Boulder Reservoir (660 ac), built and operated by the city, is fair fishing for walleye, crappie, yellow perch, largemouth bass, channel catfish and bullhead. Trolling usually gives good results. Boulder Reservoir is less than 0.5 mile from Hwy 119 northeast of Boulder on the Longmont Diagonal. Turn north at Jay Road intersection and continue to 15st Street, then east. Admission is $1.75 for adults, $1.50 for teenagers, 50 cents for children. Fishing hours are 7 a.m. until dark. Weekend and holiday boating is reserved to City of Boulder residents with boat permits. (Boating permits are $100 and up with proof of $400,000 liability insurance required.) Public boat ramp and marina are available.

Independent Reservoir is closed to public fishing.

North on I-25, and about 7 miles east of Longmont, are the nine **Barbour Ponds** (80 ac total). They are good for crappie, channel catfish, black bass, perch, bullhead and sunfish. The ponds are heavily fished, and a use permit is required. Only hand-propelled craft, sailboats and boats with electric

---

RIVERVIEW CAMPGROUND

Between Loveland & Estes Park with quarter mile frontage on the Big Thompson River.

Full Hookups • Tent Camping
Square Dancing • 23 Acres Shade Trees
Clean Showers • Open Year Round

Your Hosts: Gene & Sylvia Klonglan
Call 303-667-9910

7806 W. U.S. Hwy 34 Loveland, CO 80537

UNITED CAMPGROUND
"A Sweetheart of a Campground"

Offering lovely shaded lawns, full hookups and pull thrus, clean bathrooms, heated pool, movies, laundry facilities, propane.

(303) 667-1204
4421 E. Hwy. 34 Loveland, CO
80537

---

motors are permitted.

In the Loveland area there is good fishing in several lakes and reservoirs. Southwest of Loveland is **Boedecker Reservoir** (380 ac). It has walleye, yellow perch, crappie, largemouth bass, channel catfish, bluegill, carp and bullhead. Boats are allowed, but not available to rent. Boedecker Reservoir is reached by taking US 34 west from Loveland. Turn south at Ft. Namaqua, about a half-mile outside of town. Drive 1 mile south, then 0.5 mile west.

Lon Hagler Reservoir (250 ac) is located about a mile south of Boedecker and a mile north of Lonetree Reservoir. Lon Hagler is stocked with rainbow, channel catfish and walleye. Boat ramp and campsites are available. Fishing is prohibited in the Lon Hagler inlet structure as posted.

Lonetree Reservoir (502 ac) is excellent fishing for crappie, fair for bass, and good for perch in early spring. Lonetree also is regarded as a good ice fishing lake. Access to Lonetree is gained by turning west off US 287 about 3 miles south of Loveland. It's about 2 miles to the reservoir. There is a 5-site camping area.

Due west of Lonetree 4.5 miles is **Carter Lake Reservoir** (1158 ac). Carter has rainbow from 8 inches to 4 pounds and a few kokanee salmon 12 to 13 inches. Holders of the trout stamp may take a double rainbow trout limit. Best access to Carter is by driving 7 miles west from the town of Berthoud on Hwy. 56.

North of Berthoud, the city of Loveland surrounds **Lake Loveland** (500 ac). It is good fishing for walleye, bass, crappie, channel catfish and a few rainbow trout. A boat permit from the city is required.

Northeast of Loveland less than a half-mile, **Boyd Lake** (1674 ac), **Horseshoe Reservoir** (1800 ac) and **Equalizer Reservoir** (60 ac) offer warm water fishing with an occasional rainbow trout taken. Boyd is especially popular and offers good fishing for perch, walleye to 8 pounds and northern pike to 30 pounds. There is a boat marina and ramp on Boyd. Fishing is prohibited on the south inlet area of Boyd as posted. Horseshoe Reservoir offers fishing for walleye, crappie, largemouth and smallmouth bass and bluegill. Access to these reservoirs is by driving 2 miles east from Loveland on US 34; about 1 mile west of the US 34 and I-25 junction; turn north.

In the same area, adjacent to I-25 on the west side, **Big Thompson Ponds** (40 ac) have crappie, largemouth bass, channel catfish, bluegill, carp and bullhead. Boats or any other floating devices are prohibited. Camping is permitted.

About 5 miles east of I-25 on Hwy 392 turn north on US 257 at Windsor. Drive about 7 miles north to **Windsor Lake** (70 ac). Fishing here is for yellow perch, crappie and channel catfish.

BOB'S REEL SERVICE
A Complete Fishing Shop

Full Service Factory Warranty Center For
DAIWA, RYOBI & ZEBCO REELS
Largest Reel Parts Inventory in Colorado

(303) 667-1107
406 S. Lincoln Ave.   Loveland, CO 80537

FORT COLLINS AREA

In the Fort Collins area, **Wellington Reservoir** (100 ac) offers fishing for walleye, yellow perch, crappie, channel catfish, carp and bullhead. Take Hwy 1 north from Fort Collins about 5 miles to reach the reservoir.

River Bend Ponds, Simson Ponds, North Shields Ponds, Prospect Ponds #2 & #3 are gravel pits obtained by the Division of Wildlife for warm water fishing. They have bass, yellow perch, bluegill, catfish and crappie.

River Bend Ponds are just south of Hwy 14 between the east side of Fort Collins and I-25. There's an innocuous dirt road near the state highway patrol building, but it's not marked as access.

Simson Ponds are 2 miles west of I-25 at Exit 402. At county road 9E turn north to the ponds 0.5 mile. **North Shields Ponds** are just north of Cache la Poudre River along Shields Street in north Fort Collins. **Prospect Ponds** are on the south side of Prospect street just west of the river. Turn onto Sharp Point Drive, then go 0.5 mile south.

Watson Lake is along the Cache la Poudre River along the diagonal road off US 287 just west of LaPorte. It has stocked rainbow and some brook trout.

Southeast of Fort Collins, in the Greeley area, are several reservoirs. From Greeley, take US 85 about 10 miles north to the town of Ault. Turn west on Hwy 14 for about 5 miles to where a county road leads north to **Black Hollow Reservoir** (580 ac). This is an irrigation reservoir that is subject to weekly fluctuations. Its warm water fish include walleye, yellow perch, crappie and northern pike. Camping is allowed and a boat ramp is available.

Seeley Lake (125 ac) offers walleye, crappie, catfish, northern pike, bluegill, carp and bullheads. The lake is 9 miles east of Windsor on Hwy 392, then south 1 mile. **Riverside Reservoir** (1460 ac) is a fluctuating reservoir and offers walleye, bass, crappie and other warm water species. It is north of the South Platte River midway between Greeley and Fort Morgan. Turn north off US 34 on county road at Masters.

East of Greeley about 30 miles, in the northwest corner of Morgan County, **Jackson Reservoir** (2960 ac) was one of the better fisheries for walleye. It also contained yellow perch, crappie, largemouth bass, channel catfish, northern pike, whitebass, bluegill, carp and bullhead. The lake was nearly drained in 1984 because of a leak in an irrigation outlet gate. It has yet to be restored to the major fishery it was, despite stocking of sub-catchable size walleye and crappie. There's a huge carp population. It may be 4 or 5 years before the reservoir achieves significant fishing status. Inquire locally. Jackson is reached from Fort Morgan on I-76 by taking Hwy 144 about 15 miles west to the town of Goodrich. Turn north and drive less than 0.5 mile to reach the reservoir. A marina and boat ramp are available. Fishing is prohibited from one-half hour after sunset until one-half hour before sunrise March 15 through April 15. No overnight camping on the reservoir.

Several miles northeast of Fort Morgan, **Prewitt Reservoir** (2430 ac) lies on the Logan-Washington County line. Take US 6 about 30 miles northeast of Brush. Prewitt is fair fishing for walleye, yellow perch, crappie, largemouth bass, channel catfish, white bass, carp and bullhead. It has a boat ramp.

NORTH STERLING RESERVOIR

Twenty-five miles due north of Prewitt Reservoir is **North Sterling Reservoir** (2880 ac) with about 44 miles of jagged shoreline; about 7 miles are accessible by vehicle. There are 4 boat ramps and a marina. Fishing is for walleye to 12 pounds; crappie in May and June; and bass, channel catfish and bluegill July to September. Fishing is prohibited from one-half hour

Jim's Marine & Prop Shop

- OMC & MerCruiser Sales and Service
- MerCruiser
- Boating Accessories
- Complete Prop Repair

Jim Parsons
6580 N. Federal
Denver, CO 80221
(303) 427-0887

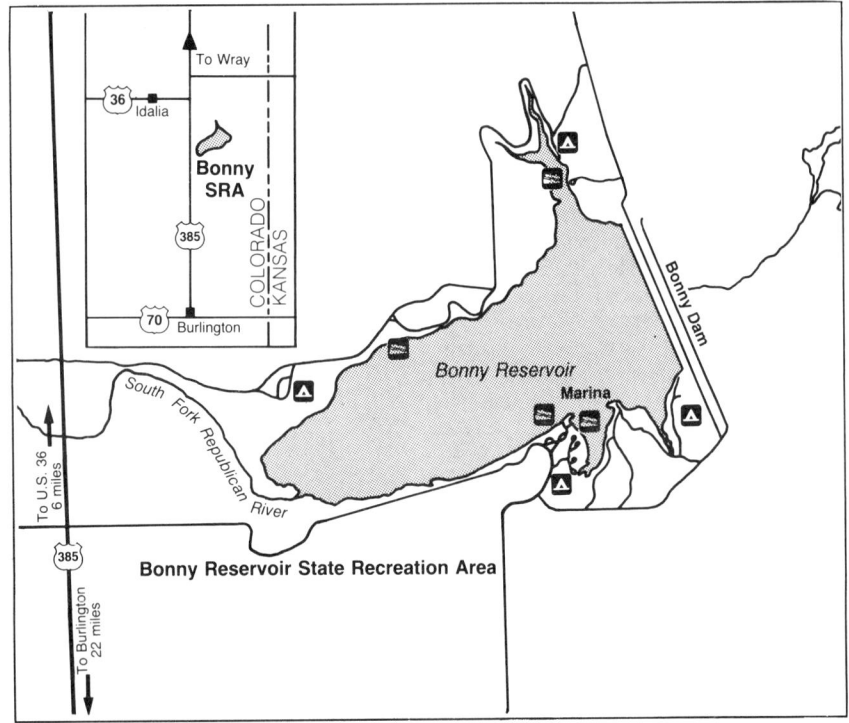

Bonny Reservoir

after sunset to one-half hour before sunrise from March 15 through April 15.

East and a bit north of North Sterling Reservoir near the Nebraska state line, **Jumbo** or **Julesburg Reservoir** (1580 ac) is 32 miles northeast of the town of Sterling and about 20 miles west of the town of Julesburg. It offers fair fishing for walleye, channel catfish, northern pike, carp and bullhead. Ice fishing often is very good. The reservoir is in the Red Lion State Wildlife Area. There is a boat ramp.

From Julesburg, take US 385 south toward the town of Wray. Northwest of Wray, **Stalker Lake** (26 ac) does not appear on most maps. Inquire in Wray for access. Stalker offers good fishing for crappie, bluegill, largemouth bass, channel catfish, and an occasional rainbow trout. Overnight camping is prohibited. A boat ramp is available. Electric-powered motors only. Black bass taken between 12 and 15 inches must be returned to the water immediately.

In the Wray vicinity there is fishing for brown trout along the **North Fork of the Republican River** on the west side of town and its tributary, **Chief Creek.** Chief Creek fishing is on state property and signed for angling.

BONNY RESERVOIR

South of Wray about 30 miles on US 385, **Bonny Reservoir** (1900 ac) is on the east side of the highway. Bonny averages 30 to 50 feet deep. It has an open shoreline lined with some willow and cottonwood. It is popular because fishing is good for walleye, yellow perch, crappie, largemouth bass, channel catfish, northern pike, whitebass, bluegill, carp and bullhead. Bonny is in the South Republican State Wildlife Area, in the southeastern corner of Yuma County. A boat ramp and marina are at the reservoir. And fishing is prohibited one-half hour after sunset until one-half hour before sunrise from March 15 to April 15. Seining of fish used as bait is prohibited in the Bonny Reservoir stilling basin and downstream as posted from October 1 through January 31. All black bass less than 15 inches in length taken at Bonny Reservoir and at the wildlife area ponds must be returned to the water immediately.

The **Bonny** or **Hale Ponds** (15 ac) located at the east end of Bonny Reservoir on the Kansas and Colorado state line offer fishing for yellow perch, crappie, largemouth bass, channel catfish, whitebass, bluegill, carp and bullhead.

Traveling south from Bonny Reservoir on US 385, turn west at the town of Burlington (20 miles south) onto Hwy 24, paralleling I-70. Drive about 32 miles west to the town of Seibert. About 6 miles west of Seibert, **Flagler Reservoir** (130 ac) is in the Flagler Reservoir State Recreation Area. Flagler Reservoir has a boat ramp and offers fishing for walleye, yellow perch, crappie, largemouth bass, channel catfish, northern pike, bluegill, carp and bullhead.

West of Flagler on I-70 is Limon. From Limon drive 19 miles southeast to Hugo. From Hugo drive due south about 5 miles on a secondary road to **Kinney Lake** (7 ac) in the Hugo SWA (State Wildlife Area). This small spring fed pond is about 20 feet deep. Kinney's best fishing is from its grassy shoreline. Fish Kinney for yellow perch, crappies, channel catfish, bluegill, carp, and bullhead. Only hand-propelled boats are allowed.

Also in the Hugo State Wildlife Area, **Hugo SWA Ponds** (20 ac) offer fishing for yellow perch, largemouth and smallmouth bass, channel catfish, bluegill, carp and bullhead. All bass taken less than 15 inches must be returned to the water immediately.

Continue 35 miles south from the town of Hugo on a secondary road across Hwy 94. About 1.5 miles southeast of the town of Karval is the Karval Reservoir State Fishing Area. **Karval Reservoir** (24 ac) is rated good fishing in the spring and fair in the summer for yellow perch, crappie, black bass, channel catfish, rock bass and rainbow. The 15-foot-deep lake is subject to some fishing restrictions, including that all black bass less than 15 inches in length must

FOR BETTER FISHING PUT 'EM BACK ALIVE...

A fish has the best chance for survival if you:
- Do not play any fish to total exhaustion.
- Keep fish in water as much as possible when handling and removing hooks.
- Remove hook gently—do not squeeze fish or put fingers in gills.
- Cut the line—do not pull hook out if fish is deeply hooked.
- Release fish only after its equilibrium is maintained. If necessary, gently hold fish and move fish slowly back and forth.
- Release fish in quiet water.

COLORADO B.A.S.S. CHAPTER FEDERATION, INC.
Pueblo: 1-542-9257   Arvada: 1-423-7606   Pine: 1-898-0137

Charles A. Walker photo

be returned to the water immediately.

About 5 miles west of Karval, Hwy 71 south leads to US 50 and several reservoirs north of the Arkansas River, many of them offering superb fishing.

Lake Henry (1120 ac) is about 3 miles northeast of Ordway. This 15-foot-deep lake offers fishing for walleye, crappie, largemouth bass, channel catfish, bluegill, carp and bullhead. Black bass less than 15 inches must be returned to the water immediately.

About 4 miles directly south of Lake Henry on the south side of Hwy 96 near Sugar City, **Lake Meredith** (1000 ac) is about 15 feet deep with a mucky bottom and a sandy shoreline fringed with tamarack and willow. Fishing here is for bluegill, carp and bullhead. Some campsites and a boat ramp are available.

About 7 miles south of Lake Meredith is **Holbrook Reservoir** (400 ac). Drive south on Hwy 71 to the intersection of US 50. Drive east 2 miles through Rocky Ford and on another 5 miles to Swink. At Swink turn north and drive about 4 miles to the Holbrook Reservoir. Holbrook has an open, sandy shoreline with cotton and tamarack. It offers fair fishing for walleye, yellow perch, crappie, smallmouth bass, channel catfish, northern pike, bluegill, carp and bullhead.

Northeast of Holbrook Reservoir, and about 7 miles northeast of the town of Cheraw on Hwy 109, is **Horse Creek Reservoir** or **Timber Lake** (2636 ac). Access from La Junta on US 50 is by driving about 10 miles to Cheraw, then northeast about 5 miles to the reservoir. Horse Creek, 35 feet deep, has a sand and cottonwood shoreline and a boat ramp. It offers good fishing for walleye, yellow perch, crappie, largemouth bass, channel catfish, northern pike, white bass, bluegill, carp and bullhead.

Northeast of Horse Creek Reservoir and due north of Las Animas about 12 miles is **Adobe Creek Reservoir** or **Blue Lake** (1200 ac) with a depth of 35 feet. It has an open, grassy shoreline with good unimproved campsites and cabins. A boat ramp is located on its south side. Adobe offers good fishing for walleye, crappie, channel catfish, northern pike, white bass, bluegill, carp, and bullhead.

JOHN MARTIN RESERVOIR

Just east of the town of Las Animas, **John**

Martin Reservoir (3000 ac) is on the Arkansas River. It offers a boat ramp and fishing for most warm water fish species. All black bass less than 15 inches must be returned to the water immediately. Fishing has been improving in recent years with a permanent pool of water.

Hasty Lake (73 ac) is at the eastern edge of John Martin Reservoir. Hasty Lake is 3 miles south of the town of Hasty by paved road. It is spring-fed, about 35 feet deep and has grassy shores. Hasty offers fishing for yellow perch, crappie, largemouth bass, channel catfish, carp, bullhead, and bluegill. A campground is located beside the lake.

Drive east beyond John Martin and Hasty Lake to the intersection of US 287, turn north about 10 miles to **North** and **South Queens Reservoirs** (1900 ac). They are fluctuating reservoirs that are sometimes at low levels and offer fair fishing for walleye, yellow perch, crappie, smallmouth bass, channel catfish, northern pike, white bass, bluegill, carp and bullhead.

Continuing north on US 287 about 3 miles, the **Nee Noshe Reservoir** (3696 ac) and several other reservoirs, including **Nee Skah, Nee Sopah** and **Nee Gronda Reser-**

Charles A. Walker photo

voirs, all are within a five-mile radius. They are part of the Queens State Wildlife Area. Nee Noshe Reservoir has a boat ramp and offers fishing for walleye, yellow perch, crappie, largemouth bass, channel catfish, northern pike, white bass, bluegill, carp and bullhead. Nee Noshe has been "hot" for wiper and other bass, and a boat is highly recommended. It is becoming a very popular fishery.

Thurston Reservoir (173 ac) is a state wildlife area with a variety of warm water species. It is 9 miles north of Lamar on Hwy 149, then east a mile on county road. **Clay Creek** also is a wildlife area 4 miles east of Lamar on US 50. The 6-acre pond has

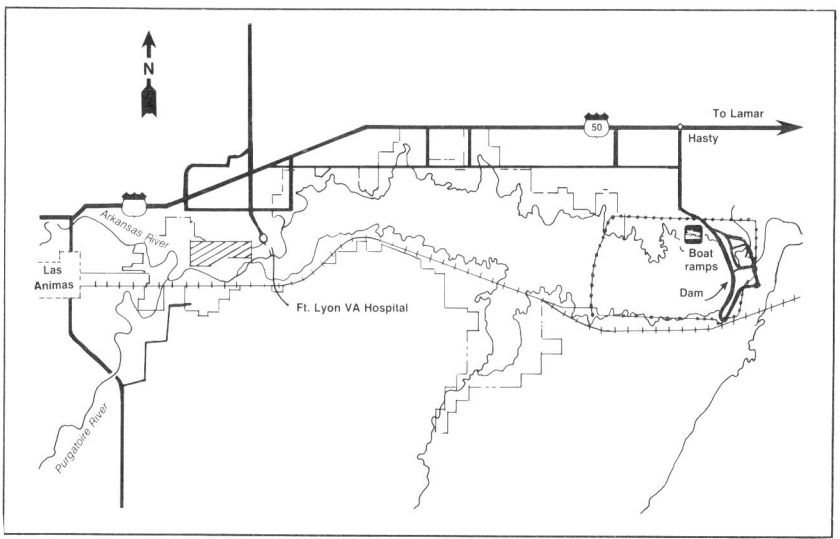
John Martin Reservoir

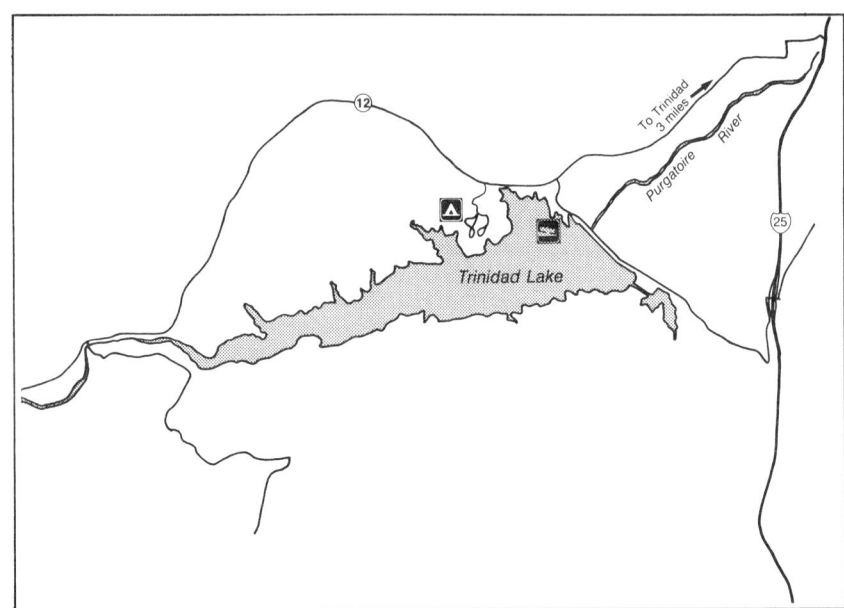

Trinidad State Recreation Area

several warm water species. No boats allowed.

Take US 287 south through Lamar about 30 miles to the **Two Buttes Reservoir** (1700 ac) on the east side of the highway. The reservoir has an open and rocky shoreline and reaches depths of 50 feet. It offers poor fishing for crappie, ling perch, bullhead, white bass, walleye and an occasional rainbow. There are two boat ramps. At the Two Buttes Ponds, below the dam, motorized boats are prohibited.

Farther south, in the arid country southwest of Springfield, **Comanche Ponds** (10 ac) are on the Oklahoma-Colorado state line. From Springfield, in the southeastern corner of the state, drive 22 miles south on US 287 to the town of Campo; inquire locally for access instructions. Comanche offers fishing for yellow perch, crappie, channel catfish, bluegill, carp and bullhead. All black bass taken less than 15 inches must be returned to the water immediately.

TRINIDAD LAKE

Trinidad Lake (800 ac) is less than 2 miles southwest of Trinidad on the Purgatoire River. It has become one of the finest bass fishing places in Colorado with 6- and 7-pound largemouth there for the catching. Avid bass fishermen have tournaments here and release their prizes after measuring and weighing.

There are 62 campsites tucked in pinion and juniper on Carpios Ridge on the west side overlooking the lake. They accommodate recreational vehicles, trailers and tents. There's room for the bass boat. Provisions for the handicapped have been designed into the campground, which boasts hot showers, coin-operated laundry, flush toilets, trailer dump station, electrical hookups and water hydrants. The only hitch to this bass utopia is the launch ramp, which is too small and located for a lower water level.

Bass fishing success is found in the Carpios and Levsa coves on the west and the cove along the east side of the dam, where the primary fish holding structures are submerged bushes and trees. Other areas to fish around the lake are sandstone ledges, flooded grass, fallen timber and islands.

Trinidad offers a boat ramp and fishing for walleye, largemouth bass, channel catfish, bluegill, carp and bullhead. All black bass less than 15 inches must be returned to the water immediately.

Lake Dorothey (4 ac) is rainbow and brook trout fishing for the adventuresome. It is on the Raton-Sugerite Wildlife Refuge southeast of Trinidad. It is reached by driving 17 miles south of Trinidad on I-25 and taking the Folsom Street Exit near Raton, N.M. Take N.M. Hwy 526 to Sugerite Canyon and then 12 miles of winding road back into Colorado. Fly and lure fishing only.

LATHROP STATE PARK

North of Trinidad 38 miles on I-25 is Walsenburg. East of town 1.5 miles on US 160 is Lathrop State Park. There are two large lakes in the park. **Martin Lake** (180 ac) is to the east and **Horseshoe Lake** (100 ac) is 1000 feet to the west. Lathrop was Colorado's first state park. It offers camping facilities complete with showers, laundry and dump stations. Martin Lake has an open grassy shoreline. It offers fair to good fishing for 8- to 12-inch rainbow. It has a boat ramp at its southwestern shore. Horseshoe Lake is about 15 feet deep and is

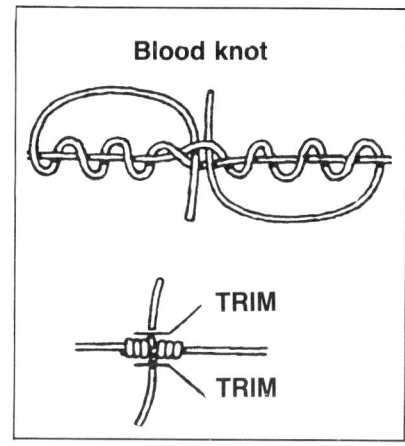

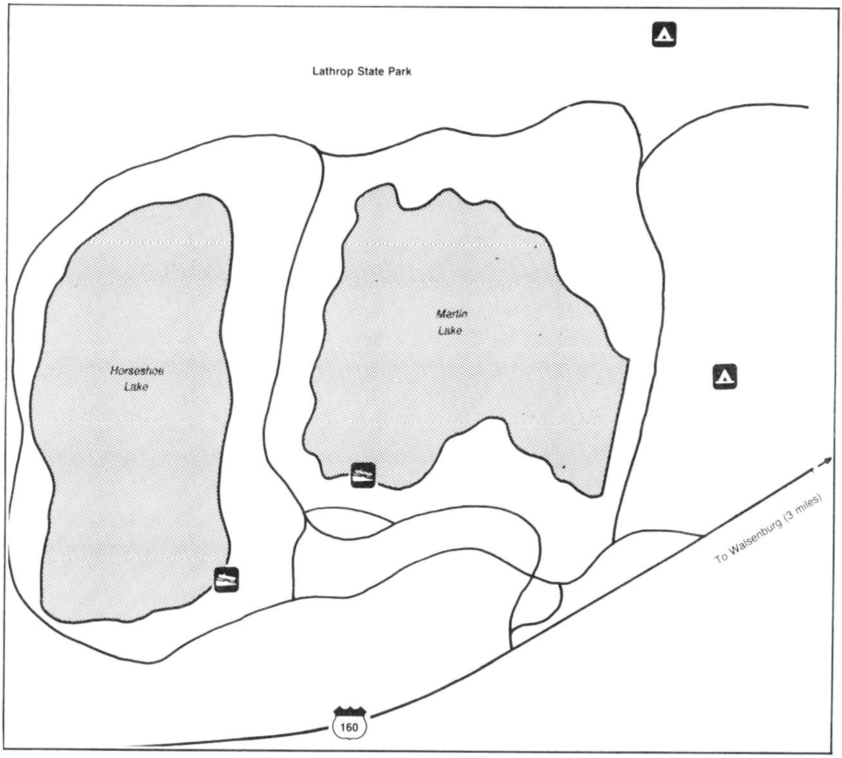

Lathrop State Park

LAKE TOPO MAPS
FOR LAKE POWELL and selected Colorado reservoirs. Contour maps show lake-bottom structure in detail. Available at local tackle, marine, diving supply and map dealers, or contact:

HYDROSURVEYS, INC.
7533 S. Ogden Way, Littleton, CO 80122
Dealer
(303) 794-0951   Inquiries Welcome

part of Walsenburg's water supply. Horseshoe offers fishing for warm water species including bass, channel catfish and bluegill. A boat ramp is located on the southeast corner of the lake. Ice fishing is marginal on the two lakes.

North of Walsenburg about 50 miles by I-25, the Pueblo area offers some fine warm water fishing. Pueblo Reservoir is top notch bass fishing. See discussion under Arkansas River. Southeast of Pueblo (inquire locally for directions) **Runyon Lake** (20 ac) offers fishing for largemouth bass and channel catfish.

Brush Hollow Reservoir (186 ac) has been leased to DOW by the Beaver Park Irrigation Co. It has some of the best channel catfish and crappie fishing some of the time. There's also largemouth bass, bluegill, carp and bullheads. There's no boat ramp yet, but one is proposed. Bass stocking is likely. The reservoir is 3.5 miles northwest of Penrose via county road F-42 via Hwy 115 from US 50 west of Pueblo.

Northeast from Colorado Springs take US 24 about 40 miles to the **Ramah Reservoir** (170 ac). This reservoir has a boat ramp and offers fishing for largemouth bass, bluegill, carp and an occasional rainbow. Ramah sometimes is drawn dry; check with the Colorado Springs office of the Division of Wildlife. Phone 473-2945.☐

Rule of thumb: Small streams have small fish. But sometimes there are surprises.

Nymph Fishing Classes
**For Beginner & Experienced Anglers
Using fly or spin gear**
- Special Nymph Fishing Equipment, Proper Rigging, Knots
- Casting, Line Control Techniques
- Insect Collection, Identification, Matching
- Important Artificial Fly Characteristics
  - On-Stream Sampling, Collecting Tools, Preservation Methods
    - Actual Fishing, Reading The Water

Individual or Group Classes Available

Tom Lentz   303/455-7278
* Colorado Licensed Outfitter #32

Ice fishing augers well for anglers

By the time winter cold rules the West and ice armors lakes and reservoirs, most fishermen have packed away their fly and spinning rods, hung up their waders and are dreaming of fairweather angling, past and future. They may even tie a few dry flies and get their tackle ready for the coming season.

Others bundle up for a whole new season—ice fishing. Depending on ice conditions, the season runs roughly from December through April in both Colorado and Wyoming. In Wyoming, some lakes and reservoirs have special ice fishing seasons, December through February, to protect quality fishing.

Check to be sure that the migratory waterfowl season on the flatland ponds and lakes is past.

Some ardent anglers head out by snowmobile. Others find snowshoes or cross-country skis helpful when roads are drifted with snow. A thermos of hot coffee, tea, lemonade or soup is welcome, but be sure to have the threaded top and cap dry so it won't freeze when capped.

Who would relish ice fishing? Fishermen who are patient and know that the chance of catching larger fish (2 pounds and up) is often good, and are willing to brave the elements to prove it.

Just like open water fishing, there's more to ice fishing than drilling a hole in the ice and hanging in there until a trout takes the lure or bait. And it's a spot the fair weather angler ought to investigate before indulging himself in an outfit that's only used a few months a year. Go out and talk to devotees of winter angling. You won't have much trouble finding one who welcomes the opportunity to share what he knows.

As far as equipment goes, ice augers or drills are far, far easier than chopping a hole in the ice. And it's worth a few minutes with a file keeping 'em sharp. An 8-inch-diameter auger is big enough.

There's nothing fancy about the tackle. There's a wooden tip-up rod with 20 feet or so of line or a sawed-off spincast rig set up so a flag will indicate a bite. Bait usually is salmon eggs or fresh (but dead) minnows. Live minnows are banned above 7000 feet in Colorado.

Ice fishermen'll try about anything. Fluorescent lures and jigs and orange-colored cheese marshmallows have produced. It's fun to invent your own lure and some shops have inexpensive kits to devise your own jigs.

Ice fishin' great, grandpa

Some general guidelines include: "think small" in terms of lures and use light tackle with 2- to 3-pound test line and a strike detector, because fish don't usually "hit & run" in winter water.

Jigs are good, and fluorescents are good fish takers, if they're fished at the right depth. It's important to know at what depth you're getting action.

A couple of the most productive colors are chartreuse and white, and chartreuse and fluorescent red. But try other colors, because it depends on what kind of fish you're after as much as what's most appealing to them.

One good way to prepare for ice fishing is to buy live minnows and freeze 'em in watertight plastic bags in the home freezer. Placed by the car heater enroute to the fishing spot they thaw and are ready to use. Worms also are good winter bait and this too takes pre-ice fishing season planning, often with basement wormbeds. Waxworm bait (bee moth larva) often is effective.

Lures, jigs and weighted ice flies are also used, but these need to be in constant motion to attract fish.

In recent years, ice fishing by sight has become popular. It involves making a low platform to lie on so one can peer through the hole in the ice to see the fish. A sleeping bag or a cover over head and hole is necessary to keep out reflection. By seeing the fish, the bait or lure can be jiggled at the proper depth and you can see when to set the hook. Most importantly, you can see if there are any fish to hook. If not, go elsewhere, bore a new hole and take another peek.

Some fishermen prefer deep water, some 12-14 feet, and some 1 to 3 feet, depending upon the lake and the kind of trout being sought. A cluster of fishermen and shanties doesn't mean that's where the fish are.

A few words of caution are in order. Wait for the ice at the edge of the lake to be at least 8 (preferably 12) inches thick before venturing out on it—especially with a vehicle. Ice thickness isn't uniform, so be wary of thin and soft spots. If you abandon a hole, mark it so another fisherman won't step in it. A pole or stick will do the job.

In Wyoming, some good winter fishing holes are Lake Hattie, Glendo Reservoir, Alcova Reservoir, Pathfinder Reservoir, Laramie Plains Lakes, Twin Butte, Saratoga Lake, Seminoe Reservoir, Lake DeSmet, Wheatland Reservoir No. 3, Goldeneye Reservoir, Pathfinder Reservoir, Healy Reservoir, Willow Lake and Halfmoon Lake, Keyhole Reservoir, Ocean Lake, Pilot Butte Reservoir, Ring Lake, Trail Lake, Torrey Lake, Boysen Reservoir, Bighorn Lake and the Bighorn River downstream from Robertson Dam, Jackson Lake, Newton Lake, and Fremont Lake. Many lakes are open to fishing year around, so inquire locally.

In Colorado, favorite ice fishing sites include Lake John, Delaney Buttes Lake Cowdrey Lake, Red Feather Lakes, Dowdy Lake, West Lake, Island Lake, Vega Reservoir, Avery Lake, Bonny Reservoir, Steamboat Reservoir, Lon Hagler Reservoir Elevenmile Reservoir, Pueblo Reservoir Lake Trinidad, Tarryall Reservoir, Terrel Reservoir, Barr Lake, Lake Dillon, Cherry Creek Reservoir, Chatfield Reservoir Green Mountain Reservoir, Blue Mesa Reservoir, and many others. □

Jiffy™
POWER ICE DRILL

The World's Champion. #1 in Power & Performance.

In 1980, 1981 and 1982 Jiffy powered the World Ice Drilling Champions to victory. Thousands in use.

Feldmann quality . . . respected, recognized for reliability since 1945.

See it at your local dealer or contact factory for product details.

Feldmann
ENGINEERING & MANUFACTURING CO., INC.
P.O. BOX 153, SHEBOYGAN FALLS, WI 53085
Telephone 414/467-6167

Wyoming fishing still makes dreams come true

Wyoming fishing has an extra "something." It's more than just the usual satisfaction of precious hours spent angling. It has to do with invisible things—the bigness of the country, the blueness of the sky, the contentment of enjoyment, the sense of being next to history.

It doesn't seem to matter where in the Cowboy State the angler is. There's a specialness whether fishing the rose-rocked canyon at Flaming Gorge or witnessing the vitality of a clear rushing mountain stream edged with wildflowers.

That "something" is enjoyed and shared by non-fishing companions, as well: the bull elk flying up a mountainside like Pegasus; a cow moose with more curiosity about us than we have for her; the basin rattlesnake that brought to an abrupt end a hunt for bait grasshoppers near Kaycee. And that shiny black bear who stole those cutthroat beauties, caught the evening before and slated for our breakfast, even though we thought they were so well-secured high between two trees.

Experiences such as these generate a Wyoming mystique. The enthusiasm of anglers in Wyoming and other states may account for the fact that more fishermen are seeking the pools and riffles of Wyoming's 416 miles of Blue Ribbon Trout Streams (compared to 158 miles of designated Gold Medal trout waters in Colorado), and probing the depths of lakes and reservoirs.

FISHING PRESSURE

The "mystique" also translates into more people wanting to fish and have a photo snapped to prove Wyoming fishing is all it's cracked up to be. That means fishing pressure—on the fish and on the fisheries managers at the State Game & Fish Department.

A more up-to-date indicator of fishing pressure is fishing license sales. A breakdown of licenses sold by the Wyoming Game and Fish Department reveals:

	Resident	Nonresident	
1980	75,965	57,716	(incl. 45,010 5-day licenses)
1981	138,119	142,965	(incl. 109,081 5-day licenses)
1982	141,941	134,641	(incl. 101,378 5-day licenses)
1983	137,529	125,434	(incl. 110,326 5-day licenses)

Total fishing licenses sold jumped from 133,681 in 1980 to more than twice that—276,582 licenses—two years later.

Reduced mining and petroleum industry employment is believed responsible for the 1983 decline in resident licenses. No 1984 data were available.

MANAGEMENT

Wyoming's fabulous Miracle Mile on the North Platte River has another kind of fantastic fishing besides that for the rainbow and brown trout for which it is famous.

It's those tasty walleyes—they're running in the 8- to 12-pound range—especially in the Chalk Cliffs area on the northwest portion of "the mile." And they'll give you a tussle before you can land 'em. In fact, a lot of the river is great walleye fishing these days.

John Baughman, head of fisheries for the Wyoming Game & Fish Department, would like to see a lot of walleyes taken. He looks back 15 years, before Seminoe Reservoir was built, and there were no walleye in that section of the North Platte. With the filling of the reservoir, walleye were introduced and eventually went over the dam and into "the mile."

"We're trading 10 trout for every walleye," he said, noting that the trout fishing "is nowhere near what it was, but it's still one of the finest natural trout fisheries on the continent."

The prolific walleye not only compete with trout for food, they find rainbows mighty fine dining in themselves. Catch-and-release fishing has kept "the mile," which is actually about 6 miles long, up to blue-ribbon levels.

A recent creel census, a key fish management tool, showed 2600 trout per mile in the catch-and-release areas, and 2000 per mile of river where legal size trout may be kept. A mid-afternoon's fishing on Miracle Mile netted Baughman 20 trout in 2 hours, including two caught on back casts. An equal number got away. The largest: 16.5 inches.

Baughman is a catch-and-release fisherman who plays the trout fast, handles 'em gently and releases them quickly. Studies have shown that fish which are played to exhaustion and mishandled die frequently after release, because their systems respond to the shock of being caught.

One of the things about walleyes: the limit is 20 *in addition* to the trout bag limit between the Colorado state line and Seminoe. Of course, you don't fish the same way for walleye; instead of using flies and spinners you're bouncing lures off the bottom. Also, instead of setting the hook right away, a walleye will want to hang on for 10 seconds or so, making a second run during which time the hook is set. (See Tom Lentz article on plastic worms and walleye elsewhere in this edition.)

The fishing for walleye and trout east of Casper is excellent for float fishermen too. For the angler seeking to put fish on the table or grill, the walleye is prime eating. Check the new regulations for limits on various stretches of the river.

GOODBYE TROUT

The walleye are literally killing a good trout fishery, the Goldeneye Reservoir north of Casper. Illegal stocking introduced the predators, perch and others. The result: a $20,000 trout improvement program conducted in the fall of 1984 is shot. There will be rainbows in Goldeneye for a while, but the forecast is that they're done for.

Illegal stocking, well intentioned or not, is a painful reality for fish managers in Colorado and Wyoming. In the Goldeneye situation, the walleye won't adapt to the habitat well and won't grow...so even the illegal stockers will suffer in the long run, Baughman said.

The same thing happens when minnows are introduced into waters where live bait is prohibited. The minnows become fish in competition with the trout and the trout fishing suffers...maybe permanently.

"It's a lot more damaging than poaching big game," Baughman explained. "The introduced species often don't have the forage fish, the plankton size may not be right and you end up with fish that don't grow though they consume food that trout need. So no one ends up with any decent sized fish." White suckers are an example of a species that will ruin trout fishing.

Yet the penalties for poaching one big game animal can be prison terms and fines, while ruining a fishery is a minor offense under the law. The consequences are far, far more devastating in the fish situation.

"We just can't tolerate these violations," Baughman said. "The fishermen have to control the situations themselves by reporting violators." Also, he'd like to see heavier penalties for violators.

HIGHLIGHTS

Wyoming anglers can look forward to more intensive fish management at reservoirs, many of which offer nearly year-round fishing except during the migratory waterfowl season.

Upper and Lower Newton Lakes near Cody, Sand Creek near Beulah, Wheatland Reservoir No. 3 west of Wheatland, Half Moon Lake and the Green River Lakes near Pinedale, Grayrocks Reservoir near Guernsey Seminoe Reservoir on the North Platte, Sulphur Creek Reservoir south of Evanston and Keyhole Reservoir near Sundance are among the 15 major bodies of water in Wyoming that are or will be getting intensive fish management.

Cooperative ventures with Trout Un-

Fly fishing isn't an exclusively male endeavor.

limited, the U.S. Soil Conservation Service, U.S. Forest Service and private landowners are improving present and future fishing in many parts of the state.

The Green River below Fontenelle Reservoir will be closed for two weeks each fall to permit kokanee salmon to spawn and to permit egg taking in order to introduce or strengthen the species elsewhere. The kokanee in this stretch average 17 to 18 inches. After the spawn, angling's open again.

Grayrocks Reservoir on the Laramie River will probably be one of the hottest and most utilized fishing holes in the state. The white crappie is joining the walleye, rainbow, channel cat and other species there.

Fishing in the Snake River is destined for improvement, thanks to one of those cooperative efforts. Stream improvements in Jackson Hole are designed to improve spawning and, eventually, mainstream fishing.

Northern Pike have been restocked in Keyhole Reservoir near Sundance. It'll be a couple of years before they reach the minimum 30 in size, but the long range picture for Keyhole is continued good fishing.

Lake DeSmet north of Buffalo is stocked with catchable size Eagle Lake Rainbow, which is known locally as Lake DeSmet Rainbow. The Eagle Lake strain is better adapted to lake fishing, reproduces more prolifically and grows faster than their cous-

Ordinary tackle nets big fish

ins. In the long run, it's hoped fishing will improve and stocking costs decline.

Flaming Gorge Reservoir is being watched for the outcome of experimental stocking of Kamloops Rainbow and Eagle Lake Rainbow. There's no certainty the efforts to improve fishing will succeed, but it's worth a try in the face of increased fishing pressure.

Slot-limit catches are destined to become more prevalent. That means only fish in certain sizes may be kept. The goal is better fishing at lower cost with expectations the fish can reproduce and keep their populations without stocking.

Inescapable seems to be the fact that fishing license fees will increase, especially for Wyoming residents who in 1985 were paying only $7.50 plus the $5 for a conservation stamp.

"Barely a third of the fishing in Wyoming is done by nonresidents," Baughman said. "Fishing always has been a kind of give away in Wyoming, but if this tradition of paying only half the cost of what it takes to provide fishing continues, the fishing is going to go down hill. It's up to the public through organized sportsman's groups to look to the future—sport fishing and the tourist business is the second biggest Wyoming business (next to minerals)."

So, as far as fishing is concerned, Mother Nature gets help from the catch-and-release anglers and fisheries managers that's to everyone's benefit.

ANGLING VARIETY

From a more subjective viewpoint, this all adds up to an appealing range and variety of angling. Quirky goldens in high alpine lakes inexplicably will ignore a Royal Wulff one evening, then attack it with a vengeance the next morning. Brown trout haunt wide murky streams, and greedy brook abound in smaller streams and beaver ponds. The Rocky Mountain whitefish, shunned by some fishermen, are in fact a lively and tasty game fish. Huge mackinaw patrol big, deep lakes, pursued by intense anglers in powerboats with deep-sea caliber fishing rigs.

High-finned and plucky grayling are taking hold in some mountain lakes, providing an alluring alternative to the acrobatic rainbow trout.

Among warm-water fish, the battling bass, walleye, channel catfish, crappie, perch and ling cod are finally getting the recognition for the fine angling they provide—often where pioneers found desert and desolation a few score years ago.

Yet, it's the cutthroat (native) with its vivid red-pink jaw that is king of the sporting coldwater species—at least in Wyoming. It all adds up to some really fine living, splendid fishing and good times. ☐

1985-1986 WYOMING FISHING LICENSE FEES

Resident	$ 7.50*
Non-Resident	35.00*
1 day	5.00
10 day	15.00*

* A $5 conservation stamp is mandatory. See regulations for military, lifetime and special situations. Fees are subject to change.

RECORD WYOMING FISH

Here are the record-size fish compiled by the Wyoming Game and Fish Department as of Spring 1985.

Fish	Weight	Length	Locality	Date	Angler
Cutthroat	15 lbs.	32"	Native Lake Sublette Co.	1959	Alan Dow
Rainbow	23 lbs.	35½"	Burnt Lake Sublette Co.	1969	Frank Favazzo
Brown	25 lbs. 13 oz.	34¼"	Anvil Draw Flaming Gorge	1982	George Rose
Lake (Mackinaw)	50 lbs.	46"	Jackson Lake Teton Co.	1983	Doris Budge
Golden	11¼ lbs.	28"	Cook's Lake Sublette Co.	1948	C.S. Read
Brook	10 lbs.	—	Torrey Lake Fremont Co.	1933	Unidentified
Kokanee	3.98 lbs.	22½"	Flaming Gorge	1983	Charles C. Kirby
Whitefish	4¼ lbs.	21"	Snake River Teton Co.	1977	Dennis Jennings
Grayling	2.36 lbs.	—	Meadow Lake Sublette Co.	1983	Robert Doak
Walleye	14¼ lbs.	—	Keyhole Res. Crook Co.	1973	Wilmer Swindler
Sauger	6 lbs. 11½ oz.	25¾"	Tongue River Sheridan Co.	1981	Tracey Smiley
Largemouth	7 lbs. 2 oz.	—	Stove Lake Goshen Co.	1942	John Tetters
Smallmouth	4¾ lbs.	—	Southeast Pit Sheridan Co.	1982	Jon Nelson
Black Crappie	2 lbs. 3 oz.	—	Crook County	1983	Mardell Palmer
Channel Catfish	22¾ lbs.	34¼"	Glendo Res.	1984	Ed Schulz
Ling	19¼ lbs.	44"	Pilot Butte Res. Fremont Co.	1965	K. E. Moreland
Northern Pike	23 lbs. 1 oz.	44⅜"	Keyhole Res. Crook Co.	1983	Keith Bower
Ohrid Trout	9 lbs. 3 oz.	28.8"	Alcova Res.	1984	Kent Erickson
Perch	1 lb. 10½ oz.	13⅜"	Glendo Reservoir	1985	Mike Laursen
Bluegill	1.06 lbs.	10.3"	Deaver Res. Park Co.	1983	Don Anderson

Weather in the West

Being ready for the elements by knowing what extremes can be encountered should be as much a part of a fishing trip as packing the rod and reel.

Weather in the West can change swiftly, drastically and relentlessly—to the point of being life-threatening and sometimes life-taking. The need for a basic awareness ap-

Gary, Bill and Charlie.

plies to mountain angler or flatlands reservoir boater alike. Here are some things to be alert to:

Dehydration: Year-round, the high altitudes of Colorado and Wyoming wring water out of your system not only through your skin but also as you breathe, especially during exertion. Headache, listlessness, irritability and tiredness are symptoms that it's time for a drink of water. Surprising what it can do. Take plenty of water along and drink it. While some streams and lakes are safe to drink from, play it safe; treat drinking water to kill disease-causing organisms that can ruin a trip.

Altitude sickness: Lightheadedness, rapid heartbeat, fatigue, inability to walk or climb without undue shortness of breath, and clumsiness, are sure signs that you need to get to a lower altitude now, before serious, incapacitating illness results. Rest doesn't help; going to a lower altitude will. Try again another day. Don't try to be a good sport and keep going.

Exposure: Getting chilled by wind, cold air or rain, or the three in combination, is a killer if body temperature cannot be maintained. A dangerous time is during the summer when temperatures are in the 40s and 50s, and there is wind and rain. Often protective warm clothes and raingear aren't along. Carrying a daypack or putting an overnight bag in the boat or Jeep with a wool cap, wool sweater, foil survival blanket, and a substantial packet of high energy rations can be a lifesaver.

Sunburn: Overcast days at high altitudes, and reflections from water can cause severe burning and aggravate other existing conditions. A wide-brimmed hat, good quality sunglasses, and an adequate amount of sunscreen are common sense. Hospitalization resulting from the effects of sunburn isn't uncommon.

Lightning: A particularly frightening occurrence in open country above timberline, in highly mineralized areas, and in the wide open spaces of prairie reservoirs. Pay attention to what the wind and clouds are doing and by all means heed that prickly, hair-raising static electricity that signals Zeus is at hand. Get off the lake, into the timber, below the crest of the ridge, and away from any prominent features.

Swift water: Water in mountain streams is deceptively fast, and even at streamside it can be perilous to small children who are subject to being swept away, their cries drowned by the noise of the water. Knee-deep streams often are unwadable. Clear water often is deeper than it looks, and far colder than it seems on first contact.

There are many measures that can be taken to increase the enjoyment and success of a fishing trip. Nature-wise sportsmen are aware and prepared to protect themselves from situations that could cause tragedy. □

Photo by Candy Moulton

Which fly to try? Give this list an eye

by Jim Kurtz
Wyoming Game & Fish Department
fish biologist, Pinedale

What fly-fishing enthusiast hasn't overheard the following pronouncements in numerous angling emporiums throughout trout country?

• "The only way to catch trout is to *match* the prevailing insect hatch."
• "All that hatch-matching is a bunch of nonsense. What one needs is a fly that will *attract* a trout into striking."
• "The best way to *deceive* a trout is to use a fly that resembles a combination of many different types of fish food."

Crackerbarrel discussions concerning fly patterns will be afloat as long as trout continue to swim. In some cases, it appears store-bought or kitchen-counter-tied flies snag more anglers than trout. Disputes over why a particular fly pattern will catch fish for one angler and will not produce a strike for another remain unsolved.

Many Rocky Mountain fishermen agree on one thing—that dry, nymph and streamer flies are more effective than wet flies.

Fishing publications suggest trying the following fly patterns in the Rockies: Adams, Royal Wulff, Humpy, Muddler Minnow, and Gold-Ribbed Hares Ear Nymph.

A recent Wyoming survey revealed some additional specifics for Wyoming fishing.

With its cutthroat trout, the **Snake River** drainage is very popular with both resident and nonresident fishermen. Patterns which seem to be favorites include:

Dry Flies
• Humpy (yellow-belly), sizes 8-18
• Adams, sizes 8-18
• Royal Wulff, sizes 8-18
• Hopper (various types), sizes 6-14

Wet Flies
• Black/Grizzly Wooly Worm, sizes 6-12

Nymphs
• Gold-Ribbed Hares Ear, sizes 8-16
• Montana (Black Stonefly) sizes 4-8
• Golden Stonefly, sizes 6-12

Streamers
• Muddler Minnow, sizes 4-8
• Olive/Grizzly Matuka, sizes 2-8
• White Maribou Muddler, sizes 2-10

Perhaps due to the great variety of water notably in the **Salt River** drainage, a number of specialty patterns have been developed

• Hank-a-hair (Dry) sizes 12-22
• Swift Creek Special (Nymph), sizes 10-16
• Shadow (Streamer), sizes 2-6
• Salt River Spuddler (Streamer), sizes 2-6

For a variety in trout species and kinds of water, the **Green River** drainage is one of the best in the state. Many similar patterns are used in both the Snake and Green River drainages. Some of the most widely used patterns are:

Dry Flies
• Humpy (yellow or red belly), sizes 8-18
• Royal Wulff, sizes 8-18
• Adams, sizes 8-18
• Hopper (various types) sizes 6-14

Wet Flies
• Black/Grizzly Wooly Worm, sizes 6-1
• Royal Coachman, sizes 8-14
• Double Renegade, sizes 6-14

Nymphs
• Golden Stonefly, sizes 6-12
• Montana, sizes 6-12
• Gold-Ribbed Hares Ear, sizes 8-16

Streamers
• Muddler Minnow, sizes 2-14
• Olive/Grizzly Matuka, sizes 2-8
• White Maribou Muddler, sizes 2-10
• Spruce Fly, sizes 6-10

Improved clinch knot

The area surrounding Lander provides good fishing in both the **Wind River** and **Sweetwater River** drainages. There also are exceptional high country lakes and small streams. Some recommended patterns for both stream and lake fishing are:

Dry Flies
- Troth Elk Hair Caddis, sizes 14-16
- Irresistible, sizes 12-18
- Humpy, sizes 12-20
- Royal Wulff, sizes 12-18
- Adams, sizes 14-20

Wet Flies
- Black Wooly Worm, sizes 2-8

Nymphs
- Trueblood Blue Gray, sizes 12-14
- Trueblood Otter Shrimp, sizes 12-14
- Kaufman Olive Scud, sizes 12-14
- Olive Green Dragon, sizes 4-8
- Montana, sizes 6-8

Streamers
- Muddler Minnow, sizes 2-10
- Spruce Fly, sizes 6-8
- Maribou Muddler, sizes 6-8

The northcentral region provides lake and stream fly fishing within the shadows of the Bighorn Mountains. The wet fly is popular in this region. Popular patterns include:

Dry Flies
- Adams
- Irresistible all-sizes 12-16
- Various Wulff Patterns

Wet Flies
- Gray Quill, size 10
- Wooly Worm (various types), sizes 6-10
- Gray-Hackle Peacock, sizes 8-10
- Rio Grande Kine, sizes 8-10

Nymphs
- Mite series, size 10
- Montana, size 10
- Girdle Bug, sizes 8-10

Streamers
- Muddler Minnow, sizes 6-8
- Platte River Special, sizes 6-8

Two specialty patterns for this region are the Cauncy Special and the Lake DeSmet Special.

Finally, the **Platte River** drainage in the vicinity of Casper provides excellent stream, lake and reservoir fishing. Perhaps the trout fishing in this area is exemplified by the renowned "miracle mile" of the Platte River. Trout fly patterns are quite diversified with agreement limited to nymph and streamers, which include:

Nymphs
- Girdle Bug, sizes 6-12
- Halfback, sizes 4-10
- Fullback, sizes 4-10

Streamers
- Platte River Special, sizes 4-8
- Muddler Minnow, sizes 4-8

The dry fly patterns include: Mosquito, Black Quill, Rio Grande King, H&L Variant and the Irresistible (sizes for all—2-18). Some suggested wet-fly patterns are the Wooly Worm, Adams, Gray-hackle Peacock, Renegade, Black Gnat and the Blue Dun (sizes for all—10-14). Specialty patterns for this area include both the Big Horn Streamer (size 4, Platte River) and the Green Drake (sizes 6-8, Goldeneye Reservoir).

A composite pattern list for Wyoming is difficult to designate. Certain famous patterns can be used with confidence throughout the state—Adams, Montana, Wooly Worm, Muddler Minnow, etc.

But if your favorite pattern isn't listed,

perhaps it may succeed where others fail.

(Adapted and reprinted with permission from *Wyoming Wildlife*.)

TOP-NOTCH BOOK

Tying and Fishing the West's Best Dry Flies by Bob Wilson and Richard Parks is a magnificent directory of top-notch dry flies and some of the principal tackle shops in the West. It also offers direct, useful information on fishing them effectively. The well-illustrated book is $9.95 plus postage and handling from Parks' Fly Shop, P.O. Box 196, Gardiner, MT 59030. □

Autumn fly fishing on the North Platte near Saratoga

Bear River fishing's only fair

ADJACENT COMMUNITIES:
Evanston, Sage, Cokeville, Kemmerer.

PRINCIPAL HIGHWAYS:
U.S. I-80, 30; Wyo. 89, 282.

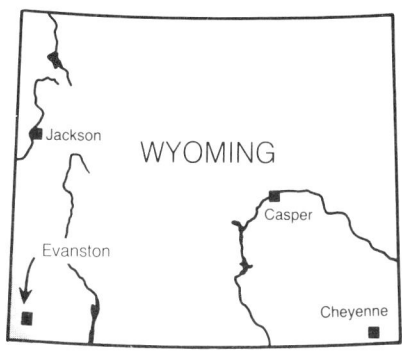

The years have not been kind to **Bear River,** which winds back and forth across the Utah-Wyoming border. Dewatering, channeling and high-water damage have taken their toll. Although there are still some brown and cutthroat, it's not great fishing.

There are a few fishing places, including **Woodruff Narrows Reservoir** (6439 ft; 2000 ac). It is private with public access allowed. There are no boat ramps (maybe in 1986), but there are places to launch boats. The reservoir has brown, cutthroat and rainbow to 20 inches with an occasional 5-pounder being hooked, but most fish are smaller. There are no camping facilities. Fishing is poor in late summer. The reservoir is on the river about 10 miles north of Evanston via Hwy 89 and US 30.

Farther downstream, near Cokeville on US 30 north from the village of Sage (24 miles west of Kemmerer), the tributaries harbor some trout.

In the **Smiths Fork,** including **Porcupine Creek,** the **Hobble Creek** drainage, **Lake Alice** and **Thomas Fork** drainage, all cutthroat under 10 inches must be returned to the water. Fishing is with flies and lures only. The Game and Fish Department is endeavoring to build the quality of the fishery with the Bonneville and Bear River cutthroat. The latter is a candidate for the endangered species list. Because the small trout are to be returned to the water doesn't mean there are big fish here. There aren't. □

Put Them Back Alive...

The following steps will help insure that a released fish has a better chance to survive—and be caught again.

• Do not play a fish to total exhaustion.
• Wet hands before touching fish.
• Keep fish in the water as much as possible when handling and removing the hook. Remove the hook gently—do not squeeze the fish or put fingers in the gills.
• If deeply hooked—cut the line. Do not pull out the hook.
• Release the fish only after it regains its equilibrium. If necessary, gently hold the fish facing upstream and move the fish back and forth.
• Release the fish in quiet water.

Wind River fisherman's dream

ADJACENT COMMUNITIES:
Dubois, Crowheart, Fort Washakie, Ethete, Lander, Riverton, Atlantic City, South Pass City.

PRINCIPAL HIGHWAYS:
U.S. 26, 287; Wyo. 28.

The cold, clear waters of the Wind River Mountains in western Wyoming give rise to two major river systems, both of them fishing wonderlands. On the west side of the Continental Divide is the fabulous Green River; on the east, the Wind River. The lakes are so numerous many never have been named.

The fishing is for the hard-to-get golden trout, the feisty rainbow, the wary brown, the brook, cutthroat, mackinaw, ling cod, splake and whitefish. At lower elevations, warm water species include walleye, perch, catfish and a variety of panfish.

Many of the high lakes and streams are reachable only on foot or horseback. Some are in established wilderness areas. Many mid-elevation waters and those in the Wind River Valley are accessible by car and recreation vehicle with boat in tow.

The discussion here is of fishing on the east side of the divide, of the Wind River and its tributary streams from the Wind River Mountains on the west and the Absaroka Mountains on the north.

From the West, Wind River fishing is reached via US 26 over Togwotee Pass, from the south out of Rock Springs US 191 and Hwy 28; from Rawlins US 287 brings the angler to the base of the Mountains. From the east visitors take US 26 out of Casper.

The logical starting points for backcountry trips are Lander, for the southern Wind River Mountains, and Dubois for the northern area.

High on the east side of the Continental Divide southeast of Yellowstone National Park, the Wind River begins a circuitous southeasterly journey. Near Riverton, it swoops north where it is dammed to form Boysen Reservoir, flows into the Owl Creek Mountains and emerges with a new name.

The primary streams feeding the Wind River are the Little Wind River from the West, and the three forks of the Popo Agie River from the southwest. Numerous small tributaries join the river in its upper reaches. The Wind River Indian Reservation encloses a major portion of the stream and of its high mountain streams and lakes. (The Indians have their own fishing rules and enforcement procedures and the visitor, fisherman or not, is wise to know what they are and to obey them. A special section in this guide discusses fishing on the reservation.)

HEADWATERS

The Wind River's origin is in the Togwotee Pass area, in the notch where US 287 crosses the Continental Divide to link the Teton Valley on the west to the Wind River Valley on the east. It flows southeasterly through the town of Dubois and into the Indian reservation.

From Togwotee Pass to Dubois and from there south another 44 miles, the Wind River closely parallels US 287. The best fishing on the main river is in the Dubois vicinity, aplenty. Dry flies are the angler's favorite in late summer and autumn. Rainbow, brown, cutthroat and whitefish, averaging 12 inches but often larger, can be caught.

At the point US 287 heads south to Lander and US 26 east to Riverton, the river follows US 26. It is about 75 feet wide in the Dubois area but broadens considerably as it meanders south, east, and then north. The river originates on Forest Service land, but enters private property about 12 miles north of Dubois. South of Dubois, signs along the highway mark several access points to good public fishing. Check with landowners to

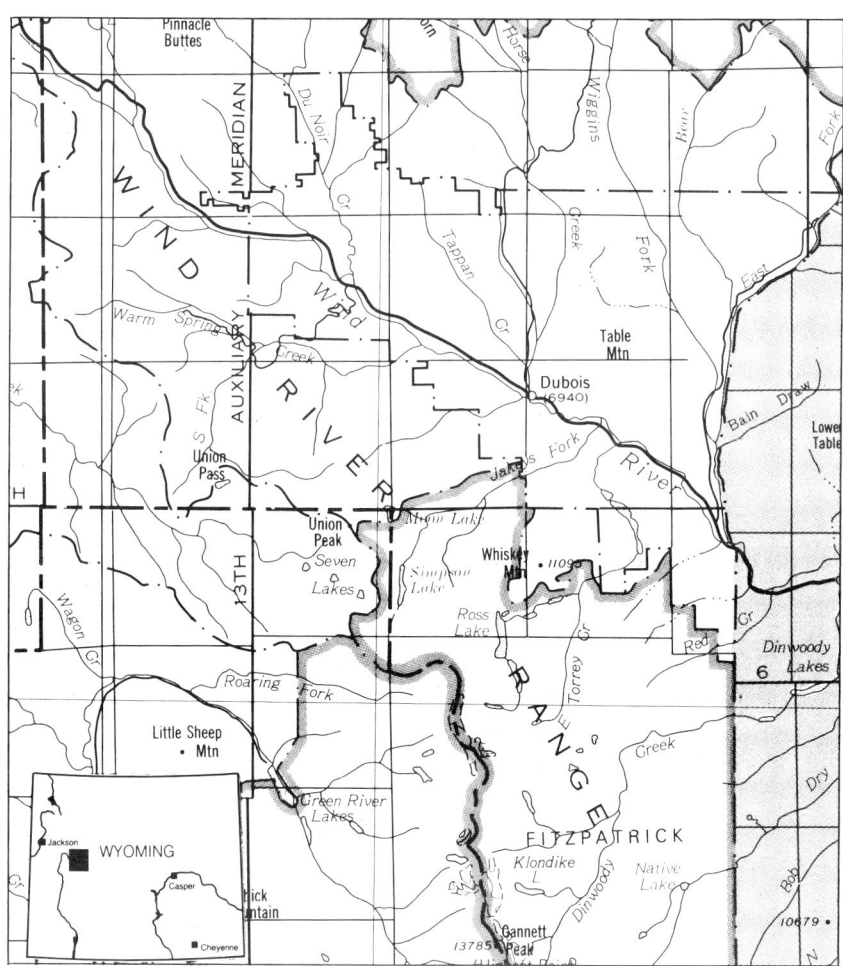

Upper Wind River

fish the river elsewhere.

The best fishing in the lakes and streams in the drainage lie west and southwest of the river. Near the headwaters and south to Dubois there also are tributaries from the southern Absaroka Mountains to the north and east. These waters are not as varied or abundant as those to the west, but there is some good fishing.

Near the top of the drainage, just east of the Continental Divide, **Wind River Lake** (9542 ft; 10 ac) lies on the north side of US 287. There is a picnic area and easy vehicle access, but no sign. Rainbow trout 9-12 inches are caught here.

Brooks Lake (9050 ft; 234 ac) lies at the end of a gravel road (marked by a sign) that exits north from US 287 about 27 miles north of Dubois. There are campgrounds and a lodge near the lake. Rainbow, small brook and mackinaw up to 20 inches are caught here. Catchable size fish are stocked regularly. Motorboats are permitted. You can also fish **Brooks Lake Creek,** which flows south from the lake, for small brook and rainbow.

Upper Brooks Lake (9100 ft; 25 ac), **Rainbow Lake** (9200 ft; 42 ac), **Lower Jade Lake** (9500 ft; 20 ac) and **Upper Jade Lake** (9600 ft; 18 ac) lie within a four-mile radius north of Brooks Lake and can be reached by trail. Upper Brooks and Rainbow have small brook; the Jade Lakes have cutthroat up to 16 inches, and mackinaw.

Still on the east side of the Wind River, **Dunoir Creek** flows south out of the Absarokas and into the river from the north about 9 miles above Dubois. A county road follows the creek for about 10 miles, mostly through private land where permission to fish is necessary. About nine miles from the highway a trail forks east along **East Dunoir Creek** to **Trail Lake** (8053 ft; 33 ac). It has brook and rainbow. The Dunoir itself offers cutthroat, with some whitefish and brook trout.

Kisinger Lakes (9400 ft; largest, 18 ac) are among several small lakes at the Dunoir headwaters with cutthroat and small brook. Follow the creek north to these lakes or reach them by hiking about 8 miles east from Brooks Lake.

DUBOIS

Horse Creek, which flows into Wind River at the town of Dubois, offers modest fishing for small brook and rainbow. The paved Horse Creek Road north from Dubois, follows Little Horse Creek, becomes a good dirt road and joins Horse Creek proper after 9 miles.

The road continues 7 to 8 miles to **Wiggins Fork,** which flows into the East Fork of the Wind River. The East Fork offers fine fishing for cutthroat, with some brown, brook, and whitefish. Wiggins Fork flows though handsome wooded country broken by steep rock outcroppings. The fish are small but plentiful, averaging 10 inches.

The **East Fork** of the Wind River joins the main stream about 10 miles below Dubois. It forms the western boundary of the Wind River Indian Reservation. The East Fork is accessible from US 287 by a road posted "Game and Fish East Fork Elk Management Area." The road runs north about 20 miles north with the stream and can be hiked farther for small cutthroat, brook and rainbow. Don't fish the reservation side without a reservation permit! Bear Creek and the East Fork of the Wind River are treated in the Indian Reservation section.

WIND RIVER

Now, let's take a look at the superb waters west of Wind River where the streams flow easterly out of the Wind River Mountains. This is some of the best fishing on the continent and it takes a real effort to get to much of it. It would take a lifetime or two to explore them all, and experienced local fishermen say this bountiful range deserves a book all its own. Fishing opportunities range from fishing from boats in the "lowlands" around 4000 feet and to the glacier-fed lakes in which golden and cutthroat trout eat heartily when the ice breaks in the summer.

Just south of Togwotee Pass, **Sheridan Creek** is reached by turning west off US 287 about 18 miles north of Dubois, just south of the Tie Hack Historical Marker. The road follows the creek, with brook and rainbow, for 2 miles, then becomes a trail. A road to **Pelham Lake** (8817 ft; 33 ac)

Wind River harvest.

forks to the north from Sheridan Creek Road about a half mile from the highway for a rugged 5 miles. The lake has fat cutthroat to 16 inches and brook to 12 inches. No motorboats are allowed. **Trout Creek Lake** (10 ac), with hatchery-raised rainbow and grayling, is reached by driving 5 miles on Sheridan Creek Road, then taking a right fork 2.5 miles to the lake.

Nine miles northwest of Dubois the Union Pass Road, marked by a sign, goes west from US 287. About 6 to 7 miles from the highway the road forks. The right fork follows Warm Springs Creek, which has brook to 8 inches, and rainbow. You may need 4-wheel drive to go the 21 miles to **Fish Lake** (9400 ft; 28 ac) for unusually good cutthroat fishing. Two-track roads of uneven quality crisscross the area, and confuse unfamiliar travelers; local inquiry and a Shoshone National Forest (south portion) map will make it easier to get where you want to go.

The Union Pass Road provides access to some good fishing along the northern boundary of the Fitzpatrick Wilderness Area. **Union Lake** and **Moon Lake** (9400 ft; 60 ac) are good for brook and some mackinaw to 16 inches. Grayling have been planted in Moon. The 4-wheel drive Moon Lake Road is marked by a sign on Union Pass Road. Several lakes to the south, and many in the Green River drainage, by trail across the Continental Divide, can be reached from here. Jakey's Fork provides alternative trail access. Just over the Divide off the Union Pass Road, **Lake of the Woods** is closed to fishermen year-round. The lake is used by Wyoming Game & Fish to raise Snake River cutthroat. As many as 2 million eggs a year are taken for planting in other Wyoming lakes and streams.

Three miles southeast of Dubois on US 287, a road leaves the highway west to the state fish hatchery on **Jakey's Fork Creek.** The stream is open to public fishing along the 1.5 miles to the hatchery and holds brook, brown and rainbow up to 12 inches.

Continuing up Jakey's Fork on the CM Trail, hikers reach the Whiskey Mountain Trail 6 miles in. This approach should not be confused with the Jakey's Fork Trail, which actually originates in Dubois and goes to the above-mentioned Union Lake. Take a right on the Whiskey Mountain Trail to reach **Soapstone Lake** (10,000 ft; 13 ac) for brook to 9 inches. Near the Continental Divide, 3 miles from Soapstone, is **Simpson Lake** (9700 ft; 170 ac) with 14-inch brook and rainbow. **Rim Lake,** still higher, and the two **Blanket Lakes,** north of Simpson, have good fishing for brook trout. Nestled right near the Divide is **Marion Lake** (10,400 ft; 18 ac) with golden trout up to 2 pounds; just below Marion are **Peat Lake** and **Dyke Lake,** both with medium-size rainbow. To the south, **Lost Lake** and **Pinto Lake** have golden; Pinto also has cutthroat.

TORREY CREEK

A half-mile south of the Jakey's Fork turnoff from US 287 is a gravel road to Whiskey Basin and **Torrey Creek,** marked by a sign. The road is rough, but cars without 4-wheel drive can make it. This is a gateway to 3 large lakes and a host of smaller ones in the wilderness. **Lower Torrey Creek** is good for rainbow and brook. **Upper Torrey Creek** has cutthroat. The creek above Torrey Lake is closed to fishing April through May.

Torrey Lake (7400 ft; 240 ac), **Ring Lake** (7400 ft; 108 ac) and **Trail Lake** (7500 ft; 130 ac) can be reached by car. Torrey and Ring have big browns; Torrey and Trail have mackinaw, some as large as 20 pounds, and good splake populations. There are crude boat ramps at Torrey and Trail, and motorboats are allowed. Campsites are available at Ring and Trail lakes and west of Trail Lake Ranch, which is owned now by the National Audubon Society. All three lakes are open for a special winter fishing season December through February.

Vehicles can negotiate most of the 2 miles above Trail Lake to the Audubon Camp, beyond which there is a parking area near the wilderness boundary. A steep trail climbs up along **East Torrey Creek** to Bomber Falls, with moderate fishing for brook and cutthroat. There are no fish above the falls. Hike the Glacier Trail, which, after 6.5 miles, crosses over into the Dinwoody creek drainage for some good fishing.

Up the very fishable **West Torrey Creek** is **Lake Louise** (8380 ft; 75 ac) with small brook trout and some cutthroat. **Hidden Lake** (9300 ft; 63 ac) has some nice rainbows and cutthroat hybrids. **Big Ross Lake** (9675 ft; 448 ac) and **Upper Ross Lake** (173 ac) have some fine rainbow-cutthroat

---

BLUE-RIBBON WATERS

The Wyoming Game and Fish Department has classified 416 miles of the state's 15,443 miles of streams as first class trout fishing waters with the designation, "Blue Ribbon Streams." Another 1181 miles are identified as second class fisheries. The blue ribbon waters are:

The **North Platte River** from the Colorado state line north to the confluence with Jack Creek north of Saratoga, and the 6-mile Miracle Mile stretch between Seminoe and Pathfinder reservoirs northeast of Rawlins.

The **Green River** south from Wagon Creek below Green River Lakes to Bronx; from the intersection of US 187 and US 189 south to the confluence with the New Fork River east of Big Piney; and from Fontenelle Dam downstream to 15 miles below Green River.

The **Snake River** below Jackson Lake Dam to the Idaho state line.

Clarks Fork of the Yellowstone River from the confluence of Sunlight Creek downstream to 10 miles below its juncture with Pat O'Hara Creek.

Timber Creek downstream from its origin to its confluence with Closed Creek in the Absaroka Wilderness.

Tongue River from its confluence with Fool Creek downstream through Tongue Canyon.

Middle Fork Powder River from its origin downstream to its juncture with Buffalo Creek.

Wind River, 10 miles downstream from Boysen Reservoir Dam.

Sand Creek from Black Hills National Forest boundary downstream to its confluence with Redwater Creek east of Beulah.

hybrids up to 20 inches. Pack in an inflatable boat to fish these lakes, but remember this is a wilderness area. Fishing is banned on Ross Lake south of P.J. Island in the stream drainage above the lake from January through July 14.

FITZPATRICK WILDERNESS

Several accesses to the wilderness in this area begin as roads on the Wind River Indian Reservation and become trails as they penetrate the back country. A gravel road leaves US 287 about 8 miles into the reservation from its western border and heads south from the highway toward the Dinwoody Lakes. Be sure to check on reservation regulations before fishing or traveling across Indian lands. Another 5 miles south, the Gannett Peak road, which becomes a trail leading to Wyoming's highest mountain (13,804 ft), leaves the highway.

The Dinwoody Trail meets the north-south Glacier Trail about 6 miles into the wilderness. Near this juncture are a group of small lakes dubbed the **Dinwoody Lakes** (not to be confused with the larger, more accessible Dinwoody Lakes on the reservation). Among these is **Honeymoon Lake** (9838 ft; 23 ac) with small cutthroat. To reach Honeymoon Lake drop down a steep embankment for small to fair-size cutthroat. **Star Lake** (10,200 ft; 15 ac) has 16-inch splake, but not in great numbers. Don't drink the water; it looks clean, but is frequented by horsepackers and game. **Golden Lake** (9900 ft; 20 ac) has good size and wily, golden trout, and **Florence Lake** (10,767 ft; 43 ac) has good size rainbow, cutthroat and hybrids. **Phillips** and **Upper Phillips** lakes offer similar opportunities. **Double Lake,** despite many visitors, is very productive and offers a host of small trout. Follow Downs Fork by horsetrail and fish for cutthroat almost to the large, but barren, **Downs Lake;** just below Downs, two small lakes, **Twin** and **Blueberry,** have small cutthroat.

DRY CREEK

The Glacier Trail is a busy thoroughfare for horsepackers and backpackers. Be prepared for rough climbing on sharp rock switchbacks since the old trail has been wiped out by a slide. It will take you south through glaciated terrain near the Continental Divide. The going is tough here, but the fish have a short and hungry feeding season that will keep hardy anglers busy.

Moving south from the Dinwoody drainage, the Dry Creek drainage has its own set of fine lakes. There are a number of ways to enter this remote area. One approach is through the reservation by taking the Gannett Peak Road, which goes southwest from US 287 about 6 miles north of the reservation town of Crowheart. It eventually becomes a trail in the reservation's Wind River Roadless Area before crossing into Shoshone National Forest.

This is open country and often hot and dry in summer. You can also reach Dry Creek by the Glacier Trail at Trail Lake south of Dubois. Head up Dinwoody Creek and pick up the Ink Wells Trail, and go over Horse Ridge. Topographic maps are very helpful.

Just before the forest boundary there is a fork. One trail forks west to the **Ink Wells Lakes** (10,200 ft), a group of small lakes with good, but small brook. The other fork goes southwest along **Dry Creek.** You can also hike into this area from Moon Lake to the north.

Two miles from the boundary of the reservation on Dry Creek Trail is **Native Lake** with primarily brook and some cutthroat, rainbow and cut-rainbow crosses up to 12 inches. In the vicinity of Native are **Horseshoe Lake, Grassy Lake** and **Phillips Lake** (10,475 ft; 45 ac), all with brook, rainbow and cutthroat to 12 inches. **Quag Lake** and **Vixen Lake** are dead. Up Grassy Creek to the south are **Marks Lake,** which also is fishless, and **Splake Lake,** which has been stocked by plane with mackinaw/brook crosses.

On the North Fork of Dry Creek is **Marten Lake** and **Lake Whitney,** both with crosses of cutthroat, rainbow and golden trout. They could use some fishing. Other lakes in the drainage like **Ugh** and **Lost Shoe** lakes are dead.

The Middle Fork of Dry Creek above Native Lake has brook and cutthroat in its lower reaches and cutthroat and golden upstream. **Moose Lake** has cutthroat under 12 inches and small brook. Two to three miles up Dry Creek, **Cub Lake** (10,380 ft; 45 ac) and **Bud's Lake** have primarily cutthroat and maybe some cutthroat/golden crosses to 14 inches. **Don Lake** (10,475; 35 ac) has golden/cutthroat crosses to 14 inches. Still higher, **Golden Lake** has healthy and wary good-sized goldens. **Lower Glacier Lake** has golden up to 14 inches. On the South Fork of Dry Creek, golden-rainbow crosses were planted in **Norman** and **Rock Lakes** in 1981.

Farther south, there are a number of lakes which drain east into Bull Creek and onto the reservation; these can be reached by crossing the reservation or by entering the Wind River Mountains from the west. Start at Elkhart Park, west of Pinedale, and pack in by horse or foot along the Hay Pass Trail across the Continental Divide.

This arduous trip will put you among what are sometimes called the **Hay Pass Lakes,** at the headwaters of Bull Lake Creek. Among them are **Dennis Lake** (10,630 ft; 60 ac), **Golden Lake** (10,155 ft; 20 ac) and **Camp Lake** (10,163 ft; 30 ac). They provide excellent fishing for golden trout up to 14 inches. Many of the best lakes in the Bull Lake Creek drainage are on the reservation. Right on the border are two sets of **Milky Lakes.** The two to the north draining into North Bull Lake Creek have small rainbow, probably stocked from the reservation; the **Southern Milky Lakes,** flowing into **Middle Bull Lake Creek,** have cutthroat and golden. Use a map to stay clear of reservation waters, or buy a reservation permit.

For a dozen or more miles south of the lakes just described, the reservation boundary reaches all the way to the Continental Divide. Most of the headwaters of the Little Wind River are entirely on the reservation.

RESERVATION BOUNDARY

Near Bonneville Peak the reservation border leaves the Divide, and some of the lakes feeding the South Fork of the Little Wind are on Forest Service land. There are a number of ways to reach this area—you'll need strong legs or a good horse. In any case, the fish are worth it.

To get to this area, turn west off US 287, 15 miles north of Lander by the Hines General Store in Fort Washakie on the Wind River Indian Reservation. There is no sign. Drive 19 miles on this road, up some steep switchbacks, to trailheads at Dickinson Park. From there you take the steep Bears Ears Trail over Adams Pass, reaching the **South Fork of the Little Wind River** after about 13 miles.

The South Fork itself has cutthroat, golden and brook in its clear, alpine waters. The lakes described here feed into the South Fork through creeks. Near the reservation border is **Grave Lake** (9900 ft; 200 ac) with mackinaw up to 18 inches, cutthroat, and occasional golden. The little lakes above Grave are barren. Four miles east, also on the reservation border, is **Gaylord Lake** (10,175 ft) with cutthroat to 2 pounds but some considerably bigger, according to Crowheart guide George Hunker. **Moss Lake** (10,000 ft), less than a mile south, has brook to 10 inches and some cutthroat. **Dutch Oven Lake** (10,600 ft; 12 ac), another mile south from Moss, has fair fishing for brook to 3 pounds.

Valentine Lake (10,400 ft; 45 ac) has slow fishing for golden and cutthroat hybrids, averaging 11 inches. **Washakie Lake,** still farther south on the Washakie Trail, has had golden-rainbow crosses landed that have been as large as 15 pounds, according to Wyoming Game & Fish Supervisor Charles A. Viox in Lander. Spawning areas around this lake are closed from January to July 14 to protect the trophy fish. **Loch Leven Lake,** a half-mile to the north, has hard-to-catch browns in the 1 pound and up range, and rainbow have been stocked. Nearby, **Spearpoint Lakes** also have been stocked with "goldbows,"—running about 14 inches.

POPO AGIE

From Dickinson Park you can also reach the more accessible headwaters of the **North Fork Popo Agie River.**

The North Popo Agie has rainbow, brook, cutthroat and whitefish as it alternately cascades and meanders its way from the mountains. There is a good deal of summer traffic along this river (particularly

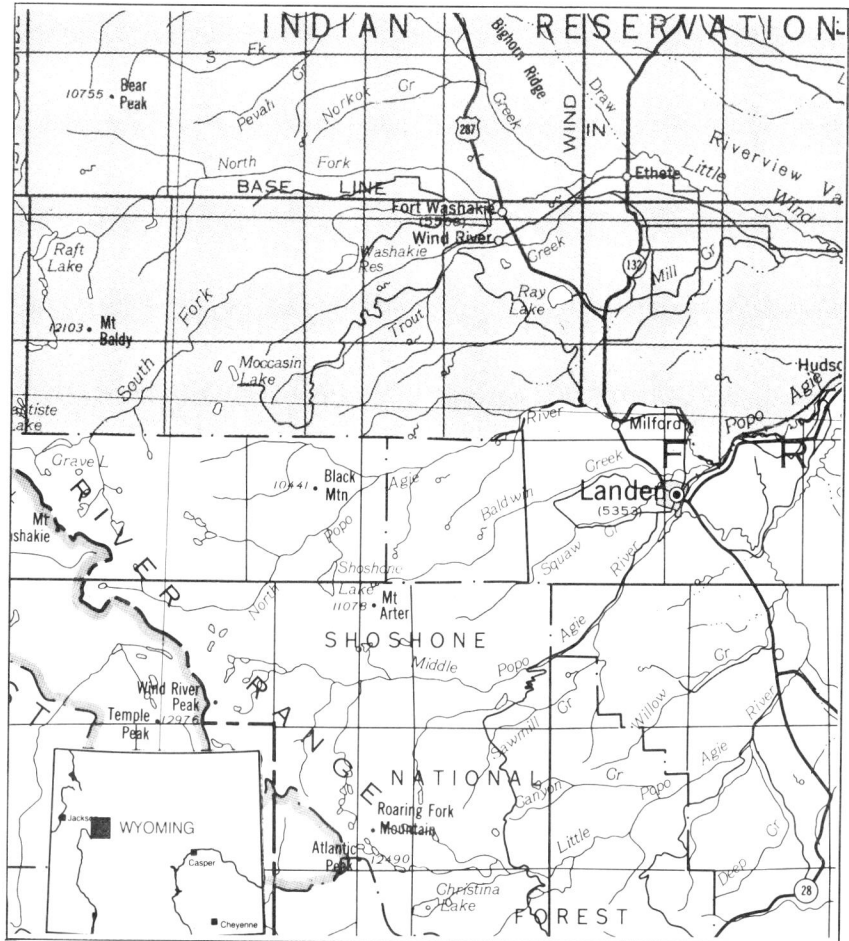

Little Wind and Popo Agie Rivers

mountain climbers headed for the "Cirque of Towers"), so you might have better luck fishing its tributaries. Nearest to Dickinson Park are **Dickinson Creek,** with brook to 7 inches, and **Sand Creek,** with the same. Near Lander, there is a marked public access, on North Second Street, two miles north of town.

Take the Smith Lake Trail south from Dickinson Park for 5 miles to **Smith Lake** (9748 ft; 58 ac), which has small brook and mackinaw to 20 inches. Just above Smith is **Middle Lake** (10,013 ft; 60 ac), with similar fishing, and above Middle is **Cathedral Lake** (10,095 ft; 30 ac), with small brook and 20-inch mackinaw swimming below a spectacular sheer rock face at the western end. Nearby **Cloverleaf Lake** (10,000 ft; 15 ac) has small brook and **Cook Lake** (10,000 ft; 38 ac) has 10-inch brook. Above Cook are **Phyllis** and **Glacier Lakes,** with more brook. Smith Lake Creek drains into the North Popo Agie.

South of the Smith Lake group, and also draining into the North Popo Agie, is **High Meadow Lake** (10,000 ft; 30 ac). It is reached by hiking from Dickinson Park to the North Popo Agie and then along the river to the signed High Meadow Trail. Or climb over a rugged saddle, with no trail, from Cook Lake. High Meadow will reward a morning fisherman with plentiful cutthroat up to 18 inches. **Cliff Lake** (9900 ft; 12 ac) just to the south offers the same, plus a scenic high waterfall. Farther down the High Meadow drainage, **Shelf** and **Gray Lakes** have grayling.

Draining into the North Popo Agie from the south are the **Bear Lakes,** with brook up to 2 pounds.

At the top of the North Fork of the Popo Agie drainage is **Bear Lake** (also known as **Lower Lizard Head**) with good cutthroat, **Lonesome Lake** (10,187 ft; 30 ac) with 12-inch cutthroat. Above Lonesome is **Hidden Lake,** recently stocked with golden-rainbow crosses.

Shoshone Lake (9500 ft; 200-500 ac) drains into the North Popo Agie and has brook to 12 inches. It is accessible with a 4-wheel drive vehicle. Take the initially-paved Baldwin Creek Road west off US 287 just north of Lander next to the Pamida store. It's about a 15-mile drive. The lake and **Shoshone Creek** are closed to fishing from September through May.

SINKS CANYON

Moving south, the **Middle Fork Popo Agie** merges from the mountain in scenic Sinks Canyon State Park, 7 miles southwest of Lander. Take the Sinks Canyon Road west from town; there is a marked public fishing access off the road. As you enter the canyon, an area between the rise and the fall of the "sinks" is closed to fishing.

The river has rainbow, brown and brook in its lower reaches. Cutthroat populations increase as altitude is gained. In the canyon a bridge spans the stream and there is a large parking area. The hiking trail up the Middle Fork leads to some excellent lake fishing. By car continue up the canyon road switchbacks. There are numerous trailheads along this road (Hwy 131), which is known as the Louis Lake or Loop Road, because it loops back to US Hwy 28 near the South Pass south of Lander.

If you want to see the biggest browns in the state, stop at the "Rise of the Sinks" on your way up the canyon. This is where the Middle Fork Popo Agie rises after an underground journey of less than a half-mile, and the fat fish feed there under the protective eyes of state park officials.

The most northerly tributary to the **Middle Fork** is **Deep Creek,** which will be a 13-mile trek from the top of Sinks Canyon, or a few miles less if you take the Loop Road to a trailhead above Frye Lake. The Middle Fork and Deep Creek have good fishing for cutthroat, brook and brown to 10 inches along here. At Three Forks Park, just within the Popo Agie Primitive Area, take the Pinto Park Trail, and now you are in lake fishing country. **Pinto Lake** has small brook trout. **Little Hart Lake** has brook; up high, sitting below Wind River Peak, are

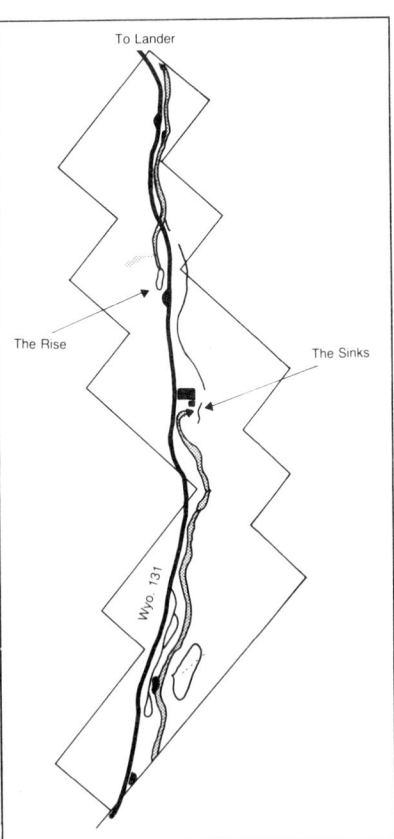

Sinks Canyon State Park

the three **Deep Creek Lakes.** The middle lake (10,700 ft) has fat golden trout to 18 inches which sometimes show a curious disdain for manmade lures and flies; the upper lake is barren; the **Lower Deep Creek Lake** has golden and golden-rainbow crosses.

Ice Creek joins Deep Creek from the south, and has small brook trout. **Park, Jug** and **Boot Lakes,** have brook. Most other lakes in the vicinity are barren.

The Middle Fork itself, above its juncture with Deep Creek, can be followed by trail to its headwaters. Near the top it is joined by **Tayo Creek** which drains **Coon Lake** (10,500 ft; 38 ac.), with golden and cutthroat-golden hybrids to 17 inches; **Mountain Sheep Lake** (10,800 ft; 28 ac), with cutthroat-golden hybrids; **Poison Lake** (10,000 ft; 40 ac), with rainbow, cutthroat, and cutthroat-golden hybrids to 12 inches. Just below the juncture of Tayo Creek and the Middle Popo Agie, and off on a creek a quarter-mile north, is **Squirrel Lake,** which has grayling to 16 inches.

Joining the Middle Fork from the south just below its juncture with Deep Creek is **Stough Creek,** which drains the many fine lakes in Stough Creek Basin. (These lakes are easier to reach from the Loop Road than by hiking up the Middle Fork.) **Toadstool** and **Upper Toadstool Lakes** have small brook; **Big Stough** and **Little Stough Creek Lakes** (10,500 ft) have brook and cutthroat. Above them, **Cutthroat Lake** has good cutthroat to 12 inches; **Shoal Lake** has excellent brook and cutthroat fishing. **Footprint** and **Zigzag Lakes** have cutthroat, and so does **Blackrock Lake.**

The Middle Fork Trail is scenic and not difficult, but many prefer to drive up the Loop Road and hike from it into the Middle Fork drainage. There are a few lakes very close to the road and its offshoots that merit mention. **Worthen Meadows Reservoir** (10 to 92 acres) is reached by taking the Townsend Creek Road west off the Loop Road for about 2 miles. It provides Lander's water supply, and the rainbow and brook here, up to 12 inches, grew up in a hatchery. A short hike up a closed jeep road is **Roaring Fork Lake,** a shallow, choking lake with small brook. In the other direction is **Frye Lake Reservoir** (up to 105 acres), built by an irrigation ditch company and located right on the Loop Road. It has rainbow, brook and grayling, from the hatchery.

The **Little Popo Agie River,** the third and southernmost fork of this drainage, is easily accessible in its upper reaches from the Loop Road. It captures the water from the southernmost lakes in the Wind River Range before it ends at the Red Desert.

Four primary drainages feed into the Little Popo Agie: **Fiddlers Creek, Silas Creek, Atlantic Creek** and **Louis Creek.** Fiddlers Creek drains **Fiddlers Lake,** (7900 ft; 56 ac), located 23 miles south of Lander on the Loop Road. It has rainbow to 14 inches.

From Fiddlers you can take the Christina Lake Trail which, in 2 miles, reaches **Silas Creek.** A trail leads up this drainage to **Lower Silas Lake** (9700 ft; 10 ac) with small brook trout. About 1.5 miles up the trail is **Upper Silas Lake** with 10- to 12-inch brook and 13-inch cutthroat. Still higher, **Island Lake** (10,500 ft; 25 ac) has good-size cutthroat, and so does **Fawn Lake** just above it; **Thumb Lake** (11,000 ft; 33 ac) contains golden up to 2 pounds. Also flowing into Lower Silas Lake is a small stream draining **Tomahawk Lake** (10,000 ft; 28 ac). It has cutthroat to 12 inches. **Little Tomahawk Lake,** a quarter-mile above, has good fishing for 8- to 10-inch cutthroat.

It's a long hike up **Atlantic Creek,** the next drainage to the south, to its alpine lakes. The creek itself has golden, cutthroat, and brook to 10 inches. **Atlantic Creek Lake** (10,200 ft; 23 ac) has small brook and cutthroat to 12 inches. Draining into Atlantic Creek from the north is **Rock Lake** with splake and brook to 11 inches. Above it is **Little Atlantic Lake,** with splake to 12 inches. Up near the top of the Atlantic Creek drainage is **Windy Lake** (10,700 ft; 30 ac) with golden averaging 14 inches.

A 4-wheel-drive road west off the Loop Road takes you to the headwaters of the Little Popo Agie at **Christina Lake** (9942 ft; 340 ac), which has 10-pound mackinaw, large rainbow and brook to 12 inches. **Gus-**

tave Lake, just below Christina, has brook and mackinaw.

Louis Creek starts near the Continental Divide and flows 8 miles to Louis Lake—it has brook trout to 8 inches. **Louis Lake** (7500 ft; 120 acres) is located just east of the Loop Road, 27 miles from Lander. It has mackinaw as big as 20 pounds, and rainbow and brook to 12 inches. A road runs around the southern end and there are campgrounds, boat launch ramps, and a lodge.

As the Little Popo Agie drops out of the mountains, there is a good public fishing area located about 14 miles south of Lander off US 28. Just beyond the juncture of US 28 and US 287 (to Rawlins) turn right on the gravelled Red Canyon Road. There is a marked fishing access with a parking area on the left less than a mile up the road.

BOYSEN RESERVOIR

The Wind River turns north near Riverton and empties into Boysen Reservoir. West of Boysen, **Ocean Lake** (6162 ac) gathers the wastewater and ditch water of the Riverton Reclamation Project before draining into Fivemile Creek, which runs into Boysen. US 26 provides paved access on the south side of the lake, or Wyoming County Roads 134 and 133 on the north and west sides. There are four boat launching and camping areas around the lake, and a resort on the south side. From the middle of May until July this shallow lake is successfully fished for walleye, bass, perch, crappie, ling, and some trout. After midsummer fishing is less successful. The once-famous black crappie fishery here has declined, apparently due to the heavy siltation.

Also west of Boysen is **Cameahwalt Lake** (4700 ft; 464 ac) with rainbow trout and some bass. A well-marked gravel road goes north from US 26, 5 miles west of Shoshoni to Cameahwalt and the west shore of Boysen Reservoir. Lodging is available and boating is allowed, but there is no boat rental here.

Finally, there is **Boysen Reservoir,** 19,000 acres of water backed up from the Wind River drainage before the Owl Creek Mountain Range. The reservoir has an electricity generating station and stores water for irrigation, but it has become a popular recreation area for boaters and fishermen. Walleye, perch, sauger, crappie, ling, cutthroat, rainbow and brown trout inhabit the lake, as well as mackinaw, splake, brook, bass and bluegill. Trout are not showing up much in Boysen—most of the catch is perch and walleye. The walleye are taking over, partly due to the successful plant of spot-tail shiners upon which they feed. They have been caught up to 13 pounds. Most of the good fishing is in June, by trolling lures from boats. Boysen and Ocean Lake are open to winter ice fishing in December, January and February, primarily for ling cod.

The fish in Boysen appear healthier than they've been in a long time as irrigators have eased up their drawdowns during spawning periods. Bill Weaver's Boysen Marina is the one resort on the lake.

US 20, from Shoshoni to Thermopolis, runs along the eastern side of the lake. Boat launching facilities are available on both sides, and campgrounds on the east side. There also are two resorts on the lake.

From Boysen Reservoir, the Wind River plunges into the Wind River Canyon of the Owl Creek Mountains and emerges on the north side as the Bighorn River. The Bighorn and its creeks and lakes are discussed in the chapter on the Bighorn River.

WIND RIVER RESERVATION

The Wind River Indian Reservation sits right in the middle of some of the best fishing country in Wyoming. Its 2.2 million acres encompass a large chunk of the Wind River Mountains' eastern slope, as well as some big lowland reservoirs and lakes. A large mountainous section of the reservation has been protected as wilderness since 1938.

US 26 from Dubois southeast to Riverton runs through the reservation and roughly parallels the Wind River. This section of the Wind River offers some of the best and most accessible fishing in the state. But the tributaries and the alpine lakes that often feed them are even better.

The reservation is the home of the Arapahoe and Shoshone Indian tribes, and their

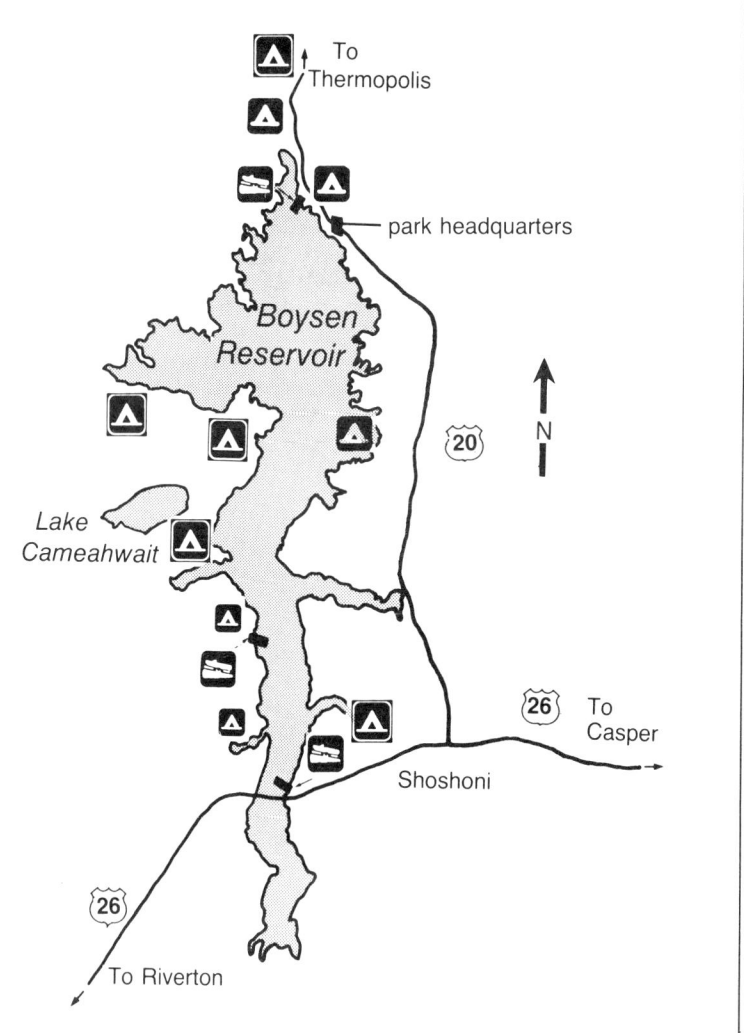

Boysen State Park

spective councils together decide what game and fish regulations apply on the reservation. Federal agencies such as the U.S. Fish and Wildlife Service act in an advisory capacity and stock fish in reservation waters with the approval of the tribes.

Indians have different perspectives on game and fish management than are common off the reservation, but the goal still is to preserve viable game and fish populations. There is a cultural heritage of unrestricted hunting by Indians on Indian land, and that attitude applies to fishing, too. Nontribe members must pay fees.

Reservation policy has not been too successful regarding game management; there have been serious declines in moose populations. But when it comes to fish, there is excellent sport and healthy populations in a variety of environments.

Wyoming streams offer blue-ribbon angling

Why is fishing so good on the reservation? One reason is the cost of a permit. In recent years, increased fishing pressure in Wyoming has come from new Wyoming residents; but they are unlikely to buy an expensive annual reservation permit ($40 one recent year) when a state fishing license costs less than $10 and there is plenty of good fishing outside the reservation. Only 82 season permits were sold on the reservation in 1981, according to Vince Underwood, director of the Fish and Game Department on the reservation.

Another factor contributing to good fishing on the reservation is that in the 1970s the reservation was closed to public fishing for about four years, stimulating fish growth and populations.

Though fishing is good on the reservation, be aware that regulations change annually, fees fluctuate, and season lengths may vary from year to year. No live bait is allowed. On certain lakes there is a special winter season.

You need a permit to cross the reservation. It is available from the Wind River Indian Reservation Fish & Game Office in Fort Washakie, on North Fork Road just across from the post office, or by writing the tribe at P.O. Box 217, Fort Washakie, Wyo. 82514. Office hours are 8 a.m. to 4:45 p.m. weekdays. Phone 307/255-8265 or 307/255-8227.

It also can be obtained from Hartman's Store in Riverton; The Outdoorsman or Hole-in-the-Wall Store in Lander; Redrocks Lodge in Dubois; and in Thermopolis at the Rexall Drug or KOA Campground. The 1985 fees are $7 for one day; $14/2 days; $21/3 days or $40 annually.

Fishing on the reservation varies from the scrappy crappie in the ample lowland reservoirs to glamorous golden trout in the Milky Lakes and brazen brook in raging rivers.

There are several lower elevation lakes that can be reached by vehicle most of the year. Two of the biggest, **Ocean Lake** (6062 ac) and **Boysen Reservoir** (18,000 ac), lie within the reservation but are managed by state and federal agencies. They are open to public fishing and are not subject to reservation regulations. Both are detailed in the Wind River section of this guide.

EAST FORK WIND RIVER

The northwestern boundary of the Wind River Reservation is the **East Fork of Wind River.** It is good for 12-inch cutthroat, especially upstream from its confluence with the Wiggins Fork. There are some brown trout below and cutthroat in beaver ponds in the upper reaches. The East Fork is easily reached from US 26-287. East bank is Indian Reservation; west is a mix of state, private and federal property. Check land ownership locally.

Bear Creek is the middle fork of the East Fork. It has good fishing for small (10-inch) cutthroat above its juncture with the East Fork. Some private land, but good public access via a 4-wheel drive road.

Downstream from the East Fork about 20 miles southeast of Dubois, a rough road runs from US 26-287 south to the **Dinwoody Lakes** (6475 ft). Boats are allowed on the lakes and ling cod and brown and mackinaw trout are caught from them.

The large Dinwoody Lakes on the reservation are not to be confused with the smaller Dinwoody lakes a dozen miles to the west at the headwaters of Dinwoody Creek in the Glacier Primitive Area.

Bull Lake (5820 ft) is a big, popular fishing lake located a couple of miles west of US 26 to the south, and east of Dubois about 40 miles. It is marked by a sign on the highway. Boats are allowed. Bull Lake has big mackinaw, browns, rainbow, and ling cod.

Farther south, near the reservation headquarters at Fort Washakie, are **Washakie Reservoir** (6359 ft), 6 miles west of the highway, with cutthroat, brook and lots of suckers, and **Ray Lake,** adjacent to US 287 south of Fort Washakie. Ray is a shallow lake with poor fishing for cutthroat and a few rainbow and brown trout. It also has lots of rough fish.

Higher in the Wind River Mountains to the southwest and accessible by vehicle is **Moccasin Lake** (9514 ft; 92 ac), open from June until September, with mackinaw and cutthroat. Boats are allowed on the lake, but motors are prohibited.

Meeting the Wind River as it winds around Riverton, the **Little Wind River** and its tributaries are affected by irrigation withdrawals and offer sporadic fishing in the spring for rainbow and brook.

Trails to the upper reaches of the Little Wind River and the reservation's back country are in poor condition; reservation officials recommend guides for anyone unfamiliar with the area. There are a number of access points, so consult with the Fish and Game Department when planning a backcountry trip. In addition, lakes and streams that are open to fishing change from year to year. Obtain a map and up-to-date information before setting out.

BACK COUNTRY LAKES

Here are some of the backcountry lakes that have good fishing: **Lake Heebeecheche** (10,360 ft; 90 ac), **Wykee Lake** (9843 ft; 50 ac), **Sonnicant Lake** (10,100 ft; 135 ac), **Lake Kagevah** (10,560 ft; 82 ac), **Lake Solitude** (10,522 ft; 110 ac), **Baptiste Lake** (10,828 ft; 200 ac), **Raft Lake** (10,154 ft; 340 ac), **Elk Lake** (10,600 ft; 35 ac), **Tigee Lake** (10,452 ft; 40 ac), **Enos Lake** (10,450 ft; 23 ac), **Hatchet Lake** (10,476 ft; 55 ac), **Steamboat Lake** (10,019 ft; 38 ac), **Kirkland Lake** (9956 ft; 63 ac), **Alpine Lake** (8957 ft; 150 ac) and **Deadman Lake** (9257 ft; 40 ac).

Most of the lakes and streams have cutthroat and brook trout. Local fishermen who get up to the higher lakes testify that the fishing can be absolutely spectacular using flies and lures and fishing from the lakeshore, especially early in the season. In recent years, the backcountry fishing season has run from June 1 to September 30—roughly corresponding to when the weather allows it.

There is private land within the reservation—a reservation permit does not give you license to cross fences and boundaries without permission. There are strict regulations governing campfires, littering and boat safety. The creel limits on reservation land differ from state regulation—most recently, the limit was 10 game fish not exceeding 8 pounds total. Regulations are strictly enforced.

Finally, it is worth remembering that this is not public land, that it belongs to, and is maintained by, the Arapaho and Shoshone Indians. Outsiders should be considerate guests, in the hope that they'll be welcome in years to come.

BLM CAMPGROUNDS

The US Bureau of Land Management operates several campgrounds convenient to fishing in Wyoming. Reservations are not accepted and use fees may be imposed.

Warren Bridge Campground: 10 miles west of Pinedale via US 187, 10 miles north on US 187. (8000 ft; open land); open June 15 to October 31; 23 tent/RV spaces; pit toilets; firewood; dump. Stream 1 mile. Boat launch; trout fishing in Green River.

Big Atlantic Gulch Campground: 6 miles southeast of Lander via US 287/WY 789, 30 miles south on WY 28. (9000 ft; forest; mountains); open June 1 to October 31; 10 tent/RV spaces; pit toilets; fishing in Sweetwater River; South Pass historic mining area.

Atlantic City Campground: 6 miles southeast of Lander via US 287/WY 789, 30 miles southwest on 28. (9000 ft; forest; mountains); open June 1 to October 31; 22 tent/RV spaces; fishing in Sweetwater River; South Pass historic mining area.

Bennett Peak Campground: 4 miles east of Riverside via WY 230, 12 miles east via Co. Rd. (French Creek Rd), 7 miles north on Bennett Peak Rd. (7500 ft; forest; riverbank); open June 1 to October 31; 14 tent/RV spaces, some shaded (RV to 18 ft); pit toilets, boat launch, trout fishing in North Platte River; difficult road access for RVs, road narrow and rough in places.

Cottonwood Campground: 6 miles east of Jeffrey City via US 287, 8 miles south on BLM road; (8500 ft; forest; mountains); open June 1 to October 31; 19 tent/RV spaces, some shaded, (RV to 18 ft); pit toilets; firewood; trout fishing in Cottonwood Creek; difficult road access for RVs, fairly steep and rough in places.

Five Springs Fall Recreation and Camping Site: 23 miles east of Lovell on US 14A. (6800 ft; forest; mountains); open June 1 to October 31; 8 tent spaces, all shaded; pit toilets; parking lot for RVs to 18 ft; Five Springs Falls 0.25 mi; Big Horn Mtns.

Fourteen-Mile Reservoir Campground: 14 miles north of Rock Springs on US 187. (6800 ft; open land); open all year; 6 tent spaces, some shaded; pit toilets; firewood; no motor boats; trout fishing in Fourteen-Mile Reservoir.

Corral Creek Campground: 4 miles east of Riverside via WY 230, 12 miles east via Co Rd 66 (French Creek Rd), 6 miles north on Bennett Peak Rd.; (7500 ft; mountains), open June 1 to October 31; 4 RV/4 comb, RV to 18 ft; pit toilets; trout fishing in North Platte River; difficult road access for RVs, road narrow and rough in places; hiking.

Lodgepole Campground: 17 miles south of Casper on county and BLM roads in Muddy Mtn. environmental education area; open July 1 to October 31; 15 tent/RV spaces; restrooms; drinking water.

U.S. Forest Service campgrounds

U.S. Forest Service compilation was current as of 1985.

Asterisks denote fee areas. Some campgrounds are open only Memorial Day weekend through Labor Day. Below freezing weather could mean no water supply.

WIND RIVER DRAINAGE

SHOSHONE NATIONAL FOREST
Headquarters: 225 W. Yellowstone Ave., Box 2140, Cody, WY 82414

Campground name	Elevation	No camp sites	Travel trailers	Drinking water	Length of stay (days)	Location and directions
Falls*	8200	44	Yes	Yes	14	On Hwy 287, 23 mi W of Dubois
Brooks Lake*	9200	13	Yes	Yes	14	28 mi NW of Dubois on Hwy 287 and forest road
Double Cabin*	8100	15	Yes	Yes	14	29 mi N of Dubois on forest road
Deer Creek	6400	7	Yes	No	14	42 mi SW of Cody on state highway
Clearwater*	6000	27	Yes	Yes	14	On US 16, 32 mi W of Cody
Horse Creek*	7900	9	Yes	Yes	14	12 mi N of Dubois on forest road
Sinks Canyon*	7000	10	Yes	Yes	14	9 mi SW of Lander, of Wyo. 701
Dickinson Creek	9400	15	Yes	No	14	37 mi W of Lander on Hwy 287 and forest roads
Fiddlers Lake*	9400	20	Yes	Yes	14	23.5 mi SW of Lander on Wyo. 701 and forest road
Popo Agie	8400	3	Yes	No	14	26.3 mi SW of Lander on Wyo. 701 and forest road
Louis Lake*	8600	9	Yes	Yes	14	30 mi SW of Lander on Wyo. 701 and forest road

Bighorn River year-round angling

ADJACENT COMMUNITIES:
Riverton, Thermopolis, Worland, Basin, Greybull, Lovell and, to the west, Cody.

PRINCIPAL HIGHWAYS:
U.S. 20, 14, 16, 310, Alt. 14; Wyo. 433, 789.

The Wind River undergoes a number of changes where it turns north from Riverton and heads into Boysen Reservoir. It has a new direction—heading north instead of southeast. It has a different environment—after rushing clear from its snowy mountainous beginnings, it surges muddy and murky into a broad arid plain. And finally, it gets a new name—the **Bighorn River.**

The change takes place after the river leaves Boysen Reservoir and tumbles through the Owl Creek Mountains in Wind River Canyon. The point where the river emerges south of Thermopolis is called the Wedding of the Waters, but nobody has the faintest idea why. A few small streams with names like **Red Canyon Creek** and **Big Draw** join the river in the vicinity.

Still, it's a good place for a new name. This part of the river, north to the Wyoming-Montana border, is less known for its fishing than the Wind River. The fish are different too: Large numbers of ling cod (burbot), second only to rainbow trout in this fishery, are caught.

The Bighorn is one of Wyoming's most accessible rivers. From Shoshoni, US 20 follows it through Wind River Canyon and north to Greybull. There US 310 leads to access roads to **Bighorn Canyon Reservoir.** Thermopolis, Worland and Lovell are good towns in which to stop and learn local conditions and hot spots.

To the west, Cody is a thriving outfitting and recreation center in the Shoshone River basin, a good fishing area.

As the Bighorn travels north it drains the west side of the Bighorn Mountains, which have some good lakes feeding into **Shell Creek, Nowood Creek** and some of the other streams. More renowned are the drainages that join the Bighorn from the west, the Absaroka Mountains. Major notable streams from this range include the **Greybull River,** the **North** and **South Forks of Shoshone River,** and the **Clarks Fork of the Yellowstone River.** The Clarks Fork disdains an early union with the Bighorn, turns northward into Montana and joins the Yellowstone near Billings.

In this section, the Bighorn River, its tributaries from the Bighorn Range (south to north), and finally its tributaries from the Absarokas (south to north) are presented.

The Bighorn runs north from the Wedding of the Waters through the towns of Thermopolis and Worland before emptying into Bighorn Lake (also called the Yellow-

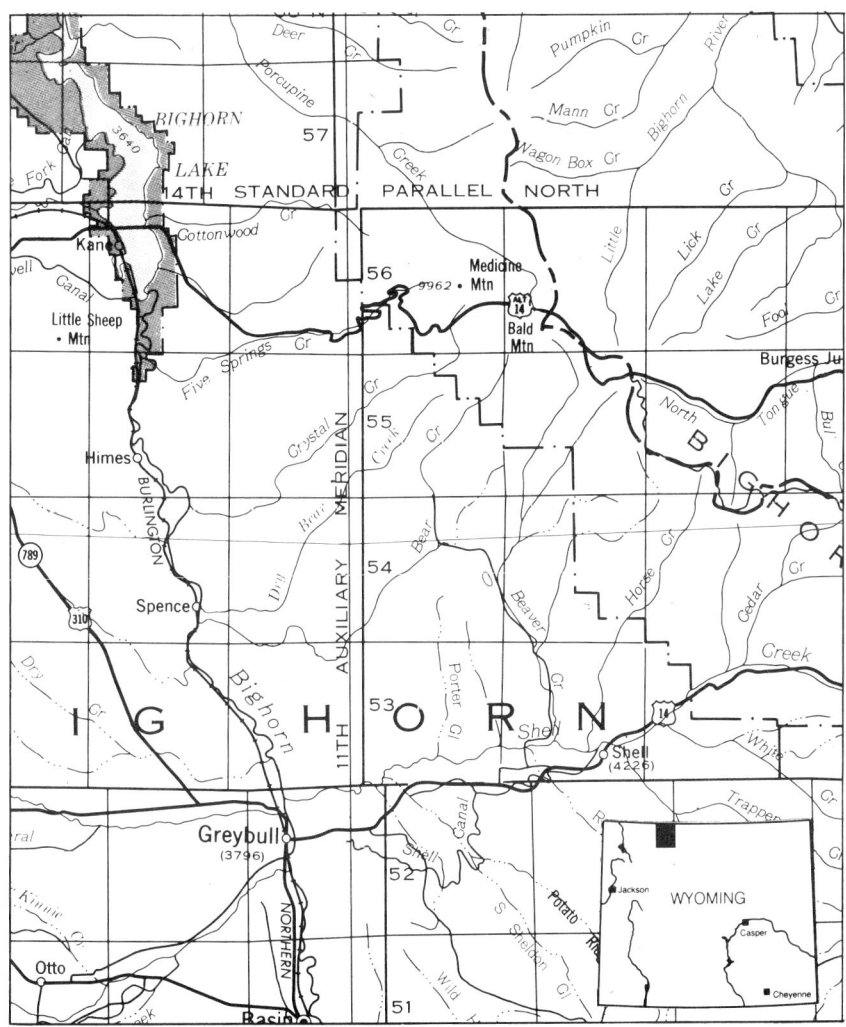

Bighorn River

tail Reservoir) in Bighorn Canyon National Recreation Area on the Montana-Wyoming border.

There is good to excellent fishing and easy access to it from the mouth of Wind River Canyon to Robertson Dam 8 miles south of Worland. Rainbow average 12 inches, but some as large as 20 inches are caught. An occasional fat brown is found lurking in the shadows. Lures and flies are successful. Ling cod are plentiful and usually are caught with minnows. There are small populations of largemouth bass and yellow perch. Cutthroat trout are being stocked in the river between the canyon and Worland.

The uppermost section of the Bighorn, putting in at Wedding of the Waters and pulling out almost 7 miles later at Thermopolis, is popular for float fishing. There are several public fishing areas north of Thermopolis—from the Harvey Public Fishing Area 4.5 miles downstream from Thermopolis to another public access 6 miles farther at the Black Mountain Road. The four public access areas within 10 miles downstream from Thermopolis are reached from US 20, which parallels the river. Signs mark put-in sites. Moss and algae sometimes accumulate in the river during summer months, but the fish don't stop feeding.

There is less public access to the lower 92 miles of river below Robertson Dam, but some landowners are willing to allow fishermen through their property. Be sure to ask. The lower stretch of the river is cooler than the upper, and it offers fishing for walleye, ling, sauger and channel catfish. Trout can be caught too, but they're not as plentiful here as they are above Robertson Dam. There is a 10-mile stretch of public fishing access just upstream of Bighorn Lake.

BIGHORN LAKE

Bighorn Lake is one of the biggest impoundments in the state, backing up 11,000 acres in Wyoming and 6000 acres in Montana. But it doesn't have the fishing reputation of, say, Flaming Gorge or Glendo Reservoir. Perhaps this is because the river filled a narrow, deep canyon. Fish are inclined to hide in canyon recesses and arms during the hot summer months and sometimes are difficult to find.

The fish here (most are caught by trolling) are similar to those in the lower stretches of the river: Walleye, sauger, ling, channel catfish, yellow perch, bullhead, stonecat and crappie. There also are trout—

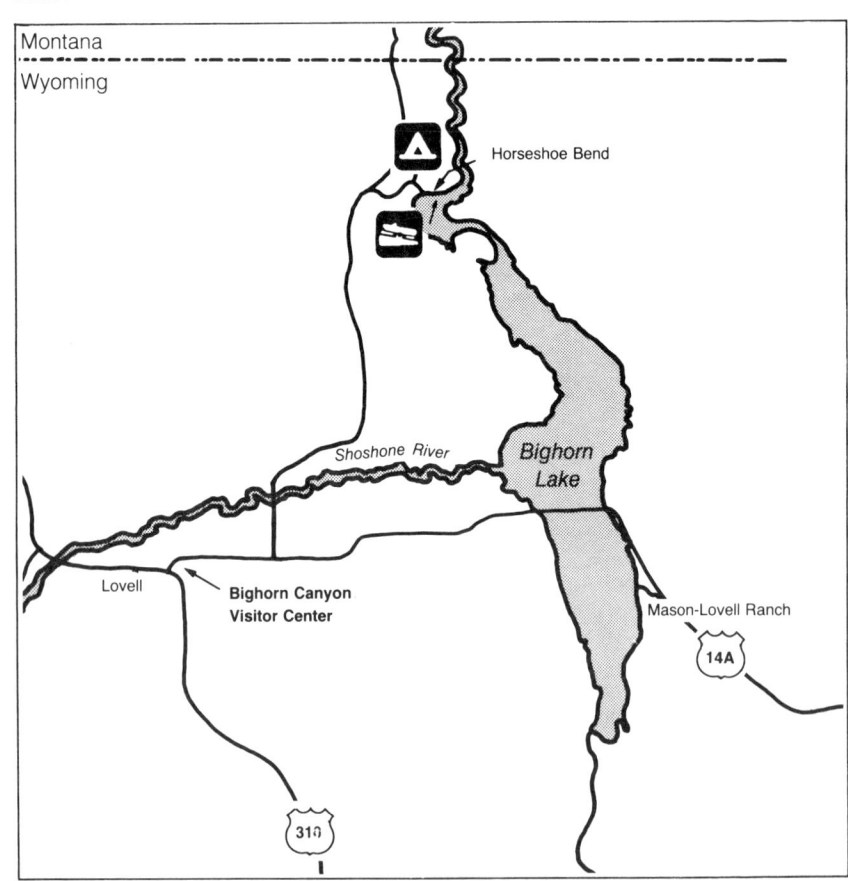

Bighorn Recreation Area

rainbow up to 20 inches, and an occasional big brown or mackinaw. Fishing is best in the early spring, before the fish retreat into nooks and crannies of the canyon, or late fall.

Walleye, averaging 14 to 19 inches, are increasingly the dominant fish in the reservoir. Channel catfish as large as 10 and 12 pounds are not uncommon, especially for night fishermen.

To reach Bighorn Lake, take US 310 north from Greybull to Lovell, then go east on US Alternate 14. State Hwy 37, which goes north from US 14A about 3 miles east of Lovell, provides access to Horseshoe Bend Campground and a boat launch, where rental boats are available. There also are boat ramps on the west side of the lake and the east side where US 14A bridge crosses the lake.

Nowood River enters the Bighorn some 20 miles north of Worland at about Manderson after draining most of the southern Bighorn Mountain Range. The upper reaches, known as **Nowood Creek,** can be reached either by driving east from Worland on US 16 to Ten Sleep then south on State Hwy 434, or by coming north from US 20-26 east of Shoshoni on the Nowood Road heading north from Moneta.

The best fishing is in the upper reaches of this creek where there are small brook and rainbow to 12 inches.

Farther downstream the fishing is only fair, with a few large browns around Ten Sleep. While the lower part of the river runs low in the summer due to irrigation diversions, it has some good size channel catfish. There is better fishing in the upper reaches of Nowood tributaries. **Trout, Deep, Lost, Otter,** and **Canyon Creeks** all have good fishing for small cutthroat and brook trout. These creeks are south of Ten Sleep and dirt roads generally follow them. These creeks run through a patchwork of state, Bureau of Land Management, and private land. Check ownership status and ask permission if necessary before fishing.

TEN SLEEP CREEK

Ten Sleep Creek enters the Nowood 24 miles east of Worland on US 16 which heads east over the Bighorns to Buffalo. Along the river in Ten Sleep Canyon are numerous campgrounds. The creek, for 7 miles upstream of Ten Sleep, is on private land where permission may be granted to fish for cutthroat and rainbow averaging 9 to 11 inches. There are browns averaging 12 inches.

Seven miles into the Bighorn National Forest is the confluence of **West** and **East Ten Sleep Creeks** which have fair fishing for 8- to 10-inch brook. There is a good road and heavy fishing pressure. Stay on the highway (3 miles along the east fork) to reach **Meadowlark Lake** (8700 ft; 182 ac), which has fair fishing for rainbow 11 to 18 inches and some brown, cutthroat and brook up to 14 inches. *Casper Star-Tribune* sports columnist and very savvy fisherman Al Novotny describes Meadowlark Lake as being comparable "to a pond in downtown Pittsburgh" on the weekend. Getting off the beaten track in the area can pay dividends.

In the fall, trolling boat fishermen sometimes pull in browns up to 6 pounds. There is a lodge, campgrounds and boat rental. This is a take-off point for hikers going into the Cloud Peak Primitive Area. A rough road goes northeast 4 miles from Meadowlark Lake to **East Ten Sleep Lake** (9735 ft; 45 ac), where there is fair to good fishing for cutthroat and rainbow averaging 12 inches. A rough trail southeast from this lake will take you to **McClain Lake** (9675 ft; 10 ac) and **Maybelle Lake** (9725 ft; 12 ac), with cutthroat averaging 12 inches, and some larger fish in Maybelle. These lakes also can be reached by a 4-wheel drive road called the Baby Wagon Road. It heads north off US 16 about 2 miles east of Meadowlark Lake.

A dirt road runs up **West Ten Sleep Creek** about 7 miles to **West Ten Sleep Lake** (9075 ft; 42 ac), which has a campground and fair fishing for brook trout 8 to 10 inches. A trail west of the lake will take you 4 miles up **Middle Ten Sleep Creek** to **Mirror Lake** (9650 ft; 18 ac), with fair to good fishing for rainbow from 14 to 18 inches, 12-inch brook and mackinaw to 22 inches early in the season. Another 2 miles upstream are the **Lost Twin Lakes,** with **Upper Lost Twin Lake** (10,400 ft; 35 ac) good for golden averaging 15 inches and the **Lower Lost**

288 BIGHORN RIVER

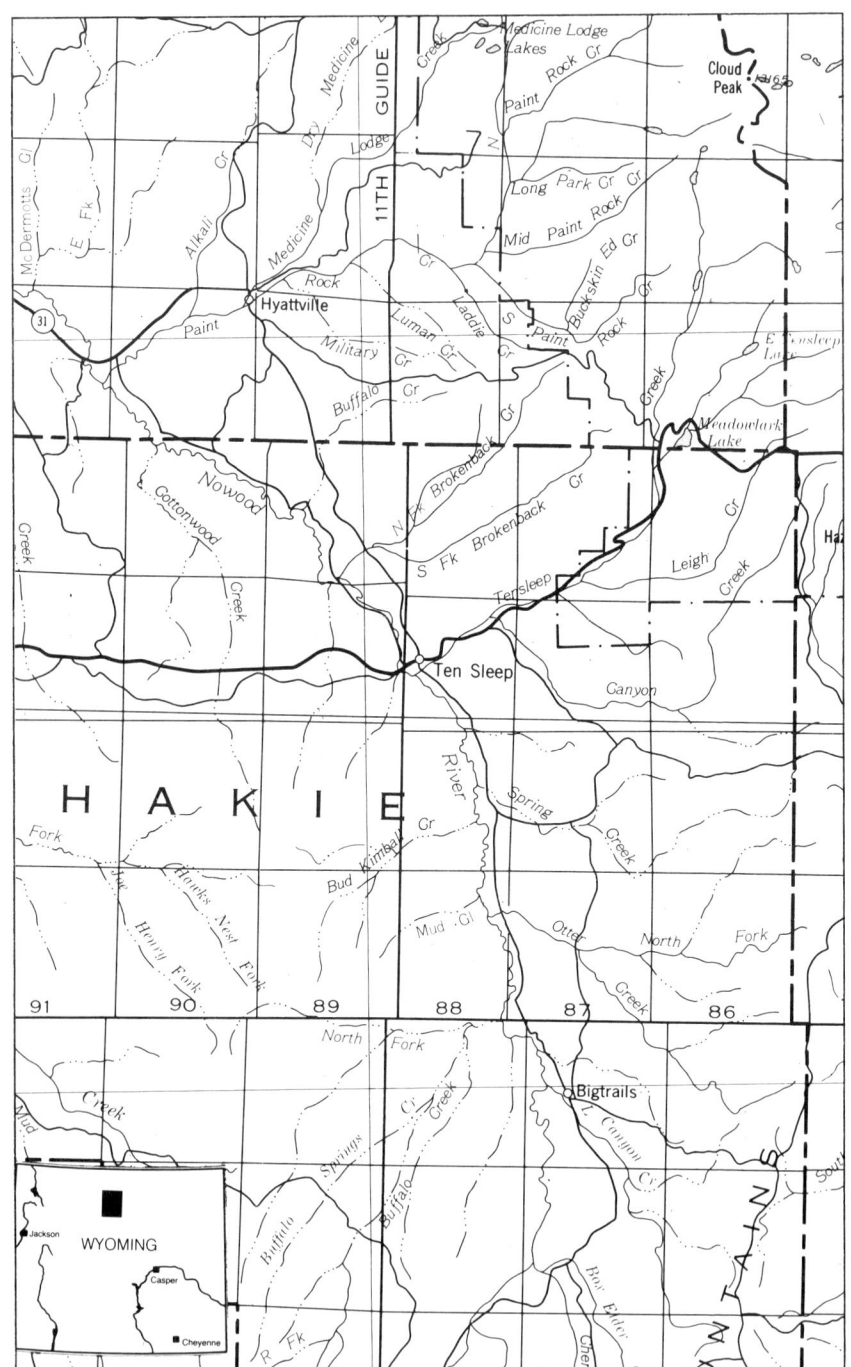

Nowood River

Twin Lake (10,350 ft; 32 ac) good for rainbow averaging 14 inches. Hike north from West Ten Sleep Lake 3.5 miles to **Lake Helen** (9968 ft; 45 ac) for good fishing for small brook; two campgrounds. The lake itself is 0.75 mile within the Cloud Peak Primitive Area.

A half-mile north of Helen is **Lake Marion** (10,100 ft; 12 ac) with good fishing for small brook. Half a mile farther is **Mistymoon Lake** (10,236 ft; 38 ac), which is over-populated with small brook. A trail west from Mistymoon leads less than a mile to the **Fortress Lakes** (10,500 ft; 2, 3, and 8 ac), and **Gunboat Lake** (10,500 ft; 16 ac) with good fishing for golden averaging 12 inches. This trail continues over Florence Pass into the Powder River drainage (see separate chapter).

From Mistymoon Lake trails go west and north to lakes which drain into **Paint Rock Creek.** The creek joins the Nowood about 13 miles above its juncture with the Bighorn River. Only 2 miles west of Mistymoon Lake is **Lake Solitude** (9274 ft; 72 ac) with an overabundance of brook trout. Some mackinaws range to 18 inches and some are larger. There are 2 campgrounds, at the west and east ends. Higher in this drainage, accessible by trail, are **Middle Cloud Peak Lake** and many other small lakes which can be fair to good for golden trout and cutthroat. A mile and a half downstream from Solitude, outside the wilderness, is **Grace Lake** (9302 ft; 13 ac), with good fishing for brook to 15 inches. Another mile downstream are the **Lost Lakes** (9399 ft) with cutthroat up to 16 inches. Lost Lakes can be reached by a rugged 4-wheel drive road beginning at Soldier Creek. Southeast of Lost Lake 2 miles, and also accessible with 4-wheel drive, is **Lily Lake** (9547 ft; 15 ac) with grayling to 16 inches.

North Paint Rock Creek drains a more northerly bunch of lakes in the Primitive Area, reachable by trail from the Medicine Lodge Lakes, which are about 2 miles outside the wilderness. **Medicine Lodge Lakes** are reached from the north by taking US 14 east from Greybull up Shell Creek

SUBSCRIBE NOW TO:

Cheyenne, Wyoming 82002

A MONTHLY STORY IN PICTURES AND WORDS OF THE WILDLIFE AND SCENIC BEAUTY IN THE STATE OF WYOMING

From_____

Address_____

City_____ State_____ Zip_____

1 Year for $8.00 ☐   SAVE—Subscribe for 3 Years for $20.00 ☐

SUBSCRIPTION FOR: (include other names on separate sheet of paper)

Name_____

Address_____

City_____ State_____ Zip_____

Wyoming Wildlife is a publication of the Wyoming Game & Fish Commission

Canyon about 30 miles to the Cabin Creek Campground, then going south approximately 20 miles on graveled Forest Service roads. Consult a map. There are several campgrounds in the area. **Upper Medicine Lodge Lake** (9265 ft; 65 ac) and **Lower Medicine Lodge Lake** (9121 ft; 45 ac) have fair to good fishing for rainbow from 10 to 12 inches.

A half-mile southeast are **Upper Paint Rock Lake** (9714 ft; 24 ac) and **Lower Paint Rock Lake** (9300 ft; 15 ac). These lakes were overcrowded with brook, but higher creel limits have brought them under control.

At this writing, the Wyoming Game and Fish Department allows more than the normal number of fish to be taken on the eastern tributaries to the Bighorn River above Nowater Creek all the way to the Montana border. The limit on trout, salmon and grayling is 12 fish per day in possession, and only one fish 20 inches or longer. Check to be sure this regulation is still in effect.

The Paint Rock Creek trail goes 2 miles and into the Cloud Peak Primitive Area. About 7 miles farther are some good alpine lakes. Along the way, the creek itself has small brook. **Cliff Lake** (9790 ft; 17 ac) has good fishing for brook to 11 inches. One-half mile northeast in **Lake Eunice** (9700 ft; 10 ac), and just to the southeast **Lake Elsie** (10,095 ft; 23 ac) is good fishing for brook to 12 inches. To the south lie the two Crater Lakes, **Upper Crater Lake** (10,515 ft; 38 ac) and **Lower Crater Lake** (10,313 ft; 22 ac) with small populations of 11-inch cutthroat and some larger mackinaw. Half a mile from Lake Elsie to the northeast is **Rainbow Lake** (10,452 ft; 18 ac) with brook to 14 inches. There are numerous smaller lakes in this area with brook trout that get as large as 15 inches. The setting is spectacular. A trail heads north over Geneva Pass to Big Goose Creek. **Robin Lake** (10,650 ft), just before the pass, has excellent fishing for 8-inch brook.

SHELL CREEK

Shell Creek flows west from the Bighorns and enters the river at Greybull. US 14 follows the stream for 22 miles from Greybull to the edge of the national forest, and for another 9 miles within the forest in Shell Canyon. Below the canyon there is spring fishing for brown trout up to 14 inches. The 10 miles of stream from the forest boundary to the Shell Creek Ranger Station has rainbow to 14 inches and some brook. Above the station the stream primarily has small brook. After US 14 turns north, gravelled Forest Service roads continue south by the stream.

The Shell Creek headwaters are in the Cloud Peak Primitive Area, north of the Paint Rock Creek headwaters. About 5 miles northeast from Paint Rock Lakes is **Emerald Lake** (10,250 ft; 33 ac) with good fishing for brook to 12 inches, rainbow somewhat larger, and a few golden. A short distance downstream from Emerald are the **Lakes of the Rough.** The lower one (9980 ft; 7 ac) and the upper (10,250 ft; 6 ac) offer good fishing for brook to 12 inches. Another 2 miles downstream, outside the wilderness, are the **Shell Lakes** (9535 ft; 32 and 5 ac) with good fishing for small brook.

From the Shell Creek Ranger Station there are rough 4-wheel drive roads leading east, north and south to lower elevation lakes. Driving south past the station for 6 miles on a gravel road, you'll find a sign for **Shell Reservoir,** which is 3 miles farther east on a poor road. The reservoir (8997 ft; 85 ac when full) has brook trout 10 to 13 inches, and is rated fair to good. Across the dam and 0.75 mile on another poor road is **Adelaide Lake** (9250 ft; 90 ac), which has rainbow to 14 inches and brook to 10 inches. Fishing quality varies with water fluctuations. Another mile along a poor road is **Mud Lake** (9250 ft; 2 ac), harboring brook to 12 inches—and some larger. Above Mud Lake is **Lake Arden** (9400 ft; 12 ac), with good fishing for brook to 10 inches.

Fishing in the Bighorn Mountains north of Shell Creek is mostly in streams flowing easterly as tributaries of the Little Bighorn and are discussed in the Powder River chapter.

ABSAROKA MOUNTAINS

Now the discussion shifts to the waters entering the Bighorn River from the west, draining the Absaroka Mountains in Shoshone National Forest. Access to the

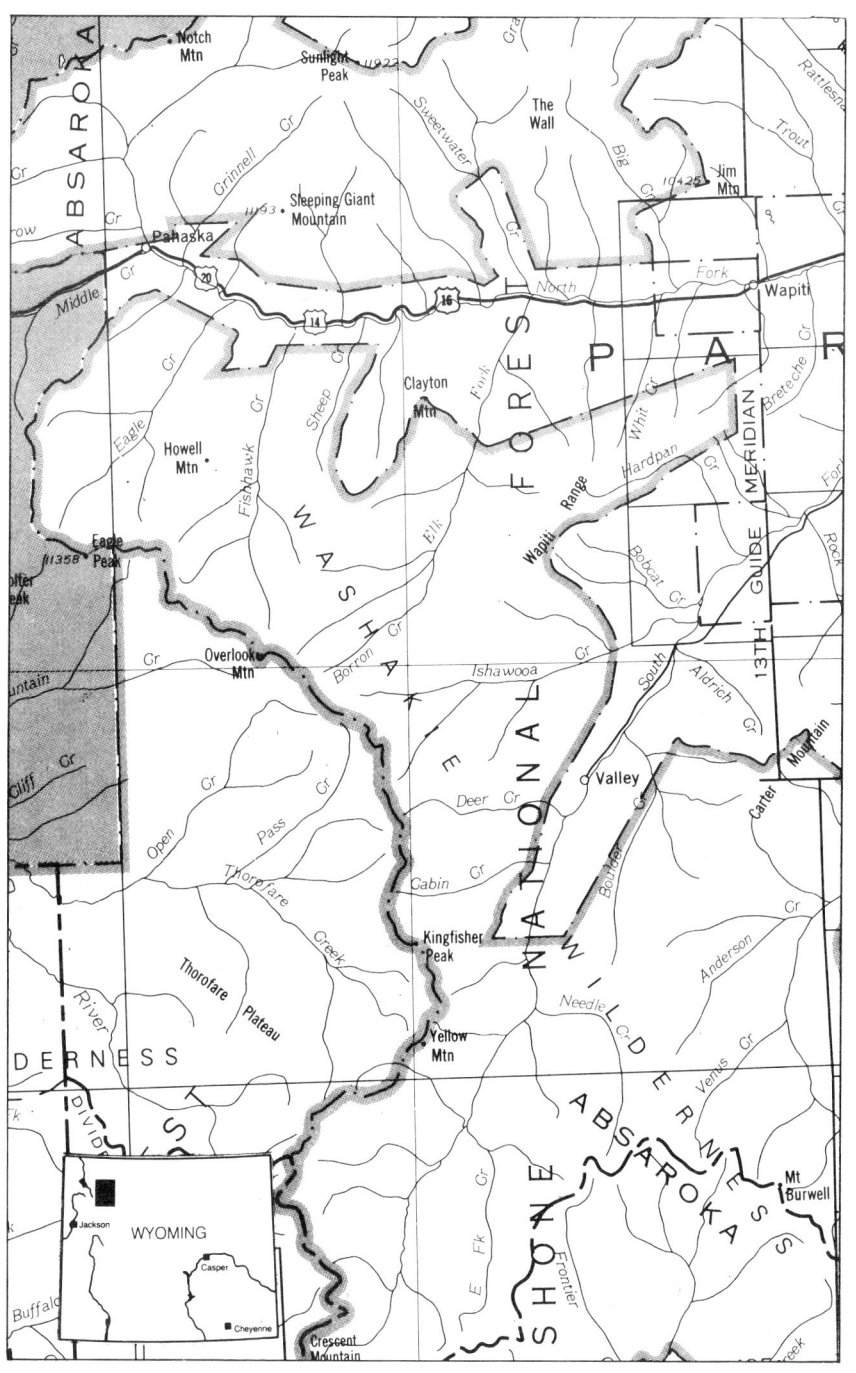

North and South Forks Shoshone River

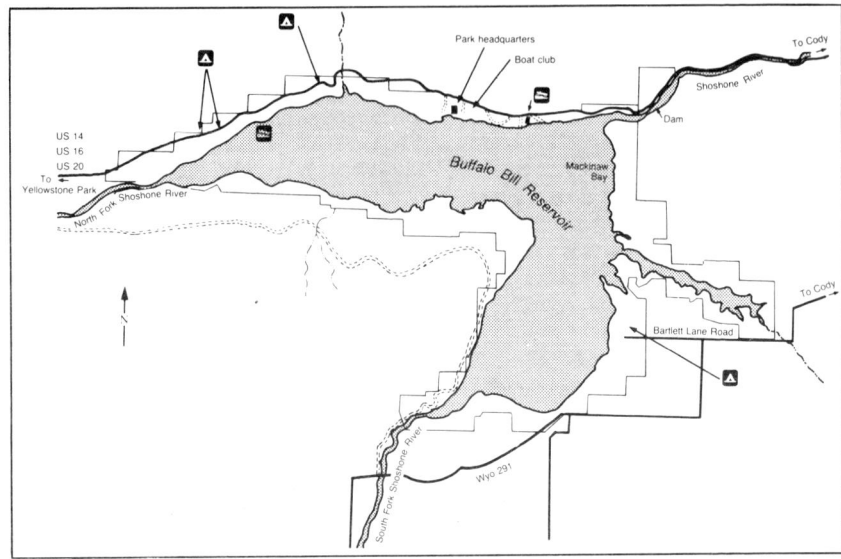

Buffalo Bill State Park

headwaters of the Yellowstone River, which drain northwest into Yellowstone Park and an area southeast of the park called Thorofare country, can be either from the park, the Jackson Hole area to the south or from the east side. The Yellowstone River flows north to Yellowstone Lake, then doubles around to the east, ultimately uniting with the Bighorn River east of Billings in Montana. **Gooseberry, Cottonwood** and **Owl Creeks** all flow from the west into the Bighorn River between Boysen Reservoir and just north of Thermopolis. They are only fair fisheries.

Southwest of Meeteetse, the **Wood River,** some 40 feet wide, flows north into the **Greybull River,** which joins the Bighorn at Greybull. There is fair fishing for cutthroat on the Wood. Take County Road 290 west of Meeteetse along the Greybull River about 7 miles to the Wood River juncture, then follow the Wood south on County Road 90. A paved, then dirt, road goes some 30 miles to the old mining town of Kirwin; private property. Just inside the Shoshone National Forest boundary the **South** and **Middle Forks of Wood River** join the Wood. Trails go up both forks, which have fair to good fishing for cutthroat and some brook. There are two campgrounds along the main river within the forest. About 5 miles within the forest and 2 miles west of Brown Mountain Campground, **Jojo Creek** flows in from the north. It is a steep four-mile trail up to **Jojo Lake** (11,000 ft; 3 ac) for good fishing for golden trout averaging 12 inches.

Also draining into the Greybull from the south is **Sunshine Creek,** draining **Sunshine Reservoir** (6691 ft; 1200 ac). There is a road off County Road 290 about 10 miles west of Meeteetse, which runs 2.5 miles to the reservoir. Fishermen troll with lures and baits, and the fishing is fair for 15-inch rainbow, and cutthroat from 16 to 24 inches. Lower reaches of the Greybull River are on private land and fishing isn't very good.

SHOSHONE RIVER

Moving north is the **Shoshone River,** which has **South** and **North Forks** emptying into **Buffalo Bill Reservoir.** The South Fork runs northeast flowing 50 to 60 feet wide in the lower reaches of its 50-mile length of mountainous fishing waters. Good roads follow the stream for more than 30 miles. There are numerous private lands for about 12 miles into the forest. The lower part of the river has brown to 18 inches and cutthroat averaging 12 inches. There are brook trout and whitefish, too. Permission from the landowners is required. The river is closed to fishing from the reservoir to Fall Creek, just above the private in-holdings, from April 1 to June 30.

Traveling upstream, vehicle traffic ends at the South Fork Ranger Station. About six miles beyond, hikers enter the Washakie Wilderness, where the fishing tends to improve. For the next 15 miles upstream on the **South Fork of Shoshone River** there are cutthroat 12 to 13 inches and some rainbow, fair to good fishing. Caddis, mayfly and grasshopper action is good from July into September. Above Bliss Creek Meadows there are mostly small brook. About 10 miles upstream from the wilderness boundary, **East Fork Creek** enters from the southeast; 4 miles later **Clark Creek** enters from the same direction; both streams have good fishing for 14- to 16-inch cutthroat.

About 3.5 miles up river from East Fork Creek a trail goes west up **Marston Creek** to Marston Pass and the Continental Divide. To the north are the headwaters of the Yellowstone River, Thorofare Plateau and **Bridger Lake,** which is on the border of Yellowstone National Park. This beautiful lake (100 ac) has good fishing for cutthroat from 16 to 18 inches, and brook. It's a long trip into this country, by foot or horse, and a guide is a good idea. Southwest from Marston Pass is the upper Snake River drainage.

Also flowing into Buffalo Bill Reservoir is the **North Fork of Shoshone River.** US Hwys 14-16-20 run 45 miles along the north side of the reservoir from Buffalo Bill to within 2 miles of the east entrance to Yellowstone National Park. There are 14 campgrounds, numerous summer homes, and even a ski area along the way. The busy highway and increasing population have diminished the quality of the fishing. The North Fork still offers fair fishing for rainbow and cutthroat, averaging 10 to 11 inches, and occasional browns. There are three well-marked public access areas through private land to the river along the 11 miles above the reservoir before it enters Shoshone National Forest. A short stretch of the river—about a mile—between the reservoir and the first bridge upstream, called the Gibbs Bridge, is closed to fishing from April 1 to July 14. Rainbows from Buffalo Bill Reservoir spawn up the North Fork in April and May, and you can do some good fishing above the juncture of **Clearwater Creek.** Upstream from this bridge another 18 miles or so to Clearwater Creek, fishing is banned from April 1 to June 30. The waters in this 50-foot stream vary from fast, whitewater stretches to a few deep pools. Among the better tributaries for fishing are **Elk Fork Creek,** entering the North Fork 6 miles west of the forest boundary from the southwest, with cutthroat to 13 inches; **Fishhawk Creek,** entering from the south 10 miles east of the Yellowstone entrance, with fair to good flyfishing for cutthroat, rainbow, brook and some brown; and **Eagle Creek,** entering from the south 6 miles from the Yellowstone entrance, with cutthroat at the lower end and brook in the upper reaches (about 6 miles by trail). These creeks often are starting points for trips southwest into Thorofare country.

BUFFALO BILL RESERVOIR

Buffalo Bill Reservoir (5350 ft; 6691 ac) is at the dammed confluence of the North and South Forks of the Shoshone River, 8 miles west of Cody. It is a big and popular fishery offering rainbow, brown, cutthroat, mackinaw, whitefish, carp, chubs, yellow dace and other junk fish. There are three boat launching ramps and several overnight camping areas in the immediate vicinity.

Fishing is usually best in early spring by trolling and from shore. Worms, nightcrawlers and sucker meat are common bait. Mackinaw run 17 to 25 inches and 25 pounders have been caught. Cutthroat run

---

Wicker creels or baskets provide good air circulation and can help keep fish from spoiling until they can be refrigerated—or eaten.

14 to 18 inches. Some big rainbow and brown are reported. Water is used for irrigation and the reservoir draws down considerably in dry years.

Northwest of Cody about 5 miles are Upper (west) and Lower Newton lakes—two very popular recreation areas for swimmers, waterskiers and boaters, as well as fishermen. **Upper Newton Lake** (16 ac) has rainbow up to 4 pounds and is seasonally good fishing. There are a few brook trout. There's no boat ramp, but small boats are readily launched. Expect the southwest side to be marked with buoys prohibiting boating in the swimming/fishing area. Boating is generally permitted from 10 a.m. and 5 p.m. **Lower Newton Lake** (30 ac) is good fishing with mostly rainbows up to 12 pounds. It's a shallow—16 feet deep—productive lake where waders are recommended and boat launching is possible, but arduous. There is no boat ramp. The lake is being eyed as a trophy fishery and restrictions to only one fish and manmade lures are being considered.

CLARKS FORK

Clarks Fork of the Yellowstone River heads in the Beartooth Mountains near the northeast corner of Yellowstone Park just north of Cooke City, Montana, dips south into Wyoming before reentering Montana to empty into the Yellowstone River. In Wyoming it offers 75 miles of river, some of it in a beautiful canyon that has earned it consideration as a possible Wild and Scenic River. It is a popular fishing river, but the steep terrain in some sections limits access. That may be what keeps the fishing quality high. The upper 16 miles, where the river is fairly small, has fair to good fishing for cutthroat, some rainbow, and a few small brook. It can be reached by taking Hwy 120 north from Cody 18 miles, then turning west on a road marked "Sunlight Basin"—Hwy 296. Except for a section over Dead Indian Hill, this road is not oiled as it travels northwest in Shoshone National Forest to meet with US 212. Along the way, it runs alongside the river's upper reaches.

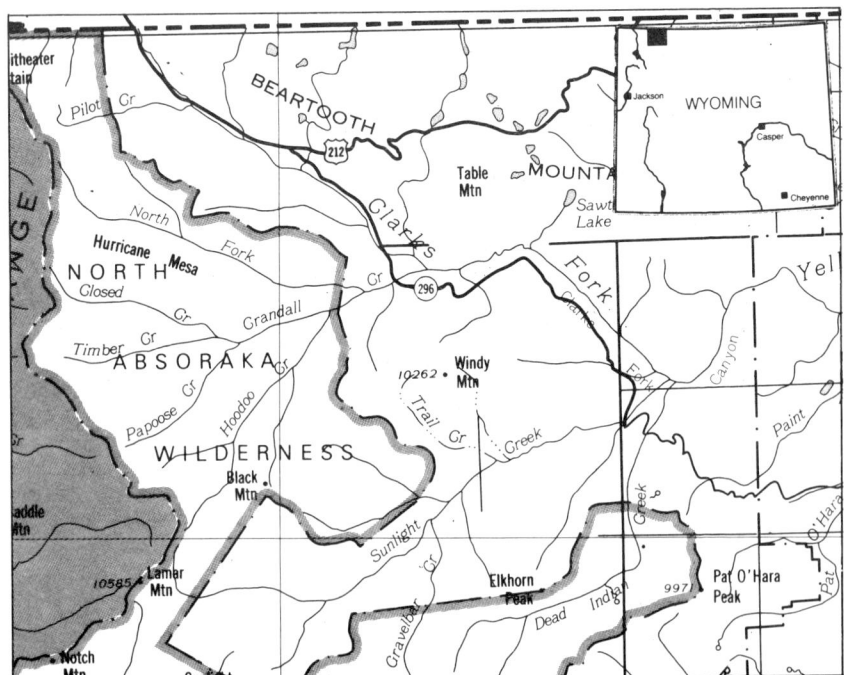

Clarks Fork Yellowstone River

The middle section of the river is in a steep canyon, limiting access. It has rainbow and cutthroat in the 14-inch range, and some brook. Expect to wade in this section. Between the canyon and the Montana line, a distance of 18 miles, the Clarks Fork has some blue-ribbon trout fishing.

The lower section of Clarks Fork, which has mostly 12-inch rainbow and some large browns, has received national publicity for its blue-ribbon quality. Consequently, fishing pressure has been heavy. Big trout to be caught on flies are there, but overall it's not a very productive fishery. There is a Clarks Fork Hunting and Fishing Area about 30 miles northwest of Cody off Hwy 120. It includes four signed access areas and about 6.4 miles of fishing water. The longest stretch of public access surrounds the Clarks Fork Fish Hatchery.

In cooperation with Park County Recreation Board, $15,000 is being spent to improve trout habitat in the stream in 1985 and 1986.

The chief tributaries of the Clarks Fork from the south are **Crandall, Sunlight** and **Dead Indian Creeks.** Trails follow these creeks, which offer good fishing for cutthroat 10 to 15 inches. Some land around Sunlight Creek is privately owned, so be sure to ask permission. A dirt road runs up Sunlight Creek to abandoned mining areas, and from the old Lee City Mining Camp a 4-mile switchback over a ridge leads to the three **Copper Lakes. Lower Copper** (9850 ft; 35 ac) and the two **Upper Copper** (10,250 and 10,100 ft) offer fair to good fishing for temperamental golden to 12 inches.

On the north side of Clarks Fork is the rugged high country of the Beartooth Plateau, bisected by the Wyoming-Montana line. The Beartooth Highway, US 212, looping to the southwest from Red Lodge, Montana, into Wyoming, over Beartooth Pass (10,947 ft), and back up again to Cooke City, Montana, provides access to this country. It skirts a couple of the larger lakes, and there you will also find trailheads to dozens of lakes in more remote areas. Large areas are very boggy; others are rocky in very rough terrain.

Brook trout were brought to the Beartooths by railroad from New England and Pennsylvania around 1900. In recent years there has been a phenomenal growth in backpacking on the plateau, which is only 8 to 10 miles wide and 25 miles long. As a result, the lakes are no longer teeming with brookies, and other trout are harder to catch.

Readily accessible and in the center of the Beartooth range is **Beartooth Lake** (8901 ft; 110 ac), north of the highway, with good rainbow, cutthroat and brook averaging 10 to 12 inches, grayling up to 15 inches at the lake's east end, and mackinaw as large as 20 pounds. Campground and boat ramps at the lake. Also easy to reach is Island Lake, about 2 miles east of Beartooth and also on the highway. **Island Lake** (9518 ft; 146 ac) has brook trout and rainbow, and a campground. Trailheads from either of these lakes go north to a variety of lakes: among them **Beauty Lake** (9400 ft; 75 ac), **Grayling Lake** (9500 ft; 20 ac), **Night Lake** (9560 ft; 60 ac), and **"T" Lake.** Rainbow and brook predominate; in the case of "T" Lake, it is overrun with grayling.

Also north of Beartooth Lake are numerous small lakes with brookies. Among them are **Lobster Claw, Elkhorn, Shallow, Marmot, Horseshoe** and **Finger lakes.** Gus Lake, on the Montana border, has larger than average brook.

Farther west, draining from the north into Clarks Fork is **Granite Lake** (8620 ft; 300 ac). It is 4 miles from US 212 by trail and has plentiful brook to 10 inches and larger rainbow. **Lake Reno** (8244 ft; 140 ac) is another 2 miles west, 4 miles from the highway. South of Reno only a mile north of US 212, is **Lily Lake** (7600 ft; 40 ac), with fair to good fishing for rainbow up to 17 inches and brook and golden to 12 inches.

Immediately south of US 212 and slightly east of Island Lake is **Rainbow Lake** (9700 ft; 20 ac), with fair to good fishing for golden 11 to 13 inches. Another mile south, reachable by vehicle, is **Sawtooth Lake** (9230 ft; 28 ac) with rainbow to 20 inches, 12- to 13-inch cutthroat, and some brook. Southeast from Sawtooth 3 miles by 4-wheel-drive road is **Deep Lake** (7992 ft; 200 ac). To reach Deep Lake hike down from the rim. It's a tough hike out, but there are brook, 13-inch cutthroat, and larger fish. ☐

If minnows are active, it's a good bet that gamefish are too, because many species of fish in a body of water start and stop activity at approximately the same time.

In 1981, 29,277,241 U.S. anglers paid almost $213 million in fishing license fees, according to the Wildlife Management Institute.

U.S. Forest Service campgrounds

U.S. Forest Service compilation was current as of 1985.

Asterisks denote fee areas. Some campgrounds are open only Memorial Day weekend through Labor Day. Below freezing weather could mean no water supply.

BIGHORN RIVER DRAINAGE

SHOSHONE NATIONAL FOREST
Headquarters: W. Yellowstone Hwy, Box 961, Cody, WY 82414

Campground name	Elevation	No camp sites	Travel trailers	Drinking water	Length of stay (days)	Location and directions
Dead Indian	6100	12	Yes	No	14	37.4 mi NW of Cody on Wyo. 120 and forest roads
Hunter Peak*	6500	9	Yes	Yes	14	19 mi SE of Cooke City, MT on Hwy 212 and forest road
Reef Creek	6700	4	Yes	Yes	14	27 mi SE of Cooke City, MT on Hwy 212 and forest road
Lake Creek*	6900	6	Yes	Yes	14	15.5 mi SE of Cooke City MT on Hwy 212 and forest road
Fox Creek*	7100	27	Yes	Yes	14	On Hwy 212, 7.5 mi SE of Cooke City, MT
Crazy Creek*	6900	16	Yes	Yes	14	On Hwy 212, 12 mi E of Cooke City, MT
Beartooth Lake*	9000	17	Yes	Yes	14	On US 212, 24.2 mi E of Cooke City, MT
Island Lake*	9600	20	Yes	Yes	14	On US 212, 27.5 mi E of Cooke City, MT
Wood River*	7300	5	Yes	Yes	14	22 mi SW of Meeteetse on Wyo. 290 and county hwy
Brown Mountain*	7600	6	Yes	Yes	14	25 mi SW of Meeteetse on Wyo. 290 and county hwy

BIGHORN NATIONAL FOREST
Headquarters: 23 N. Scott, Box 2046, Sheridan, WY 82801

Campground name	Elevation	No camp sites	Travel trailers	Drinking water	Length of stay (days)	Location and directions
Bald Mountain	9200	15	Yes	Yes	14	On US 14, 26.4 mi E of Lovell
Porcupine	8900	12	Yes	Yes	14	Near US 14A, 26.3 mi E of Lovell

Cabin Creek Trailer Camp	7500	26	Yes	Yes	30	On US 14, 12.3 mi NE of Shell
Ranger Creek*	7600	10	Yes	Yes	14	2 mi S of US 14, 16 mi NE of Shell
Ranger Creek #2	7800	11	Yes	Yes	14	12 mi SW of Big Horn
Upper Paint Rock Lake	9300	10	No	No	14	26 mi SE of US 14, 16 mi NE of Shell
Medicine Lodge Lake	9300	8	No	No	14	25 mi SE of US 14, 16 mi NE of Shell
Deer Park	8900	5	Yes	No	14	6 mi N of US 16 on forest roads, 20 mi NE of Ten Sleep
Island Park	8600	10	Yes	No	14	4 mi N of US 16 on forest roads, 20 mi NE of Ten Sleep
Sitting Bull*	8600	43	Yes	Yes	14	1 mi N of US 16, 23 mi NE of Ten Sleep
Ten Sleep Creek	5400	5	Yes	No	14	Off US 16, 8 mi N of Ten Sleep
Lakeview*	8300	11	Yes	Yes	14	Off US 16, 15 mi NE of Ten Sleep
Boulder Trailer Park*	8000	34	Yes	Yes	14	Off US 16, 13 mi NE of Ten Sleep
West Ten Sleep Lake	9100	7	Yes	Yes	14	7.5 mi NE of US 16 on forest road, from 20 mi NE of Ten Sleep
Leigh Creek	5400	11	Yes	No	14	1 mi E of US 16, 8 mi NE of Ten Sleep
Cabin Creek*	7400	4	Yes	Yes	14	16 mi NE of Shell on US 14
Shell Creek*	7500	11	Yes	Yes	14	17 mi NE of Shell on US 14 and forest road
Hanging Rock*	5800	4	No	Yes	14	On US 16, 26.3 mi W of Cody
Big Game*	5900	17	Yes	Yes	14	On US 16, 28.6 mi W of Cody
Wapiti*	6000	41	Yes	Yes	14	On US 16, 29.4 mi W of Cody
Elk Fork*	6000	12	Yes	Yes	14	On US 16, 29.5 mi W of Cody
Newton Creek*	6300	31	Yes	Yes	14	On US 16, 37.3 mi W of Cody
Eagle Creek*	6500	20	Yes	Yes	14	On US 16, 44.7 mi W of Cody
Sleeping Giant*	6600	6	Yes	Yes	14	On US 16, 47.6 mi W of Cody
Three Mile*	6700	55	Yes	Yes	14	On US 16, 48.6 mi W of Cody
Pahaska*	6800	24	Yes	Yes	14	On US 16, 49.6 mi W of Cody

Yellowstone National Park has exceptional angling

ADJACENT COMMUNITIES:
Cody, Wyo.; Jackson, Wyo.; Cooke City, Mont.; West Yellowstone, Mont.; Gardiner, Mont.

PRINCIPAL HIGHWAYS:
U.S. 287, 89, 14, 20, 16, 212, 191. Roads through the park are closed in winter, except U.S. 212 from Cooke City to Gardiner, Mont.

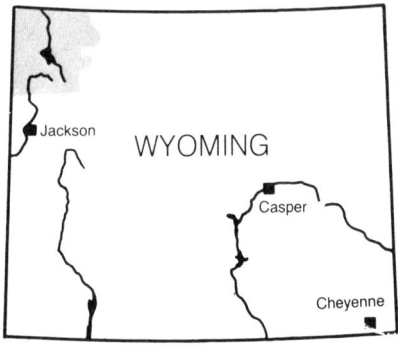

Yellowstone National Park is a mecca for fishermen from around the country. Lured by wild trout and pristine settings, well over 100,000 anglers visit the park each year. Even so, there are many streams and lakes in the 2.2-million-acre wonderland that see few, if any, fishermen in an entire season.

In spite of the numbers of fishermen, the Park remains an excellent fishery. The average size fish landed was 13.4 inches, according to a recent survey. One lake had an *average* size of landed fish of more than 18 inches.

Preservation of the park's sport fishery has been accomplished through intense management, utilizing a complex set of regulations. Anglers must take time to become thoroughly acquainted with those regulations before fishing. The park opens for fishing in late May (the Saturday before Memorial Day) and closes the end of October. But some waters, including Yellowstone Lake and parts of the Yellowstone River, open later. Fishing generally is restricted to flies and lures only; however several streams and lakes have fly-fishing-only and catch-and-release regulations.

No license is necessary within the park, but a fishing permit is required. The permit and accompanying regulations are available free at entrances and ranger stations. Boating is allowed on lakes, but a permit is required for that activity also. Permits are available free from ranger stations at Lewis Lake and Yellowstone Lake.

Man isn't the only one fishing in Yellowstone National Park for its grayling, brook, brown cutthroat, lake and rainbow trout. The grizzly bear, osprey, bald eagle, kingfisher, otter and other creatures dine there regularly.

Yellowstone is bear country. Since anglers and bears frequent the same habitat, some caution is required. Roadside anglers are not likely to see bear, but, in some areas, back country anglers almost certainly will. A list of recent bear sightings and incidents is available at ranger stations and may aid in planning trips. All fishermen should follow Park Service suggestions and regulations carefully.

FOUR MAJOR DRAINAGES

There are four major drainages within the park. The Snake River and its tributaries flow south out of the park into Wyoming and Idaho. The Madison River drainage covers a large part of the west side of the

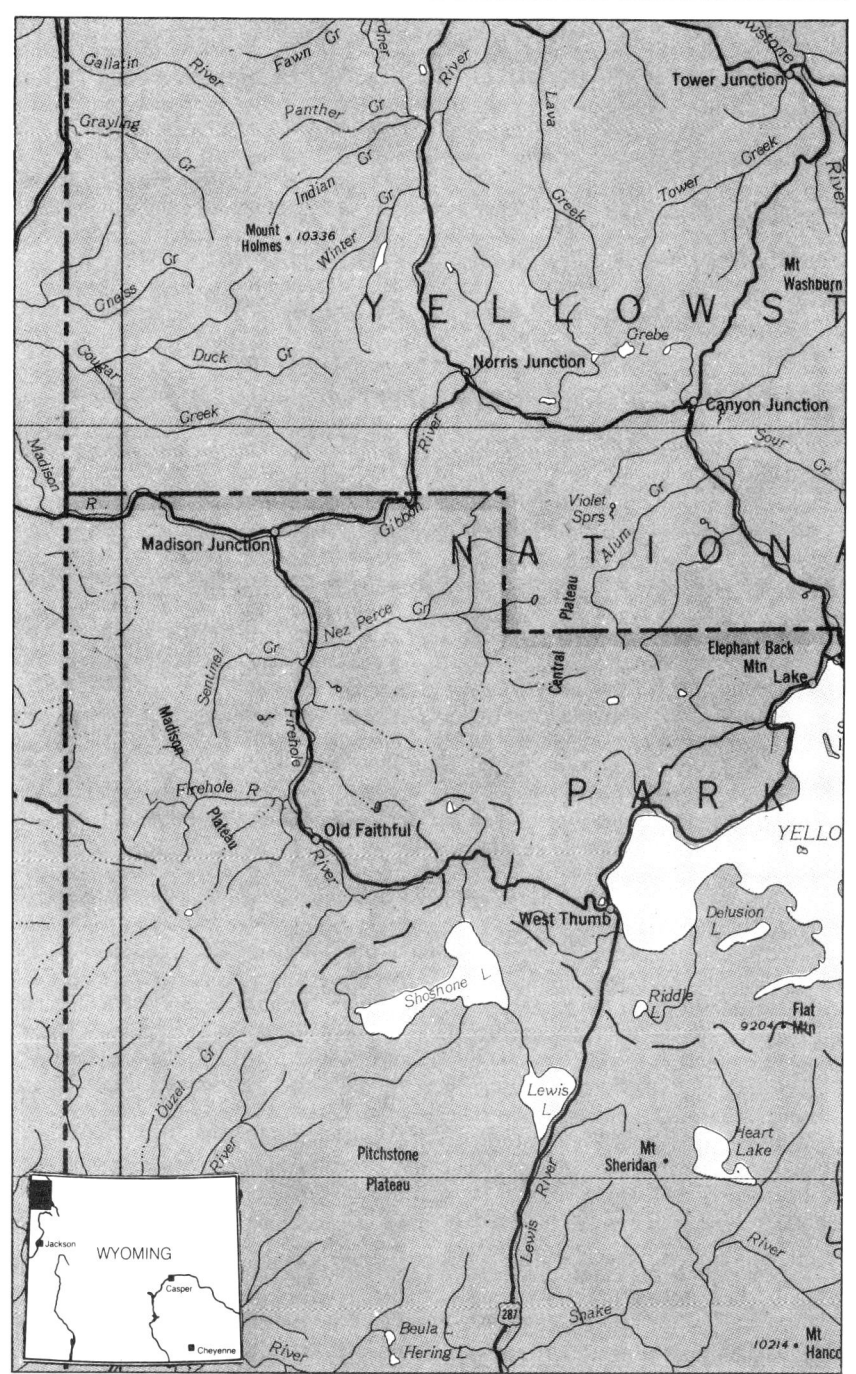

West side Yellowstone National Park

park. The Gallatin River drains the park's northwest corner. Finally, the Yellowstone River, the park's most famous fishing attraction, flows north into Montana. Its drainage includes more than half the Park's 3500 square miles.

After a brief description of the drainage, this guide follows each river from its headwaters to its confluence with another river or to the park boundary. A Yellowstone National Park topographic map will aid the fisherman in locating individual streams and lakes.

SNAKE RIVER

Tourists who enter Yellowstone National Park by the South Entrance are, for the most part, unimpressed by the roadside scenery. A few may stop to admire the deeply carved Lewis Canyon; and some may stop at **Lewis Lake,** the park's third largest lake, to stretch their legs and enjoy the expanse of water. Lewis offers excellent fishing. But almost everyone is eager to get on to Old Faithful.

So it is with fishermen. They stop at the South Entrance Station to wonder what the **Snake River** is like after it winds away from the road into the back country, and they slow down at Lewis Lake to see whether fish are rising. But they, too, are eager to try Yellowstone Lake and Yellowstone River.

By ignoring the southern section of the park, fishermen have bypassed a lake that produced the park record lake trout—a 43-pound monster. They have overlooked another lake that boasts the largest average sized fish in the park—18.3 inches. And they've missed miles and miles of beautiful back country stream fishing.

Except for the extreme southeastern corner, the southern part of the park is in the Snake River drainage. The Snake River flows from the east past the South Entrance Station on Hwy 89-287 through more than 30 miles of roadless back country from its headwaters along the park boundary. Well to the west of South Entrance Road, the **Falls River** collects water from the Pitchstone Plateau.

Two main tributaries, carrying water from three major lakes, feed the Snake: the Heart River flows from Heart Lake and joins the Snake in the back country; and the Lewis River, bringing water from Lewis and Shoshone lakes, meets the Snake near the South Entrance. Except for Lewis Lake and those portions of the Lewis River accessible from the road, fishing requires walking. Some of the water is definitely only for the physically fit, dedicated backpacker.

The Falls River also has two main tributaries, **Mountain Ash Creek** and the **Bechler River.** There are few lakes in the area. The Falls River drainage is considered some of the most remote in the park. It's lower in elevation and wetter than other areas, causing lush growth and greater variety of plant life. Browsing deer, elk and moose are common companions of fishermen along the rivers and streams. The most singular feature of the Falls River drainage is the number of waterfalls. There are 21 of them, more than half the total for the entire park. Twister, Rainbow, Silver Scarf and Collinade waterfalls are on trout streams with deep pools holding some good sized fish.

Trails into the Falls River area are located along the Reclamation Road and at the Cave Falls Road. The Reclamation Road, a 45-mile dirt road paralleling, in part, the southern park boundary, begins just south of the park entrance. Take the Huckleberry Hot Springs turn and stay on the road to Grassy Lake Reservoir. The road comes out at Marysville, on State Hwy 47, east of Ashton, Idaho. Since the road is primitive, local inquiry is suggested, and large RVs and vehicles with trailers are not recommended. The Cave Falls Road exits Hwy 47 a few miles east of Marysville. It dead-ends in the park's southwest corner. This is the best access to most of the area. From there it's walk or ride horseback.

After leaving the South Entrance Road, the Snake River winds through 30 miles of the back country. It's accessible from the South Boundary Trail and adjoining trails. No other stream holds such a variety of fish life. Snake River cutthroat, browns and rainbows make up a large portion of the catch, but lake trout, brook trout and whitefish are available in some sections. However, both angler success and the average size of fish caught were below park averages. Angling is fair to good for fish averaging 10 inches.

Near the southeast corner of the park and the headwaters of the Snake is **Mariposa Lake** (9100 ft), a 28-mile walk or ride by way of the South Entrance Trail. It offers fair fishing for cutthroats to 14 inches. **Crooked Creek** and **Sickle Creek,** tributaries located downstream from Mariposa along the difficult Snake River Trail (25 miles from the entrance station), offer fair fishing for small cutthroats and rainbows.

The first major tributary of the Snake, the **Heart River,** joins it about 20 miles in. It provides good fishing for cutthroats and other species. Four miles up Heart River, **Outlet Creek** and its tributary, **Surprise Creek,** are both good for small cutthroats and other species. Three miles up Outlet Creek, **Outlet Lake** (7800 ft) is fair for small cutthroat.

Immediately upriver of the Outlet Creek confluence is **Heart Lake** (7450 ft). This large lake is an excellent fishery. The average size fish, a recent survey shows, is 16 inches, but many larger cutthroats and lake trout are taken each year. The park record lake trout (43 pounds) was taken from Heart Lake. It also contains cutthroat, rainbow, brook and brown trout. Heavy spoons, spinners and weighted streamers are good for lake trout; best results are had early and late in the season when they are in shallow water. Dry flies and nymphs work for rising trout. The lake usually is reached by an 8-mile trail from the South Entrance Road. The trailhead is located 14.3 miles north of the entrance station; trail goes through bear country. Near the lake, the trail crosses **Witch Creek,** one of two inlet streams. **Beaver Creek** enters the lake on the north shore. Both are rated good for small cutthroat and other species; best fishing is found near the lake.

Two miles southwest of Heart Lake on Heart Lake Trail is **Sheridan Lake.** Along with **Basin Creek Lake,** two miles farther, they feed **Basin Creek,** which flows into the Snake below the Heart River confluence. Creek and lakes are rated good for small cutthroat.

About six miles from the entrance, **Red Creek** enters the Snake from the north. Four miles in, **Forest Creek** joins the Snake, also from the north. Both hold small cutthroats and rainbows, but Forest Creek is considered better fishing.

Lewis River enters the Snake near the South Entrance Station. The highway follows the river for about 11 miles to a point a mile below Lewis Lake. One mile north of the entrance station, **Crawfish Creek** enters the Lewis. Crawfish is a tempting stream with good-looking water, yet it is rated poor for small cutthroats.

In the lower 7 miles, Lewis River flows through a steep-walled canyon. It is beautiful water, made even more so by its inaccessibility. If trout in the meadow section above the canyon are any indication, it's not worth the trip in; however, the river might hold some very large browns. From the canyon upstream to Lewis Falls, the Lewis is a meadow stream averaging 75 feet in width. Many very small fish, mostly browns, are in this stretch; good insect hatches.

From the falls to Lewis Lake outlet, the river has varied water ranging from long riffles to deep runs. Many small browns are here, too, but an occasional large fish drifts down from the lake. This section holds larger browns and lake trout during fall spawning. **Aster Creek,** a small meadow stream, enters the Lewis immediately downstream of the highway bridge below the falls. Aster is fair for small trout.

Lewis Lake, located along the South Entrance Road, contains brook, browns and lake trout averaging 15 inches. Lakers over 30 pounds have been taken. Trolling is most effective except during the fall when fish are in shallows. Motorized boats are allowed, but a boat permit (free) is required. Ranger station, boat ramp and campground are located at the southeast corner of lake. Browns rise to evening caddis hatch in July and August. The lake is easily fished with chest waders, especially along the eastern shore.

At the northwest corner of Lewis Lake is its main inlet, the **Lewis-Shoshone Chan-**

nel, four miles of slow-moving water between Lewis and the back country Shoshone Lake. The channel is reached by boat or by a 2.5 mile trail that parallels the north shore. Only hand-propelled craft are allowed in the channel, where there is very good fishing for browns averaging 17 inches. Try a size 12 Adams or large caddis patterns. Fish are spooky in the clear, calm water, which is difficult to fish from the bank since wading is nearly impossible.

Shoshone Lake, second largest in the park, is accessible by boat through the channel (some pulling or portaging is necessary) or by trail. Trail to the channel continues up to Shoshone. Other trails head along Old Faithful Road. Shoshone had the biggest average size of fish caught for the park in 1980—18.3 inches. It contains browns and lake trout with some brook trout. Fall fishing is excellent. Motorless craft are allowed, but sudden storms make boating hazardous. **DeLacy Creek** on the north shore, **Shoshone Creek** on the west shore, and **Moose Creek** on the south shore provide fair to good fishing for small browns and brook trout. **Pocket Lake,** a small lake west of Shoshone, holds small cutthroat.

Joining the Snake below the Lewis River confluence, **Polecat Creek** parallels the highway for three miles west and enters the Snake outside the park. Access is from Moose Falls just north of the South Entrance or along Reclamation Road. The road crosses the creek about one mile from South Entrance Road, but at that point, the creek is not within the park, so regulations should be checked. Fishing is rated poor to fair for small cutthroat.

Located west of Polecat Creek in the Falls River drainage are **Beula Lake** and **Hering Lake.** They can be reached by a 2.5-mile trail from near the inlet to **Grassy Lake Reservoir** on Reclamation Road. They provide good fishing for cutthroats to 14 inches, but Beula is considered better. **South Boundary Lake,** 1.5 miles east from the junction of Beula Lake Trail on South Boundary Trail, is reported to contain small cutthroat. The outlet of Beula Lake is part of the headwaters of Falls River, which flows through back country along the south boundary; it is accessible by trails from Reclamation Road and Cave Falls Road.

Since nearly all the trails to the falls and other streams and lakes in the area require crossing boggy meadows and fording rivers, trips into this area are better planned for after spring runoff, usually after the first week in July. If wet feet and mosquitoes don't bother you, the scenery is magnificent. The area is known for its many waterfalls and lush plant growth. The **Falls River** is rated good for rainbows and cutthroats averaging 10 inches, with the upper reaches considered better.

Mountain Ash Creek, a tributary entering Falls River about four miles above Cave Falls, is rated very good for cutthroat and rainbows averaging 12 inches. **Proposition Creek** joins Mountain Ash about two miles upstream and is good for small cutthroat and rainbow. The other main tributary of the Falls, the **Bechler River,** enters at Cave Falls from the north. It, too, is good fishing for cutthroats and rainbows averaging 10 inches. **Boundary Creek** joins the Bechler 3.5 miles upstream. Rated good for cutthroats and rainbows to 14 inches. Another 4 miles upstream, **Ouzel Creek** flows into Bechler. It's fair for small cutthroats and rainbows. **Lilypad Lake,** located west of Bechler River, approximately 2 miles from Cave Falls, is rated good for 10- to 12-inch rainbows.

Robinson Lake lies two miles west of Bechler River Ranger Station along the West Boundary Trail. The lake and its outlet, **Rock Creek,** provide fair to good fishing for small cutthroats and rainbows. Two miles past the lake, the trail crosses **Little Robinson Creek** and then follows **Robinson Creek** north. Cutthroats and rainbows to 12 inches are found in these small streams. **Buffalo Lake,** 12 miles north, holds no fish.

MADISON RIVER

The headwaters of one of the best-known trout streams in the country are found in Yellowstone National Park. The **Madison River** is one of Montana's blue-ribbon trout streams, and many waters within its drainage in the park are worthy of that designation.

Big water can mean big fish, like this brown trout

Fish the Madison for grayling, brown and rainbow.

From **Grebe Lake** near Canyon, the **Gibbon River** flows through high meadows and down over Gibbon Falls to meet the **Firehole River.** The Firehole heads at Madison Lake near Shoshone Lake and flows north through one of the park's most extensive thermal areas. From there it rushes through Firehole Canyon and meets the Gibbon at Madison Junction. Their confluence forms the Madison.

Three smaller streams, **Cougar Creek, Duck Creek** and **Grayling Creek,** flow west out of the park directly into **Hebgen Lake.** They are north of the Madison, and access is easiest from Hwys 287 and 191 north from West Yellowstone, Montana. Hebgen Lake is good fishing for rainbow and browns from April into October, but you'll need a Montana fishing license.

Fly fishermen are attracted to this area because much of the water, including the Madison, the Firehole, and the Gibbon below Gibbon Falls, is restricted to flyfishing. Some of the most challenging fishing in the country is found on the Firehole and Madison.

Anglers with limited time, who wish to catch grayling, would do well to concentrate on two lakes at the headwaters of the Gibbon River: **Grebe Lake** and **Wolf Lake** have grayling and rainbow. **Ice Lake** froze out and offers no fishing, because the park does not stock it (or any other waters). From Ice Lake trailhead, 3 miles east of Norris on the road to Canyon, Ice Lake is a quartermile. Wolf Lake is 3 miles farther, and Grebe Lake is 1 mile more. Grebe also can be reached by an easy 3-mile trail beginning 3 miles west of Canyon. Wolf Lake is rated good for grayling and rainbows to 12 inches. Grebe is the best with fish to 18 inches. All grayling caught in the park must be returned immediately to the water. The numerous mosquitoes, however, may be killed at will. Bring lots of repellent.

The **Gibbon River,** 38 miles of stream averaging 25 feet in width, provides good fishing for browns and brook trout averaging 9 inches. Larger fish are taken below Gibbon Falls. Some rainbows, grayling and whitefish also are caught. There's easy fishing for small brook trout in the meadow sections of Elk Park and Gibbon Meadows, 3 miles west of Norris on Madison Junction Road. There are many elk (and more tourists) in the meadows, so watch your backcast. Fly-fishing-only is permitted below Falls River. **Solfatara Creek** enters Gibbon at Norris, and is reached by trail from the ranger station. Fair for small brook trout. **Lake of the Woods** at headwaters is barren. **Canyon Creek** enters Gibbon from the south below falls. Grayling have been reintroduced here, so the stream may be closed to fishing. Check regulations.

For being one of the best-known trout streams in the country, the **Firehole River** has rather inauspicious beginnings. It heads at **Madison Lake** located a few miles west of **Shoshone Lake.** Madison Lake contains no permanent fish population, and the stream below it all the way to Old Faithful is unremarkable. In this section, it's a pleasant mountain stream with small rainbows, browns and brook trout. **Spring Creek,** a tributary that follows the Old Faithful Road near **Scaup Lake** (which contains no fish), enters the Firehole about 1.5 miles in from the road. Spring Creek provides fair fishing for browns and rainbows.

A transformation begins as the Firehole flows past Old Faithful and the underlying thermal features. It picks up warm water overflow from the thermals along with minerals that are beneficial to insect growth. For the next 12 miles, the Firehole provides some of the most challenging dry-fly fishing and some of the most unique fishing experiences found anywhere. Then it becomes more normal again and flows through the 2-mile-long Firehole Canyon, after which it joins with the Gibbon to form the Madison River.

In those 12 miles, the river is generally a flat, meadow stream. Fishing there requires stealth, long leaders and small flies. Only experienced fly fishermen need apply. The rewards can be great, for there are grayling and many very large rainbows and browns here. Often, however, catching one or two small fish will make the angler feel triumphant. Occasionally, an elk or even a buffalo will join the angler at streamside, watching with what always seems a critical eye. Geysers, hot springs, and fumaroles next to the river create an atmosphere not found elsewhere. They also create hazards, and anglers should take care where they wade in the stream and where they walk on the bank.

In **Firehole Canyon,** anglers will find pocket water and deep swift runs. Here, streamers and nymphs work well, and although there are not as many large fish, it's good fishing. Avoid the swimming hole near the top of the canyon. Fishing success in all parts of the Firehole tends to drop off in July and August due to warm water temperatures. It resumes in the autumn.

Two tributaries enter the Firehole in the Bisquit Basin area, 14 miles from Madison Junction. **Iron Spring Creek** enters above the bridge, and the **Little Firehole River** enters below the bridge. Both offer good fishing for 9- to 11-inch rainbows, browns and brook trout. The Little Firehole is considered better, however. Iron Spring holds bigger fish during hot summer months, but it's difficult to fish. **West Fork,** a tributary of Iron Spring Creek, enters at Black Sand Geyser Basin. It's considered fair for smaller rainbows and browns. **Summit Lake,** in the back country southwest of Bisquit Basin, and **Mallard Lake,** east of Bisquit Basin, are barren.

North of Midway Geyser Basin, the Firehole leaves the main highway. Access is from Fountain Freight Road, which exits 5.5 miles south of Madison Junction. This road ends at **Goose Lake,** a small lake with rainbow to 14 inches. West of the lake, **Fairy Creek** parallels the road on its way to the Firehole below Ojo Caliente Spring. It's only about 5 feet wide, but holds some small rainbows and browns. **Sentinel Creek** enters a quarter-mile downstream from the west. A meandering meadow stream, 6 to 10 feet in width, it has fair fishing for small rainbows and browns.

The major tributary of the Firehole is **Nez Perce Creek** which enters near the Fountain Freight Road exit. A fairly shallow creek, 15 feet wide, it's rated poor for 9- to 11-inch rainbows, browns and brook trout. Three tributaries enter the Nez Perce starting about 5 miles in by trail. **Magpie, Spruce** and **Cowan Creeks** are fair for small trout. Above Cowan Creek confluence, the creek and its headwater lake, **Mary Lake,** are barren.

One seldom sees many fishermen on the Madison River, which runs for about 12 miles along the West Entrance Road and then 4 more miles into the Madison Valley before leaving the park. The absence of fishermen is due, in part, to the fly-fishing-only regulations. More than that, though, the fishing simply is difficult, especially for visiting anglers unfamiliar with the river. In nature, the Madison is much like the Firehole, only bigger. And like the Firehole, there are very good fish in the river. In a recent survey, a 13-inch average was reported for the Madison. However, only 52% of the anglers surveyed caught any fish (and most of them probably were local fishermen).

The stretch of river that angles across a corner of the Madison Valley is accessible from a dirt road north from the West Entrance Road about a mile from the entrance. Follow the road about a half-mile to the river. This area is known as the Barns, and it's a good place to try a large nymph or streamer. Bears are occasionally seen.

Two streams flow out of the Madison Valley into Hebgen Lake. **Cougar Creek** and **Duck Creek** are reached by driving about 8 miles north of West Yellowstone, Montana, on US 287. The turn east on a dirt road may or may not be marked. Watch for Highway Department buildings on the east side or backtrack from Duck Creek bridge to the dirt road east. Private homes are on the left as you drive in. Continue until you reach the posts marking the park boundary; follow the road to the right for Cougar Creek, left for Duck Creek. Rainbows, browns, cutthroats and brook trout are the most common species in both streams. Both are meadow streams averaging 15 feet in width.

Cougar Creek and its tributary, **Maple Creek** (located about three miles upstream), are fair for trout to 16 inches and contain many smaller fish. **Campanula, Gneiss,** and **Richards Creeks** converge about one mile in to form **Duck Creek.** Fishing in these streams is good but difficult for trout to 18 inches. Since many bears, including grizzlies, frequent the meadows of both creeks, caution is required. Moose also are seen here and are dangerous if surprised or approached too closely.

Stay on Hwy 191 north to reach **Grayling Creek,** the northernmost stream in the Madison drainage within the park. Don't be fooled by the name. The stream holds rainbows, cutthroats, browns and some whitefish. The highway follows the stream for several miles, then leaves it when the stream bends east. There is some good fishing off the road but, generally, the higher sections have smaller fish. A few miles past Grayling Creek, the highway passes Divide Lake and enters the Gallatin River Drainage.

GALLATIN RIVER

The Gallatin River drainage covers the extreme northwest corner of Yellowstone National Park. Highway 191 meets the Gallatin about 20 miles north of West Yellow-

Firehole River trout fishing is a Yellowstone National Park delight

stone, Montana. A few high country lakes and four tributaries make up the fishery. Most fishing is on the portions of the river next to the road.

The **Gallatin River** flows north alongside Hwy 191 for about 10 miles. Most fishing occurs in that stretch. From the road to its headwaters, **Gallatin Lake** (8900 ft) is another 10 miles of river that provide better fishing. The river is a typical mountain stream with varied water. The average size fish is about 12 inches. The river contains grayling, rainbows, browns, cutthroats, brook trout and some whitefish. Gallatin Lake is fair to good for small cutthroat.

Fan Creek, one of four tributaries, is about 2 miles downstream from where the highway meets the Gallatin. The fishing is slow in this small stream, but the fish—cutthroats—average 10-12 inches. All the back country streams in this area, but especially Fan Creek, flow through excellent grizzly bear habitat. Extreme caution is suggested. A good bear bell is as essential as a fly rod in this country.

Four miles downstream from Gallatin Lake, **Specimen Creek** enters the Gallatin River. It's rated fair for browns and cutthroats averaging 10 inches. Two miles in, the creek splits into the **North Fork** and the **East Fork,** both rated good for small cutthroat. There are high country lakes at the heads of each fork. **Shelf Lake** (9200 ft) is located on one branch of the North Fork, a long 8 miles in. It also can be reached by trail from Black Butte Creek, but that trail is difficult, even perilous in sections, and is not recommended just for the fair fishing for small cutthroats found in the lake. Another branch of the North Fork leads to **Crescent, Sedge** and **Crag Lakes,** about 7 miles in. These are all beautiful lakes, but their status as fisheries is unclear. Crescent may be barren, although it once held fish. The others may hold small cutthroats. At the head of the East Fork is **High Lake** (8774 ft), about 9 miles in. It provides fair fishing for small cutthroat. None of the lakes in the drainage can be recommended for their fishing alone. All are a long hike in, and the trails involve a significant elevation gain.

Black Butte Creek is the next tributary downstream from Specimen Creek. It's a small stream with 9- to 11-inch cutthroats and some browns. The same holds true for **Daly Creek,** which is the last tributary to enter the Gallatin before it leaves the park. Daly joins the river about 30 miles north of West Yellowstone.

YELLOWSTONE RIVER

The Yellowstone River drainage is the most extensive in the park. Beginning at the southeast corner of the park, near its headwaters, the river winds through the Thorofare Region, one of the most remote and scenic areas of Yellowstone, and empties into Yellowstone Lake, a main attraction for many fishermen. From Fishing Bridge at the lake's outlet, the river flows along the Grand Loop Road. There are few other angling attractions in this section, but the river itself is enough to excite any fisherman.

From that roadside run, the Yellowstone breaks free of civilization at Canyon, site of the spectacular Upper and Lower Falls, and runs north through some of the most rugged country in the park, the Grand Canyon of the Yellowstone. There are few tributaries here and little water close to any road. To reach the river, the angler must work, and work hard, for the canyon is deep and steep.

The Yellowstone briefly meets civilization again just east of Tower Junction. It then flows through the Black Canyon of the Yellowstone on its way to Gardiner, Montana, near the North Entrance to the park. A major tributary, the Lamar River, has its confluence in this section. The Lamar and its tributaries, Soda Butte Creek, Cache Creek and Slough Creek, drain the northeast section of the park and offer some fine fishing. There are many other noteworthy tributaries in this section of Yellowstone. Only a few are near roads.

From Gardiner, the Yellowstone flows west for a few miles on the northern boundary before it leaves the park. There are a few minor tributaries. The Gardner River is an extensive watershed with some good angling opportunities. It enters the Yellowstone just south of the North Entrance.

More than 50% of the fishing pressure in

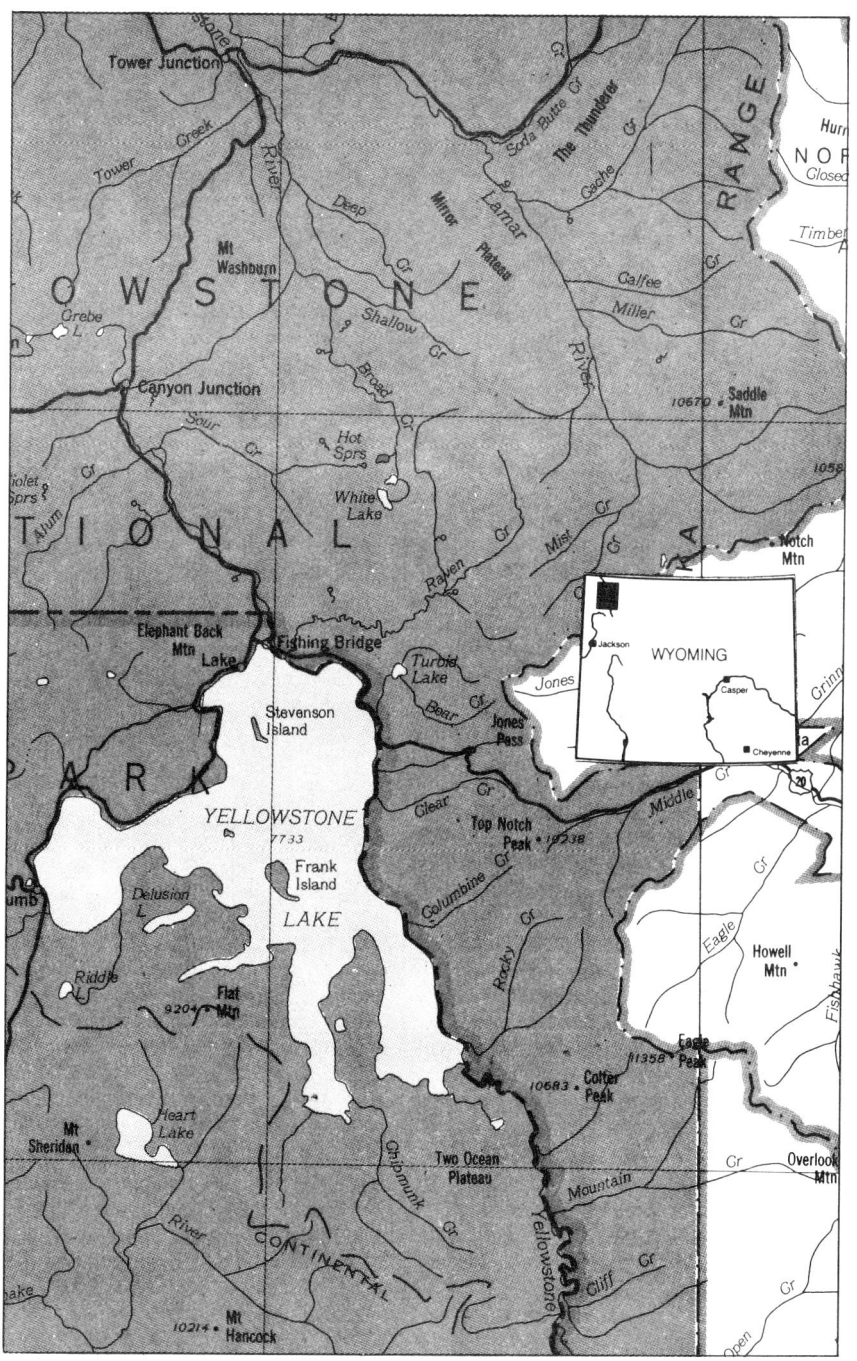

East side Yellowstone National Park

the park is concentrated in Yellowstone Lake and the few miles of roadside river below it. But this drainage also contains many streams that may go several seasons without seeing an angler. It is, indeed, a diversified and beautiful area in which to seek trout.

The most prominent body of water in the park is **Yellowstone Lake** (7733 ft). It's a large lake, covering about 150 square miles. The lake, its inlet streams, and the Yellowstone River downstream to the Upper Falls represent the largest pure-strain cutthroat fishery in the world. No other species of gamefish are found in this region. The lake has been under strict regulation for several years after it was determined that overfishing was causing the fishery to decline seriously. Check current regulations closely. The lake is not open to fishing until mid-June to protect spawning fish. Streams in the area are closed until mid-July. A 13-inch *maximum* length is in effect for fish creeled; consequently, fishing has improved to the place where it's often difficult to catch a keeper. Fish caught averaged 14.6 inches in 1980, but fish to 20 inches are taken (and returned to the water) routinely. Boating is allowed, but a permit is required and some areas of the lake are restricted. Many areas along the shore are wadable, and fly fishermen enjoy casting for cruising trout.

Beginning at Fishing Bridge (the lake's outlet and a once-famous fishing spot now closed to all angling), the road toward the East Entrance provides access to several streams as it follows the north shore of the lake. The road crosses **Pelican Creek** 1.4 miles from the bridge. This is a good spot to see moose, but a poor place to fish since the creek is closed for the first two miles. It's better to take the trail from near Squaw Lake, about 3 miles from the bridge. Pelican Creek always gets a high rating from fishermen, and the average size of the cutthroats taken in 1980 was 14 inches.

Two tributaries, **Raven Creek** and **Astringent Creek,** are good for small trout. **Squaw Lake,** across the road from the trailhead, has cutthroat to 15 inches. About 8 miles from the bridge, **Sedge Creek** enters Yellowstone Lake. It flows out of **Turbid Lake,** a thermal lake 2 miles in by trail. **Sedge Creek** above and below Turbid Lake and **Bear Creek,** another inlet to Turbid, contain small cutthroats.

Shortly after it crosses Sedge Creek, the road leaves the lake and begins to climb Sylvan Pass. About 13 miles from Fishing Bridge, the road crosses **Cub Creek,** a small stream holding 10-inch trout. About 3 miles farther, **Sylvan Lake** (8414 ft) lies just south of the road. It's under catch-and-release regulations to improve the 10-inch average size of trout found there. (On the other side of Sylvan Pass and out of the Yellowstone River drainage, **Middle Creek** flows alongside the highway as it nears the East Entrance. It contains small cutthroats.)

Cub Creek is the first of several streams that enter Yellowstone Lake on the east shore, south of the highway. Boating across the lake and hiking the Thorofare Trail (which heads at Lake Butte, 10 miles southeast from Fishing Bridge) provide access to these streams and to the headwaters of the Yellowstone River. The trail runs 32 miles to the south park boundary. At 1.5 miles from Lake Butte it crosses Cub Creek. At the 3-mile point, the trail crosses **Clear Creek,** a major stream for spawning cutthroats that flows from near Sylvan Lake. Clear Creek is excellent for 10- to 12-inch trout with some larger fish, especially early in the season. Remember that the streams and the lake shore within 100 yards of them are closed until mid-July. Check regulations for openings.

The next stream south is **Meadow Creek,** near Park Point. The inlet area can be good, especially early in the season. At 9 miles, the trail crosses **Columbine Creek,** which is good for small cutthroats. Along the southeast arm of Yellowstone, the trail reaches **Beaverdam Creek,** 17 miles in. Beaverdam is considered excellent for trout averaging 12 inches. **Rocky Creek,** a tributary 2 miles upstream, is good for 10-inch cutthroats.

At this point the Thorofare Trail heads in a southerly direction, climbing toward the headwaters of the Yellowstone River and into some of the most remote and wild areas in the park. The main river is excellent fishing, with trout averaging 14-16 inches. Many small streams enter the river along this valley. **Badger, Phlox,** and **Lynx Creeks** enter from the west. **Cabin, Trappers, Mountain** (and its tributary **Howell**), **Cliff** and **Escarpment Creeks** enter from the east side. All are good for small cutthroats. Thorofare Creek flows into the Yellowstone just inside the south boundary, 32 miles by trail from the East Entrance Road. It provides excellent fishing for trout to 16 inches.

The south shore of Yellowstone Lake from the Yellowstone River to Grant Village on the South Entrance Road provides limited fishing potential. **Trail Creek,** the outlet of **Trail Lake** (7748 ft), flows from the south into the bottom of the Southeast Arm. Both are good for 10- to 12-inch cutthroats. Access is by boat or by the Trail Creek Trail which begins near Cabin Creek, 20 miles in by Thorofare Trail. Obviously it's a remote area. Trail Creek is about 2 miles from **Cabin Creek.** Lake is 1 mile upstream of creek crossing. About 6 miles farther west is **Chipmunk Creek,** which flows into the South Arm. Fish here average 10-14 inches. **Passage Creek,** a tributary, has smaller fish. On the Promontory, the extension of land separating the Southeast Arm and the South Arm is **Alder Lake** (7752 ft), which has small cutthroats to 12 inches. Four more miles brings the angler to **Grouse Creek,** a small stream holding 8- to 10-inch trout. All the streams in this area are frequented by grizzlies, especially during cutthroat spawning when the bears help themselves to the fishing. Trail Creek Trail continues over the Continental Divide to Outlet Lake (see Snake River drainage) and down to the Heart Lake area.

Between the South Arm and West Thumb, Delusion Lake (7822 ft) holds small cutthroats. On the east shore of West Thumb, **Solution Creek** enters the lake. It provides very good fishing for cutthroats averaging 11 inches. **Riddle Lake,** the headwaters of Solution Creek, is fair for cutthroats averaging 14 inches. The lake and the upper reaches of the creek usually are reached by a 2.5-mile trail that heads at the east end of the Grant Campground area about 4 miles south of West Thumb Junction.

Only four small creeks enter the lake on the west shore between Grant Village and Fishing Bridge: **Big Thumb Creek,** just north of Grant Village; **Arnica Creek** 6 miles north of West Thumb Junction; **Weasel Creek** 2 miles south of Bridge Bay; and **Bridge Creek** just south of Bridge Bay. All offer fair to good fishing for small cutthroats.

More than 13,000 anglers fish the **Yellowstone River** annually, most of them concentrating on the 9 miles of river from Lake Junction to Canyon. Some sections are closed and posted. The remaining miles of the Yellowstone within the park are in rugged back country. Beginning at the outlet of Yellowstone Lake at Fishing Bridge, the river is large; much of it is also deep and swift. It's necessary to wade the river in order to fish it properly, and chest waders are best. Because of the depth and swiftness of the current and the loose bottom gravel in many parts, caution is required. Many anglers have been baptized challenging this river.

The section of stream from **Fishing Bridge** near Lake Junction to **Chittenden Bridge** near Canyon is catch-and-release and has a later opening (usually July 15) than lower sections to protect spawning cutthroats. The river is favored by fly fishermen. Stoneflies are effective early. Late season angling requires matching the caddis and mayfly hatches carefully. Later in the season, the fishing can be tough but the rewards are high. Fish average about 15 inches, and 20 inchers are taken regularly.

Buffalo Ford, 5 miles north of Lake Junction, is a popular spot and a good place to check what's happening on the river. About 4 miles of river, from **Sulphur Cauldron** to **Alum Creek,** is closed permanently to fishing, as is the first mile downstream from the lake.

Several tributaries enter the Yellowstone from Fishing Bridge to Canyon, but most of them are in the Hayden Valley, which is closed to fishing. These include **Alum,**

Trout and **Elk Antler Creeks** from the west, and **Sour** and **Cottongrass Creeks** from the east. All contain small cutthroats. **Wrangler Lake** is near Sour Creek. It contains small cutthroats. Check with rangers to see if it's open to fishing, since regulations are unclear. Just below LeHardy Rapids, 3 miles from Lake Junction, **Thistle Creek** enters from the east. It contains 9- to 11-inch trout, but since the Yellowstone cannot be crossed safely nearby, the creek can only be reached by walking down the Howard Eaton Trail from Fishing Bridge or by crossing the Yellowstone at Buffalo Ford and walking upstream. **Otter Creek** enters the Yellowstone River from the west about 12.5 miles north of Lake Junction. A shallow stream averaging 10-15 feet in width, it's poor to fair for small cutthroats. **Cascade Creek** meets the Yellowstone near the Lower Falls. It holds small cutthroats. Two

Grizzly bear

trails lead to **Cascade Lake,** which is good to excellent for cutthroats and grayling from 10 to 12 inches. One trail follows the creek to where it heads on the Canyon-Norris Road about a quarter-mile from Canyon. The other begins at the picnic area 1.25 miles north of Canyon. The trail continues on to Grebe and Wolf Lakes, which also have grayling (see Madison River section).

From Canyon to Tower Junction, the river runs through the precipitous Grand Canyon of the Yellowstone. There's great fishing, but you have to be part mountain goat to reach it. Few established trails travel near the canyon, and only one spur trail leads to the water 1200 feet below the canyon rim. That trail leads off the Howard Eaton Trail from near Canyon. Fishing is reputed to be excellent in the canyon, with cutthroat trout the predominant species. The other common access is where the road between Tower Junction and the Northeast Entrance crosses the river. The farther from the road, the better the fishing. Besides the tributaries entering the Yellowstone in this stretch, there are two small lakes. **Ribbon Lake,** reached by trail from Artist Point, is fair for small rainbows. At the other end, **Lost Lake** near Roosevelt Lodge at Tower, has small brook trout.

Broad Creek enters the Yellowstone from the east about halfway between Canyon and Tower. It and its tributary, **Shallow Creek,** hold 12-inch cutthroats and some rainbows. Access is from the Wapiti Lake Trail near Upper Falls or by the trail up Astringent Creek near Pelican Creek (see Yellowstone Lake section). Three lakes at the headwaters, **Fern, Tern** and **White** contain no fish. **Deep Creek** and its **Burnt Creek, Agate Creek** and **Quartz Creek** tributaries all enter from the east, downstream of **Broad Creek.** Each is good to excellent for cutthroats to 15 inches. No established trails service these streams directly, but they can be reached from along the river or from the Specimen Ridge Trail that begins near Tower Junction. **Antelope Creek,** the most accessible water in this area, flows along the roadside south of Tower Falls. Fishing is poor. **Tower Creek** and its tributary, **Carnelian Creek,** have brook and rainbow to 12 inches and are considered to have good fishing. A trail up the creek begins at Tower Falls, 3 miles south of Tower Junction.

The Yellowstone River from Tower to the North Entrance at Gardiner, Montana, flows through the back country in an area known as the Black Canyon of the Yellowstone. It's just as wild as the Grand Canyon area described above but less remote. Three major trails reach the river. The Yellowstone River Trail heads at Gardiner and follows the river along its north bank. Blacktail Trail begins along the Mammoth-Tower Road about 7 miles from Mammoth. Finally, Hellroaring Creek Trail begins just north of Floating Island Lake, 3.3 miles west of Tower Junction. There are bridges across the Yellowstone at the bottom of both trails.

For an angler familiar with map and compass, other routes are possible. Elevation differences between road and river are between 700 and 1,000 feet. The fishing (and the wildlife viewing) is excellent, especially during the stonefly hatch in early season. Cutthroats are the dominant trout, but rainbows, browns and brook trout can play a significant part in the angler's day on the river. The river in this section is big and wild, with lots of boulders and swift runs.

LAMAR RIVER

The **Lamar River** joins the Yellowstone two miles downstream from Tower. The Lamar River and its major tributaries, Cache Creek, Soda Butte Creek and Slough Creek, are excellent fisheries. They drain the northwest quarter of the park. The Lamar flows alongside the Northeast Entrance Road for about 7 miles, beginning about 3 miles above its confluence with the Yellowstone. Then it bends south for nearly 30 miles to its headwaters. Near the road from the confluence upstream to Cache Creek, catch-and-release regulations have been in effect. Fish in this stretch of the river average 12 inches, with larger fish taken. Upstream the fish get smaller, averaging 11 inches. Cutthroats and rainbows are the major species. The river can flow high well into July, so it's considered a better stream for later in the season.

The **Little Lamar River** is the first tributary to join the Lamar near its headwaters. Reached by the Lamar River Trail, it's about a 14-mile hike and holds small cutthroat. **Cold Creek** joins the Lamar from the south a few miles downstream. **Mist Creek** flows into Cold Creek. Both streams have small cutthroats to 10 inches. At the top of Mist Creek, the angler is only about eight miles from the East Entrance Road.

As the Lamar takes a northerly route, **Willow** and **Timothy Creeks** enter from the west. Both are fair for small cutthroats. At the 8.5-mile point on the trail, **Miller Creek** joins the Lamar. Like the other streams, it holds small cutthroats. A trail follows the creek to its headwaters at **Canoe Lake** near the park boundary. The lake is barren. Between Miller Creek and Cache Creek, **Calfle Creek** enters from the east and **Flint Creek** enters from the west. Both are small streams containing small cutthroats. The best tributary is probably **Cache Creek,** 3.3 miles in by trail. The Cache Creek Trail follows the stream for about 15 miles. Surveys consistently rank this stream high. It provides excellent fishing for cutthroats averaging 12 inches, with many larger fish reportedly taken. Two small streams, **Opal** and **Chalcedony Creeks,** enter the Lamar from the west before the river meets the Northeast Entrance Road. Both are considered fair for small cutthroats.

As the Northeast Entrance Road leaves the Lamar River, it follows **Soda Butte Creek** 14 miles to the park boundary. Soda Butte is very good for cutthroats averaging 11 inches and a few rainbows. Nine miles from the entrance, **Amphitheater Creek** enters Soda Butte Creek from the east. It provides good fishing for small cutthroats. Ten miles from the entrance, **Pebble Creek** flows into Soda Butte Creek. A trail upstream takes the angler into country of rugged beauty. The fishing's not bad either, with cutthroats and a few rainbow averaging 10 inches. An unmarked trail along the highway at about 12.7 miles from the entrance leads the angler a quarter-mile west to **Trout Lake** (7000 ft). It contains some large rainbows and a few cutthroats. The fishing is slow for these temperamental lunkers. Two smaller lakes nearby, **Shrimp** and **Buck,** offer marginal fishing for small rainbows.

Three minor tributaries of the Lamar River enter it between the confluences of Soda Butte Creek and Slough Creek. **Amethyst, Jasper,** and **Crystal Creeks** all are small streams holding small cutthroats. **Slough Creek** is the last major tributary entering the Lamar before it joins the Yellowstone. A dirt road leaves the highway heading north about 6 miles east from Tower Junction; it goes 2 miles to a campground. A trail follows an old wagon road 11 miles up Slough Creek to the north boundary. Slough Creek is a meandering meadow stream with slow-moving, difficult to assess currents. The valley through which it runs is one of the most beautiful in the park. Wildflowers and wildlife can be as much a part of a fishing trip here as are the cutthroats and rainbows in the stream. Catches average 13 inches, but trout of 20 inches are taken from Slough Creek by experienced anglers. **Buffalo Creek,** a small tributary, enters from the north near the campground. It contains small cutthroats.

McBride Lake is located about 3 miles up the valley. Praised for its back-country beauty, the lake also provides very good fishing for cutthroats to 14 inches. Eight miles in, **Elk Tongue Creek** joins Slough Creek. It's good for small cutthroats. Finally, 11 miles up the valley and very near the north boundary is **Cutoff Creek,** which is good for small cutthroats. All the waters in the Slough Creek drainage, including McBride Lake, are catch-and-release.

About 4 miles downstream from Tower, the first of several tributaries enters this section of Yellowstone River. **Little Buffalo Creek** flows into the river from the north. Access to this small stream, rated good for small cutthroats, is from Hellroaring Creek Trail described previously. The Mammoth-Tower Road crosses **Lost Creek** just outside of Tower Junction and **Elk Creek** about 2 miles farther west. Both are poor to fair for small brook trout. Like the other tributaries, better fishing is found closer to the Yellowstone. **Hellroaring Creek,** entering from the north, provides excellent fishing for 12-inch cutthroats and rainbows. Hellroaring Creek Trail crosses the Yellowstone and meets the creek about 1 mile to the west. **Coyote Creek,** a tributary of Hellroaring Creek, is good for 9- to 11-inch cutthroats and rainbows. About 2 miles down the Yellowstone are **Little Cottonwood Creek** and **Cottonwood Creek.** Both have cutthroats and rainbows to 14 inches. Little Cottonwood is considered the better of the two. Both are accessible from the Yellowstone River Trail on the north side of the river.

Oxbow Creek, a small stream holding 9- to 11-inch brook trout, leaves the highway from **Phantom Lake.** As with other streams, it's better in the lower reaches.

> *Allow ample time to drive in the park. Besides heavy traffic, many miles of road are narrow and in poor condition. Reduced speeds result. Numerous road projects often delay traffic. Keep drinking water handy to prevent heat exhaustion and dehydration.*

Blacktail Deer Creek, a major tributary located about 7 miles southeast of Mammoth, provides excellent fishing for brook trout averaging 10 inches. A trail at the highway follows the creek north to the river. Blacktail Ponds, north of the highway near the creek, have beaver pond fishing for 10-inch brook trout and a few cutthroats. **Crevice Creek** enters the Yellowstone from the north about 1 mile downstream from where Blacktail Creek meets the river. It's fair for small cutthroats and rainbows.

The Yellowstone River from Gardiner, Montana, downstream to the northwest forms part of the park's northern boundary. The river here is much like the section immediately upstream from Gardiner and, like that section, receives a lot of fishing pressure and is not rated as good by fishermen as other sections within the park. Browns, rainbows, cutthroats, and brook trout all are available.

The highway from Gardiner gives access to the north bank, and a dirt road follows the south bank. Three small tributaries join the Yellowstone in this section. **Landslide, Stephens, Reese Creek** and **Cache Lake** at the headwaters of Reese Creek have few, if any, fish.

Mol Heron Creek is farther west. It joins the Yellowstone outside the park. At its head is **Sportsman Lake** (8300 ft). The creek has small cutthroats; the lake provides excellent fishing for cutthroats to 12 inches. Access is difficult. The strenuous Sportsman Lake Trail leads to the lake. Another trail follows Mol Heron Creek 8 miles to the lake; it heads in the Gallatin National Forest outside the park.

GARDNER RIVER

The most prominent tributary in this region is the Gardner River which meets the Yellowstone at Gardiner, Montana. The river heads near Electric Peak, west of Mammoth. It meanders south through back country until it meets the Mammoth-Norris Road at the Indian Creek Campground, 8.5 miles south of Mammoth. It then flows northeast around Bunsen Peak and drops over Osprey Falls, east of the peak. The Mammoth-Tower Road crosses the Gardner downstream, and the highway between Mammoth and the North Entrance follows it for several miles. Access to the upper part is by any one of several trails, although no trail follows it directly. The rest is reached by short hikes from the highways or from the Bunsen Peak Road, a one-way dirt road leaving the Mammoth-Norris Road near the Golden Gate, 4.7 miles south of Mammoth. The river is divided into two sections by Osprey Falls.

Downstream the Gardner contains that mixture of species common to the Yellowstone in its lower reaches: browns, rainbows, cutthroats and brook trout. Some larger trout are available. Above the falls, the river is primarily a brook trout fishery. It provides better fishing in terms of the numbers caught, but the fish are smaller.

One access to the upper Gardner is the Fawn Pass Trail. It leaves from near Mammoth Hot Springs and reaches the river in about 5 miles. About a half-mile past the river, the trail meets **Fawn Creek**, a tributary rated fair for small brook trout. The trail follows the creek to Fawn Pass, an area known for its grizzlies. Another similarly rated tributary, **Panther Creek,** enters about a half-mile north of the Indian Creek campground. The Big Horn Pass Trail follows it upstream. Fishing is fair for small brook. There are no fish in the unnamed lakes seen near the pass, but there may be grizzlies around them, so be cautious. **Indian Creek** enters the Gardner River near the campground, 8.5 miles south of Mammoth.

For an extra-tasty fish fillet, brush it with Italian dressing before broiling.

It has good fishing for small brook trout if you get away from the campground. South from the campground, the highway follows **Obsidian Creek.** There's good fishing for small brook trout in the next few miles of meadow. Moose are often seen among the willows here. Hooking one is the experience of a lifetime, especially if done on the backcast. Above the confluence of Winter and Straight Creeks, about 11 miles south of Mammoth, Obsidian Creek becomes too small for good fishing. Both **Winter** and **Straight Creeks** are good to excellent for 8- to 10-inch brook trout. A trail follows Winter Creek for about a mile and a half. At that point, Winter Creek winds away to the west and another trail follows Straight Creek south to **Grizzly Lake** (7058 ft), a mile and a half farther. A new trail leaves the highway about 1 mile south of Beaver Lake and goes more directly to Grizzly Lake. The lake is considered excellent for brook trout that average nine inches.

Two tributaries of the Gardner have their confluence below Osprey Falls. **Glen Creek** joins the river north of Bunsen Peak. It's fair for small brook trout. The Sportsman Lake Trail from Mammoth Hot Springs reaches the upper section of Glen Creek, and the Mammoth-Norris Road crosses it near Rustic Falls, 4.7 miles south of Mammoth. **Lava Creek** joins the Gardner downstream from where the Mammoth-Tower Road crosses the river. The highway follows the creek for a few miles before the creek bends south into the back country. In its lower sections, Lava Creek provides the angler with an opportunity to catch several species including browns, rainbows and brook trout. The back country stretches primarily have brook trout. **Lupine Creek** meets Lava Creek immediately after it leaves the highway. A second tributary, **Arrow Canyon Creek,** enters far upstream near the creek's headwaters. Both are good for small brook trout.

Two other fishing opportunities are present in the Gardner River drainage before the river's confluence with the Yellowstone. **Slide Lake** and the **Mammoth Beaver Ponds** (so named for their proximity to Mammoth rather than their size) are west of the highway between Mammoth and the North Entrance. Both are reached by trails from the old dirt road between Mammoth and Gardiner, Montana, or by bushwhacking from the highway. They contain a few rainbows, some of them large, but fishing is considered only poor to fair.

The use of topographic maps is recommended in hiking and fishing in Yellowstone Park. □ —Scott Roederer

> *The free permit necessary to fish in the park is available at all ranger stations, entrance stations, visitor centers, Hamilton Stores and most fishing tackle shops adjacent to the park. Anglers should be sure to obtain a copy of the current regulations.*

FISHING MAJOR STREAMS AND LAKES IN YELLOWSTONE NATIONAL PARK

STREAM OR LAKE	SPECIE OF FISH						BEST TIME OF YEAR											
	C	R	B	EB	G	M	J	F	M	A	M	J	J	A	S	O	N	D
Yellowstone River above Canyon	●												●	●				
Canyon to Gardiner	●	●	●										●	●	●	●		
Pelican Creek	●												●	●				
Lamar River	●	●											●	●	●			
Slough Creek	●	●											●	●				
Soda Butte Creek	●	●											●	●				
Gardner River	●	●	●	●									●	●	●	●		
Madison River in Park		●	●		●							●			●	●		
Gibbon River		●	●									●	●		●	●		
Firehole River		●	●	●	●							●	●		●	●		
Snake River		●	●															
South Snake in Park	●	●											●	●	●			
Gallatin River in Park	●	●			●								●	●	●	●		
Yellowstone Lake	●											●	●		●			
Trout Lake	●	●											●	●		●		
Blacktail Lakes				●									●			●	●	
Shoshone Lake			●	●		●							●			●	●	
Lewis Lake			●	●		●							●			●	●	
Heart Lake	●		●			●							●	●		●	●	
Grebe Lake			●		●								●	●	●	●	●	

Key
C—Native Cutthroat Trout
R—Rainbow Trout
B—Brown Trout (Loch Leven)
EB—Eastern Brook Trout
G—Montana Grayling
M—Mackinaw or Lake Trout

Chart courtesy of Parks' Fly Shop, Gardiner, Montana.

FOR BACK COUNTRY FISHERMEN BEAR FACTS

Bears may be encountered along trails, streams or lakeshores. Make enough noise while hiking so bears can hear and avoid you. That means talking, singing, jangling equipment, whistling.

To keep from attracting bears, dispose of fish entrails in the back country by puncturing the air bladder and dropping fish guts in a deep hole in the lake or stream. Dispose of suckers and other unwanted fish in the stream.

Avoid bears if they are seen. If charged by a bear, climb a tree. If caught by a bear, play dead. Even Olympic sprinters can't outrun a bear, so don't try. It will only excite it if you do, and the results would be unbearable.

Yellowstone Park campgrounds

Yellowstone Park campgrounds are actually small communities. Some have several thousand campers nightly in mid-season. The park campground maps are helpful in finding your site again, once you've become established and left to return later, particularly after dark.

YELLOWSTONE RIVER DRAINAGE
YELLOWSTONE NATIONAL PARK

Campground name	No. camp sites	Water and toilet	Showers	Length of stay (days)	Location
Bridge Bay	438	Yes	Yes	14	3 mi SW of Lake Junction
Canyon	280	Yes	Yes	14	¼ mi E of Canyon Junction
Fishing Bridge	308	Yes	Yes	14	1 mi E of Lake Junction
Grant Village	438	Yes	Yes	14	2 mi S of West Thumb Junction
Indian Creek	78	Yes	No	14	7 mi S of Mammoth
Lewis Lake	100	Yes	No	14	10 mi S of West Thumb
Madison	292	Yes	No	14	¼ mi W of Madison Junction
Norris	116	Yes	No	14	1 mi N of Norris Junction
Pebble Creek	36	Yes	No	14	7 mi SW of Northeast Entrance
Slough Creek	30	Yes	No	14	10 mi E of Tower Falls Junction
Tower Falls	37	Yes	No	14	3 mi E of Tower Junction

Snake River— big water; big fish

ADJACENT COMMUNITIES:
Moran Junction, Wilson, Jackson, Hoback Junction, Alpine Junction.

PRINCIPAL HIGHWAYS:
U.S. 287, 89, 26, 191; Wyo. 390, 22.

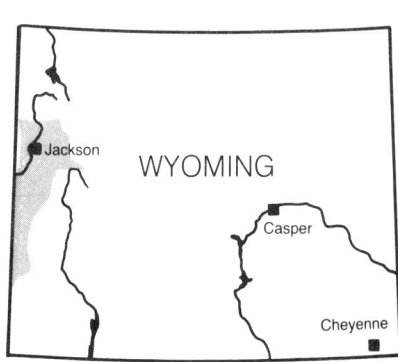

Flowing from its headwaters in Yellowstone National Park past the resort town of Jackson and west to the Palisades Reservoir, the **Snake River** is one of the most popular fishing rivers in the country. Heavy fishing pressure has reduced the number of trophy-sized fish, but the river clears and comes to life every year after the traditionally heavy spring runoff is over.

The river is too fast and deep to wade, and surrounded by private land in several sections, so fishermen often float it, using Jackson-area guides. Excellent fly fishing starts in April and early May, with time out for the runoff and occasional fluctuations in releases from Jackson Lake Dam. Humpys and Hoppers are two favorite dry flies. The catch is likely to be cutthroat trout, though whitefish are also plentiful, and there are some brown and a few brook trout in the river.

Not only sportsmen, but also fishery biologists, admire this river. It is one of the few Wyoming fisheries where the state's one indigenous fish—the cutthroat (native) trout—thrives with little assistance from man, despite the heavy pressure. Snake River cutthroat range up to 20 inches, though a 12-inch fish is more common.

The river passes through Jackson Lake, in Grand Teton National Park. Below the lake, you have to watch conditions carefully, waiting for clear water and insect hatches. Besides the heavy spring runoff, there are fluctuations in Jackson Lake Dam releases, where the Bureau of Reclamation controls the spigot.

The Snake River drainage is one of the chief elements in Wyoming's biggest regional tourist attraction, the area that includes Yellowstone and Grand Teton national parks and the town of Jackson. There are camping facilities and numerous motels in and near the parks, and in the Bridger-Teton National Forest. Guides and outfitters offer horsepacking into the wilderness back country and float trips on the Snake.

HEADWATERS

Snake River headwaters lie in the Teton Wilderness and Yellowstone National Park. The river's major downstream tributaries are the Gros Ventre, the Hoback, the Greys, and Salt rivers.

The Snake and its tributaries from Hoback Junction upstream are closed to fishing from November 1 through May 20.

Some tributaries, including **Cottonwood Creek** and **Flat Creek,** are closed even longer. Check current regulations.

Three streams on the Yellowstone-Teton Wilderness border in the Absaroka Range north of Jackson form the Snake's starting point. They are **Fox** and **Plateau Creeks** and the Snake itself. Pack trails from the west and south require a trip of 20 miles or more. Among the trails into this area are the Snake River Trail, the South Boundary Trail, and cutoffs from the Atlantic-Pacific Trail. The headwater drainages have good fishing for cutthroat trout to 15 inches.

For 2 miles from the Yellowstone Park border, south to the Flagg Ranch, US 287 parallels the river. This section of the river is, for the most part, within Grand Teton National Park. The park requires a Wyoming fishing license and prohibits fishing with real or artificial fish eggs. Park regulations on fishing may vary. Check with the Wyoming Game & Fish office in Jackson or park officials to be sure.

Polecat Creek enters the Snake about 1 mile west of Flagg Ranch. A dirt road crosses

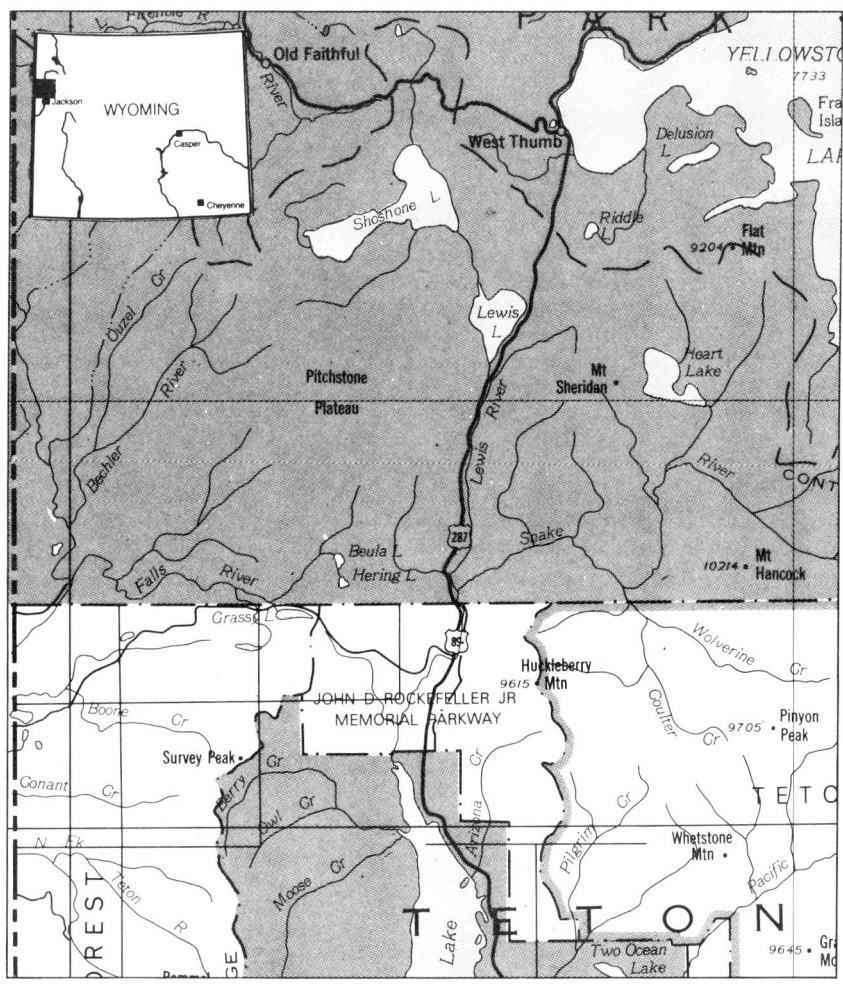

Southwest Yellowstone Park and Upper Snake River

the creek from the ranch. Hike 2 miles upcreek for a 10-foot-wide stream that offers fair fishing for 12-inch cutthroat and brown. About a mile down this trail, turn left and travel 4 miles to **Glade Creek,** which has small brook and some cutthroat. **Grassy Lake** (7,200 ft; 346 ac), a reservoir 9 miles from the ranch, has cutthroat, some rainbow, and mackinaw from 13 to 16 inches. Fishing for mackinaw is best along the north shore early in the summer when the ice first breaks.

Two miles beyond Grassy is **Lake of the Woods** (7,300 ft; 245 ac), with fair fishing for rainbow averaging 10 inches.

JACKSON LAKE

Jackson Lake (6,770 ft; 17,800 to 25,730 ac) produced a record-setting 44-pound mackinaw in 1967. The possibility of trophy fish attracts thousands of anglers.

The dam at the southeast end of the lake was built by the Bureau of Reclamation to provide irrigation water for Wyoming and Idaho. In addition to mackinaw, Jackson Lake has cutthroat, brown trout and mountain whitefish. Ten-pound macks are not as common as they once were, but fishermen armed with lead core and steel lines and with ocean-scale trolling rigs ply the deeper water of the lake and sustain its reputation by pulling in an occasional 20- to 30-pound fish. Bank fishermen have good luck right after the ice breaks in the spring.

WYOMING STATE PARKS

Overnight camping permits are required in Wyoming State Parks. The fee has been $2 per night. Annual permits costing $10 permit up to 14 days camping at any one time in any park. Overnight permits are available at campsite entrances. Annual permits are available from concessionaires, park headquarters or Wyoming State Recreation Commission, 1920 Thomas Ave, Cheyenne, WY 82002.

Jackson Lake will be a different place for the rest of the 1980s. The lake is lowered to a third of its maximum capacity to allow repairs on the dam. This means the fish will redistribute themselves and may not be where they used to predominate. They'll have less room and for a while at least anglers' success rates should be higher. And it certainly won't be as beautiful with its shores laid bare.

Fishing below the dam should not change much, unless the demands of Idaho irrigators strain the lake's lowered capacity. Bank fishermen find great casting just below the dam, but construction may interfere there, too.

Expect flies and lures on the river only from 500 yards below Jackson Lake dam to the bridge at Moose with 11- to 15-inch trout being released unharmed. The limit has gone from 2 to 6 fish, with only one keeper over 15 inches allowed. There's a 2-cutthroat limit within Teton National Park.

Campgrounds, fine lodgings and boat rentals are available by the lake; boat launch facilities are at Colter Bay, Leeks Marina and Signal Mountain, all located on the east side of the lake. Catches here, and on Jenny and Leigh lakes, are limited to 6 fish per day and only 1 trout 24 inches or longer. To get to the lake, take US 287-89 north from Moran Junction; exits are well-marked. Jackson Lake is closed to fishing from October 1 to October 31.

Just to the south lie **Leigh Lake, String Lake** and **Jenny Lake,** draining south into Cottonwood Creek, which later joins the Snake. Jenny Lake (6,780 ft; 1,200 ac) has the Tetons for a backdrop, a fine lodge, cutthroat 12 to 16 inches, and mackinaw averaging 18 inches. Brook trout are marginal in this lake, and rainbow-cutthroat hybrid make rare appearances. Take the Teton Park road south from Jackson Lake to reach Jenny.

You can canoe up this little chain of lakes—from Jenny to String Lake to Leigh Lake—with a short but steep portage to Leigh. Leigh Lake (6,870 ft; 1,200 ac) has a fish population similar to Jenny, but takes hiking a mile from the trail head or a canoe

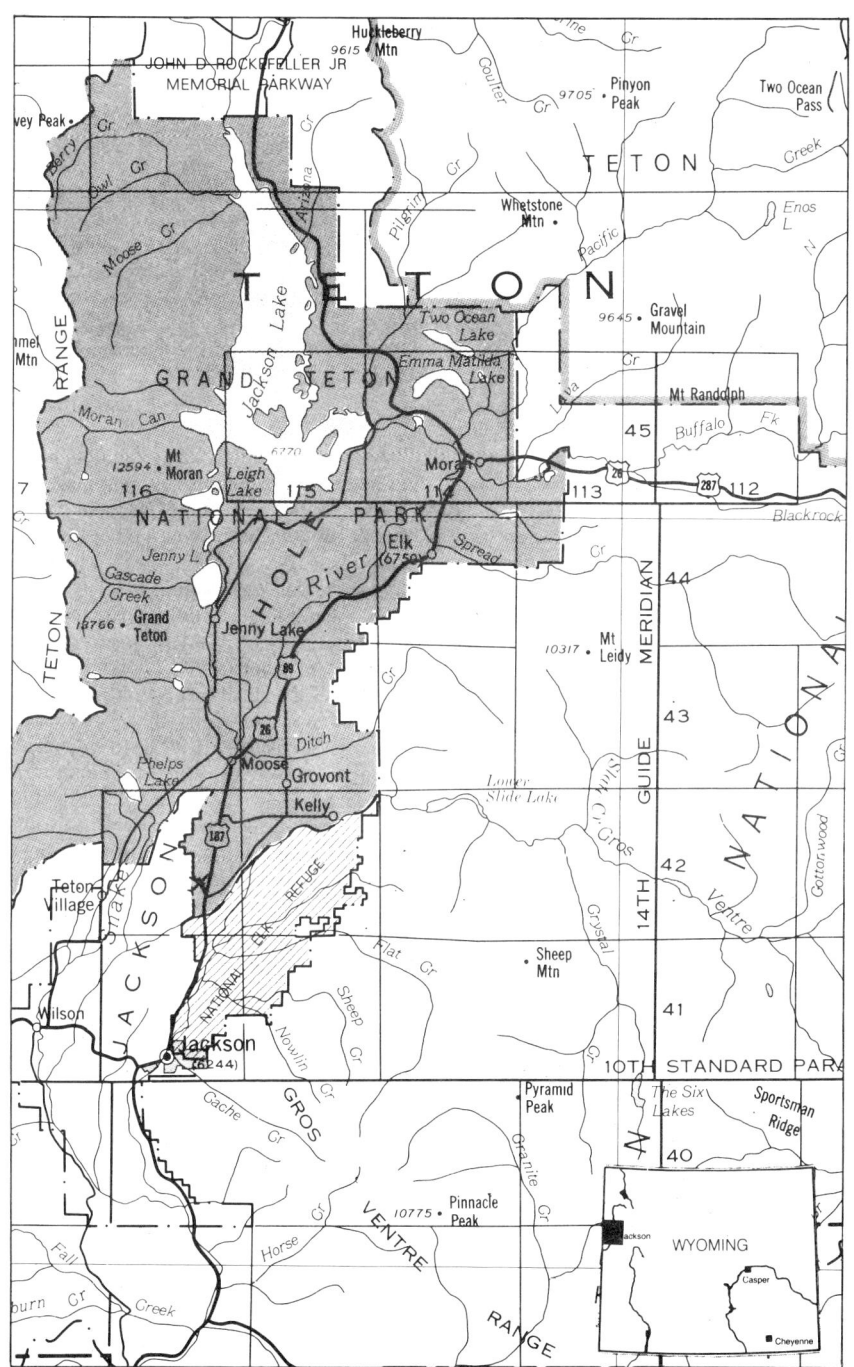

Snake River, Grand Teton National Park

> *The transition zone between the warmer top layer and the cooler bottom layer of water in a lake is called the thermocline.*

to get there. Motors up to 7.5 horsepower are allowed on Jenny Lake, but no motorcraft are allowed on String or Leigh lakes. Leigh and Jenny Lakes are open to fishing the year around.

The high alpine lakes in the park west of these big lakes are mostly sterile—the ice stays on them much of the year and there is little food. Park policy is to let nature take its course, and since reproduction and growth is limited by the high, cold waters many of the stocked fish of the 1950s have died out. There is not much fishing pressure on those lakes that still have cutthroat populations. The best among them are **Lake Solitude, Holly Lake** and **Surprise Lake,** reachable from the trailhead between Leigh and Jenny lakes.

The Jenny Lake outlet, **Cottonwood Creek,** runs through parklands and private lands south, 7 miles to the Snake. It holds cutthroat to 12 inches with an average stream width of 12 feet.

Two miles west of Cottonwood Creek via marked trails are **Bradley Lake** (7,000 ft; 60 ac) and **Taggart Lake** (6,900 ft; 115 ac) with fair fishing for small cutthroat.

Arizona Creek enters Jackson Lake on the east side of the drainage, flowing into the park from Teton National Forest. It is fair for cutthroat and brook trout. It is marked by a sign on US 287. A trail following the stream also skirts **Bailey Creek** where there are small cutthroat. **Pilgrim Creek** enters the lake farther south; it has small cutthroat in its lower section. The fishing is better higher up, by the trail.

One mile west of Moran Junction a marked road travels north 3 miles to the south end of **Two Ocean Lake** (6,900 ft; 580 ac), where there's fair fishing for 10- to 12-inch cutthroat. You can also reach **Emma Matilda Lake** (6,870 ft; 890 ac), but the cutthroat population in this lake has given way to the Utah chub. No motors are allowed and no boat rental is available at either lake.

A few miles below Jackson Lake, **Pacific Creek** enters the Snake just west of Moran Junction. A marked dirt road from US 287 follows the creek 7 miles; a trail goes on from there. The 4 miles of stream within the park can be fished only with flies or lures. About 6 miles up the Pacific Creek Trail you can take the Enos Creek cutoff east to Enos Lake. **Enos Lake** (7,750 ft; 170 ac) has cutthroat trout, but shoals make shore fishing difficult; waders are recommended. The cutthroat here have been crowded in recent years by a growing population of chub.

Gravel Creek flows into Pacific 4 miles from the Pacific trailhead. You can take the Gravel Creek trail north to fish for cutthroat averaging 11 inches. About 4 miles from the trail fork is 20-acre **Gravel Lake,** which has plentiful small cutthroat.

The guides and wildlife experts who travel in the Teton Wilderness along these Snake River tributaries are concerned about overuse of the small and fragile streams in this area, and they argue strongly for catch and release fishing. This is rugged back country, but it gets a lot of summer pressure. Amid the lush meadows and snow covered rockfaces above the North Buffalo Fork falls, you may encounter dozens of horsepackers and hikers, only a few of whom may fish.

Buffalo Fork Creek empties into the Snake at Moran Junction after a sinuous journey west from headwaters near the Continental Divide in the Absaroka Mountains. The lower 9 miles of the river, from the Snake to Turpin Meadows, is the Teton Wilderness; fishing waters are reached by foot or horseback. To get to the river's lower reaches, turn off US 287 north on the marked Buffalo Valley Ranch Road 3 miles east of Moran Junction, or turn north to Turpin Meadows at the Fourmile Meadow picnic area, halfway between Togwotee Lodge and the Blackrock Ranger Station.

At Turpin Meadows, the south and north branches of the Buffalo Fork join. Trails follow both forks. The south is the larger, a favorite of outfitters, but heavy runoff in recent years and channel changing has taken its larger fish. Brook and cutthroat are likely to average under 10 inches, though some are larger. Above South Fork Falls, about a 11-mile hike, there are some rainbow.

Two Ocean-North Buffalo Fork trail heads north from the Turpin Meadows trailhead. **North Buffalo Fork** has some 8- to 10-inch brook and small cutthroat. **Soda Fork Creek** enters North Buffalo Fork from the east about 4 miles from the trailhead. Game & Fish biologist Ralph Huddleston notes there are a great many whitefish in this stream, as well as cutthroat. The big meadows through which these streams flow often get nearly fished out in the fall; the steep canyons, more difficult to reach, do not.

Crater Lake (9,300 ft; 240 ac) lies at the head of the Soda Fork drainage and has nice cutthroat up to 12 inches.

The South Buffalo Fork trail follows the creek for 15 miles. The fork has cutthroat averaging 10 inches and a few brook. There are also some rainbow in the upper reaches. About 8 miles upstream is the confluence with **Cub Creek,** which has brook and cutthroat for the first 2 miles and strictly brook (up to 10 inches) above the junction with Trail Creek.

Farther up the drainage, go north up the steep Lake Creek drainage to **Ferry Lake** (9,900 ft; 45 ac) which has average fishing for 10-inch cutthroat. A south fork in the trail will take you to the 5 **Angle Lakes** (8,500 ft; 2-4 ac) which have cutthroat averaging 12 inches, and some rainbow—particularly in Rainbow Lake.

The better known Angle Lakes—**Rainbow, Johnson** and **Mackinaw**—are reached by trail from Turpin Meadows to the west or Brooks Lake to the south and are heavily fished. Fishermen who leave the mail trail to try the smaller, lesser known lakes in the area will find an abundance of brook and cutthroat, though they tend to be small.

Blackrock Creek flows into the Buffalo Fork near the Blackrock Ranger Station after running next to US 287 from very near the top of Togwotee Pass. It has cutthroat to 10 inches in the beaver ponds near Togwotee Lodge.

Spread Creek enters the snake from the east 3 miles south of Moran Junction after crossing under US 187-26-89. A dirt road south from the Hatchet Campground (right across from Blackrock Ranger Station) off US 287 travels 6 miles to the upper part of the creek. A trail leads from here up the North Fork, which has 10-inch cutthroat; the road farther along the south fork has the same kind of fishing. A 4-wheel-drive road continues from the end of this road for 4 miles to **Leidy Lake** (8,700 ft; 8 ac), for small cutthroat.

Returning to the west side of the Snake River, **Phelps Lake** (6,600 ft; 450 ac) is located off the Moose-Wilson Road about 4 miles south of Moose. There is a road access on private land; the public must hike 1 mile on a marked trail to fish for brook and cutthroat (averaging 14 inches) and some mackinaw. Motors are allowed but there is no boat rental.

GROS VENTRE RIVER

The **Gros Ventre River** enters the Snake about 9 miles north of Jackson, crossing under US 187-26-89 from the east. A paved road follows the river to **Slide Lake;** there are good gravel roads for another 35 miles, and trails beyond that. This river has cutthroat averaging 12 inches. **Lower Slide Lake** (6,900 ft; 1,300 ac), which was formed by a landslide across Gros Ventre Canyon, is 12 miles by good road from the highway. It has cutthroat averaging 12 inches and some mackinaw. Motors are allowed, and there are launching facilities,

---

HITCHING RAIL

Fishing Tackle
Bait
Licenses
Fishing Float Trips
Sporting Goods

**(307) 883-2302
Thayne, WY**

Small streams can be excellent fisheries

but there are no boats for rent. Two campgrounds are located within 3 miles upstream of the lake. **Crystal Creek** enters the Gros Ventre River 4 miles above the lake; a road follows the creek for 2 miles and then there is a trail. It has small cutthroat and whitefish. Just above the Crystal Creek Campground, **Slate Creek** enters the Gros Ventre from the north, offering small cutthroat. Another 3 miles up the river road is **Upper Slide Lake.** It has cutthroat. **Cottonwood** and **Fish Creeks** enter the river from the north about 4 miles above Upper Slide Lake. Some 4-wheel drive trails provide access to fish for cutthroat averaging 10 inches.

At the headwaters of the south fork of Fish Creek are the many **Fish Creek Lakes** (above 9,000 ft; 20-90 ac) with good fishing for cutthroat and brook averaging 10 inches. The best way to get there is to take the good gravel road from the west side of the Continental Divide—take the turnoff from US 287 on the west side of Togwotee Pass. There are 4-wheel-drive roads and horse trails from the east side.

From the Grand Teton Park downstream to the South Park Elk Feed Ground, the Snake River is about 150-175 feet wide, much of it flowing through private land. There is a lot of floating and fishing pressure on this river, yet guides say the fishing remains good and exciting. Limited public access is available along the flood control dikes at the US 22 bridge east of Wilson.

A second **Fish Creek,** which joins the Snake 4 miles south of Wilson, offers 6 miles of fishing water north and south of Wilson, but these are private lands and permission to fish is required. The stream has cutthroat (averaging 12 inches) and some brook.

Flat Creek flows through the town of Jackson and enters the Snake 8 miles to the south. In its journey through the National Elk Refuge, north of Jackson, only fly fishing is allowed above Crawford Bridge.

The lower part of the stream in the South Park Elk Feeding Ground off US 187 is open to the public; the rest requires access permission from private landowners. It has cutthroat about 10 inches and small brook.

The Jackson Hole Chapter of Trout Unlimited raised about $20,000 for stream improvement within the refuge. Some 83 boulders and structures will be placed during the next three or four years, usually in the autumn when stream flows are down.

Above the National Elk Refuge, the creek is open to the public and accessible for 3 miles with a 4-wheel-drive vehicle. A trail continues up the drainage. This stream is good for cutthroat up to 12 inches and small brook. Vehicle traffic stops at the entrance to a private ranch, which adjoins **Flat Creek Lake.** You can hike 1.5 miles around the ranch to the lake (7,460 ft; 100 ac), which has cutthroat averaging 11 inches and small brook.

From the South Park feeding ground to Palisades Reservoir, the Snake is on National Forest lands and open to the public. Check for any special regulations.

The **Hoback River** flows from the south into the Snake 14 miles below Jackson. It drains the west side of the Gros Ventre Mountains. US 187 runs alongside the river for 30 miles south from Hoback Junction. It has long riffles and deep pools with fair to good cutthroat averaging 10 inches. There are two campgrounds off the road upriver from the Snake, 7 and 12 miles from Hoback Junction. **Granite Creek,** the largest tributary, is 12 miles above Hoback Junction. A good gravel road runs 9 miles along the stream to a campground and hot spring-fed swimming pool. The stream is heavily fished and has only fair cutthroat to about 10 inches. **Turquoise Lake** (9,500 ft; 12 ac) is 10 miles beyond the Granite Creek campground by trail. It has cutthroat to 12 inches.

Farther upriver, **Cliff, Dell, Jack** and **Fisherman Creeks** are marked at the highway and have dirt roads that follow them. They have small cutthroat trout, but fishing is only fair.

Fall Creek enters the Snake less than a mile below Hoback Junction from the west. Ranging in width from 15 to 20 feet, it offers 6 miles of fishing for small cutthroat. You can reach it by dirt road from Wilson south or go north on a road that leaves the highway one mile below Astoria Hot Springs. There is some posted land, so be sure to inquire if you think you are on private land.

GREYS, SALT RIVERS

The **Greys River** splits the Wyoming Mountain Range from the Salt River Range and empties into the Palisades Reservoir near Alpine Junction on US 26-89. A gravel road follows the river for its full 55 miles. The stream can be waded above the juncture with the **Little Greys River,** 9 miles from the Palisades. The stream has 10- to 16-inch cutthroat and is especially good for fly

---

ALPINE SPORTS CENTER
on Palisades Reservoir
"Ask us about fishing conditions"
- Fishing Tackle & Bait
- Fishing & Hunting Licenses
- Camping Equipment
- Guns & Ammunition
- Buy, Sale & Trade

on Hwy 26 North of Junction of Hwy 26 & Hwy 89
Alpine WY   (307) 654-7788

---

fishing. Wyoming Game & Fish biologists say it is delicate and should not be fished too heavily. Catch and release fishing is encouraged.

The **Salt River** meanders through the rich bottomlands of the Star Valley and joins the Snake drainage at the Palisades Reservoir, which it enters from the south. US 89 runs along this stream from the reservoir to the south end of the Star Valley, which has been called the "Little Switzerland" of Wyoming for its mountainous beauty and dairy industry.

These two rivers in extreme western Wyoming have been getting heavy fishing pressure, and the confluence of the two, before they join the Snake, can be fabulous angling for brown and cutthroat according to Hal Taylor at the Three Rivers Motel in Alpine. In the autumn, it's particularly beautiful, and because many anglers have swapped their fishing gear for hunting outfits the fishing pressure is down.

The browns and cutthroat are getting larger and more numerous in the Salt River. There is a lot of bait fishing, but flies and lures work well. A possible difficulty: heavy runoffs in recent years and habitat improvement by Wyoming Game & Fish have changed flow patterns so some savvy fish-hunting may be required.

It has spots of excellent fishing after spring runoff for cutthroat, browns, some brook and rainbow, and whitefish. Upstream from Afton, the fish population is mostly cutthroat. Paul Stauffer of Afton reports that when the fish are biting they are "not usually selective . . . any pattern near the size of the insect will usually produce." Stauffer also says that trophy browns can be caught in the fall using large streamers and sunken lines.

The Salt River downstream from the Upper Narrows Bridge on Hwy 238 near Afton is open all year. In the fall and winter the big browns from Palisades Reservoir come up the Salt to spawn. They run 3 to 6 pounds and can get to 12 pounds.

Willow Creek enters the Salt from the east between Thane and Afton. Five miles of dirt road follow the creek, with a parking area at the end. It has small cutthroat. There are brook, cutthroat and brown in this stream and its tributaries. Get permission before fishing on private lands.

Cottonwood Lake (6,000 ft; 35 ac) lies eight miles east of Smoot. A good gravel road from US 89 runs seven miles to the lake. Motors are allowed and there is a campground, but no boat rental. Cutthroat and brook around 10 inches are caught here.

Palisades Reservoir (700 ac when full) is another BuRec reservoir that fluctuates as it serves irrigation needs in Wyoming and Idaho. The mackinaw population in the lake has been growing; there are now macks up to 5 pounds and 16-inch fish are average. There are also 10- to 12-inch cutthroat. Fishing is good from the shore at the mouths of the Snake, Greys, and Salt rivers. Trolling is best in midsummer and fall, when sufficient water is held. □

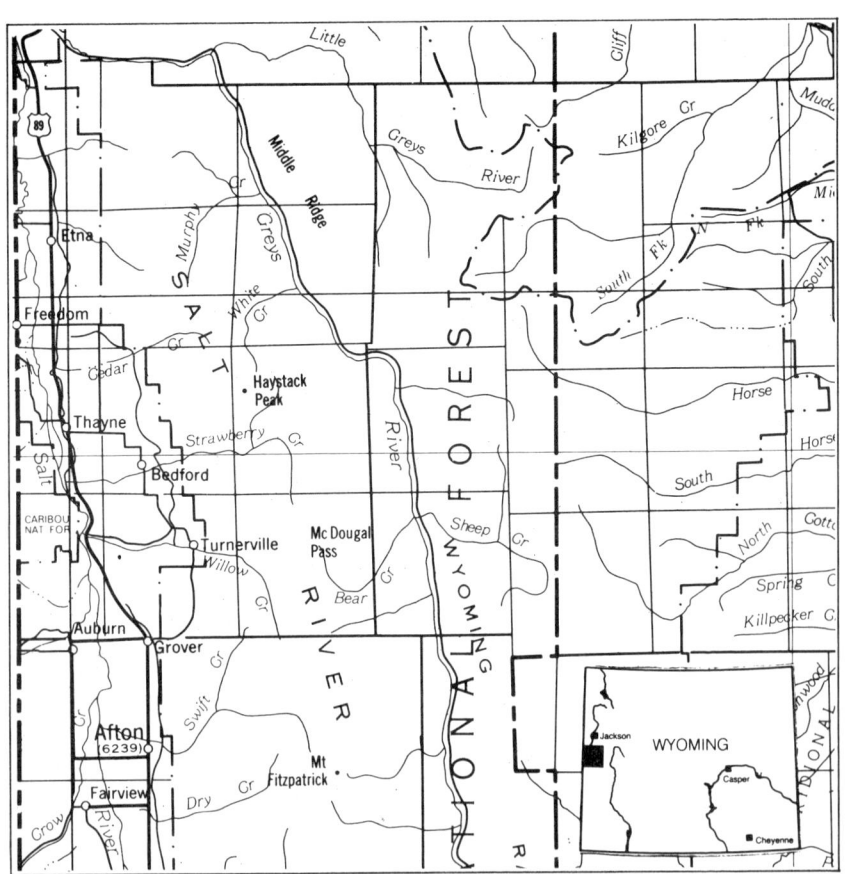

Salt and Greys Rivers

CHECK THIS

The Snake River area fishing seasons vary widely. The Wyoming Game & Fish office in Jackson has current regulations as do most tackle shops.

Snake River: Most of this river, and its major tributaries, are closed to trout fishermen from November 1 to March 31. The exceptions are:

• 150 feet below Jackson Lake Dam on the Snake River, closed to fishing year-round.

• The river is open to whitefish fishermen all year long.

Palisades Reservoir; Jenny, Leigh, Two Ocean, Phelps, and **Lower Slide Lakes;** and **Flat Creek** between the federal Elk Refuge and Hwy 187: These waters are open to fishing year-round. The section of Flat Creek described is open only to those under 14 years old.

Jackson Lake: The lake is closed from October 1 to October 31; open the rest of the year.

Salt River: This drainage is open year-round below the Narrows Bridge, where US 238 crosses the river near Afton. Above the Narrows Bridge the drainage is closed November 1 through December 31.

Snake River drainage: Tributaries to the Snake upstream from Hoback Junction are closed to fishing from November 1 to March 31, with these exceptions: Cottonwood, Blacktail, Spring, and Upper Bar BC creeks in Grand Teton National Park; Lower Bar BC Spring and Flat creeks between the Old Crawford Bridge and McBride Bridge on the elk refuge are closed from November 1 through July 31. Flat Creek within the refuge from the Old Crawford Bridge to the refuge boundary is closed all year. So is Nowlin Creek.

Hoback and Greys Rivers: These and other waters draining the west side of the Teton Range are closed November 1 through March 31.

FISHING · HUNTING
HIKING · BOATING
Fine Living at Fair Rates
Mr. & Mrs. Hal Taylor - Owners
654-7551
1/4 Mile S. of Junction of US Hwy. 89 & 26
P.O. Box 27   Alpine, WY

U.S. FOREST SERVICE DISTRICT RANGER STATIONS

Below are listed forest headquarters offices and ranger district stations for U.S. Forest Service operations west of the Continental Divide in Wyoming. Stations in adjacent states close to Wyoming are cited for convenience since they have information on western Wyoming facilities.

BRIDGER-TETON NATIONAL FOREST

Headquarters
340 North Cache
P.O. Box 1888
Jackson, WY 83001
307/733-2752

Greys River Ranger District
125 Washington
P.O. Box 338
Afton, WY 83110
307/886-3166

Hoback Ranger District
140 East Broadway
P.O. Box 1689
Jackson, WY 83001
307/733-4755

Gros Ventre Ranger District
140 East Broadway
P.O. Box 1689
Jackson, WY 83001
307/733-3381

Buffalo Ranger District
Blackrock Ranger Station
Hwy 26-287
P.O. Box 278
Moran, WY 83013
307/543-2386

CARIBOU NATIONAL FOREST

Soda Springs Ranger District
421 West 2nd South
P.O. Box 635
Soda Springs, ID 83276
208/547-4356

Montpelier Ranger District
431 Clay
Montpelier, ID 83254
208/847-0375

TARGHEE NATIONAL FOREST

Island Park Ranger District
Highway 20
Island Park, ID 83429
208/558-7301

Ashton Ranger District
30 Yellowstone Highway
P.O. Box 228
Ashton, ID 83420
208/652-7442

Teton Basin Ranger District
Driggs, ID 83422
208/354-2431

U.S. Forest Service campgrounds

U.S. Forest Service compilation was current as of 1985.
Asterisks denote fee areas. Some campgrounds are open only Memorial Day weekend through Labor Day. Below freezing weather could mean no water supply.

SNAKE RIVER DRAINAGE

BRIDGER-TETON NATIONAL FOREST
Headquarters: Forest Service Bldg., Jackson, WY 83001

Campground name	Elevation	No camp sites	Travel trailers	Drinking water	Length of stay (days)	Location and directions
Forest Park	7000	13	Yes	No	10	28.6 mi SE of Alpine by forest road
Lynx Creek	6200	14	Yes	No	—	9.6 mi SE of Alpine by forest road
Atherton Creek*	7200	20	Yes	Piped	10	On forest road 7.3 mi E of Kelly
Red Hills	7300	5	Yes	Well	10	9.3 mi E of Kelly on forest road
Crystal Creek	7300	6	Yes	Well	10	9.5 mi E of Kelly on forest road
Granite Creek*	6900	53	Yes	Piped	10	8 mi NE off US 189, 10.1 mi NW of Bondurant
Hoback*	6200	28	Yes	Piped	10	Along US 189, 10.2 mi NW of Bondurant
Kozy	6400	8	Yes	No	10	6.9 mi NW of Bondurant on US 189

SNAKE RIVER

Curtis Canyon*	7000	12	Yes	Piped	10	5.6 mi NE of Jackson on forest roads
Hatchet*	7000	9	Yes	Well	10	8 mi E of Moran on US 26

GRAND TETON NATIONAL PARK

Campground name	No. camp sites	Water and toilet	Showers	Length of stay (days)	Location
Lizard Creek	60	Yes	No	14	17 mi NW of Moran
Colter Bay	350	Yes	Yes	14	9 mi NW or Moran
Signal Mountain	86	Yes	No	14	7 mi SW of Moran
Jenny Lake	49	Yes	No	7	7 mi N of Moose
Gros Ventre	360	Yes	No	14	10 mi SE of Moose

TARGHEE NATIONAL FOREST
St. Anthony, Idaho (Admin. By Bridger-Teton, Jackson, Wyo.)

Campground name	Elevation	No camp sites	Travel trailers	Drinking water	Length of stay (days)	Location and directions
Cave Falls*	6200	16	Yes	Faucet	16	21 mi E. of Highway 47, 5 mi N of Ashton, Idaho
Teton Canyon*	7200	9	Yes	Faucet	16	10.9 mi E. of Driggs, Idaho on county hwys and forest road
Trail Creek*	6600	11	Yes	Faucet	16	5.9 mi E of Victor, Idaho, off State Hwy 33
Alpine*	5800	33	Yes	Faucet	16	Off US 89, 2.9 mi NW of Alpine
Cabin Creek*	5800	10	Yes	Faucet	10	16.4 mi E of Alpine on US 89
Elbow*	5800	17	Yes	Faucet	10	13.7 mi E of Alpine on US 89
Station Creek*	5800	14	Yes	Faucet	10	11 mi E of Alpine on US 89
East Table Creek*	5800	18	Yes	Faucet	10	12.7 mi E of Alpine on US 89
Little Cottonwood	5800	10	Yes	Faucet	10	5.2 mi E of Alpine on US 89
Ham's Fork*	8000	10	Yes	Piped	10	17.0 mi NE of Cokeville on state hwy and forest road
The Bridge	5800	5	Yes	No	10	3.5 mi SE of Alpine
Cottonwood Lake*	7600	12	Yes	No	10	8.8 mi E of Smoot off US 89
Swift Creek*	6000	26	Yes	Faucet	—	1.8 mi E of Afton on county hwy
Murphy Creek	6300	10	Yes	No	10	15.1 mi SE of Alpine by forest road
Allred Flat*	7000	48	Yes	Piped	10	9.2 mi S of Smoot on US 89

Green River & Flaming Gorge

ADJACENT COMMUNITIES:
Cora, Daniel, Pinedale, Boulder, Marbleton, Big Piney, La Barge, Farson, Green River.

PRINCIPAL HIGHWAYS:
U.S. 189, 191; Wyo. 351, 372, 530, 374.

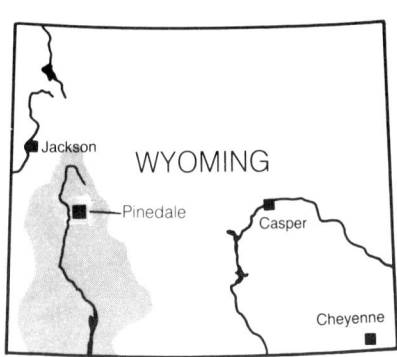

Gannet Peak, 13,804 feet above sea level and Wyoming's highest point, serves as a beacon to some of the best fishing in the West—the **Green River.**

The river flows south from high streams, lakes and glaciers, through high desert for more than 150 miles before leaving the state's southwest corner among the red-hued rocks and canyons of Flaming Gorge Reservoir.

Sections of the Green are a floater's dream—if he knows what he's doing.

These are brook, cutthroat, rainbow, and the elusive golden trout. Increasingly, grayling are added to the angler's creel in the mountain waters. The open reservoirs offer many of these varieties plus whitefish, walleye, catfish, mackinaw and several warm water species.

Regulations limiting fishing have become more strict in recent years as population in the area grows and the Green's reputation for thrilling fly fishing spreads.

The upper waters of the Green run south for 20 miles in the national forest from Lower Green River Lake to privately owned ranch lands.

Fishing regulations are among the most complex in the state. On the Green between Kendall Warm Springs and the Bridger-Teton National Forest boundary, the creel limit is two fish a day and only one may be over 20 inches and none under 10 inches. Fishing is with artificial lures and flies only. There are various creel limits, size restrictions, bait rules and seasons, so it's essential to get a copy of the current regulations before fishing the Green.

The size of fish you're likely to take on the Upper Green will be smaller than they were just a few years ago. The trout rarely exceed 12 inches—9 inches is average—and, though there must be some larger ones in there, they are fewer in number than they once were. Fishing pressure and natural conditions are responsible. These upper reaches offer rainbow, cutthroat and brown.

Guide Robbie Garrett of Pinedale notes that this great rainbow fishery can provide catches of 40 or more trout in a day's fishing, but, like everyone else familiar with the river, he thinks fishing pressure is taking its toll because fewer and smaller fish are being caught.

Successful fishermen are using elk hair caddis, humpies and Wulffs, with muddler variations and attractor patterns. Lures work less well and nymphs produce uneven

GREEN RIVER 329

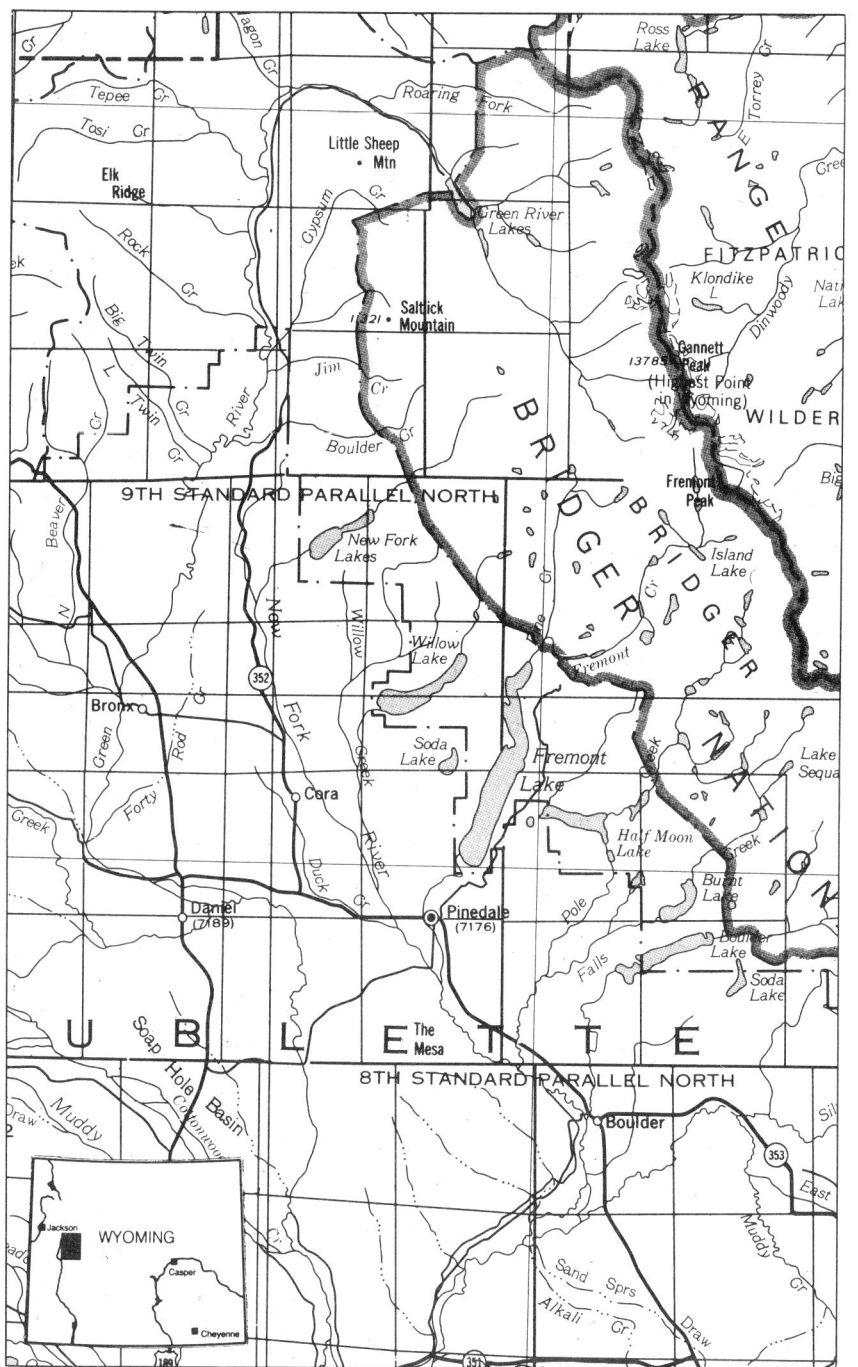

Upper Green River, Wind River Mountains

results. Streamers and dry flies are the most generally used and successful.

The river can be fast and deep, and is often floated, particularly in areas where access to the stream is a problem—and those places are many.

To get to this reach of the Green, drive 5 miles west of Pinedale on US 187; turn north on Hwy 352 and drive about 25 miles on paved road to the forest boundary. Good forest roads go to the lower end of the Green River Lakes. There are campgrounds at Whiskey Grove, below Kendall Warm Springs, and at the lake.

From the forest boundary south, there are 17.3 river miles of private land to the beginning of the Warren Bridge Easement, an area open to public fishing managed by the U.S. Bureau of Land Management. You can't float the 17.3 miles in one day, and you won't be allowed to step out of your boat.

This underlines a problem that exists all along the Green above Fontenelle Reservoir. The ranchers who own much of the surrounding land are not friendly to fishermen. There are three primary reasons: there are just too many fishermen; many of them have no respect for land or property; and ranchers are getting into the fishing and dude ranching business themselves and are simply protecting their territory.

The **Warren Bridge Easement,** managed by the U.S. Bureau of Land Management, runs for 10 miles upstream from US 187. A road runs along the west side of the river with over a dozen access points and campsites. The fishing quality in this much-used area is fair to good.

Wind River Sporting Goods
234 Pine St.
Pinedale, WY 82941
307-367-2419
Jack Ely

For your quality fishing and hunting supplies

"Hunting & Fishing Licenses"

A popular floating area starts at the Warren Bridge and runs downstream toward Daniel. There are two access points between the Warren Bridge and Daniel Junction: one is west of Daniel Junction and the other is near the Daniel Fish Hatchery. Again, floating is through private lands, and landowners will not hesitate to have you arrested for trespassing. For this reason, those not familiar with the river should have a guide and a good set of BLM land ownership maps. Below Daniel, there is a pullout at Trappers Point, and another between there and the Green's confluence with the New Fork River, a stretch of more than 20 miles. This is a long float. You will need maps and help from Wyoming Game and Fish, BLM officials, or a guide to locate pull-outs. This area has rainbow and brown trout and whitefish. Dry flies still produce an occasional brown to 4 pounds.

There are several public access points along the river between the Green's confluence with the New Fork and its arrival at Fontenelle Reservoir about 40 miles farther downstream. These can be reached from the west side off US 189 and from BLM roads to the east. The water is deep, fairly fast, and has numerous holes, but the fishing is not as good as upstream. Rainbow and brown up to 14 inches are caught. Be careful of trespassing on private land.

FONTENELLE RESERVOIR

The Green empties into **Fontenelle Reservoir,** 20 miles long with depths to 100 feet and covers about 8000 acres when full. From I-80, the reservoir can be reached by turning north on US 189, 12 miles east of Evanston. The reservoir is 35 miles east of Kemmerer on this highway.

The future of Fontenelle is in doubt for the moment. It has been lowered 25 feet so that repairs can be made to the dam. The fish will be more concentrated and, for a while, anglers' "luck" should be good, but the Bureau of Reclamation hasn't ruled out lowering the water even more and possibly draining the reservoir. Check in advance for conditions.

There are campgrounds and a boat launch area on the west side of Fontenelle, and a small bait and tackle store 4 miles south of the dam; but no boat rental. The lake produces brown and some rainbow, generally weighing 1-2 pounds. Boat fishermen troll with bait such as cheese and nightcrawlers and flatfish lures; ice fishing in the winter occasionally produces a brown up to 4 pounds. An occasional mackinaw appears. Fishing is fair.

Repairs could be affecting downstream fishing as well, although Wyoming Game & Fish has worked valiantly to improve fishing below the dam. Blue-green algae from the lowered reservoir is floating downstream, inhibiting fish development. If the reservoir is lowered even more, silt also may be flushed out. If the Lower Green is the color of pea soup, you can hope for better fishing sometime in the future. With the lower water, the downstream Green will be subject to irregular, natural flows. Nonetheless, fishing should improve, especially for cutthroat. But check the water color first.

The lower Green River below Fontenelle is no match for the upper Green, but recent work by the Wyoming Game and Fish Department to improve game fish habitat should increase fish populations in coming years. Boulders have been placed in large flatwater areas of the river in the 29 miles between Fontenelle and the confluence with the Big Sandy River.

It is hoped that this will help game fish to displace the suckers and other garbage fish that crowd trout in this stretch of river. The nongame species have proliferated since the mid-1960s when the river was chemically treated from Pinedale down to Utah to clear them out. This is an extremely delicate fishery, primarily for rainbow averaging 14 to 16 inches. In the past, dry fly fishing has been good in the fall with browns as large as 8 pounds caught above the Big Sandy confluence. Kokanee salmon from Flaming Gorge were making appearances as far upriver as Fontenelle Dam. They make a spawning run in the fall that lasts about a month; the fish average 16 to 18 inches. Whitefish are plentiful, too.

Access to the lower Green is no problem—it runs mostly through BLM land;

LAIN'S SPORTS CENTER AND MOTEL

Fishing Equipment
Hunting & Fishing Licenses
Outdoor Clothing
Camping & Backpacking
Guns & Ammunition

We Honor Visa & Mastercard
307-276-3303
If No Answer Call 307-276-3304
200 Budd Ave. • Downtown • Big Piney, WY

however, it's easy to get lost, even with maps.

FLAMING GORGE RESERVOIR

The Green leaves Wyoming via **Flaming Gorge Reservoir** (6040 ft; 42,000 acres). Flaming Gorge has a little bit of everything, and a lot of the kind of trophy fishing that attracts anglers from afar. Flaming Gorge National Recreation Area is administered by the Forest Service and there is a road around the reservoir. Red and Horseshoe canyons in the south, and rolling sagebrush country and occasional abrupt cliffs and promontories to the north make it a classic western scene.

Flaming Gorge has abundant rainbow, but anglers are increasingly attracted by the big browns and mackinaw. The rainbow average 16 to 18 inches. At depths of 40 to 60 feet, they are caught with bait; near the surface, best success is with flies; from a boat or the shoreline, one can fish with rapallas and flatfish. A record for brown trout was set in 1982 when a New Mexico dentist pulled out a 25-pound, 13-ounce fish. You can bet that many fishermen dream of such a catch. The brown population is growing, and many anglers have a chance at one over 10 pounds. The browns were introduced in 1967 to control the Utah chub.

Fishermen come to Flaming Gorge for mackinaw, often bringing electronic sounding devices and heavy-duty deepwater fishing gear. You're not likely to catch a 30-pound fish, but anglers are landing 20 pounders; most mackinaw are in the 16- to 18-inch range.

Flaming Gorge offers more than trout. Kokanee salmon populations in the reservoir are up, and fishermen are catching them with pop gear and worms. The fish sometimes weigh in at more than 3 pounds. Fishermen should be aware that the kokanee's mouth is soft and the fish must be handled gently.

Smallmouth bass are in Flaming Gorge, but they're rarely over 12 inches. Bass fishing is improving and the Lowell Canyon area and near the pipeline at the lower narrows are popular bass sites. The bass picture could be surprisingly bright. A few largemouth bass also have turned up. Channel catfish have been planted at the northern end of the reservoir to help control the suckers and chubs, and they are now being caught up to 12 inches in length at places like the Firehole Canyon boat ramp.

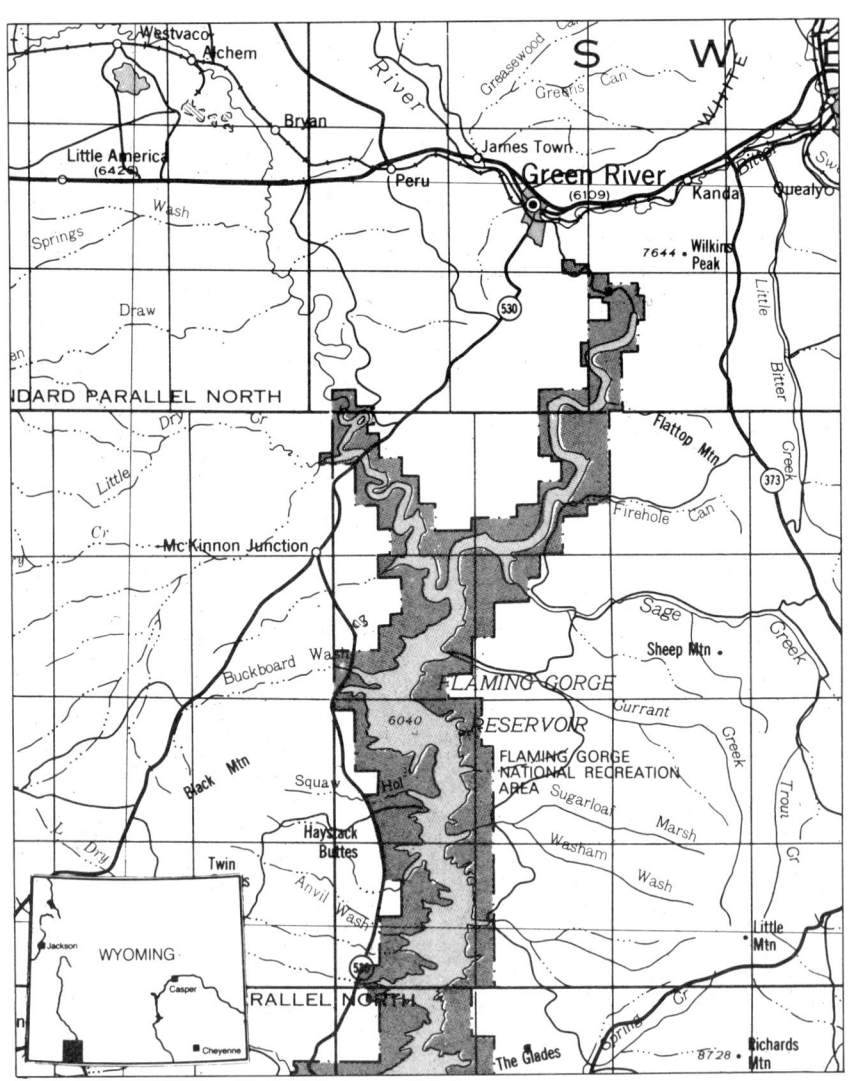

Flaming Gorge Reservoir

WYOMING

HUNTING-
Elk, Deer, Moose, Sheep, Bear, Antelope. We operate three camps in the famous Wind River Range. Excellent success in all hunts. Six and nine day guided hunts from tent camps by horse.

SUMMER-
Gear Drops, Spot Packs, Guided horseback trips for fishing & sightseeing throughout the Bridger Wilderness Area. Golden, Rainbow, Brookie, Cutthroat, Grayling, Brown & Mackinaw.

ELK

FISH

BRIDGER WILDERNESS OUTFITTERS

P.O. Box 561 K   Pinedale, WY 82941   (307) 367-2268

Greg Tanner, of Buckboard Marina, says to fish the gravel banks and sandbars near stream inlets in the spring and fall, especially on drainages where the kokanee spawn. The big browns and macs like to snack at these spawning runs. Later in the year, after the water has warmed, big ones hang around the steep ledges near channels at depths of 60 to 80 feet, sometimes deeper. There's a persistent rumor of scuba divers encountering huge trout—record busters. To hear them talk, you'd need deep sea tackle; there's no question of big fish in Flaming Gorge.

To reach the east side of the reservoir, take Hwy 373 south from I-80, 4 miles west of Rock Springs. At County Road 4-33 to Firehole Canyon, where there is a campground and boat ramp, turn south along the reservoir and reach another campground and boat ramp at Upper Marsh. The west side of Flaming Gorge is reached by turning south from I-80 west of Green River on Hwy 530. It runs along the west side of the reservoir. There are campgrounds and boat ramps about 22 miles from Green River at Buckboard Crossing, and also at Squaw Hollow, another 10 miles south. There is a commercial marina at Buckboard Crossing.

Either a Wyoming or Utah fishing license is required at Flaming Gorge. To fish in the other state's waters, an inexpensive stamp from that state is necessary. The limit is 8 trout or salmon (only one 20 inches or longer) and no more than 2 mackinaw. Use of corn, live fish, or game fish or their parts as bait is prohibited.

UPPER GREEN RIVER

Returning to near Pinedale, focus is put on the Upper Green River, its tributary and associated lakes and streams within the Bridger-Teton National Forest. The Whiskey Grove Campground is a starting point for fishing the Green and creeks that run into it between Kendall Warm Springs and the Green River Lakes to the north. Cross the bridge over the Green at the campground to the west side of the river and travel south on a dirt road 2.5 miles to **Rock Creek,** which joins the Green at the forest border. Follow this 10- to 15-foot-wide stream for several miles by 4-wheel-drive road, and farther by trail, for fair to good fishing for brook and rainbow to 12 inches.

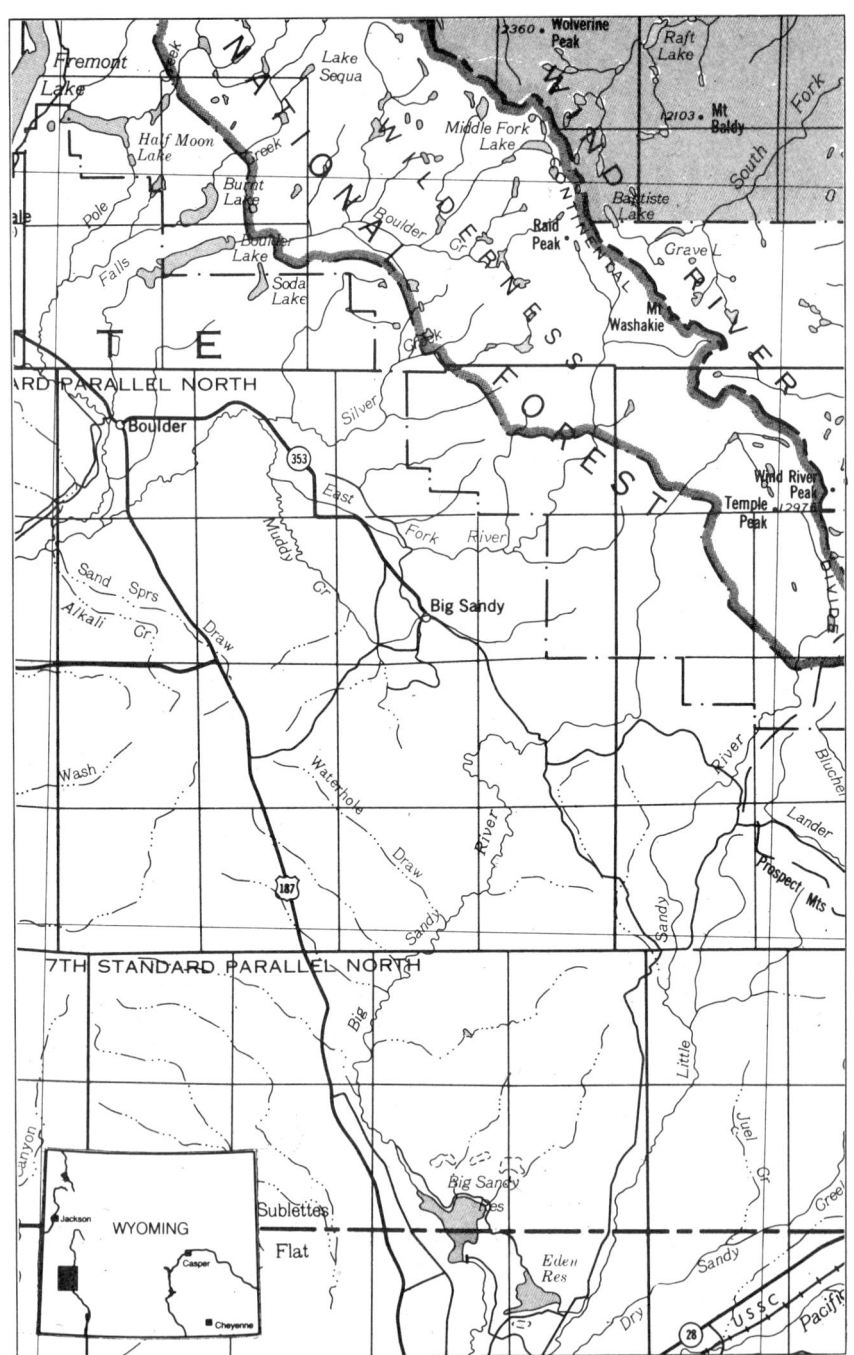

Green River Tributaries, Wind River Mountains

Also very near the forest border is a 4-wheel-drive road leading east along **Gypsum Creek.** This 10- to 15-foot-wide creek provides 8 miles of fishing for cutthroat and brook. It heads at **Big Sheep Mountain Lake** (10,007 ft; 6 ac), which has small cutthroat.

Three miles northwest of the Kendall Bridge on a good gravel road is **Tosi Creek,** which can be followed west on a rough road. Fishing is fair for rainbow and brook to 12 inches. A tributary to Tosi, joining it 3 miles west of the Green, is **Tepee Creek,** a fair to good fishing stream for brook to 10 inches and occasional cutthroat.

Fourteen miles from the forest boundary, **Roaring Fork Creek** drains into the Green from the east. The creek offers good fishing for brook and cutthroat. A 4-wheel-drive road (closed within the Bridger Wilderness) follows it much of the way. It's about 15 miles to the headwaters (5 of them in wilderness) where **Native Lake** (9925 ft; 14 ac) is located. It is good for golden and rainbow to 10 inches, with some larger. Still higher in the Roaring Fork drainage are **Crescent Lake** (10,730 ft; 13 ac) and **Upper Crescent Lake** (10,770 ft; 6 ac) with plentiful small cutthroat.

Eighteen miles from the forest boundary by good gravel road lies **Lower Green River Lake** (7961 ft; 453 ac). The lake lies on the edge of the Bridger Wilderness. Trails into the back country originate here. The lake has rainbow from 10 to 17 inches, and brook and cutthroat occasionally. There are good mackinaw as large as 4 pounds. This is also a popular ice fishing lake in the winter. To the south is **Upper Green Lake** (7965 ft; 135 ac) with cutthroat and rainbow to 15 inches.

WILDERNESS

The Bridger Wilderness, like the Fitzpatrick Wilderness on the east slope of the Wind River Mountains, has a plethora of alpine lakes. A guide or outfitter is a good idea if you are not familiar with the area—the weather can be quirky and dangerous, and a guide can steer you away from some of the barren mountain lakes that might look tempting on a map. In addition, trails often are poorly marked or nonexistent. Topographic maps are vital for backpacking fishermen.

There are at least six approaches to the wilderness. Lower Green River Lake is the northernmost entry. The trip can originate at New Fork Lake by turning west on Forest Road 107, 7 miles north of Cora. Three miles to the south is the Willow Creek trailhead. The Elkhart trailhead lies 12 miles north of Pinedale and can be reached by taking the paved road around the east side of Fremont Lake. The Boulder Lake entrance is reached by turning off US 187, 1 mile north of Boulder, then driving 8 miles on a dirt road to the lake and trailhead. The southernmost entrance is the Big Sandy, reached by driving east of Boulder on Forest Road 911 for 45 miles.

Between Lower and Upper Green River Lakes, **Clear Creek** runs into the river from the east. A trail follows the creek 3 miles to Clear Creek Natural Bridge. Another 3 miles up the drainage is **Clear Lake** (8800 ft; 53 acres), with golden to 12 inches. One mile northeast of Clear Lake is **Faler Lake** (10,185 ft; 13 acres) with 10- to 12-inch golden. Two miles east from Clear Lake is **Bear Lake** (10,500 ft; 107 acres), a very good rainbow fishery with 12-inchers. Less than a half-mile north of Bear is **Daphne Lake** (11,202 ft; 80 ac) with decent rainbow fishing. Only a mile above the Green River, Clear Creek is joined by **Slide Creek,** which drains **Slide Lake** (9400 ft; 75 ac), 3 miles up the trail. Fishing is fair to good for brook to 10 inches in the lake. The creek has small brook and rainbow.

Flowing from the west into the Green between Upper and Lower Green Lake is **Porcupine Creek.** A little more than a mile from the Green the trail forks; by bearing west you will climb some switchbacks to several small lakes with cutthroat. They include **Twin Lakes** (9820 ft; 12 ac), **Shirley Lake** (9980 ft; 4 ac), **Valiate Lake** (10,075 ft; 4 ac), and **Gadsby Lake** (10,270 ft; 10 acres), all within a one-mile radius.

About 5 miles up the Green River from Lower Green River Lake, a small stream enters from the southwest, draining **Granite Lake** (9247 ft; 15 ac) which is good fishing for brook to 10 inches and some cutthroat. Another mile up the Green, **Elbow Creek** enters from the east, draining the three little **Golden Lakes** (9800 ft), which have golden up to 12 inches. Neither of these drainages has a maintained trail.

Another mile along the Green River Trail, **Martin Creek** enters the river from the southeast. It heads at **Kenny Lake** (10,925 ft; 47 ac), which is good to very good for 10-inch brook.

This is an area that is accessible not only from Green River Lakes but also by trail from New Fork Lakes. The New Fork trailhead is about 15 miles west of the Green River's upper reaches and goes along the New Fork River.

Two miles upstream from the confluence of Martin Creek and the Green, the trail from Green River Lakes bends west, following **Trail Creek.** A mile along Trail Creek, the New Fork Trail comes in from the west. Take the New Fork Trail west up the **Clark Creek** drainage to **Clark Lake** (10,275 ft; 4 ac) for small rainbow. The creeks are fair to good for rainbow.

About 1.5 miles up the trailless banks of the Green River above Trail Creek, an unnamed creek enters from the east. Half a mile up this creek is **Stonehammer Lake** (10,250 ft; 17 ac), which has excellent fishing for goldens averaging 10 inches. Another half-mile up the drainage is **Peak Lake** (10,515 ft; 32 ac) with small, healthy golden.

NEW FORK RIVER

This is the area of the New Fork River drainage. The **New Fork River** flows west out of the mountain about 10 miles north of Cora. The two **New Fork Lakes** (7820 ft; combined size 1250 ac) lie outside the wilderness and have a boat launch and several campgrounds. With depths as great as 200 feet, the lakes have mackinaw 20 inches and up plus brookies and kokanee to 12 inches and fair fishing for rainbow in the 10- to 15-inch range. The New Fork Lakes are easily reached by driving 14 miles north from US 187 on paved Forest Service Road 160, which leaves US 187, about 5 miles west of Pinedale. At 14 miles, turn east and drive 2.5 miles to the lake.

Remote lakes offer golden to 5 pounds, but often a guide from Pinedale, such as Tim Singewald or Robbie Garrett, is the way to make the most of a fishing trip.

The New Fork River flows out of Bridger National Forest just below the lakes and turns south for more than 30 miles to its confluence with the East Fork River. It then turns west another 20 miles to merge with the Green just east of Big Piney.

The New Fork River is, like the Green, a popular floating river in its lower reaches. The fishery here leans more toward browns than rainbows, but with some brook. The trout average 12-14 inches, but there are some 4-pound browns taken. Small hairwings and dry flies are successful.

North of the junction with the East Fork, the New Fork is surrounded mostly by private land, and the same hostility found among Green River landowners toward fishermen prevails. Floaters often put their craft in at Boulder, then pull out on the BLM lands below the New Fork and East Fork confluence. Careful attention to land ownership—or better yet, a guide—is important. Floaters also pull out at the Big Piney cutoff. Local fishermen say that this river, like the Green, receives heavy fishing pressure.

Above New Fork Lakes, almost 8 miles up the drainage, lie a group of lakes called the **Hidden Lakes** (10,720-10,900 ft; ranging from 12 to 13 ac) with good to very good fishing for brook to 10 inches.

WILLOW CREEK

The next few drainages south are reached primarily from the Willow Creek trailhead. **Willow Creek** heads about 3 miles in from the Willow Creek Guard Station at **Rainbow Lake** (10,190 ft; 8 ac), which has good fishing for rainbow and some brook.

Several miles south is **Willow Lake** (7745 ft; 1805 ac), about 14 miles north of Pinedale on the Willow Lake road. There are campgrounds on this big lake, but no adequate boat launching sites. It has mackinaw and rainbow from 10 to 20 inches and a few browns. A mile and a half above Willow on **Lake Creek** is **Snake Lake** (7795 ft;

18 ac) with small brook trout. Trails above Snake Lake are poor, but there is good fishing in lakes scattered higher in the drainage. North of Snake Lake (4.5 miles) on **Park Creek** is **Lost Camp Lake** (9812 ft; 12 ac) where there is good fishing for brook to 12 inches. Also on this drainage, 2 miles south of Lost Camp Lake, is **Section Corner Lake** (9245 ft; 56 ac), with brook and grayling to 9 inches and some brown as long as 15 inches. This lake can be reached from the Willow Creek Trailhead by hiking 6 miles on the Section Corner Lake Trail. A trail north from Section Corner follows Lake Creek 1 mile to **Coyote Lake** (9678 ft; 10 ac), which has grayling. A trail east from Section Corner leads 1 mile to **Trapper Lake** (9682 ft; 58 ac) with good fishing for cutthroat to 9 inches. North of Trapper 1 mile by trail is **Trail Lake** (9753 ft; 20 ac) with grayling to 10 inches. Two miles north of Section Corner Lake on the Lake Trail is **Round Lake** (9952 ft; 22 ac) with brook trout to 11 inches. Continue another mile north and you'll reach **Palmer Lake** (10,165 ft; 19 ac) with good fishing for brook to 10 inches. Just above Round Lake, a trail forks east to **Dean Lake** (10,165 ft; 19 ac) with small brook.

PINE CREEK

The next drainage to the south is **Pine Creek,** which empties dozens of high mountain lakes and delivers their waters and some brook, cutthroat and rainbow to **Fremont Lake** (7420 ft; 5000 ac), a popular lake that gets a lot of fishing pressure. It has depths to 600 feet, so mackinaws and browns as big as 20 pounds are occasionally taken. There also are small rainbow and brown. Kokanee salmon are stocked sporadically.

The lake is located 3 miles north of Pinedale by paved Forest Service Road 111. There is a boat launch at the south end and campgrounds on the east and north sides. Fishermen troll from boats and spin-cast from the shore. Large numbers of fishermen ice fish here in the winter.

Soda Lake (7500 ft; 312 ac) lies about 7 miles north of Pinedale by the gravel Willow Lake Road. The brook trout average 10

GREAT OUTDOOR SHOP
Rex & Linda Poulson, Props.
FISHING • BACKPACKING
Cortland Pro Shop
Wilderness Experience
Lowe Alpine Systems
Patagonia
In Pinedale on Hwy 191
**332 W. Pine St. Pinedale, WY
307-367-2440**

to 15 inches, and the brown fishing is good for fish 2 to 3 pounds, with some trophy-size fish of 7 pounds. A bad winter kill a few years ago may have reduced their number somewhat, but they're still there and obtainable from boat or shore. Motors are allowed but launching sites are in poor condition. The best fishing here is just after the ice-off in spring. The lake is closed from October 1 through May 9.

At the northeastern end of the lake is the Elkhart Park trailhead on the Bridger Wilderness boundary. Four miles north, up some steep switchbacks, is **Gimpse Lake** (9373 ft; 11 ac) with good fishing for small brook. Farther up **Pine Creek,** a number of lakes drain from east and west into the creek, which can be approached from Lake Trail to the west or the Highline Trail from the Green River Lakes in the north.

Going north up Pine Creek 5.5 miles from Fremont Lake is **Neil Lake** (9730 ft; 9 ac) with very good fishing for cutthroat and rainbow to 14 inches. Another half-mile northwest is **Gottfried Lake** (9800 ft; 3 ac) with cutthroat and rainbow of the same size. Still higher up this tributary is **Heart Lake** (10,014 ft; 23 ac) with rainbow to 14 inches.

Draining into Pine Creek from the east are the three **Sauerkraut Lakes** (about 10,200 ft; 4 to 16 acres), with cutthroat. Farther north on Pine Creek's east side are **Twin Lakes** (10,350 ft; 4 and 11 ac), with good fishing for cutthroat, golden and cutthroat-golden crosses. About 7 miles up the Pine Creek drainage, **Borum Lake** (10,145 ft; 35 ac) drains from the west with cutthroat to 13 inches. Northwest from Borum another 1.5 miles is **Cutthroat Lake**

(10,595 ft; 23 ac) with cutthroat trout to 12 inches. Half a mile north of Cutthroat, draining into Pine Creek, are the **No Name Lakes** (10,600 ft; 18 and 23 ac) with good to very good fishing for cutthroat up to 14 inches. **Thompson Lake,** off the trail to the north of No Name Lakes, has lots of small brook. Two miles east of No Name Lakes is **Summit Lake** (10,324 ft; 37 ac) with cutthroat to 14 inches.

Two miles east of Pine Creek on the Highline Trail is **Elbow Lake** (10,777 ft; 80 ac) offering good fishing for golden to 15 inches.

At the northern tip of Fremont Lake, Pine Creek is joined from the east by **Bridger Creek,** a fast stream with 8- to 14-inch brook, cutthroat and rainbow. The **Bridger Lakes,** with no trail, lie about 5 miles northeast of Fremont Lake at elevations from 10,100 to 10,500 feet. There are a half-dozen lakes ranging in size from 5 to 36 acres. The highest of these lakes have brook to 10 inches and excellent fishing; the lower lakes have excellent fishing for goldens to 12 inches.

Only 2 miles east of the confluence of Bridger Creek and Pine Creek is **Triangle Lake** (8895 ft; 55 ac) with excellent fishing for golden 8-10 inches.

FREMONT CREEK

Before Bridger Creek joins Pine Creek and Fremont Lake, **Fremont Creek** flows into it from the southeast. Fremont Creek drains a big chunk of the Wind River Mountains' high lakes. Only 2 miles from the Elkhart Park entrance is **Long Lake** (7875 ft; 125 ac) with fair to good fishing for cutthroat, and brook and rainbow, too; **Upper Long Lake** (7945 ft; 35 ac) offers similar fishing. Two miles above Upper Long is **Gorge Lake** (8870 ft; 60 ac) with rainbow and brook around 10 inches. Two miles north of Gorge is **Lost Lake** (9755 ft; 52 ac) with good to excellent angling for brook and rainbow 10-12 inches.

Five miles east from Elkhart Park, the Pole Creek Trail meets the Seneca Lake Trail which is a good approach to the Fremont Creek drainage. One mile north from this juncture on the Seneca Lake Trail is **Hobbs Lake** (10,075 ft; 20 ac). It has good fishing for rainbow to 14 inches. Another 2 miles north is **Seneca Lake** (10,270 ft; 159 ac) with good fishing for rainbow to 14 inches. Northeast is **Little Seneca Lake** (10,350 ft; 11 ac) with small rainbow. Another 1.5 miles northeast is **Island Lake** (10,346 ft; 118 ac) with good to very good fishing for rainbow, cutthroat and golden. This lake can be circled on the east side; then up the Titcomb Basin Trail, it is 2 miles to **Upper Titcomb Lake** (10,598 ft; 106 ac) and **Lower Titcomb Lake** (10,575 ft; 106 ac), where there is good fishing for golden up to 15 inches. Nearby to the east is **Mistake Lake** (10,782 ft; 23 ac) with good-size golden trout.

On the Highline Trail 4 miles north of Little Seneca Lake is **Lower Jean Lake** (10,651 ft; 57 ac) and **Upper Jean Lake** (10,799 ft; 17 ac), both with good fishing for cutthroats to 14 inches. From Upper Jean, a trail leads northwest to the Pine Creek drainage.

Less than 2 miles southeast of Fremont Lake sits **Half Moon Lake** (7500 ft; 900 ac). With depths to 282 feet, Half Moon has developed into a mackinaw fishery with macks primarily in the 15-inch range, but some are larger. There are some rarely-caught browns and rainbows up to 6 pounds lurking here. There is a campground and an adequate boat launching ramp at the southwest end of the lake. Take paved Forest Road 111 north from Pinedale to the south end of Fremont Lake, then follow Forest Road 134 four miles north and turn east to Half Moon Lake.

Line-to-leader knot

Wyoming lakes and reservoirs provide top-notch fishing

The drainage that feeds Half Moon Lake, **Pole Creek,** is closed to fishing from April 1 through June 30. A short distance below Half Moon Lake is **Little Half Moon Lake** (90 ac) with rainbow, brook and brown averaging 10 inches.

Up Pole Creek one mile east is **Fayette Lake** (7800 ft; 300 ac) with rainbow, brook and cutthroat to 14 inches, some larger. The lakes a few miles above Fayette Lake do not have established trails, but they do have fish. **Dollar Lake** (8545 ft; 14 ac) has brook trout around 10 inches. **Junction Lake** (9048 ft; 100 ac), 1.5 miles northeast of Dollar, has good fishing for rainbow, brook, cutthroat, and cutthroat-rainbow crosses to 15 inches. South of Junction Lake up **Spruce Creek** is **Sturrey Lake** (9155 ft; 24 ac) with good brook fishing; **Emma Lake** (9053 ft; 6 ac), a short distance north of Junction, has rainbow, cutthroat and brook.

Above Sturrey Lake on Spruce Creek is **Spruce Lake** (9797 ft; 98 ac) with good fishing for rainbow and cutthroat around 14 inches; above Spruce near the Highline Trail are the three **Chain Lakes** (about 9800 ft; 21 to 67 ac) with rainbow, cutthroat and crosses to 14 inches. A mile north of Upper Chain Lake is **Upper Pole Creek Lake** (9731 ft; 52 ac) with good fishing for brook and cutthroat; above Pole Creek Lake to the west is **1000 Island Lake** (9580 ft; 70 ac) with the same fish.

Two miles east of Pole Creek Lake are the Pole Creek headwaters: **Upper Cook Lake** (10,170 ft; 163 ac) and **Lower Cook Lake** (10,143 ft; 82 ac); still farther north, **Wall Lake** (10,450 ft; 105 ac). Wall has very good fishing for golden; the Cook Lakes (there are several small ones) have good fishing for brook of 8-10 inches, with some golden and cutthroats. Southwest 0.5 mile is **Don Lake** (10,220 ft; 19 ac), with mackinaw, golden and brook; nearby **Peter Lake** (10,175 ft; 32 ac) has similar fishing.

Flowing into Pole Creek from the south just above Fayette Creek is a creek from **Trophy Lake** (9430 ft; 22 ac) with brook trout, and **Belford Lake** (9550 ft; 28 ac) with good to very good fishing for brook to 9 inches.

Baldy Creek flows into Sturrey Lake from **Barnes Lake** (9747 ft; 66 ac) (with cutthroat to 14 inches), which lies a half-mile south of Chain Lakes on the Highline Trail. Above Barnes is **Bell Lake** (10,010 ft; 15 ac) with good fishing for cutthroat to 12 inches. At the top of this drainage is **Baldy Lake** (10,350 ft; 30 ac) with cutthroat to 14 inches.

The next drainage to the south is **Fall Creek,** which comes down from the mountains into 1000-acre **Burnt Lake,** which produced a 23-pound rainbow in 1969—a record at the time. Outside the Bridger Wilderness, this lake has rainbows averaging 12 inches, small brook and mackinaws to 3 pounds. It can be reached by road 10 miles west of Pinedale.

Meadow Lake is 0.5 mile northwest of Burnt Lake, with excellent fishing on flies and lures for grayling. There is a boat ramp, and shore fishing is difficult. A boat or float tube is a good way to fish here. Meadow and Burnt lakes are closed to fishing December 1 through April 30. A trail from the east side of the lake leads 6 miles north to **Horseshoe Lake** (9457 ft; 100 acres) where fishing is for small brook. Two miles northeast on **Little Fall Creek** is **Lake Sequa** (9940 ft; 106 ac), offering excellent fishing for small brook. These lakes also can be approached from the north by the Highline Trail. At the top of the drainage, around 10,200 feet, are the three **Fall Creek Lakes,** with small brook trout. A mile south of Burnt Lake is **Boulder Lake** (7300 ft; 1200 ac), 7 miles north of Boulder by dirt road. The fish in this lake include rainbow 10-15 inches and some larger mackinaw. Campsites and a trailhead lie at the east end of the lake. A trail heads north 2 miles to **Lake Ruff (Blueberry Lake)** (8476 ft; 55 ac), with good fishing for brook and grayling. Two miles northeast of Ruff is **Lovatt Lake** (9456 ft; 70 ac), with good fishing for brook and golden averaging 14 inches. Half a mile farther north is **Cross Lake** (9550 ft; 13 ac) with brook and grayling; a short distance farther is **Coyote Lake** (9515 ft; 23 ac) with graylings 8-12 inches. One mile northeast from Coyote is **Lake George** (9679 ft; 16 ac) with excellent fishing for brook 8-10 inches. Farther along this trail is **Edmond Lake,** but it is barren.

BOULDER CREEK

Boulder Creek is a rapid flowing stream with good fishing for rainbow and brook. About 5 miles east from Boulder Lake, a trail leads north to **Ethel Lake** (8660 ft; 27 ac) where cutthroat average 12 inches. Another 2 miles northwest is **Christine Lake** (9255 ft; 27 ac) with small brook trout. Half a mile farther lies **Mac's Lake** (9382 ft; 9 ac) with excellent fishing for small brook. Another 2 miles northeast is **North Fork Lake** (9754 ft; 163 ac) with good fishing for cutthroat averaging 12 inches and sometimes larger. Still farther north on the **North Fork of Boulder Creek** is **Lake Victor** (9834 ft; 139 ac) with cutthroat up to 16 inches. Several more miles up the North Fork of Boulder Creek is **Barber Lake** (10,322 ft; 25 ac) with cutthroat. Also draining into Victor Lake is **Long Lake** (10,683 ft; 55 ac), and the lakes up **Europe Creek,** all of which have cutthroat. The creeks as well as the lakes in this area are good fishing for cutthroat.

Below North Fork Lake in the **Pipestone Creek** drainage is **Lake Winona** (9688 ft; 26 ac), with good to very good fishing for cutthroat to 16 inches. A trail goes southeast from the lower end of this lake 1 mile to **Lake Isabella** (9719 ft; 51 ac), a narrow lake with very good cutthroat fishing. Above Isabella are the **Pipestone Lakes** (10,125 ft; 9 and 21 ac) with good cutthroat to 13 inches. One-half mile northeast of Isabella is **Howard Lake** (10,013 ft; 45 ac), with good to very good fishing for 15-inch cutthroat.

The three **Firehole Lakes** drain into Pipestone Creek. They are at about 9600 feet and range in size from 23 to 30 acres. All three have good fishing for cutthroat to 12 inches. Just south is **Lake Vera** (9625 ft; 8 ac) with cutthroat to 14 inches.

The **Middle Fork of Boulder Creek** has a passel of lakes that contain primarily brook trout. Hike a mile south from Lake Vera to **Junction Lake** (9575 ft; 79 ac) for brook 10 inches and larger. Just north of Junction are **Sandpoint Lake** (9810 ft; 32 ac) and **Bob's Lake** (9875 ft; 70 ac), each with very good fishing for small brook. Five miles northeast from Junction Lake along the creek brings you to **Middle Fork Lake** (10,252 ft; 257 ac) where there is excellent fishing for small brook. Two miles to the northwest is **Halls Lake** (10,602 ft; 206 ac) with more excellent brook, and above Halls is **Howe Lake** (10,655 ft; 51 ac) with more of the same. **Smaller Middle Fork Lakes** lie below the big one on the drainage; brook are predominant in them. To the south is **Rainbow Lake** (10,341 ft; 76 ac) with excellent rainbow to 16 inches. Also in this drainage, just south of Rainbow, is **Sunrise Lake** (10,380 ft; 28 ac), with cutthroat. Flowing out of Rainbow is **Dream Creek,** which flows 2 miles southwest to **Dream Lake** (9842 ft; 63 ac) with good fishing for brook and cutthroat averaging 9 inches. Dream Creek joins the **South Fork of Boulder Creek.** Up the South Fork 1 mile from this juncture is **Raid Lake** (9946 ft; 131 ac), with excellent fishing for brook 9 inches and larger, and some mackinaw. The South Fork provides good fishing for small brook. Northeast in the drainage, with no established trails, is **Jim Harrower Lake** (10,521 ft; 16 ac), about 3 miles northeast from Raid Lake. It contains golden trout. **Bonneville Lake** (10,521 ft; 16 ac) is a mile downstream and also has good golden. Draining into Raid Lake from a half-mile to the southeast is **Cross Lake** (10,087 ft; 83 ac), which offers excellent fishing for brook to 10 inches and mackinaw.

Below the juncture of Dream Creek and the South Fork lies, just to the north, **Crescent Lake** (9751 ft; 16 ac) with excellent small brook trout fishing.

Divide Creek enters **Boulder Creek** 5 miles east of the Boulder Lake trailhead. **Divide Lake** (9668 ft; 134 ac) has good fishing for rainbow to 14 inches, and **Little Divide Lake** (9603 ft; 14 ac) is excellent for small brook. Half a mile to the south by trail from Divide Lake is **Monroe Lake** (9570 ft; 20 ac), which drains into **Silver Creek** to

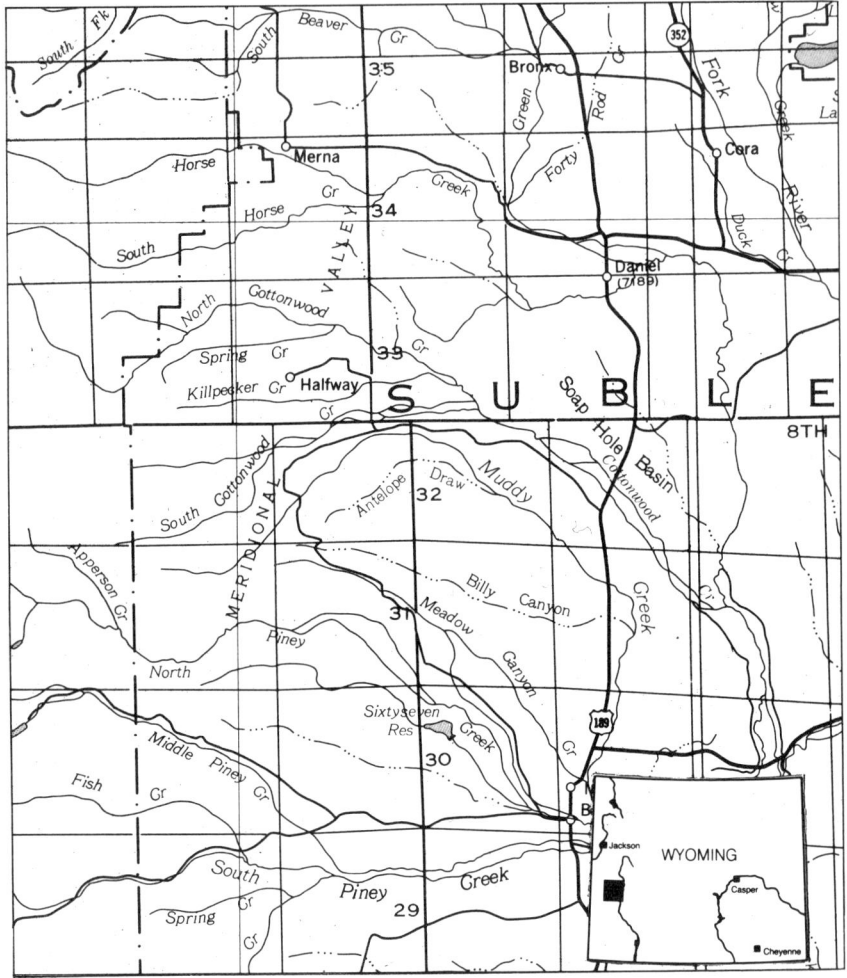

Green River Western Tributaries

the south and has brook to 12 inches and some cutthroat. Four miles to the east in another fork of this drainage (1.5 miles south of Cross Lake) are **Silver Lake** (9928 ft; 171 ac) and **Upper Silver Lake** (9967 ft; 66 ac) with good to very good fishing for brook to 12 inches. **Jessie Lake** (20 ac), with a small creek, lies a mile south of Silver.

EAST FORK RIVER

Moving south, the next major drainage is the **East Fork River,** which flows south and then west out of the national forest and across a patchwork of private and public land before joining the New Fork River 4 miles south of Boulder, just west of US 187. The East Fork has brown and rainbow in the 8- to 15-inch range; here, as elsewhere, respect the private ownership along the river. Most lakes in the East Fork drainage are on Forest Service land and are reached by way of the Big Sandy Road.

Close to the forest boundary and outside the Bridger Wilderness is **Boulter Lake** (9225 ft; 31 ac), with good fishing for 12-inch cutthroats and brook. One mile on the other side of the East Fork from Boulter

Lake is **Poston Lake** (9350 ft; 13 ac) with small brook. About six miles from the forest boundary and then two miles west of the river is **Dad's Lake** (9740 ft; 53 ac) with brook and cutthroat averaging 10 inches. One mile north of Dad's Lake is **Marm's Lake** (9880 ft; 33 ac), with good fishing for 12- to 14-inch brook trout. Draining into Dad's from a mile west is **Donald Lake** (10,153 ft; 25 ac) with cutthroat to 12 inches.

Farther up the drainage, **Washakie Creek** enters the East Fork from the east, draining **Shadow Lake** (10,338 ft; 44 ac), which has small brook; still higher on Washakie is **Billy's Lake** (10,717 ft; 22 ac). Each has small brook.

Far up on the East Fork, tucked next to the Continental Divide, is **Pyramid Lake** (10,570 ft; 55 ac), with temperamental golden from 12 to 22 inches. Half a mile down the drainage from Pyramid is **Maes Lake** (10,343 ft; 26 ac), with rainbow, brook and mackinaw.

BIG SANDY RIVER

The **Big Sandy River** at the southern end of the Wind River Mountains collects waters from the high peaks and dumps them some 60 miles to the south in turbid and unattractive **Big Sandy Reservoir** (6500 ft; 3000 ac). It is 9 miles northeast of Farson and east of US 287. The reservoir has campgrounds and a boat launching area on the west shore; fishing with trolled lures and bait fish for brown trout is fair. There are some cutthroat, rainbow, brook and whitefish, and abundant suckers.

Before it leaves the mountains, the Big Sandy drains some good fishing lakes. The Big Sandy entrance is accessible from Boulder by going about 20 miles east and south on Hwy 353 to Big Sandy village. The entrance is another 8 miles south and 14 miles more east and north. From the Big Sandy entrance, it is a 5-mile trek to **Big Sandy Lake** (9690 ft; 57 ac), not to be confused with the reservoir. The lake has excellent fishing for small brook and some cutthroat. From there you can hike a mile east to **Clear Lake** (10,012 ft; 44 ac) with good to very good fishing for small brook. Still another mile east is **Black Joe Lake** (10,550 ft; 76 ac), with cutthroat from 10 to 14 inches. Above Clear Lake, **Deep Lake** (10,526 ft; 62 ac) has good fishing for brook to 12 inches. Closer to the Big Sandy entrance, and therefore more often fished, are **Diamond Lake** (12 ac) with fair to poor fishing for cutthroat 12-14 inches; **"V" Lake** (9420 ft; 42 ac) with rainbow from 10 to 15 inches, and sometimes larger; and **Meeks Lake** (9303 ft; 11 ac) with brook to 10 inches.

At the southernmost end of the western slope of the Wind River Mountains, **Little Sandy Creek** drains **Little Sandy Lake** (9479 ft; 94 ac), with small cutthroat and brook trout.

The Big Sandy and Little Sandy creeks converge at Farson and then flow more than 30 miles southwest through high desert to enter the Green River in the badlands of Seedskadee National Wildlife Refuge. Fishing is not recommended in this section.

Following is a review of streams west of the Green River.

WESTERN STREAMS

North, Middle and South Piney Creeks enter the Green River from the west near Big Piney. They drain part of the eastern face of the Wyoming Mountains in Bridger-Teton National Forest. **North Piney Creek** has fair to good fishing for brook and cutthroat to 12 inches. It drains **North Piney Lake** (8700 ft; 50 ac), which has cutthroat and some brook to 12 inches. The upper part of this stream, as well as the lake, can only be fished with artificial flies and lures, and cutthroat 10 inches or less must be returned to the water. North Piney Lake and upstream tributaries in Sublette County are closed June 1 to July 15 to fishing. The same limits on cutthroat catches apply to several streams north of the Piney Creeks, all of which have fair fishing for cutthroat and occasional brook. They are **North and South Cottonwood Creeks,** reached by county and Forest Service roads west of US 189 between Daniel and Big Piney, and **North and South Horse Creeks** west of Daniel.

Middle Piney Creek ranges in width

from 10 to 20 feet and has fair to good rainbow and brook trout fishing for 8- to 10-inch fish. It drains **Middle Piney Lake** (8820 ft; 150 ac), which has rainbow, brook and cutthroat to 12 inches, some larger browns, and mackinaw up to 5 pounds. Take County Road 41 west of Big Piney, and subsequent Forest Service dirt road, to the lakeside. There are campsites. Just beyond the forest boundary on 41, a road forks to the south; it goes 9 miles to **South Piney Creek,** which has fair fishing for rainbow, brook and cutthroat averaging 10 inches.

Farther south, **La Barge Creek** has fair fishing for 10-inch brook and rainbow. County Road 315, which leaves US 189 two miles south of La Barge, follows the creek northwest over a natural divide to the headwaters of **Greys Fork** (see Snake River drainage). Stretches of the creek near La Barge are on private land.

Fontenelle Creek runs into Fontenelle Reservoir from the west and a county road runs along its lower stretch where there is fair angling for brook and rainbow in the 10-inch range. Take County Road 306 north of Kemmerer to reach the upper part of the creek, where fishing is best.

The **Hams Fork River** comes out of the southern end of the Wyoming Range and flows south through the coal-mining town of Kemmerer before turning east to join **Blades Fork** and empty into Flaming Gorge Reservoir. State Hwy 233 follows the stream north from Kemmerer to the forest boundary, and Forest Service roads continue along the stream for several miles more. Below Viva Naughton Reservoir and the Kemmerer Reservoir there is fair to good fishing in the stream for rainbow averaging 11 inches. Between Kemmerer Reservoir and **Viva Naughton Reservoir** (7240 ft; 458 ac), a stretch of about a mile, no fishing is allowed from October 1 to July 14. Viva Naughton Reservoir, 16 miles north of Kemmerer, is a Utah Power and Light reservoir. It has boat launching facilities and a campground, both of which charge fees. This is primarily a rainbow fishery with catches averaging 16 inches. There are a few browns and big whitefish, as well as some cutthroat and brook. Shoreline fishing produces decent catches, but most fishermen troll using lures and worms. No live fish bait is allowed. Ice fishing is also popular here.

The Hams Fork upstream to **Corral Creek** is closed April 1 through June 30, as are all sloughs and tributaries to Viva Naughton Reservoir. Cutthroat and small brook are found on Hams Fork in the Bridger-Teton National Forest. The lower reaches of the creek below Kemmerer have fair to good fishing for rainbow and browns to 16 inches.

Blacks Fork, which drains a portion of Utah's Uinta Mountain Range, flows north from Meeks Cabin Reservoir on the Utah-Wyoming border through Lyman, eventually turns east and, joined by Hams Fork, loops south into the northern end of Flaming Gorge reservoir southwest of Green River. **Meeks Cabin Reservoir** fluctuates with irrigation use, but it has fair fishing for cutthroat up to 16 inches, averaging 8 to 10 inches. Two public fishing areas are 3 and 4 miles below the reservoir on Blacks Fork, reached by county roads south of I-80 about 28 miles southwest of Lyman. Blacks Fork, about 40 feet in width, is fair to good for 8- to 12-inch brook, cutthroat and rainbow, with an occasional large brown taken between Lyman and Fort Bridger. Much of this vicinity is private land, requiring landowner's permission to fish.

Henrys Fork also comes out of the Uinta Mountains in Utah just north of the Wyoming-Utah border and flows east to Flaming Gorge. State Hwy 414 runs near it much of the way. It offers fair fishing for rainbow, brown and cutthroat to 12 inches. □

Kendall Warm Springs, some 35 miles north of Pinedale on the Green River, is the only place in the world where the Kendall Dace is found. Barely 2 inches long when fully grown, the fish spends its entire life in the springs where the water temperature is 84.4°F year-round. At breeding time the males are purple, the females green.

GREEN RIVER

U.S. FOREST SERVICE DISTRICT RANGER STATIONS

Below are listed forest headquarters offices and ranger district stations for U.S. Forest Service operations west of the Continental Divide in Wyoming. Stations in adjacent states close to Wyoming are cited for convenience since they have information on western Wyoming facilities.

BRIDGER-TETON NATIONAL FOREST

Headquarters
340 North Cache
P.O. Box 1888
Jackson, WY 83001
307/733-2752

Kemmerer Ranger District
Hwy 189
P.O. Box 31
Kemmerer, WY 83101
307/877-4415

Pinedale Ranger District
210 West Pine
P.O. Box 220
Pinedale, WY 82941
307/367-4326

Big Piney Ranger District
Hwy 189
P.O. Box 218
Big Piney, WY 83113
307/276-3375

ASHLEY NATIONAL FOREST
437 East Main
Vernal, UT 84078
801/789-1181

Flaming Gorge Ranger District
Headquarters
P.O. Box 278
Manila, UT 84046
801/784-5445

Flaming Gorge Ranger District
Dutch John Office
P.O. Box 157
Dutch John, UT 84023
801/885-3838

Vernal Ranger District
650 North Vernal Avenue
Vernal, UT 84078
801/789-0323

WASATCH NATIONAL FOREST

Evanston Ranger District
Federal Building
221 10th Street
P.O. Box FS
Evanston, WY 82930
307/789-3194-Winter
801/642-6662-Summer

Mountain View Ranger District
Lone Tree Road, Hwy 44
Mountain View, WY 82939
307/782-6555

U.S. Forest Service campgrounds

U.S. Forest Service compilation was current as of 1985.
Asterisks denote fee areas. Some campgrounds are open only Memorial Day weekend through Labor Day. Below freezing weather could mean no water supply.

GREEN RIVER DRAINAGE

BRIDGER-TETON NATIONAL FOREST
Headquarters: Forest Service Bldg.; Jackson, WY 83061

Campground name	Elevation	No camp sites	Travel trailers	Drinking water	Length of stay (days)	Location and directions
Middle Piney Lake	8600	5	No	Well	10	25.5 mi W of Big Piney off county hwy

Campground name	Elevation	No camp sites	Travel trailers	Drinking water	Length of stay (days)	Location and directions
Sacajawea	8200	26	Yes	Piped	10	23.8 mi W of Big Piney off county hwy
Green River Lake*	8000	27	Yes	Piped	10	26.4 mi N of Cora on county hwy and forest road
New Fork Lake	7800	15	Yes	No	10	7.4 mi E off county hwy, 11 mi N of Cora
Whiskey Grove*	7800	9	Yes	Piped	10	25.8 mi N of Cora by county hwy and forest road
Willow Lake	7700	9	No	No	10	8.5 mi N of Pinedale by dirt road
Trails End*	9100	8	Yes	Piped	10	14 mi NE of Pinedale on forest road
Fremont Lake*	7600	54	Yes	P	10	7.6 mi NE of Pinedale
Half Moon	7600	8	Yes	No	10	6.8 mi NE of Pinedale
Big Sandy	9100	12	Yes	No	10	42 mi SE of Boulder by state and county hwys
Moose Flat	6400	10	Yes	No	10	23.9 mi SE of Alpine by forest road
Spring Lake Creek	7300	4	No	No	10	24.0 mi NE of Cokeville on county hwy and forest roads
Narrows*	7800	19	Yes	Piped	10	7.1 mi E off county hwy, N of Cora
New Fork Group	7900	1	Yes	No	—	18.4 mi NE of Cora on county hwys and forest road

U.S. Forest Service compilation was current as of 1985.

Asterisks denote fee areas. Some campgrounds are open only Memorial Day weekend through Labor Day. Below freezing weather could mean no water supply.

LOWER GREEN RIVER DRAINAGE

ASHLEY NATIONAL FOREST
Headquarters: 434 E. Main St.; Vernal, UT 84078

Campground name	Elevation	No camp sites	Travel trailers	Drinking water	Length of stay (days)	Location and directions
Buckboard Crossing*	6100	68	Yes	Faucet	14	24.8 mi SW of Green River
Squaw Hollow	6100	12	Yes	No	—	18 mi NE of Manila, Utah, on state hwys
Upper Marsh Creek	6100	3	Yes	No	—	18 mi NE of Manila, Utah, on state hwys
Fire Hole	6100	40	Yes	Yes	—	29.9 mi SW of Rock Spring on I-180, state hwy and forest roads

Sweetwater River's headwaters best bet

ADJACENT COMMUNITIES:
South Pass City, Atlantic City, Jeffrey City.

PRINCIPAL HIGHWAYS:
U.S. 28, 287; Wyo. 220, 789.

The Wind River Mountains produce numerous prolific fishing streams—so many that some, like **Sweetwater River,** are almost overlooked.

The Sweetwater offers neither the best nor the worst of Wyoming's stream fishing. Portions of its upper reaches, where it drops out of the Jim Bridger Wilderness at the southern end of the Winds, attract serious fly fishermen, especially in spring and fall. The river journeys more than 100 miles through a confusing mixture of private, U.S. Bureau of Land Management and state lands to Pathfinder Reservoir on the North Platte River. The Oregon and Mormon trails of the 1840s and later follow much of its length. It is a historic area.

Gamefish are not abundant in the Sweetwater, partly because it runs low in the late summer and the water becomes too warm in its lower reaches. The best fishing it and its tributaries have to offer—for browns, rainbows, brook and cutthroat—lies northwest of Hwy 28 between Lander and Rock Springs.

About an hour's drive south of Lander, at South Pass, Hwy 28 crosses the Sweetwater less than two miles from the Continental Divide. Just beyond the river the highway intersects the Lander Cutoff, a well-maintained gravel road that follows the river west and north. This road (C.R. 23-132) parallels first the Sweetwater and then one of its tributaries, **Lander Creek.** There are numerous jeep roads heading north from the cutoff into the mountain drainages.

The alpine lakes that feed into the Sweetwater are for the most part barren, because of the altitude and shallow waters. However, **Blucher Lake** has brook and a small cutthroat population, and Needles Lake has small brook trout. These are in the Bridger Wilderness Area; trails are poorly marked, so good maps are advisable. **Needles Lake** is reached by the Sweetwater Gap Trail. A shorter route, though harder, is to hike over the Continental Divide from the Sandy Creek Road. Local inquiry is recommended because most maps (other than USGS topographic) are vague.

Blucher Creek, the **Little Sweetwater** and **Jack Creeks,** all of which feed into the upper Sweetwater drainage from Forest Service land above Hwy 28, have small brook trout and are accessible to the wilderness border by jeep roads, and from there by foot. The upper reaches of the Sweetwater itself, as well as its East Fork (also above the highway), have brown, brook and stocked rainbow to 12 inches; the East Fork also has cutthroat.

After the Sweetwater runs under the highway, it crosses a mixture of private, BLM and state lands in the high desert, draining the old gold mining region of South Pass. From the many dirt roads that etch this barren landscape, the river appears like a meandering oasis, winding along and lined by low brush and some trees. The river bottom land gives refuge to antelope, waterfowl and moose. You will need maps and a careful eye for property markers to distinguish public and private land along this part of the river. Don't expect great numbers of fish, but there are a few large browns and rainbows.

Willow Creek, which empties into the Sweetwater from the north near Atlantic City, has brook and cutthroat and is accessible by dirt roads. **Rock Creek,** much of it located on private land below Atlantic City, has brook, brown and rainbow—some of good size. A higher section of Rock Creek can be reached above Hwy 28 by taking the **Louis Lake** "Loop" Road running north from the highway near Atlantic City. Big Atlantic Gulch, also on BLM land near Atlantic City, offers only 2.7 miles of access to fishermen, and is heavily used by locals, but in recent years it produced a 7-pound cutthroat.

There's private land south from Atlantic City at the Phelps Dodge Bridge over the Sweetwater to the steep Sweetwater Canyon, where the brown trout reach a good size.

As the river flows to the Pathfinder Reservoir, there is more private than public land along its banks. There are brown and rainbow trout up to 16 inches, and there is not much fishing pressure, but reaching the river can be difficult. Be sure to check with landowners before crossing private land. There are also carp and suckers in this part of the river.

The river ends its journey at the Pathfinder Reservoir 45 miles southwest of Casper. Reservoir is described in Wyoming chapter on the North Platte River system. □

North Platte River blue-ribbon fishing

ADJACENT COMMUNITIES:
Riverside, Saratoga, Rawlins, Sinclair, Casper, Glenrock, Douglas, Guernsey, Lingle, Torrington.

PRINCIPAL HIGHWAYS:
U.S. I-80, I-25, 26, 20; Wyo. 230, 130, 220.

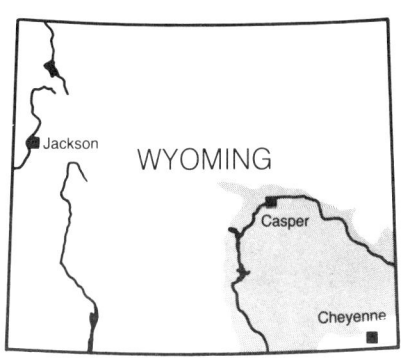

Some of Wyoming's most renowned fishing is not in the streams and lakes of the state's western mountains; it is in the southeast, where the **North Platte River** flows north out of Colorado, drains the Snowy Mountain Range, nourishes three major reservoirs, loops east through Casper and southeast out of the state at Torrington. Its Wyoming reaches have some of the finest blue-ribbon fly fishing in the country. At lower elevations, it supplies bass and walleye angling.

The upper North Platte is more than 120 miles of good quality free-flowing stream in Colorado and Wyoming, a favorite of floaters, that has much private land but also several public access areas. South of the town of Saratoga, it is fed by numerous mountain streams favored by spawning trout. North of Interstate 80, it enters a series of reservoirs and tucked amidst them is the famous Miracle Mile, which draws fly fishermen from around the country, who crave a sporting tussle with big rainbow and browns.

The river curls east near Wyoming's largest city, Casper, and thereafter offers less spectacular fishing, but it's still very good in some sections, such as Government Bridge.

Discussion of the North Platte River picks up at the Colorado State line and goes to I-80. Then the fishing in lakes and streams west of the Snowy Range is presented. Then the big reservoirs north of I-80—Seminoe, Pathfinder, Alcova and Glendo—are described. The description then turns to the Laramie River and the lakes on the east side of the Snowy Range.

The Wyoming portion of the upper North Platte has managed to hold its own as a fine fishery in recent years despite heavy fishing pressure. Special regulations have enabled the state Game and Fish Department to keep most of the fishery "wild" and productive, although there is some stocking of rainbow.

Brown and rainbow trout predominate in the river; they average 14 inches, but often come in larger sizes. There are some walleyes, too, especially east of Casper. From the Colorado-Wyoming border to Saratoga, only artificial flies and lures can be used, only one fish over 16 inches may be kept, and all trout 10 to 16 inches must be returned immediately to the water. This may deprive some fishermen of good eating, but it's helped the North Platte maintain its reputation as a great sport fishery.

Streamers have proven to be fish-getters with the tried-and-true North Platte Special, a brown and yellow streamer available in the area—and a favorite. In the vicinity of Casper, cheese-flavored salmon eggs have been productive in the murky waters of spring.

From the Colorado border, the North Platte runs within Medicine Bow National Forest for about 13 miles. In south-central Wyoming, State Highway 130 leaves I-80 about 20 miles east of Rawlins and heads south toward Saratoga. Twenty miles south on Hwy 130 is Saratoga, which serves as headquarters for many fishing guides who know the North Platte. Between Saratoga and Riverside, Hwy 130 heads east across the river and over Snowy Range Pass (10,800 ft) to Laramie. Hwy 230 continues south at the town of Riverside, and then heads southeast, roughly parallel but not close to the North Platte, to Colorado.

SIX MILE GAP

Trails and 4-wheel drive roads east from Hwy 230 lead to the river at the state line and also about 4 miles downstream at Six Mile Gap Campground. Signs on the highway alert motorists to the access. Floaters use this stretch of the river and also put in some 20 miles downstream at Sanger Bridge 9 miles east of Encampment, which

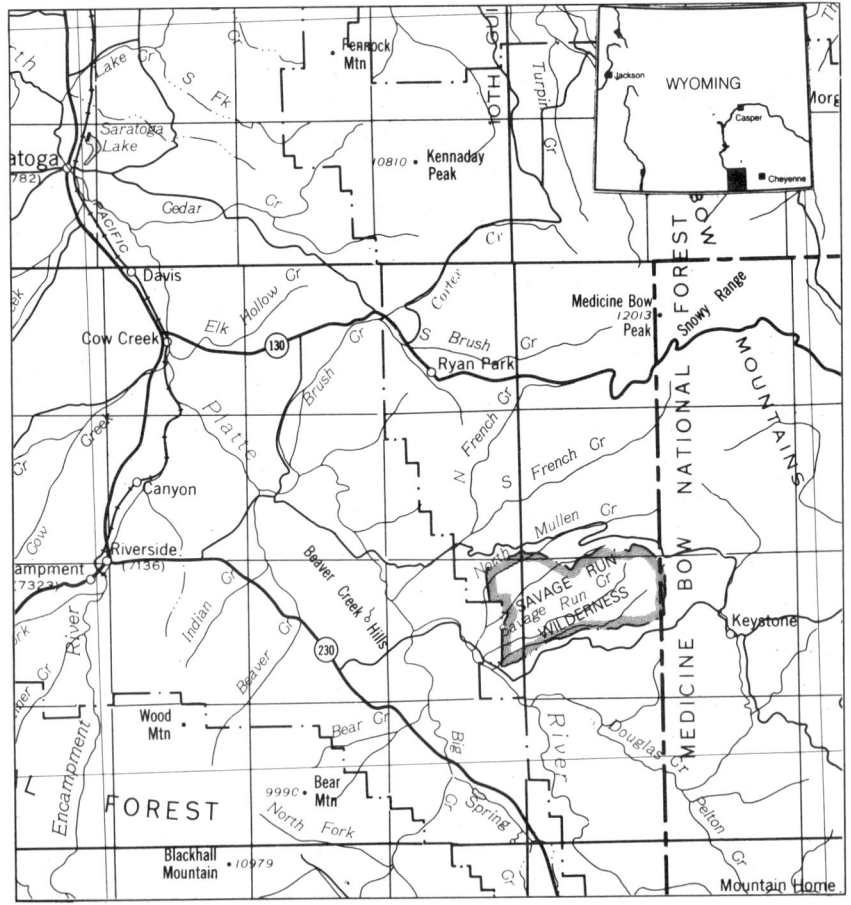

North Platte and Encampment Rivers

WOLF ADVENTURES and the WOLF HOTEL

Located just a block from the famous North Platte River in Saratoga, Wyoming. Economical accommodations; delicious cuisine/steaks a specialty; bar and lounge; and headquarters for expert fishing and hunting guide service. Float the Platte with us for a memorable Wolf Adventure.

Ph. 307/326-5525 (Doug Campbell) or 307/326-5736 (Stu McClelland)

---

is reached on county roads. A put-in fee is charged. Crossing the North Platte eastbound on the French Creek Road (County Road 660) it is 3 miles farther north to a lefthand turn, a gravel road to the Bennett Peak area, where there are campgrounds, a mile of fishing on public land, and launching sites.

The main river has excellent fly fishing, particularly during the fall, according to Stuart McClelland of Wolf Adventures in Saratoga. Prime spincast fishing with lures is during June and July, he says. Browns and rainbow in the river average 12-14 inches, but remember the special "slot limit" requires fish between 10 and 16 inches be landed promptly and returned to the river. Outfitters say the regulations are helping fishermen have a good shot at trout larger than that.

A listing and description of public access points on the North Platte is available for $2 from the Wyoming Game & Fish Department, 5400 Bishop Blvd., Cheyenne, Wyo. 82002. Or check locally with outfitters like Rick Hughes, Debbie and Stuart McClelland, or Great Rocky Mountain Outfitters, all of Saratoga.

A number of creeks entering the North Platte from the east offer fair to good fishing. **Douglas Creek** flows southwest out of the Snowy Range, joining the river 8 miles downstream from Sixmile Gap. It has good fishing for brown, brook and rainbow averaging 10 inches.

County and Forest Service roads provide access (see Medicine Bow National Forest Map; inquire locally) almost to the creek. Two tributaries of Douglas Creek, **Pelton Creek** and **Muddy Creek,** offer fair fishing for brown and rainbow. There is camping at Pelton Creek and at the Douglas Creek-North Platte confluence.

High up in the Douglas Creek drainage is **Rob Roy Reservoir** (150 ac) with fair to good fishing for brown, brook and rainbow averaging 12 inches. Motorboats are allowed. Rob Roy is reached from the east via an intricate network of roads from either

---

FIND YOUR WAY TO BLUE RIBBON FISHING
with
A Fisherman's & Riverrunner's
Map to
THE UPPER NORTH PLATTE RIVER*

River Access
Camping
Trails
Roads
Land Ownership

**Dick Prouty Associates
1780 Glen Dale Dr.
Lakewood, CO 80215**

$4.95 + 1.00 postage and handling

*prepared by the Wyoming Game & Fish Department

Albany or Centennial. From the west it is about 20 miles east of French Creek Campground on the French Creek Road.

French Creek, reached by County Road 660, flows west out of the Snowies and joins the North Platte 14 miles east of Encampment. Brook and rainbow average 10 inches and, in the lower reaches, chances of catching a 12-inch or larger brown are decent. French Creek Campground is on the edge of the national forest. **Cottonwood Creek,** flowing into the Platte between French and Douglas Creeks, offers only fair fishing.

Entering the North Platte from the south and west only 1.5 miles upstream from the French Creek juncture is **Big Creek,** which originates in Colorado. Hwy 230 crosses the creek about 8 miles from the Colorado-Wyoming border and about 6 miles south of the confluence with the North Platte. There is a mile of public fishing downstream from this point; upstream, the creek runs mostly on private land for 3 miles to Medicine Bow National Forest where it is open to the public. The creek is 15-20 feet wide and has good fishing for brook, rainbow and brown to 12 inches.

ENCAMPMENT RIVER

Also entering the upper North Platte from the south and west is the **Encampment River,** which enters Wyoming from Colorado and flows 40 miles to the North Platte. The lower reaches of this river run on private land, limiting public access. There is a public access area just south of the town of Encampment, and then a trail follows the river upstream across state and public lands into the Medicine Bow National Forest, where there are 12 miles of good fishing for brook, brown and rainbow trout that average 12 inches. A good road south from Encampment leads 25 miles to **Hog Park Reservoir** (150 ac). The reservoir was recently enlarged and restocked with brook and brown trout. Motorboats are allowed.

When the North Platte rolls out of the Medicine Bow National Forest near its juncture with Cottonwood Creek, it runs primarily on private lands to Saratoga. Landowners, many of whom run fishing clubs and dude ranches, are quite protective of their stretches of the river. A little over 9 miles upstream from Saratoga, just south of the junction of Hwys 130 and 230, the Treasure Island Public Fishing and Hunting Area opens over a mile of the river to bank fishermen. There is a campground and a launching area for floaters.

Spring Creek enters the North Platte from the southwest on the southern outskirts of Saratoga. Most of its lower portions are on private land where permission to fish is necessary. Fishing is fair to good in the upper reaches along the **North** and **South Forks of Spring Creek** in Medicine Bow National Forest for brook and rainbow averaging 10 inches. The South Fork of Spring Creek heads at **South Spring Creek Lake** (12 ac), at the foot of Bridger Peak. The lake is privately owned, and permission must be asked. The creek has brook and rainbow, and can be reached by trail from the Jack Creek Campground, 8 miles to the northwest. A better bet might be **North Spring Creek Lake** (20 ac), 6 miles from the Jack Creek Campground on the same trail, with the same fish species.

North Platte River Trips

Fishing on a blue ribbon trout stream • white water floats • scenic trips
Half day, full day and overnite trips available.

ELK MOUNTAIN SAFARI INC.

P.O. Box 188 Saratoga, WY 82331
Ed Beattie, Mgr. 307/326-8773

The Saratoga Inn,
Wyoming's finest hunting-fishing camp.

Lots of Wyoming's celebrated fishing is just a few feet from our lodge on the beautiful North Platte River in Southern Wyoming.
Cozy Bar and Lounge, delightful meals in our dining room, (we have a helluva staff of camp cooks). If you wish, do your fishing here beside our golf course, and ease those tired muscles in our giant-size natural hot water swimming pool.
It's all here for you at the **SARATOGA INN**, P.O. Box 869, Saratoga, Wyoming 82331, Ph. **(307) 326-5261.** See ya!

Check about unrestricted fishing at the Saratoga Inn in Saratoga, where the North Platte swirls along the 9-hole golf course.

The town of Saratoga, "where the fish jump on Main Street," actually has excellent fishing right in town. In most places no permission is needed, just a valid fishing license and conservation stamp.

SARATOGA LAKE

Saratoga Fishing Lake (300 ac) at the northeast edge of town boasts 12- to 14-inch rainbow, boat launching facilities, campgrounds, and great popularity as a winter fishing spot.

Jack Creek heads near Bridger Peak and runs north 10 miles before swinging northeast to join the main river from the west, 3 miles north of Saratoga. It offers fair fishing for small brown and brook. This water runs mostly on private land. Its headwaters can be reached by taking a county road west from Saratoga that swings southwest along Jack Creek to the forest boundary. The Jack Creek Campground is about 27 miles southwest of Saratoga.

Two roads head west from Hwy 130 north of Saratoga to about 10 miles of river open to public fishing. The first access road is 4 miles north of Saratoga, the second 6.5 miles north. Fishing is for brown and rainbow.

The North Platte runs under I-80 about 2 miles south of Fort Steele (a historic monument) 14 miles east of Rawlins. The river is open to fishermen for 11 miles south of Fort Steele, with paved and graveled roads and trails to various sections. No overnight camping is allowed. The fishing here is for good-size rainbow and brown.

Pass Creek lazily joins the North Platte in this public fishing area. It meanders northwest out of the Snowy Range to its juncture with the Platte. Its lower portions are mostly on private land, where permission to fish must be received. Take the Pass Creek Road (County Road 404) off Hwy 130 about 11 miles north of Saratoga, or, to reach Pass Creek's upper stretches in Medicine Bow National Forest, take County Road 504 east of Saratoga to the forest boundary and proceed from there on Forest Service roads. The creek offers fair to good fishing for 8- to 10-inch brook in beaver ponds; there are brown and rainbow from 10-12 inches in its lower reaches.

North of I-80, there are stretches of excellent river fishing, but first a look at the many lakes in the Snowy Range which contribute to it. Those that drain west swell several of the creeks described above. The lakes on the Snowy Range's eastern slopes drain into the Laramie River and its tributaries, or flow north to join the North Platte itself.

SNOWY RANGE LAKES

The Snowy Range comprises more than 500,000 acres of mountainous and heavily timbered land broken by grassy mountain meadows. The maximum elevation is 12,500 feet. Small streams abound, most of them dammed by beavers, and contain small brook trout. Much of the range is Forest Service land, though there is some private ownership. The mountain range is bisected east to west by Hwy 130, and there are numerous campgrounds, a ski area and easy access to lakes by 4-wheel-drive vehicles,

> *Usually, very fast or very slow retrieval of a cast gets better results than the middle-of-the stream speed most anglers use.*

cars, or short hikes. There is tremendous fishing pressure because of the concentration of population in this corner of the state and visitors from Colorado. Most lake fishing is maintained by stocking. Some 32 square miles of the forest have been closed to motor vehicles, and only two lakes, Sand Lake and Rob Roy Lake, can be fished from motorboats.

One mile west from the Snowy Range Pass on Hwy 130 are **Lake Marie** (10,500 ft; 24 ac) and **Mirror Lake** (10,530 ft; 18 ac) within a half mile of each other. They contain brook and rainbow averaging 10 inches. Lying at the foot of Medicine Bow Peak (12,006 ft) at the head of South French Creek, they are heavily fished. Just north is **Lookout Lake** (10,600 ft; 35 ac), with the same fishing but less pressure.

The marked Twin Lakes-Gold Hill Road, heads north about 6 miles west of Hwy 130's summit. A mile from the highway the road forks; to the left along South Brush Creek, but a mile farther on this 4-wheel drive road, turn north for another mile to **Lower Missouri Lake** (10,200 ft; 4 ac), a shallow lake which has fair fishing for small brook. North of it is **Stamp Mill Lake** (9900 ft; 4 ac) with similar fishing. Still another mile north is **Arrastre Lake** (10,220 ft; 10 ac) with small brook. A mile southwest is **Phantom Lake** (10,050 ft; 18 ac), with good fishing for small brook.

The first right fork from Hwy 130 on the Twin Lakes-Gold Hill Road leads 0.5 mile to **South Twin Lake** (10,282 ft; 22 ac) and **North Twin Lake** (10,400 ft; 20 ac), both with small brook. A 4-wheel drive road heads north 1.5 miles to **Dipper Lake** (10,650 ft; 11 ac), with good fishing for decent-sized rainbow and cutthroat. North of Dipper is **Quealy Lake** (10,340 ft; 10 ac) on a 4-wheel drive road. Another 0.5 mile by trail southeast leads to **Vagner Lake** (10,460 ft; 15 ac). Both lakes have good fishing for brook averaging 10 inches. Another 2 miles north is **Cascade (Campbell) Lake** (10,980 ft; 12 ac) with good fishing for 10- to 12-inch brook; a mile farther is **North Banner Lake** (9940 ft; 12 ac), with the same. Nearby are **East Banner Lake** (10,050 ft; 11 ac) and **South Banner Lake** (9960 ft; 4 ac) with more small brook. These lakes also can be approached from the north by driving south from I-80 on the Elk Mountain Road (County Road 101) and into the forest to within a half-mile of Cascade Lake.

Libby Lake (10,750 ft; 26 ac) and **Lewis Lake** (10,750 ft; 19 ac) are located a mile north of Hwy 130, following a signed road just west of the summit. Both lakes contain brook; Lewis also has rainbow to 13 inches, and campgrounds. This marks a popular starting point for hikes to other lakes. Northwest of Lewis are the three **Klondike Lakes, East, North** and **South** (10,760 ft; 2-11 ac), all with brook trout. Another half-mile north by trail are **North Gap Lake** (10,970 ft; 32 ac) and **South Gap Lake**

LEGENDARY FISH

The first account of the pyrite perch was published in the summer of 1887 after Sir Jacob Kant Foole, a geologist, mentioned it in an account on contemporary prospecting. Prospectors offered Sir Jacob a fish when he happened upon their camp at mealtime. Observing its particularly succulent flesh, he inquired of its origin and was shown to a stream near the camp.

"A most careful eye could scarcely discern a naturally disguised fish among pyrite deposits evident in the stream bed," he wrote, also noting the fish was much in favor among the populace. A bright orange-yellow mottled with brown, the perch died in great numbers early in the 20th century as a result of improved chemical ore processing methods. Some may remain today in remote areas in the central Rocky Mountains and Alaska, where it was known as "Foole's Goldfish."

NORTH PLATTE RIVER 355

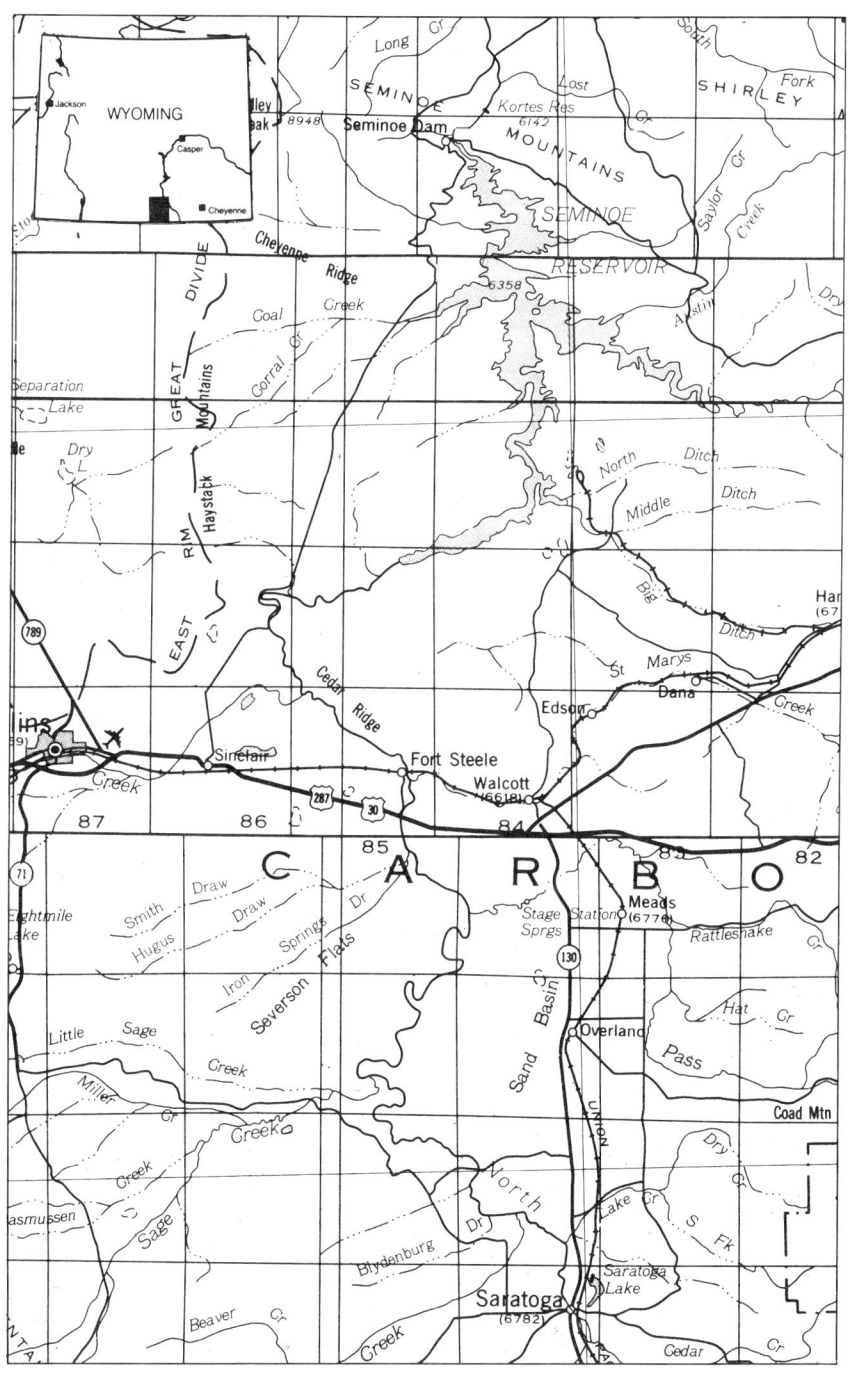

North Platte River, Seminoe Reservoir

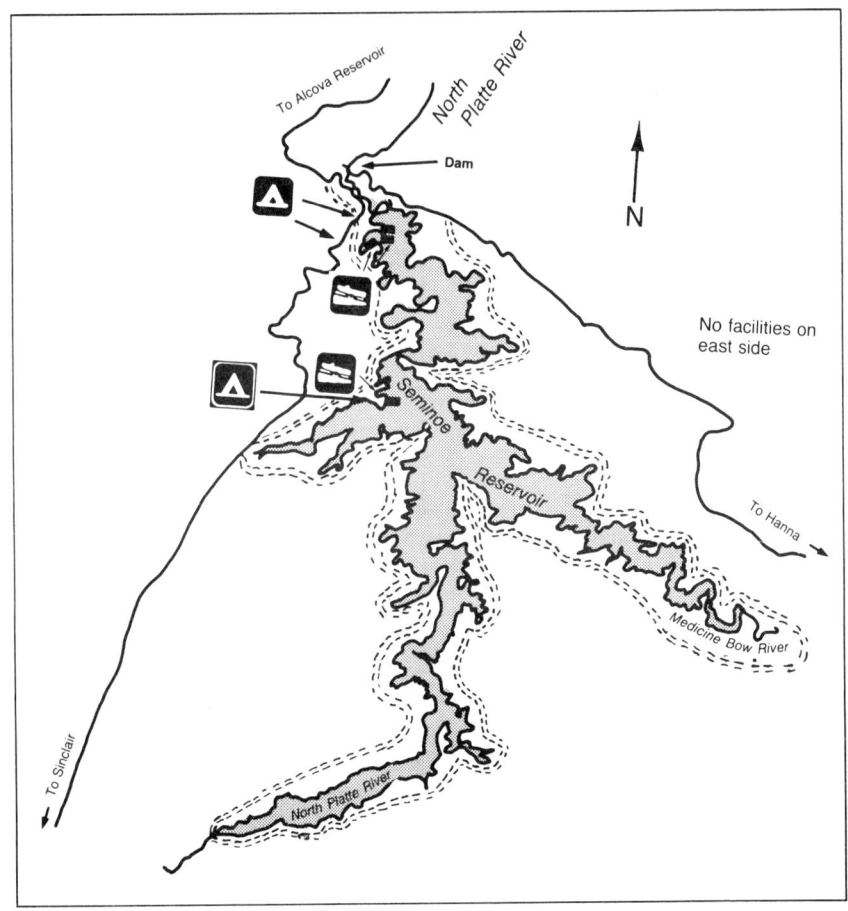

Seminoe Reservoir

(10,970 ft; 30 ac). There is good fishing for cutthroat to 12 inches in South, and brook and some golden of similar size in North. The four **Arrow (Shelf) Lakes** (10,970 ft; 1-7 ac) lie directly east of North Gap on the north side of Brooklyn Ridge.

East of the summit on Hwy 130 about 3.5 miles, only 9 miles west of the town of Centennial, a well-marked road goes north to **Brooklyn Lakes.** After one mile, the road forks. On the lefthand fork is **Little Brooklyn Lake** (10,350 ft; 7 ac) with brook averaging 9 inches, and some brown. Along the righthand fork 0.75 mile is **Big Brooklyn Lake** (10,526 ft; 22 ac) with rainbow and brook 12-14 inches. There is a campground and a road encircling the lake. The lake is heavily fished.

North by trail 0.5 mile from Big Brookyn are **East Glacier Lake** (10,730 ft; 6 ac), with good fishing for cutthroat to 12 inches, and **West Glacier Lake** (10,730 ft; 8 ac), where fishing is poor. One mile east of Big Brooklyn by trail is **South Twin lake** (10,650 ft; 10 ac), with cutthroat to12 inches. Just to the north is **North Twin Lake** (4 ac), which cannot sustain fish through the winter and is not stocked.

Still more lakes can be reached by taking a trail to the sterile **Sheep Lake** and beyond. Two to 3 miles above Sheep Lake are **North** and **South Meadow Lakes** (10,600 ft; 4 and

9 ac) with brook; **Garden Lakes** (10,700 ft; 5 and 10 ac) with brook; **Reservoir Lake** (10,760 ft; 25 ac) with brook; **Crescent Lake** (10,850 ft; 8 ac) with brook; and **Cutthroat Lake** (10,680 ft; 8 ac) with brook and cutthroat. East of Cutthroat is **Arrowhead Lake** (10,760 ft; 9 ac) with brook. And north of Sheep is **Mutt Lake** (10,625 ft; 25 ac) and **Jeff Lake** (10,620 ft; 12 ac) with brook. Still north of these lakes are **Grassy Lake** (10,650 ft; 2 ac) with small brook, and up Lindsey Creek, **Golden Lake** (10,450 ft; 10 ac) with good fishing for cutthroat to 16 inches.

A trail west beyond Little Brooklyn Lake leads a mile to **Big Telephone Lake** (10,750 ft; 9 ac), with good fishing for brook to 14 inches. **Scott Lake** (10,900 ft; 2 ac) and **Lost Lake** (10,900 ft; 17 ac), on the south side of Brooklyn Ridge, both have cutthroat to 12 inches.

SEMINOE RESERVOIR

Now back to the North Platte as it surges north of I-80 towards Casper. Live bait fishing is allowed in the river from I-80 north to **Seminoe Reservoir.** The reservoir is about 20 miles long, comprising about 13,000 acre feet of water. It fluctuates considerably and fishing can be poor when there are big irrigation drawdowns. The wind, too, can be fierce, but bays can offer protection to boaters.

The reservoir has become primarily a walleye fishery, with some rainbow and brown. The walleye limit is 10 in addition to a regular limit of trout. Lures with bait can be trolled for walleye from the middle of May to July.

The Eagle Lake strain of rainbow trout has been introduced into Seminoe downstream, as well as into Alcova Reservoir. This long-lived and voracious fish should be tipping the scales regularly at 5 pounds before long.

There are boat ramps on the west side, campgrounds, and a mile of shoreline is open to public use; adjacent landowners are often cooperative about access when asked. Trout average 11-16 inches, with some larger. Ice fishing is popular in the winter. The reservoir is reached by driving north on a county road from I-80 at Sinclair east of Rawlins. It also can be approached from the north by driving southwest from Casper to Alcova on Hwy 220, then taking the Kortes Road (County Road 291) south to the Kortes Dam, and from there on south on the Seminoe Road.

Seminoe and the two large reservoirs below it, Pathfinder and Alcova, have a special winter fishing season from December through February. Winter regulations are available from the Wyoming Game and Fish Department.

The **Medicine Bow River** and the **Little Medicine Bow River** join northeast of the town of Medicine Bow and flow into the southeast arm of Seminoe Reservoir. The rivers have only fair fishing for 10 inch brown, with larger trout near its juncture with Seminoe. Much of the flow is on private land, where permission is required. They drain the northern end of the Snowy Range, and headwater streams have good populations of brook trout in beaver ponds. County Road 101 south from Elk Mountain on I-80 follows them onto Forest Service land. Follow this road to **Sand Lake,** which drains into Rock Creek, where there are rainbow and brook 8-12 inches. Motors are allowed.

Just north of Seminoe Reservoir is the two-mile-long 920-acre **Kortes Reservoir,** which fills a deep canyon and offers only fair fishing for the trollers who ply its waters. The browns and rainbows average 15 to 18 inches; occasionally large browns are taken. Access is only from the south end and is difficult. Inquire locally.

MIRACLE MILE

Downstream from Kortes, the North Platte enters its famous **Miracle Mile** section—which actually is about 6 miles. This area is heavily fished. Despite the pressure, it lives up to its name, producing browns 10-14 inches and rainbow up to 2 pounds and sometimes larger, though not in great numbers. The area is easily accessible and there are several campgrounds. Drive about 30 miles south of Casper on Hwy 220, then south on Kortes Road another 30 miles from its exit near Alcova. The fishing is best with large wet flies, streamers and Mepps spinners.

There are two times a year when the Miracle Mile warrants special attention—May and June when many other streams are roily with runoff and during the fall hunting season when the crowds thin out and the fish are as hungry as they'll ever get.

One strange autumn twist is that "the mile" will sometimes be turbid if runoff was particularly heavy the previous spring. It takes that long for the silt suspended in the water to work its way through Seminoe Reservoir. A recent creel census by Wyoming Game & Fish showed rainbows averaging 14.7 inches, with almost a third of them over 17 inches. The average brown was 15.2 inches and the average cutthroat was nearly 17.5 inches.

"The mile" and reservoirs down and upstream have been planted with some challenging and fast-growing trout—Ohrid browns from Yugoslavia and Eagle Lake rainbows, which reputedly grow to enormous size. In 1984 a Colorado Golden of 7 pounds was taken from the mile.

PATHFINDER

Below Miracle Mile is **Pathfinder Reservoir** (5850 ft; 23,000 ac when full; 18 mi long). This impoundment is also subject to high winds and big drawdowns by irrigators—as much as 80-90 feet in dry years. Cutthroat 16-17 inches are commonly caught, as well as browns and walleyes up to 21 inches, and occasionally larger, and walleyes of 7 pounds are being challenged by the Ohrid browns for the angler's attention. A 6-pound Ohrid was landed at Pathfinder in 1984. There is a designated public use area and boat launching facilities. Be careful with lightweight boats when the wind is blowing. Trolling is best in the summer; bank fishing using lures and pop gear with worms is fair to good in the spring and fall. Live bait restrictions have been

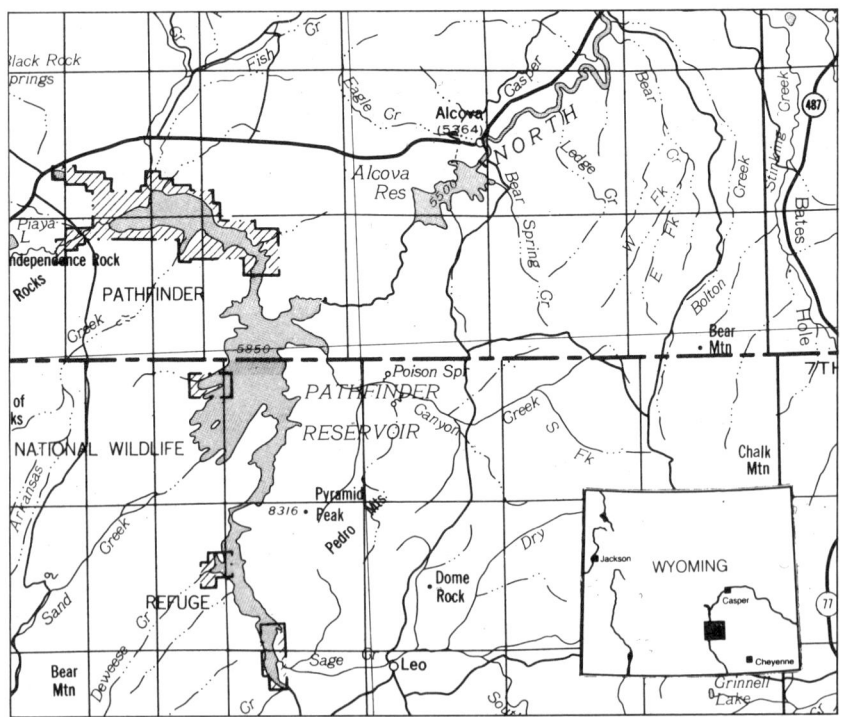

North Platte River, Pathfinder and Alcova Reservoirs

NORTH PLATTE RIVER 359

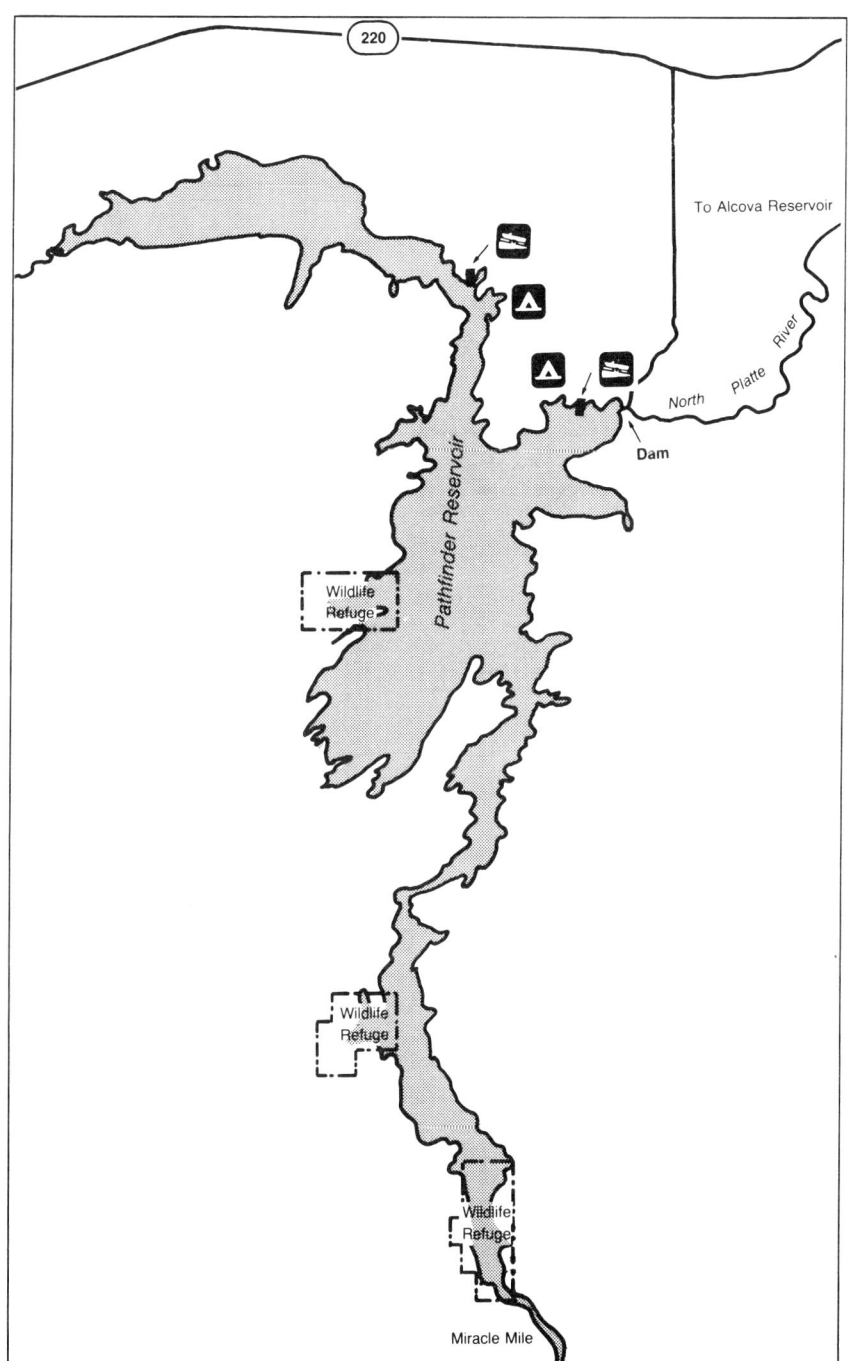

Pathfinder Reservoir

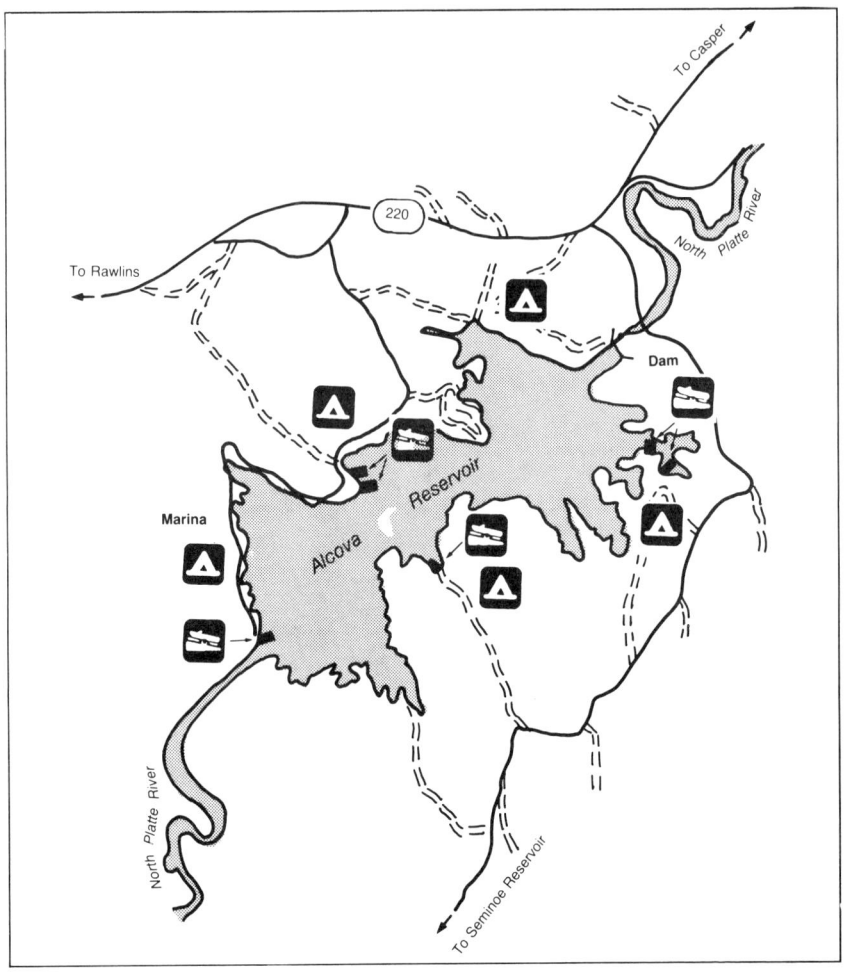

Alcova Reservoir

eased and minnows and spoons with pork strips are permissible.

The big spring runoff in 1983 swept substantial numbers of cutthroat over the dam and they're now spawning in some of the larger and deeper holes downstream. Some 4-pounders have been reported.

ALCOVA RESERVOIR

Alcova Reservoir (5000 ft), downstream from Pathfinder, is a better fishery than its upstream neighbors. It is 5 miles long, 2500 acres, and has several boat ramps, boat rental and supplies. The rainbow run 10-16 inches, with some cutthroat and the occasional brown as large as 5 pounds. A special regulation allows 12 trout per day, including one over 20 inches. Shore fishing is good in the spring and fall; trolling with lures and pop gear with worms is good in the summer. There are campgrounds. Fremont Canyon at the southwest end of Alcova is a miniature Grand Canyon and well worth a visit although there's no fishing.

Below Alcova, the North Platte is no

longer a top-notch fishery. There are several posted access areas, and there is lots of competition for 10- to 14-inch browns and stocked rainbow that are generally fished out by midsummer. Sections of the river here can be floated. Hwy 220 generally follows the river from Alcova to Casper.

Goldeneye Reservoir on Casper Creek just north of Casper was recently cleared of suckers and carp by chemical kill. It's been restocked with rainbow, which won't last long because of illegal stocking of walleye, yellow perch and ling.

Grey Reef Reservoir (182 ac when full), 30 miles southwest of Casper on Hwy 220 to County Road 412, is a regulating reservoir below Alcova. It has rainbow and brown in the channel, which can be hard to get to. Fishing upstream and down can be good for rainbow, Eagle Lake rainbow, brown, Ohrid brown and a few cutthroat. There's two miles of public access to the pools and rapids below Grey Reef, then a half mile or so of private land and then more public access. Fishermen park at the reservoir parking area and then walk.

North of Casper are several small ponds on BLM land. Some have trout and others have illegally introduced bass and perch. There are lots of them, but none of any size.

Bates Creek drains an area southwest of Casper and enters the North Platte 11 miles northeast of Alcova. Turn east off Hwy 220 on Hwy 487; after 9 miles County Road 141 follows the creek east. The creek has fair fishing for brook averaging 8 inches. Much of it is on private land, requiring owners' permission.

Twenty miles downstream from Casper, near the town of Glenrock, **Deer Creek** joins the North Platte from the south. It runs through a hodgepodge of state, federal and private lands from its source in the Deer Creek Range of the Medicine Bow National

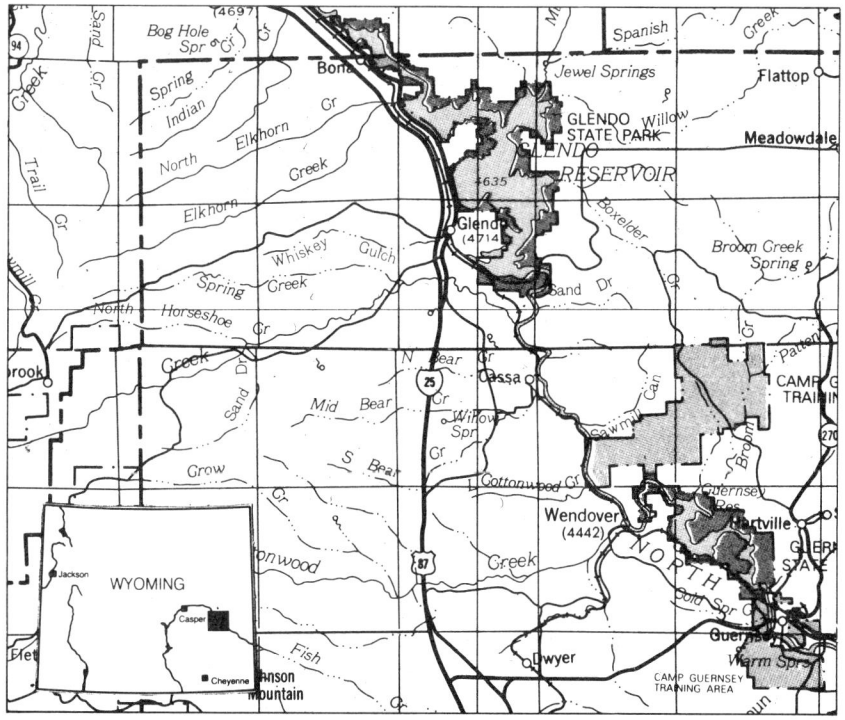

North Platte River, Glendo Reservoir, Guernsey State Park

Alcova Reservoir
Photo courtesy Wyo Travel Commission

Forest. It has good fly fishing for 10- to 15-inch browns and smaller rainbow, with brook in the headwaters. Avoid the lower 2 miles, where fishing is poor. Access to the upper stretches is by driving south from I-25 at Glenrock on the Mormon Canyon Road or the Deer Creek Road. Its middle section can be reached by taking the Hat Six Road from I-25 south, 2 miles east of Casper, 20 miles to the forest boundary.

La Prele Creek offers fair to good fishing for brown, brook and rainbow above **La Prele Reservoir,** which is located 5 miles south of I-25 about 12 miles west of Douglas on the Natural Bridge Road. Via the Cold Springs Road, it is west from Douglas. South of Douglas along the Esterbrook Road is **La Bonte Creek,** which has fair to good fishing for 10-inch brook in its upper portions.

Still farther south and east, running into the North Platte below the town of Glendo, is **Horseshoe Creek,** with fair to good fishing for brown and rainbow averaging 10

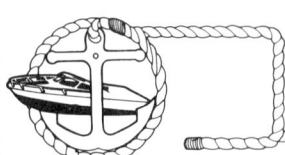

Glendo Marina
Your Recreation Headquarters

- Boat Sales & Service
- Tackle Shop
- Motel
- Restaurant

"Ask us about current fishing conditions"
Bill and Charlotte White

307-735-4216 • *Lake Shore Drive* • *P.O. Box 187* • *Glendo, Wyoming 82213*

inches. A county road one mile south of Glendo follows the creek. Much of it is on private land, where permission to fish is necessary.

Glendo Reservoir is the last large impoundment of interest to fishermen on the Platte—it has walleye, rainbow and perch.

Channel catfish have been introduced and there are good rainbow just below the Glendo Dam. Access is blocked in many areas by private landowners.

Seven- to eight-pound channel cat were being caught in the river upstream from Glendo before ice-out in 1985.

Glendo covers about 12,000 acres, but, like the other reservoirs on the river, it is subjected to considerable drawdowns by irrigators. The lake produces walleye predominantly; there is a full service marina with boat rentals at Glendo; there are several boat ramps, too. Trolling in the mornings and evenings is usually the most successful. After the ice is out, rainbow are caught near the dam on spinners and spoons, and the perch average 8 to 12 inches. Ice fishing is popular here. There is a three-month special winter season from December through February.

Glendo Reservoir

Above and around Glendo there are several small tributaries that offer good angling. Try the **Roaring Fork, Ashenfelder, Friend** and **Boxelder** creeks for rainbow, especially in the spring.

The North Platte flows another 80 miles to the Nebraska-Wyoming Line, but the water and fishing quality suffer from irrigation drawdowns, and the water is too warm for trout.

LOWER NORTH PLATTE

The **Laramie River** flows north and east from the Snowy Range across the Laramie Plain to enter the North Platte at Fort Laramie. The upper stream has excellent fly fishing; much of the river is heavily fished. Where access is possible there is good fishing for browns 12-14 inches and larger, and some rainbow. Take Hwy 230 west from Laramie. The road leaves the river to follow Woods Creek up Medicine Bow National Forest and provide access to the small creeks and beaver ponds that feed into the Laramie.

Fishermen in the Laramie area can get expert advice from Phil Hicks at the West Laramie Fly Store. His enthusiasm is contagious, his knowledge astonishing.

Draining the Snowies to the north is the **Little Laramie River** which joins the bigger river northwest of Laramie on the north side of I-80. Take Hwy 130 about 21 miles west from Laramie and then turn south on County Road 11. Most of the river is on private land, but there is some signed public access before it enters the forest, including a half-mile of public fishing off Hwy 130, 16 miles west of Laramie. The **North, Middle** and **South Forks** of the Laramie River all flow from the forest. They offer small brook and a few brown and rainbow. A Forest Service road leaves Hwy 130, 4 miles northwest of Centennial and follows the North Fork for several miles; a road leaves Hwy 11 at Albany and follows the South Fork. By following this road about 8 miles from Albany, you will reach Rob Roy Reservoir (150 ac), which drains south and west into Douglas Creek (described previously).

Lake Owen (100 ac) is a popular fishery 3 miles south of Albany. It is reached by county and Forest Service roads. It produces mostly small brook but occasionally a large rainbow. There is a campground.

On the Laramie, 10 miles above its confluence with the North Platte, is the **Grayrocks Reservoir** (3500 ac). This water body has walleye to 2 pounds and probably some of the best perch fishing in the state, as well as rainbow averaging 12 inches, and some brown trout. The trout are declining in the warm water, and walleye, perch, largemouth bass and channel catfish are fished with bait, jigs, minnows and lures. There is camping on the southside and a boat ramp, and more access is planned. No fishing or boats are allowed near the dam.

Take Hwy 160 east off I-25 at the North Wheatland exit; or go west on 160 from US 26 at Fort Laramie to reach Grayrocks.

East of the Snowy Range, in the open spaces that feed the Laramie as it meanders towards the North Platte, there are a number of aptly named "plains" reservoirs and lakes, some of which provide good fishing. They get fished heavily, and require stocking. They are often treeless, shallow and fluctuating because of agricultural draw downs, but their popularity has sparked efforts to improve the fishing.

Very popular is **Lake Hattie** (2900 ac when full), 18 miles west of Laramie. The lake has good fishing for brown, rainbow, yellow perch and some cutthroat to 15 inches, with an occasional lunker. There are campsites and boat launching areas. This lake is supplied irregularly with water from the Laramie River by canal, and it sometimes runs low. Access is attained by driving 8 miles southwest from Laramie on Hwy

---

HAIR & FUR SUPPLY

QUALITY - QUANTITY - VARIETY
For The Tyer Who Demands
The Best

Box 3531   University Station
Laramie, WY 82071
(307) 721-2837

Charles A. Walker photo

230 the turning west on Pahlow Lane (County roads 41 and 422) for another 10 miles.

Also on Pahlow Lane, closer to Laramie, is **Meeboer Lake** (115 ac). This shallow lake has good fishing for planted rainbow trout. A half-mile west of Meeboer is **Gelatt Lake** (34 ac), with rainbow averaging 10 inches and grayling. **Sodergreen Lake,** located along Hwy 230 about 17 miles southwest of Laramie, has fair fishing for 10-inch rainbow and an occasional big brown. The lake provides municipal water storage for Laramie. There are boat launching sites. **Twin Buttes Lake** (300 ac) is a mile from Gelatt Lake on Pahlow Lane, and it has good fishing for brown and rainbow despite plentiful chubs and suckers—which youngsters delight in at an age when a fish is a fish. **Diamond Lake** is probably the most popular lake in the area.

Alsop Lake (40 ac) is 14 miles northwest of Laramie, north of I-80, and is reached by taking Herrick Lane Road off Hwy 130 west of Laramie. The lake is surrounded by private land, but the owners allow fishing for rainbow trout from May 1 through October 31. There are a lot of suckers here. Splake have been planted. A second lake in this area, **West Carroll lake** (70 ac), was previously listed in this guide, but now is owned by a private fishing club. Another previously listed lake, **Ione Lake** (130 ac) was once a good rainbow fishery but has lost its water supply and is becoming a "mud puddle."

One large body of water 40 miles north of Laramie—**Wheatland Reservoir No. 2** —shows up on most maps, but is closed to fishing.

East Allen Lake (160 ac) lies 2 miles south of Medicine Bow. The lake has abundant small rainbow and cutthroat. Boat launching facilities are available.

Guernsey Reservoir, on the North Platte north of Guernsey, is not good fishing. It fluctuates greatly and is usually very low late in the year.

Near Wheatland, just off I-25, 5 miles north of town, there is **Wheatland Reservoir No. 3,** one of three irrigation impoundments, with good fishing for walleye and rainbow. Cutthroat are also now stocked. **Festo Lake** (50 ac) is 3 miles northwest of Wheatland, with largemouth bass and channel catfish. No motors are allowed. There is winter and night fishing. Ten miles north of Wheatland on I-25 is **Joe Johnson Reservoir** (200 ac) with good fishing for bullheads and rainbow trout. **Rock Lake** (45 ac) is 4 miles south and 4 miles west of Wheatland, and has bass, walleye and crappie. There are boat launching facilities.

Crystal Reservoir (100 ac), **Granite Reservoir** (100 ac) and **North Crow Reservoir** (90 ac) are 25 miles west of Cheyenne on the Happy Jack Road. There is heavy fishing pressure from Cheyenne for rainbow averaging 10 inches. Boat permits from the city (this is their drinking supply) must be obtained.

Leazenby Lake (25 ac) is about 10 miles south of Laramie off US 287. It has good fishing for 9- to 12-inch rainbow and yellow perch. □

"Some people go fishing in a stream full of fish and don't catch a darned one. People who just don't know how to fish always swear there's not a fish in the water."—Jess Hackstaff, 86, talking about the Laramie River.

U.S. Forest Service campgrounds

U.S. Forest Service compilation was current as of 1985.
Asterisks denote fee areas. Some campgrounds are open only Memorial Day weekend through Labor Day. Below freezing weather could mean no water supply.

NORTH PLATTE RIVER DRAINAGE

MEDICINE BOW NATIONAL FOREST
Headquarters: 605 Skyline Drive, Laramie, WY 82070

Campground name	Elevation	No camp sites	Travel trailers	Drinking water	Length of stay (days)	Location and directions
Battle Creek	7800	4	Yes	Yes	14	23 mi E of Savery on Wyo. 401
Little Sandstone	8400	9	Yes	Yes	14	15.6 mi NE of Savery on Wyo. 401
Bottle Creek	8800	16	Yes	Yes	14	7 mi SW of Encampment on Wyo. 70
Six Mile Gap	8000	7	Yes	Yes	14	26.6 mi SE of Encampment on Wyo. 230 and forest road
French Creek	8000	15	Yes	Yes	14	15.5 mi E of Encampment on Wyo. 230 and county hwy
Lakeview	8400	34	Yes	Yes	14	28 mi SW of Encampment by Wyo. 70 and forest road
Lost Creek	8800	14	Yes	Yes	14	14 mi SW of Encampment on Wyo. 401
Haskins Creek	9000	10	Yes	Yes	14	15.3 mi SW of Encampment on Wyo. 401
South Brush Creek*	7900	21	Yes	Yes	14	Off Wyo. 130, 23 mi SE of Saratoga
Jack Creek	8500	12	Yes	Yes	14	27 mi SW of Saratoga on county hwy 500 and forest road
Ryan Park Trailer Camp	8000	49	Yes	Yes	14	On Wyo. 130., 18.8 mi SE of Saratoga
Lincoln Park*	7800	6	Yes	Yes	14	Off Wyo. 130, 25.5 mi E of Saratoga
Bow River*	8600	13	Yes	Yes	14	15.5 mi S of Elk Mt. on county hwy and forest road
Deep Creek	10,200	12	Yes	Yes	14	25.3 mi SE of Elk Mt. on county hwy and forest roads
Campbell Creek	8200	9	Yes	Yes	14	32.4 mi SW of Douglas on Wyo. 501 and forest road
Esterbrook	6500	12	Yes	Yes	14	24 mi SW of Douglas on Wyo. 503 and forest road

Curtis Gulch	7500	6	Yes	Yes	14	27.6 mi SW of Douglas on Wyo. 501, county highway and forest road
Pole Creek*	8300	18	Yes	Yes	14	3 mi off I-80, 8 mi SE of Laramie
Yellow Pine*	8400	19	Yes	Yes	14	3 mi off I-80, 14 mi SE of Laramie
Tie City*	8600	26	Yes	Yes	14	Off I-80, 9.2 mi SE of Laramie
Woods Creek	8900	9	Yes	Yes	14	On Wyo. 230, 31 mi SW of Laramie
Holmes	9700	11	Yes	Yes	14	44 mi W of Laramie on Wyo. 130 and forest roads
Boswell Creek	8900	9	Yes	Yes	14	Off Wyo. 230, 41 mi SW of Laramie
Vedawoo*	8200	11	Yes	Yes	14	Off I-80, 15.5 mi SE of Laramie
Pelton Creek*	8100	15	Yes	Yes	14	8 mi NW of Wyo. 230, 40 mi SW of Laramie
Rob Roy*	9500	20	Yes	Yes	14	42 mi W of Laramie on Wyo. 130 and forest road
Libby Creek—Spruce*	8600	8	Yes	Yes	14	2 mi NW of Centennial on Wyo. 130
Libby Creek—Aspen*	8600	8	Yes	Yes	14	Off Wyo. 130, 2 mi NW of Centennial
Libby Creek—Pine*	8600	6	Yes	Yes	14	Off Wyo. 130, 2.1 mi NW of Centennial
Brooklyn Lake*	10,500	17	Yes	Yes	14	Off Wyo. 130, 11.5 mi NW of Centennial
Sugar Loaf*	10,700	16	Yes	Yes	14	Off Wyo. 130, 14 mi NW of Centennial
Nash Fork*	10,200	29	Yes	Yes	14	Off Wyo. 130, 13.6 mi W of Centennial
Silver Lake*	10,400	21	Yes	Yes	14	On Wyo. 130, 16 mi W of Centennial
Lake Owen*	9000	38	Yes	Yes	14	5 mi NE of Foxpark on forest roads
Bobbie Thompson*	8800	10	Yes	Yes	14	11 mi NW of Foxpark on forest road
Miller Lake*	9100	7	Yes	Yes	14	Off forest road, .8 mi S of Foxpark
Pickaroon	7800	7	Yes	Yes	14	23 mi W of Foxpark on forest road 512
Pike Pole	7800	6	Yes	No	14	23.5 mi W of Foxpark on forest road 512
Evans Creek*	9000	12	Yes	Yes	14	.6 mi S of Foxpark on forest roads

Northeast Wyoming
Keyhole Reservoir

ADJACENT COMMUNITIES:
Sheridan, Story, Buffalo,
Kaycee, Moorcroft, Sundance.

PRINCIPAL HIGHWAYS:
U.S. I-25, I-90, 87, 14; Wyo. 331, 335, 24.

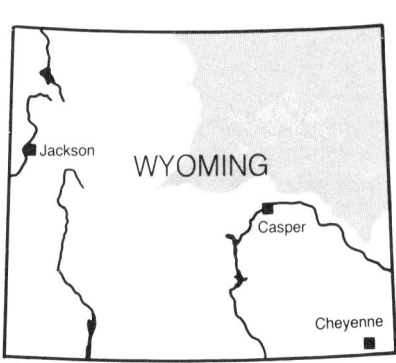

Fishing in northeast Wyoming focuses on two principal areas: the east side of the Bighorn Mountains west of Buffalo and Sheridan, and Keyhole Reservoir near Moorcroft, more than 100 miles to the east. And the fishing can be extra fine in both areas.

In between, the rolling, grassy Powder River Basin just doesn't stack up for fishing—unless it's for broken drillpipe downhole in an oil or gas well. The Powder River itself has been described as a mile wide and an inch deep—until it stops raining.

Keyhole Reservoir, described at the end of this chapter, is one of the most popular, productive and promising fisheries around.

POWDER RIVER

Streams flowing out of the Bighorns from the Middle Fork of the Powder River and northward offer fishing, if any, only at their headwaters. The **South Fork of the Powder River** and its tributaries aren't worth a fisherman's time.

West of I-25 at Kaycee, via Hwys 190 & 191, some good fishing can be found in the upper reaches of the **Middle Fork** and **North Fork of the Powder River.** In fact, Outlaw Canyon on the Middle Fork is designated blue ribbon trout fishing by the Wyoming Game and Fish Department. Access is tricky, so inquire in Kaycee at the cafe. The state and Bureau of Land Management have negotiated access across private land. Fishing is for brown trout, mostly, and includes stretches of **Buffalo, Beaver, Blue** and **Red Fork Creeks.**

The North Fork Powder River, reached by Hwy 191, is good fishing, but once again it is mostly on private property. It has a canyon area that offers good fishing, but it's private, so get permission. The North Fork is fair for 8- to 12-inch rainbow and brown. Near its headwaters, **Dullknife Reservoir** is a fluctuating irrigation reservoir on private land. Dullknife is rated good for 10- to 15-inch brook, brown, rainbow and cutthroat. Access to the reservoir is by taking US 16 west from Buffalo about 27 miles to the Hazelton Road intersection. Turn south and drive 12 miles to the reservoir.

Pass and **Dry Creeks,** tributaries of the North Fork, are usually dry by summer and offer no fishing.

Moving north on the Powder, several tributaries enter the Powder below the forks: **Salt, Fourmile, Soldier, Willow, Nine-**

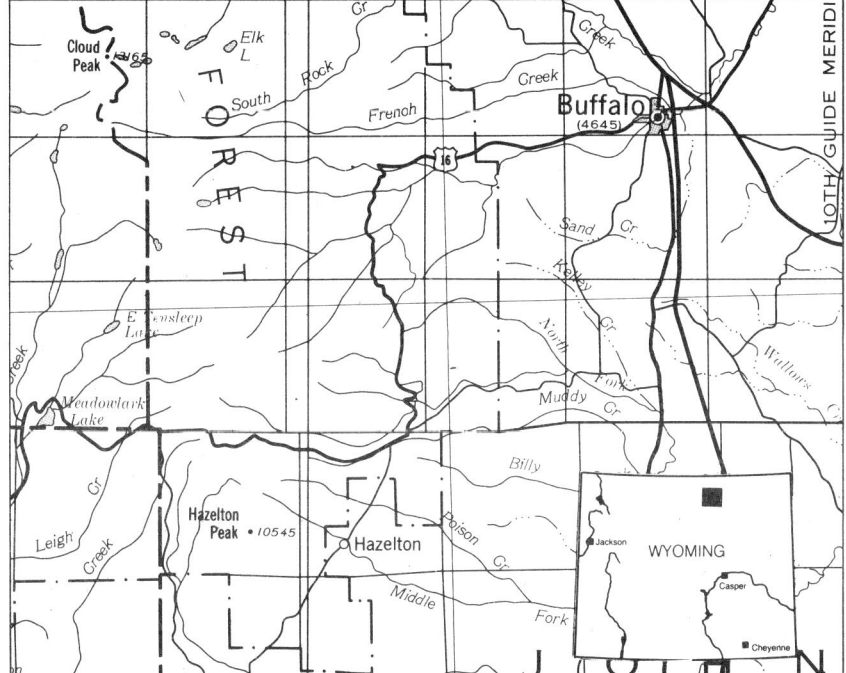

Bighorn Mountains, French Creek

mile, **Pumpkin** and **Deadhorse Creeks** are fishless.

CRAZY WOMAN CREEK

The headwaters of **Crazy Woman Creek** are just north of the Powder River forks. Crazy Woman and its **South Fork** offer virtually no fishing. The shovel-nose sturgeon is being caught on Crazy Woman and Clear Creek as they come up to spawn. Check regulations.

The **Middle Fork Crazy Woman Creek** meanders about 10 miles, mostly through private land. It is a ponded stream with good brown fishing. It can be reached by I-25 and Hwy 196 from where they cross the creek. Its headwaters are accessible from Hazelton in the national forest, about 30 miles southwest of Buffalo.

North Fork Crazy Woman, with its headwaters in the Bighorn National Forest, offers good fishing for 8- to 10-inch brown and rainbow. A road follows the stream through the canyon where fishing is good for rainbow. Check at Buffalo or Hazelton on access.

CLEAR CREEK

The headwaters of **Clear Creek** lie north of the Crazy Woman Creek headwaters. It has good fishing for brown and rainbow from 8 to 12 inches from about 5 miles east of Buffalo upstream to its forks in the national forest. This is mostly private land; seek permission. Most of the stream west of Buffalo is on public land.

To reach the alpine lakes of the southern Cloud Peak Primitive Area, drive 12 miles west on US 16 from Buffalo to Hunter Creek. Four-wheel drive roads lead west following North Clear Creek to the primitive area boundary. Or continue on US 16 to Middle Fork or South Fork campgrounds. Both camping areas have trails and rough roads leading to the nearby primitive area boundary.

South Clear Creek is crossed by US 16. The stream is good for rainbow and brown to 8 inches. At its headwaters are several lakes in the Cloud Peaks. These lakes include: **Lame Deer Lakes** which have rainbow; **Chill Lakes** with no fish; **Firehole Lakes** (9500 ft; 8 and 18 ac) with mackinaw to 17 inches, rainbow and brook; **South Fork Ponds,** with brook and rainbow to 8 inches. **Mabel Lake** has no fish.

Sourdough Creek is a southern tributary of South Clear Creek, entering near Tie Hack Campground just off US 16 at South Fork Campground. Sourdough is rated fair to good for 6-inch brook and some rainbow.

Duck Creek enters the South Clear Creek west of the South Fork Campground. The stream is good for small rainbow and brook. At its headwaters, which are near the South Clear Creek headwaters, are **Brown Bear Lake** (5 ac) and **Magdalene Lake** (10 ac) which have cutthroat from 10 to 14 inches, and **Trigger Lake** (10 ac) with 10- to 12-inch cutthroat. Access is by 4-wheel drive road to the west about a mile south of South Fork Campground.

Middle Clear Creek enters Clear Creek about 3 miles east of Middle Fork Campground. The stream is good for brown and brook below the campground, and good for brook above it. At its headwaters in the primitive area about 7 miles west of the campground, is **Lake Angeline** (10,700 ft; 56 ac). The lake is good for cutthroat 10 to 14 inches. Access is by a 4-wheel-drive road that runs 5 miles to the primitive area boundary, then 3 more miles by trail to the lake.

North Clear Creek has good access by road and then by trail into the primitive area. The stream has rainbow and brook to 8 inches. A small tributary, **Hunter Creek,** which enters from the north at North Fork Campground, is rated good for brook.

At the headwaters of North Clear Creek are several lakes near the center of the primitive area. **Florence Lake** (11,100 ft; 18 ac) is good fishing for cutthroat from 9-14 inches. **Powell Lakes** (12 and 16 ac) are good for cutthroat 10 to 16 inches. Farther downstream, still in the primitive area, **Seven Brothers Creek** enters North Clear from the southwest. This stream is overpopulated with small brook averaging 5 inches. At the headwaters of Seven Brothers Creek are **Seven Brothers Lakes** (9600 ft; 5 to 20 ac). The seven lakes have mackinaw and rainbow. Lake No. 6 has cutthroat.

Frozen Lakes are south of Seven Brothers Lakes about 2 miles. They are less than a half-mile north of Lake Angeline at the headwaters of Middle Clear Creek. There are two lakes, with the lower having golden. There are no fish in the upper lake.

French Creek enters Clear Creek from the west less than 5 miles west of Buffalo. The lower reaches are on private property and the upper ones are in the forest. The stream is rated fair to good for rainbow and brook to 12 inches. Check locally for access.

Rock Creek enters Clear Creek just east of Buffalo. It flows from the northwest to meet Clear Creek. Rock is primarily a brown trout stream and most of it flows through private property. The upper forks, **North** and **South Rock Creeks,** have brook.

Healy Reservoir (250 ac) is 6 miles east of Buffalo on old highways 14-16. It's stocked with rainbow and, although owned by Texaco, Inc., is open to the public. No boats. It is scheduled to be lowered in the fall of 1985 and treated chemically for suckers and other trash fish. It's to be refilled and restocked in late fall with rainbow.

PINEY CREEK

South Piney and **Kearny Creeks** in the national forest offer fishing for rainbow and brook. Access to these streams and their headwater lakes is complex; inquire at Buffalo, Kearny or Story.

North Piney Creek enters Piney near the town of Story. It offers good fishing for rainbow and brook.

Access to the Cloud Peak Primitive Area and its northern lakes is from Sheridan by driving 17 miles southwest through the town of Big Horn along the Red Grade Road to Little Goose Campground. From Little Goose Campground, the road stretches 5 miles, and then a trail leads another 3 miles to the primitive area boundary and the Highland Park area. This is the best access to Kearny Lakes despite what appears to be a 4-wheel drive road from Banner. This road is on private property and cannot be used.

Another route into the north end of the Cloud Peak Primitive Area is by driving about 20 miles from Sheridan through Big Horn on the Red Grade Road to Big Goose Campground. From Big Goose Campground, drive south to Bighorn Reservoir. Four-wheel drive vehicles can drive as far as the footbridge over Cross Creek, midway between Cross Creek Reservoir and Bighorn Reservoir. From the footbridge, hike west about 5 miles to Highland Park in the Cloud Peak Primitive Area.

At the headwaters of Kearny and North and South Piney Creeks, several lakes straddle the primitive area boundary. They include: **Diamond, Glacier** and **Mead Lakes** with rainbow and brook; **Cloud Peak Reservoir** (100 ac) with cutthroat and rainbow; **South Piney** and **Flatiron Lakes** (16 ac) with cutthroat and brook to 11 inches; **Frying Pan Lake** (10 ac) with 7- to 10-inch cutthroat and rainbow; **Kearny Lakes** (100 ac) with mackinaw and rainbow. Inside the primitive area are **Sawtooth Lakes** with rainbow; **Bard Lake** (10,600 ft; 8 ac) and

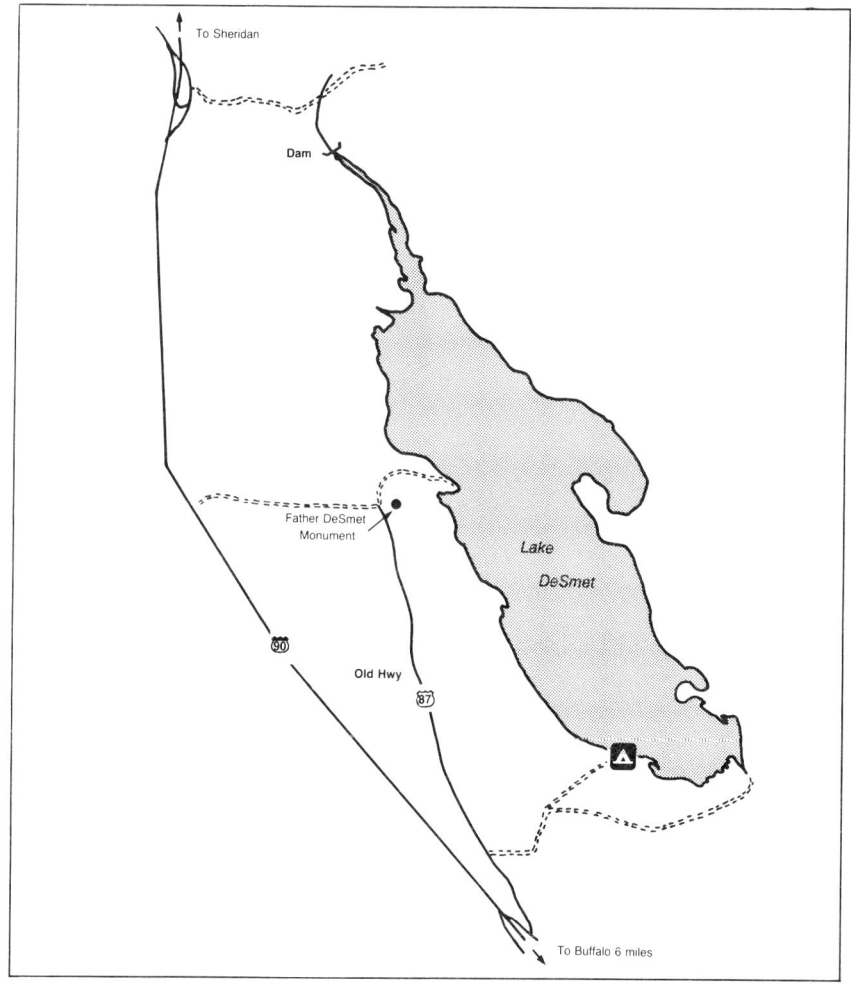

Lake De Smet

Loomis Lake with cutthroat; **Spear Lake** with brook; **Myrtle** and **Elephant Head Lakes** with golden; **Lake Silver** with no fish; and **Highland Park,** and **Peggy Lakes** with brook and rainbow.

East of that group of lakes and outside the primitive area, **Willow Park Reservoir** (8600 ft; 150 ac) is one of the largest waterbodies in the area. It is on South Piney Creek and is fair to good fishing for brook, cutthroat and rainbow to 10 inches.

Fishing is looking up at **Lake DeSmet** on Piney Creek just east of I-90, 10 miles northeast of Buffalo. DeSmet has been enlarged from 2300 acres to 3600 acres when full. It's 110 feet deep at an elevation of 4620 feet. An ongoing stocking program is emphasizing the Eagle Lake Rainbow, a fast growing, scrappy trout that's a little easier to catch than its rainbow relative. There also are perch, crappie and rock bass. A boat ramp is on the south end. Fishing is best by trolling or fishing from shore.

GOOSE CREEK

The Tongue River drains the northern end of the Bighorn Mountains. Its principal tributary is **Goose Creek** which enters from the south just north of Sheridan.

To the southwest, **Big Goose Creek** flows through 20 miles of rough country. It offers good fishing for brown and rainbow west of Beckton (10 miles west of Sheridan on Hwy 331) to the headwaters of East and West Forks Big Goose Creek in the Bighorns.

East Fork Big Goose Creek flows from the south to enter Big Goose Creek about 7 miles southwest of Beckton. From its confluence with Big Goose Creek to its headwaters, East Fork offers about 20 miles of good fishing for brook and rainbow. Access to the headwaters is by turning south from Big Goose Creek Ranger Station, about 12 miles southwest of Beckton.

At the headwaters of East Fork Big Goose Creek, inside Cloud Peak, are several lakes including **Lake Geneva** (9200 ft; 27 ac), which is good for brook and mackinaw, and **Crystal Lake** (9600 ft; 9 ac), rated fair to good for small rainbow.

Edelman Creek is a small tributary of the East Fork and is rated good for small brook. It enters East Fork near Coffeen Park Campground on the primitive area border, about 2 miles south of Park Reservoir.

At the headwaters of Edelman Creek, **Thayer Lake** (8800 ft; 4 ac) is good to excellent for small brook. **Devils Lake** (9000 ft; 10 ac) is rated good for small brook.

At Park Reservoir, **Cross Creek** enters the East Fork Big Goose Creek. There are several lakes at the headwaters of Cross Creek including **Cross Creek Lakes** which are good for brook and rainbow to 10 inches. **Cross Creek Reservoir** (8900 ft; 20 ac) is fair to good fishing for brook, rainbow and brown to 12 inches. **Bighorn Reservoir** is surrounded by private property and is often drained dry during the summer.

Park Reservoir (8400 ft) fluctuates greatly. It is rated fair for brook and some rainbow. On the west side of the reservoir, **Patricia Lake** (8500 ft; 5 ac) is fair to good for 10-inch cutthroat.

West Fork Big Goose Creek is less than 5 miles west of Park Reservoir. The stream offers fishing for brook and rainbow to 10 inches. Access is by good road from Ranger Creek Campground, just north of Park Reservoir.

There are several lakes at the headwaters of West Fork including **Lake Buffalo** (9900 ft; 3.5 ac), which is good fishing for small brook. **Geddes Lake** (9300 ft; 20 ac) offers excellent fishing for small brook. **Dome, Heart** and **Crescent Lakes,** near Twin Lakes Campground, are private and closed to fishing.

North of Dome Lake, **Coney Creek** enters West Goose from the west. At its headwaters are **Coney Lake** (9100 ft; 19 ac), good for small brook to 10 inches, and **Stull Lakes** (8900 ft; 15 and 3 ac). The larger Stull Lake is good for brook and rainbow to 10 inches, and the smaller is good for small brook.

Sawmill Creek enters the West Goose north of Coney Creek from the west. The stream is rated good to excellent for small brook. Near the end of the 4-wheel-drive road that provides access are the **Sawmill Lakes** (8000 ft; 14 ac each). The Upper and Lower lakes have splake and cutthroat to 12

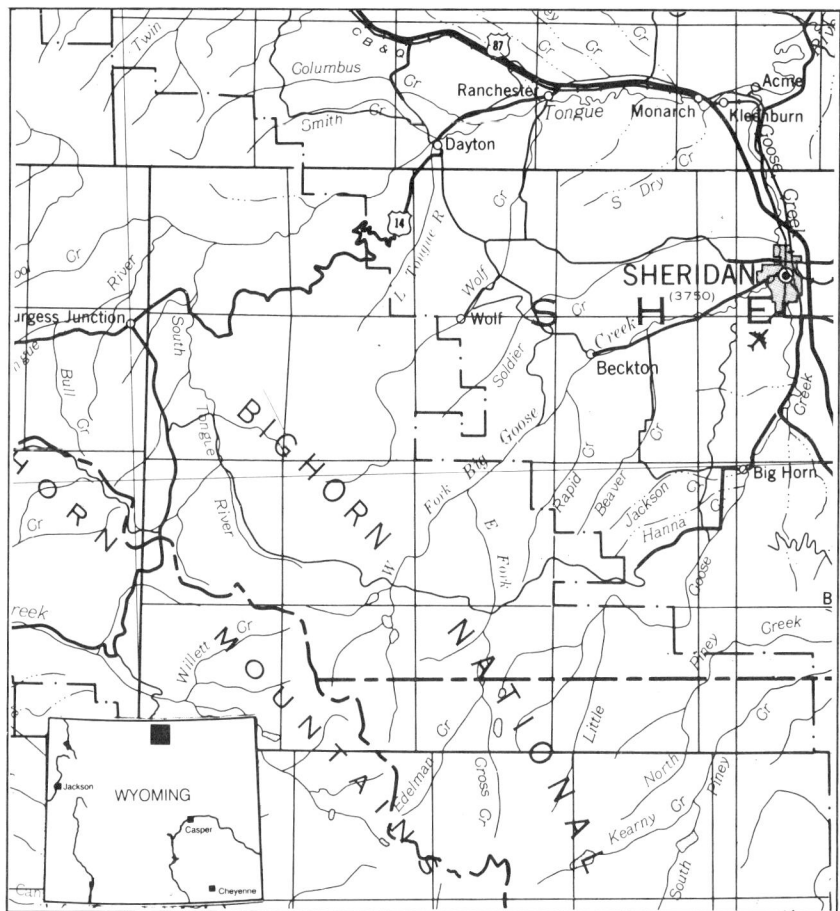

Bighorn Mountains, Tongue River

inches. Above the lakes, **Sawmill Reservoir** has brook.

TONGUE RIVER

The **Tongue River** drains the northern end of the Bighorn National Forest. It flows 60 miles from the west, just north of Sheridan, into Montana. US 14 parallels the streams most of its way through the national forest. Only the stretches west of Dayton in the forest are open to public fishing.

The **North Tongue River** is the farthest west tributary on US 14. It provides fair fishing for rainbow, brook and some brown.

Bull Creek enters North Tongue from the south about 4 miles west of Burgess Junction on US 14. Bull is a small stream that is rated fair for cutthroat and brook. **Big Willow Creek** also enters North Tongue from the south at North Tongue Campground near Burgess Junction. It is a small stream with fishing for rainbow in its upper reaches, and brook in its lower portions.

East of Burgess Junction, the **South Tongue River** stretches about 15 miles from the south to enter the Tongue north of Pine and Prune Creek campgrounds on US 14. South Tongue offers good fishing for rainbow and brown 6 to 12 inches, and small brook at its headwaters.

The South Tongue forks about 7 miles south of US 14 at Dead Swede Camp-

IT'S BEAUTIFUL WATER, BUT DOES IT HAVE FISH?

Nature is not always kind to fishermen. Even in wilderness some clear lakes and streams, or portions of them, are sterile or barren. Others are not naturally productive enough to warrant wasting precious hours on a fishing trip.

Experienced fishermen look for a range of natural life to determine whether a fishing spot is worth angling over. Insects, plants, birds, the nature of stream bottom in both fast and quiet water, and small creatures' signs are good indicators that fishing may be productive.

Man isn't the only polluter, especially in the mineral-rich areas of the Rocky Mountain West. Natural deposits of arsenic and other heavy metals, and radioactive materials can limit or curtail fish productivity. Mine drainage also pollutes streams, but usually it is easier to detect mine-related water discoloration and heavy sediment levels. Yet brook trout have been able to adapt and even reproduce in some mineral-rich waters.

Lakes and stretches of streams that once were stocked may no longer be part of a fish management program. So there's nothing like local inquiry and talking with fellow anglers to enhance fishing opportunities.

On the other hand, don't overlook the mountain meadow streams that race clear and narrow, and often are a deceptive two to four feet deep. Sometimes you can step across them—they might be just irrigation channels—but fat, vigorous browns, rainbows and sometimes cutthroats waft their fins in the shadows of the undercut banks.

On hands and knees, the stealthy angler—wary of making sound and casting shadow—can flip a tiny fly or grasshopper impaled on a hook to tempt a 1.5- to 2-pounder. Using hand-held leaders, anglers of all ages can enjoy this particularly delightful method of fishing. □

ground. The **West Fork South Tongue River** has several tributaries including the small **Prospect** and **Bruce Creeks.** They are rated fair for small brook. Access is by turning south at Burgess Junction. Drive 8 miles south. The tributaries are on the northeast side of Granite Pass.

East Fork South Tongue River also has several tributary streams including **Graves, Mohawk** and **Woodchuck Creeks,** which are small with fair fishing for brook to 8 inches. Access is by turning south at Burgess Junction on US 14 about 5 miles to Owen Campground. At Owen Campground, turn east to Tie Flume Campground where the road drops south and crosses the tributaries.

North of the confluence of the West and East forks, **Bonanza, Sucker, Copper, Owen** and **Sheeley Creeks** enter the South Tongue. These streams are fair to good fishing for small rainbow, with brook in their upper sections.

Eastward along US 14, **Prune Creek** enters the South Tongue from the east. It is fair to good fishing for brown, brook and rainbow to 9 inches. Seven miles from the confluence of South Tongue and Prune, **Sibley Lake** (7950 ft; 33 ac) is along the south side of US 14 as the highway turns northward. It offers fishing for rainbow and some brook. Prune Creek above the lake has small brook.

The **Little Tongue River,** just east of South Tongue, meanders northeast and enters the Tongue at Dayton from the southwest. About half of the stream is on private land and is good fishing for brown. The upper section is on public land. It can be reached by foot from US 14.

LITTLE BIGHORN

The **Little Bighorn River** flows 17 miles from the northern end of the Bighorn Mountains into Montana. It has brown, rainbow and whitefish. In the canyon area north of US 14A, it has cutthroat from 8 to 12 inches. Above the canyon are rainbow and brook from 5 to 10 inches. Access is by taking US 14 west from Sheridan until the highway drops south to Greybull.˙ From there continue west on US 14A until reaching the Medicine Wheel Ranger Station Road. Turn north to the headwaters of the Little Bighorn. Two tributaries of the Little Bighorn River, **Dry Fork** and **Pumpkin Creek,** have cutthroat. Dry Fork also has brook and rainbow to 12 inches. Access is by rough 4-wheel drive or trail from Medicine Wheel Ranger Station. Inquire locally.

EASTERN STREAMS

East of the Bighorns, the Powder River drainage is open, sparsely populated country. The **Little Powder River,** about 30 miles east of the Powder River, is 40 miles long and flows through private property. Word from a state game and fish official is "don't send anyone out there." The tributaries are usually dry and the main stream offers only marginal fishing for channel catfish, but not without permission.

Farther east, the **Belle Fourche River,** stretching about 100 miles to the northeast, flows east of Gillette toward the famed Black Hills and into South Dakota. Most of the stream is on private property and is not worth the bother of getting permission to fish.

However, **Sand Creek,** one of Wyoming's blue-ribbon fisheries, is absolutely loaded with brown trout this spring of 1985. The sparkling waters flow out of the Black Hills and into the Belle Fourche in Beulah, Wyo., by Hwy 111. The limit on the spring-fed stream is 12 trout, double the usual limit. The trout are mostly 9 to 12 inches long.

Turn off I-90 at Beulah and take the well marked Sand Creek Road. Public fishing is signed and begins about a mile south of town and continues for about 4 miles. Then there's a private stretch through Country Club subdivision, and about 10 miles from town is Ranch A, a U.S. Fish and Wildlife Service property. This section of Sand Creek, a little more than a mile long, has never been open to public fishing. It will be open in 1985 from May 1 through August 31 for fly and lure fishing only for the 14- to 16-inch browns. But it doesn't take much action to alert the wily trout that something's amiss. It can be a tough place to fish despite the exceptional numbers of trout.

Hay, Raven and **Inyan Kara Creeks** offer no fishing.

The **Keyhole Reservoir** (7000 ac), northeast of Moorcroft; is rated fair for walleye, northern pike, yellow perch, smallmouth bass, channel catfish with an occa-

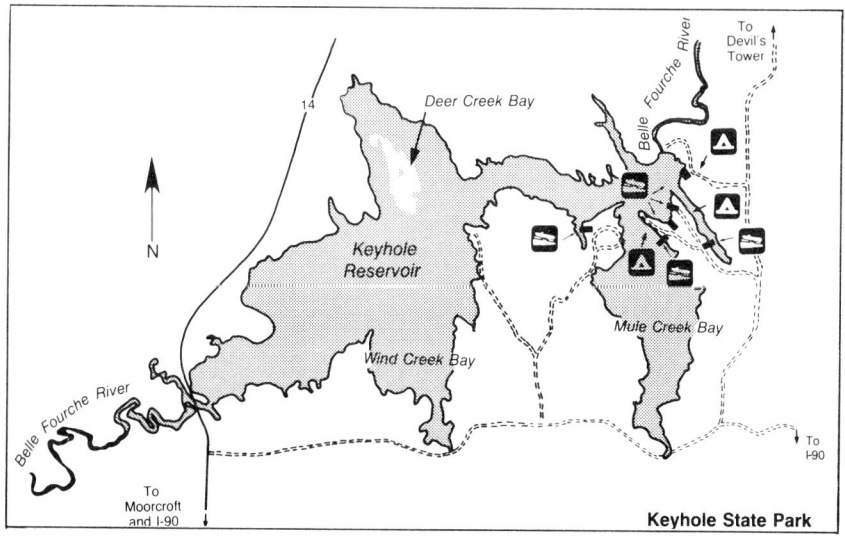

Keyhole Reservoir

sional 10-pounder taken. It is in the Keyhole State Park.

The state record walleye was caught at Keyhole, and a 23-pound Northern Pike landed there in 1983 holds the state record for that species. There are a few rainbow too big for the pike to swallow. The north shore and around the sand bars in Deer Creek Bay are good for walleye. Northerns in the vicinity of Eagle Creek Bay have caused a stretch to be named "Pike Alley."

Campgrounds, boat ramp and bait, tackle, supplies and boat rental are available. From Gillette, take I-90 east about 25 miles to the town of Moorcroft; turn north on Hwy 14 for 8 miles.

Other streams in eastern Wyoming might harbor a catfish or two, but the advice here is to stick to the high country fishing found to the west or try the Black Hills in South Dakota. Small streams there often have rainbow or brook. □

U.S. Forest Service campgrounds

U.S. Forest Service compilation was current as of 1985.
Asterisks denote fee areas. Some campgrounds are open only Memorial Day weekend through Labor Day. Below freezing weather could mean no water supply.

POWDER RIVER DRAINAGE
(Northeast Wyoming)

BIGHORN NATIONAL FOREST
Headquarters: 23 N. Scott, Box 2046, Sheridan, WY 82801

Campground name	Elevation	No camp sites	Travel trailers	Drinking water	Length of stay (days)	Location and directions
Canyon	7400	4	No	No	14	2 mi E of US 16, 25.5 mi W of Buffalo
Circle Park*	7900	10	Yes	Yes	14	2.5 mi W of US 16, 14.5 mi W of Buffalo
Crazy Woman	7600	6	No	Yes	14	Off US 16, 16.5 mi SW of Buffalo
Doyle	8100	18	Yes	No	14	5.8 mi SW of US 16, 27 mi W of Buffalo
Middle Fork*	7400	9	Yes	Yes	14	Off US 16, 12.8 mi W of Buffalo
South Fork*	7800	13	Yes	Yes	14	On US 16, 13.3 mi SW of Buffalo
Tiehack	7500	9	Yes	Yes	14	1.6 mi E of US 16, 14.5 mi SW of Buffalo
Cross Creek	8400	3	No	No	14	14 mi S of county hwy, 9.3 mi SW of Big Horn
Ranger Creek	7800	11	No	Yes	14	10 mi SW of county hwy, 18 mi SW of Big Horn
North Tongue	7900	11	No	No	14	1 mi N of US 14, 29 mi SW of Dayton

Owen Creek*	8400	7	No	Yes	14	On US 14, 34.2 mi SW of Dayton
Prune Creek*	7700	21	No	Yes	14	On US 14, 12.2 mi SW of Dayton
Sibley Lake*	7900	10	No	Yes	14	On US 14, 11.6 mi SW of Dayton
Dead Swede*	8400	22	No	Yes	14	4 mi SE of US 14, 34 mi SW of Dayton
Tie Flume*	8400	25	Yes	Yes	14	34 mi SW of Dayton, then 2 mi E of US 14 on forest road
Little Goose	7000	3	No	No	14	2.5 mi SW of county hwy, 12 mi SW of Big Horn
Coffeen Park	8500	5	No	No	7	7 mi SW of county hwy, 17 mi SW of Big Horn
East Fork	7600	11	Yes	No	7	1 mi SW of county hwy, 17 mi SW of Big Horn

A scrappy crappie's fishin' fun

Photo courtesy Charles A. Walker

Finding your way is easier with a map

There's a wealth of information available to Colorado and Wyoming anglers from a host of guidebooks, pamphlets and maps. Most are available free or at modest cost. This listing describes what's available. The range of helpfulness varies widely and none offers an ideal glimpse of a stream, lake or reservoir. Some of the publications are inconsistent in what they offer, and it is suggested the prospective user examine the materials prior to purchase. *Tim Kelley's Fishing Guide* does not endorse any of the maps, although obviously some are better than others.

RECREATION & TRAVEL MAP OF COLORADO

SIZE: 39.75" × 29.25"
SCALE: 1' = 30 miles
HOW TO OBTAIN: Available in many tackle shops, book stores, etc. and from Adventure, Inc., 6105 W. 83rd Pl., Arvada, CO 80003, 303/423-5710. Each mail order map costs $3.95 plus $1 for tax, postage and handling.

INFORMATION INCLUDED: This is a good general map of the heart of Colorado recreation lands in four colors. It features national forests, parks, monuments and major fishing waters, principal mountain peaks, ski areas, wilderness areas and highways. Many features are cited by number only for reference to descriptive tables. Climatic extremes, mountain passes, public campgrounds, ghost town sites also are listed.

COLORADO LAKES AND RESERVOIRS RECREATIONAL GUIDE

SIZE: 11" × 15", bound, 148 pp.
STYLE: Atlas, 2-color.
HOW TO ORDER: Available at many retail outlets, including boat stores, fishing and sporting goods stores, book outlets, and U-Haul rental outlets. Can also be obtained from the addresses below for $12.95 plus $2.00 postage and handling. MasterCard, VISA, personal check or money order are accepted.

DELIVERY TIME: Ten to 14 days.

INFORMATION INCLUDED: 50 lakes and reservoirs in Colorado, five in Wyoming, and Lake McConaughy in Nebraska. Any body of water larger than 500 acres, especially warm water lakes permitting power boats, is particularly covered. Information includes boating regulations; fishing records; fees; general information; size, elevation, and depth information; information and emergency telephone numbers; uses; fishing comments; camping data; location maps; campgrounds; restrictions; general history on each reservoir; diving tables; fish species, food and habitat; hypothermia and cold water drowning first aid instructions; thunderstorm suggestions; fishing regulations and statutes; boat ramps and rentals; picnic areas; toilets; dumping stations; horseback riding, trails, and hiking; showers; drinking water; marinas; concessions; RV camping; swimming and water skiing; marinas; first aid stations; Ranger stations; airstrips; and other general recreation information.

MAPS & GUIDES

LOCATIONS INCLUDED:

COLORADO
Adobe Creek Reservoir
Antero Reservoir
Barbour Ponds
Barr Lake
Black Hollow Reservoir
Blue Mesa Reservoir
Bonny Reservoir
Carter Lake
Chatfield Reservoir
Cherry Creek Reservoir
Dillon Reservoir
Eleven Mile Reservoir
Grand Lake
Ground Hog Reservoir
Green Mountain Reservoir
Horse Creek Reservoir
Horsetooth Reservoir
Jackson Reservoir
John Martin Reservoir
La Jara Reservoir
Lake Granby
Lake John
Lathrop State Park
Lone Tree Reservoir
McPhee Reservoir
Meredith Reservoir
Monarch Lake
NeeNoshe Reservoir
North Sterling Reservoir
Paonia Reservoir
Platoro Reservoir
Pueblo Reservoir
Queens Reservoir
Rifle Gap Reservoir
Rio Grande Reservoir
Ruedi Reservoir
Sanchez Reservoir
Shadow Mountain Reservoir
Smith Reservoir
Spinney Mountain Reservoir
Steamboat Lake
Taylor Park Reservoir
Trinidad Lake
Turquoise Lake
Twin Lakes Reservoir
Two Buttes Reservoir
Vallecito Reservoir
Vega Reservoir
Williams Fork Reservoir
Willow Creek Reservoir

WYOMING
Flaming Gorge Reservoir
Glendo Reservoir
Guernsey Reservoir
Pathfinder Reservoir
Seminoe Reservoir

NEBRASKA
Lake McConaughy

SOON TO BE AVAILABLE: Aquamaps Inc. is updating this guide. An expanded second edition is to be available in 1985 for $12.95.

Aquamaps Inc.
1915 Clarkson Street
PO Box 417
Denver, CO 80201
303/534-2090

DEPARTMENT OF HIGHWAYS, STATE OF COLORADO, ROAD MAP

SIZE: $33\frac{1}{2}"$ × 22", flat; $3\frac{3}{4}"$ × $7\frac{3}{8}"$, folded.

SCALE: 1" = 15 miles.

HOW TO OBTAIN: The first map is free, each additional is 10¢. This map can be obtained by contacting either the office listed below or the Colorado Tourism Board. If ordering more than one map, prepayment is required. Make remittance payable to Department of Highways, State of Colorado.

DELIVERY TIME: Seven to 10 days.

INFORMATION INCLUDED: All types of roads, ranging from multi-lane divided to unimproved; access points; hospitals; points of interest; mountain passes; Forest Ranger headquarters; roadside parks; rest areas; campgrounds; passenger train routes; distance mileage; national or state forests; national parks or monuments; Indian reservations; government reservations; airports; outdoor recreation areas; cities, towns, and counties; lakes, reservoirs, streams, and lakes; motorist information; colleges and universities; museums and zoos; selected historic districts; ski and winter sport areas; selected Denver sites; AM radio station information; Colorado mountain peaks;

Colorado State Patrol offices, with telephone numbers; runaway truck ramps; and outdoor recreation sites with the following information about each site indicated: fees, sanitary dumping sites, toilets, camping, picnicking, hiking, swimming, and boating. Sites listed include: Antero, Arapaho (USFS), Barbour Ponds, Barr Lake, Bents Old Fort, Black Canyon of the Gunnison, Bonny, Boyd, Castlewood Canyon, Chatfield, Cherry Creek, Colorado, Crawford, Curecanti, Dinosaur, Eldorado Canyon, Eleven Mile, Flagler, Florissant Fossil Beds, Golden Gate Canyon, Great Sand Dunes, Highline, Hovenweep, Island Acres, Jackson, Lake Hasty (Corps of Engineers), Lathrop (Martin Lake), Lory, Mesa Verde, Miramonte, Navajo, Paonia, Pueblo, Ramah, Rifle Gap/Falls, Rocky Mountain, Roxborough, State Forest, Steamboat Lake (Pearl Lake), Sweitzer Lake, Tarryall, Trinidad, Vega, Arapaho, Browns Park, Monte Vista, and Alamosa.

State of Colorado
Department of Highways
4201 East Arkansas Avenue
Denver, CO 80222
303/757-9313

1985 GUIDE TO COLORADO'S STATE PARKS AND RECREATION AREAS

SIZE: 16" × 27", flat; 4" × 9", folded.
STYLE: Road map, 4-color.
HOW TO OBTAIN: Available free from the address below.

DELIVERY TIME: Seven to 10 days.

INFORMATION INCLUDED: General location map, showing major highway access to state parks or recreation areas; general information about each park or recreation area; park regulations, including park pass fees, boat and snowmobile registration, campground fees, and instructions on ordering park passes by mail. Chart giving specific information about each park and recreation area, including which of the following facilities each area has: visitor center, dump station, number of campsites (indicates additional fees), group campsites, flush or vault toilets, laundry equipment, showers, group picnic shelters, nature trails, horseback riding, hiking, climbing, snowmobile/ski touring, motorized trails, primitive/back country, bathhouse, swimming, boat rental, boat ramps, water skiing, boating, boat mooring/docking, electrical hookups (indicates additional fees), concessions, airstrips, distances to the nearest store, gasoline, town and hospital, land and water acreage, elevation, handicap access. NOTE: Camping and running water are seasonal at many parks.

PARK NAMES, LOCATIONS, AND TELEPHONE NUMBERS:

Barbour Ponds	Loveland	303/669-1739
Barr Lake State Park	Brighton	303/659-6005
Bonny	Idalia	303/354-7306
Boyd	Loveland	303/669-1739
Castlewood	Parker	303/690-1166
Chatfield	Denver	303/797-3986
Cherry Creek	Denver	303/690-1166
Crawford	Crawford	303/921-5721
Eldorado	Eldorado Springs	303/494-3943
Eleven Mile	Lake George	303/748-3401
Golden Gate Canyon State Park	Denver	303/592-1502
Highline	Fruita	303/858-7208
Island Acres	Palisade	303/464-7297
Jackson	Goodrich	303/645-2551
Lathrop State Park	Walsenburg	303/738-2376

Lory State Park	Bellevue	303/493-1623
Navajo	Allison	303/883-2208
Paonia	Crawford	303/921-5721
Pueblo	Pueblo	303/561-9320
Rifle Gap/Falls	Rifle	303/625-1607
State Forest	Gould	303/723-8366
Steamboat Lake State Park/ Pearl Lake	Steamboat Springs	303/879-3922
Sweitzer Lake	Delta	303/874-4258
Trinidad	Trinidad	303/846-6951
Vega	Collbran	303/487-3407

REGIONAL DPOR OFFICES:
DPOR South Region Office
2126 North Weber
Colorado Springs, CO 80907
303/471-0900

DPOR North Region Office
1720 West Mulberry, #B-10
Fort Collins, CO 80525
303/482-2602

DPOR West Region Office
Room 410, State Services Building
Sixth and Ute
Grand Junction, CO 81501
303/248-7319

CAMPSITE RESERVATIONS: To reserve a campsite in the Colorado State Park system, call the Select-A-Seat Corporation at 1-800/421-2435 (Colorado residents) or 1-303/778-6691 (nonresidents).

Colorado Division of Parks and Outdoor Recreation (DPOR)
Department of Natural Resources
1313 Sherman, Room 618
Denver, CO 80203
303/866-3437

COLORADO TROUT STREAMS OPEN FOR PUBLIC ACCESS

SIZE: 8½" × 11" maps, photocopied.
HOW TO ORDER: Free. At the listed address only.

INFORMATION INCLUDED: All information pertains to river fishing on easements, leased properties, DOW-owned land, or wildlife areas. Information contains a description of the location. Maps are updated at each printing, ensuring current information regarding leased waters.

LOCATIONS INCLUDED: Blue River; Cochetopa and Pauline creeks; Eagle River; North Park, including Brownlee, Butte Land & Cattle Company, MacNaughton, Manville, Murphy, North Park Angus, Peterson, Verner & Brownlee, and Willford leases; Rio Grande; Saguache Creek; San Miguel River; South Park, including Buffalo Peaks Ranch, Knight/Imler Wildlife Area, Tomahawk Ranch, and Tarryall Creek leases.

Colorado Division of Wildlife
Department of Natural Resources
6060 Broadway
Denver, CO 80216
303/297-1192

COLORADO FISHING MAP

SIZE: 33½" × 22", flat; 3¾" × 7⅜", folded.
STYLE: Road map format, 4-color.
HOW TO ORDER: Send a stamped, self addressed #10 envelope with 39¢ postage to address below.

DELIVERY TIME: Seven to 10 days.

INFORMATION INCLUDED: Type of highway ranging from multi-lane divided to unimproved; mountain passes; Forest Ranger headquarters; rest areas; roadside parks; some campgrounds; national and state forests; national parks and monuments; airports; outdoor recreation areas; short descriptions of major sport fish in Colorado; list of popular fishing spots in metropolitan Denver; major fishing waters for both warm and cold water fish; gold medal streams; wild trout waters; fish hatcheries and rearing units; Colorado record-size fish.

Colorado Division of Wildlife
Department of Natural Resources
6060 Broadway
Denver, CO 80216
303/297-1192

COLORADO ADVENTURE GUIDE

SIZE: 11" × 8½", bound pamphlet, 51 pp.
HOW TO OBTAIN: Available free from the office listed below.
DELIVERY TIME: Seven to 10 days.

INFORMATION INCLUDED: General tourist information including simple location maps; points of interest; general history and background; places to see and things to do.
ALSO AVAILABLE: The Colorado Tourism Board will include in the package a pamphlet of mini-tours that can be taken in Colorado, a list of dude ranches in Colorado, and a road map of Colorado from the Department of Highways.

Colorado Tourism Board
550 South Syracuse Street, Suite 267
Englewood, CO 80111
303/779-1067

USGS STANDARD TOPOGRAPHIC QUADRANGLES

SIZE: 7.5" × 7.5" (latitude and longitude).
SCALE: Range from 1:24,000 to 1:63:360.
HOW TO OBTAIN: Request an index for either Colorado or Wyoming from U.S. Geological Survey, Denver Federal Center, Box 25286, Denver, CO 80225, 303/236-7477. You will receive an index, order form and explanation brochure. Each standard topographic quadrangle map costs $2.25. Orders under $10.00 must include $1.00 for shipping and handling. Maps of the area may be purchased over-the-counter or at many local retail outlets.

INFORMATION INCLUDED: The detailed maps include boundaries, land survey systems, roads and related features, buildings and related features, railroads and related features, transmission lines and pipelines, mines and caves, surface features, vegetation, marine shoreline, rivers, lakes, canals, glaciers and permanent snowfields, submerged areas and bogs. Maps are too numerous to list.
SALES COUNTERS:
U.S. Geological Survey Map Sales
Building 41, Denver Federal Center (off W. Sixth Ave. Freeway). Take Kipling Exit south to Fourth Ave. to center entrance.
Denver, CO 80225

U.S. Geological Survey
Room 169, Federal Building
1961 Stout Street
Denver, CO 80202

THE FLOATER'S GUIDE TO COLORADO

SIZE: Book, 296 pp.
HOW TO OBTAIN: Check your local sporting goods outlet or bookstore. If not available, contact the company below for information.

INFORMATION INCLUDED: As the title indicates, this book contains detailed information for the person using water craft on the rivers of Colorado and the southern Rocky Mountains. Although the book contains little specific information for anglers, it does contain a wealth of information about rivers, including location maps, history, geological formations and uses. A valuable source of information, as well as being interesting and enjoyable.

Falcon Press Publishing Company Inc.
PO Box 279
Billings, MT 59103
406/245-0550

COLORADO MAP SERIES

SIZE: Each map of a lake or reservoir is a slightly different size, depending on what would be the best presentation.
SCALE: Ranges from 800' to 1500' = 1".
STYLE: Road map, 1-color.

HOW TO OBTAIN: Check your local sporting goods outlet, tackle store, boat dealer, or diving shop. Individual maps are sold at these locations for $3.99 each. If not available locally, write or call the address or telephone number listed below for information on ordering.

INFORMATION INCLUDED: Lake bottom topography; old river channels, streams, and dry washes; submerged features, including old highways and railroads; shoals; access points (ways); marinas; boat ramps; campgrounds; forest ranger stations; RV dumping stations and floating dump stations for boats; picnic areas; toilets, including vault, flush, and privy notations; camper services; fish cleaning stations; drinking water; suggested fishing areas; highways and roads, including dirt, gravel, and paved; visitor centers; reservoir project data; type of fish likely to be found in reservoir; location map; brief explanation of how to use contour information; and specification of contour intervals.

AVAILABLE FOR: Each map is separate and must be purchased individually.
Blue Mesa Reservoir, CO-11 (HydroSurveys' code number—can be eliminated if necessary)
Bonny Reservoir, CO-12
Carter Lake, CO-9
Chatfield Reservoir, CO-1
Cherry Creek Reservoir, CO-2
Dillon Reservoir, CO-5
Eleven Mile Reservoir, CO-6
Granby Lake, CO-4
Green Mountain Reservoir, CO-7
Horsetooth Reservoir, CO-3
Pueblo Reservoir, CO-8
Trinidad Lake, CO-10

SOON TO BE AVAILABLE: HydroSurveys Inc. is preparing a collection of maps on Lake Powell. The first of a series of areas to be presented is the Bullfrog-Halls Creek area. An 11" × 14" atlas format will be used.

HydroSurveys Inc.
7533 South Ogden Way
Littleton, CO 80122
303/794-0951

CAMPING IN THE NATIONAL PARK SYSTEM

SIZE: 8" × 9¼", bound pamphlet.
HOW TO OBTAIN: Available free of charge from the office below.

DELIVERY TIME: Seven to 10 days.

INFORMATION INCLUDED: General information about camping in national parks; specific information about individual campsites within each park, including camping season; limit of stay; campground type; number of sites or spaces; group camps; campsite fees; water; toilets; sanitary stations; trailer village vehicle sites and fees; showers and laundry facilities; handicapped access; swimming; boating; fishing; and general notes. A simplified location map shows park locations nationwide.
AREAS INCLUDED:
Curecanti National Recreation Area
PO Box 1040
Gunnison, CO 81230
303/641-2337

Grand Teton National Park
PO Drawer 170
Moose, WY 83012
307/733-2880

Rocky Mountain National Park
Estes Park, CO 80517
303/586-2371

Yellowstone National Park
PO Box 168
Yellowstone National Park, WY 82190
307/344-7381

National Park Service
655 Parfet Street
PO Box 25287
Denver, CO 80225
303/236-4648

USER'S GUIDE TO OUTDOOR RECREATION ON THE PUBLIC LANDS IN COLORADO

SIZE: 7" × 8½," bound, 31 pp, pamphlet.
HOW TO ORDER: Free by writing or calling BLM.

INFORMATION INCLUDED: Pamphlet is divided into three sections. They are: I. Using the Public Lands for Outdoor Recreation; II. Available Recreation Opportunities; III. Developed Recreation Sites on the Public Lands in Colorado. Sections I and II include general information of value to anyone using outdoor recreation sites. Type of information ranges from environmental hazards to forms of available recreation.

Section III is composed of a Colorado map showing public lands, National Forests, National Grasslands, National Wildlife Refuges, National Parks and Monuments, Indian Reservations, State Land, cities, towns, major highways, and BLM Developed Recreation Sites.

Also included in Section III are small maps of and directions to each of the following BLM recreation sites: Pumphouse, Bishop, Rocky Reservoir, Calloway, Irish Canyon, Little Dolores Falls, Mud Springs, Miracle Rock, Big Dominguez, Anvil Points, Gypsum, East Fryingpan Rest Stop, West Fryingpan Rest Stop, Catamount Bridge, Red Bridge, Mill Creek, Cebolla Creek, Escalante Ruins, Dolores River Overlook, Lowry Pueblo Ruins, Five Points, Hecla Junction, Fisherman's Bridge, and De Weese Reservoir.

A chart indicates which of the following facilities, associated activities, and/or limitations and restrictions apply to the above-listed sites: single family or group camping, trailer/camper/tent usage, drinking water, other water, tables, grills or fire rings, toilets, garbage cans, fishing, river rafting, raft launching, hunting, hiking, sightseeing, boating, camping and/or parking in designated areas only, pack out trash, 14-day limit, no camping allowed, and no boat launching allowed.

ADDITIONAL INFORMATION INCLUDED: Names, addresses, and telephone numbers of helpful Colorado agencies and Bureau of Land Management offices in Colorado.

U.S. Bureau of Land Management
Colorado State Office
1037 20th Street
Denver, CO 80202
303/294-7557—Public Service Unit

SURFACE MANAGEMENT QUAD

SIZE: 16" × 21" (surface ownership).
SCALE: ½" = 1 mile and each map covers approximately 1000 square miles.
HOW TO ORDER: There is a total of 88 maps in this series. Write for a map index. Each map is $2.00. Make remittance payable to Bureau of Land Management.

INFORMATION INCLUDED: These maps are color-coded and show the public lands managed by the Bureau of Land Management, National Park Service, Forest Service, Fish and Wildlife Service, etc.; lands managed by the state, and private lands. The maps also show major highways, some trails, rivers, streams; section, township and range designations.

ADDITIONAL INFORMATION AVAILABLE: A resource map of the entire state of Colorado showing private, Forest Service, and Bureau of Land Management lands, in color, also is available for $3.50. Overall size is 52" × 44". The map also shows township and range designations.

U.S. Bureau of Land Management
Colorado State Office
1037 20th Street
Denver, CO 80202
303/294-7557—Public Service Unit

30 × 60 MINUTE QUADRANGLE MAPS/COLORADO

SIZE: 40" × 30".
HOW TO ORDER: Send $3.25 for each map. Make remittance payable to Bureau of Land Management.

DELIVERY TIME: Four weeks.

INFORMATION INCLUDED: Contours and elevations (in meters); highways, roads, and other manmade structures; water features; geographic names; surface and mineral ownership; townships; range and section designations.

AVAILABLE FOR:
Canyon of Lodore
Rangely
Douglas Pass
Grand Junction
Delta
Dove Creek
Cortez
Meeker
Glenwood Springs
Carbondale
Montrose
Walden
Steamboat Springs
Vail
Saguache
Del Norte
Fort Collins
Canon City
Blanca Peak
Eaton
Greeley
Colorado Springs
Pueblo
Walsenberg
Trinidad
Sterling
Fort Morgan
Last Chance
Las Animas
La Junta
Kim
Julesburg
Wray
Bonny Reservoir
Burlington
Cheyenne Wells
Lamar
Two Buttes
Springfield

U.S. Bureau of Land Management
Colorado State Office
1037 20th Street
Denver, CO 80202
303/294-7557—Public Service Unit

PUBLIC LAND USER MAPS WYOMING

SIZE: 40″ × 25″, flat.
SCALE: 1″ = 3 miles.
HOW TO OBTAIN: Contact the above office for an index. Ten of 14 maps currently are available. Each map costs $1.00, including postage and handling. Send check or money order, payable to the Bureau of Land Management. Remittance must accompany order for maps.

DELIVERY TIME: Seven to 10 days.

INFORMATION INCLUDED: Historical sites and trails; rest areas; fishing waters; scenic roads and overlooks; ski and snowmobile areas; campgrounds and picnic areas; boat ramps; canoe and rafting waters; rockhounding areas; and other recreation information. In addition, color-coded land ownership status information is depicted for private, state, public, and other federal lands. Also included is information about safe enjoyment of the lands, wildlife habitat, environment, transportation, water activities, weather conditions, and other outdoor tips for the land user.

MAPS AVAILABLE:
Bighorn Mountains
Dull Knife
Devil's Gate
Fort Steele
Flaming Gorge
South Pass
Wind River
Heart Mountain
Grand Teton
Fossil Butte
SOON TO BE AVAILABLE: These maps are currently in process and should be available in the future. They also will cost $1.00 each.
Chugwater
Fort Laramie
Thunder Basin
Devil's Tower

U.S. Bureau of Land Management
2515 Warren Avenue
PO Box 1828
Cheyenne, WY 82001
307/772-2334

WYOMING VACATION GUIDE

SIZE: 10" × 8", bound pamphlet, 36 pp.
HOW TO OBTAIN: Available free of charge from the offices below.

DELIVERY TIME: Seven to 10 days.

INFORMATION INCLUDED: Special events of interest; general history and background on Wyoming; brief description of self-guided tours in Wyoming; short discussion of state parks and historical sites; wildlife information; list of campsites in national forests and Wyoming counties, including information such as location, tent sites, trailer sites, season, limit, fees, toilets, showers, hook-ups, drinking water, dumping stations, facilities for handicapped, and nearest town; names, addresses, and phone numbers of hotels and motels throughout the state; list of dude ranches and resorts; and general location map.

ALSO AVAILABLE: Included in the mailing are general information brochures with the following titles:
Where to Get More Information
Recreation on Public Land
Rockhounding on Public Land
Hunting and Fishing on Public Land
What to Do and Where to Go in Wyoming
Public Land Terminology

BLM OFFICES IN WYOMING:
U.S. Bureau of Land Management
2515 Warren Avenue
PO Box 1828
Cheyenne, WY 82001
307/772-2334

Worland District Office
PO Box 119
1700 Robertson Avenue
Worland, WY 82401
307/347-9871

Rawlins District Office
PO Box 670
1300 Third Street
Rawlins, WY 82301
307/324-7171

Rock Springs District Office
PO Box 1869
Highway 191 North
Rock Springs, WY 82901
307/382-5350

Casper District Office
951 Rancho Road
Casper, WY 82601
307/261-5101

FOREST AND GRASSLAND VISITOR MAPS

SIZE: 25¾" × 44½", flat; 5" × 8¾", folded, or 26" × 56½", flat; 6½" × 8¾", folded.
SCALE: ½" = 1 mile.
STYLE: Large road map, 4-color.
HOW TO OBTAIN: Visitor maps cost $1.00 each and prepayment is required. Make your check or money order payable to USDA Forest Service. Send remittance for the amount of the total cost only; do not include postage.

DELIVERY TIME: Two to 3 weeks.

INFORMATION INCLUDED: National forest, county, reservation, and wilderness or primitive area boundaries; roads, highways, and trails; Forest supervisor headquarters and ranger stations; recreation sites; ski areas; points of interest; mountain passes; wells and springs; national park, BLM, and state lands; recreation directory; streams, lakes, and reservoirs; and general data concerning parks.

MAPS AVAILABLE: Each of the following is a separate map and costs $1.00.
Arapaho National Forest
Bighorn National Forest
Black Hills National Forest
Buffalo Gap National Grassland
Cimarron National Grassland
Grand Mesa National Forest
Gunnison National Forest
Medicine Bow National Forest
Pike National Forest
Rio Grande National Forest
Roosevelt National Forest
Routt National Forest

San Isabel National Forest
Shoshone National Forest-North half
Shoshone National Forest-South half
Uncompahgre National Forest
White River National Forest

ALSO AVAILABLE: The Colorado Wilderness Map shows wilderness areas in the state as designated by Congress through December 20, 1980. The map scale is 1:1,000,000. Cost is 50¢ each.

NATIONAL FOREST HEADQUARTERS:
Arapaho and Roosevelt National Forests
240 West Prospect Road
Fort Collins, CO 80526
303/221-4390

Bighorn National Forest
1969 South Sheridan Avenue
Sheridan, WY 82801
307/672-0751

Bridger-Teton National Forest
Forest Service Building
340 North Cache
PO Box 1888
Jackson, WY 83001
307/733-2752

Flaming Gorge National Recreation Area
PO Box 178
Dutch John, UT 84023
801/885-3315

Grand Mesa, Uncompahgre, and Gunnison National Forests
2250 Highway 50
Delta, CO 81416
303/874-7691

Medicine Bow National Forest
605 Skyline Drive
Laramie, WY 82070
307/745-8971

Pike and San Isabel National Forests
1920 Valley Drive
Pueblo, CO 81008
303/545-8737

Rio Grande National Forest
1803 West Highway 160
(1.3 miles west on U.S. 160)
Monte Vista, CO 81144
303/852-5941

Routt National Forest
29587 West U.S. 40
Steamboat Springs, CO 80487
303/879-1722

San Juan National Forest
Federal Building
701 Camino del Rio
Durango, CO 81301
303/247-4874

Shoshone National Forest
225 West Yellowstone Avenue
PO Box 2140
Cody, WY 82414
307/527-6241

White River National Forest
Old Federal Building
9th and Grand
Glenwood Springs, CO 81602
303/945-2521

U.S. Forest Service, Rocky Mountain Region
11177 West 8th Avenue
PO Box 25127
Lakewood, CO 80225
303/236-9431

FOREST TRAVEL MAPS COLORADO

SIZE: 35" × 23", flat; 8¾" × 7¾", folded.
SCALE: 2¼" = 5 miles.
HOW TO OBTAIN: Free.

DELIVERY TIME: Two to 3 weeks.

INFORMATION INCLUDED: Areas closed to motorized vehicles and areas where motorized vehicles are allowed only on designated roads or trails. Persons with motorcycles, trail bikes, 4-wheel-drive vehicles, all-terrain vehicles, and snowmobiles should find these maps useful in planning trips. Maps also include all infor-

mation listed on Forest and Grassland Visitor maps. Information on travel maps is smaller and more difficult to read.
MAPS AVAILABLE:
Arapaho National Forest
Bighorn National Forest
Black Hills National Forest
Grand Mesa National Forest
Gunnison National Forest
Medicine Bow National Forest
Pike National Forest
Rio Grande National Forest
Roosevelt National Forest
Routt National Forest
San Isabel National Forest
San Juan National Forest
Shoshone National Forest-North half
Shoshone National Forest-South half
Uncompahgre National Forest
White River National Forest

U.S. Forest Service, Rocky Mountain Region
11177 West 8th Avenue
PO Box 25127
Lakewood, CO 80225
303/236-9431

MAPS OF NATIONAL FORESTS OF THE INTERMOUNTAIN REGION

SIZE: ⅜" × ½" = 1 mile, 1" = 6 miles.
STYLE: Some come folded in road map format, others are flat and are folded for mailing.
HOW TO OBTAIN: Each map costs $1.00. Send check or money order payable to USDA Forest Service.

INFORMATION INCLUDED: The maps are planimetric and show roads, trails, streams, lakes, recreation sites, and forest boundaries.

AVAILABLE FOR:
Ashley National Forest
Boise National Forest
Bridger-Teton/Pinedale Ranger District
Bridger-Teton/Gros Ventre/Teton Wilderness
Bridger-Teton/West Division
Targhee National Forest/East
Targhee National Forest/West
Targhee National Forest (Complete)
Teton National Forest
Teton Wilderness
Uinta National Forest
Wasatch-Cache National Forest

INTERMOUNTAIN REGIONAL OFFICES:

Flaming Gorge Ranger District
Headquarters
PO Box 278
Manila, UT 84046
801/784-5445

Flaming Gorge Ranger District
Dutch John Office
PO Box 157
Dutch John, UT 84023
801/885-3838

Bridger-Teton National Forest
Forest Service Building
340 North Cache
PO Box 1888
Jackson, WY 83001
307/733-2752

Kemmerer Ranger District
Highway 189
PO Box 31
Kemmerer, WY 83101
307/877-4415

Big Piney Ranger District
Highway 189
PO Box 218
Big Piney, WY 83113
307/276-3375

Greys River Ranger District
125 Washington
PO Box 338
Afton, WY 83110
307/886-3166

Jackson Ranger District
140 East Broadway
PO Box 1689
Jackson, WY 83001
307/733-3381, 307/733-4755

Buffalo Ranger District
Blackrock Ranger Station
Highway 26-287
Moran, WY 83013
307/543-2386

Pinedale Ranger District
210 West Pine
PO Box 220
Pinedale, WY 82941
307/367-4326

Targhee National Forest
420 North Bridge Street
PO Box 208
Saint Anthony, ID 83445
208/624-3151

Wasatch National Forest
8226 Federal Building
125 South State Street
Salt Lake City, UT 84138
801/524-5030

Wasatch National Forest
Evanston Ranger District
103 Highway 150 South, Suite A
PO Box FS
Evanston, WY 82930
307/789-3194 (winter)
801/642-6662 (summer)

United States Department of Agriculture
Forest Service,
Intermountain Region Information Center
Room 1407, Ogden Federal Building
324 25th Street
Ogden, UT 84401
801/625-5182

A FISHERMAN'S AND RIVER RUNNER'S MAP/GUIDE TO THE UPPER NORTH PLATTE RIVER

SIZE: 14½" × 37", flat; 3-color. (Prepared by the Wyoming Game & Fish Department with the cooperation of the United States Forest Service and the Bureau of Land Management.)

HOW TO ORDER: This map is available in several sporting goods stores. If not available locally, send $4.95 plus $1.00 shipping and handling in money order or check to the address listed below.

DELIVERY TIME: Seven to 10 days.

INFORMATION INCLUDED: River access; land ownership; whitewater ratings; parking; camping; put-in and take-out sites; trails; type of roads and trails; easement information; relative river distances; specific information regarding the river; national forest boundaries; public lands.

LOCATIONS INCLUDED: Routt, Colorado to Pickaroon; Pickaroon to Bennett Peak; Bennett Peak to Treasure Island; Treasure Island to Foote; Foote to Eagle's Nest; Eagle's Nest to I-80; and I-80 to Seminoe Reservoir.

Dick Prouty Associates
1780 Glen Dale Drive
Lakewood, CO 80215
303/233-9696

WYOMING STREAM FISHERY CLASSIFICATION

SIZE: 27" × 22", flat; 5½" × 11", folded.
STYLE: Heavy paper, road map.
HOW TO ORDER: Available free of charge by writing or calling the address or telephone number below.

INFORMATION INCLUDED: Wyoming streams and rivers are presented in the following color-coded system:
Class 1-Blue: Premium trout waters
Class 2-Red: Very good trout waters
Class 3-Yellow: Important trout waters
Class 4-Gray: Low production waters
Class 5-Black: Very low production waters

General information regarding the rating systems contains comments about the esthetics, availability and productivity of the streams. Map also indicates nine drainage areas of Wyoming, including Snake River, Wind River-Big Horn River, Tongue River-Powder River, Green River, North Platte River, Belle Fourche River-Cheyenne River, Little Snake River, Yellowstone

River-Clark's Fork River, and Bear River Drainages.

NOT CLASSIFIED: Reservoirs, lakes, Wind River Indian Reservation and Yellowstone National Park.

Game & Fish Department
5400 Bishop Boulevard
Cheyenne, WY 82002
307/777-7735

WYOMING FISHING REGULATIONS (1984-1985) (1986-1987)

SIZE: 4" × 9", 32 pp, pamphlet.
HOW TO ORDER: Pamphlet is mailed with all maps requested from the Wyoming Game & Fish Department. If you want only this brochure and license applications, write or call the address or telephone number listed below.

INFORMATION INCLUDED: License fees; definitions; game fish and legal tackle; prohibited fishing methods; trespass; watercraft restrictions; fishing rules; area rules; special regulations for wilderness areas, Wind River Indian Reservation, Yellowstone National Park, and Grand Teton National Park.

ADDITIONAL INFORMATION: Specific rules governing each of five drainage areas are covered. Additional information can be obtained by contacting the Area Fisheries Supervisor as listed below:
Drainage Area I—Includes the Snake River, Salt River, Greys River, Hoback River, Gros Ventre River and Buffalo Fork River, plus all drainages west of the Teton Range. Contact: Jon Erickson, Area Fisheries Supervisor, Box 67, Jackson, WY 83001.
Drainage Area II—Includes the Wind River, Big Horn River (which starts at the Wedding of the Waters' sign at the mouth of the Wind River Canyon), Shoshone River, Clark's Fork, and Yellowstone River. Contact: Charles A. Voix Jr., Area Fisheries Supervisor, 260 Buena Vista, Lander, WY 82520, or Louis S. Pechacek, Area Fisheries Supervisor, Box 988, Cody, WY 82414.

Drainage Area III—Niobrara River, Cheyenne River, Stockade-Beaver Creek, Sand Creek, Belle Fourche River, Little Missouri River, Little Powder River, Powder River, Tongue River, and Little Horn River. Contact: John W. Mueller, Area Fisheries Supervisor, Box F, Buffalo, WY 82834.
Drainage Area IV—Includes the Green River, Little Snake River, Bear River, and Great Divide Basin drainages. Contact: Glen Dunning, Area Fisheries Supervisor, Box 860, Pinedale, WY 82941, or David Dufek, Area Fisheries Supervisor, 351 Astle Avenue, Green River, WY 82935.
Drainage Area V—Includes the North Platte River, Sweetwater River, and Laramie River. Contact: Don D. Miller, Area Fisheries Supervisor, Route 2, Box 25, Laramie, WY 82070 or Larry Peterson, Area Fisheries Supervisor, 3535 CY Avenue, Casper, WY 82601.

Game & Fish Department
5400 Bishop Boulevard
Cheyenne, WY 82002
307/777-7735

WYOMING STATE PARKS INFORMATION BROCHURE

SIZE: 15" × 18" flat; 3¾" × 9½", folded.
STYLE: Road map, 2-color brochure.
HOW TO OBTAIN: Available free.

DELIVERY TIME: Seven to 10 days.

INFORMATION INCLUDED: General information brochure regarding Wyoming State Parks and historic attractions. Individual brochures on each Wyoming State Park are available and include information about fishing; camping; boating, boat ramps, and boat rentals; snowmobile permits; picnic areas; marinas; toilets; roads and highways; general location map; reservoir or park data; camping fees; and fishing license information.

AVAILABLE FOR:
Boysen State Park
Buffalo Bill State Park
Curt Gowdy State Park
Glendo State Park

Guernsey State Park
Keyhole State Park
Seminoe State Park
Sinks Canyon State Park

Wyoming Recreation Commission
Herschler Building
122 West 25th
Cheyenne, WY 82002
307/777-7550

FAMILY WATER SPORTS IN BIG WYOMING

SIZE: 20″ × 32″, flat; 4″ × 10″, folded.
STYLE: Road map, 4-color.
HOW TO OBTAIN: Available free of charge either from address listed below or the Wyoming Game & Fish Department.

DELIVERY TIME: Seven to 10 days.

INFORMATION INCLUDED: General map showing access points; national forests, parks, and wilderness areas; cities; counties; roads; rivers, streams, reservoirs, and lakes; marinas; and specific fishing holes. Fishing chart lists the following information on each of 62 streams, lakes, and reservoirs: lodging, camping, guide service, bait/tackle, boats for hire, surface acres or length in miles, and nearest town. Also indicated on the chart is which of the following types of fish are available in each location: Rainbow Trout, Cutthroat Trout, Brown Trout, Brook Trout, Lake Trout, Grayling, Whitefish, Walleye, Bass/Crappie, Yellow Perch, Channel Catfish and Ling.

Separate charts list information on types of water activities and facilities for national parks, forests, and recreation areas, plus state water parks and water sports areas. Information listed includes fishing; type of boating; boat rental, repairs and ramps; food service; camping; picknicking; swimming; and miscellaneous activities.

LOCATIONS INCLUDED:
Snake River
Gros Ventre River
Hoback River
Jackson Lake
Grey's River
Salt River
Clark's Fork River
Buffalo Bill Reservoir
North Fork Shoshone River
Beartooth Lake
Shell Creek
Ten Sleep Creek
Meadowlark Lake
North Tongue River
South Tongue River
Little Horn River
Wind River
North Fork Popo Agie
Middle Fork Popo Agie
Louis Lake
Big Horn River
Big Horn Lake
Boysen Reservoir
Ocean Lake
Tongue River
Clear Creek
Lake DeSmet
Middle Fork Powder River
Sand Creek
Lake Cook
Keyhole Reservoir
Green River
New Fork River
Meadow Lake
Fremont Lake
Willow Lake
Half Moon Lake
Middle Piney Lake
Fontenelle Reservoir
Lake Cameahwait
Hams Fork River
Viva Naughton Reservoir
Big Sandy Lake
Flaming Gorge Reservoir
Seminoe Reservoir
North Platte River
Saratoga Lake
Encampment River
Medicine Bow River
Laramie River
Lake Hattie
Lake Ione
Granite Lake
Crystal Reservoir
North Laramie River
Johnson Lake
Festo Lake
Packer's Lake

Glendo Lake
Alcova Reservoir
Pathfinder Reservoir
Teton Reservoir
WATER ACTIVITIES AND FACILITIES
Grand Teton National Park and Jackson Hole
Yellowstone National Park
Black Hills National Forest
Bridger National Forest
Medicine Bow National Forest
Shoshone National Forest
Teton National Forest
Big Horn Canyon National Recreational Area
Wyoming Water Parks; Alcova Park, Big Sandy, Boysen State Park, Buffalo Bill State Park, Glendo State Park, Guernsey State Park, Keyhole State Park, Seminoe State Park, Curt Gowdy State Park, Sinks Canyon State Park, Fontenelle Reservoir, Viva Naughton, Lake Hattie, Saratoga Lake, Springer Reservoir, Lake DeSmet, Big Horn River, and Ocean Lake.

Wyoming Travel Commission
Interstate 25 and Etchepare Circle
Cheyenne, WY 82001
307/777-7777

YOUR SELF-GUIDED TOUR TO WYOMING

(Central, Northern, Southern, and Western).
SIZE: 22¾" × 34¾", flat; 5" × 7½", folded.
STYLE: Road map, 2-color.
HOW TO OBTAIN: Available free of charge by contacting the address below.

DELIVERY TIME: Seven to 10 days.

INFORMATION INCLUDED: Wyoming has been divided into four sections for the purpose of these brochures and a brochure is available for each. Information includes: brief descriptions of major cities, towns, points of interest, state parks, zoos, museums, historical sites, etc.; major events; recreation sites; sources of additional information, and location and key maps.
CENTRAL WYOMING: Includes information on Converse, Fremont, Goshen, Platte, Natrona, and Niobrara counties. Also includes general data on Guernsey State Park; Glendo State Park; Medicine Bow National Forest, Laramie Peak District; Dan Speas Fish Hatchery; Alcova Lake; Pathfinder Lake; Shoshone and Boysen Lake State Parks; Ocean Lake; Sinks Canyon State Park; and parts of the Bridger, Shoshone, and Teton National Forests.

NORTHERN WYOMING: Includes information on Big Horn, Campbell, Crook, Hot Springs, Johnson, Park, Sheridan, and Weston counties. Also includes general data on Black Hills National Forest; Keyhole State Park; Big Horn National Park; Cloud Peak Primitive Area; Lake DeSmet; Big Horn Canyon National Recreation Area; Ten Sleep Creek; Hot Springs State Park; Wind River Canyon; Boysen State Park; Shoshone National Forest; and Buffalo Bill State Park.

SOUTHERN WYOMING: Includes information on Albany, Carbon, Laramie, Sweetwater, and Uinta counties. Also includes general data on: Curt Gowdy State Park; Medicine Bow National Forest, Pole Mountain and Snowy Range divisions; Sierra Madre Mountain Range; Battle Lake; Seminoe Lake State Park; and Flaming Gorge National Recreation Area.

WESTERN WYOMING: Includes information on Lincoln, Sublette, and Teton counties, plus Yellowstone National Park. Also includes general data on: the Mammoth Hot Springs, Norris Junction, Madison Junction, Old Faithful, Tower Junction, Canyon, Lake Junction, and West Thumb areas of Yellowstone National Park; Grand Teton National Park; Jackson Lake; Two Ocean Lake; Jenny Lake; National Fish Hatchery; Bridger-Teton National Forest; Gros Ventre Slide Geological Area; Targhee National Forest; Jackson Hole; Fremont Lake; Bridger Wilderness Area; Green River; Salt River; Fontenelle Reservoir; Viva Naughton; Fossil Butte National Monument; and Kemmerer.

Wyoming Travel Commission
Interstate 25 and Etchepare Circle
Cheyenne, WY 82001
307/777-7777

Recognizing and catching cold water fish

Fishermen in the Rockies should be familiar with nine species of cold water fish, most of them trout.

Trout are easier to catch than many warm water species. The major differences are in the methods used. Trout essentially are sight feeders rather than smell feeders, such as catfish. This means that moving bait or a bait that attracts attention produces results. Even in a lake, trout are attracted by movement of the lure in trolling, casting, etc. In the stream, the bait or fly is carried to the fish in the current in as natural a manner as possible.

The trout is one of the lowest forms of animal life. It has a small brain for its bulk, but keen eyesight. It has a short memory and stays close to home during its lifespan. Primarily a bottom feeder, the trout eats when hungry or strikes when provoked.

Time of day plays an important part in trout fishing. Basically trout feed at three periods of the day although they can be caught around the clock. Morning feeding commences around 5:00 a.m. and continues until 9:00 or 10:00. A lag usually ensues until midday. There is a short midday feeding period from about noon to 2:30 p.m. Midafternoon is the most unproductive time to fish. Evening feeding begins about sundown and sometimes continues into the night. (Hours cited are approximate and are not hard and fast rules.)

An expert does not rely on color alone to identify trout, as coloration is affected by surroundings. Trout in large lakes tend to be silvery in color, while lava rock streams will produce dark fish. Trout show distinct vivid color variations in their spawning season. The general coloration, spots and marks are still a good means of identification, however.

The **brown trout** often is confused with the **Loch Leven.** The brown was introduced into the United States from Europe in 1883 and planted in the Rockies soon afterwards. Two species were introduced, the Loch Leven brown and the German brown. These have become so intermixed that it is generally accepted that only one form now exists in Wyoming and Colorado.

This golden-brown trout lacks the vivid coloration of other trouts. It has many dark spots with some reddish-orange specks surrounded by faint halos. The tail usually has no spots and the back edge is straight. The lower fins are a pale yellow to white. Browns may weigh up to 40 pounds although stream fish seldom exceed 10 pounds.

Because it is highly adaptable and often harder to catch than other trout, the brown has survived in many streams to the exclusion of other species; thus it has continued to offer good fly fishing. They are probably the most tolerant of high water temperatures and muddy stream conditions of all the trout species, but they seem to thrive best in larger bodies of slower water with deep quiet pools. Unless they are feeding in shallow riffles, browns usually hide in heavy cover, shadows under banks or in deep pools.

Brown trout have a reputation for being difficult to catch, especially in lakes. This is probably true because most of its feeding is done at night, especially during the summer months. Fishing early morning, late in the evening, or just after a good rain can produce good results. In streams, fish every hole with overhanging brush or cut bank while casting up and quartering across streams. The brown is primarily a bottom feeder, it also is the most predatory of trout. It is versatile in its feeding, taking most aquatic forms and even some mice and small birds.

Experienced anglers call the brown the wisest of trout. It is a shy and wary fish, and if mature, probably "educated." Seldom does a brown rise a second time for a fly. It is probably the least sporting of trout because it does not break water, dart and resist like other species; when hooked he reacts stubbornly but with little finesse.

Browns are fall spawners and prefer headwater streams from 10 to 30 feet wide for spawning. Depending on the size, the female produces 200 to 600 eggs. Because browns are fall spawners, when water levels are fairly stable, a large number of eggs usually hatch.

Experienced fishermen can identify the **rainbow trout** as soon as it takes the lure because it will make a swift run, then leap out of the water. Scrappiness makes them a favorite of anglers. The rainbow is native to West Coast streams and was introduced in Colorado and Wyoming in the 1880s. Colorado and Wyoming rivers and streams are stocked annually with millions of rainbow at least 8 inches long. They constitute 75% of the fish caught in Colorado and a major percentage of the fish landed in Wyoming.

A classic rainbow has a dark back, light belly and a rose-color band on each side. The lateral stripes are especially evident during spawning season.

A rainbow is not especially difficult to catch, for it acts the way a trout is expected to act. The strike is swift and hard. It habitually seeks swift, heavy water. Fish the edges of the swiftest waters.

Rainbows are attracted to bright colors and, as do all trout, feed very actively after heavy rain. The largest rainbows are usually snagged in lower, warmer and food-filled waters.

Rainbows usually seek small headwaters for spring spawning. They scour into the gravel of the river bed to lay 200 to 9,000 eggs.

Brook trout originally were native to the eastern United States. It now can be found in all parts of the country. It differs from other trout mainly in the structure of a tooth-bearing bone in the center of the roof of the mouth.

Brook trout do not generally put up a good fight when hooked, and it is undoubtedly the easiest of the trout species to lure to a fly. Rather greedy, the brook fights deep and rarely breaks water. Brook normally constitute about 15% of the annual cold water catch of the two states.

Brook are readily distinguished by sides spattered with red and white spots on a background of darker color. It is best identified by the pure white leading edge of the lower fins and the mottled "worm track" pattern on the back. Scales of the brook are numerous, small and deeply embedded, giving the skin a soft, fine-textured appearance. The scales don't rub off as readily as they do from other trout. Brooks live about 4 years and average 7 to 10 inches. They usually weigh less than 0.5 pound. However, brook twice that size have been caught.

They generally like the gravelly bottom of cold-water streams or spring-fed lakes with a moderate current. They are most active in 48°F water. Look for the brook near the bottom of eddies, pools, under banks and logs, and behind rocks.

The brook feeds on aquatic and terrestrial insects and will rise to a large range of small lures, baits and flies.

In October or November, brook seek cold spring-fed tributaries with gravel bottoms to spawn. The female usually travels upstream leaving nests of 100 to 5,000 eggs in the gravel bottom along the way.

The **cutthroat,** also known as the native, is the only trout indigenous to the central Rockies. It is sometimes called a black-spotted trout. Pure strains of cutthroat are rare today because hatcheries have interbred species.

The dash of red found between the gills and the body gives the cutthroat its name. Sometimes it is necessary to separate the folds about the gills on the bottom side of the fish to see this feature.

Cutthroats often are heavily spotted on a background of a lighter color. There may be a reddish wash along the length of the body during the spawning season. Cutthroat seem more slimey than other trout and are considered a more difficult fish to keep firm and fresh for the trip home. Cutthroat-rainbow hybrids are common, identified by both the red slash on the throat and the rainbow stripe down the side.

Found mostly in the upper stretches of cold, clear streams and mountain lakes, the cutthroat seems to do best in waters not subject to heavy siltation. Consequently the range of the cutthroat has been reduced throughout the West because most major streams carry a substantial silt load at sometime during the year.

Cutthroat head for the bottom when hooked and usually fight hardest when brought in close. Flies and spinning gear are most commonly used to catch them.

Cutthroat spawn in the spring between April and June in clear headwater streams. They have no success reproducing in lakes if there is no entering stream.

Three subspecies of the cutthroat, the Rio Grande, Colorado River, and Greenback, are protected in Colorado. The Snake River cutthroat, Yellowstone cutthroat or variations are the most prevalent of the species.

The **mackinaw,** or lake trout, is found in many of the deeper cold water lakes of Wyoming and Colorado. It is the largest of all trout, reaching 60 pounds. The mack is an excellent food fish, although more oily than other trout. It is so closely related to the brook trout that the two can be successfully crossed. The result is a **splake.**

The mack is a long, slender fish that can be readily distinguished from other trout by its deeply forked tail. Its color varies from gray to almost black with light gray spots. Its pelvic and pectoral fins are bordered with a light gray. Its head is very long and flattened with a large toothy mouth.

Macks spend a great part of the year in the deep waters. There is a period in the spring and again during the fall spawning when they move to shallower waters.

Small fish make up most of the mature mack's diet, but some Colorado macks continue to eat insects throughout their life. Because it is a cold water fish, it is slow growing. Mature 6-year-old macks may average 17 inches and 1.5 pounds.

Very few macks are caught by the average fisherman. Catching the mack requires special planning and equipment. Successful techniques vary, but for deep water fishing try salmon eggs. Trolling gear usually is regarded as essential. The key is patience, and knowledge of the lake bottom and currents helps.

Macks spawn at age 3 in shallow waters. In October or early November they leave 1500 to 2500 eggs in gravel beds and rocky areas. They tend to be very mobile during this time.

The **grayling** is a favorite of the fisherman who knows the species. Rising readily to the fly, it is not as easily hooked as the trout, due partially to its smaller mouth and quick movements. It will often dart repeatedly after a fly only to return swiftly to deep water without taking it. Grayling are found in Wyoming mountain lakes and some Colorado waters. They are no longer stocked in Colorado.

The grayling can be distinguished by its large, colorful dorsal fin, patterned with pink and black stripes and green, orange, or pink spots. Its torso is grayish to silver with purplish dark spots. Grayling may reach 20 inches and 4 pounds.

Grayling usually are found in schools. They like cool, clear streams with gravelly bottoms. Their principal food is aquatic insects.

Grayling are often taken on spinners, bait, or other lures, but small flies seem best.

Grayling migrate to tributary streams from March to June to spawn. The female lays about 6,000 eggs.

The **kokanee salmon** is the landlocked cousin of the Pacific sockeye salmon. It was introduced to Colorado and Wyoming waters in the early 1950s. Since it inhabits many of the same waters as trout, it is often taken by trout fishermen.

The kokanee has a rich metallic blue back upon which there are a few black spots. Its sides and belly are silvery. During its immature years it has a weak jaw and its scales can be removed easily. By the end of its third summer, its jaw becomes stronger. As maturity is reached by mid-fall, the kokanee goes through numerous physical changes as it prepares to spawn. The male kokanee becomes brick red, develops a hump before its dorsal fin, and its scales become difficult to remove. The female changes color to a reddish gray.

The number of kokanee inhabiting a given body of water determines their size more so than the food supply.

Studies in Colorado show that the kokanee feeds near the surface from dawn to dusk. It drops down about 60 feet or more as night sets in. It feeds mostly on plankton. When fishing for kokanee, it will take flies, but few are caught in this manner; trolling and bait land the bulk of the catch.

During the spawning season, mid-October through December, the kokanee begin to school up. As the salmon look for spawning places, they can be snagged with a treble hook and molded weight. After spawning the kokanee dies.

The **mountain whitefish** is a native of Colorado found mainly in the Yampa and White rivers. They have been introduced in the Colorado River and Cache la Poudre drainages. Its weak mouth makes it a difficult fish to hook and land. Although slightly more bony than trout, whitefish are good to eat.

This white, soft-fleshed fish cannot be mistaken for a trout, but it is sometimes called a grayling. It can reach 18 inches and 4 pounds.

The whitefish lives in fast, clear waters. It prefers large rivers with good pools, 3 to 4 feet deep with riffles and gravel bottoms.

The whitefish feeds on the bottom at dusk and during the night. Its main diet consists of insects, particularly caddisflies and other larvae. When fishing try bait or flies, but take care in setting the hook or it will pull out.

Whitefish also make good winter sport by ice fishing.

The whitefish spawns in the fall, moving only a short distance from the pools to riffles to scour nests and lay eggs. □

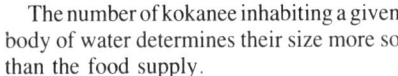

Recognizing and catching warm water fish

Colorado and Wyoming fishermen consider themselves fortunate to have such a variety of fresh water fishing packed into their backyards. Whether stalking trout in high alpine lakes or luring pike in a neighborhood reservoir, the fisherman is rarely more than a cast away from good fishing.

Some of the nation's best reservoir fishing is on the plains. Boats provide access to areas unfishable from the shore and permit a greater range of fishing methods.

Reservoir fishing is best in the spring and fall; summer fishing generally is slow. Water level fluctuations, water turbidity, and sudden temperature changes all tamper with the fisherman's luck.

As cold weather rolls in from the north, four-seasoned anglers edge out on frozen reservoirs in pursuit of the slow-moving yellow perch, crappie and walleye.

Some of the warm water fish are:

The **bluegill,** introduced to Colorado in the 1920s, can be found in many water impoundments and lower elevation streams. Bluegills provide both fast-paced fishing and tasty dinners. This scrappy little fish, also known as the bream, will fight deep, running at right angles to your rod.

Known for both tenacity and an appetite limited to anything handy, bluegills are best caught in the morning or evening using small tackle ranging from a cork and a worm on a hook to delicate dry flies. Once one bluegill is located, others are usually in the immediate vicinity. As summer heat becomes extreme, bluegills move to deeper water and the shade of weed beds.

The bluegill varies in coloration, but can be distinguished from other sunfish relatives by the 6 to 8 vertical bars on its sides, the long black earflap which has no trim, and a black spot which is present on the posterior of the dorsal fin. The maximum length is usually 12 inches and weight about 1 pound. The primary food of the bluegill is insects. But when available, fish eggs or smaller fish are also a part of their diet. They tend to live and feed in shallower waters, close to shore. They are rather easy to catch and will take a wet or dry fly, worm, grasshopper or other live bait.

Spawning season for the bluegill is from late spring through August. Nests are built in colonies by the males on sandy or gravelly bottoms in 1 to 4 feet of water. Males guard their nests from predator fish and viciously strike at anything that comes close . . . especially a carefully placed lure.

The **walleye pike** is actually not a pike but the largest member of the perch family. Even experienced anglers find it difficult to take this wily fish which is confined primarily to large irrigation reservoirs. Seasonal changes in water levels result in different behavior.

The walleye varies in color depending on where it is found, but it is usually dark-olive green or gold speckled with yellow. Walleye can vary in length depending on the character of the water, but mature fish (about 2 years) are usually more than 12 inches and weigh 7 to 9 pounds. Distinctive characteristics include well-developed canine teeth and large eyes with milky white corneas. Its eyes are extremely sensitive to light, so it seeks out cool, dimly lit waters during the day. At night it will prowl the shallows in search of food.

WARM WATER FISH

The walleye is a schooling fish that stays near the bottom in both deep and shallow waters. It forages for food around sandy bars and rocky reefs. It often frequents the waters off dams, particularly if numerous small fish can be found there.

The walleye's diet is mainly fish, but it will eat crayfish, frogs and snails. Minnows, suckers, sunfish, and yellow perch are most frequently found in the walleye's stomach.

Trolling with assorted artificial lures and lures combined with live and cut bait has produced the best results for walleye. Casting with lures and live bait off sandbars and rocky reefs also has produced fair results. Use deep and medium running lures about 6 to 18 inches off the bottom.

Shortly after ice is out in the early spring, the walleye will find a shallow gravelly area or rocky reef to spawn. Both the male and female move around a lot at this time and may be taken near the spawning areas.

The **yellow perch** is a controversial fish, mainly because it overproduces to such an extent that many have become stunted. However, in waters where adequate natural or artificial control is applied, many nice-size fish are harvested. It has adapted well to fluctuating reservoirs and also is found in major drainages. It is most at home in a lake environment with young perch preferring the shallows and the adults preferring deeper waters.

The yellow perch has a white belly and golden-yellow to olive-green sides with 6 to 8 evenly spaced dark stripes. Spawning males have bright reddish-orange lower fins. Perch rarely exceed more than 12 inches or weigh more than 1 pound. It lives in a large school, spending the entire day in deep waters and moving to shore to feed in the late afternoon or evening.

Perch will eat nearly anything that moves that will fit into its mouth. Food includes aquatic insects, clams, snails, and even its own young.

Perch bite best around noon and toward evening and are fun fish to catch. Small flies and spinners or natural bait fished a foot or two off the bottom are time-proven techniques. During the summer, worms appear to be the best bait. If possible, fish in a shaded area and do not hesitate to give the worm some action. Larger perch often are taken by slow trolling lures near the bottom.

Winter ice fishing probably produces good catches and often larger fish. When ice fishing, seek out the deepest areas of the lake. But since the fish continue to move out even during the winter, it may be necessary to cut several holes before finding a school. A small minnow fished near the bottom is the best bet.

The yellow perch spawns in the spring at age 3. Its eggs are laid in gobs attached by ribbons to bottom vegetation; but in reservoirs without rooted vegetation, the eggs are laid on the bottom and drift with the water.

The **white crappie** was introduced in the West in the 1880s and now is abundant in eastern Wyoming and Colorado waters. It is tolerant of warm, muddy waters. This gregarious fish gathers in large schools during the spring. Small jigs cast around submerged brush piles are an effective method for catching them. Flies or a popper at dusk also are good.

The white crappie has silvery-olive sides shading into olive green on its back, with eight to nine dark vertical side bands. It usually has six distinguishing dorsal fin spines.

In large reservoirs, crappie reach 9 to 12 inches at the mature age of 4.

The crappie is attracted to submerged brushy, weedy and rocky areas. The dams of most reservoirs are favorite areas of concentration. In deep water, the crappie seeks irregular bottom areas, rock ledges or other

types of cover.

The crappie feeds on smaller fish, competing directly with the black bass.

During the summer crappie are usually found in depths of 15 to 25 feet. Trolling or drifting with minnows in the spring is a favorite technique for catching this fish. A bobber with a small live minnow hung 5 to 8 feet below the surface is another popular method. The crappie can often be hooked with a porkrind hanging a foot or so from the surface.

The crappie spawns in the spring generally in water 3 to 8 feet deep. It prefers spawning sites near brush piles, stumps or rock outcroppings.

The **channel catfish** is a native of eastern Colorado and Wyoming and is stocked in warm water rivers and reservoirs in other parts of the states. Night fishing provides the best sport. A variety of bottom bait—night crawlers, minnows, crayfish, chicken innards, and flavored dough balls—all work well. Many fishermen will let this wary, flavorful fish run several seconds on an open bail before setting the hook.

The channel catfish has a forked tail and is greenish-colored with small irregular dark spots. It has a gray or dusky-brown spine. Channel catfish more than 50 pounds have been captured, but few weigh over 20 pounds. Most Colorado channel cats weigh less than 5 pounds.

The channel catfish is attracted to muddy bottoms, however, it also frequents areas containing heavy vegetation growth. The crayfish is the choice diet of the channel catfish, but it also feeds on minnows.

With the exception of certain periods, channel catfish are night fish and anglers who expect to take them on a regular basis must fish well into the night hours. In reservoirs, the channel cat tends to concentrate in the deep midsection or deep narrow bays. Its high smell sensitivity draws it to rotten chicken innards, a variety of cheese or licorice-flavored dough balls.

When you hook a bass, prepare for a battle. The **largemouth bass** hits hard, leaps furiously and twists wildly when airborne. It was the first fish introduced in Colorado in the late 1800s. The largemouth bass, or black bass, is the largest member of the sunfish family. It gets its name from the upper jaw bone which extends under and behind the eye. The **smallmouth bass,** introduced in Colorado in 1951, differs from the largemouth in that its upper jaw extends to under the middle of the eye.

The largemouth has a lustrous yellow-green body laced with dark, horizontal bars. The mature western largemouth is 8 to 10 inches long and weighs 3 to 5 pounds. The smallmouth is a golden-bronze or copper color with dark vertical bars and weighs 1 to 1.5 pounds.

Bass can adapt to almost any type of fresh water, but are most often found in shallow, weedy lakes with soft bottoms and sparse vegetation.

Young bass feed mostly on plankton, but as it matures, its diet changes to fish, crayfish, frogs, tadpoles and larger insects.

Spring is one of the best seasons for bass fishing. Work the shorelines and shallows that have shade. Try to lure them from beneath fallen trees, lily pads and boat docks. Smallmouth lie in slack water and dart into fast current for food, so look for a combination of current and cover.

Largemouth bass are probably the most prized of the warmwater fish. They will strike throughout the day, but early morning and evening fishing are best.

Casting and spin fishing are the two best methods for snagging a bass. A wide assortment of artificial lures can be used. Although bass stay deep in the summer, they lurk around submerged objects and can be caught by fishing deep with live minnows, crayfish or frogs. Most bass fishermen prefer to work the shores, but many bass are taken from boats by casting towards the shore and retrieving the lure to the boat.

The bass builds a nest in late May or June for spawning. The nest is a cleared area in shallow water on sand, gravel, roots, or vegetation.

The **northern pike** is a fierce-looking predator that eats other fish up to one-half its own size and may grow 15 inches in one year. Stocking this aggressive predator since 1956 in several plains and mountain reservoirs has possibly made Colorado second only to Minnesota in fishing for big pike in the Lower 48 states. It also is in large Wyoming reservoirs.

Pike originally were stocked in mountain reservoirs to control heavy populations of suckers. This appears to have backfired; pike prefer small trout and kokanee salmon.

The northern has a long-tapered body and pointed nose lined with needle-sharp teeth. It has light-green sides marked with white or pale yellow spots. Its belly usually is yellow or white. A mature pike weighs 3 to 10 pounds and is 15 or more inches long.

Pike seek shallow (1-5 ft) water with abundant vegetation during most of the year; however, they move into deeper water during extremely warm or cold weather. The pike is attracted to weedy or grassy areas.

The best time to hook a northern is right after the ice breaks in the reservoirs—usually early June. Trollers working the rocky points and edges of weed beds take pike on bit spoons and plugs. Weedless hooks and snag-resistant gear often is desirable.

Northern pike spawn immediately after the ice leaves the reservoir. Short, dense vegetation is preferred for egg laying.

(Information on fish species was compiled from personal experience and data from the Colorado Division of Wildlife and the Wyoming Game & Fish Department.) ☐

HOW TO CLEAN A TROUT

The adage "you catch it, you clean it" is easier to follow if you know the simple steps it takes to dress a trout. Fish taste better if they are cleaned within a few minutes of being caught.

• Using a sharp knife, split the fish up the belly from the anal opening to within a quarter-inch of the gills. An upward motion minimizes the risk of cutting the inside and makes a cleaner cut.

• Cut away the gills from the lower jaw.

• Pinch gills and pull them out with the entrails in one motion.

• Using thumb nail or gentle knife pressure, scrape away the membrane and blood under the backbone. Be careful not to sever bones if a knife is used. Scrape clean.

• Wash inside of fish and dry thoroughly with cloth, paper or soft, dry grass.

• Refrigerate, pack in ice or snow or place in creel with wet grass or cloth to provide evaporative cooling.

• Put fish entrails on land where scavengers can eat them; do not throw entrails in water.

SOME COLORADO AND WYOMING TACKLE SHOPS

These tackle shops are listed as a convenience to the reader. It is not an all-inclusive list, but these shops offer helpful and friendly people, fishing know-how and appropriate tackle. While we have visited nearly all of them, this listing is not an endorsement. We surmise some first class shops have been omitted and we would appreciate hearing about them.

Colorado tackle shops

ASPEN
Chuck Fothergill's
ARVADA
Al's Sporting Goods
BASALT
Roaring Fork Anglers
BOULDER
Creative Anglers
Front Range Anglers
Hank Roberts
BRIGHTON
Bait 'N' Bullet
BUENA VISTA
Hi Rocky Store
COLORADO SPRINGS
Angler's Covey
Fish 'n Hole
CREEDE
Ramble House
DEL NORTE
M & M Sporting Goods
DENVER & SUBURBS
The Flyfisher
The Trout Fisher
The Complete Angler
Colorado Angler
Angler's All
High Country Bass Pro Shop
The Fisherman
Uncle Milty's
All Pro Fish 'N Sport
Bob's Rod & Tackle
J & A Sports
DURANGO
The Outdoorsman
Gardenswartz Sporting Goods
EAGLE
Game & Fish Depot
ESTES PARK
The Fisherman's Fly
FRISCO
Frisco Sporting Goods
GLENWOOD SPRINGS
Army & Factory Surplus
Roaring Fork Anglers
GRANBY
Fletcher's Sporting Goods
GRAND JUNCTION
Gene Taylor's Rod & Gun
Beaver Creek Sports
GRAND LAKE
Grand Lake Marina
Lake Kove Marina
GUNNISON
Elmer's Sporting Goods
Elk Creek Marina
LAKE CITY
The General Store
LA PORTE
Vern's Place
LEADVILLE
Buckhorn Sporting Goods
PAGOSA SPRINGS
Shive's Custom Flies
Pagosa Trading Post
Pagosa Sports
PUEBLO
T & M Sporting Goods
RIFLE
Buckhorn Sports
STEAMBOAT SPRINGS
Clark Store
Straightline Fly & Tackle
TABERNASH
Nelson Fly & Tackle Shop

Wyoming tackle shops

ALPINE
Alpine Sports Center
Palis Sports
BIG PINEY
Lain's Sports Center
BOYSEN RESERVOIR
Boysen Reservoir Marina
CASPER
Dean's Sporting Goods
Coast To Coast Store
CHEYENNE
Cheyenne Trading Post
CODY
Compleat Angler
Wyoming Waters Fly Shop
FLAMING GORGE RESERVOIR
Buckboard Marina
FONTENELLE RESERVOIR
Painter's Store
GARDINER, MT
Parks' Fly Shop
GREEN RIVER
Hillcrest Drug

ADVERTISERS' INDEX

JACKSON
Jack Dennis Outdoor Shop
High Country Flies
Stone Drug
KEYHOLE RESERVOIR
Keyhole Marina
LANDER
The Outdoorsman
LARAMIE
West Laramie Fly Store
Rocky Mountaineering
Lou's Sport Shop
OCEAN LAKE
Little's Place
PINEDALE
Garrett's Outdoor Shop
Great Outdoor Shop
Faler's General Store
Wind River Sporting Goods
RAWLINS
Bi Rite Drugs
SARATOGA
Great Rocky Mountain Outfitters
Wolf Adventures
Pat Hughes
THAYNE
Hitching Rail
WEST YELLOWSTONE, MT
Artful Angler
Bud Lilly Trout Shop

ADVERTISERS' INDEX

Adams' Fishing and Hunting Lodge	90
Admiral's Bridge	244
Alpine Sports Center	323
Arkansas Adventures	198
Aspen Basalt KOA Campground	167
Bait 'N' Bullet Shop	207
Bear Paw Lodge	52
Best Western Aspenalt Lodge	171
Big J Camper Court	67
Bob's Reel Service	246
Bridger Wilderness Outfitters	333
Buckhorn Sporting Goods II	176
Cabela's	14
Cannova, Tony Taxidermy & Sculpture Studio	7
Canty's, Del Museum Quality Taxidermy	10
Clark Store	106
Colorado AMC Jeep/Renault	9
Colorado Angler	409
Colorado B.A.S.S.	249
Colorado Outdoors	114
Colorado School of Flyfishing	235
Colorado Tent Company	434
Driftwood Lodge	144
Eagle Claw	BC
Elk Mountain Safari	352
Feldmann Engineering & Manufacturing	256
Fisherman's Fly	240
Fletcher's Gun Repair & Sporting Goods	145
Flyfisher, The	11
Frisco Sporting Goods	149
Generator City	227
Generator City	407
Glendo Marina	362
Grand Lake Tackle Co.	140
Great Outdoor Shop	337
Hair & Fur Supply	364
Hitching Rail	321
HydroSurveys	254
Jim's Marine & Prop Shop	247
Keith's Taxidermy Studio	37
Lain's Sports Center & Motel	331
Lake Kove Marina	147
Lazy J Resort	196
Mariner	6
Nymph Fishing Classes	254
Outdoorsman	45
Outdoor Specialists	148
Pagosa Sports	147
Pikes Peak Traveland Inc.	14
Pine River Lodge	49
Prouty, Dick, Associates	351
Rainbow Falls Park	211
Ramble House	31
Rancho Del Rio	151
Rimrock Wildlife & Taxidermy	101
Riverview Campground	245
Riverwood	85
Roaring Fork Anglers	166
Rocky Mountain News	IFC
Saratoga Inn	353
Sportsman Quik Stop	156
Sportsman's Supply	120
Straightline Fly & Tackle	103
Sugar Loafin'	191
Sunnyside Campground	75
3 Rivers Motel	325
Topper Mfg.	231
Trophy Taxidermy	48
Trout Fisher, The	233
Trout Haven Ponds	241
Uncle Milty's	8
United Campground	246
Western Slope Homes	68
Wilderness Sports	150
Wind River Sporting Goods	330
Winding River Campground	142
Wolf Adventures & Hotel	351
Wyoming Wildlife	289

Index

The streams, lakes and reservoirs in Tim Kelley's Fishing Guide are indexed alphabetically by name. The chapter in which they are mentioned is abbreviated immediately after the listing. The state is indicated by a "CO" or a "WY" prior to the page number. If a lake or reservoir has two names, both are listed. Often there are several lakes in the same chapter with the same name. The description in the text differentiates among them.

COLORADO

South Platte River	SP
Front Range Streams	FRS
Cache la Poudre	POU
Laramie River	LAR
North Platte River	NP
Rocky Mountain National Park	RMNP
Colorado River	COLO
White River	WHR
Yampa River	YAM
Flat Tops Wilderness	F-W
Gunnison River	GUNN
San Miguel River	SM
Dolores River	DOL
Southwest Rivers	SWR
Rio Grande	RG
Arkansas River	ARK
Eastern Colorado	E-C
Urban Fishing	URB
San Luis Valley	SLV

WYOMING

Wind River	WIND
Sweetwater River	SWT
Bighorn River	BHR
Yellowstone National Park	YNP
Snake River	SN
Green River	GRN
North Platte River	NP
Wind River Indian Reservation	WRIR
Northeast Wyoming	NEW
Bear River	BR

Stream name	Chapter	State	Page
A			
Abyss Lake	SP	CO	213
Adams County Lake	URB	CO	222
Adams Fork	RG	CO	34
Adams Lake	COLO	CO	175
Adelaide Lake	BHR	WY	290
Adobe Creek Reservoir	E-C	CO	250
Agate Creek	YNP	WY	310
Alamosa Reservoir	RG	CO	33
Alamosa River	RG	CO	33
Alan Lake	ARK	CO	193
Albert Lake	NP	CO	117
Alberta Park Reservoir	RG	CO	31
Alcova Reservoir	NP	WY	360
Alder Creek	RG	CO	32
Alder Creek	SLV	CO	41
Alder Lake	NP	CO	116
Alder Lake	YNP	WY	309
Alexander Lake	COLO	CO	181
Allen Basin Reservoir	YAM	CO	104
Alpine Lake	WIND	WY	282
Alsop Lake	NP	WY	365
Alta Lakes	SM	CO	62
Alum Creek	YNP	WY	309
American Lake	COLO	CO	168
Amethyst Creek	YNP	WY	311
Amphitheater Creek	YNP	WY	311
Anderson Lake	COLO	CO	168
Anderson Lake	F-W	CO	96
Andrews Lake	SWR	CO	54
Anglemeyer Lake	ARK	CO	194
Angles Lakes	SN	WY	321
Animas River	SWR	CO	53
Antelope Creek	YNP	WY	310
Antero Reservoir	SP	CO	208
Anthracite Creek	GUNN	CO	83
Antone's Cabin Creek	COLO	CO	165
Antone's Cabin Lakes	COLO	CO	165
Arapaho Creek	COLO	CO	144
Arapaho Creek	FRS	CO	236
Arapaho Creek	NP	CO	116
Arapaho Lakes	FRS	CO	236
Arapaho Lakes	NP	CO	116
ARAPAHO NATIONAL RECREATION AREA		**CO**	**139**
Arch Lake	COLO	CO	181
Archuleta Creek	RG	CO	31
Archuleta Lake	RG	CO	31
Arizona Creek	SN	WY	320
ARKANSAS RIVER		**CO**	**188**
Armstrong Creek	YAM	CO	109
Arnica Creek	YNP	WY	309
Arrastre Lake	NP	WY	354
Arrow Canyon Creek	YNP	WY	313
Arrow Lakes	NP	WY	356
Arrowhead Lake	NP	WY	357
Arrowhead Lake	RMNP	CO	136

404 LAKES & STREAMS INDEX

Stream name	Chapter	State	Page
Ashenfelder Creek	NP	CO	364
Aster Creek	YNP	WY	301
Astringent Creek	YNP	WY	308
Atlantic Creek	WIND	WY	277
Atlantic Creek Lake	WIND	WY	277
Avalanche Creek	COLO	CO	174
Avalanche Lake	COLO	CO	169
Avalanche Lake	COLO	CO	174

B

Stream name	Chapter	State	Page
Badger Creek	YNP	WY	309
Bail Lakes	F-W	CO	99
Bailey Creek	SN	WY	320
Bailey Lake	WHR	CO	91
Bailey Lakes	COLO	CO	158
Baker Creek	COLO	CO	142
Baldwin Creek	ARK	CO	194
Baldwin Lake	ARK	CO	194
Baldy Creek	GRN	WY	340
Baldy Lake	GRN	WY	340
Baldy Lake	SLV	CO	41
Balman Reservoir	ARK	CO	197
Balsam Lake	SWR	CO	54
Balsam Park Pond	URB	CO	222
Banana Lake	FRS	CO	237
Banjo Lake	ARK	CO	198
Baptiste Lake	WIND	WY	282
Barber Lake	GRN	WY	340
Barbour Ponds	E-C	CO	245
Bard Creek	FRS	CO	233
Bard Lake	NEW	WY	371
Barker Reservoir	FRS	CO	239
Barlow Creek	DOL	CO	59
Barnes Lake	GRN	WY	340
Barnes Meadow Reservoir	POU	CO	129
Barnes Reservoir	COLO	CO	180
Barnum Park Lake	URB	CO	223
Baron Lake	COLO	CO	182
Barr Lake	SP	CO	218
Barr Lake	URB	CO	223
Basin Creek	YNP	WY	301
Basin Creek Lake	YNP	WY	301
Bass Lake	URB	CO	223
Bates Creek	NP	WY	361
Battle Creek	COLO	CO	147
Bear Creek	COLO	CO	169
Bear Creek	DOL	CO	60
Bear Creek	GUNN	CO	71
Bear Creek	NP	CO	118
Bear Creek	RG	CO	25
Bear Creek	SLV	CO	41
Bear Creek	SM	CO	62
Bear Creek	SP	CO	216
Bear Creek	WIND	WY	281
Bear Creek	YNP	WY	308
Bear Creek Ponds	URB	CO	223
Bear Creek Reservoir	SP	CO	215
Bear Creek Reservoir	URB	CO	223
Bear Lake	ARK	CO	194

Stream name	Chapter	State	Page
Bear Lake	ARK	CO	191
Bear Lake	GRN	WY	335
Bear Lake	RG	CO	35
Bear Lake	WIND	WY	276
Bear Lakes	NP	CO	118
Bear River	YAM	CO	101
BEAR RIVER		**WY**	**267**
Bear Track Lakes	SP	CO	216
Beartooth Lake	BHR	WY	295
Beauty Lake	BHR	WY	295
Beaver Creek	ARK	CO	196
Beaver Creek	COLO	CO	164
Beaver Creek	COLO	CO	146
Beaver Creek	GUNN	CO	75
Beaver Creek	GUNN	CO	79
Beaver Creek	NP	CO	121
Beaver Creek	POU	CO	130
Beaver Creek	POU	CO	130
Beaver Creek	NEW	WY	368
Beaver Creek	RG	CO	32
Beaver Creek	SM	CO	63
Beaver Creek	SP	CO	212
Beaver Creek	SP	CO	206
Beaver Creek	SWR	CO	47
Beaver Creek	YAM	CO	111
Beaver Creek	YNP	WY	301
Beaver Creek Reservoir	RG	CO	32
Beaver Lake	COLO	CO	180
Beaver Lake	COLO	CO	164
Beaver Lake	COLO	CO	172
Beaver Lake	GUNN	CO	80
Beaver Lake	RG	CO	37
Beaver Lake	YAM	CO	107
Beaver Reservoir	FRS	CO	240
Beaver-Mandall Lake	YAM	CO	104
Beaverdam Creek	YNP	WY	308
Bechler River	YNP	WY	302
Belford Lake	GRN	WY	340
Bell Lake	GRN	WY	340
Bell Roth Park Pond	URB	CO	223
Bellaire Lake	POU	CO	130
Belle Fourche River	NEW	WY	375
Bellows Creek	RG	CO	30
Bench Lake	LAR	CO	124
Bench Lake	RMNP	CO	138
Berkeley Hills Pond	URB	CO	223
Berkeley Lake	URB	CO	223
Betty Lake	FRS	CO	238
Beula Lake	YNP	WY	302
Big Battlement Lake	COLO	CO	181
Big Blue Creek	GUNN	CO	80
Big Branch Creek	SWR	CO	49
Big Brooklyn Lake	NP	WY	356
Big Cottonwood Creek	ARK	CO	197
Big Creek	NP	WY	352
Big Creek	YAM	CO	108
Big Creek Lakes	NP	CO	121
Big Creek Lakes	YAM	CO	109
Big Creek Reservoir No. 1	COLO	CO	183
Big Draw Creek	BHR	WY	284
Big Dutch Creek	RMNP	CO	138

LAKES & STREAMS INDEX

Stream name	Chapter	State	Page	Stream name	Chapter	State	Page
Big Emerald Lake	SWR	CO	51	Blue Creek	GUNN	CO	80
Big Fish Creek	F-W	CO	96	Blue Creek	NEW	WY	368
Big Fish Creek	WHR	CO	90	Blue Lake	ARK	CO	192
Big Fish Lake	F-W	CO	96	Blue Lake	COLO	CO	153
Big Flint Creek	SWR	CO	51	Blue Lake	COLO	CO	142
Big Goose Creek	NEW	WY	372	Blue Lake	COLO	CO	175
Big Horn Lake	NP	CO	119	Blue Lake	E-C	CO	250
Big Kline Creek	COLO	CO	174	Blue Lake	FRS	CO	240
Big Lake	COLO	CO	164	Blue Lake	GUNN	CO	74
Big Lake	RG	CO	35	Blue Lake	LAR	CO	124
Big Meadows Reservoir	RG	CO	31	Blue Lake	NP	CO	119
Big Pine Lake	COLO	CO	164	Blue Lake	RG	CO	35
Big Rainbow Lake	LAR	CO	125	Blue Lake	YAM	CO	104
Big Ross Lake	WIND	WY	272	Blue Lakes	COLO	CO	149
Big Sandy Lake	GRN	WY	343	Blue Lakes	GUNN	CO	85
Big Sandy Reservoir	GRN	WY	343	Blue Mesa Reservoir	GUNN	CO	75
Big Sandy River	GRN	WY	343	Blue River	COLO	CO	148
Big Sheep Mountain Lake	GRN	WY	335	Blue River	COLO	CO	154
Big Spring Creek	RG	CO	28	Blueberry Lake	GRN	WY	340
Big Spruce Lake	COLO	CO	164	Blueberry Lake	WIND	WY	273
Big Squaw Creek	RG	CO	26	Bluebird Lake	RMNP	CO	135
Big Stough Creek Lake	WIND	WY	277	Bob Lake	FRS	CO	238
Big Telephone Lake	NP	WY	357	Bob's Lake	GRN	WY	341
Big Thompson Ponds	E-C	CO	246	Bobtail Creek	COLO	CO	147
Big Thompson River	FRS	CO	240	Boedecker Reservoir	E-C	CO	245
Big Thompson River	RMNP	CO	135	Bonanza Creek	NEW	WY	374
Big Thumb Creek	YNP	WY	309	Bonham Reservoir	COLO	CO	183
Big Union Creek	ARK	CO	192	Bonita Reservoir	COLO	CO	182
Big Willow Creek	NEW	WY	373	Bonneville Lake	GRN	WY	341
Bighorn Creek	COLO	CO	164	Bonny Ponds	E-C	CO	249
Bighorn Lake	BHR	WY	286	Bonny Reservoir	E-C	CO	248
Bighorn Reservoir	NEW	WY	372	Boot Lake	WIND	WY	277
BIGHORN RIVER		**WY**	**284**	Booth Creek	COLO	CO	164
Bilk Creek	SM	CO	62	Booth Lake	COLO	CO	164
Bill Moore Lake	FRS	CO	233	Borah Lake	COLO	CO	165
Billy's Lake	GRN	WY	343	Borns Lake	SWR	CO	47
Birdland Lake	URB	CO	223	Borum Lake	GRN	WY	337
Bison Lake	COLO	CO	159	Boss Lake Reservoir	ARK	CO	196
Black Butte Creek	YNP	WY	306	Boulder Creek	COLO	CO	153
Black Canyon Creek	SLV	CO	42	Boulder Creek	F-W	CO	96
Black Creek	COLO	CO	153	Boulder Creek	GRN	WY	341
Black Gore Creek	COLO	CO	163	Boulder Lake	COLO	CO	153
Black Hollow Reservoir	E-C	CO	247	Boulder Lake	F-W	CO	96
Black Joe Lake	GRN	WY	343	Boulder Lake	GRN	WY	340
Black Lake	COLO	CO	163	Boulder Lake	GUNN	CO	68
Black Lake	RMNP	CO	136	Boulder Reservoir	E-C	CO	245
Black Lakes	COLO	CO	163	Boulter Lake	GRN	WY	342
Black Mandall Lake	YAM	CO	103	Boundary Creek	YNP	WY	302
Blackman Reservoir	COLO	CO	183	Bowen Creek	COLO	CO	142
Blackrock Creek	SN	WY	321	Bowen Lake	COLO	CO	142
Blackrock Lake	WIND	WY	277	Bowl of Tears	COLO	CO	163
Blacks Fork	GRN	WY	344	Bowles Grove Pond	URB	CO	223
Blacktail Creek	COLO	CO	156	Bowman Creek	GUNN	CO	69
Blacktail Deer Creek	YNP	WY	312	Box Creek	YAM	CO	111
Blades Fork	GRN	WY	344	Box Lake	RMNP	CO	135
Blair Lake	F-W	CO	98	Boxelder Creek	NP	WY	364
Blanket Lakes	WIND	WY	271	Boyd Lake	E-C	CO	246
Blodgett Lake	COLO	CO	163	Boysen Reservoir	WIND	WY	278
Blucher Creek	SWT	WY	347	Bradley Lake	SN	WY	320
Blucher Lake	SWT	WY	347	Brady Lake	COLO	CO	161

406 LAKES & STREAMS INDEX

Stream name	Chapter	State	Page
Brainard Lake	FRS	CO	239
Brewery Creek	SLV	CO	42
Bridge Creek	YNP	WY	309
Bridger Creek	GRN	WY	338
Bridger Lake	BHR	WY	293
Bridger Lakes	GRN	WY	338
Broad Creek	YNP	WY	310
Brook Creek	RMNP	CO	136
Brooklyn Lakes	NP	WY	356
Brooks Lake	WIND	WY	370
Brooks Lake Creek	WIND	WY	370
Broomfield Park	URB	CO	224
Brown Bear Lake	NEW	WY	370
Brown Lake	RG	CO	28
Browns Canyon	ARK	CO	194
Browns Creek	ARK	CO	195
Browns Lake	POU	CO	130
Browns Park NWR	YAM	CO	112
Bruce Creek	NEW	WY	374
Brush Creek	COLO	CO	165
Brush Creek	COLO	CO	169
Brush Creek	GUNN	CO	78
Brush Creek	GUNN	CO	72
Brush Hollow Reservoir	E-C	CO	254
Buchanan Creek	COLO	CO	144
Buck Creek	RG	CO	27
Buck Lake	YNP	WY	311
Buckeye Lake	ARK	CO	190
Buckles Reservoir	SWR	CO	49
Buckskin Creek	SP	CO	206
Bud's Lake	WIND	WY	274
Buffalo Bill Reservoir	BHR	WY	293
Buffalo Creek	NEW	WY	368
Buffalo Creek	SP	CO	215
Buffalo Creek	YNP	WY	312
Buffalo Fork Creek	SN	WY	320
Buffalo Lake	YNP	WY	302
Bull Basin Reservoir	COLO	CO	180
Bull Creek	NEW	WY	373
Bull Creek Resvs.	COLO	CO	180
Bull Lake	WIND	WY	281
Bull Run Creek	COLO	CO	147
Bundy Lake	NP	CO	116
Burn Creek	YAM	CO	107
Burning Bear Creek	SP	CO	212
Burns Reservoir	NP	CO	117
Burnt Creek	YNP	WY	310
Burnt Lake	GRN	WY	340
Burro Creek	RG	CO	33
Bushnell Lakes	ARK	CO	197
Butcherknife Creek	YAM	CO	106
Button Rock Reservoir	FRS	CO	240
Butts Lake	COLO	CO	181
Butts Park Pond	URB	CO	224
Byers Canyon	COLO	CO	146
Byron Lake	FRS	CO	233

C

Stream name	Chapter	State	Page
Cabin Creek	COLO	CO	145
Cabin Creek	YNP	WY	309
Cache Creek	YNP	WY	311
Cache Lake	YNP	WY	312
CACHE La POUDRE		**CO**	**127**
Cache la Poudre River	RMNP	CO	137
Calfie Creek	YNP	WY	311
California Gulch	ARK	CO	191
California Gulch Creek	SLV	CO	41
Cameahwalt Lake	WIND	WY	278
Camenisch Park Pond	URB	CO	224
Cameron Creek	GUNN	CO	71
Camp Creek	NP	CO	121
Camp Lake	WIND	WY	274
Campanula Creek	YNP	WY	305
Campbell Lake	NP	WY	354
Canadian River	NP	CO	120
Canoe Lake	YNP	WY	311
Canon Paso Creek	SWR	CO	51
Canyon Creek	BHR	WY	287
Canyon Creek	COLO	CO	156
Canyon Creek	COLO	CO	175
Canyon Creek	GUNN	CO	66
Canyon Creek	GUNN	CO	84
Canyon Creek	SWR	CO	54
Canyon Creek	YNP	WY	303
Canyon Rincon Creek	RG	CO	35
Canyon Verde Creek	RG	CO	35
Capitol Creek	COLO	CO	169
Capitol Lake	COLO	CO	169
Carbon Creek	GUNN	CO	75
Carey Lake	LAR	CO	124
Carl Park Pond	URB	CO	224
Carmody Park Pond	URB	CO	224
Carnelian Creek	YNP	WY	310
Carnero Creek	SLV	CO	41
Carp Lake	COLO	CO	181
Carson Lake	COLO	CO	181
Carter Lake	COLO	CO	171
Carter Lake Reservoir	E-C	CO	246
Cascade Creek	COLO	CO	145
Cascade Creek	GUNN	CO	79
Cascade Creek	GUNN	CO	84
Cascade Creek	POU	CO	127
Cascade Creek	RMNP	CO	137
Cascade Creek	SWR	CO	54
Cascade Creek	YNP	WY	310
Cascade Lake	NP	WY	354
Cascade Lake	YNP	WY	310
Castillo Lake	SWR	CO	53
Castle Creek	COLO	CO	168
Castle Creek	GUNN	CO	75
Castle Rock Lake	RG	CO	27
Cataract Creek	COLO	CO	153
Cataract Creek	GUNN	CO	77
Cataract Lake	GUNN	CO	77
Cathedral Lake	COLO	CO	168
Cathedral Lake	WIND	WY	275
Causeway Lake	YAM	CO	110
Cave Creek	SLV	CO	41
Ceanothuse Lake	NP	CO	118
Cebolla Basin	GUNN	CO	75
Cebolla Creek	GUNN	CO	76

LAKES & STREAMS INDEX 407

Stream name	Chapter	State	Page
Cebolla Creek	GUNN	CO	78
Cedar Mesa Reservoir	COLO	CO	182
Cement Creek	GUNN	CO	72
Centennial Park Lake	URB	CO	224
Chain Lakes	GRN	WY	339
Chain of Lakes	COLO	CO	161
Chalcedony Creeks	YNP	WY	311
Chalk Creek	ARK	CO	194
Chama Lakes	RG	CO	37
Chama River	RG	CO	37
Chambers Lake	LAR	CO	123
Chambers Lake	POU	CO	128
Chapin Creek	POU	CO	127
Chapin Creek	RMNP	CO	137
Chapman Creek	COLO	CO	172
Chapman Dam	COLO	CO	172
Chapman Lake	COLO	CO	172
Chapman Reservoir	YAM	CO	105
Chasm Lake Pool	RMNP	CO	135
Chatfield Ponds	YAM	CO	104
Chatfield Reservoir	SP	CO	215
Chatfield Reservoir	URB	CO	224
Chatfield Reservoir	YAM	CO	104
Chedsey Creek	NP	CO	117
Cheesman Reservoir	SP	CO	211
Cherry Creek Reservoir	SP	CO	211
Cherry Creek Reservoir	URB	CO	224
Cherry Lake	SLV	CO	42
Chicago Creek	FRS	CO	234
Chihuahua Creek	COLO	CO	151
Chief Creek	E-C	CO	248
Chihuahua Lake	COLO	CO	151
Chill Lakes	NEW	WY	370
Chinns Lake	FRS	CO	234
Chipmunk Creek	YNP	WY	309
Chiquita Lake	RMNP	CO	137
Christina Lake	WIND	WY	277
Christine Lake	COLO	CO	169
Christine Lake	GRN	WY	340
Cimarron Creek	SWR	CO	47
Cimarron River	GUNN	CO	80
Circle Creek	YAM	CO	109
Cirque Lake	POU	CO	130
City Park Lake	URB	CO	225
City Reservoir	SWR	CO	53
Clark Creek	BHR	WY	293
Clark Creek	GRN	WY	336
Clark Lake	GRN	WY	336
Clarks Fk Yellowstone R	BHR	WY	294
Clay Creek	E-C	CO	251
Clayton Lake	FRS	CO	236
Clear Creek	ARK	CO	193
Clear Creek	FRS	CO	231
Clear Creek	GRN	WY	335
Clear Creek	NP	CO	120
Clear Creek	NEW	WY	369
Clear Creek	RG	CO	27
Clear Creek	YNP	WY	308

SMOOTH CURRENT. FROM HONDA.

We've got the full line of unbeatable Honda 4-cycle outboards and portable AC/DC generators at hard to beat prices! See us first—for "watt-ever" you need!

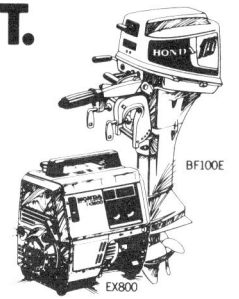

BF100E

EX800

SALES • SERVICE • RENTALS • PARTS

Generator City
Your power products supercenter!

1700 N. Federal Blvd.
Denver, Colorado 80204
Next to Mile High Stadium

9625 E. Arapahoe Rd.
Englewood, Colorado 80112
Arapahoe at Dayton

Monday-Friday 8-5, Saturday 9-4

455-2800 790-4900
TOLL FREE IN COLORADO 1-800-521-1511

408 LAKES & STREAMS INDEX

Stream name	Chapter	State	Page
Clear Creek Pond	URB	CO	225
Clear Creek Reservoir	ARK	CO	193
Clear Creek Reservoir	FRS	CO	233
Clear Fork Creek	GUNN	CO	83
Clear Lake	GRN	WY	335
Clear Lake	GRN	WY	343
Clear Lake	NP	CO	121
Clear Lake	SWR	CO	54
Clearwater Creek	BHR	WY	293
Cleveland Lakes	COLO	CO	161
Cliff Creek	GUNN	CO	84
Cliff Creek	SN	WY	323
Cliff Creek	YNP	WY	309
Cliff Lake	BHR	WY	290
Cliff Lake	COLO	CO	153
Cliff Lake	NP	CO	116
Cliff Lake	WIND	WY	276
Cliff Lakes	COLO	CO	175
Clinton Reservoir	COLO	CO	150
Cloud Peak Reservoir	NEW	WY	371
Clover Creek	SLV	CO	41
Cloverleaf Lake	WIND	WY	275
Cloyses Lake	ARK	CO	193
Coal Creek	COLO	CO	174
Coal Creek	DOL	CO	59
Coal Creek	GUNN	CO	74
Coal Creek	GUNN	CO	79
Coal Creek	GUNN	CO	84
Cochetopa Creek	GUNN	CO	67
Coffin Lake	F-W	CO	96
Coke Oven Creek	DOL	CO	59
Colby Horse Park Res	COLO	CO	183
Cold Creek	DOL	CO	60
Cold Creek	YNP	WY	311
Cole Reservoir No. 1	COLO	CO	182
Colorado Creek	NP	CO	116
COLORADO RIVER		**CO**	**142**
Columbine Creek	YNP	WY	308
Columbine Lake	COLO	CO	145
Columbine Lake	SWR	CO	52
Columbine Lake	SWR	CO	53
Columbine Pond	URB	CO	225
Comanche Lake	ARK	CO	199
Comanche Ponds	E-C	CO	252
Comanche Reservoir	POU	CO	130
Cone Lake	FRS	CO	233
Conejos River	RG	CO	33
Coney Creek	FRS	CO	240
Coney Creek	NEW	WY	372
Coney Lake	NEW	WY	372
Continental Reservoir	RG	CO	27
Conundrum Creek	COLO	CO	168
Cony Creek	RMNP	CO	135
Cony Lake	RMNP	CO	135
Cook Lake	WIND	WY	275
Coon Lake	WIND	WY	277
Cooney Lake	SP	CO	206
Cooper Creek	GUNN	CO	76
Cooper Lake	GUNN	CO	76
Copper Creek	COLO	CO	147
Copper Creek	COLO	CO	169

Stream name	Chapter	State	Page
Copper Creek	GUNN	CO	74
Copper Creek	NEW	WY	374
Copper Lake	GUNN	CO	74
Copper Lakes	BHR	WY	295
Cornelius Creek	POU	CO	130
Corona Lake	COLO	CO	146
Corral Creek	GRN	WY	344
Corral Creek	POU	CO	128
Costo Lake	GUNN	CO	75
Cotton Creek	SLV	CO	42
Cotton Lake	SLV	CO	42
Cottongrass Creek	YNP	WY	310
Cottonwood Creek	ARK	CO	193
Cottonwood Creek	ARK	CO	199
Cottonwood Creek	GUNN	CO	77
Cottonwood Creek	NP	WY	352
Cottonwood Creek	SLV	CO	42
Cottonwood Creek	SN	WY	317
Cottonwood Creek	SN	WY	320
Cottonwood Creek	YAM	CO	109
Cottonwood Creek	YNP	WY	312
Cottonwood Creek	BHR	WY	292
Cottonwood Lake	ARK	CO	194
Cottonwood Lake	SLV	CO	42
Cottonwood Lake	SN	WY	324
Cottonwood Lakes	COLO	CO	183
Cottonwood Park Lake	URB	CO	225
Cougar Creek	YNP	WY	305
Cougar Creek	YNP	WY	303
Cow Creek	GUNN	CO	70
Cow Creek	GUNN	CO	85
Cow Lake	GUNN	CO	70
Cowan Creek	YNP	WY	304
Cowdrey Lake	NP	CO	119
Coyote Creek	YNP	WY	312
Coyote Lake	GRN	WY	337
Coyote Lake	GRN	WY	340
Crag Lake	YNP	WY	306
Crandall Creek	BHR	WY	295
Crater Lake	COLO	CO	168
Crater Lake	COLO	CO	145
Crater Lake	F-W	CO	98
Crater Lake	GUNN	CO	84
Crater Lake	SN	WY	321
Crater Lake	SWR	CO	46
Crater Lakes	FRS	CO	236
Crawfish Creek	YNP	WY	301
Crawford Lake	COLO	CO	144
Crawford Reservoir	GUNN	CO	82
Crazy Woman Creek	NEW	WY	369
Creedmore Lakes	POU	CO	130
Crescent Lake	COLO	CO	158
Crescent Lake	GRN	WY	341
Crescent Lake	GRN	WY	335
Crescent Lake	NP	WY	357
Crescent Lake	NEW	WY	372
Crescent Lake	YNP	WY	306
Crevice Creek	YNP	WY	312
Crooked Creek	COLO	CO	146
Crooked Creek	RG	CO	27
Crooked Creek	YNP	WY	301

LAKES & STREAMS INDEX   409

Stream name	Chapter	State	Page	Stream name	Chapter	State	Page
Crosby Creek	NP	CO	117	Cub Lake	WIND	WY	274
Crosho Lake	YAM	CO	104	Culebra Creek	RG	CO	33
Cross Creek	COLO	CO	163	Cunningham Creek	COLO	CO	171
Cross Creek	NEW	WY	372	Cunningham Creek	SWR	CO	53
Cross Creek	RG	CO	32	Curecanti Creek	GUNN	CO	80
Cross Creek Lakes	NEW	WY	372	Currier Reservoir	COLO	CO	183
Cross Creek Reservoir	NEW	WY	372	Cushing Park Pond	URB	CO	225
Cross Lake	GRN	WY	340	Cutoff Creek	YNP	WY	312
Cross Lake	GRN	WY	341	Cutthroat Lake	GRN	WY	337
Cross Mountain Creek	GUNN	CO	71	Cutthroat Lake	NP	WY	357
Crown Hill Lake	URB	CO	225	Cutthroat Lake	WIND	WY	277
Crystal Creek	GUNN	CO	71				
Crystal Creek	SN	WY	322	**D**			
Crystal Creek	YNP	WY	311				
Crystal Lake	ARK	WY	192	Dad's Lake	GRN	WY	343
Crystal Lake	ARK	CO	192	Dallas Creek	GUNN	CO	85
Crystal Lake	COLO	CO	149	Daly Creek	YNP	WY	306
Crystal Lake	GUNN	CO	68	Daphne Lake	GRN	WY	335
Crystal Lake	GUNN	CO	78	Davis Creek	NP	CO	121
Crystal Lake	NEW	WY	372	DeLacy Creek	YNP	WY	302
Crystal Lake	RMNP	CO	136	DeWeese Reservoir	ARK	CO	198
Crystal Lake	SWR	CO	53	Dead Indian Creek	BHR	WY	295
Crystal Lake Creek	ARK	CO	192	Deadhorse Creek	NEW	WY	369
Crystal Lakes	RG	CO	32	Deadman Creek	LAR	CO	125
Crystal Reservoir	GUNN	CO	81	Deadman Creek	RG	CO	27
Crystal Reservoir	NP	WY	365	Deadman Creek	SLV	CO	42
Crystal River	COLO	CO	172	Deadman Creek	SWR	CO	50
Cub Creek	SN	WY	321	Deadman Lake	COLO	CO	146
Cub Creek	YNP	WY	308	Deadman Lake	SLV	CO	42

THE Colorado Angler

"Fly Fishing Specialty Shop"   LAKEWOOD, CO

(303) 232-8298

"The Finest and Most Complete Fly Shop in the west"

We offer quality name brands in fly fishing equipment and fly tying materials. We will help you select proper equipment, provide up-to-date fishing reports and give you the service you expect.

Join our classes and learn the art of fly tying, fly fishing and rod building.

Conveniently located on the west side. Stop in on your way to the mountains for all your fishing needs. (Coffee's always on).

Put your trust in The Colorado Angler
1457 Nelson Street   Lakewood, CO 80215
(½ block south of Westland Shopping Center)

LAKES & STREAMS INDEX

Stream name	Chapter	State	Page
Deadman Lake	WIND	WY	282
Dean Lake	GRN	WY	337
Deckers Lake	ARK	CO	190
Deep Creek	BHR	WY	287
Deep Creek	COLO	CO	159
Deep Creek	COLO	CO	155
Deep Creek	RG	CO	29
Deep Creek	SM	CO	62
Deep Creek	WIND	WY	276
Deep Creek	YNP	WY	310
Deep Creek Lakes	WIND	WY	277
Deep Lake	BHR	WY	289
Deep Lake	COLO	CO	159
Deep Lake	GRN	WY	343
Deep Slough Res	COLO	CO	181
Deer Creek	COLO	CO	151
Deer Creek	NP	WY	361
Deer Creek	SP	CO	213
Deer Creek Lakes	GUNN	CO	78
Deer Lake	COLO	CO	158
Deer Lake	F-W	CO	99
Delaney Butte Lakes	NP	CO	118
Dell Creek	SN	WY	323
Delusion Lake	YNP	WY	309
Dennis Lake	WIND	WY	274
Denny Creek	ARK	CO	194
Denny Lake	DOL	CO	61
Denver Lake	SWR	CO	53
Derby Creek	COLO	CO	156
Derby Creeks	F-W	CO	99
Devil's Thumb Lake	FRS	CO	238
Devils Lake	NEW	WY	372
Diamond Lake	FRS	CO	237
Diamond Lake	GRN	WY	343
Diamond Lake	NEW	WY	371
Diamond Lake	NP	WY	365
Dickinson Creek	WIND	WY	275
Diemer Lake	COLO	CO	171
Dillon Reservoir	COLO	CO	149
Dinkle Lake	COLO	CO	169
Dinwoody Lakes	WIND	WY	281
Dinwoody Lakes	WIND	WY	273
Dipper Lake	NP	WY	354
Disappointment Creek	DOL	CO	60
Disappointment Lake	NP	CO	116
Divide Creek	GRN	WY	341
Divide Lake	GRN	WY	341
Divide Lake	SWR	CO	51
Dogfish Reservoir	GUNN	CO	84
Dollar Lake	GRN	WY	339
Dollar Lake	GUNN	CO	84
Dollar Lake	SWR	CO	51
DOLORES RIVER		CO	**58**
Dome Lake	NEW	WY	372
Dome Lake	YAM	CO	107
Don Lake	GRN	WY	339
Don Lake	WIND	WY	274
Donald Lake	GRN	WY	343
Donut Lake	RMNP	CO	136
Dora Lake	COLO	CO	153
Double Lake	WIND	WY	273
Douglas Creek	NP	WY	351
Dowdy Lake	POU	CO	131
Downs Lake	WIND	WY	273
Dream Creek	GRN	WY	341
Dream Lake	GRN	WY	341
Dream Lake	RMNP	CO	136
Drink Creek	LAR	CO	125
Dry Creek	ARK	CO	199
Dry Creek	NEW	WY	368
Dry Creek	WIND	WY	273
Dry Fork Creek	NEW	WY	375
Dry Lakes	ARK	CO	199
Duck Creek	NEW	WY	370
Duck Creek	YNP	WY	303
Duck Creek	YNP	WY	305
Duck Lake	RG	CO	37
Duck Lake	SP	CO	213
Dugout Creek	NEW	CO	368
Dullknife Reservoir	NEW	WY	368
Dunoir Creek	WIND	WY	270
Dutch Creek	SWR	CO	55
Dutch Creek	YAM	CO	108
Dutch Oven Lake	WIND	WY	274
Dyke Lake	WIND	WY	272

E

Stream name	Chapter	State	Page
EASTERN COLORADO		**CO**	**243**
Eagle Creek	BHR	WY	293
Eagle Lake	COLO	CO	171
Eagle Lake	RMNP	CO	135
Eagle River	COLO	CO	159
Eaglesmere Lakes	COLO	CO	154
East Allen Lake	NP	WY	365
East Anthracite Creek	GUNN	CO	83
East Banner Lake	NP	WY	354
East Beaver Creek	GUNN	CO	72
East Bellows Creek	RG	CO	30
East Brush Creek	COLO	CO	165
East Brush Creek	GUNN	CO	72
East Canyon Creek	COLO	CO	175
East Creek	COLO	CO	174
East Cross Creek	COLO	CO	163
East Dunoir Creek	WIND	WY	270
East Elk Creek	GUNN	CO	79
East Fork Arkansas River	ARK	CO	190
East Fork Big Goose Creek	NEW	WY	372
East Fork Cimarron River	GUNN	CO	80
East Fork Creek	BHR	WY	293
East Fork Dallas Creek	GUNN	CO	85
East Fork Eagle River	COLO	CO	159
East Fork Muddy Creek	GUNN	CO	83
East Fork Piney River	COLO	CO	156
East Fork River	GRN	WY	342
East Fork San Juan River	SWR	CO	46
East Fork San Miguel River	SM	CO	62
East Fork South Tongue R	NEW	WY	374
East Fork Specimen Creek	YNP	WY	306
East Fork Trout Creek	RG	CO	28
East Fork Williams Fork R	YAM	CO	110
East Fork Wind River	WIND	WY	281

LAKES & STREAMS INDEX

Stream name	Chapter	State	Page
East Fork Wind River	WIND	WY	270
East Fork of Hermosa Creek	SWR	CO	55
East Fork of Homestake Ck	COLO	CO	160
East Fork of Miller Creek	WHR	CO	92
East Fork of Powderhorn Ck	GUNN	CO	79
East Fork Piedra River	SWR	CO	50
East Fork Williams Fork	YAM	CO	110
East Glacier Lake	NP	WY	356
East Inlet Creek	RMNP	CO	138
East Klondike Lake	NP	WY	354
East Lake Creek	COLO	CO	164
East Lost Lakes	YAM	CO	110
East Maroon Creek	COLO	CO	168
East Maroon Lake	GUNN	CO	74
East Marvine Creek	F-W	CO	97
East Marvine Creek	WHR	CO	90
East Meadow Creek	COLO	CO	156
East Middle Creek	SLV	CO	41
East Reservoir	URB	CO	226
East Rifle Creek	COLO	CO	176
East River	GUNN	CO	72
East Snowmass Creek	COLO	CO	169
East Ten Sleep Creek	BHR	WY	287
East Ten Sleep Lake	BHR	WY	287
East Tennessee Creek	ARK	CO	190
East Torrey Creek	WIND	WY	272
East Ute Lake	RG	CO	26
East Willow Creek	GUNN	CO	70
East Willow Creek	RG	CO	29
Eastern Hohnholz Lake	LAR	CO	126
Echo Canyon Reservoir	SWR	CO	48
Edelman Creek	NEW	WY	372
Edge Lake	COLO	CO	158
Edge Lake	F-W	CO	99
Edmond Lake	GRN	WY	340
Eggleston Lake	COLO	CO	182
El Rito Azul Creek	RG	CO	34
Elbert Creek	SWR	CO	55
Elbow Creek	GRN	WY	336
Elbow Lake	GRN	WY	338
Electra Lake	SWR	CO	54
Elephant Head Lake	NEW	WY	372
Elevenmile Canyon	SP	CO	210
Elevenmile Reservoir	SP	CO	209
Elk Antler Creek	YNP	WY	310
Elk Creek	COLO	CO	146
Elk Creek	COLO	CO	175
Elk Creek	RG	CO	35
Elk Creek	SP	CO	215
Elk Creek	SWR	CO	54
Elk Creek	YNP	WY	312
Elk Fork Creek	BHR	WY	293
Elk Lake	SWR	CO	51
Elk Lake	WHR	CO	90
Elk Lake	WIND	WY	282
Elk Lakes	F-W	CO	98
Elk River	YAM	CO	106
Elk Tongue Creek	YNP	WY	312
Elkhead Creek	YAM	CO	109
Elkhead Reservoir	YAM	CO	109
Elkhorn Creek	POU	CO	130
Elkhorn Gulch Creek	SLV	CO	42
Elkhorn Lake	BHR	WY	295
Elliott Creek	COLO	CO	155
Embargo Creek	RG	CO	32
Emerald Lake	ARK	CO	191
Emerald Lake	BHR	WY	290
Emerald Lake	COLO	CO	158
Emerald Lake	GUNN	CO	73
Emerald Lake	RMNP	CO	136
Emma Lake	GRN	WY	339
Emma Matilda Lake	SN	WY	320
Emmaline Lake	POU	CO	130
Encampment River	NP	CO	121
Encampment River	NP	WY	352
Engineers Lake	URB	CO	226
English Creek	YAM	CO	106
Enos Creek	SN	WY	320
Enos Lake	SN	WY	320
Enos Lake	WIND	WY	282
Envy Lake	FRS	CO	240
Equalizer Reservoir	E-C	CO	246
Escarpment Creek	YNP	WY	309
Esther Lake	COLO	CO	161
Ethel Lake	GRN	WY	340
Eureka Lake	ARK	CO	199
Europe Creek	GRN	WY	340
Evelyn Lake	COLO	CO	147
Evergreen Lake	SP	CO	216
Exposition Park Pond	URB	CO	226

F

Stream name	Chapter	State	Page
Fairview Lake	COLO	CO	170
Fairview Reservoir	GUNN	CO	85
Fairy Creek	YNP	WY	304
Faler Lake	GRN	WY	335
Fall Creek	COLO	CO	162
Fall Creek	GRN	WY	340
Fall Creek	GUNN	CO	80
Fall Creek	LAR	CO	123
Fall Creek	LAR	CO	123
Fall Creek	POU	CO	130
Fall Creek	SM	CO	62
Fall Creek	SN	WY	323
Fall Creek Lakes	GRN	WY	340
Fall River	FRS	CO	233
Fall River	RMNP	CO	136
Fall River Reservoir	FRS	CO	234
Falls River	YNP	WY	302
Falls River	YNP	WY	300
Fan Creek	YNP	WY	306
Fancy Creek	COLO	CO	161
Fancy Lake	COLO	CO	161
Farmer's Union Reservoir	RG	CO	25
Farris Creek	GUNN	CO	72
Fawn Creek	YNP	WY	313
Fawn Lake	WIND	WY	277
Fay Lakes	RMNP	CO	137
Fayette Lake	GRN	WY	339
Fehling's Reservoir	ARK	CO	195
Fern Creek	RG	CO	28

412 LAKES & STREAMS INDEX

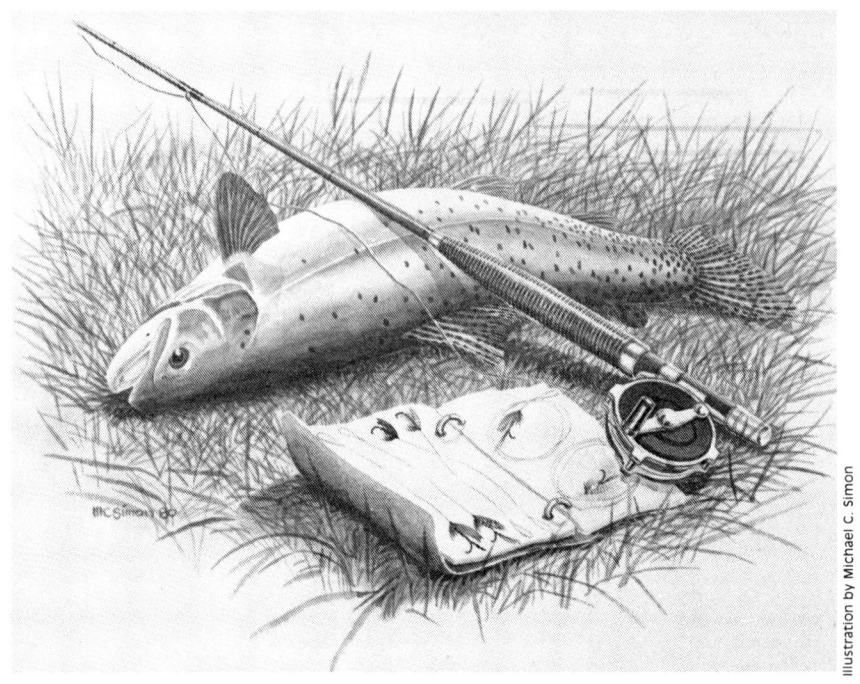

Illustration by Michael C. Simon

Stream name	Chapter	State	Page
Fern Creek	RMNP	CO	136
Fern Lake	RMNP	CO	136
Fern Lake	YNP	WY	310
Ferry Lake	SN	WY	321
Festo Lake	NP	WY	365
Fiddlers Creek	WIND	WY	277
Fiddlers Lake	WIND	WY	277
Fifth Lake	RMNP	CO	138
Finger Lake	BHR	WY	295
Finney Cuts Lakes	COLO	CO	182
Firehole Lakes	GRN	WY	340
Firehole Lakes	NEW	WY	370
Firehole River	YNP	WY	303
Firehole River	YNP	WY	304
First Creek	YAM	CO	109
Fish Creek	LAR	CO	126
Fish Creek	SN	WY	322
Fish Creek	SWR	CO	48
Fish Creek	YAM	CO	105
Fish Creek	YAM	CO	109
Fish Creek	DOL	CO	60
Fish Creek Lakes	SN	WY	322
Fish Creek Reservoir	YAM	CO	105
Fish Creek Reservoirs	GUNN	CO	81
Fish Hawk Lake	YAM	CO	109
Fish Lake	SWR	CO	48
Fish Lake	WIND	WY	271
Fisher Creek	RG	CO	30
Fisherman Creek	SN	WY	323
Fishhawk Creek	BHR	WY	293
Fishhawk Lake	YAM	CO	109
Fishhook Creek	YAM	CO	105

Stream name	Chapter	State	Page
Fishhook Lake	YAM	CO	105
Fishing Bridge	YNP	WY	309
Flagler Reservoir	E-C	CO	249
Flaming Gorge Reservoir	GRN	WY	331
Flat Creek	SN	WY	317
Flat Creek	SN	WY	322
Flat Creek Lake	SN	WY	322
FLATTOPS WILDERNESS		**CO**	**94**
Flatiron Lake	NEW	WY	371
Flint Creek	SWR	CO	51
Flint Creek	YNP	WY	311
Flood Lake	RMNP	WY	136
Florence Lake	NEW	WY	370
Florence Lake	WIND	WY	273
Florida River	SW	CO	53
Floyd Creek	YAM	CO	108
Fontenelle Creek	GRN	WY	344
Fontenelle Reservoir	GRN	WY	330
Fooses Creek	ARK	CO	196
Footprint Lake	WIND	WY	277
Ford Creek	SLV	CO	41
Forest Creek	YNP	WY	301
Forest Lakes	FRS	CO	236
Forester Creek	NP	CO	118
Forrest Lake	COLO	CO	181
Forrester Creek	LAR	CO	126
Fortification Creek	YAM	CO	109
Fortress Lakes	BHR	WY	289
Fourmile Creek	ARK	CO	196
Fourmile Creek	ARK	CO	193
Fourmile Creek	FRS	CO	238
Fourmile Creek	NEW	WY	368

LAKES & STREAMS INDEX

Stream name	Chapter	State	Page	Stream name	Chapter	State	Page
Fourmile Creek	SP	CO	207	Gold Dust Lakes	COLO	CO	164
Fourmile Creek	SWR	CO	48	Golden Gate Can St. P.	FRS	CO	236
Fourmile Creek	YAM	CO	111	Golden Lake	NP	WY	357
Fourth Lake	RMNP	CO	138	Golden Lake	WIND	WY	273
Fox Creek	SN	WY	317	Golden Lake	WIND	WY	274
Fraser River	COLO	CO	145	Golden Lakes	GRN	WY	336
Freeman Reservoir	YAM	CO	109	Goldeneye Reservoir	NP	WY	361
Fremont Creek	GRN	WY	338	Goodenough Reservoir	GUNN	CO	84
Fremont Lake	GRN	WY	337	Goodwin Creek	ARK	CO	199
French Creek	COLO	CO	161	Goodwin Lakes	ARK	CO	199
French Creek	NP	WY	352	Goose Creek	NP	CO	118
French Creek	NEW	WY	370	Goose Creek	NEW	WY	372
Friend Creek	NP	WY	364	Goose Creek	RG	CO	30
FRONT RANGE STREAMS		**CO**	**231**	Goose Lake	FRS	CO	239
Frozen Lakes	NEW	WY	370	Goose Lake	RG	CO	31
Frye Lake Reservoir	WIND	WY	277	Goose Lake	YNP	WY	304
Frying Pan Lake	NEW	WY	371	Gooseberry Creek	BHR	WY	292
Fryingpan Lakes	COLO	CO	171	Gore Creek	COLO	CO	163
Fryingpan River	COLO	CO	169	Gore Lake	COLO	CO	163
Fuchs Reservoir	RG	CO	33	Gorge Lake	GRN	WY	338
Fuller Lake	SWR	CO	54	Gorge Lakes	RMNP	CO	136
G				Gottfried Lake	GRN	WY	337
				Gould Reservoir	GUNN	CO	83
Gadsby Lake	GRN	WY	335	Gourd Lake	COLO	CO	145
Galena Lake	ARK	CO	191	Grace Creek	LAR	CO	126
Galena Lake	COLO	CO	172	Grace Lake	BHR	WY	289
Gallatin Lake	YNP	WY	306	Granby Reservoirs	COLO	CO	181
Gallatin River	YNP	WY	306	Grand Lake	COLO	CO	143
Garden Lakes	NP	WY	357	Granite Creek	COLO	CO	171
Gardner Park Reservoir	YAM	CO	104	Granite Creek	SN	WY	323
Gardner River	YNP	WY	312	Granite Lake	BHR	WY	295
Garfield Park Lake	URB	CO	226	Granite Lake	GRN	WY	335
Garland Park Lake	URB	CO	226	Granite Lake	SWR	CO	51
Garner Creek	SLV	CO	42	Granite Lakes	COLO	CO	171
Gas Creek	ARK	CO	196	Granite Reservoir	NP	WY	365
Gaylord Lake	WIND	WY	274	Grape Creek	ARK	CO	198
Geddes Lake	NEW	WY	372	Grape Creek	ARK	CO	200
Gelatt Lake	NP	WY	365	Grass Lake	ARK	CO	196
Gem Lake	NP	CO	122	Grassy Lake	WIND	WY	273
Geneva Creek	SP	CO	212	Grassy Lake	NP	WY	357
Geneva Lake	COLO	CO	172	Grassy Lake	SN	WY	318
George Creek	POU	CO	130	Grassy Lake Reservoir	YNP	WY	302
Georgetown Lake	FRS	CO	232	Grave Lake	WIND	WY	274
Ghost Lake	RG	CO	29	Gravel Creek	SN	WY	320
Gibbon River	YNP	WY	303	Gravel Lake	SN	WY	320
Gibralter Lake	FRS	CO	240	Graves Creek	NEW	WY	374
Gibson Lake	SP	CO	212	Gray Lake	WIND	WY	275
Gimpse Lake	GRN	WY	337	Gray's Lake	COLO	CO	151
Glacier Creek	RMNP	CO	136	Grayling Creek	YNP	WY	303
Glacier Lake	FRS	CO	238	Grayling Creek	YNP	WY	305
Glacier Lake	NEW	WY	371	Grayling Lake	BHR	WY	295
Glacier Lake	RG	CO	35	Grayrocks Reservoir	NP	WY	364
Glacier Lake	WIND	WY	275	Grays Creek	ARK	CO	196
Glacier Springs Pond	COLO	CO	180	Grebe Lake	YNP	WY	303
Glade Creek	SN	WY	318	Green Creek	ARK	CO	196
Glass Lake	RMNP	CO	136	Green Creek	YAM	CO	105
Glen Creek	YNP	WY	313	Green Gables Park Pond	URB	CO	226
Glendo Reservoir	NP	WY	363	Green Lake	GUNN	CO	74
Gneiss Creek	YNP	WY	305	Green Lake	RG	CO	35
Goldbolt Lake	RMNP	CO	136	Green Lakes	FRS	CO	239
Gold Creek	GUNN	CO	68	Green Mountain Reservoir	COLO	CO	154

Stream name	Chapter	State	Page
GREEN RIVER		**WY**	**328**
Green River	YAM	CO	111
Greenhorn Creek	ARK	CO	201
Grey Reef Reservoir	NP	WY	361
Greybull River	BHR	WY	292
Greys Fork	GRN	WY	344
Greys River	SN	WY	323
Griffith Lake	COLO	CO	180
Grizzly Creek	ARK	CO	195
Grizzly Creek	COLO	CO	159
Grizzly Creek	COLO	CO	166
Grizzly Creek	COLO	CO	168
Grizzly Creek	NP	CO	115
Grizzly Lake	ARK	CO	195
Grizzly Lake	COLO	CO	159
Grizzly Lake	COLO	CO	167
Grizzly Lake	YNP	WY	313
Grizzly Reservoir	COLO	CO	167
Gros Ventre River	SN	WY	321
Gross Reservoir	FRS	CO	237
Ground Hog Creek	DOL	CO	60
Ground Hog Reservoir	DOL	CO	60
Grouse Creek	COLO	CO	163
Grouse Creek	COLO	CO	144
Grouse Creek	YNP	WY	309
Grouse Lake	COLO	CO	163
Guernsey Reservoir	NP	WY	365
Gunboat Lake	BHR	WY	289
GUNNISON RIVER		**CO**	**66**
Gurley Reservoir	SM	CO	63
Gus Lake	BHR	WY	295
Gustave Lake	WIND	WY	277
Guthrie Lake	F-W	CO	98
Gutzler Lakes	COLO	CO	156
Gwendolyn Lake	F-W	CO	96
Gypsum Creek	COLO	CO	165
Gypsum Creek	GRN	WY	335

H

Stream name	Chapter	State	Page
Hagerman Lake	ARK	CO	191
Hague Creek	POU	CO	127
Hague Creek	RMNP	CO	137
Hahns Peak Lake	YAM	CO	107
Hale Ponds	E-C	CO	249
Half Moon Lake	GRN	WY	338
Half Moon Lake	SWR	CO	51
Halfmoon Creek	ARK	CO	191
Halfmoon Lake	COLO	CO	170
Halligan Reservoir	POU	CO	130
Halls Lake	GRN	WY	341
Hamilton Creek	COLO	CO	145
Hampton Lake	GUNN	CO	81
Hams Fork River	GRN	WY	344
Hancock Creek	ARK	CO	195
Hancock Lake	ARK	CO	195
Handcart Gulch	SP	CO	212
Hang Lake	LAR	CO	124
Hansen Creek	RG	CO	35
Hardscrabble Lake	COLO	CO	169
Harris Reservoir	SWR	CO	49

Stream name	Chapter	State	Page
Harrison Creek	YAM	CO	105
Harrison Flats Lake	ARK	CO	193
Hartenstein Lake	ARK	CO	194
Harvey Gap Reservoir	COLO	CO	175
Harvey Lake	COLO	CO	163
Harvey Park Lake	URB	CO	226
Hassell Lake	FRS	CO	233
Hasty Lake	E-C	CO	251
Hatcher Lakes	SWR	CO	47
Hatchet Lake	WIND	WY	282
Haviland Lake	SWR	CO	55
Hawk Creek	COLO	CO	174
Hay Creek	NEW	WY	375
Hay Lake	GUNN	CO	78
Hay Pass Lakes	WIND	WY	274
Hay Press Lake	RG	CO	30
Hayden Creek	ARK	CO	197
Hazel Lake	SWR	CO	52
Healy Reservoir	NEW	WY	104
Heart Lake	COLO	CO	159
Heart Lake	FRS	CO	236
Heart Lake	GRN	WY	337
Heart Lake	NEW	WY	372
Heart Lake	RG	CO	27
Heart Lake	YAM	CO	104
Heart Lake	YNP	WY	301
Heart River	YNP	WY	301
Hebgen Lake	YNP	WY	303
Heflin Creek	SWR	CO	50
Hell Canyon Creek	COLO	CO	144
Hellroaring Creek	YNP	WY	312
Henderson Lake	SWR	CO	54
Henry Lake	GUNN	CO	68
Henrys Fork	GRN	WY	344
Henson Creek	GUNN	CO	78
Hering Lake	YNP	WY	302
Herman Lake	FRS	CO	232
Hermit Lake	ARK	CO	199
Hermit Lake	RG	CO	28
Hermosa Creek	SWR	CO	55
Hidden Lake	SWR	CO	52
Hidden Lake	WIND	WY	275
Hidden Lake	WIND	WY	272
Hidden Lakes	GRN	WY	336
Hidden Lakes	NP	CO	117
High Lake	YNP	WY	306
High Meadow Lake	WIND	WY	275
Highland Mary Lakes	SWR	CO	53
Highland Park Lake	NEW	WY	372
Highline Lake	COLO	CO	179
Hill Creek	NP	CO	118
Hinman Creek	YAM	CO	107
Hoback River	SN	WY	323
Hobbs Lake	GRN	WY	338
Hog Park Reservoir	NP	WY	352
Hohnholz Lake	LAR	CO	126
Holbrook Park Pond	URB	CO	226
Holbrook Reservoir	E-C	CO	250
Hole-in-the-Wall Creek	YAM	CO	109
Holly Lake	SN	WY	320
Home Lake	RG	CO	33

LAKES & STREAMS INDEX

Stream name	Chapter	State	Page
Homestake Creek	COLO	CO	160
Homestake Lake	ARK	CO	190
Homestake Reservoir	COLO	CO	160
Honeymoon Lake	WIND	WY	273
Hooper Lake	COLO	CO	158
Hooper Lake	F-W	CO	99
Hope Creek	RG	CO	31
Horn Creek	ARK	CO	199
Horn Fork Creek	ARK	CO	193
Horse Creek	SP	CO	212
Horse Creek	WIND	WY	270
Horse Creek Reservoir	E-C	CO	250
Horse Shoe Creek	NP	WY	362
Horseshoe Creek	COLO	CO	156
Horseshoe Lake	ARK	CO	199
Horseshoe Lake	COLO	CO	164
Horseshoe Lake	E-C	CO	253
Horseshoe Lake	GRN	WY	340
Horseshoe Lake	COLO	CO	147
Horseshoe Lake	WIND	WY	273
Horseshoe Reservoir	E-C	CO	246
Horsetooth Reservoir	POU	CO	131
Hotel Twin Lake	COLO	CO	181
Hourglass Reservoir	POU	CO	130
House Creek	RG	CO	27
Howard Creek	ARK	CO	197
Howard Fork San Miguel R	SM	CO	62
Howard Lake	GRN	WY	340
Howe Lake	GRN	WY	341
Howell Creek	YNP	WY	309
Hubbard Creek	GUNN	CO	84
Hugo SWA Ponds	E-C	CO	249
Hunky Dory Lake	COLO	CO	161
Hunkydory Lake	ARK	CO	196
Hunt Creek	YAM	CO	104
Hunt Lake	ARK	CO	196
Hunter Creek	COLO	CO	168
Hunter Creek	NEW	WY	370
Hunters Lake	RG	CO	31
Hunts Lake	ARK	CO	197
Hurd Creek	COLO	CO	145
Huston Park Lake	URB	CO	226
Hutcheson Lakes	RMNP	CO	135

I

Ice Creek	WIND	WY	277
Ice Lake	FRS	CO	234
Ice Lake	SWR	CO	53
Ice Lake	YNP	WY	303
Iceberg Lake	LAR	CO	126
Iceberg Lakes	FRS	CO	236
Idaho Springs Reservoir	FRS	CO	234
Illinois Creek	GUNN	CO	69
Illinois Lake	GUNN	CO	69
Illinois River	NP	CO	120
Independence Creek	YAM	CO	111
Independence Lake	COLO	CO	166
Independent Reservoir	E-C	CO	245
Indian Creek	SLV	CO	41
Indian Creek	SWR	CO	50

Stream name	Chapter	State	Page
Indian Creek	YNP	WY	313
Indian Lake	COLO	CO	158
Indian Run Creek	YAM	CO	111
Ink Wells Lakes	WIND	WY	273
Inyan Kara Creek	NEW	WY	375
Iola Basin	GUNN	CO	75
Ione Lake	NP	WY	365
Iron Spring Creek	YNP	WY	304
Irving Creek	SWR	CO	51
Irving Hale Creek	COLO	CO	144
Irving Lake	SWR	CO	52
Island Lake	ARK	CO	196
Island Lake	BHR	WY	295
Island Lake	COLO	CO	181
Island Lake	COLO	CO	174
Island Lake	COLO	CO	145
Island Lake	FRS	CO	239
Island Lake	GRN	WY	338
Island Lake	LAR	CO	124
Island Lake	SWR	CO	54
Island Lake	WIND	WY	277
Isle of the Pine Lake	F-W	CO	97
Isolation Lakes	COLO	CO	160
Italian Creek	GUNN	CO	69
Ivanhoe Creek	COLO	CO	171
Ivanhoe Lake	COLO	CO	171
Ivy Creek	RG	CO	29

J

Jack Creek	NP	CO	120
Jack Creek	NP	WY	353
Jack Creek	SN	WY	323
Jack Creek	SWT	WY	347
Jack Lake	COLO	CO	167
Jackson Gulch Reservoir	SWR	CO	55
Jackson Lake	SN	WY	318
Jackson Reservoir	E-C	CO	247
Jade Lakes	WIND	WY	270
Jakey's Fork Creek	WIND	WY	271
James Creek	FRS	CO	239
James Peak Lake	FRS	CO	236
Jarosa Creek	RG	CO	33
Jasper (Reservoir) Lake	FRS	CO	238
Jasper Creek	FRS	CO	238
Jasper Creek	YNP	WY	311
Jeff Lake	NP	WY	357
Jefferson Creek	SP	CO	211
Jefferson Lake	SP	CO	211
Jenny Lake	FRS	CO	236
Jenny Lake	SN	WY	318
Jessie Lake	GRN	WY	342
Jet Lake	F-W	CO	98
Jewel Lake	RMNP	CO	136
Jewell Lake	SWR	CO	54
Jewell Park Pond	URB	CO	226
Jim Creek	RG	CO	33
Jim Harrower Lake	GRN	WY	341
Joe Johnson Reservoir	NP	WY	365
Joe Moore Reservoir	SWR	CO	55
Joe Wright Creek	LAR	CO	123

416 LAKES & STREAMS INDEX

Stream name	Chapter	State	Page
Joe Wright Creek	POU	CO	128
Joe Wright Reservoir	POU	CO	128
John Martin Reservoir	E-C	CO	251
Johns Creek	SLV	CO	41
Johnson Creek	LAR	CO	126
Johnson Creek	SWR	CO	51
Johnson Lake	F-W	CO	98
Johnson Lake	SN	WY	321
Johnson Pond	URB	CO	228
Johnson Reservoir	COLO	CO	182
Jojo Creek	BHR	WY	292
Jojo Lake	BHR	WY	292
Jonah Lake	NP	CO	117
Jones Creek	GUNN	CO	83
Jones Hole Creek	YAM	CO	112
Jug Lake	WIND	WY	277
Julesburg Reservoir	E-C	CO	248
Julian Lake	RMNP	CO	138
Jumbo Lake	COLO	CO	180
Jumbo Reservoir	E-C	CO	248
Junction Creek	SWR	CO	55
Junction Lake	GRN	WY	339
Junction Lake	GRN	WY	341

K

Stream name	Chapter	State	Page
Kannah Creek	COLO	CO	181
Karval Reservoir	E-C	CO	249
Katherine Lake	NP	CO	119
Kearny Creeks	NEW	WY	370
Kearny Lakes	NEW	WY	371
Keener Lake	COLO	CO	158
Keener Lake	F-W	CO	99
Kelly Creek	NP	CO	120
Kelly Lake	NP	CO	121
Kendrick Lake	URB	CO	228
Kenny Creek Reservoir	COLO	CO	183
Kenny Lake	GRN	WY	336
Kenosha Creek	SP	CO	212
Kerber Creek	SLV	CO	41
Kerr Lake	RG	CO	34
Ketring Park Lake	URB	CO	228
Keyhole Reservoir	NEW	WY	375
Keyser Creek	COLO	CO	147
Keystone Creek	COLO	CO	151
Kilpacker Creek	DOL	CO	60
King Lake	FRS	CO	238
King Solomon Creek	YAM	CO	111
Kinney Creek	COLO	CO	147
Kinney Lake	E-C	CO	249
Kirkland Lake	WIND	WY	282
Kiser Creek	COLO	CO	182
Kiser Slough Reservoir	COLO	CO	182
Kisinger Lakes	WIND	WY	270
Kite Lake	SP	CO	206
Kitson Reservoir	COLO	CO	183
Kitty Creek	RG	CO	27
Kiwanis Park Pond	URB	CO	228
Kline's Folly Lake	COLO	CO	159
Knowles Creek	YAM	CO	109
Kortes Reservoir	NP	WY	357

Stream name	Chapter	State	Page
Kroenke Creek	ARK	CO	194
Kroenke Lake	ARK	CO	194

L

Stream name	Chapter	State	Page
La Barge Creek	GRN	WY	344
La Bonte Creek	NP	WY	362
La Garde Creek	LAR	CO	126
La Garita Creek	SLV	CO	41
La Jara Creek	RG	CO	33
La Jara Reservoir	RG	CO	33
La Manga Creek	RG	CO	37
La Plata River	SWR	CO	55
La Prele Creek	NP	WY	362
La Prele Reservoir	NP	WY	362
Lake Adams	RMNP	CO	138
Lake Albion	FRS	CO	239
Lake Angeline	NEW	WY	370
Lake Ann	ARK	CO	193
Lake Arbor	URB	CO	228
Lake Arden	BHR	WY	290
Lake Avery	WHR	CO	91
Lake Buffalo	NEW	WY	372
Lake Caroline	FRS	CO	234
Lake Charles	COLO	CO	165
Lake Constantine	COLO	CO	162
Lake Creek	ARK	CO	192
Lake Creek	ARK	CO	197
Lake Creek	COLO	CO	164
Lake Creek	GRN	WY	336
Lake Creek	NP	CO	118
Lake Creek	RG	CO	31
Lake Creek	SWR	CO	51
Lake Cristobal	GUNN	CO	78
Lake DeSmet	NEW	WY	372
Lake Dinosaur	YAM	CO	105
Lake Dorothy	E-C	CO	237
Lake Dorothey	E-C	CO	253
Lake Dorothy	FRS	CO	237
Lake Elbert	YAM	CO	109
Lake Elmo	YAM	CO	105
Lake Elsie	BHR	WY	290
Lake Emma	SP	CO	206
Lake Estes	FRS	CO	241
Lake Estes	FRS	CO	241
Lake Ethel	FRS	CO	233
Lake Eunice	BHR	WY	290
Lake Fork	SM	CO	62
Lake Fork Arm	GUNN	CO	76
Lake Fork Creek	ARK	CO	191
Lake Fork Creek	ARK	CO	190
Lake Fork Conejos	RG	CO	34
Lake Fork Crestone Creek	SLV	CO	42
Lake Fork Gunnison	GUNN	CO	76
Lake Fork San Miguel R	SM	CO	62
Lake Geneva	NEW	WY	372
Lake Geneva	URB	CO	228
Lake George	GRN	WY	340
Lake George	SP	CO	210
Lake Granby	COLO	CO	144
Lake Haiyaha	RMNP	CO	136

LAKES & STREAMS INDEX

Stream name	Chapter	State	Page
Lake Hattie	NP	WY	364
Lake Heebeecheche	WIND	WY	282
Lake Helen	BHR	WY	289
Lake Henry	E-C	CO	250
Lake Humphreys	RG	CO	30
Lake Husted	RMNP	CO	137
Lake Irwin	GUNN	CO	74
Lake Isabel	ARK	CO	201
Lake Isabella	GRN	WY	340
Lake Isabelle	FRS	CO	239
Lake John	NP	CO	119
Lake Josephine	COLO	CO	171
Lake Kagevah	WIND	WY	282
Lake Louise	WIND	WY	272
Lake Loveland	E-C	CO	246
Lake Margaret	YAM	CO	109
Lake Marie	NP	WY	354
Lake Marion	BHR	WY	289
Lake Meridith	E-C	CO	250
Lake Nanita	RMNP	CO	138
Lake Nokoni	RMNP	CO	138
Lake Owen	NP	WY	364
Lake Patricia	COLO	CO	163
Lake Quivira	FRS	CO	234
Lake Reno	BHR	WY	295
Lake Ridge Lakes	COLO	CO	174
Lake Ruff	GRN	WY	340
Lake Sequa	GRN	WY	340
Lake Silver	NEW	WY	372
Lake Solitude	BHR	WY	289
Lake Solitude	RMNP	CO	136
Lake Solitude	SN	WY	320
Lake Solitude	WIND	WY	282
Lake Thomas	COLO	CO	164
Lake Vera	GRN	WY	340
Lake Verna	RMNP	CO	138
Lake Victor	GRN	WY	340
Lake Whitney	WIND	WY	273
Lake Winona	GRN	WY	340
Lake Woebegon	MISS	MN	603
Lake of the Clouds	RMNP	CO	138
Lake of the Crags	YAM	CO	109
Lake of the Woods	F-W	CO	96
Lake of the Woods	SN	WY	318
Lake of the Woods	WIND	WY	271
Lake of the Woods	YNP	WY	303
Lakes of the Clouds	ARK	CO	198
Lakes of the Rough	BHR	WY	290
Lamar River	YNP	WY	311
Lame Deer Lakes	NEW	WY	370
Lander Creek	SWT	WY	347
Landslide Creek	YNP	WY	312
Laramie Lake	LAR	CO	123
LARAMIE RIVER		**CO**	**123**
Laramie River	NP	WY	364
Larson Creek	YAM	CO	108
Larson Lakes	GUNN	CO	78
Last Chance Creek	COLO	CO	171
Lava Creek	YNP	WY	313
Lawn Lake	RMNP	CO	136
Leazenby Lake	NP	WY	365
Lede Reservoir	COLO	CO	165
Lee Creek	GUNN	CO	83
Left Hand Creek	FRS	CO	239
Left Hand Park Reservoir	FRS	CO	239
Leidy Lake	SN	WY	321
Leigh Lake	SN	WY	318
Lemon Reservoir	SWR	CO	53
Leon Lake	COLO	CO	182
Leopard Creek	SM	CO	63
Leroux Creek	GUNN	CO	84
Lester Creek Reservoir	YAM	CO	108
Leviathan Creek	SWR	CO	51
Lewis Lake	NP	WY	354
Lewis Lake	YNP	WY	300
Lewis River	YNP	WY	301
Lewis-Shoshone Channel	YNP	WY	301
Libby Lake	NP	WY	354
Lily Lake	BHR	WY	289
Lily Lake	BHR	WY	295
Lily Lake	COLO	CO	174
Lily Lake	COLO	CO	183
Lilypad Lake	YNP	WY	302
Lime Creek	COLO	CO	170
Lime Creek	RG	CO	29
Lime Creek	SWR	CO	54
Lincoln Creek	COLO	CO	167
Lincoln Lake	SP	CO	217
Link Creek	LAR	CO	125
Linkins Lake	COLO	CO	166
Little Atlantic Lake	WIND	WY	277
Little Battlement Lake	COLO	CO	181
Little Bear Creek	YAM	CO	109
Little Bighorn River	NEW	WY	374
Little Brooklyn Lake	NP	WY	356
Little Buffalo Creek	YNP	WY	312
Little Cabin Creek	COLO	CO	145
Little Causeway Lake	YAM	CO	103
Little Cimarron River	GUNN	CO	80
Little Coal Creek	GUNN	CO	82
Little Cochetopa Creek	ARK	CO	196
Little Cottonwood Creek	YAM	CO	109

418 LAKES & STREAMS INDEX

Stream name	Chapter	State	Page
Little Cottonwood Creek	YNP	WY	312
Little Crystal Lake	RMNP	CO	136
Little Divide Lake	GRN	WY	341
Little Echo Lake	FRS	CO	236
Little Emerald Lake	SWR	CO	54
Little Emerald Lake	SWR	CO	51
Little Fall Creek	GRN	WY	340
Little Firehole River	YNP	WY	304
Little Fish	DOL	CO	60
Little Flint Creek	SWR	CO	51
Little Gem Lake	COLO	CO	172
Little Gem Reservoir	COLO	CO	181
Little Greys River	SN	WY	323
Little Grizzly Creek	NP	CO	117
Little Grizzly Creek	NP	CO	315
Little Gunnison Creek	GUNN	CO	84
Little Half Moon Lake	GRN	WY	339
Little Hart Lake	WIND	WY	276
Little Hohnholz Lake	LAR	CO	126
Little Horn Lake	ARK	CO	199
Little Ice Lake	SWR	CO	54
Little James Creek	FRS	CO	239
Little Lamar River	YNP	CO	311
Little Laramie River	NP	WY	364
Little Medicine Bow River	NP	WY	357
Little Molas Lake	SWR	CO	54
Little Morrison Creek	YAM	CO	104
Little Muddy Creek	COLO	CO	147
Little Popo Agie River	WIND	WY	277
Little Powder River	NEW	WY	375
Little Rainbow Lake	LAR	CO	125
Little Red Park Creek	YAM	CO	111
Little Robinson Creek	YNP	WY	302
Little Rock Lake	RMNP	CO	136
Little Ruby Lake	RG	CO	28
Little Sand Creek	ARK	CO	200
Little Sand Creek Lake	SLV	CO	42
Little Sand Creek Lakes	ARK	CO	200
Little Sandy Creek	GRN	WY	343
Little Sandy Lake	GRN	WY	343
Little Seneca Lake	GRN	WY	338
Little Skillet Lake	YAM	CO	103
Little Snake River	YAM	CO	111
Little Squaw Creek	RG	CO	27
Little St. Charles River	ARK	CO	201
Little Stough Creek Lake	WIND	WY	277
Little Sweetwater Creek	SWT	WY	347
Little Tomahawk Lake	WIND	WY	277
Little Tongue River	NEW	WY	374
Little Trappers Creek	F-W	CO	96
Little Trappers Lake	F-W	CO	96
Little Wind River	WIND	WY	281
Little's Creek Pond	URB	CO	228
Lizard Head Creek	DOL	CO	59
Lizard Lake	COLO	CO	172
Lobster Claw Lake	BHR	WY	295
Loch Leven Lake	WIND	WY	274
Loch Lomond	FRS	CO	234
Lon Hagler Reservoir	E-C	CO	246
Lone Lick Lakes	COLO	CO	156
Lone Pine Creek	NP	CO	118
Lone Pine Creek	POU	CO	130
Lone Pine Lake	RMNP	CO	138
Lonesome Lake	COLO	CO	160
Lonesome Lake	WIND	WY	276
Lonetree Reservoir	E-C	CO	246
Long Draw Creek	POU	CO	128
Long Draw Reservoir	POU	CO	128
Long Lake	COLO	CO	144
Long Lake	FRS	CO	239
Long Lake	GRN	WY	338
Long Lake	GRN	WY	340
Long Lake	NP	CO	116
Long Lake	YAM	CO	105
Longs Lakes	NP	CO	120
Lookout Lake	NP	WY	354
Loomis Lake	NEW	WY	372
Loomis Lake	RMNP	CO	135
Los Pinos Creek	GUNN	CO	67
Los Pinos River	SWR	CO	50
Lost Camp Lake	GRN	WY	337
Lost Canyon Creek	DOL	CO	60
Lost Creek	BHR	WY	287
Lost Creek	COLO	CO	147
Lost Creek	YNP	WY	312
Lost Dog Creek	YAM	CO	106
Lost Lake	COLO	CO	151
Lost Lake	COLO	CO	165
Lost Lake	COLO	CO	180
Lost Lake	COLO	CO	164
Lost Lake	FRS	CO	238
Lost Lake	GRN	WY	338
Lost Lake	GUNN	CO	84
Lost Lake	LAR	CO	123
Lost Lake	NP	CO	116
Lost Lake	NP	WY	357
Lost Lake	RG	CO	28
Lost Lake	RMNP	CO	137
Lost Lake	SWR	CO	52
Lost Lake	SWR	CO	53
Lost Lake	WIND	WY	272
Lost Lake	YAM	CO	105
Lost Lake	YNP	WY	310
Lost Lake Slough	GUNN	CO	84
Lost Lakes	BHR	WY	289
Lost Lakes	COLO	CO	161
Lost Man Creek	COLO	CO	166
Lost Man Lake	COLO	CO	166
Lost Man Reservoir	COLO	CO	166
Lost Shoe	WIND	WY	273
Lost Solar Creek	F-W	CO	98
Lost Trail Creek	RG	CO	26
Lost Twin Lakes	BHR	WY	287
Lottis Creek	GUNN	CO	71
Louis Creek	WIND	WY	277
Louis Lake	WIND	WY	278
Lovatt Lake	GRN	WY	340
Love Lake	RG	CO	29
Loveland Lake	FRS	CO	231
Lower Big Creek Lake	NP	CO	121
Lower Brush Creek Lake	ARK	CO	198
Lower Camp Lake	LAR	CO	125

LAKES & STREAMS INDEX 419

Stream name	Chapter	State	Page
Lower Cataract Lake	COLO	CO	153
Lower Chicago Lake	FRS	CO	234
L Cochetopa Dome Res	GUNN	CO	67
Lower Coney Lake	FRS	CO	240
Lower Cook Lake	GRN	WY	339
Lower Copper Lake	BHR	WY	295
Lower Crater Lake	BHR	WY	290
Lower Deep Creek Lake	WIND	WY	277
Lower Eaglesmere Lake	COLO	CO	154
Lower Fourmile Lake	SWR	CO	48
Lower Glacier Lake	WIND	WY	274
Lower Green River Lake	GRN	WY	335
Lower Island Lake	COLO	CO	158
Lower Island Lake	F-W	CO	99
Lower Jade Lake	WIND	WY	270
Lower Jean Lake	GRN	WY	338
Lower Lake Agnes	NP	CO	120
Lower Lamphier Lake	GUNN	CO	68
Lower Lizard Head Lake	WIND	WY	276
Lower Lost Twin Lake	BHR	WY	289
Lower Marvine Lake	F-W	CO	97
L Medicine Lodge Lake	BHR	WY	290
Lower Michigan Lake	SP	CO	211
Lower Missouri Lake	NP	WY	354
Lower Mitchell Lake	FRS	CO	240
Lower Muskrat Lakes	F-W	CO	99
Lower Newton Lake	BHR	WY	294
Lower Notch Lake	ARK	CO	191
Lower Paint Rock Lake	BHR	WY	290
Lower Sand Creek Lake	SLV	CO	42
Lower Sand Creek Lake	ARK	CO	200
Lower Sandbar Lake	LAR	CO	125
Lower Silas Lake	WIND	WY	277
Lower Slide Lake	SN	WY	321
Lower Smith Lake	YAM	CO	103
Lower Titcomb Lake	GRN	WY	338
Lower Torrey Creek	WIND	WY	272
Lower Twin Lake	LAR	CO	126
Lower Twin Mandall Lake	YAM	CO	104
Luna Lake	YAM	CO	109
Lupine Creek	YNP	WY	313
Lyle Creek	COLO	CO	171
Lyle Lake	COLO	CO	171
Lynch Creek	SP	CO	207
Lynx Creek	WHR	CO	89
Lynx Creek	YNP	WY	309

M

Mabel Lake	NEW	WY	370
Mac's Lake	GRN	WY	340
Macey Creek	ARK	CO	199
Machin Lake	SLV	CO	40
Mack Mesa Lake	COLO	CO	179
Mackinaw Lake	SN	WY	321
Mackinaw Lake	COLO	CO	158
Mad Creek	YAM	CO	108
Madison Lake	YNP	WY	304
Madison River	YNP	WY	302
Maes Lake	GRN	WY	343
Magdalene Lake	NEW	WY	370

Stream name	Chapter	State	Page
Magpie Creek	YNP	WY	304
Mahan Lake	COLO	CO	154
Main Elk Creek	COLO	CO	175
Main Horn Lake	ARK	CO	199
Main Reservoir	URB	CO	228
Main Ute Lake	RG	CO	26
Major Creek	SLV	CO	42
Mallard Lake	YNP	WY	304
Mammoth Beaver Ponds	YNP	WY	313
Mammoth Creek	FRS	CO	237
Mammoth Reservoir	FRS	CO	236
Manazares Lake	NP	CO	122
Mancos River	SWR	CO	55
Mandall Creek	YAM	CO	103
Mandall Lakes	YAM	CO	103
Manitou Lake	SP	CO	212
Maple Creek	YNP	WY	305
Marion Lake	WIND	WY	272
Mariposa Lake	YNP	WY	301
Marks Lake	WIND	WY	273
Marm's Lake	GRN	WY	343
Maroon Creek	COLO	CO	117
Marmot Lake	BHR	WY	295
Maroon Creek	COLO	CO	168
Maroon Lake	COLO	CO	168
Marshall Creek	GUNN	CO	66
Marston Creek	BHR	WY	293
Marten Lake	WIND	CO	273
Martha Lake	NP	CO	117
Martin Creek	COLO	CO	155
Martin Creek	COLO	CO	171
Martin Creek	GRN	WY	336
Martin Lake	E-C	CO	253
Martinez Creek	SWR	CO	50
Marvine Creek	F-W	CO	97
Marvine Creek	WHR	CO	90
Marvine Lakes	F-W	CO	97
Mary Lake	YNP	WY	304
Mary Loch Lake	F-W	CO	98
Mary's Lake	FRS	CO	240
Matt Arch Slough Lake	COLO	CO	181
Maybelle Lake	BHR	WY	287
McBride Lake	YNP	WY	312
McClain Lake	BHR	WY	287
McCullough Gulch Lakes	COLO	CO	149
McGinnis Lake	WHR	CO	90
McIntyre Creek	LAR	CO	125
McIntyre Lake	LAR	CO	126
McJunkin Creek	DOL	CO	59
McKee Pond	COLO	CO	174
McMillan Lake	COLO	CO	158
McPhee Reservoir	DOL	CO	58
McQueary Creek	COLO	CO	147
McQueary Lake	COLO	CO	147
Mead Lake	NEW	WY	371
Meadow Creek	COLO	CO	175
Meadow Creek	COLO	CO	145
Meadow Creek	COLO	CO	156
Meadow Creek	DOL	CO	60
Meadow Creek	YNP	WY	308
Meadow Creek Lake	COLO	CO	175

LAKES & STREAMS INDEX

Stream name	Chapter	State	Page
Meadow Creek Reservoir	COLO	CO	145
Meadow Lake	GRN	WY	340
Meadowlark Lake	BHR	WY	287
Medano Creek	SLV	CO	42
Medano Lake	SLV	CO	42
Medicine Bow River	NP	WY	357
Medicine Bow River	NP	WY	357
Medicine Lodge Lakes	BHR	WY	289
Medicine Lodge Lake	BHR	WY	290
Meeboer Lake	NP	WY	365
Meeks Cabin Reservoir	GRN	WY	344
Meeks Lake	GRN	WY	343
Meridian Lake	GUNN	CO	74
Mesa Creek	COLO	CO	179
Mesa Creek	RG	CO	28
Mesa Lakes	COLO	CO	179
Michigan Creek	SP	CO	211
Michigan River	NP	CO	119
Middle Anthracite Creek	GUNN	CO	83
Middle Boulder Creek	FRS	CO	237
Middle Brush Creek	ARK	CO	198
Middle Brush Creek	GUNN	CO	72
Middle Bull Lake Creek	WIND	WY	274
Middle Clear Creek	NEW	WY	370
Middle Cloud Peak Lake	BHR	WY	289
Middle Cottonwood Creek	ARK	CO	194
Middle Creek	RG	CO	28
Middle Creek	SLV	CO	41
Middle Creek	YNP	WY	308
Middle Fork Arapaho Creek	NP	CO	116
Middle Fork Boulder Creek	GRN	WY	341
Middle Fork Cimarron R	GUNN	CO	80
Middle Fork Conejos	RG	CO	34
Mid Fk Crazy Woman Ck	NEW	WY	369
Middle Fork Derby Creek	COLO	CO	158
Middle Fork Derby Creek	F-W	CO	99
Middle Fork Fish Creek	YAM	CO	105
Middle Fork Lake	GRN	WY	341
Middle Fork Laramie River	NP	WY	364
Middle Fk Little Snake R	YAM	CO	111
Middle Fork Michigan R	NP	CO	120
Middle Fork Miller Creek	WHR	CO	92
Middle Fork Piedra River	SWR	CO	50
Middle Fk Popo Agie R	WIND	WY	276
Middle Fork Powder River	NEW	WY	368
Middle Fk Powderhorn Ck	GUNN	CO	79
Middle Fork Ranch Creek	COLO	CO	145
Middle Fk S. Arkansas R	ARK	CO	196

Stream name	Chapter	State	Page
Middle Fk Saguache Ck	SLV	CO	40
Middle Fk S Platte R	SP	CO	206
Middle Fork Williams Fork	COLO	CO	147
Middle Fork Wood River	BHR	WY	292
Middle Griffith Lake	COLO	CO	180
Middle Hunt Creek Fork	YAM	CO	104
Middle Lake	COLO	CO	165
Middle Lake	WIND	WY	275
Middle Mancos River	SWR	CO	55
Middle Piney Creek	GRN	WY	343
Middle Piney Lake	GRN	WY	344
Middle Quartz Creek	GUNN	CO	67
Middle Rifle Creek	COLO	CO	176
Middle Sandbar Lake	LAR	CO	125
Middle St. Vrain Creek	FRS	CO	240
Middle Taylor Creek	ARK	CO	199
Middle Ten Sleep Creek	BHR	WY	287
Middle Thompson Creek	COLO	CO	174
Middle Ute Lake	RG	CO	26
Middle Willow Creek	GUNN	CO	70
Middle Willow Creek	COLO	CO	153
Milky Lakes	WIND	WY	274
Mill Creek	FRS	CO	233
Mill Creek	GUNN	CO	78
Mill Creek	GUNN	CO	75
Mill Creek	SWR	CO	53
Mill Creek	SWR	CO	48
Mill Creek	YAM	CO	108
Mill Lake	GUNN	CO	68
Miller Creek	WHR	CO	92
Miller Creek	YNP	WY	311
Millions Reservoir	RG	CO	32
Mills Lake	RMNP	CO	136
Mineral Creek	SWR	CO	53
Mineral Creeks	GUNN	CO	78
Miners Creek	RG	CO	29
Miners Creek	SLV	CO	41
Miracle Mile	NP	WY	357
Miramonte Reservoir	SM	CO	63
Mirror Creek	F-W	CO	96
Mirror Lake	BHR	WY	287
Mirror Lake	COLO	CO	154
Mirror Lake	COLO	CO	145
Mirror Lake	F-W	CO	96
Mirror Lake	GUNN	CO	70
Mirror Lake	NP	WY	354
Mirror Lake	POU	CO	127
Mirror Lake	YAM	CO	109
Mishak Lakes	SLV	CO	41
Missouri Lakes	COLO	CO	161
Mist Creek	YNP	WY	311
Mistake Lake	GRN	WY	338
Mistymoon Lake	BHR	WY	289
Mix Lake	RG	CO	34
Moccasin Lake	WIND	WY	281
Mohawk Creek	NEW	WY	374
Mohawk Lakes	COLO	CO	149
Mol Heron Creek	YNP	WY	312
Molas Lake	SWR	CO	54
Monarch Lake	ARK	CO	196
Monarch Lake	COLO	CO	144

LAKES & STREAMS INDEX 421

Stream name	Chapter	State	Page
Monroe Lake	GRN	WY	341
Monroe Reservoir	COLO	CO	180
Monte Cristo Creek	COLO	CO	149
Montgomery Reservoir	SP	CO	206
Monument Creek Reservoir	COLO	CO	183
Monument Lake	COLO	CO	159
Moody Creek	YAM	CO	104
Moon Lake	COLO	CO	169
Moon Lake	SWR	CO	51
Moon Lake	WIND	WY	271
Moose Creek	YNP	WY	302
Moose Lake	WIND	WY	273
Moraine Lake	FRS	CO	239
Mormon Creek	COLO	CO	171
Mormon Lake	COLO	CO	171
Morrow Point Reservoir	GUNN	CO	80
Mosquito Creek	SP	CO	206
Mosquito Lake	COLO	CO	181
Mosquito Lake	YAM	CO	103
Moss Lake	WIND	WY	274
Mountain Ash Creek	YNP	WY	302
Mountain Ash Creek	YNP	WY	300
Mountain Creek	YNP	WY	309
Mountain Home Reservoir	SLV	CO	42
Mountain Sheep Lake	WIND	WY	277
Mt. Massive Lakes	ARK	CO	192
Muckie's Lake	COLO	CO	165
Mud Lake	BHR	WY	290
Mud Lake	COLO	CO	158
Mud Mandall Lakes	YAM	CO	104
Muddy Creek	COLO	CO	155
Muddy Creek	GUNN	CO	83
Muddy Creek	NP	WY	351
Muddy Pass Lake	NP	CO	116
Mule Creek	COLO	CO	147
Mulhall Lakes	COLO	CO	161
Murray Lake	FRS	CO	233
Music Pass Creek	ARK	CO	200
Muskrat Lake	COLO	CO	158
Mutt Lake	NP	WY	357
Myrtle Lake	NEW	WY	372
Mystery Lake	SWR	CO	52
Mystic Island Lake	COLO	CO	165

N

Stream name	Chapter	State	Page
Narraguinnep Reservoir	DOL	CO	60
Native Lake	ARK	CO	191
Native Lake	GRN	WY	335
Native Lake	WIND	WY	273
Navajo Lake	DOL	CO	60
Navajo Reservoir	SWR	CO	44
Navajo River	SWR	CO	44
Naylor Lake	FRS	CO	233
Nee Gronda Reservoir	E-C	CO	251
Nee Noshe Reservoir	E-C	CO	251
Nee Skah Reservoir	E-C	CO	251
Nee Sopah Reservoir	E-C	CO	251
Needle Creek	GUNN	CO	67
Needle Creek	SWR	CO	54
Needle Creek Lakes	SWR	CO	54

Stream name	Chapter	State	Page
Needle Creek Reservoir	GUNN	CO	67
Needles Lake	SWT	WY	347
Neil Lake	GRN	WY	337
Neva Lakes	FRS	CO	237
Neversweat Reservoir	COLO	CO	183
New Fork Lakes	GRN	WY	336
New Fork River	GRN	WY	336
New York Lake	COLO	CO	164
Newcomb Creek	NP	CO	117
Newton Lakes	BHR	WY	294
Nez Perce Creek	YNP	WY	304
Nicholson Lake	GUNN	CO	74
Night Lake	BHR	WY	295
Ninemile Creek	NEW	WY	368
No Name Lake	RG	CO	35
No Name Lakes	GRN	WY	338
Nolan Creek	COLO	CO	165
Nolan Lake	COLO	CO	165
Noname Creek	SWR	CO	54
Norman Lake	WIND	WY	274
North Anthracite Creek	GUNN	CO	83
North Banner Lake	NP	WY	354
North Boulder Creek	FRS	CO	239
North Brush Creek	ARK	CO	197
North Buffalo Fork Creek	SN	WY	321
North Clear Creek	FRS	CO	234
North Clear Creek	NEW	WY	370
North Clear Creek	RG	CO	27
North Colony Creek	ARK	CO	199
North Colony Lakes	ARK	CO	199
North Cottonwood Creek	ARK	CO	193
North Cottonwood Creek	GRN	WY	343
North Crestone Creek	SLV	CO	42
North Crestone Lake	SLV	CO	42
North Crow Reservoir	NP	WY	365
North Elk Creek	WHR	CO	91
North Empire Creek	FRS	CO	233
North Fk Big Thompson R	FRS	CO	241
North F Big Thompson R	RMNP	CO	137
North Fork Boulder Creek	GRN	WY	340
North Fork Cache la Poudre	POU	CO	130
North Fork Chalk Creek	ARK	CO	195

422 LAKES & STREAMS INDEX

Stream name	Chapter	State	Page
North Fork Clear Creek	ARK	CO	193
North Fork Colorado River	RMNP	CO	137
North Fork Conejos River	RG	CO	34
North F Crazy Woman Ck	NEW	WY	369
North Fork Creek	SWR	CO	51
North Fork Derby Creek	COLO	CO	158
North Fork Derby Creek	F-W	CO	99
North Fork Elk River	YAM	CO	106
North Fork Elkhead Creek	YAM	CO	109
North Fork Fish Creek	YAM	CO	105
North Fork Fryingpan River	COLO	CO	171
North Fork Gunnison River	GUNN	CO	83
North Fork Lake	ARK	CO	196
North Fork Lake	GRN	WY	340
North Fork Laramie River	NP	WY	364
North Fork Michigan River	NP	CO	119
North Fk Mid Boulder Ck	FRS	CO	237
North Fk North Platte R	NP	CO	118
North Fork Piney River	COLO	CO	156
North Fork Popo Agie R	WIND	WY	274
North Fork Powder River	NEW	WY	368
North Fork S. Arkansas R	ARK	CO	196
North Fork Shoshone R	BHR	WY	293
North Fork Saguache Ck	SLV	CO	40
North Fk South Platte R	SP	CO	212
North Fork Specimen Creek	YNP	WY	306
North Fork Spring Creek	NP	WY	352
North Fork Swan Creek	COLO	CO	149
North Fk W Branch Creek	LAR	CO	124
North Fork White River	F-W	CO	95
North Fork of Crystal River	COLO	CO	172
North Fork of Elk River	YAM	CO	106
North Fork of Elkhead Ck	YAM	CO	109
North Fork of Fish Creek	SWR	CO	48
North Fork of Fish Creek	YAM	CO	105
North Fork of Mad Creek	YAM	CO	108
North Fork of Ranch Creek	COLO	CO	145
North Fork of South Platte	SP	CO	212
North Gap Lake	NP	WY	354
North Halfmoon Creek	ARK	CO	192
North Halfmoon Lakes	ARK	CO	192
North Henson Creek	GUNN	CO	78
North Horse Creek	GRN	WY	343
North Hunt Creek Fork	YAM	CO	104
North Inlet Creek	RMNP	CO	138
North Klondike Lake	NP	WY	354
North Lake	YAM	CO	107
North Lake Creek	ARK	CO	197
North Leviathan Lake	SWR	CO	52
North Lottis Creek	GUNN	CO	70
North Meadow Lake	NP	WY	356
North Michigan Lake	NP	CO	119
North Paint Rock Creek	BHR	WY	289
North Piney Creek	GRN	WY	343
North Piney Creek	NEW	WY	370
North Piney Lake	GRN	WY	343
NORTH PLATTE RIVER		**CO**	**115**
NORTH PLATTE RIVER		**WY**	**349**
North Prong Creek	ARK	CO	197
North Prospect Lake	URB	CO	228
North Quartz Creek	GUNN	CO	68
North Queens Reservoir	E-C	CO	251
North Rock Creek	NEW	WY	370
North Rock Creek	COLO	CO	153
North Shields Ponds	E-C	CO	247
North Spring Creek Lake	NP	WY	352
North St. Vrain Creek	FRS	CO	240
North St. Vrain Creek	RMNP	CO	135
North Sterling Reservoir	E-C	CO	247
North Taylor Creek	ARK	CO	199
North Tenmile Creek	COLO	CO	150
North Thompson Creek	COLO	CO	174
North Tongue River	NEW	WY	373
North Twin Lake	NP	WY	356
North Twin Lake	NP	WY	354
North Willow Creek	COLO	CO	153
NORTHEAST WYOMING		**WY**	**368**
Nowood Creek	BHR	WY	287
Nowood River	BHR	WY	287
Nunn Creek	LAR	CO	125

O

O'Haver Lake	ARK	CO	196
Oak Creek	YAM	CO	105
Oat Lake	YAM	CO	105
Obsidian Creek	YNP	WY	313
Ocean Lake	WIND	WY	278
Odessa Lake	RMNP	CO	136
Officer's Gulch Pond	COLO	CO	151
Oh Be Joyful Creek	GUNN	CO	74
Ohio Creek	GUNN	CO	74
Ohman Lake	FRS	CO	234
Oliver Twist Lake	SP	CO	206
Olsen Lake	COLO	CO	163
Onahu Creek	RMNP	CO	138
Opal Creek	YNP	WY	311
Opal Lake	SWR	CO	49
Ophir Creek	ARK	CO	201
Otter Creek	BHR	WY	287
Otter Creek	COLO	CO	153
Otter Creek	YNP	WY	310
Ouray Creek	ARK	CO	196
Outlet Creek	YNP	WY	301
Outlet Lake	YNP	WY	301
Ouzel Creek	RMNP	CO	135
Ouzel Creek	YNP	WY	302
Ouzel Lake	RMNP	CO	135
Overland Pond	URB	CO	228
Overland Reservoir	GUNN	CO	84
Owen Creek	NEW	WY	374
Owl Creek	BHR	WY	292
Oxbow Creek	YNP	WY	312

P

Pacific Creek	SN	WY	320
Pagoda Lake	WHR	CO	90
Pagosa Creek	SWR	CO	50
Paint Rock Creek	BHR	WY	289
Palisades Reservoir	SN	WY	324
Palmer Lake	COLO	CO	159

LAKES & STREAMS INDEX 423

Stream name	Chapter	State	Page
Palmer Lake	GRN	WY	337
Panhandle Creek	POU	CO	130
Panhandle Reservoir	POU	CO	130
Panther Creek	YNP	WY	313
Paonia Reservoir	GUNN	CO	83
Parachute Creek	COLO	CO	176
Paradise Creek	RMNP	CO	138
Paradise Lakes	COLO	CO	160
Parika Lake	COLO	CO	142
Park Creek	GRN	WY	337
Park Creek	RG	CO	31
Park Lake	WIND	WY	276
Park Reservoir	NEW	WY	372
Parvin Lake	POU	CO	131
Pass Creek	ARK	CO	196
Pass Creek	COLO	CO	146
Pass Creek	GUNN	CO	75
Pass Creek	GUNN	CO	70
Pass Creek	NP	WY	353
Pass Creek	NEW	WY	368
Pass Creek	RG	CO	31
Pass Creek Lake	ARK	CO	196
Pass Creek Lake	RG	CO	31
Passage Creek	YNP	WY	309
Pastorius Reservoir	SWR	CO	55
Pathfinder Reservoir	NP	WY	358
Patricia Lake	NEW	WY	372
Patterson Creek	F-W	CO	98
Pauline Creek	GUNN	CO	67
Pawnee Lake	COLO	CO	145
Peacock Pool	RMNP	CO	135
Peak Lake	GRN	WY	336
Pear Reservoir	RMNP	CO	135
Pearl Lake	RG	CO	27
Pearl Lake	SWR	CO	54
Pearl Lake	YAM	CO	108
Peat Lake	WIND	WY	272
Pebble Creek	COLO	CO	153
Pebble Creek	YNP	WY	311
Peeler Creek	GUNN	CO	74
Peeler Lake	GUNN	CO	74
Peggy Lake	NP	CO	119
Peggy Lake	NEW	WY	372
Pelham Lake	WIND	WY	270
Pelican Creek	YNP	WY	308
Peltier Lake	WHR	CO	91
Pelton Creek	NP	WY	351
Pennsylvania Creek	SP	CO	206
Percy Lake	NP	CO	116
Peru Creek	COLO	CO	151
Peter Lake	GRN	WY	339
Peterson Lake	POU	CO	129
Petroleum Lake	COLO	CO	168
Phantom Lake	NP	WY	354
Phantom Lake	YNP	WY	312
Phelps Lake	SN	WY	321
Phillips Creek	YAM	CO	104
Phillips Lake	WIND	WY	273
Phillips Lake	WIND	WY	273
Phlox Creek	YNP	WY	309
Phyllis Lake	WIND	WY	275
Piedra River	SWR	CO	50
Pierre Lakes	COLO	CO	169
Pika Lake	FRS	CO	240
Pilgrim Creek	SN	WY	320
Pine Creek	ARK	CO	193
Pine Creek	COLO	CO	168
Pine Creek	FRS	CO	234
Pine Creek	GRN	WY	337
Pine Creek	GUNN	CO	69
Pine Creek	YAM	CO	111
Piney Lake	COLO	CO	156
Piney River	COLO	CO	156
Pinkham Creek	NP	CO	121
Pinos Creek	RG	CO	33
Pinto Lake	WIND	WY	272
Pinto Lake	WIND	WY	276
Pipestone Creek	GRN	WY	340
Pipestone Lakes	GRN	WY	340
Pitkin Creek	COLO	CO	164
Pitkin Lake	COLO	CO	164
Plateau Creek	COLO	CO	177
Plateau Creek	SN	WY	317
Platoro Reservoir	RG	CO	34
Plumtaw Creek	SWR	CO	50
Poage Lake	RG	CO	32
Pocket Lake	YNP	WY	302
Poison Lake	WIND	WY	277
Pole Creek	COLO	CO	146
Pole Creek	GRN	WY	339
Pole Creek	LAR	CO	126
Pole Creek	RG	CO	26
Pole Mountain Reservoir	NP	CO	117
Polecat Creek	SN	WY	317
Polecat Creek	YNP	WY	302
Pomeroy Lakes	ARK	CO	195
Pomoma Lake	URB	CO	229
Poncha Creek	ARK	CO	196
Poose Creek	YAM	CO	110
Porcupine Creek	GRN	WY	335
Possum Creek	COLO	CO	175
Poston Lake	GRN	WY	343
Pot Hole Lakes	GUNN	CO	69
Potato Lake	SWR	CO	54
Poudre Lake	POU	CO	127
Poudre Lake	RMNP	CO	137
Powder River	NEW	WY	368
Powderhorn Creek	GUNN	CO	79
Powderhorn Lakes	GUNN	CO	79
Powell Lakes	NEW	WY	370
Prewitt Reservoir	E-C	CO	247
Priest Gulch Creek	DOL	CO	60
Prince Creek	COLO	CO	174
Pristine Lake	YAM	CO	107
Proposition Creek	YNP	WY	302
Prospect Creek	NEW	WY	374
Prospect Park Lake	URB	CO	229
Prospect Ponds #2&3	E-C	CO	247
Prune Creek	NEW	WY	374
Ptarmigan Creek	ARK	CO	194
Ptarmigan Creek	RMNP	CO	138
Ptarmigan Lake	ARK	CO	194

424 LAKES & STREAMS INDEX

Stream name	Chapter	State	Page
Ptarmigan Lake	GUNN	CO	69
Ptarmigan Lake	RMNP	CO	138
Ptarmigan Lake	YAM	CO	107
Pueblo Reservoir	ARK	CO	202
Puett Reservoir	DOL	CO	61
Puett Reservoir	SWR	CO	55
Pumphouse Lake	COLO	CO	146
Pumpkin Creek	NEW	WY	369
Pumpkin Creek	NEW	WY	375
Pyramid Lake	GRN	WY	343
Quag Lake	WIND	WY	273
Quartz Creek	GUNN	CO	67
Quartz Creek	SWR	CO	46
Quartz Creek	YNP	WY	310
Quartz Lake	SWR	CO	46
Quartzite Creek	RG	CO	25
Quealy Lake	NP	WY	354
Queens Reservoirs	E-C	CO	251
Quincy Reservoir	URB	CO	229
Quincy Reservoir	SP	CO	218
Quivira Lake	FRS	CO	248

R

Stream name	Chapter	State	Page
Race Creek	RG	CO	32
Raft Lake	WIND	WY	282
Ragged Lakes	COLO	CO	165
Raid Lake	GRN	WY	341
Rainbow Falls	SP	CO	212
Rainbow Lake	ARK	CO	194
Rainbow Lake	ARK	CO	193
Rainbow Lake	ARK	CO	191
Rainbow Lake	ARK	CO	197
Rainbow Lake	BHR	WY	290
Rainbow Lake	BHR	WY	295
Rainbow Lake	COLO	CO	149
Rainbow Lake	F-W	CO	98
Rainbow Lake	GRN	WY	336
Rainbow Lake	SN	WY	321
Rainbow Lake	GRN	WY	341
Rainbow Lake	WIND	WY	270
Rainbow Lake	YAM	CO	103
Rainbow Lakes	FRS	CO	239
Rainbow Lakes	NP	CO	118
Ralph Price Reservoir	FRS	CO	240
Ralph White Lake	YAM	CO	109
Ramah Reservoir	E-C	CO	254
Rams Horn Lake	YAM	CO	104
Ranger Lakes	NP	CO	120
Raspberry Creek	NP	CO	117
Rat Creek	RG	CO	29
Raven Creek	NEW	WY	375
Raven Creek	YNP	WY	308
Rawah Creek	LAR	CO	125
Rawah Lakes	LAR	CO	125
Ray Lake	WIND	WY	281
Razor Creek	GUNN	CO	67
Red Canyon Creek	BHR	WY	284
Red Creek	COLO	CO	165
Red Creek	GUNN	CO	79
Red Creek	YNP	WY	301
Red Deer Lake	FRS	CO	240
Red Feather Lakes	POU	CO	131
Red Fork Creek	NEW	WY	368
Red Lake	COLO	CO	165
Red Lake	RG	CO	37
Red Mountain Creek	GUNN	CO	69
Red Mountain Creek	RG	CO	29
Red Rock Lake	FRS	CO	239
Red Sandstone Creek	COLO	CO	164
Reed Reservoir	COLO	CO	182
Reese Creek	YNP	WY	312
Regan Lake	RG	CO	27
Republican River	E-C	CO	248
Reservoir Lake	NP	WY	357
Reynolds Lake	FRS	CO	234
Reynolds Reservoir	COLO	CO	151
Ribbon Lake	YNP	WY	310
Rich Creek	SP	CO	207
Richards Creek	YNP	WY	305
Riddle Lake	YNP	WY	309
Ridgeview Park Pond	URB	CO	229
Rifle Creek	COLO	CO	175
Rifle Gap Reservoir	COLO	CO	175
Rim Lake	COLO	CO	165
Rim Lake	COLO	CO	158
Rim Lake	F-W	CO	98
Rim Lake	WIND	WY	271
Rim Rock Lake	COLO	CO	181
Rincon La Osa Creek	SWR	CO	51
Rincon La Vaca Creek	SWR	CO	51
Ring Lake	WIND	WY	272
Rio Blanco Reservoir	WHR	CO	92
Rio Blanco River	SWR	CO	48
RIO GRANDE		**CO**	**24**
Rio Grande Reservoir	RG	CO	25
Rio de Los Pinos	RG	CO	37
Ripple Creek	WHR	CO	90
Rito Alto Creek	SLV	CO	42
Rito Alto Lake	SLV	CO	42
Rito Blanco Creek	SWR	CO	48
Rito Hondo Reservoir	RG	CO	27
River Bend Ponds	E-C	CO	247
Riverside Reservoir	E-C	CO	247
Road Canyon Reservoir	RG	CO	27
Roan Creek	COLO	CO	177
Roaring Creek	POU	CO	129
Roaring Fork Cabin Creek	RMNP	CO	135
Roaring Fork Creek	COLO	CO	144
Roaring Fork Creek	DOL	CO	60
Roaring Fork Creek	NP	WY	364
Roaring Fork Creek	GRN	WY	335
Roaring Fork Lake	WIND	WY	277
Roaring Fork North Platte	NP	CO	117
Roaring Fork River	COLO	CO	166
Roaring River	RMNP	CO	136
Rob Roy Reservoir	NP	WY	351
Robin Lake	BHR	WY	290
Robinson Creek	GUNN	CO	84
Robinson Creek	YNP	WY	302
Robinson Lake	YNP	WY	302
Rock Creek	GRN	WY	333

LAKES & STREAMS INDEX

Stream name	Chapter	State	Page
Rock Creek	NEW	WY	370
Rock Creek	SWR	CO	51
Rock Creek	SWT	WY	348
Rock Creek	YNP	WY	302
Rock Hole Lake	LAR	CO	124
Rock Lake	NP	WY	365
Rock Lake	RG	CO	37
Rock Lake	RG	CO	35
Rock Lake	RMNP	CO	136
Rock Lake	WIND	WY	277
Rock Lake	WIND	WY	274
Rocky Brook Creek	GUNN	CO	71
Rocky Creek	YNP	WY	308
Rocky Mountain Lake	URB	CO	229
ROCKY MOUNTAIN NATIONAL PARK		**CO**	**133**
Rogers Pass Lakes	FRS	CO	236
Rosa Lake	YAM	CO	109
Rosedale Lake	ARK	CO	195
Ross Lakes	WIND	WY	272
Rotary Park Pond	URB	CO	229
Rotella Park Pond	URB	CO	229
Rough Creek	GUNN	CO	78
Rough and Tumbling Creek	SP	CO	207
Round Lake	GRN	WY	337
Round Lake	NP	CO	116
Round Lake	NP	CO	116
Round Lake	YAM	CO	110
Round Mountain Lake	NP	CO	117
Roxy Ann Lakes	NP	CO	118
Ruby Anthracite Creek	GUNN	CO	83
Ruby Creek	RG	CO	27
Ruby Creek	SWR	CO	54
Ruby Jewel Lake	NP	CO	120
Ruby Lake	F-W	CO	97
Ruby Lake	RG	CO	28
Ruby Lake	SP	CO	207
Ruby Lake	SWR	CO	54
Ruby Lakes	COLO	CO	168
Ruedi Reservoir	COLO	CO	170
Runyon Lake	E-C	CO	254
Russell Lakes	SLV	CO	41
Ruybalid Lake	RG	CO	35
Ryman Creek	DOL	CO	60

S

Stream name	Chapter	State	Page
Sacramento Creek	SP	CO	206
Saddle Creek	RG	CO	35
Saguache Creek	SLV	CO	40
Salmon Lake	COLO	CO	153
Salt Creek	NEW	WY	368
Salt River	SN	WY	323
Saltada Creek	SM	CO	63
San Isabel Creek	SLV	CO	42
San Isabel Lake	SLV	CO	42
San Juan River	SWR	CO	45
San Luis Creek	SLV	CO	41
SAN LUIS VALLEY		**CO**	**40**
SAN MIGUEL RIVER		**CO**	**62**
Sanchez Creek	YAM	CO	106
Sanchez Lakes	YAM	CO	107
Sanchez Reservoir	RG	CO	33
Sand Creek	ARK	CO	200
Sand Creek	LAR	CO	126
Sand Creek	SLV	CO	42
Sand Creek	SWR	CO	46
Sand Creek	WIND	WY	275
Sand Creek	NEW	WY	375
Sand Creek Lakes	ARK	CO	200
Sand Creek Lakes	SLV	CO	42
Sand Lake	NP	WY	357
Sandbeach Lake	RMNP	CO	135
Sandpoint Lake	GRN	WY	341
Santa Marie Reservoir	RG	CO	29
Sapinero Basin	GUNN	CO	75
Saratoga Fishing Lake	NP	WY	353
Sauerkraut Lake	GRN	WY	337
Savage Lakes	COLO	CO	171
Sawhill Ponds	E-C	CO	244
Sawmill Creek	NEW	WY	372
Sawmill Lake	NP	CO	117
Sawmill Lakes	NEW	WY	372
Sawmill Reservoir	NEW	WY	373
Sawtooth Lake	BHR	WY	295
Sawtooth Lakes	NEW	WY	371
Sawyer Lake	COLO	CO	172
Scaup Lake	YNP	WY	304
Scotch Creek	DOL	CO	59
Scott Gomer Creek	SP	CO	212
Scott Lake	COLO	CO	167
Scott Lake	NP	WY	357
Scott Run Creek	YAM	CO	107
Seaman Reservoir	POU	CO	131
Section Corner Lake	GRN	WY	337
Sedge Creek	YNP	WY	308
Sedge Lake	YNP	WY	306
Seeley Lake	E-C	WY	247
Seepage Creek	RG	CO	29
Seepage Lake	RG	CO	29
Sellar Lake	COLO	CO	171
Seminoe Reservoir	NP	WY	357
Seneca Lake	GRN	WY	338
Sentinel Creek	YNP	WY	304
Service Creek	YAM	CO	104
Seven Brothers Creek	NEW	WY	370
Seven Brothers Lakes	NEW	WY	370
Seven Lakes	NP	CO	121
Seven Sisters Lakes	COLO	CO	161
Seymour Reservoir	NP	CO	116
Shadow Lake	F-W	CO	98
Shadow Lake	GRN	WY	343
Shadow Mountain Lake	COLO	CO	143
Shafer Creek	NP	CO	118
Shallow Creek	YNP	WY	310
Shallow Lake	F-W	CO	98
Shallow Lake	BHR	CO	295
Shamrock Lake	F-W	CO	97
Shaw Reservoir	RG	CO	31
Sheeley Creek	NEW	WY	374
Sheep Creek	POU	CO	129
Sheep Creek	POU	CO	130

426 LAKES & STREAMS INDEX

Stream name	Chapter	State	Page	Stream name	Chapter	State	Page

Stream name	Chapter	State	Page
Sheep Creek	SLV	CO	41
Sheep Lake	GUNN	CO	84
Sheep Lake	NP	WY	356
Sheephorn Creek	COLO	CO	156
Shelf Lake	RMNP	CO	136
Shelf Lake	SP	CO	213
Shelf Lake	WIND	WY	276
Shelf Lake	YNP	WY	306
Shelf Lakes	NP	WY	356
Shell Creek	BHR	WY	290
Shell Lakes	BHR	WY	290
Shell Reservoir	BHR	WY	290
Shepherd Lake	COLO	CO	158
Sheridan Creek	WIND	WY	270
Sheridan Lake	YNP	WY	301
Sheriff Reservoir	YAM	CO	105
Sherman Lake	RG	CO	33
Sherry Lake	COLO	CO	170
Sherwin Lake	FRS	CO	234
Shingle Lake	COLO	CO	165
Shirley Lake	GRN	WY	335
Shoal Lake	WIND	WY	277
Short Creek	SLV	CO	42
Shoshone Creek	WIND	WY	276
Shoshone Creek	YNP	WY	302
Shoshone Lake	WIND	WY	276
Shoshone Lake	YNP	WY	302
Shoshone Lake	YNP	WY	304
Shoshone River	BHR	WY	292
Shrimp Lake	YNP	WY	311
Sibley Lake	NEW	WY	374
Sickle Creek	YNP	WY	301

LAKES & STREAMS INDEX

Stream name	Chapter	State	Page
Sierra Vandera Creek	SWR	CO	51
Silas Creek	WIND	WY	277
Silas Lakes	WIND	WY	277
Silex Lake	SWR	CO	52
Silver City Creek	YAM	CO	111
Silver Creek	ARK	CO	196
Silver Creek	GRN	WY	341
Silver Creek Lakes	ARK	CO	196
Silver Dollar Lake	FRS	CO	233
Silver Jack Reservoir	GUNN	CO	80
Silver King Lake	ARK	CO	193
Silver Lake	ARK	CO	197
Silver Lake	COLO	CO	183
Silver Lake	FRS	CO	239
Silver Lake	GRN	WY	342
Simpson Lake	WIND	WY	271
Simson Ponds	E-C	WY	247
Skillet Lake	YAM	CO	103
Skinny Fish Creek	WHR	CO	89
Sky Pond	RMNP	CO	136
Skylark Creek	COLO	CO	147
Skyscraper Reservoir	FRS	CO	238
Slate Creek	DOL	CO	59
Slate Creek	SN	WY	322
Slate Lake	COLO	CO	153
Slate River	GUNN	CO	74
Slater Creek	YAM	CO	111
Slater Lake	FRS	CO	234
Slaughterhouse Creek	SLV	CO	42
Slide Creek	GRN	WY	335
Slide Lake	ARK	CO	190
Slide Lake	F-W	CO	97
Slide Lake	GRN	WY	335
Slide Lake	SN	WY	321
Slide Lake	YNP	WY	313
Slide Lakes	NP	CO	118
Slide Mandall Lake	YAM	CO	103
Sloan Lake	GUNN	CO	76
Sloans Lake	URB	CO	229
Slough Creek	YNP	WY	311
Smaller Middle Fork Lakes	GRN	WY	341
Smith Creek	YAM	CO	111
Smith Creek	YAM	CO	103
Smith Fork Creek	GUNN	CO	82
Smith Lake	WIND	WY	275
Smith Lake	YAM	CO	103
Smith Reservoir	SLV	CO	42
Smith Reservoir	URB	CO	229
Snake Lake	GRN	WY	336
Snake River	COLO	CO	151
SNAKE RIVER		**WY**	**316**
Snake River	YNP	WY	300
Snell Creek	WHR	CO	90
Snow Spur Creek	DOL	CO	59
Snowball Creek	SWR	CO	48
Snowdrift Lake	RMNP	CO	138
Snowfield Lake	COLO	CO	172
Snowmass Creek	COLO	CO	169
Snowmass Lake	COLO	CO	169
Snowslide Creek	SWR	CO	51
Snyder Creek	SP	CO	211
Soap Creek	GUNN	CO	79
Soapstone Lake	WIND	WY	271
Soda Butte Creek	YNP	WY	311
Soda Creek	COLO	CO	151
Soda Creek	YAM	CO	106
Soda Fork Creek	SN	WY	321
Soda Lake	GRN	WY	337
Sodergreen Lake	NP	WY	365
Soldier Creek	GUNN	CO	80
Soldier Creek	NEW	WY	368
Solfatara Creek	YNP	WY	303
Solitary Lake	COLO	CO	158
Solution Creek	YNP	WY	309
Sonnicant Lake	WIND	WY	282
Sopris Creek	COLO	CO	174
Sopris Creek	COLO	CO	169
Sopris Creek	COLO	CO	161
Sopris Lake	COLO	CO	161
Sour Creek	YNP	WY	310
Sourdough Creek	NEW	WY	370
Sourdough Lake	COLO	CO	165
South Arkansas River	ARK	CO	196
South Banner Lake	NP	WY	354
South Beaver Creek	GUNN	CO	75
South Boulder Creek	FRS	CO	236
South Boundary Lake	YNP	WY	302
South Branch Lake	ARK	CO	198
South Brush Creek	ARK	CO	198
South Clear Creek	NEW	WY	369
South Clear Creek	RG	CO	28
South Colony Creek	ARK	CO	199
South Colony Lakes	ARK	CO	199
South Cottonwood Creek	ARK	CO	194
South Cottonwood Creek	GRN	WY	343
South Crestone Creek	SLV	CO	42
South Crestone Lake	SLV	CO	42
South Elk Creek	RG	CO	37
South Fork Big Creek	NP	CO	121
South Fork Boulder Creek	GRN	WY	341
South Fork Cache la Poudre	POU	CO	129

428 LAKES & STREAMS INDEX

Stream name	Chapter	State	Page
South Fork Carnero Creek	SLV	CO	41
South Fork Clear Creek	ARK	CO	193
South Fork Clear Creek	FRS	CO	232
South Fork Conejos River	RG	CO	35
South Fk Crazy Woman Ck	NEW	WY	369
South Fork Crystal River	COLO	CO	172
South Fork Derby Creek	COLO	CO	156
South Fork Eagle River	COLO	CO	159
South Fork Elk River	YAM	CO	107
South Fk Fryingpan R	COLO	CO	171
South Fk Hog Park Ck	NP	CO	122
South Fork Lake Creek	ARK	CO	192
South Fork Laramie River	NP	WY	364
South Fk Little Snake R	YAM	CO	111
South Fk Little Wind R	WIND	WY	274
South Fork Mad Creek	YAM	CO	108
South Fork Michigan River	NP	CO	120
South Fk Mid Boulder Ck	FRS	CO	237
South Fork Mineral Ck	SWR	CO	53
South Fork Ponds	NEW	WY	370
South Fork Powder River	NEW	WY	368
South Fork Ranch Creek	COLO	CO	145
South Fork Rio Grande	RG	CO	31
South Fork Saguache Creek	SLV	CO	40
South Fork San Miguel R	SM	CO	62
South Fork Shoshone R	BHR	WY	293
South Fork Snake River	COLO	CO	151
South Fk South Platte R	SP	CO	207
South Fork Spring Creek	NP	WY	352
South Fork White River	F-W	CO	98
South Fork White River	WHR	CO	90
South Fork Williams Fork	COLO	CO	147
South Fk Williams Fork R	YAM	CO	110
South Fork Wood River	BHR	WY	292
South Gap Lake	NP	WY	354
South Grizzly Creek	COLO	CO	159
South Hardscrabble Creek	ARK	CO	201
South Horse Creek	GRN	WY	343
South Klondike Lake	NP	WY	354
South Leviathan Lake	SWR	CO	52
South Lottis Creek	GUNN	CO	71
South Meadow Lake	NP	WY	356
South Mesa Lake	COLO	CO	180
South Piney Creek	GRN	WY	343
South Piney Creek	NEW	WY	371
South Piney Lake	NEW	WY	371
SOUTH PLATTE RIVER		**CO**	**205**
South Platte River Canyon	SP	CO	215
South Quartz Creek	GUNN	CO	67
South Queens Reservoir	E-C	CO	251
South Rock Creek	NEW	WY	370
South Rock Creek	COLO	CO	153
South Spring Creek Lake	NP	WY	352
South St. Vrain Creek	FRS	CO	239
South Twin Lake	NP	WY	356
South Twin Lake	NP	WY	354
South Willow Creek	COLO	CO	153
Southern Milky Lakes	WIND	WY	274
SOUTHWEST RIVERS		**CO**	**44**
Spanish Creek	SLV	CO	41
Spear Lake	NEW	WY	372
Spearpoint Lakes	WIND	WY	274
Specimen Creek	YNP	WY	306
Spectacle Lake	RG	CO	35
Spencer Lake	GUNN	CO	72
Spinney Mountain Res	SP	CO	209
Spirit Lake	RMNP	CO	138
Splake Lake	WIND	WY	273
Sportsman Lake	YNP	WY	312
Sprague Lake	RMNP	CO	136
Spread Creek	SN	WY	321
Spring Creek	ARK	CO	197
Spring Creek	COLO	CO	155
Spring Creek	GUNN	CO	71
Spring Creek	GUNN	CO	79
Spring Creek	GUNN	CO	83
Spring Creek	NP	WY	352
Spring Creek	SLV	CO	41
Spring Creek	YAM	CO	106
Spring Creek	YNP	WY	304
Spring Creek Reservoir	GUNN	CO	71
Spruce Creek	ARK	CO	197
Spruce Creek	COLO	CO	155
Spruce Creek	GRN	WY	339
Spruce Creek	RMNP	CO	135
Spruce Creek	YNP	WY	304
Spruce Lake	GRN	WY	339
Spruce Lake	RMNP	CO	135
Square Top Lakes	SP	CO	213
Squaw Lake	RG	CO	27
Squaw Lake	YNP	WY	308
Squirrel Lake	WIND	WY	277
St. Charles River	ARK	CO	201
St. Kevin Lake	ARK	CO	191
St. Louis Creek	COLO	CO	146
St. Louis Lake	COLO	CO	146
St. Mary's Lake	FRS	CO	234
Stalker Lake	E-C	CO	248
Stambaugh Reservoir	NP	CO	117
Stamp Mill Lake	NP	WY	354
Standley Lake	SP	CO	218
Standley Lake	URB	CO	229
Stapp Lakes	FRS	CO	240
Star Lake	WIND	WY	273
Starvation Creek	ARK	CO	196
Steamboat Lake	WIND	WY	282
Steamboat Lake	YAM	CO	108
Steelman Creek	COLO	CO	147
Stephens Creek	YNP	WY	312
Sterne Pond	URB	CO	230
Steuart Lake	FRS	CO	234
Steuben Creek	GUNN	CO	79
Stillwater Creek	COLO	CO	143
Stillwater Reservoir	YAM	CO	103
Stollsteimer Creek	SWR	CO	50
Stone Lake	COLO	CO	144
Stonehammer Lake	GRN	WY	336
Stoner Creek	DOL	CO	60
Storm King Creek	SWR	CO	51
Storm King Lake	SWR	CO	52
Storm Lake	FRS	CO	238

LAKES & STREAMS INDEX

Stream name	Chapter	State	Page
Stough Creek	WIND	WY	277
Stout Creek Lakes	ARK	CO	197
Straight Creek	YNP	WY	313
Strawberry Creek	COLO	CO	145
Strawberry Lake	COLO	CO	145
Strawberry Lakes	COLO	CO	170
String Lake	SN	WY	318
Stub Creek	LAR	CO	125
Stuck Creek	LAR	CO	126
Stukey Creek	YAM	CO	109
Stull Lakes	NEW	WY	372
Stump Lake	SWR	CO	53
Sturrey Lake	GRN	WY	339
Sucker Creek	NEW	WY	374
Sugar Bowl Lake	LAR	CO	126
Sugarloaf Lake	COLO	CO	165
Sullenburger Reservoir	SWR	CO	50
Summit Creek	YAM	CO	111
Summit Lake	GRN	WY	338
Summit Lake	NP	CO	117
Summit Lake	SP	CO	216
Summit Lake	YNP	WY	304
Summit Reservoir	DOL	CO	61
Summit Reservoir	SWR	CO	55
Sunlight Creek	BHR	WY	295
Sunlight Creek	SWR	CO	51
Sunlight Lakes	SWR	CO	52
Sunrise Lake	GRN	WY	341
Sunset Lake	COLO	CO	180
Sunshine Creek	BHR	WY	292
Sunshine Reservoir	BHR	WY	292
Supply Basin Lake	COLO	CO	159
Supply Creek	COLO	CO	143
Surprise Lake	COLO	CO	153
Surprise Lake	SN	WY	320
Surprise Creek	YNP	WY	301
Surprise Lake	F-W	CO	96
Swan River	COLO	CO	149
Swede Lake	WHR	CO	91
Sweetwater Creek	COLO	CO	158
Sweetwater Creek	F-W	CO	98
Sweetwater Lake	COLO	CO	158
SWEETWATER RIVER		**WY**	**347**
Sweitzer Lake	GUNN	CO	85
Swift Creek	ARK	CO	198
Sylvan Lake	COLO	CO	165
Sylvan Lake	YNP	WY	308
Sylvan Lakes	ARK	CO	190

T

Stream name	Chapter	State	Page
T Lake	BHR	WY	295
Tabor Creek	COLO	CO	168
Tabor Lake	COLO	CO	168
Taggart Lake	SN	WY	320
Tarryall Creek	SP	CO	210
Tarryall Reservoir	SP	CO	211
Taylor Creek	DOL	CO	60
Taylor Lake	GUNN	CO	69
Taylor Reservoir	GUNN	CO	68
Taylor River	GUNN	CO	70
Tayo Creek	WIND	WY	277
Teal Lake	NP	CO	117
Teller Lake	FRS	CO	236
Tellurium Creek	GUNN	CO	69
Tellurium Lake	COLO	CO	171
Tellurium Lake	GUNN	CO	69
Ten Sleep Creek	BHR	WY	287
Tenmile Creek	COLO	CO	150
Tenmile Creek	SWR	CO	54
Tennessee Creek	ARK	CO	190
Tepee Creek	GRN	WY	335
Tern Lake	YNP	WY	310
Texas Creek	ARK	CO	197
Texas Creek	GUNN	CO	69
Texas Creek	RG	CO	28
Texas Creek Lakes	GUNN	CO	69
Thayer Lake	NEW	WY	372
The Loch	RMNP	CO	136
Thistle Creek	YNP	WY	310
Thomas Lakes	COLO	CO	174
Thompson Lake	GRN	CO	338
Three Island Creek	YAM	CO	107
Three Island Lake	YAM	CO	107
Threemile Creek	SP	CO	212
Thumb Lake	WIND	WY	277
Thunder Lake	RMNP	CO	135
Thurston Reservoir	E-C	CO	251
Tiago Lake	NP	CO	117
Tigee Lake	WIND	WY	282
Timber Creek	RMNP	CO	138
Timber Lake	E-C	CO	250
Timber Lake	LAR	CO	124
Timber Lake	RG	CO	35
Timber Lake	RMNP	CO	138
Timberline Lake	ARK	CO	190
Timberline Lake	POU	CO	130
Timothy Creek	YNP	WY	311
Tipperary Lake	COLO	CO	154
Toadstool Lakes	WIND	WY	277
Tobacco Lake	RG	CO	35
Tomahawk Lake	WIND	WY	277
Tomichi Creek	GUNN	CO	66
Tonahutu Creek	RMNP	CO	138
Tongue River	NEW	WY	373
Torrey Creek	WIND	WY	272
Torrey Lake	WIND	WY	272
Torsido Creek	RG	CO	33

LAKES & STREAMS INDEX

Stream name	Chapter	State	Page
Torso Creek	YAM	CO	109
Tosi Creek	GRN	WY	335
Totten Reservoir	DOL	CO	61
Tower Creek	YNP	WY	310
Trail Creek	COLO	CO	145
Trail Creek	GRN	WY	336
Trail Creek	YAM	CO	106
Trail Creek	YNP	WY	309
Trail Lake	GRN	WY	337
Trail Lake	RG	CO	35
Trail Lake	WIND	WY	270
Trail Lake	WIND	WY	272
Trail Lake	YNP	WY	309
Trap Creek	LAR	CO	123
Trap Creek	POU	CO	129
Trap Lake	POU	CO	129
Trapper Lake	GRN	WY	337
Trappers Creek	YNP	WY	309
Trappers Lake	F-W	CO	95
Trappers Lake	WHR	CO	89
Treasure Vault Lake	COLO	CO	163
Triangle Lake	GRN	WY	338
Trickle Park Reservoir	COLO	CO	182
Trigger Lake	NEW	WY	370
Trinchera Creek	SLV	CO	42
Trinidad Lake	E-C	CO	252
Triple Lakes	FRS	CO	239
Trophy Lake	GRN	WY	340
Troublesome Creek	COLO	CO	148
Trout Creek	ARK	CO	194
Trout Creek	BHR	WY	287
Trout Creek	RG	CO	28
Trout Creek	SP	CO	212
Trout Creek	SP	CO	209
Trout Creek	YAM	CO	109
Trout Creek	YNP	WY	310
Trout Creek Lake	WIND	WY	271
Trout Lake	RG	CO	28
Trout Lake	SM	CO	62
Trout Lake	YNP	WY	311
Trujillo Meadows Res	RG	CO	37
Truro Creek	COLO	CO	167
Truro Lake	COLO	CO	167
Tucker Ponds	RG	CO	31
Tuhare Lakes	COLO	CO	162
Tunnel Lake	ARK	CO	195
Turbid Lake	YNP	WY	308
Turkey Creek	SWR	CO	47
Turkey Creek Lake	SWR	CO	48
Turquoise Lake	ARK	CO	190
Turquoise Lake	SN	WY	323
Turquoise Lakes	COLO	CO	163
Turquoise Lakes	COLO	CO	164
Turret Creek	COLO	CO	158
Turret Creek	F-W	CO	98
Tuttle Creek	SLV	CO	41
Twelvemile Creek	SP	CO	207
Twelvemile Lakes	SP	CO	207
Twilight Peaks Lake	SWR	CO	54
Twin Buttes Lake	NP	WY	365
Twin Crater Lakes	LAR	CO	124
Twin Lake	WIND	WY	273
Twin Lakes	COLO	CO	182
Twin Lakes	GRN	WY	335
Twin Lakes	GRN	WY	337
Twin Lakes	GUNN	CO	72
Twin Lakes	NP	CO	119
Twin Lakes	RG	CO	26
Twin Lakes	RG	CO	35
Twin Lakes Park Ponds	URB	CO	230
Twin Lakes Reservoir	ARK	CO	192
Two Buttes Reservoir	E-C	CO	252

Bob Salle photo

LAKES & STREAMS INDEX

Stream name	Chapter	State	Page
Two Ocean Lake	SN	WY	320

U

Stream name	Chapter	State	Page
Ugh Lake	WIND	WY	273
Uncompahgre River	GUNN	CO	84
Union Lake	WIND	WY	271
Union Square Ponds	URB	CO	230
Upper Bear Creek	SP	CO	216
Upper Big Creek Lake	NP	CO	121
Upper Brooks Lake	WIND	WY	270
Upper Brush Creek Lake	ARK	CO	198
Upper Camp Lake	LAR	CO	125
Upper Cataract Lake	COLO	CO	154
Upper Chicago Lake	FRS	CO	234
Up Cochetopa Dome Res	GUNN	CO	67
Upper Coney Lake	FRS	CO	240
Upper Cook Lake	GRN	WY	339
Upper Copper Lake	BHR	WY	295
Upper Crater Lake	BHR	WY	290
Upper Crescent Lake	GRN	WY	335
Upper Crystal Lake	COLO	CO	149
Upper Diamond Lake	FRS	CO	237
Upper Eaglesmere Lake	COLO	CO	154
Upper Eggleston Lake	COLO	CO	182
Upper Fourmile Lake	SWR	CO	48
Upper Geneva Lake	COLO	CO	172
Upper Green Lake	GRN	WY	335
Upper Hancock Lake	ARK	CO	195
Upper Homestake Res	COLO	CO	160
Upper Hotel Lake	COLO	CO	181
Upper Island Lake	COLO	CO	158
Upper Island Lake	F-W	CO	99
Upper Jade Lake	WIND	WY	270
Upper Jean Lake	GRN	WY	338
Upper Kerber Creek	SLV	CO	42
Upper La Jara Creek	RG	CO	33
Upper Lake	COLO	CO	144
Upper Lake Agnes	NP	CO	120
Upper Lamphier Lake	GUNN	CO	68
Upper Long Lake	GRN	WY	338
Upper Lost Twin Lake	BHR	WY	287
Upper Marvine Lake	F-W	CO	97
Upper Medicine Lodge Lk	BHR	WY	290
Upper Mitchell Lake	FRS	CO	240
Upper Muskrat Lakes	F-W	CO	99
Upper Newton Lake	BHR	WY	294
Upper Notch Lake	ARK	CO	191
Upper Paint Rock Lake	BHR	WY	290
Upper Phillips Lake	WIND	WY	273
Upper Pole Creek Lake	GRN	WY	339
Upper Pomeroy Lake	ARK	CO	195
Upper Pomeroy Lake	WIND	WY	272
Upper Ross Lake	WIND	WY	272
Upper Sand Creek Lake	SLV	CO	42
Upper Sand Creek Lake	ARK	CO	200
Upper Sandbar Lake	LAR	CO	125
Upper Silas Lake	WIND	WY	277
Upper Silver Lake	GRN	WY	342
Upper Slate Lake	COLO	CO	153
Upper Slide Lake	SN	WY	322
Upper Stillwater Reservoir	YAM	CO	103
Upper Titcomb Lake	GRN	WY	338
Upper Toadstool Lake	WIND	WY	277
Upper Torrey Creek	WIND	WY	272
Upper Twin Lake	LAR	CO	126
Upper Twin Mandall Lake	YAM	CO	104
Upper West Ute Lake	RG	CO	26
Urad Reservoir	FRS	CO	233
URBAN FISHING		**CO**	**222**
Ute Creek	COLO	CO	147
Ute Creek	F-W	CO	98
Ute Creek	NP	CO	118
Ute Creek	RG	CO	26
Ute Lake	NP	CO	119

V

Stream name	Chapter	State	Page
V Lake	GRN	WY	343
Vagner Lake	NP	WY	354
Valentine Lake	WIND	WY	274
Valiate Lake	GRN	WY	335
Vallecito Creek	SWR	CO	51
Vallecito Reservoir	SWR	CO	52
Valmont Reservoir	E-C	CO	245
Valmont Reservoir	FRS	CO	245
Vanderbilt Park Pond	URB	CO	230
Vasquez Creek	COLO	CO	146
Vaughn Lake	YAM	CO	110
Vega Reservoir	COLO	CO	177
Vela Reservoir	COLO	CO	182
Venable Creek	ARK	CO	199
Venable Lakes	ARK	CO	199
Verde Lakes	SWR	CO	53
Virginia Lake	ARK	CO	190
Viva Naughton Reservoir	GRN	WY	344
Vixen Lake	WIND	WY	273

W

Stream name	Chapter	State	Page
Wall Lake	F-W	CO	96
Wall Lake	GRN	WY	339
Walters Lake	COLO	CO	156
Walton Creek	YAM	CO	105
Wannamaker Creek	SLV	CO	40
Ward Creek Reservoir	COLO	CO	181
Ward Lake	COLO	CO	181
Ward Road Pond	URB	CO	230
Warren Bridge Easement	GRN	WY	330
Washakie Creek	GRN	WY	343
Washakie Lake	WIND	WY	274
Washakie Reservoir	WIND	WY	281
Washington Gulch Creek	GUNN	CO	74
Washington Park Lakes	URB	CO	230
Watanga Creek	COLO	CO	144
Watanga Lake	COLO	CO	144
Water Dog Lake	COLO	CO	180
Waterdog Lake	GUNN	CO	78
Waterdog Lakes	ARK	CO	196
Watson Creek	YAM	CO	104
Watson Lake	POU	CO	131
Watson Lake	URB	CO	230

LAKES & STREAMS INDEX

Stream name	Chapter	State	Page
Watson Lake	E-C	CO	247
Weasel Creek	YNP	WY	309
Webb Lake	SWR	CO	54
Webster Lake	URB	CO	230
Weir Reservoir	COLO	CO	182
Weller Lake	COLO	CO	168
Wellington Lake	SP	CO	215
Wellington Reservoir	E-C	CO	246
Weminuche Creek	RG	CO	26
Weminuche Creek	SWR	CO	50
West (Twin) Lake	POU	CO	131
West Alder Creek	RG	CO	32
West Bellows Creek	RG	CO	30
West Branch Creek	LAR	CO	124
West Brush Creek	COLO	CO	165
West Brush Creek	GUNN	CO	72
West Carroll Lake	NP	WY	365
West Creek	SP	CO	212
West Cross Creek	COLO	CO	163
West Cross Creek Lakes	COLO	CO	163
West Elk Creek	GUNN	CO	79
West Fork Arapaho Creek	NP	CO	116
West Fork Big Goose Creek	NEW	WY	372
West Fork Cimarron River	GUNN	CO	80
West Fork Clear Creek	FRS	CO	233
West Fork Dallas Creek	GUNN	CO	85
West Fork Dolores River	DOL	CO	60
West Fork Encampment	NP	CO	122
West Fork Lake	NP	CO	122
West Fork Powderhorn Ck	GUNN	CO	79
West Fork San Juan River	SWR	CO	47
West Fork South Tongue R	NEW	WY	374
West Fork Trout Creek	RG	CO	28
West Glacier Lake	NP	WY	356

Stream name	Chapter	State	Page
West Griffith Lake	COLO	CO	180
West Grouse Creek	COLO	CO	163
West Lake Creek	COLO	CO	164
West Lost Lakes	YAM	CO	110
West Lost Trail Creek	RG	CO	26
West Mancos River	SWR	CO	55
West Maroon Creek	COLO	CO	168
West Marvine Creek	F-W	CO	98
West Marvine Creek	WHR	CO	90
West Muddy Creek	GUNN	CO	83
West Prospect Lake	URB	CO	230
West Rifle Creek	COLO	CO	176
West Snowmass Creek	COLO	CO	169
West Sopris Creek	COLO	CO	169
West Ten Sleep Creek	BHR	WY	287
West Ten Sleep Lake	BHR	WY	287
West Tenmile Creek	COLO	CO	150
West Tennessee Creek	ARK	CO	190
West Tennessee Lakes	ARK	CO	190
West Torrey Creek	WIND	WY	272
West Ute Creek	RG	CO	26
West Ute Lake	RG	CO	26
West Willow Creek	GUNN	CO	70
West Willow Creek	RG	CO	29
Whale Lake	NP	CO	117
Whalen Creek	NP	CO	117
Wheatland Reservoir No. 2	NP	WY	365
Wheatland Reservoir No. 3	NP	WY	365
Wheeler Lakes	COLO	CO	151
Wheeler Lakes	SP	CO	206
Whiskey Creek	YAM	CO	111
White Creek	SWR	CO	49
White Lake	YNP	WY	310
White Owl Lake	COLO	CO	159
WHITE RIVER		**CO**	**89**
Whitney Lakes	COLO	CO	161
Wiggins Fork Wind River	WIND	WY	270
Wild Cherry Creek	SLV	CO	42
Wildcat Creek	GUNN	CO	74
Williams Creek	SWR	CO	50
Williams Creek Reservoir	SWR	CO	50
Williams Fork Lake	SWR	CO	50
Williams Fork Reservoir	COLO	CO	147
Williams Fork River	COLO	CO	147
Williams Fork River	YAM	CO	109
Williams Lake	COLO	CO	169
Willis Gulch	ARK	CO	192
Willis Lake	ARK	CO	192
Willow Creek	COLO	CO	146
Willow Creek	COLO	CO	168
Willow Creek	DOL	CO	60
Willow Creek	GRN	WY	336
Willow Creek	GUNN	CO	79
Willow Creek	GUNN	CO	70
Willow Creek	GUNN	CO	84
Willow Creek	NP	CO	120
Willow Creek	NEW	WY	368
Willow Creek	RG	CO	32
Willow Creek	RG	CO	29
Willow Creek	RMNP	CO	137
Willow Creek	SN	WY	324

LAKES & STREAMS INDEX

Stream name	Chapter	State	Page
Willow Creek	SP	CO	207
Willow Creek	SWT	WY	348
Willow Creek	YAM	CO	107
Willow Creek	YAM	CO	111
Willow Creek	YNP	WY	311
Willow Creek Lake	SLV	CO	42
Willow Creek Reservoir	COLO	CO	146
Willow Lake	COLO	CO	169
Willow Lake	GRN	WY	336
Willow Lake	NP	CO	116
Willow Lake	RG	CO	26
Willow Lakes	COLO	CO	153
Willow Park Reservoir	NEW	WY	372
Wind River Lake	WIND	WY	270
WIND RIVER		**CO**	**268**
Windsor Lake	ARK	CO	191
Windsor Lake	E-C	CO	246
Windy Lake	WIND	WY	277
Winter Creek	YNP	WY	313
Witch Creek	YNP	WY	301
Wolf Lake	YNP	WY	303
Wolverine Creek	YAM	CO	107
Wolverine Lake	YAM	CO	107
Wood River	BHR	WY	292
Woodchuck Creek	NEW	WY	374
Woodland Lake	FRS	CO	238
Woodruff Narrows Res	BR	WY	267
Woods Creek	FRS	CO	233
Woods Lakes	COLO	CO	171

Stream name	Chapter	State	Page
Woods Lake	FRS	CO	233
Woods Lake	SM	CO	63
Woody Creek	COLO	CO	169
Worthen Meadows Res	WIND	WY	277
Wrangler Lake	YNP	WY	310
Wykee Lake	WIND	WY	282

Y

Stream name	Chapter	State	Page
Yamcollo Reservoir	YAM	CO	104
Yampa Reservoir	YAM	CO	104
YAMPA RIVER		**CO**	**101**
Yankee Doodle Lake	FRS	CO	236
Yellowstone Lake	YNP	WY	308
YELLOWSTONE NATIONAL PARK		**WY**	**298**
Yellowstone River	YNP	WY	307-9
Youngs Creek Reservoir	COLO	CO	182
Youngs Lake	COLO	CO	183
Ypsilon Lake	RMNP	CO	137
Yule Creek	COLO	CO	172
Yule Lakes	COLO	CO	172

Z

Stream name	Chapter	State	Page
Zimmerman Lake	POU	CO	128
ZigZag Lake	WIND	WY	277

Catch the best in an Arcticreel®

You're fishing your favorite stream. By mid-morning you've netted your "keepers." And your Arcticreel stores your catch right up to frying pan time. Flax canvas imported from Scotland keeps them firm and cool. And a washable plastic liner insures a clean, sweet creel after years of use.

Arcticreel. The original self-cooling creel. It captures the pure enjoyment of the sport. Three models available, plus an optional snap-on Tackle Pocket. You can find the Arcticreel at better sporting goods dealers and tackle shops throughout the Rockies.

Night falls. You return to camp and fry your catch on the camp stove. As you crawl into your sleeping bag, you know you'll be protected all night long by the common-sense construction of your sturdy, spacious wall tent.

Colorado Tent Company: The finest in outdoor living equipment for 80 years. When the West was still a frontier, Colorado Tent earned its reputation as supplier to big game hunters, guides, outfitters and sportsmen.

Today Colorado Tent still carries the equipment you need:
- Wall tents
- Camp stoves
- Pack sacks
- Feed bags
- Saddle bags

Manufacturers of Herder Tents, Range Tents and Indian Teepee Tents as well as traditional Western-style Wall Tents.

Please write or call for a free illustrated catalog.

Colorado Tent Company
2228 Blake St., Denver, CO 80205
Phone (303) 294-0924